Romania

THE ROUGH GUIDE

There are more than one hundred Rough Guide titles
covering destinations from Amsterdam to Zimbabwe

Forthcoming titles include
Bangkok • Barbados
Japan • Jordan • Syria

Rough Guide Reference Series
Classical Music • European Football • The Internet • Jazz
Opera • Reggae • Rock Music • World Music

Rough Guide Phrasebooks
Czech • French • German • Greek • Hindi & Urdu • Indonesian • Italian
Mandarin Chinese • Mexican Spanish • Polish • Portuguese
Russian • Spanish • Thai • Turkish • Vietnamese

Rough Guides on the Internet
http://www.roughguides.com

ROUGH GUIDE CREDITS

Text editor: Judith Bamber
Series editor: Mark Ellingham
Editorial: Martin Dunford, Jonathan Buckley, Samantha Cook, Jo Mead, Kate Berens, Amanda Tomlin, Ann-Marie Shaw, Paul Gray, Sarah Dallas, Chris Schüler, Julia Kelly, Helena Smith, Caroline Osborne, Kieran Falconer, Olivia Eccleshall, Orla Duane (UK); Andrew Rosenberg (US)
Production: Susanne Hillen, Andy Hilliard, Judy Pang, Link Hall, Nicola Williamson, Helen Ostick

Cartography: Melissa Flack, Maxine Burke
Picture research: Eleanor Hill
Online editors: Alan Spicer (UK); Geronimo Madrid (US)
Finance: John Fisher, Celia Crowley, Catherine Gillespie, Neeta Mistry
Marketing & Publicity: Richard Trillo, Simon Carloss, Niki Smith (UK); Jean-Marie Kelly, SoRelle Braun (US)
Administration: Tania Hummel, Alexander Mark Rogers

ACKNOWLEDGEMENTS

Tim would like to thank Emil Silvestru, Mircea Pîrlog, the Farcaş family, Isolde, Marie Ciceu, Cristi and Teddy and all at the Bucovina Estur, Ildiko Mitru, Mihail Pop, Mihail Ghizaru, Yves Prescott, Julian Ross, Simon Broughton, Martin Barlow, David Turnock, Dennis Deletant, Tom Gallagher, Michelle Bonnel, Brenda Walker, Christoph Machat, Peter Domokos, Bobby Barth, Andrei Blumer, Sarah Roe, Jeroen van Marle and James Brabazon.

Many thanks also to Narrell Leffman; Nick Thomson; David Callier, Melissa Flack and Maxine Burke for cartography; Helen Ostick for typesetting; and Susannah Walker for proofreading.

PUBLISHING INFORMATION

This third edition published March 1998 by Rough Guides Ltd, 1 Mercer St, London WC2H 9QJ. Distributed by the Penguin Group:
Penguin Books Ltd, 27 Wrights Lane, London W8 5TZ
Penguin Books USA Inc., 375 Hudson Street, New York 10014, USA
Penguin Books Australia Ltd, 487 Maroondah Highway, PO Box 257, Ringwood, Victoria 3134, Australia
Penguin Books Canada Ltd, 10 Alcorn Avenue, Toronto, Ontario, Canada M4V 1E4
Penguin Books (NZ) Ltd, 182–190 Wairau Road, Auckland 10, New Zealand
Typeset in Linotron Univers and Century Old Style to an original design by Andrew Oliver.
Printed in England by Clays Ltd, St Ives PLC
Illustrations in Part One and Part Three by Edward Briant.

Illustrations on p.1 & p.341 by Henry Iles
© Tim Burford and Dan Richardson 1998.

432pp – Includes index
A catalogue record for this book is available from the British Library
ISBN 1-85828-305-1

Romania

THE ROUGH GUIDE

written and researched by

Tim Burford and Dan Richardson

THE ROUGH GUIDES

THE ROUGH GUIDES

TRAVEL GUIDES • PHRASEBOOKS • MUSIC AND REFERENCE GUIDES

 We set out to do something different when the first Rough Guide was published in 1982. Mark Ellingham, just out of university, was travelling in Greece. He brought along the popular guides of the day, but found they were all lacking in some way. They were either strong on ruins and museums but went on for pages without mentioning a beach or taverna. Or they were so conscious of the need to save money that they lost sight of Greece's cultural and historical significance. Also, none of the books told him anything about Greece's contemporary life – its politics, its culture, its people, and how they lived.

So with no job in prospect, Mark decided to write his own guidebook, one which aimed to provide practical information that was second to none, detailing the best beaches and the hottest clubs and restaurants, while also giving hard-hitting accounts of every sight, both famous and obscure, and providing up-to-the-minute information on contemporary culture. It was a guide that encouraged independent travellers to find the best of Greece, and was a great success, getting shortlisted for the Thomas Cook travel guide award, and encouraging Mark, along with three friends, to expand the series.

The Rough Guide list grew rapidly and the letters flooded in, indicating a much broader readership than had been anticipated, but one which uniformly appreciated the Rough Guide mix of practical detail and humour, irreverence and enthusiasm. Things haven't changed. The same four friends who began the series are still the caretakers of the Rough Guide mission today: to provide the most reliable, up-to-date and entertaining information to independent-minded travellers of all ages, on all budgets.

We now publish 100 titles and have offices in London and New York. The travel guides are written and researched by a dedicated team of more than 100 authors, based in Britain, Europe, the USA and Australia. We have also created a unique series of phrasebooks to accompany the travel series, along with an acclaimed series of music guides, and a best-selling pocket guide to the Internet and World Wide Web. We also publish comprehensive travel information on our web site:

http://www.roughguides.com

HELP US UPDATE

We've gone to a lot of effort to ensure that this new edition of The Rough Guide to Romania is accurate and up-to-date. However, things change – places get "discovered", opening hours are notoriously fickle, restaurants and rooms raise prices or lower standards, extra buses are laid on or off. If you feel we've got it wrong or left something out, we'd like to know, and if you can remember the address, the price, the time, the phone number, so much the better.

We'll credit all contributions, and send a copy of the next edition (or any other Rough Guide if you prefer) for the best letters. Please mark letters: "Rough Guide Romania Update" and send to:
Rough Guides, 1 Mercer St, London WC2H 9QJ, or
Rough Guides, 375 Hudson St, 9th floor, New York NY 10014.
Or send email to: mail@roughguides.co.uk
Online updates about this book can be found on Rough Guides' Web site at http://www.roughguides.com

THE AUTHORS

Tim Burford studied languages at Oxford University. He first visited East-Central Europe in 1988 and has travelled widely in the region over the last ten years, researching and writing hiking guides to Romania, Poland and Ukraine, and, with Dan Richardson, the Rough Guide to Romania. Tim has also led hiking groups in Romania and Slovakia, as well as writing specialist hiking and eco-travel guides to Mexico, Central America, Chile and Argentina.

Dan Richardson was born in England in 1958. Before becoming a Rough Guides' author in 1984, he worked as a sailor on the Red Sea, and as a commodities dealer in Peru. Since then he has travelled extensively in Egypt and Eastern Europe. He first went to Romania in 1984 and has been back many times since. While researching the Rough Guide to St Petersburg in 1992, he met his future wife, Anna; they now have a daughter, Sonia, aged three.

READERS' LETTERS

Marie Adamson, Andy Ashton, David Boulton, Shane Bryans, J. Bushey, Karel Berkhout, Helen Carpenter and Adam Kawecki, Elizabeth M. Cooper, Kirsty Crocket, "Duns Scotus", Mrs J. Eden, Hugh Finsten, Mike Frost, Rob Hale, Derek Henderson, Phil Hewitt, Mary Hoskins, Philip Howell, Edward Johnson, Angela Lepper, Giovanni Lupetin, Tommy McGibney, Esther McLean, Pat Patterson, Bee Patterson, Andrew Plummer, Brian D. Price, Kristina Pommert, Jenny Scotcher, Cameron Scott, Barbara Simmonds, Stephen Skinner, Barry Smith, Nick Steumacher, K. B. Stoddart, Fran Tattersall and Peter Schofield, Mark Throop, Paola Vallerga Marzollo, Patrick van der Hofstad, Laura Viñas, Agueda Gota and Ana Moral, Will Werley.

CONTENTS

Introduction ix

PART ONE   BASICS   1

Getting there from Britain 3
Getting there from Ireland 9
Getting there from North America 10
Getting there from Australia and New Zealand 13
Visas and red tape 15
Insurance 17
Travellers with disabilities 19
Costs, money and banks 20
Health 21
Information 23

Getting around 26
Accommodation 32
Eating and drinking 35
Post and phones 39
The media 41
Opening hours, shops and monuments 42
Festivals and public holidays 43
Sports and outdoor pursuits 46
Police, trouble and harassment 49
Directory 51

PART TWO   THE GUIDE   53

• CHAPTER 1: BUCHAREST 55–91

Arrival, information and city transport 57
Accommodation 61
Piaţa Revoluţiei 66
The Royal Palace 67
Calea Victoriei 70
The Centru Civic 73
The Palace of Parliament 73
The historic centre 76
Around Piaţa Unirii 75

The Botanic Gardens 77
Piaţa Victoriei 78
The Village Museum 79
Eating 81
Drinking 84
Nightlife and entertainment 84
Listings 86
Snagov 88
Mogoşoaia and Potlogi 89

• CHAPTER 2: WALLACHIA 92–121

Ploieşti 94
Tîrgovişte 98
Piteşti 100
Cîmpulung 103
Curtea de Argeş 104
Dracula's Castle 105

The Olt valley 106
Tîrgu Jiu 109
Drobeta-Turnu Severin 114
The Iron Gates 115
Scorniceşti 119
Giurgiu 119

• CHAPTER 3: TRANSYLVANIA 122–218

The Prahova valley and the Bucegi mountains 126
Braşov 133
Bran castle 140

Făgăraş 142
The Saxon Villages 145
Sighişoara 148

Sibiu 153
The Cindrel and Lotrului mountains 161
Sebeş 163
Alba Iulia 165
Orăştie 169
Deva 170
Hunedoara 172
Haţog 173

The Retezat mountains 174
The Székely Land 178
The Upper Mureş valley 184
Tîrgu Mureş 187
Cluj-Napoca 190
The Transylvanian Heath 200
The Apuseni mountains 202
Northern Transylvania 211

● CHAPTER 4: MOLDAVIA 219–263

Brăila 221
Galaţi 223
The Csángó region 225
Neamţ county 227

Iaşi 233
Suceava 242
The Painted Monasteries 252
Cîmpulung Moldovenesc and the Rarău Massif 259

● CHAPTER 5: MARAMUREŞ 264–285

Satu Mare 266
Baia Mare 268
Southern Maramureş 271

The Iza valley 280
The Vişeu valley and the Rodna mountains 282

● CHAPTER 6: THE BANAT 286–311

Oradea 286
Arad 294
Timişoara 300
The Timiş valley 305

The Cerna valley 307
Reşiţa and the Semenic range 308
Oraviţa 309

● CHAPTER 7: THE DELTA AND THE COAST 312–340

Tulcea 315
Into the Delta 319
The Dobrogea and the Danube–Black Sea Canal 326

Constanţa 328
Mamaia 334
Agigea to Vama Veche 335

PART THREE **CONTEXTS** **341**

The historical framework 343
Chronology of monuments 361
Romania's minorities 364
Environmental and social problems 368
Wildlife 372
Music 375

Dracula and vampires 384
Books 388
Language 395
Romanian terms: a glossary 399
An A–Z of Romanian street names 401

Index 403

LIST OF MAPS

Romania	x–xi	Approaches to the Retezat mountains	175
Romanian rail lines	28–29	Miercurea Ciuc	183
Chapter divisions	53	Tîrgu Mureş	188
Bucharest and Around	56	Cluj	192–193
Bucharest metro	60	Apuseni mountains	204–205
Around the Gara de Nord	62	Bisriţa	214
Bucharest	68–69	Moldavia	220
Downtown Bucharest	71	Piatra Neamţ	228
Wallachia	93	Iaşi	234
Ploieşti	95	Suceava	243
Tîrgovişte	99	Southern Bucovina	253
Piteşti	101	Maramureş	265
Tîrgu Jiu	109	Satu Mare	267
Drobeta–Turnu Severin	114	Baia Mare	268
Transylvania	124–125	The Banat	287
Sinaia	128	Oradea	290
Bucegi mountains	131	Arad	295
Braşov	134	Timişoara	301
Făgăraş mountains	143	The Delta and the coast	313
Sighişoara	149	Tulcea	316
Sibiu	154	The Delta	320
Alba Iulia	165	Constanţa	329
Deva	171		

MAP SYMBOLS

━━	Railway	⬙	Refuge
▬▬	Motorway	◠	Cave
═══	Road	▲	Peak
- - - -	Path	ⵢⵢⵢ	Gorge
– – –	Ferry route	⊐	Pass
────	Waterway	✈	Airport
▬ ▬ ▬	Chapter division boundary	✕	Waterfall
▬▬ ▬▬	International borders	〰	Marshland
········	Cable car	ⓘ	Tourist office
────	Wall	⊠	Post office
⛪	Monastery	Ⓜ	Underground station
✡	Synagogue	∷∷∷	Pedestrianised area
♜	Castle	★	Bus stop
♟	Museum	■	Building
∴	Ruins	➕	Church
⌂	Campsite	⁺⁺	Cemetery
◎	Hotel	▨	Park
▣	Restaurant	▩	National park

INTRODUCTION

Travel in **Romania** is as rewarding as it is challenging. The country's mountain scenery and great diversity of wildlife, its cultures and people, and a way of life that at times seems out of the last century, leave few who visit unaffected. However, although not as impoverished as Albania and most of the countries of the former Soviet Union, it is still one of the hardest countries of Eastern and Central Europe to travel in. The regime of Nicolae Ceauşescu drove the country to the brink of bankruptcy, and Ion Iliescu's efforts to provide tangible fruit of 1989's revolution further disrupted the economy; as a consequence Emil Constantinescu's government has had to embark on a savage austerity programme which has led to big cuts in real earnings. Coming here on a package deal – to the Black Sea or Poiana Braşov, or on a "Dracula Tour" – will effectively shield you from such realities. Travelling independently will have its frustrating moments, balancing inclinations and plans against practicalities. However, it would be a shame to let such factors deter you from at least a brief independent foray. Much of Romania's charm lies in the remoter, less-visited regions, and it's the experience of getting there that really gives you an insight into the country. Rather than expecting an easy ride, try to accept whatever happens as an adventure – encounters with Gypsies, wild bears, oafish officials and assorted odd characters are likely to be far more interesting than anything purveyed by the tourist board.

Romanians (the country's largest ethnic group) trace their ancestry back to the Romans, and have a noticeable Latin character. They are generally warm, spontaneous, anarchic, and appreciative of style and life's pleasures – sadly, in contrast to the austerity with which they're saddled. In addition to ethnic Romanians, one and a half million Magyars pursue a traditional lifestyle long since vanished in Hungary, while dwindling numbers of Transylvanian Germans (Saxons) reside around the fortified towns and churches their ancestors built in the Middle Ages to guard the mountain passes. Along the coast, in the Delta and in the Banat there's a rich mixture of Russians, Ukrainians, Serbs, Slovaks, Bulgars, Gypsies, Turks and Tatars.

Bucharest has lost much of its charm – its wide nineteenth-century Parisian-style boulevards are choked with traffic, once-grand *fin-de-siècle* buildings are crumbling and the suburbs are dominated by grim apartment blocks – but it remains the centre of the country's commercial and cultural life. Many of Romania's other cities are blighted by industry and best avoided, but Braşov, Sibiu, Cluj, Oradea and other historic towns still show glimpses of past glories. To the north and west of the country, Transylvania and Banat are the provinces that are most western in feel and allow the easiest travelling, with private hotels, buses and taxis, and information more readily available. Coming from the capital, Braşov is the gateway to Transylvania; just twelve kilometres from the ski resort of Poiana Braşov, its medieval old town is a good introduction to the Saxon architecture of the region, which reaches its peak in the fortified town of Sibiu and the jagged skyline of Sighişoara. Further north and west, the great Magyar cities of Tîrgu Mureş, Cluj and Oradea have retained a wealth of medieval churches and streets, as well as impressive Baroque and Secession edifices. All these cities are served by international trains from Budapest, and any could be your first taste of Romania if you're arriving overland.

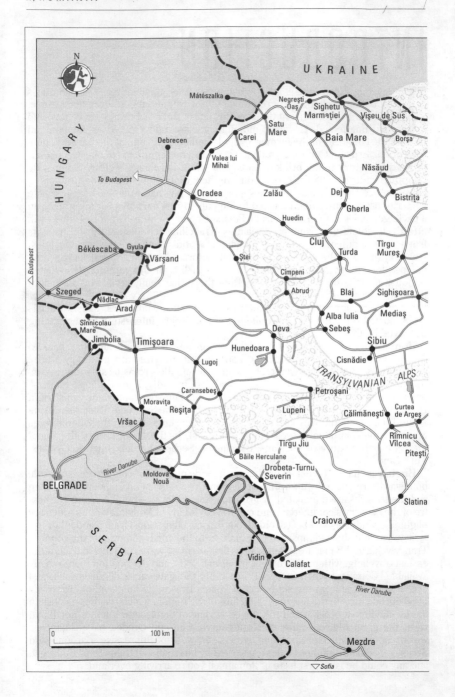

UKRAINE

HUNGARY

Mátészalka

Negreşti
-Oaş
Sighetu
Marmaţiei
Vişeu de Sus

Satu
Mare
Carei
Baia Mare
Borşa

Debrecen

Valea lui
Mihai

Năsăud

To Budapest

Oradea
Zalău
Dej
Bistriţa

Gherla

Huedin

△ Budapest

Békéscaba
Gyula
Vărşand
Cluj
Tîrgu
Mureş

Ştei
Turda

Cîmpeni

Szeged
Abrud
Blaj
Sighişoara

Nădlac
Arad

Sînnicolau
Mare
Alba Iulia
Mediaş

Jimbolia
Deva
Sebeş

Timişoara
Sibiu

Lugoj
Hunedoara
Cisnădie

Caransebeş
TRANSYLVANIAN ALPS

Moraviţa
Reşiţa
Petroşani

Vršac
Lupeni
Curtea
de Argeş

Călimăneşti
Rîmnicu
Vîlcea

Tîrgu Jiu
Piteşti

Băile Herculane

River Danube
Drobeta-Turnu
Severin

BELGRADE
Moldova
Nouă

Slatina

SERBIA
Craiova

Vidin
Calafat

River Danube

0   100 km

Mezdra

▽ Sofia

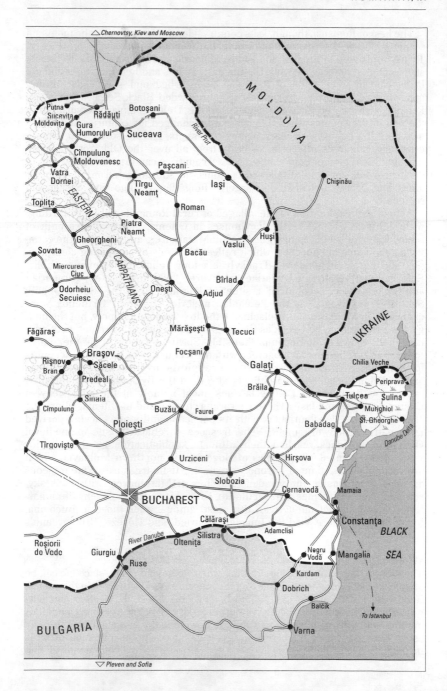

The best of Romania, though, is its countryside, and in particular the mountain scenery. The wild Carpathians, forming the frontier between the province of Transylvania and, to the east and south, Moldavia and Wallachia, shelter bears, stags, chamois and eagles; while the Bucegi, Făgăraş and Retezat ranges and the Padiş plateau offer some of the most undisturbed and spectacular **hiking** opportunities in Europe. In contrast to the crowded Black Sea beaches along Romania's east coast, the waterlogged **Danube Delta** is a place set apart from the rest of the country where life has hardly changed for centuries and where boats are the only way to reach many settlements. During spring and autumn especially, hundreds of species of birds from all over the Old World migrate through this region or come to breed. Few countries can offer such a wealth of distinctive folk music, festivals and customs, all still going strong in remoter areas like Maramureş and the largely Hungarian Csángó and Székelyföld regions.

Almost any exploration of the villages of rural Romania will be rewarding, with sights as diverse as the log houses in Oltenia, Delta villages built of reeds, watermills built entirely of wood in Maramureş, and above all the country's abundance of churches, which reflect a history of competing communities and faiths. In medieval Transylvania four religions (Roman Catholic, Reformat, Lutheran and Unitarian) and three "nations" (Saxon, Hungarian and Székely) were recognized, a situation stigmatized as the "Seven Deadly Sins of Transylvania" as the Romanian majority and their Orthodox were excluded. In Moldavia and Wallachia Orthodoxy had a monopoly, but the clergy were as likely to be Greek as Romanian, and as late as the nineteenth century held services in incomprehensible Slavonic rather than the native tongue. This religious mix, together with the frequency of invasions, accounts for Romania's extraordinary diversity of **religious architecture**. In Moldavia and Wallachia masons and architects absorbed the Byzantine style and then ran riot with ornamental stone facades, most notably at the monastery of Curtea de Argeş and Iaşi's Three Hierarchs church, and in Oltenia, where the "Brîncoveanu style" flourished, with its porticoes and stone carving derived from native woodwork motifs. The frescoes so characteristic of medieval Orthodox churches reached their ultimate sophistication on the exterior walls of the Painted Monasteries of Bucovina, in northern Moldavia, which are recognized as some of Europe's greatest artistic treasures. Fine frescoes are also found inside the wooden churches of Maramureş, with their skyscraping Gothic steeples. The Orthodox Church maintains dozens of monasteries (many in fact nunneries), the most famous, after those in Bucovina, being Snagov, where Vlad the Impaler is buried, and Horezu, Brîncoveanu's masterpiece.

When to go

The **climate** is pretty crucial in deciding where to go and when, since life can be literally at risk during **winter** unless you come fully equipped. Even in the capital, Bucharest, it's not always easy to find hotel rooms where the heating functions properly, and in winter, temperatures regularly fall well below freezing. Conditions improve with **spring**, bringing rain and wildflowers to the mountains and the softest of blue skies over Bucharest, and prompting the great migration of birds through the Delta. By May the lowlands are warming up and you might well find strong sunshine on the coast before the hordes arrive in July. **Summer** or **early autumn** is the perfect time to investigate Transylvania's festivals and hiking trails, and to see the Painted Monasteries of Bucovina, while flocks of birds again pass through the Delta towards the end of autumn.

AVERAGE TEMPERATURE (°C) (°F)

	The Banat	Bucharest	The coast	The mountains
January	−2 (28)	−3 (26)	−1 (31)	1 (34)
February	1 (34)	−1 (31)	1 (34)	1 (34)
March	5 (41)	4 (40)	3 (39)	6 (42)
April	11 (52)	11 (52)	13 (55)	11 (52)
May	16 (61)	17 (62)	19 (66)	16 (61)
June	20 (67)	21 (69)	24 (75)	19 (66)
July	20 (67)	23 (71)	26 (79)	21 (69)
August	18 (65)	22 (70)	26 (79)	21 (69)
September	18 (65)	18 (65)	22 (70)	18 (65)
October	12 (53)	12 (53)	17 (62)	13 (55)
November	6 (43)	5 (41)	11 (52)	7 (45)
December	1 (34)	1 (34)	6 (43)	2 (36)

These are average temperatures – they can rise or fall 5°C (10°F) at midday or nightfall. Spring is short and changeable; brief showers or thunderstorms are common in the Carpathians during summer, whereas the Banat and Wallachian lowlands are prone to drought. In winter a strong, icy wind (the *crivaţ*) sweeps down from Russia and snow blankets most of Romania.

PART ONE

THE

BASICS

GETTING THERE FROM BRITAIN

Deciding how to get to Romania is in large part a question of choosing between package and independent travel arrangements. If Romania is your sole destination, packages are certainly worth considering as a useful means of circumventing the hassles and frustrations of bureaucracy.

Only TAROM and British Airways offer **direct flights** to Romania, taking 3 hours 20 minutes, compared with around a day and a half by train. With so many discount deals, flying is almost certainly the cheapest way of reaching the country and probably the best option if Romania is your only destination. However, if you are planning on including Romania as part of a wider trip, or intend to travel extensively in the country on arrival, you may wish to consider an **InterRail pass**, which covers travel to and around Romania and is a more economical way of getting there than buying a return train ticket.

BY PLANE

Some charter flights are available to Romania during summer and the skiing season but you'll mostly be looking at **scheduled flights**. They are rarely the least expensive alternative, but give you the flexibility you may need. The Romanian national airline is **TAROM**, long a typical Soviet-bloc operation with little interest in its customers, but now being forced to compete and to offer a decent standard of service. It currently flies daily from London Heathrow direct to **Bucharest**. **British Airways** flies daily from London Gatwick

to Bucharest. Other European airlines serving Romania from London (Air France, Alitalia, Austrian Airlines, ČSA, KLM, LOT, Lufthansa, Malév Hungarian Airlines and Swissair) require a change of plane on route. KLM (with Air UK) and Austrian Airlines (with British Midland) also offer departures from most regional airports. Austrian Airlines flies to **Timişoara** five times a week.

An **Apex** ticket is usually the cheapest way to travel on a scheduled flight and must be reserved fourteen days in advance and include one Saturday night. Your return date must be fixed when purchasing and no subsequent changes are allowed. Currently, an Apex fare to Bucharest will cost you £349 midweek with British Airways and only slightly less with TAROM. Eastern European airlines like ČSA, Malév and LOT are often cheaper – around £240 return – but making connections in Prague, Budapest and Warsaw means you're more likely to be delayed.

If you shop around, you should be able to come up with a cheaper **discounted fare** – around £190 plus £16 in taxes for a Pex one-month return with TAROM to Bucharest. A good place to look for discount fares is the classified travel section of papers like the *Daily Telegraph* and the *Independent* on Saturdays, or the *Observer*, *Sunday Times* and *Independent on Sunday*, where agents advertise special deals, which can be as low as £150. If you're in London, check the *Evening Standard*, *Time Out* or the free travel mag *TNT* found outside mainline train stations. Independent travel specialists STA Travel and Campus Travel do deals for students and anyone under 26, and can also sell a scheduled ticket at a discount price. See the box overleaf for details of specialist Romanian flight agents.

Charter flights are in theory supposed to be sold with accommodation, but it is occasionally possible just to buy the air ticket at a discount through a travel agent. Charters have fixed and unchangeable outward and return dates, and usually a maximum stay of one month. TAROM sometimes offers charter flights from London Gatwick and Manchester to Constanţa in summer for the Black Sea beaches, and to Bucharest in winter for skiing, but you will need to check availability as they can be suspended for a season. Through an agent charter deals should cost £150–160, from Gatwick or Manchester. Jaro's fares are much

AIRLINES

Air France ☎0181/742 6600.
Alitalia ☎0171/602 7111.
Austrian Airlines ☎0171/434 7300, fax 434 7363; www.aua.com/aua
British Airways ☎0345/222111; www.british-airways.com
ČSA Czechoslovak Airlines ☎0171/255 1898, fax 323 1633; ☎0161/498 8840.
Jaro Air ☎0171/287 1700, fax 287 3310.

KLM Royal Dutch Airlines ☎0990/750900, fax 750909; www.klm.nl
LOT Polish Airlines ☎0171/580 5037.
Lufthansa ☎0345/737747; www.lufthansa.com
Malév Hungarian Airlines ☎0171/439 0577, fax 734 8116.
Swissair ☎0171/434 7200, fax 434 7233; www.swissair.com
TAROM ☎0171/224 3693, fax 487 2913.

DISCOUNT FLIGHT AGENTS

ACE Travel, Phoenix House, Desborough Park Rd, High Wycombe, Bucks HP12 3BQ (☎01494/463324, fax 464434). Romanian flight specialist offering good deals on scheduled and charter flights. Also a Bucharest office arranging accommodation, car rental and internal travel.

Campus Travel, 52 Grosvenor Gardens, London SW1W 0AG (☎0171/730 3402, fax 730 6893; www.campustravel.co.uk) and three other London sites; offices in Birmingham, Brighton, Bristol, Cambridge, Manchester, Oxford, Edinburgh and Glasgow, and in YHA shops and on university campuses all over Britain. Student/youth travel specialists.

Council Travel, 28a Poland St, London W1V 3DB (☎0171/437 7767, fax 287 9414). Flights and student discounts.

North South Travel, Moulsham Mill Centre, Parkway, Chelmsford, Essex CM2 7PX (☎01245/492882, fax 356612). Friendly agency for competitive discount fares – profits are used to support projects in the developing world, especially the promotion of sustainable tourism.

Nouvelles Frontières, 2/3 Woodstock St, London W1R 1HE (☎0171/629 7772). Long-established discount flight agent.

Romania Travel Centre, Clayfield Mews, Newcomen Rd, Tunbridge Wells, Kent TN4 9PA (☎01892/516901, fax 511579; james@romtrav.demon.co.uk). Romanian flight agents also offering tailor-made accommodation deals.

Russian–Romanian Travel, 13B Addison Crescent, London W14 8JR (☎0171/371 6367). Discount flight agent for all of Eastern Europe.

South Coast Student Travel, 61 Ditchling Rd, Brighton BN1 4SD (☎01273/570226). Student experts but plenty to offer non-students as well.

STA Travel, 86 Old Brompton Rd, London SW7 3LH (☎0171/361 6161; www.statravel.co.uk) and three other London sites; offices in Birmingham, Brighton, Bristol, Cambridge, Canterbury, Cardiff, Coventry, Durham, Leeds, Loughborough, Manchester, Newcastle, Nottingham, Oxford, Sheffield, Warwick and Glasgow. Discount fares, with good deals for students and young people.

Trailfinders, 215 Kensington High St, London W8 6BD (☎0171/937 5400) and two other London sites; offices in Birmingham, Bristol, Manchester and Glasgow. One of the best informed and most efficient discount agents.

more expensive at over £300 return, although they have recently offered some competitive deals, through Intra Travel in particular.

PACKAGE AND ORGANIZED TOURS

The main advantages of **package deals** are cheap flights, free visas and assured lodgings and meals, but you have to accept that your itinerary will be planned for you and that you'll be screened from many Romanian realities. Several

British tour operators offer beach holidays to the Black Sea Coast (see box on p.5); these packages are well worth considering if it's sun and sand you're after, since it can be time-consuming and costly to arrange the same holiday independently, especially in high season. However, even if the idea of a package fills you with horror, many of the tours described below can be good springboards for independent travel, particularly during May and late September, when they're cheapest.

SKI PACKAGES

Almost all foreigners ski at **Poiana Braşov**, 150km north of Bucharest, where there is little for advanced skiers, but facilities for beginners are good, with around a hundred English-speaking instructors. Excursions are available to Braşov and "Dracula's Castle" at Bran and sleigh rides can also be arranged. **Prices** are very reasonable, with one-week packages from Crystal, Inghams and Neilson costing between £200 and £400. Charter flights depart from London Gatwick or Manchester (£11–22 supplement), with scheduled flights running from Heathrow; the bus transfer from Bucharest's Otopeni airport to Poiana

---

SPECIALIST TOUR OPERATORS

Avian Adventures, 49 Sandy Rd, Norton, Stourbridge DY8 3AJ (☎01384/372013). Birding tours.

Balkan Holidays, 19 Conduit St, London W1R 9TD (☎0171/543 5555, fax 543 5577). Local specialist offering holidays in the Carpathians, Transylvania, the Black Sea resorts, and city breaks.

British Trust for Conservation Volunteers, 36 St Mary's St, Wallingford, Oxon OX10 0EU (☎01491/839766, fax 839646; *www.btcv.org.uk*). Projects in the Carpathians and the Danube Delta.

Crystal, Crystal House, Arlington Rd, Surbiton, Surrey KT6 6BW (☎0181/399 5144, fax 390 6952; *travel@crystalholidays.co.uk*). Skiing packages to Poiana Braşov.

Cyclists' Touring Club, Cotterell House, 69 Meadrow, Godalming, Surrey GU7 3HS (☎01483/417217, fax 426994; *cycling@ctc.org.uk*). Cycling trips, information and insurance for members.

Discover the World, 29 Nork Way, Banstead, Surrey SM7 1PB (☎01737/218800, fax 362341; *sales@arctic-discover.co.uk*). Mountain wildlife tours.

Exodus, 9 Weir Rd, London SW12 0LT (☎0181/675 5550, fax 673 0779; *sales@exodustravels.co.uk*). Hiking in the Carpathians.

Explore, 1 Frederick St, Aldershot, Hants GU11 1LQ (☎01252/319448, fax 343170; *info@explore.co.uk*). Guided tours to Maramureş, the Delta and Bucovina including some hiking.

Footprint Adventures, 5 Malham Drive, Lincoln LN6 0XD (☎01522/690852, fax 501396; *sales@footventure.co.uk*). Walking in the Carpathians and Bucovina, and bird-watching in the Delta.

High Places, The Globe Works, Penistone Rd, Sheffield S6 3AE (☎0114/275 7500, fax 275 3870; *highpl@globalnet.co.uk*). Hiking in the Carpathians.

Inghams, 10–18 Putney Hill, London SW15 6AX (☎0181/780 4455, fax 780 4470; *travel@Inghams.co.uk*). Ski packages.

Intra Travel, 44 Maple St, London W1P 5GD (☎0171/323 3305, fax 637 1425). Hotel breaks and fly-drive deals in Eastern Europe.

Naturetrek, Chautara, Bighton, near Alresford, Hants SO24 9RB (☎01962/733051, fax 733368). Wildlife-watching holidays in the Delta and Poiana Braşov.

Neilson Ski, 71 Houghside Rd, Pudsey, Leeds LS28 9BR (☎0990/994444, 0113/239 4555). Ski packages.

Ornitholidays, 1/3 Victoria Drive, Bognor Regis, West Sussex PO21 2PW (☎01243/821230). Birding tours.

Peltours, Sovereign House, 11 Ballards Lane, Finchley, London N3 1UX (☎0181/346 9144, fax 343 0579). Dracula tours, city breaks and customized packages.

Prospect Music and Art Tours, 454 Chiswick High Rd, London W4 5TT (☎0181/995 2151, fax 742 1969). Cultural tours of Transylvania.

Ramblers Holidays, PO Box 43, Welwyn Garden City, Herts AL8 6PQ (☎01707/331133, fax 333276; *ramhols@dial.pipex.com*). Relatively gentle walking in the Carpathians.

Sherpa Expeditions, 131a Heston Rd, Hounslow, Mddx TW5 0RD (☎0181/577 2717, fax 572 9788; *sherpa.sales@dial.pipex.com* or *www.sherpa-walking-holidays.co.uk*). Hiking in the Carpathians.

The Travelling Naturalist, 9 Little Britain, Dorchester, Dorset DT1 1NN (☎01305/267994, fax 265506; *travelnat@lds.co.uk*). Birding tours.

Waymark Holidays, 44 Windsor Rd, Slough SL1 2EJ (☎01753/516477, fax 517016). Mountain walking tours.

WildWings, International Hse, Bank Rd, Kingswood, Bristol BS15 2LX (☎0117/984 8040, fax 967 4444; *www.wildwings.co.uk*). Birding tours.

Braşov takes three and a quarter hours. The only package available from Ireland is with Balkantours and costs from £448 including ski-pack; flights are from Belfast only.

The Ski Hotline (☎0891/881900, code 153) and Snow Line (☎0660/617086 or 617087) give up-to-date information on snow conditions in Poiana Braşov; calls are charged at premium rate.

Ski equipment for rent at the resorts is slightly antiquated compared to the latest Western models, though otherwise serviceable; package tourists, however, get priority, so independent skiers should, if possible, bring their own gear. A lift pass will cost £34–37, ski rental £19–36, boots £19–20, lessons £40, and a package including all of the above £69–90; all prices quoted are for six-days' hire. A private snowboard centre has now opened in Poiana Braşov, charging around £10 an hour for rental and tuition.

WALKING AND WILDLIFE TOURS

Seven-night holidays in the **Carpathian mountains**, based at Poiana Braşov, are offered by Balkan Holidays (£319–399). Intra Travel offers three nights in Bucharest and seven in Poiana Braşov from £512 each. To really see the Carpathians, you might like to try one of the **hiking tours**, such as those operated by Exodus (15 days for £580), Footprint Adventures (15 days from £454 plus flights), High Places (13 days for £740) and Sherpa (15 days for £627–670). High Places prices are relatively steep, but include more meals and extras than the others. Footprint offer walking trips to the painted monasteries of Bucovina – rather easier going, with more culture thrown in. In addition Explore offers ten-day trips which rush through Maramureş, Bucovina and the Delta (with a few half-day hikes) from £375, plus a mere £120 for flights.

Organized **cycling holidays** are rare; the Cyclists' Touring Club runs them, but for members only, and not necessarily every year. **Wildlife holidays** are available from Naturetrek (£990 for ten days in the Delta and Poiana Braşov) and Discover the World (£940 for ten days, mainly spent tracking wolves in the mountains), as well as specifically ornithological holidays from Avian Adventures, Footprint, The Travelling Naturalist and Wildwings, which mostly use the same excellent Romanian naturalist guides. The British Trust for Conservation Volunteers organizes working conservation holidays in the mountains and the Delta.

DRACULA TOURS

Peltours offer **Dracula tours**, with visits to Bucharest, Snagov, Braşov, Bran, Tîrgu Mureş and Bistriţa. The Transylvanian Society of Dracula, which takes a suitably ironic approach to Gothic horror, organizes more genuine Dracula tours – contact them at B-dul Primăverii 47, Bucharest (☎1/679.57.42), or through Bravo SA, Piaţa Unirii 1, Bucharest (☎1/614.58.03).

CITY BREAKS AND FLY-DRIVES

City breaks are available to Bucharest, costing from £460 for three nights bed and breakfast for two with Balkan Holidays, Intra Travel and Peltours, using hotels such as the *Ambasador*, *Bucureşti* and *Intercontinental*. Intra Travel also has a Bucharest and Constanţa package at £520 for two for a week.

Fly-drive deals vary greatly and you'll need to shop around to find something worthwhile. Intra Travel has a £772 deal for two people for eight days; this includes two return air fares from London or regional airports. See "Driving" (p.30) for information on driving conditions in Romania.

BY TRAIN

Travelling **by train** takes around 39 hours from Britain to Bucharest, with standard return tickets costing more than discounted flights. However, the train tickets are valid for two months, with unlimited stopovers allowed en route. The cheapest way to get there by train is an **InterRail** pass, which you can also use to include Romania in a wider tour of Europe.

From much of Western Europe the fastest and simplest option is to reach **Munich** in time for the 11pm *Kalman Imre* to Budapest, continuing to Bucharest as part of the *Pannonia*. From London an early morning Eurostar train through the Channel Tunnel to Brussels or Paris will get you there in time. Alternatively the overnight *Donauwalzer* from Ostend (Brussels in winter) to **Vienna** is the best way to cross Germany without paying the InterCity/EuroCity supplement (*Zuschlag*); from London take an afternoon Eurostar, or the 11am train to Ramsgate and the Seacat to Ostend (leaving earlier in the morning you can take the cheaper ship, or a Citysprint or Eurolines bus). The *Dacia* doesn't leave Vienna (Wien Westbahnhof) until 8pm, and the *Kalman Imre* calls at Wien Hütteldorf at 4am, so you may prefer to take an earlier train to Budapest (Keleti

RAIL TICKET OFFICES

Eurostar, Eurostar House, Waterloo Station, London SE1 8SE, and 102 Victoria St, London SW1 5JL (reservations ☎0345/303030 or 01233/617575; *www.eurostar.com/eurostar*).
Eurotrain, 52 Grosvenor Gardens, London SW1W 0AG (☎0171/730 3402, fax 730 5739).
International Rail Centre, Victoria Station (by platform 2), London SW1V 1JY (☎0990/848848

or 0171/834 2345, fax 0171/922 9874; *www.britrail.com*).
Rail Europe, 179 Piccadilly, London W1V 0BA (☎0990/300003 or 0171/203 7000, fax 0171/633 9900).
Wasteels, Victoria Station (by platform 2), London SW1V 1JT (☎0171/834 7066, fax 630 7628).

BUS TICKET OFFICES

Atlas Reisen, Wohlhauszentrum, Heilbronn, Germany (☎7131/963405, fax 993801).
Bohemian Express, Unit 18, Colonnade Walk, Victoria Green Line Station, Buckingham Palace Road, London SW1V 9SH (☎0171/828 9008). London to Prague.
Citysprint, Victoria Coach Station, London, or through Hoverspeed. London to Brussels and Paris.

Hoverspeed City Sprint (☎0990/240241). London to Brussels and Paris.
Deutsche Touring Büro Frankfurt am Main, Germany (☎69/790350).
Eurolines, London (☎0990/143219; *www.eurolines.co.uk*).
Mihu Reisen, Düsseldorf, Germany (☎211/737 0480 or 323 9255, fax 460144).

station) and then an afternoon train to Arad or a bus to Oradea. Slightly slower possibilities involve the overnight *Orient Express* from Paris to Budapest, another night train from Paris to Munich and the *Bártok Béla* to Budapest, or the Paris–Vienna day train.

There are seven trains from **Budapest Keleti** to Bucharest and all run via Arad. There's also the Intercity *Ady Endre*, from Keleti to Oradea and Cluj, and others from **Budapest Nyugati** to Oradea, Cluj, Tîrgu Mureş and Braşov (via the Székely Land), and to Baia Mare by a minor border crossing from Debrecen to Valea lui Mihai, for Maramureş.

It's cheaper to buy a ticket from London to Prague and rebook there for points east – Prague can also be reached by buses, and Vienna, Prague and Budapest all now benefit from cheap airfares, though generally only for short stays.

TICKETS AND PASSES

A **standard return ticket** from London to Bucharest costs £365 and is valid for two months (£475 by Seacat, £498 by Eurostar). If you're under 26 you can get a discounted **BIJ** ticket from Eurotrain or Wasteels for £323, also valid for two months, which allows you to stop off along a pre-determined route.

For under-26s, the most flexible way of getting from London to Romania is with an **InterRail** pass, allowing the holder free travel on most European rail lines, including Romania's. A one-month pass costs £279 including the Channel crossing. Travellers aged 26 or over can buy a more limited **InterRail 26+** ticket for £215 for fifteen days, or £275 for a month.

An InterRail pass covers all services, including the supplement for faster (accelerat, rapid and InterCity) trains, but you won't have a seat reservation, so you'll either have to queue at the ticket window or take pot luck – there are no labels on reserved seats, so you will have to give up your seat if someone turns up with a reservation for it. There is a Romanian rail pass, but it has the same disadvantage – and at about £40, it's desperately overpriced as well.

BY BUS

The Eurolines consortium offers a **bus service** from **Britain to Romania**, although you'll need to change vehicles in Frankfurt and it's horribly slow and smoky. The service leaves London at 10.30pm on Sundays and reaches Bucharest by 2am on Wednesday; in summer there's an additional bus on Thursdays. Fares start at £130 single, £208 return (valid for six months). Another service, from **London to Budapest**, leaves at 10am three times a week (five times in summer), taking a mere 27 hours; return fares are £109–119. Once in Budapest you can take less pricey local trains or buses to many points within Romania. Services from the west arrive at the Erzébet tér bus station in the city centre; those to Romania leave from the **Népstadion** bus station, four stops away by metro. The key route is via Oradea, Cluj, Tîrgu Mureş and Miercurea Ciuc, and most buses leave at about 8pm or there-abouts.

There are also many services **from Germany to Romania**. Fares are low, and airlines such as British Midland (☎0345/554554), Air UK (☎0345/666777) and Debonair (☎0541/500300) now offer such cheap fares to Germany that this may be a convenient route to Romania. The bus services through Germany call at Dortmund, Düsseldorf, Cologne, Frankfurt, Nürnberg and Regensburg, and in Romania at Arad, Deva, Sibiu, Braşov, Ploieşti and Bucharest.

BY CAR

Driving to Romania is really only worth consider-ing if you have at least a month to spare, are going to Romania for an extended period, or want to take advantage of various stopovers en route.

It's important to plan ahead. The **AA** (☎0990/655555, other services 0900/500600; *www.theaa.co.uk/theaa*) and **RAC** (☎0900/ 275600, other services 0800/550055) provide a comprehensive service offering general advice on all aspects of driving to Romania and the names and addresses of useful contact organizations. The AA's European route-planning services can arrange a detailed print-out of the most appropri-ate route to follow (£14.95, with a £2 supplement for non-members). Driving licence, vehicle regis-tration documents and insurance are essential. Many car insurance policies cover only Western Europe; check with your insurer while planning your trip. Either way, it is advisable to take out extra cover for breakdown assistance.

The best **route** is through France and Germany, Austria and Hungary, passing Frankfurt, Nürnberg, Regensburg, Linz, Vienna and Budapest, and then taking the E60 down to the Borş frontier-crossing near Oradea or the E75/E68 near Nădlac near Arad. With the closure of former Yugoslavia these **crossing points** are now very busy with trucks

for Bulgaria and Turkey. New crossings are being opened for cars and buses only, of which the most useful is from Battonya to Turnu, just west of Arad. Most trucks use the main crossing at Arad, so this is best avoided; the surface of the route from Oradea to Cluj, to the north, is in better con-dition and it's more scenic. There are lesser cross-ing points, particularly from northern Hungary towards Satu Mare, but these are less accus-tomed to anything but locals. Major border cross-ings are open 24 hours a day.

CROSSING THE CHANNEL

The fastest crossing is by the Channel Tunnel; **Le Shuttle** carries vehicles and their passengers from Folkestone to Calais in 35 minutes. It oper-ates 24 hours a day, 365 days a year: services run at least hourly through the night, and every 15 minutes at peak times, which makes advance booking unnecessary. Return **fares** are £149–199 per vehicle (passengers included) from May to August, depending on the time of day you want to travel, and much less during the low season.

Many travellers use the **ferry** and **hovercraft** links from Dover or Folkestone to Calais or Boulogne, and from Ramsgate to Dunkerque or Ostend. Fares, particularly from Dover, often undercut Le Shuttle, starting at about £116 return low season, £200 return high season for a car with up to five passengers.

CROSS-CHANNEL TICKETS

Hoverspeed ☎0990/240241, fax 01304/240088; *www.hoverspeed.co.uk* Dover to Calais, Folkstone to Boulogne.

Le Shuttle ☎0990/353535. Folkestone to Calais.

P&O European Ferries ☎0990/980980; *www.poef.com* Dover to Calais.

Holyman Sally Line ☎0345/160000, 0990/595522 or 01843/595522, fax 01843/589329). Ramsgate to Ostende and Dunkerque.

SeaFrance ☎0990/711711; *www.seafrance.co.uk* Dover to Calais.

Stena Line reservations ☎0990/707070, infor-mation ☎0990/755755. Dover to Calais, Harwich to the Hook of Holland.

GETTING THERE FROM IRELAND

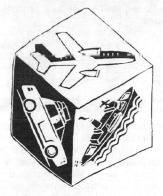

There are no direct flights from Ireland to Romania, but good connections are available via other European cities.

From **Dublin**, Aer Lingus, KLM and Swissair co-operate to offer daily services via Amsterdam or Zurich to Bucharest, costing from IR£271 through discount agents. British Airways'

Dublin–Gatwick service connects with their Bucharest flight for the same fare. British Midland and Austrian Airlines offer a route with two changes, at London Heathrow and Vienna, which also allows you to fly to Timişoara.

From **Belfast International**, British Airways flies you to London Heathrow and lets you make your own way to Gatwick for the connection to Bucharest, for £234 return; it's far easier to use the Air UK/KLM service via Amsterdam, from £265, but you won't reach Bucharest until 11pm. British Midland, Austrian Airlines and Swissair offer routings with two changes, at London Heathrow and Vienna or Zurich.

Balkantours are your best bet for **discounted tickets** (via London with TAROM, or Amsterdam with KLM). They also offer one-week ski packages from Belfast to Poiana Braşov for £448 and during the winter can offer flight-only charter tickets. **Students** and anyone under the age of 31 should contact USIT, which generally has the best discount deals on flights and train tickets. For InterRail details see "Getting There from Britain" (p.7).

AIRLINES

Aer Lingus Dublin ☎01/844 4777; Belfast ☎0645/737747; Cork ☎021/327155; Limerick ☎061/474239.

Austrian Airlines Dublin ☎01/608 0099, fax 660 1655; www.aua.com

British Airways reservations in the Republic ☎1800/626747 and through Aer Lingus. Belfast ☎0345/222111; www.british-airways.com

Swissair Dublin ☎01/677 8173, fax 679 3976; www.swissair.com

AGENTS AND OPERATORS

Balkantours, 37 Ann St, Belfast BT1 4EB (☎01232/246795, fax 234581); 5 South Great George's St, Dublin 2 (☎01/679 4415). Ski packages and budget flights.

Joe Walsh Tours, 34 Grafton St, Dublin 2 (☎01/671 8751); 8 Baggot St, Dublin 2 (☎01/676 3053); 69 Upper O'Connell St, Dublin 2 (☎01/872 2555); 117 St Patrick St, Cork (☎021/277959); 31 Castle St, Belfast (☎01232/241144). General budget fares agent.

Thomas Cook, 118 Grafton St, Dublin 2 (☎01/677 1721); 11 Donegall Place, Belfast (☎01232/242341). Package holiday and flight agent, with occasional discount offers.

Trailfinders, 4 Dawson St, Dublin 2 (☎01/677 7888). Competitive fares out of all Irish airports, as well as deals on hotels, insurance and car rental.

USIT, O'Connell Bridge, 19 Aston Quay, Dublin 2 (☎01/679 8833); Fountain Centre, College St, Belfast BT1 6ET (☎01232/324073); 10 Market Parade, St Patrick St, Cork (☎021/270900); Victoria Place, Eyre Square, Galway (☎091/565177); Central Buildings, O'Connell St, Limerick (☎061/415064); 36–37 Georges St, Waterford (☎051/872601); 33 Ferryquay St, Derry (☎01504/371888). Student and youth specialist for flights and trains.

GETTING THERE FROM NORTH AMERICA

TAROM is the only airline offering direct flights to Romania from North America, but only from New York and Chicago. Using a European carrier to get to Europe is probably your best bet as you get a good choice of departure cities, reliable and comfortable service, and direct flights to London, Paris or Frankfurt with connections to Romania. All the American airlines use European car-

riers for the final leg of their services to Romania.

Eurail train passes are not valid in Romania itself, but North Americans are eligible to purchase five-day **rail passes** for travel within Romania, available in advance before you travel or at any major Romanian train station.

SHOPPING FOR TICKETS

Barring special offers, the cheapest fare is usually an **Apex** ticket, although this will carry certain restrictions: you have to book – and pay – at least 21 days before departure, spend at least seven days abroad (maximum stay three months), and you tend to get penalized if you change your schedule. There are also winter **Super Apex** tickets, sometimes known as "Eurosavers" – slightly cheaper than an ordinary Apex, but limiting your stay to between 7 and 21 days. Some airlines also issue **Special Apex** tickets to people younger than 24, often extending the maximum stay to a year. Many airlines offer youth or student fares to **under-25s**; a passport or driving licence are sufficient proof of age, though these tickets are subject to availability and can have eccentric booking

AIRLINES

Air Canada Canada ☎1-800/555-1212 and ask for local toll-free number; USA ☎1-800/776-3000. Flights from major Canadian cities to London, Frankfurt, Paris and Amsterdam with connections to Bucharest.

Air France USA ☎1-800/237-2747; Canada ☎1-800/667-2747. Flights from Chicago, Houston, Los Angeles, Miami, Newark, New York, and San Francisco to Paris with connections to Bucharest.

British Airways USA ☎1-800/247-9297; Canada ☎1-800/668-1069; *www.british-airways.com* Flights from most major US and Canadian cities to London with connections to Bucharest.

Canadian International USA ☎1-800/426-7000; Canada ☎1-800/665-1177. Flights from major Canadian cities to London, Frankfurt, Paris and Amsterdam with connections to Bucharest.

ČSA Czechoslovak Airlines USA ☎1-800/223-2365. New York to Prague with connections to Bucharest.

Delta Airlines US ☎1-800/241-4141; in Canada call directory inquiries and ask for local toll-free number. Flights from New York to Frankfurt with connections to Bucharest.

LOT Polish Airlines USA ☎1-800/223-0593; Canada ☎1-800/361-1017. New York and Chicago to Warsaw with connections to Bucharest.

Lufthansa USA ☎1-800/645-3880; Canada ☎1-800/563-5954. New York, Chicago and Toronto to Frankfurt with connections to Bucharest.

Malév Hungarian Airlines USA ☎1-800/223-6884. New York to Budapest, with connections to Bucharest.

TAROM USA ☎212/687-6013. Twice a week from New York and Chicago direct to Bucharest.

United Airlines USA ☎1-800/538-2929. New York to London with connections to Bucharest.

DISCOUNT AGENTS, CONSOLIDATORS AND TRAVEL CLUBS

Council Travel, 205 E 42nd St, New York, NY 10017 (☎1-800/226 8624 or 212/822-2700; *cts@ciee.org*). Nationwide student travel organization with 60 branches all over the US.

Encore Travel Club, 4501 Forbes Blvd, Lanham, MD 20706 (☎1-800/444-9800). Discount travel club.

Interworld Travel, 800 Douglass Rd, Coral Gables, FL 33134 (☎1-800/468 3796 or 305/443-4929). Consolidator.

Last Minute Travel Club, 100 Sylvan Rd, Suite 600, Woburn, MA 01801(☎1-800/LAST MIN). Travel club specializing in stand-by deals.

Moment's Notice, 7301 New Utrecht Ave, Brooklyn, NY 11204 (☎718/234-6295 or 212/486-0500). Discount travel club.

New Frontiers/Nouvelles Frontières, 12 E 33rd St, New York, NY 10016 (☎1-800/366-6387 or 212/779-0600); 1180 Drummond St, Suite 330, Montréal PQ, H3G 2S1 (☎514/871-3030). French wholesale travel firm. Other branches in LA, San Francisco and Québec City.

Rail Europe, 226 Westchester Ave, White Plains, NY 10604 (☎1-800/438-7245 in USA; ☎1-800/361-7245). Can provide rail passes valid throughout all of Romania.

STA Travel, 10 Downing St, New York, NY 10014 (☎1-800/777-0112 or 212/627-3111). Worldwide specialist in independent travel with branches in Los Angeles, San Francisco and Boston.

TFI Tours International, 34 W 32nd St, New York, NY 10001 (☎1-800/745-0000 or 212/736 1140). Consolidator; other offices in Las Vegas, San Francisco, Los Angeles and Miami.

Travac, 989 6th Ave, New York NY 10018 (☎1-800/872-8800). Consolidator and charter broker; another branch in Orlando.

Travel Avenue, 10 S Riverside, Suite 1404, Chicago, IL 60606 (☎1-800/333-3335). Discount travel agent.

Travel CUTS/Voyages Campus, 187 College St, Toronto ON, M5T 1P7 (☎1-800/667 2887 or 416/979-2406). Canadian student travel organization with branches all over the country.

Travelers Advantage, 3033 S Parker Rd, Suite 900, Aurora, CO 80014 (☎1-800/548-1116). Discount travel club.

UniTravel, 1177 N Warson Rd, St Louis, MO 63132 (☎1-800/325-2222). Consolidator.

Worldwide Discount Travel Club, 1674 Meridian Ave, Miami Beach, FL 33139 (☎305/534-2082). Discount travel club.

conditions. It's worth remembering that most cheap return fares involve spending at least one Saturday night away and that many will only give a percentage refund if you need to cancel or alter your journey, so make sure you check the restrictions carefully before buying a ticket.

You can normally cut costs further by going through a **specialist flight agent** – either a **consolidator**, who buys up blocks of tickets from the airlines and sells them at a discount, or a **discount agent**, who wheels and deals in blocks of tickets offloaded by the airlines, and often offers special student and youth fares and a range of other travel-related services such as travel insurance, train passes, car rentals, tours and the like. Bear in mind, though, that penalties for changing your plans can be stiff. Remember, too, that these companies make their money by dealing in bulk – don't expect them to answer lots of questions. Some agents specialize in **charter flights**, which may be cheaper than anything available on a scheduled flight, but again departure dates are fixed and withdrawal penalties are high (check

the refund policy). If you travel a lot, **discount travel clubs** are another option – the annual membership fee may be worth it for benefits such as cut-price air tickets and car rental.

Regardless of where you buy your ticket, the **fare** will depend on the season. Fares to Europe are highest from around early June to mid-September, when the weather is best; they drop during the "shoulder" seasons (mid-September to November and mid-April to early June) and you'll get the best prices during the low season, November through to April (excluding Christmas and New Year when prices are hiked up and seats are at a premium). Note also that flying on weekends ordinarily adds $20–60 to the round-trip fare; the prices quoted below assume midweek travel and are exclusive of taxes.

FLIGHTS FROM THE USA

Although the major European carriers offer a good choice of departure points in the US, **New York JFK** is the primary gateway. TAROM, offering the only direct service to Bucharest, flies out of New York for

$463 low season ($563 high season). United's low season fare via London is $638 (high season $838). British Airways and Lufthansa offer the same low-season fare but rise to $898 in summer. ČSA is always worth trying for competitive rates, currently $598 low season ($858 high). Malév Hungarian Airlines charges the same fare to Budapest, which is just 5 hours and $15 from Oradea by train. Onward flights from Budapest to Bucharest are $258.

From **Chicago** expect to pay around $578 low season ($968 high) on TAROM, and $968 low season ($1028 high) on the major European carriers. LOT is a good bargain possibility with a low season fare of $752 ($952 high). On the West Coast, British Airways and Air France fly out of **Los Angeles** for $858 low season ($1118 high) via London and Paris respectively.

FLIGHTS FROM CANADA

Air Canada and **Canadian** have so many gateways in Canada that it's always worth checking out fares to London, Frankfurt, Paris or Amsterdam, and then picking up a European carrier to get you to Bucharest. Otherwise, British Airways and Lufthansa offer the most frequent flights, with good direct flights to London and Frankfurt from several departure cities and easy, short-layover connections to Bucharest.

British Airways serves Toronto, Vancouver and **Montréal**, with a Montréal–Bucharest fare via

London of CDN$1248 low season (CDN$1388 high season). Lufthansa flies out of **Toronto** to Bucharest via Frankfurt for CDN$1248 low season (CDN$1418 high season).

PACKAGES AND ORGANIZED TOURS

Package tours may not sound like your kind of travel, but don't dismiss the idea out of hand. If your trip is geared around special interests, packages can avoid a lot of the hassles you might incur making the same arrangements on arrival in Romania. A package can also be great for your peace of mind, if only to ensure a worry-free first week while you're finding your feet on a longer tour.

City breaks to Bucharest can start at around $300 (not including air fare). Quest Tours And Adventures offer a tour including three nights' accommodation in a 3/4 star hotel (something like a Days Inn) and a half-day's guided sightseeing starting at $321. They also offer 14 day **spa packages** starting at $900 (once again, excluding air fare). The self-proclaimed health resort specialist is Health Tours International which offers the "original guaranteed Gerovital H3 and Aslavital treatment" at the deluxe *Flora* hotel.

There are plenty of **Transylvania** tours on offer. Quest Tours and Adventures' 10-day "Romanian Experience" departs from Bucharest, takes in Sinaia, Braşov (including nearby Bran Castle), Sighişoara, Bistriţa and the Birgau Valley

---

SPECIALIST TOUR OPERATORS

Adventures Abroad, 20800 Westminster Highway, Suite 2148, Richmond BC, V6V 2W3, Canada (☎1-800/665-3998). Small-group trips including Bucovina and the Danube Delta.

Carpaţi International, Gypsy Trail Rd, Carmel NY 10512 (☎1-800/447-8742 or 766-2642 (ROMANIA), fax 1-914/225-2215; *carpati@aol.com* or *www.users.aol.com/carpati*).Offers an extensive variety of city packages, spa packages, seaside resort plans, tours of the Carpathian mountains and a tour which follows Dracula's footsteps.

Eastern Europe Tours, 600 Stewart St, Suite 524, Seattle, WA 98101 (☎1-800/641-3456). City packages to Bucharest and Dracula-themed tours.

Elderhostel, 75 Federal St, Boston, MA 02110 (☎617/426-8056). Specialists in educational and

activity programmes, cruises and homestays for senior travellers (companions may be younger).

Delta Dream Vacations Eastern Europe, 53 Summer St, Keene, NH 03431 (☎1-800/872-7786). Individual itineraries and hotel packages.

Health Pleasure Tours International, 25 West 43rd St, Suite 805, New York, NY 10036 (☎212/997-8510). Specializes in packages to Black Sea resorts and Romania's most famous health resorts.

Questers Worldwide Nature Tours, 381 Park Avenue South, Suite 1201 New York NY 10016 (☎1-800/468-8668 or 212/251-0444). Wildlife tours.

Quest Tours And Adventures, 1 World Trade Center, 121 SW Salmon St, Suite 1100, Portland, OR 97204 (☎1-800/621-8687, fax 1-503/777-0224; *www.romtour.com//@tour*). A wide variety of set tours and fully customized packages.

and costs from $750 (depending on the size of the group). Of the **Dracula-related tours**, visiting places popularized in Bram Stoker's book, Quest Tours and Adventures' eight-day "Halloween Tour", starting at $1757, including round-trip air fare, accommodation, meals, deluxe coach tour, masked ball and "other surprises" sounds the most fun, while Eastern Europe Tours offers a more personalized version with private car and driver starting from $1919.

GETTING THERE FROM AUSTRALIA & NEW ZEALAND

From Australia and New Zealand, there are reasonable connecting services to Bucharest via Bangkok, Moscow, Rome, Athens and Singapore. The national airline, TAROM, has an agent in Australia only – the Eastern Europe Travel Bureau (see box for details).

Another option is to fly to any other European city, such as Frankfurt or Vienna, and travel overland to Romania. All destinations in Europe are "common rated" – you pay the same fare whatever your destination – so this option rarely works out cheaper than buying a discounted airfare all the way, but can be a good idea if you are visiting Romania as part of a longer trip around Europe. Eurail passes can be used for overland travel to countries bordering Romania but not within the country itself.

Round-the-world tickets which take in Bucharest are limited. Qantas–British Airway's "Global Explorer" fare starting at A$2599/NZ$3089 is probably the most versatile allowing

AIRLINES

Aeroflot Australia ☎02/9262 2233. No NZ office. Several flights a week to Moscow from Sydney and twice weekly from Perth, with onward connections to Bucharest.

Air France Australia ☎02/9321 1000; New Zealand ☎09/303 3521. Several flights a week to Paris with onward connections to Bucharest from Sydney, Brisbane, Cairns and Perth via Singapore.

Alitalia Australia ☎02/9247 1308; New Zealand ☎09/379 4457. Several flights a week to Rome via Bangkok with onward connections to Bucharest from Sydney.

British Airways Australia ☎02/9258 3300; New Zealand ☎09/356 8690. Code share with Qantas to offer their "Global Explorer" round-the-world ticket

Garuda Australia ☎02/9334 9944 or 1800/800873; New Zealand ☎09/366 1855. Several flights a week to Paris/Rome/Zurich/Frankfurt from major Australian cities and Auckland via either a transfer or stopover in Denpasar or Jakarta.

Japan Airlines Australia ☎02/9272 1111; New Zealand ☎09/379 9906. Several flights a week to Paris/Zurich/Frankfurt via an overnight stopover in either Tokyo or Osaka from Sydney, Brisbane and Auckland.

Lufthansa Australia ☎02/9367 3888; New Zealand ☎09/303 1529. Several flights a week to Frankfurt via Bangkok and Vienna from Sydney, Melbourne and Auckland with onward connections to Bucharest with TAROM.

Malaysia Airlines Australia ☎1300/2627; New Zealand ☎09/373 2741. Several flights a week to Vienna from major Australian and New Zealand cities via Kuala Lumpur.

Olympic Airlines S.A. Australia ☎02/9251 2044; no NZ office. Twice weekly service to Bucharest from Sydney via Singapore and Athens.

Qantas Australia ☎1300/1211; New Zealand ☎09/357 8900 or 0800/808767. Daily flights to Frankfurt via Bangkok from major Australian cities and via Sydney and Bangkok from Auckland.

TAROM Australia ☎02/9262 1144; no NZ office. Twice weekly flights from Bangkok to Bucharest; code share with Qantas/Thai from Major Australian and New Zealand Cities.

Thai Airways Australia ☎1300/1960; New Zealand ☎09/377 3886. Several flights a week to Zurich and Frankfurt via either a transfer or stopover in Bangkok from Sydney, Brisbane, Melbourne, Perth and Auckland four sectors within Europe and routing via the US, Asia and Africa.

Whatever kind of ticket you're after, your first call should be to one of the specialist travel agents listed in the box below. If you're a student or under 26, you should be able to undercut the fares quoted below; STA is a good place to start.

Each airline has its own fare structure, though high season is usually mid-May to the end of August and December to mid-January; shoulder seasons are March to mid-May and all of September.

FLIGHTS FROM AUSTRALIA

TAROM flies twice weekly to Bucharest, using Qantas, British Airways or Thai Airways for the first leg to Bangkok, for A$1900 low season A$2200 high season. However the lowest fares, starting around A$1750–2300, are with Olympic

DISCOUNT AND SPECIALIST AGENTS

Anywhere Travel, 345 Anzac Parade, Kingsford, Sydney (☎02/9663 0411).

Brisbane Discount Travel, 260 Queen St, Brisbane (☎07/3229 9211).

Budget Travel, 16 Fort St, Auckland, plus branches around the city (☎09/366 0061 or 0800/808040).

Destinations Unlimited, 3 Milford Rd, Auckland (☎09/373 4033).

Flight Centres Australia: 82 Elizabeth St, Sydney, plus branches nationwide (☎1300/1600). New Zealand: 205 Queen St, Auckland (☎09/309 6171), plus branches nationwide. Good discounts on flights.

Northern Gateway, 22 Cavenagh St, Darwin (☎08/8941 1394).

STA Travel, Australia: 702 Harris St, Ultimo, Sydney; 256 Flinders St, Melbourne; other offices in state capitals and major universities (nearest branch ☎13 00/1776, fastfare telesales ☎1300/360960). New Zealand: 10 High St, Auckland (☎09/309 0458, fastfare telesales ☎09/366 6673), plus branches in Wellington, Christchurch, Dunedin, Palmerston North, Hamilton and at major universities. Web site *www.statravelaus.com.au* Discount flights for students and under 26s.

Thomas Cook, Australia: 175 Pitt St, Sydney; 257 Collins St, Melbourne; plus branches in other state capitals (local branch ☎1300/1771, Thomas Cook Direct telesales ☎1800/063913); New Zealand: 96 Anzac Ave, Auckland (☎09/379 3920).

SPECIALIST AGENTS AND OPERATORS

As yet there are no air-tour packages to Romania from Australasia, so the tours listed below are land only; however, most agents will also be able to arrange flights.

Adventure World, 73 Walker St, North Sydney (☎02/956 7766); 8 Victoria Ave, Perth (☎09/221 2300); 101 Great South Rd, Remuera, Auckland (☎09/524 5118). Agents for Explore's ten-day escorted tours through the Maramureş and Danube Delta regions.

Eastern Europe Travel Bureau, 75 King St, Sydney (☎02/9262 1144, fax 9262 4479); 343 Little Collins St, Melbourne (☎03/9600 0299, fax 9670 1793); 131 Elizabeth St, Brisbane (☎07/3229 9716); also branches in Adelaide and Perth. Bucharest stopovers, 5- to 8-day tours of Romania's medieval monasteries and castles. TAROM's sales agents.

Eastern Eurotours, Seabank Centre, 12–14 Marine Parade, Southport (☎07/5591 0326). Transylvanian ski and snowboarding holidays, and Dracula tours from Poiana Braşov.

Eurolynx, 3/20 Fort St, Auckland (☎09/379 9716). Bucharest accommodation and city sightseeing tours.

Gateway Travel, 5/75 King St, Sydney (☎02/9745 3333). Can arrange accommodation and tours.

Passport Travel, 320b Glenferrie Rd, Malvern, Melbourne (☎03/9824 7183). Agents for Sherpa's 15-day escorted walks in the Carpathian Mountains.

Thor Travel, 228 Rundle St, Adelaide (☎08/232 3155). Walking holidays in the Carpathian Mountains and Transylvania Alps.

Topdeck Travel, 8th floor, 350 Kent St, Sydney. (☎02/9299 8844 or 1800/800724). Agents for Exodus's 15-day treks in the Transylvanian Alps.

Travel Plan, 72 Chandos St, St Leonards, Sydney (☎02/9438 1333). Skiing in Transylvania.

Airways via Athens, Lufthansa via Frankfurt and Alitalia via Rome, while Aeroflot flies to Bucharest via Moscow for A$1900. For a little more (A$1950–2300) Ansett–Swiss Air fly to Bucharest via Zurich. Both Aeroflot and Lufthansa code share with an Asian carrier for the first leg.

If you're planning to travel overland via another European city, the best deals are with Garuda, to Frankfurt via Jakarta or Denpasar (A$1550–2000), and with Malaysia Airlines to Vienna via Kuala Lumpur from around A$1850.

Flights from eastern cities are common rated, but if you're travelling from Perth deduct A$300–400.

FLIGHTS FROM NEW ZEALAND

From New Zealand, Alitalia flies to Bucharest via Rome from NZ$2499. There's also a Qantas–Lufthansa combination via Singapore starting at NZ$2350. You'll get good-value flights to a range of other European destinations with Japanese Airlines (overnight wait in Tokyo) and Garuda, starting from around NZ$2099; Thai from NZ$2200, and Malaysia Airlines from NZ$2400.

All flights, except Qantas, serve Auckland only, so you'll need to add on around NZ$90 for Christchurch connections.

VISAS AND RED TAPE

You'll need a full passport to enter Romania, plus a visa unless you're a citizen of the USA, one of the formerly socialist states or a very few other countries such as Cyprus, Mexico, Tunisia or Turkey. Visas are included (nominally at £6/$10) in the cost of package holidays, and you may get in for free even if you just have a hotel reservation. Otherwise, you can obtain your visa in advance from a consulate or embassy, or on arrival at the country's borders or the airport.

A **tourist visa** is valid for thirty days within three months of issue and costs £33/A$50/NZ$50 if issued in advance; applications can either be lodged in person at the embassy or by post. You will need to show a current passport and proof of adequate funds, and if you're applying by post

you'll also need to enclose a money order for the full amount along with an SAE. If you buy your visa on arrival, it is usually cheaper, costing about £21/$33 on entry.

Transit visas, valid for three days' stay within one month of issue, cost £20/$30 at the border (£25/$45 at an embassy); double transit visas (two three-day visas) cost £33/$55.

US citizens simply need to fill in an immigration form on arrival at the airport.

Overstaying is an offence generally solved by means of a "tip" to the (notoriously corrupt) border police, but it is preferable to obtain a **visa extension** from any *judeţ* (county) police headquarters or the seedy, unmarked office on the first floor at Str. Nicolae Iorga 27 in Bucharest (Mon, Wed & Fri 9.30am–1pm, Tues 5.30pm–10pm, Thurs 9.30am–2pm & 5.30–8pm, Sat 9.30am–1pm). In Bucharest, you'll be sent to the CEC bank on Piaţa Amzei to pay your fee (another $25 plus $6 for "urgent" service, in lei with a bank receipt for hard currency, and then you must return with the receipt to Strada Iorga; here they may tell you to return in a day or two, although there is no reason for this and a few dollars will speed things up.

CUSTOMS

Romanian customs don't generally search tourists' luggage very closely, but they do have some byzantine **regulations**. You can import reasonable quantities of food, clothing and medica-

ROMANIAN EMBASSIES AND CONSULATES ABROAD

Britain 4 Palace Green, London W8 4QD (☎0171/937 9667); *visa@roemb.demon.co.uk*

Australia 4 Balmainn Cresent, O'Malley, Canberra ACT (☎02/6290 2442).

Austria Prinz-Eugen-Strasse 60, 1040 Vienna (☎1/505 3227).

Belgium 105 Rue Gabrielle, 1180 Brussels (☎2/345 2680).

Bulgaria Sitnyakovo 4, Sofia (☎2/70.70.47).

Canada 655 Rideau St, Ottawa, ON K1N 6A3 (☎613/232-5345); 111 Peter St, Suite 530, Toronto ON, M5V 2H1 (☎416/585-5802); 1111 St Urbain, Suite M-01, Montréal PQ, H2Z 1Y6 (☎514/876-1793).

Czech Republic Nerudova 5, 12544 Prague 1 (☎02/53.30.59).

France 5 Rue de l'Exposition, 75007 Paris (☎01.40.62.22.02).

Germany Legionsweg 14, 5300 Bonn 1 (☎228/555 860).

Hungary Thököly útca 72, 1146 Budapest (☎1/268 0271).

Ireland 60 Merrion Rd, Ballsbridge, Dublin 4 (☎01/668 1336).

Republica Moldova Vlaicu Pîrcălab 39, Chişinău (☎3732/22.75.83).

USA 200 East 38th St, New York, NY 10016 (☎212/682-9122); 1607 23rd Street NW, Washington DC 20008-2809 (☎202/232-4747 or 232-3694, fax 232-4748, *www.embassy.org/romania*).

tion (including contraceptives) for personal use, two cameras and one video camera, with film. If the details of your camera get written in your passport, you will have to produce it (or a police theft report) when you leave.

On **departure**, you can carry enough food and medicine for a 24-hour journey and up to L500,000; valuable souvenirs must be supported by exchange documents to show that they were purchased by legitimate means. Carpets and works of art can be taken out as long as they don't appear to be antiques. With the closure of Serbia, drug-runners from Turkey and Asia now often pass through Romania, and checks are being tightened up.

INSURANCE

Most people will find it essential to take out a good travel insurance policy. Many bank and credit cards (particularly American Express and Barclaycard) offer some degree of medical or other insurance, especially if you use them to pay for your trip. This can be quite comprehensive, anticipating anything from lost or stolen baggage and missed connections to charter companies going bankrupt; however, certain policies (notably in North America) only cover medical costs.

Note that very few insurers will arrange on-the-spot payments in the event of a major expense or loss; you will usually be reimbursed only after going home. In all cases of loss or theft of goods, you will have to contact the local police to have a **report** made out so that your insurer can process the claim. This can be a tricky business in Romania since many officials outside the big cities may not be accustomed to the process or may expect a tip, and making yourself understood can be a problem, but be persistent.

A standard insurance policy may not cover you for **water sports**, **hiking**, **climbing** or **skiing**; check carefully to see if you should pay an extra premium. Snowcard Insurance Services (Freepost 4135, Lower Boddington, Daventry, Northants NN11 6BR; ☎01327/262 805) specialize in mountaineering and activity holiday travel insurance.

EUROPEAN COVER

In Britain and Ireland, travel insurance schemes (from around £21 a month) are sold by almost every travel agent or bank, and by specialist insurance companies. Cover varies, but a standard policy will cover the cost of cancellation and curtailment of flights, medical expenses, travel delay, accident, missed departures, lost passport, personal liability and legal expenses. If you have a good "all risks" home insurance policy it may well cover your possessions against loss or theft even when overseas, or your insurer may be willing to extend your cover, for another £5 or so. Many private medical schemes also cover you when abroad – make sure you know the procedure and the helpline number.

Policies issued by Campus Travel or STA (see p.4 for addresses), Columbus Travel Insurance (17 Devonshire Square, London EC2M 4SQ; ☎0171/375 0011), Endsleigh Insurance (97 Southampton Row, London WC1B 4AG; ☎0171/436 4451), Frizzell Insurance (Frizzell House, County Gates, Bournemouth, Dorset BH1 2NF; ☎01202/292 333) and Worldwide (Elm Lane, Tonbridge, Kent TN10 3XS; ☎01732/773366) are all good value.

Some insurance companies will not offer cover to **travellers over 65**, and most that do charge hefty premiums. The best policies for the older traveller are offered by Age Concern (☎01883/346964), Inter Assurance (☎01252/717766), and Club Direct (☎01243/787838).

NORTH AMERICAN COVER

In the US and Canada, insurance tends to be much more expensive, and may include medical cover only. Before buying a policy, check that you're not already covered by existing insurance plans. **Canadians** are usually covered by their provincial health plans; **students** and other holders of ISIC/teacher/youth cards are entitled to $3000 worth of accident coverage and sixty days ($100 per day) of in-patient hospital treatment for the card's period of validity. Student health coverage often extends during the vacations and for one term beyond the date of last enrolment. **Household** insurance often covers theft or loss of documents, money and valuables while overseas, though conditions and maximum amounts vary from company to company.

Only after exhausting the possibilities above might you want to contact a **specialist travel**

insurance company; your travel agent can usually recommend one. Isis (through travel agencies) charges $50 for fifteen days, $80 for a month and $150 for three months. Two companies also worth trying are Access America, 6600 West Broad St, Richmond, VA 23230 (☎1-800/955-4002 or 804/285-2300), and Travel Guard, 1145 Clark St, Stevens Point, WI 54481 (☎1-800/826-1300 or 715/345-0505). Frequent travellers get a good deal from Travel Assistance International (☎1-800/821-2828), which charges $200 for a whole year's coverage (90 days maximum per trip).

None of these policies insure against **theft** of anything while overseas. North American travel policies apply only to items **lost** from, or **damaged** in, the custody of an identifiable, responsible third party – hotel porter, airline, luggage consignment, etc.

AUSTRALASIAN COVER

As in Europe, travel insurance policies are widely available through your travel agent and offer cover for periods ranging from a few days to a year or even longer. Most policies are similar in premium and coverage – typically costing A$100/NZ$110 for 2 weeks, A$170/NZ$190 for 1 month and A$250/NZ$275 for 2 months. Two **companies** worth trying are Cover More (9/32 Walker St, North Sydney; ☎02/9202 8000 & 1800/251 881) and Ready Plan, with offices in Australia (141 Walker St, Dandenong, Melbourne; ☎03/9791 5077 & 1800/337 462) and New Zealand. (10/63 Albert St, Auckland; ☎09/379 3208).

As with all policies, make sure that you are covered for any sporting or outdoor activities you might be planning.

TRAVELLERS WITH DISABILITIES

Very little attention has been paid to the needs of the disabled in Romania, as in the rest of Eastern Europe. There is little sign of any major change in attitudes, and not much money to do a lot anyway. Perhaps the best solution is to book a stay in a spa (see p.22), where there should at least be a degree of level access and some awareness of the needs of those in wheelchairs.

Transport is a major problem, as public transport is often inaccessible and cars with hand controls are not available from the car rental companies. However, it should be possible to reach Arad, Alba Iulia, Sighişoara, Braşov, Sinaia and Bucharest relatively easily by train, reserving a place in Austrian carriages, for instance on the *Dacia* (see p.6).

As with any trip abroad, read your **travel insurance** small print carefully to make sure that people with a pre-existing medical condition are not excluded. Use your travel agent or tour operator to make your journey simpler: airlines or bus companies can cope better if they are expecting you. A **medical certificate** of your fitness to travel, provided by your doctor, is also extremely useful; some airlines or insurance companies may insist on it. Make sure you carry a **prescription** for any drugs you need, including the generic name in case of emergency, and spares of any special clothing or equipment as it's unlikely you'll find them in Romania.

CONTACTS

BRITAIN

Holiday Care Service, 2 Old Bank Chambers, Station Rd, Horley, Surrey RH6 9HW (☎01293/774535). Information on all aspects of travel.

Mobility International, 228 Borough High St, London SE1 1JX (☎0171/403 5688). Information, access guides, tours and exchange programmes.

RADAR (Royal Association for Disability and Rehabilitation), 12 City Forum, 250 City Rd, London EC1V 8AF (☎0171/250 3222; Minicom ☎0171/250 4119). Limited information on travel in Romania.

Tripscope, The Courtyard, Evelyn Rd, London W4 5JL (☎0181/994 9294). National telephone information service offering free advice on international transport and travel for those with a mobility problem.

NORTH AMERICA

Directions Unlimited, 720 N Bedford Rd, Bedford Hills, NY 10507 (☎914/241-1700). Travel agency specializing in custom tours for people with disabilities.

Jewish Rehabilitation Hospital, 3205 Place Alton Goldbloom, Chomedy Laval, Quebec PQ, H7V 1RT (☎514/688-9550, ext. 226). Guidebooks and travel information.

Mobility International USA, PO Box 10767, Eugene, OR 97440 (Voice and TDD: ☎541/343-1284). Information and referral services, access guides, tours and exchange programmes. Annual membership $25 (includes quarterly newsletter).

SATH (Society for the Advancement of Travel for the Handicapped), 347 5th Ave, Suite 610, New York, NY 10016 (☎212/447-7284; www.sittravel.com). Non-profit travel-industry referral service that passes queries on to its members as appropriate; allow plenty of time for a response.

Travel Information Service (☎215/456-9600). Telephone information and referral service.

Twin Peaks Press, Box 129, Vancouver, WA 98666 (☎360/694-2462 or 1-800/637-2256). Publisher of the *Directory of Travel Agencies for the Disabled* ($19.95), listing more than 370 agencies worldwide; *Travel for the Disabled* ($19.95); the *Directory of Accessible Van Rentals* ($9.95) and *Wheelchair Vagabond* ($14.95), loaded with personal tips.

AUSTRALIA

ACROD (Australian Council for Rehabilitation of the Disabled), PO Box 60, Curtin, ACT 2605 (☎02/6282 4333).

NEW ZEALAND

Disabled Persons Assembly, 173–175 Victoria St, Wellington (☎04/811 9100).

COSTS, MONEY AND BANKS

Travellers will find costs low in Romania, and even when prices rise, the exchange rate soon tends to compensate. The more expensive hotels, flights, car rental and ONT excursions are priced in US dollars, but must be paid for in lei, together with a receipt to show that the money has been exchanged officially. You may also need to show an exchange receipt in order to buy international train tickets.

Travelling independently, a few **savings and reductions** are possible. InterRail passes are valid; **students** studying in Romania can claim a 30 percent discount on international rail and air fares, while ISIC and IUS student cards theoretically entitle you to a reduction of up to 50 percent on the price of camping, and free or reduced admission to museums. In practice the relevant officials may say no, and there's little you can do about it.

BASIC COSTS

Accommodation is likely to be your main expense, although the lowest-grade hotels charge from just £2.50/$4 for a single room, £4/$6 for a double and you could pay as much as $250 for a room in the most expensive hotels. ACR vouchers (see p.32) will guarantee you a good room in some of the better hotels. For rock-bottom budget travellers, the alternatives are *cabanas* (£2/$3 per bed), or campsites (around £2/$3 per person; slightly less with a student card). Such accommodation is usually situated

out of town, and can be awkward to reach by public transport.

The cost of eating out varies considerably, but you can get a **meal** with a glass of wine or beer for between £1.50/$2 and £7/$10 providing you avoid restaurants in the most expensive hotels, imported drinks (especially whisky) or such delicacies as caviar or sturgeon – and providing that there's a restaurant to be found. **Public transport** is cheap – it costs less than £3/$5 to take an express train from one side of Romania to the other – but car rental involves various charges on top of the basic rate of £12/$21 a day.

MONEY

Romania's **currency** is the leu (meaning lion; plural **lei**), which comes in coins of denominations up to 100 lei and notes up to 50,000 lei. Theoretically the leu is divided into 100 bani, but these fiddly little coins are no longer used and should be refused, as should any remaining L100 notes.

The exchange rate is currently around L12,000 to the pound sterling (L8000 to the US dollar), and the rate seems to have stabilized at last. The leu is not an international currency, but if you want to check the current rate, the *Thomas Cook European Timetable* and *The European* are good places to look.

BANKS AND EXCHANGE

Changing money involves least hassle at the private exchange offices (*casa de schimb valuta*) found in most towns, or at ONT offices and major hotels. Queuing and piles of documents are the norm in any bank (*banca*), and they're usually only open for a few hours on weekday mornings anyway, usually 9am–noon. Avoid the sharks hanging around the tourist hotels and exchange counters, as the risks outweigh the slim gains.

Keep your exchange receipts (*borderou de schimb*), since you may need to show them before you can use your cash for accommodation or international tickets, or to obtain a refund in hard currency (*valuta*) when leaving Romania. Note that few places will exchange lei for hard currency, and you cannot spend your lei in the duty-free shop at Otopeni airport – so it's advisable to change only small amounts of hard currency into lei at a time. It's safest to carry some of your money in **travellers' cheques**, but also wise to take plenty of **dollar bills**, some in small denominations; **Deutschmarks** are also in demand, with sterling and other currencies less welcome. The private counters much prefer cash and are only just beginning to accept travellers' cheques. Even in a bank you may have to show the receipt from the issuing bank, or another cheque to prove continuity of serial numbers; in any case rates are far better for cash. American Express and Thomas Cook are the only brands of travellers' cheques that are generally recognized, and only the former has a Romanian agent (see Bucharest listings) and can guarantee a speedy refund in case of loss.

Hotels, airlines, the big car rental companies and the more upmarket stores and restaurants will usually accept **credit cards** – Amex, MasterCard, Visa and perhaps Diners Club – but elsewhere, plastic money is useless. Visa **cash machines** (Bancomat) are now to be found in major towns (usually at the Banca Comercială Română); these should accept cards from almost any Western bank and are well worth seeking out (most are listed in the guide). If you can draw money from a current account you'll get a good rate and pay just £1.50/$2 per transaction. Credit-card cash withdrawals tend to be more expensive; an over the counter cash advance will cost you at least 4.25 percent in commission plus high daily interest charges and the bank will probably insist on giving you dollars or Deutschmarks and then changing them into lei, charging you each time. Hotels and the like will add a credit-card surcharge of between 5 and 20 percent.

THE BLACK MARKET

There is now little profit to be made by changing money on the **black market**. The exchange rate at the street kiosks is almost as good as with the black marketeers, and it's a *much* safer deal – the police do not inspire as much fear as before 1989, so rip-off merchants are common.

If you do need to raise extra funds, you could do as the locals do, and sell your foreign goods at one of the many *consignaţie* shops. Obviously, things like personal stereos fetch a good price, as do unused trainers and other trendy gear.

HEALTH

No vaccinations are required to visit Romania, but hepatitis A, polio and typhoid boosters would be wise if you're planning to stay in remote areas where cooking and sanitation are sometimes none too hygienic. There's a reciprocal health agreement between Romania and Western countries, so that emergency treatment (excluding drugs) is free. Don't forget to take out travel insurance (see p.17) in case of serious illness or accident. Keep all receipts so you can reclaim the money later.

SPECIFIC HAZARDS

Beyond an occasional sore throat from traffic fumes, Romania's pollution and other environmental problems are unlikely to have much effect on any short-term visitor. **Diarrhoea** can be a problem, so stock up with Lomotil before you leave (remember that this treats only symptoms, not causes), besides any specific medication required. Bring **tampons and contraceptives** with you, since these are hard to find in Romania. In summer you'll also need a strong **sun block**, and very strong **insect repellent** if visiting the Danube Delta. **Dogs** should be avoided (there's a slight risk of rabies), but **tap water** is safe to drink practically everywhere, and you'll find taps or drinking fountains at many train stations. However, there have recently been isolated outbreaks of cholera in Tîrgu Mureş and on the coast. Bottled water (*apă minerala*) is widely available.

HIV AND AIDS

AIDS (SIDA) was first identified in Romania in 1984, but the government refused to admit its existence until 1987, and took no effective measures to control the re-use of hypodermic needles before the revolution. In 1990 there were officially 1000 AIDS cases, and in late 1994, 3136 cases

SPAS

Spa holidays are much favoured by Romanians, following the Hapsburg tradition, and the country boasts one third of all Europe's mineral springs, and 160 spa resorts (*băile*). The theory is that you stay in a resort for about eighteen days, following a prescribed course of treatment, and ideally return regularly over the next few years.

However, for the tourist, if you can get cheap accommodation (best booked at a travel agency in almost any town) a spa can be a good base for a leisurely holiday. In any case it's worth bearing in mind that even the smallest spas have campsites and restaurants.

The basic treatment naturally involves drinking the **waters**, which come in an amazing variety: alkaline, chlorinated, radioactive, carbogaseous, and sodium-, iodine-, magnesium-, sulphate- or iron-bearing. In addition you can bathe in hot springs or sapropelic muds, breath in foul fumes at mofettes, or indulge in a new generation of complementary **therapies** such as ultrasound and aerosol treatment, ultraviolet light baths, acupuncture and electrotherapy. A great

deal of work has been done to put a scientific gloss on spa treatment, and drugs such as Pellamar, Gerovital H3 and Aslavital, said to stop and even reverse the ageing process, have been developed here. Treatment is available at all major spas, and at the *Flora* hotel in Bucharest and the *Otopeni* clinic, 2km from the airport.

The spas all have their own areas of specialization: Sovata is the best place for **gynaecological problems**; Covasna, Vatra Dornei and Buziaş deal with **cardiovascular complaints**; Călimăneşti-Căciulata, Slănic Moldova, Sîngeorz-Băi and Băile Olăneşti with the **digestion**; and others (notably Băile Herculane and Băile Felix) with a range of **locomotive and rheumatic ailments**. Mountain resorts such as Sinaia, Băile Tuşnad and Moneasa treat **nervous complaints**, not with water but with fresh air that has an ideal balance of ozone and ions.

ONT distributes a booklet and makes bookings from abroad, although given current levels of business, you can save money by booking in Romania if you have time.

of HIV infection were admitted; but these are certainly underestimates, as random samples suggested a figure of 130,000. These are almost all children, infected by the perverse custom of giving babies "microtransfusions", usually with dirty needles, to fortify them.

PHARMACIES,DOCTORS & HOSPITALS

In case of minor complaints, go to a **pharmacy** (*farmacie*), where the staff are usually well trained and have the authority to prescribe drugs, and – in the big towns at least – may understand English, French or German. In theory, one pharmacy in each town should be open 24 hours, or at least display in the window an emergency number – these are listed in the guide.

In Bucharest, the British and American embassies can supply the address of an English-speaking **doctor or dentist**, and there's a special clinic for treating foreigners. In **emergencies dial ☎961** or ask someone to contact the local casualty (*stația de salvare*) or first aid (*prim ajutor*) stations, which should have ambulances. Each county capital has a fairly well-equipped County Hospital (*Spital Judeţean*), but **hospitals** and health centres (*policlinics*) in smaller towns can be dire, and most places suffer from demoralized staff and a shortage of drugs. Foreigners are likely to receive preferential treatment, but Romanians routinely pay large tips to doctors and nurses to ensure that they're well cared for.

INFORMATION AND MAPS

Romania's national tourist office – the ONT, sometimes known abroad as Carpaţi – produces a range of maps, brochures and special interest booklets (on spas and folklore, for example), distributed in the appropriate

ROMANIAN TOURIST OFFICES ABROAD

Britain, 83A Marylebone High St, London WIM 3DE (☎ & fax 01/1/224 3692).
USA, 342 Madison Ave, #210, New York, NY 10173 (☎212/697-6971, fax 697-6972; *rnto@mail.idt.net*).

languages through their offices abroad (see box below). During the summer, ONT operates special tours for visitors including transport and accommodation, along popular routes. For more details see "Getting Around", p.26.

TOURIST OFFICES

In Romania, almost all of the **county tourist offices** (OJT) have been privatized: this hasn't made a huge difference, as they have always been more concerned with selling package trips to spas and beach resorts than with providing information.

ROMANIA ONLINE

As you might expect, there is not a great deal of information about Romania on the Internet, but the following sites might be useful.

The Embassy of Romania – Travel and Tourism
http://www.embassy.org/romania/travel/travel.html
Besides the reams of diplomatic information and the rhetoric on the "vibrant new post-revolutionary country", there are some useful addresses and tips for the would-be tourist in Romania.

Quest Tours and Adventures
http://www.teleport.com/~tour/
Web site of the US tour operator, with some interesting accounts of specialized Romanian trips, details on car rental and booking accommodation, as well as a look at the country and its history and culture.

Radio Romania International
http://indis.ici.ro/romania/news/rador.html
Daily Romanian news in English.

Romania – Encyclopedic Survey
http://indis.ici.ro/romania/romania.html
A dull name for a fairly interesting site – with pages on the history, culture and politics of Romania as well as many aspects of tourism, including a **Dracula home page**, which gives information on tourist destinations for the Dracula freak.

Romanian Press Review
http://www.halcyon.com/rompr
An in-depth look at Romanian life, politics, business and economy.

Romanian Students' Association
http://students.missouri.edu/~romsa
Written by Romanian students in America wishing "to make Romania known and loved by as many people as possible". Provides a good overview of the country, its history and culture, and has many suggestions for excursions throughout Romania.

MAP OUTLETS

BRITAIN

Stanfords in London is the UK's largest map sellers, and operates a mail order service. The UK-wide general booksellers Waterstone's and Dillons usually have comprehensive map departments, as do the less widely found Blackwell's, dotted around the country.

Aberdeen Map Shop, 74 Skene St, Aberdeen, AB10 1QE (☎01224/637999). Mail order.

Blackwell's, 156–160 West St, Sheffield, S1 3ST (☎0114/273 8906). General bookshop selling a big range of foreign maps; mail order service. Also 13–17 Royal Arcade, Cardiff, CF1 2PR (☎01222/395036); Blackwell's University Bookshop, Alsop Building, Brownlow Hill, Liverpool, L3 5TX (☎0151/709 8146); 53 Broad St, Oxford OX1 3BQ (☎01865/792792); 32 Stonegate, York YO1 2AP (☎01904/624531).

Call of the Wild, 21 Station St, Keswick, Cumbria CA12 5HH (☎01768/771014). Adventure travel with international maps reflecting the mountaineering/walking slant; some more general maps available.

Heffers Map Shop, 3rd Floor, in Heffers Stationery Department, 19 Sidney St, Cambridge, CB2 3HL (☎01223/568467). Mail order available from here; more maps and travel literature at their excellent bookshop at 20 Trinity Street.

James Thin Melven's Bookshop, 29 Union St, Inverness, IV1 1QA (☎01463/233500). Established 1849; map department with all foreign maps; mail order specialist.

John Smith and Sons, 57–61 St Vincent St, Glasgow, G2 5TB (☎0141/221 7472). Specialist map department in long-established booksellers. Full range of foreign maps; mail order service.

The Map Shop, 30a Belvoir St, Leicester, LE1 6QH (☎0116/2471400); 15 High St, Upton-upon-Severn, Worcestershire WR8 0HJ (☎01684/593146). Domestic and foreign maps; mail order available.

National Map Centre, 22–24 Caxton St, SW1H 0QU (☎0171/222 2466).

Newcastle Map Centre, 55 Grey St, Newcastle upon Tyne, NE1 6EF (☎0191/261 5622). Ordnance survey stockists; also keep a good range of foreign maps.

Stanfords, 12–14 Long Acre, WC2E 9LP (☎0171/836 1321); map by mail or phone order are available on this number. Other branches in London are located within Campus Travel at 52 Grosvenor Gardens, SW1W 0AG (☎0171/730 1314), and within the British Airways offices at 156 Regent St, W1R 5TA (☎0171/434 4744); also at 29 Corn Street, Bristol BS1 1HT (☎0117/929 9966).

The Travel Bookshop, 13–15 Blenheim Crescent, W11 2EE (☎0171/229 5260).

Opening hours are, in theory, Mon–Fri 9am–4pm and Sat 9am–noon, but they are pretty unreliable and you'll generally have to take pot luck.

MAPS

A number of maps appear in the guide section of this book, but it's always worth asking at tourist offices and hotel reception desks for a **town plan** (*plan oraşului*) or **county map** (*hartă judeţean*). They are usually of pre-revolutionary vintage, and thus feature various Communist-era street names

which have since changed, but these maps detail everything from monuments to filling stations, and though most are only in Romanian, they aren't hard to understand.

Among maps published outside Romania, the Cartographia and Falk maps of Bucharest are the most useful. Their maps of Romania (Falk's at 1:1,000,000 and Cartographia's at 1:750,000), along with the Kümmerley & Frey map of Romania and Bulgaria (1:1,000,000) are also good, while The GeoCenter Euromap (1:800,000) includes the Republica Moldova. The most

Waterstone's, 91 Deansgate, Manchester, M3 2BW (☎0161/832 1992). Particularly good map department in this branch of the UK-wide chain of bookshops; mail order service.

Whiteman's Bookshop, 7 Orange Grove, Bath BA1 1LP (☎01225/464029). General bookshop with an extensive range of maps; special orders taken and available by mail.

IRELAND

Easons Bookshop, 40 O'Connell St, Dublin 1 (☎01/873 3811).

Fred Hanna's Bookshop, 27–29 Nassau St, Dublin 2 (☎01/677 1255).

Hodges Figgis Bookshop, 56–58 Dawson St, Dublin 2 (☎01/677 4754).

Waterstone's, Queens Bldg, 8 Royal Ave, Belfast BT1 1DA (☎01232/247355); 7 Dawson St, Dublin 2 (☎01/679 1260); 69 Patrick St, Cork (☎021/ 276522).

USA

The Complete Traveller Bookstore, 199 Madison Ave, New York, NY 10016 (☎212/685-9007).

Map Link, 30 S La Petera Lane, Unit #5, Santa Barbara, CA 93117 (☎805/692-6777).

The Map Store Inc., 1636 1st St, Washington DC 20006 (☎202/628-2608).

Phileas Fogg's Books & Maps, #87 Stanford Shopping Center, Palo Alto, CA 94304 (☎1-800/533-FOGG).

Rand McNally, 444 N Michigan Ave, Chicago, IL 60611 (☎312/321-1751); 150 E 52nd St, New York, NY 10022 (☎212/758-7488); 595 Market St, San Francisco, CA 94105 (☎415/777-3131); call ☎1-800/333-0136 (ext 2111) for other locations, or for maps by mail order.

Traveler's Bookstore, 22 W 52nd St, New York, NY 10019 (☎212/664-0995).

CANADA

Open Air Books and Maps, 25 Toronto St, Toronto ON, M5R 2C1 (☎416/363-0719).

Ulysses Travel Bookshop, 4176 St-Denis, Montréal (☎514/843-9447).

World Wide Books and Maps, 736 Granville St, Vancouver, BC V6Z 1E4 (☎604/687-3320).

AUSTRALIA

The Map Shop, 16a Peel St, Adelaide (☎08/8231 2033).

Bowyangs, 372 Little Bourke St, Melbourne (☎03/9670 4383).

Perth Map Centre, 891 Hay St, Perth (☎08/9322 5733).

Travel Bookshop, 20 Bridge St, Sydney (☎02/9241 3554).

NEW ZEALAND

Specialty Maps, 58 Albert St, Auckland (☎09/307 2217).

---

detailed map of all Romania is that published at 1:500,000 by the ADAC (the German motorists' association) and the best for Transylvania is the Erdély map published by DIMAP. This and the Cartographia maps are published in Hungary and cost less there, but are available through good map outlets abroad.

ONT produces free maps of the country (just about adequate for **motoring**), and others of campsites (*popasuri turistice*) and *cabanas* (*cabane turistice*), which are useful for hikers. Hikers are also advised to seek out the booklet

Invitație în Carpați; the text is Romanian, but it contains detailed maps of the 24 main hiking areas, showing trail markings, huts, peaks etc. There are also good **hiking maps** (*hartă turistică*) of the major mountain massifs, now being reissued by Editura pentru Turism and Abeona in Bucharest and Editura Focul Viu in Cluj, and as likely to be found in bookstores as in tourist offices. See p.46 for more information on hiking. In Bucharest, street stalls outside the university are the best places for buying maps, particularly the excellent new maps of the Danube Delta.

GETTING AROUND

Major Romanian towns, and a huge number of small towns and villages, are most easily reached by train. The system, although more confusing than in Western Europe, is far more user-friendly than the bus network, which is best used for reaching local villages around the main towns.

TRAINS

Although the number of cars on the roads is increasing, and bus services are widening their range, trains remain the best means for most people to get around. The 11,300-kilometre network of the SNCFR (*Societatea Naţională a Căilor Ferate Române*, still generally known as the **CFR** or *ChéFéRé*) covers most of the country. Tickets are amazingly cheap, which is not necessarily to say that they are good value – some travellers may find the derelict trains, bizarre timetable and lengthy ticket queues too much to take. What's more, they are often crowded which, combined with the frequent lack of light, heat and water, may make long journeys somewhat purgatorial; but those who use the trains regularly often end up very much in sympathy with their rough-and-ready spirit and the generally excellent time-keeping. Many routes are extremely scenic, particularly in Transylvania, and as train journeys are good occasions to strike up conversation with Romanians, you'll gain a lot out of ignoring any discomforts and making an effort.

Fares are low, about $1 for 200km. You have a choice of paying more to travel fast or less to

travel more slowly, although if your ticket was issued abroad it will already include the express supplement. **Rapid** and **Intercity** services, halting only at major towns, are the most expensive types of train, while **accelerats** are only slightly slower, with more frequent stops, but far cheaper and the standard means of inter-urban travel. The painfully slow **personal** trains should be avoided as a rule, unless you're heading for some tiny *halta*. Each service has a number prefixed by a letter denoting its type – R, IC, A, or P. See below for information on **rail passes**.

TIMETABLES AND ROUTES

Trains generally conform pretty well to the **timetables** (*orar trenurilor*) displayed in stations and CFR offices (see below). The key terms are *sosire* (sos.) and *plecare* (pl.), arrival and departure times; *de la...* (from) and *pînă la...* (to) (*opire*); the duration of the train's stop in the station; and (*linia*) the platform or track, counting outwards from the main building. Also watch for *anulat* (cancelled), and services that only run – *circulă numai* – during certain months (eg *între 9.V şi 8.IX* – between May 9 and September 8), or only on particular days (1 represents Monday, 2 represents Tuesday; *nu circula Sîmbata şi Duminica* means the service doesn't run on Saturday or Sunday). If you're planning to travel a lot by train, try to get hold of the national CFR timetable, the *Mersul Trenurilor*, which is very cheap; it's issued in May, but likely to be sold out by July or August. A standby is the *Thomas Cook European Timetable*, published monthly, which lists the main Romanian services.

Details of main **routes** are given in the text, and summarized at the end of each chapter in the travel details: note that we give the total number of trains, fast and slow, in a 24-hour period, and give the totals for winter and summer where

> Bear in mind that in official publications such as timetables "î" has been replaced by "â", so that Cîmpulung appears as Câmpulung, Sfîntu Gheorghe as Sfântu Gheorghe, and Tîrgovişte as Târgovişte. The intention in making this change is to strip out the artificially Slavic forms imposed on the language under Stalin. For more details see the box on p.395.

these differ greatly. As there have been cuts in services and many trains run at night there may be gaps of up to seven hours in the daytime.

TICKETS AND RESERVATIONS

Advance bookings for fast services are recommended, and on most such trains you're required to have a seat reservation, although if you board at a relatively minor stop you may have to take pot luck. Thus your ticket (*bilet*) will usually be accompanied by a second piece of card, indicating the service (*nr. trenului*), your carriage (*vagon*) and reserved seat (*loc*); in Bucharest ticket issue has been computerized, with all information on one paper ticket. Return tickets (*bilet dus întors*) are rarely issued except for international services. Many long-distance overnight trains have **sleeping cars** (*vagon de dormit*) and couchettes (*cuşete*), for which a surcharge of a few thousand lei is levied.

With the exception of *personal* trains, tickets are sold at stations only an hour before departure time, and usually at specific windows for each train; these are not always clearly marked, so buying a ticket can lead to quite a scrum. Far easier, if time permits (although you'll pay four percent extra for the privilege), is to book tickets at the local **Agenţia CFR** a day in advance – allow seven days for services to the coast during summer. Addresses of offices are given in The Guide, and in the CFR timetable; opening hours vary widely, but few are open at weekends. Should you fall victim to double-booking, ticket collectors are notoriously corrupt and a small tip can work wonders. Indeed some people never buy tickets, simply paying off the conductor every time.

It's well worth having a return ticket into the country, as buying **International tickets**, except in Bucharest and a few other centres, is a pain, and virtually impossible at weekends. You can buy them only at major ticket offices and at the actual border crossings (if the border guards allow you off the train); they can't be bought at other stations. International seat reservations are relatively expensive, but in fact you don't need a reservation beyond Arad or Oradea on lines to Hungary.

Before leaving home you can buy a **Freedom Pass** (or Eurodomino), which offers free travel on Romania's railways, but it is ludicrously expensive; given that you'll have to queue for seat reservations in any case, you may as well just buy your tickets on the spot as well. Prices start at about $60.

PLANES

TAROM's domestic services depart most days from Bucharest's Băneasa airport to Arad, Baia Mare, Cluj, Constanţa, Craiova, Iaşi, Oradea, Satu Mare, Sibiu, Suceava, Timişoara, Tîrgu Mureş and Tulcea. The older Russian-made planes are now being replaced by modern ATR-42 aircraft.

Fares for foreigners are fixed at the lei equivalent of between $33 and $65, and you'll usually need your exchange receipt to prove that the money was acquired legally. Bookings should be made – preferably 36 hours in advance – at TAROM offices, the addresses of which appear in the guide.

The private **DacAir** flies from Bucharest to Timişoara, Cluj and Oradea (and to Munich, Venice, Bologna and Istanbul) – see the relevant city accounts.

BUSES AND TAXIS

Bus services (run by regional ITAs) now reach virtually every village (having almost dried up before 1989, due to fuel shortages) and with a little patience will usually get you anywhere you want to go. Timetables are usually out of date, and can only be found at urban bus stations. In the countryside, knowing when and where to wait for the bus is a local art form, and on Sundays many regions have no local buses at all (whereas trains run to much the same timetable seven days a week). Private buses run to Bucharest from many Wallachian towns, such as Cîmpulung and Rîmnicu Vîlcea.

All towns have **local bus services**, and in the main cities you'll also find **trams** and **trolley buses** (*tramvai* and *troleibuz*). Tickets for urban buses, trolley buses and trams are normally sold in pairs from street kiosks. Punch them yourself aboard the vehicle, if you can get to the machine through the crush. Most locals use season tickets, checked by plain-clothes inspectors. In Hungarian areas tickets are often sold by a conductor on the bus, rather than at a kiosk. **Information** about services seemed almost a state secret under Communism, and is only slightly easier to find now. In Bucharest new bus shelters, with city transport maps, are slowly being installed, and some stops list bus frequencies too.

Taxis are easy to find in towns, with lots of private taxis as well as state-owned vehicles. As fuel prices rise towards levels found elsewhere,

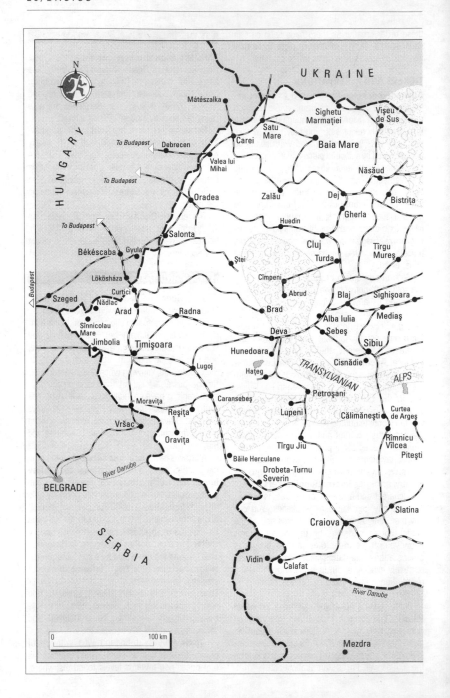

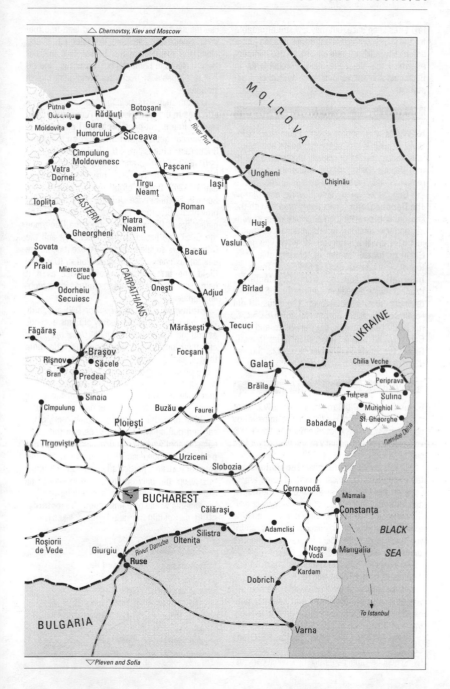

taxi fares keep pace, but they are still affordable for the visitor, with city-centre trips costing just a dollar or two. **Maxitaxis** are shared taxi minibuses which run along the main thoroughfares in Bucharest and link various towns with their train stations.

BOATS

NAVROM, the national shipping company, maintains a small fleet of passenger boats and hydrofoils which operate principally along the arms of the Danube Delta. If the situation in Serbia remains quiet, there should be regular services on the Danube between Turnu Severin and Ostrov. The **Danube Delta** services vary greatly with the season, only operating on alternate days in winter, and you can't buy tickets in advance – you'll just have to make arrangements when you get to Galaţi or Tulcea. Smaller motorboats also carry tourists around Lake Bicaz in Moldavia. There are **international** services from Constanţa to Istanbul (twice a week in summer, from $40 for a reclining seat; book through Danubius, B-dul Ferdinand 36, 8700 Constanţa; ☎041/61.58.36, fax 61.80.10) and along the Danube to and from Germany and Vienna (Transocean Tours Touristik GmbH, Bredenstr. 11, Bremen; ☎0421/3336-0, fax 333 6200).

DRIVING

Given the state of the roads and the low cost of public transport, it makes little sense to travel by car unless you have a lot of ground to cover in a very short time – especially as the queues for fuel can be lengthy.

If you do choose to drive, **regulations** are fairly standard. The most important rules are to drive on the right and overtake on the left side, and for traffic on a roundabout to give way to traffic entering. Seats belts are required outside towns. A national driving licence suffices, and if you don't have Green Card insurance, a month's cover can be purchased at the border, or from ADAC agencies (German Motorists' Association). If you have an **accident**, you're legally obliged to await the arrival of the *Poliţia*; drinking and driving is absolutely prohibited and severely punished. The police are now empowered to levy on-the-spot fines of up to L100,000.

There are often queues for **fuel** at PECO and Competrol stations, especially when rumours are flying about an imminent price rise. Most cars just use regular benzine, but super and lead-free fuel (*fără plomb*) are available in major cities and along the main highways. Diesel cars are not manufactured in Romania, but diesel fuel (*motorină*) is available at truck stops and some petrol stations.

Foreign motorists belonging to organizations affiliated to the **ACR** (Romanian Automobile Club) receive free or cut-price **technical assistance**; and you can get motoring **information** from their Bucharest offices at Str. Tache Ionescu 27 (☎01/650.25.95) and Str. Cihoski 2 (☎01/611.04.08). For ACR breakdown services dial ☎12345. Details of car repair depots (Auto-Service, Dacia-Service, Automechanica etc) and provincial ACR offices are given in *The Guide*. The mainstays of Romanian motoring, the Dacia and the Oltcit, are based on the Renault 12 and the Citroen Visa, so spare parts for these models are easiest to come by; the new Rodae (Daewoo) Cielo, the first Romanian car to look as if it belongs in the late twentieth century, is no problem either.

Highways (*Drum Naţional* or DN) are fairly well maintained, but the quality of roads declines as you move onto county roads (*Drum Judeţean*) and then local roads, which can be little more than tracks. In rural areas the danger isn't so much about other motorized traffic as the risk of hitting waggons, drunks on cycles and various animals that have yet to accept the impact of the motor age. It's wise not to drive after dark or in winter.

Other precautions include always locking the car and putting windscreen wipers in the glove compartment when not in use, since **theft of car parts** is commonplace. If asked to pay to have your car watched, particularly overnight, it's wiser to pay up; the only alternative is to stay in an expensive hotel with supervised parking.

Romania would be a fine country for **motorcycling**, except that the speed limit for bikes is ludi-

SPEED LIMITS	
Type of car	**Speed limit**
	(built-up areas/open road)
over 1800cc	60/90 kph
1100–1800cc	60/80 kph
under 1100cc	60/70 kph
jeep-type, spark ignition	60/70 kph
jeep-type, diesel	60/60kph

CAR RENTAL AGENCIES

BRITAIN		AUSTRALIA	
Avis	☎0990/900500	Avis	☎1800/225 533
Budget	☎0800/181181	Budget	☎13 2727
Eurodollar	☎01895/233300	Hertz	☎13 3039
Europcar/InterRent	☎0345/222525		
Hertz	☎0990/996600	**NEW ZEALAND**	
		Avis	☎09/526 2847
NORTH AMERICA		Budget	☎09/375 2222
Hertz US	☎1-800/654-3001	Hertz	☎09/309 0989
Hertz Canada	☎1-800/263-0600		

crously low: 40kph in built up areas and only 50kph (30mph) on the open road. Helmets are compulsory and you're advised to bring vital spares as well as a tool kit.

CAR RENTAL

Western **car rental** companies such as Avis, Budget, Eurodollar, Europcar and Hertz are now present in Bucharest (with branches at Otopeni airport) and other major cities. Budget and Eurodollar have the lowest rates, starting at $21 per day ($17/day for a week or more), topped up by a distance charge of $0.25 per kilometre or $70 a day ($51/day for a week or more) with unlimited mileage. A hefty deposit (around $500) is required, best paid by credit card.

Most rental firms use only imported vehicles, from Ford Fiestas up to minibuses, although Avis, Hertz and Romanian firms like JET Turist, Mercedes and Sebastian (see Bucharest listings) may be able to lay their hands on a less conspicuous Cielo. Renting direct from Romanian companies will save you about 20 percent on the prices quoted above.

Fly-drive deals are not good value, but may be worth considering if the convenience of a car on arrival is more important than cheap travel. See p.6.

CYCLING

Given the mountainous terrain and the poor state of many roads, you'll need to be fit and self-reliant to **cycle** around Romania. Bike stores are few and far between, although most village mechanics can manage basic repairs. You're strongly advised to carry a spare tyre and a few spokes, and to check carrier nuts regularly, as the potholes and corrugations will rapidly shake them loose. A touring bike is better than a mountain bike unless you want to go off road; with the immense network of forestry roads (*Drum Forestiere*) and free access to the hills, genuine mountain biking is wonderful here.

If you do bring your bike, avoid cycling in **Bucharest**, where the roads are so hazardous that you won't see other cyclists and drivers will have little idea how to avoid you. Carrying your bike by train is simplest on slow services, as on

ONT TOURS

Between mid-June and the end of September, ONT organizes **tours**, including weekends at Sinaia, Predeal and the seaside; two- or three-day excursions to Maramureş, the old Wallachian capitals, the monasteries of Bucovina, the Delta and the Prahova and Olt valleys; and jaunts around the country lasting 3, 5 or 7 days.

The three-day tour takes in Curtea de Argeş, Cozia Monastery, Sibiu, Sibiel, Braşov and Sinaia; five-day excursions add Bran Castle, Tîrgu Mureş, Sighişoara and Sovata to this list; while the week-

long itinerary also includes Alba Iulia, Cluj, Bistriţa, Bicaz, and several of the Moldavian monasteries. Prices depend on the number of participants and on the types of transport and accommodation required, but as an example, three people spending three days touring the Bucovina monasteries by car would pay $224 each plus either $27 by sleeper train or $88 by air from Bucharest to Suceava and back; it will always be cheaper to make your own way to Suceava and book a tour there, with the possibility of latching on to a bus party.

expresses it'll have to be carried in the guard's van – a good tip should ensure it's properly guarded.

HITCH-HIKING

Hitch-hiking (*autostop* or *occasie*) is an integral part of the Romanian transport system to supplement patchy or nonexistent services on backroads. It's common even on the *autostrada*, although illegal there, and it's accepted practice to pay for lifts, although this is often waived for foreigners. Hitch-hiking, however, is a risky business in any country and if you decide to travel this way, take all sensible precautions. Women should never hitch alone, nor is hitching at night advisable.

ACCOMMODATION

Privatization and semi-privatization (state-owned hotels being rented out to their managers) have begun to introduce a note of realism into the Romanian hotel industry; for a long time hotels had pretensions, and prices, way beyond their merits, but these days hotels with an intermittent water supply and no curtains now charge more appropriate rates. At the top end there are some excellent hotels which charge international rates to their business clientele. New private hotels are appearing in some towns, especially in Transylvania, and private rooms are common in tourist centres.

In summer it's safer, though only really essential on the coast, to make advance **reservations**. The Romanian Automobile Club (ACR) sell **ACR coupons** through tourist offices abroad and their own offices in Romania. The coupons are a system of prepaid vouchers for certain international hotels throughout Romania which entitle you to one of the better rooms in a participating hotel – and you don't need to book ahead as these hotels have to keep a certain number of rooms free every day until 7pm. You will usually save money by simply paying in cash, but coupons can help to get you a room in a hotel which is otherwise full. We've indicated which hotels accept these vouchers in hotel listings throughout the guide.

ACCOMMODATION PRICES

Hotels listed in this guide have been price-graded according to the scale below. Prices given are those charged for the cheapest **double room** available, which in the less expensive places usually comes without private bath or shower and without breakfast. Price codes are expressed in US dollars as the Romanian leu is not a stable currency, but you will generally pay for your room in lei.

Note that some hotels are currently closed for modernization, and others, now open, will no doubt follow in the near future. This is bound to result in higher rates when they reopen, so the prices quoted should be taken only as a guideline.

① $10 and under	④ $20–25	⑦ $40–50
② $10–15	⑤ $25–30	⑧ $50–65
③ $15–20	⑥ $30–40	⑨ $65 and over

HOTELS

Hotels were previously graded as deluxe, first or second class, but now boast between one and five stars; however these bear little relation to the star ratings of Western hotels and have therefore not been included in our listings. All but the most luxurious of establishments display their prices in lei; the top hotels show a price in dollars which is converted into lei at the daily rate. You may have to show your exchange receipt (*buletin de schimb*), to prove that you're not paying with black-market cash.

Single rooms generally cost around two-thirds of the price of a double; where no single is available, expect to pay anything from half the cost of a double room to the full whack. Penny-pinching couples are sometimes permitted to share a single, while **children** sleeping in their parents' room pay half to two-thirds of the "third person" tariff. Ask if there's constant hot water; if it's only available for a few hours a day (*cu program*), you may choose not to pay extra for a private bathroom, although this is likely to be far cleaner than shared facilities. In smaller towns the hotel restaurant may double as the local nightclub (featuring dancing at the weekends), and it's likely to be busy with boozers at any hour.

MOTELS AND SPORT HOTELS

Motels (*han*) have similar facilities and prices to the better hotels, but since they're situated along main highways or beyond urban ring roads, they're not much use unless you have your own transport. **Sport hotels** are an East European institution, intended for visiting teams and school groups, but now generally willing to let other tourists in. You may have to share a room, and washing facilities are likely to be primitive, but you can't argue with the bargain-basement prices (under $10 a night).

STUDENT ACCOMMODATION

The youth tourism company **CTT** (often still known by its old name of **BTT**) operates hotels which are now open to all ages, although groups get preference. The CTT head office is at Str. Mendeleev 7 in Bucharest (☎01/614.42.00), and we've listed regional offices in the guide; it may be worth checking them out personally, but be aware that they close very early – usual office hours are 8am to 3pm. CTT may also be able to advise you of student dormitories (*internats*) open to tourists from July 15 to August 31, and may be willing to book beds for you; otherwise you can book in person at the addresses they give. Having an ISIC student card may help, but charges are minimal anyway, well under $1 a night.

CABANAS

In the countryside, particularly in the mountainous areas favoured by hikers, there are well over a hundred **cabanas** or hikers' huts, ranging from chic alpine villas with dozens of bedrooms to fairly primitive chalets with bunk beds, a rudimentary bar and cold running water – these are the nearest equivalent to youth hostels in Romania.

The hikers' *cabanas* are generally friendly and useful places where you can pick up information about trails and the weather. Some *cabanas* (mainly in the Bucegi range) can be easily reached by cable car from a train station, while others are situated on roads just a few miles from towns; however, the majority are fairly isolated and accessible only by mountain tracks or footpaths. The location of the *cabanas* is shown rather vaguely on an ONT map, *Cabane Turistice*, and more precisely on hiking maps. Mountain *cabanas* are supposed not to turn hikers away, but in the Făgăraş mountains, in particular, it might be wise to book in advance, by phone or through a local agency. Beds in remoter areas cost about $3, but rather more if in a private room or in one of the plusher *cabanas*.

CAMPING

Romania has well over a hundred **campsites**, situated all over the country. You'll pay about $2 – an ISIC student card may secure a thirty to fifty percent reduction. Second-class campsites are rudimentary, usually with filthy toilets, but first-class sites often have **cabins** or bungalows (*căsuţe*) for rent (about $5 for a two bed cabin), hot showers and even a restaurant. However, water shortages seem to hit campsites especially hard, while along the coast overcrowding is a major drawback. In the mountains, certain areas may be designated as a camping area (*loc de campare*), but there are not many of these. However, providing you don't light fires in forests, leave litter or damage nature reserves, official-

HOMESTAY SCHEMES

Three organizations provide what coordination there is in the homestay sector in Romania. The nearest to an official nationwide body is **ANTREC** (the National Association of Rural, Ecological and Cultural Tourism), PO Box 22-259, Bucharest (☎ & fax 222.83.22); **Eurogites**, 7 Place des Meuniers, 67000 Strasbourg, France (☎33/88.75.56.60 or 88.75.60.19, fax 88.23.00.97) offers the best way to make reservations from outside Romania; their members are mostly in the Bran area and in the Székely land. The other two are based outside of Romania – the offices of **Opération Villages Roumains** (☎2/640 5003, fax 640 2946, *ovrcc@mail.interpac.be*) are in Brussels, but bookings can be made through Andrei Mahalnischi, at Str. Grozavescu 13, 3400 Cluj (☎064/42.05.16); while the Amsterdam-based **ECEAT** (the European

Center for Eco-Agro Tourism, ☎20/668 1030, fax 463 0594, *eceat@antenna.nl*), with a less structured network in Alba, Mureș, Harghita and Bucovina counties, is coordinated by the Focus Eco-Center in Tîrgu Mureș (Str Belsugului 6; ☎065/13.10.80 or 16.36.92, fax 16.12.55).

In addition, there's a network of **Gästehäuser in the Saxon villages**, not exactly homestays, but still village accommodation; these are coordinated by Kilian Dörr, Piața Castelului 2, Mediaș (☎069/81.33.12) and Hugo Schneider, Str. Gh. Doja 23, Mediaș (☎069/82.86.05).

Finally, **Women Welcome Women**, 88 Easton St, High Wycombe, HP11 1LT, UK (☎ & fax 01494/465441) is a scheme whereby members (women only) can stay with women in other countries, including Romania.

dom turns a blind eye to tourists **camping wild**, or, at the worst, may tell you to move along.

PRIVATE ROOMS AND OTHER POSSIBILITIES

Since the revolution private accommodation has become available to foreigners and now, six years later, **village homestays** (*agroturism*) have really begun to take off. Many villages now have projects, offering private rooms, all meals, lashings of booze and sometimes even excursions or dances, all for about $12–15 a night. These are being expanded with aid both from the government and from foreign NGOs, and 8500 households should be involved by the year 2000. In the countryside there is a strong tradition of hospital-

ity, and people may take you in and refuse payment; but you should offer a few dollars anyway, or come armed with a few packets of coffee (easily obtained in the towns), which make welcome presents.

If you're desperate to save money on accommodation and you're travelling around a lot, you can use the **trains** to your advantage. On the long overnight journeys by *rapid* or *accelerat* train, it only costs a couple of dollars to book a comfortable couchette (*cușete*), allowing you to save the cost of a hotel and arrive refreshed the following morning. Couchettes (and the costlier sleeping cars, *vagon de dormit*) can be booked up to ten days in advance through the CFR agencies found in most towns.

EATING AND DRINKING

Under Communism the only people not driven to the black market for food were package tourists, fed huge meals to obscure the
realities of life in Romania, and the Party
elite, who had their own supply network.
Visitors can still opt for the security of a
package tour and confine themselves to eating in tourist hotels, or come prepared to forage for themselves. Winter is tough everywhere, but in large towns and agricultural
areas the availability and variety of food
improves as the months pass, so that you
can eat relatively well during the summer
and autumn. Imported foods such as
oranges, bananas and German yoghurts are
also available, at a price. Nevertheless, it
might be wise to bring some concentrated,
non-perishable food with you.

BREAKFAST AND SNACKS

Staying in a hotel, you'll normally be guaranteed
breakfast on the premises or in a nearby café,
the cost of which will be included in the charge
for accommodation. Typically it's a light meal of
rolls and butter (sometimes known as *ceai com-
plet*), to which an omelette or long, unappealing-
looking skinless sausages can be added. This is
washed down with a large white coffee or a cup
of tea.

Should you rise late, or not fancy the above,
then look out for **snacks**, known as *gustări* (also
the Romanian word for hors d'oeuvres). The most

common are flaky pastries (*pateuri*) filled with
cheese or meat, often dispensed through hatches
in the walls of bakeries; brioche, a Moldavian
speciality, sandwiches, a variety of spicy grilled
sausages and meatballs, normally sold by street
vendors and in beer gardens; and small pizzas
topped with cheese and salami.

RESTAURANT MEALS

Outside the cities, you'll find most **restaurants**
are in hotels or attached to them, although small
private cafés are springing up in many towns. It's
best to go upmarket if you can, since the choice of
dishes in cheaper restaurants is limited to cutlet
(*cotlet*) and chips, and they tend to be thinly disguised beer halls. At least the grisly self-service
Autoservire canteens that Ceauşescu intended to
make the mainstay of Romanian catering have
largely vanished; unfortunately they've been
replaced for the most part by burger bars which
are little better. Lacto-Vegetarian restaurants are
also vanishing – these were in any case never
particularly vegetarian, but they can offer affordable food in reasonably congenial surroundings.
Whatever place you settle on, always enquire
"*Care feluri le serviţi astazi, ve rog?*" ("What do
you have today?") or "*Ce îhmi recomandaţi?*"
("What do you recommend?") before taking the
menu too seriously, for sometimes the only thing
going is the set menu (*un meniu fix*), usually dominated by pork.

However, at smarter restaurants and *hans*
(motels, which are actually more like traditional
inns with olde-worlde decor), there's a fair
chance of finding **authentic Romanian dishes**,
which can be delicious. The best known is *sarmale* – cabbage leaves stuffed with rice, meat
and herbs, usually served (or sometimes baked)
with sour cream or horseradish; they are sometimes also made with vine leaves (*sărmăluţe in
foi de viţă*) or with corn (*sarmale cu pasat*), as in
Maramureş. *Mămăligă*, maize mush or polenta,
often served with sour cream, is especially associated with shepherds and the authentic outdoor
life. Stews (*tocane*) and other dishes often feature a sclerotic combination of meat and dairy
products. *Muşchi ciobanesc* (shepherd's sirloin)
is pork stuffed with ham, covered in cheese and
served with mayonnaise, cucumber and herbs;

Vegetarians will have a tough time in a country where voluntarily doing without meat is simply beyond comprehension. It's hard even to get a pizza that's meat-free. You could try asking for *ghiveci* (mixed stewed veg); *ardei umplue* (stuffed peppers); *ouă umplute picante* or *ouă umplute cu ciuperci* (eggs with a spicy filling or mushroom stuffing); *ouă româneşti* (poached eggs); or vegetables and salads (see box overleaf). However, in practice, you're likely to end up with omelette, *mămăligă* (maize mush and polenta) or *caşcaval pané* (cheese fried in breadcrumbs). You can try asking for something "*fără carne, vă rog*" ("without meat, please"), or check "*este cu carne?*" ("does it contain meat?"), but you're unlikely to get very far. Watch out, too, for the ubiquitous meat stock.

while *muşchi poiana* (meadow sirloin) is beef stuffed with mushrooms, bacon, pepper and paprika, served in a vegetable purée and tomato sauce.

Wherever you are, keep an eye out for **regional specialities** (*specialităţile regiunii*). Moldavian cooking is reputedly the best in Romania, featuring rissoles (*pîrjoale*), and more elaborate dishes such as *rasol moldovenesc cu hrean* (boiled pork, chicken or beef, with a sour cream and horseradish sauce), *tochitură moldovenească* (a pork stew, with cheese, *mămăligă*, and a fried egg on top), *rulade de pui* (chicken roulade), and *pui Cîmpulungean* (chicken stuffed with smoked bacon, sausage, garlic and vegetables). Because of Romania's Turkish past, you may come across moussaka and varieties of pilaf, while the German and Hungarian minorities have contributed such dishes as smoked pork with sauerkraut and Transylvanian hotpot.

CAFÉS

Establishments called **cofetărie** serve **coffee**, soft drinks, cakes, ice cream, and even beer. Romanians usually take their coffee black and sweet in the Turkish fashion; ask for *cafea cu lapte* if you prefer it with milk or *fără zahăr* for no sugar. The instant varieties are called *Ness*. **Cakes and desserts** are sticky and very sweet, as throughout the Balkans. Romanians enjoy pancakes and pies with various fillings, and Turkish-influenced *baclava* and *cataif cu frisca* (crisp pastry soaked in syrup, filled with whipped cream).

BARS

Bars are generally men-only places and range from dark rough-and-ready dives to places with a rather chintzy ice cream-parlour atmosphere. They're all usually open well into the small hours, except in smaller towns. A *crama* is a wine cellar, while a *gradina de vară* is a terrace or garden, usually offering *mititei* (spicy sausages) as well as beer.

There is a great deal of drinking in Romania, as you will soon notice, and most crime is alcohol-related. Non-drinkers will meet with the same incomprehension as vegetarians, but could try saying "*nu consum băuturi alcoolice*" ("I don't drink alcohol").

DRINKS

The national drink is *ţuică*, a tasty, powerful brandy usually made of plums, taken neat. In rural areas, homemade spirits can be fearsome stuff, often twice distilled (to over 50 percent strength, even when diluted) to yield *palincă*, and much rougher than the grape brandy (*rachiu* or *coniac*) drunk by urban sophisticates. All spirits are alarmingly cheap (and served in large measures, usually 10cl; ask for a *mic*, 5cl, if you want less), except for whisky, which retails for around $12 a bottle.

Most **beer** is European-style lager (*bere blondă*). Silva from Reghin, Valea Prahova from Azuga, Ciucaş from Braşov and Ursus from Cluj are probably the best regional brews, while Bergenbier and Eggenburger are acceptable mass-produced brands – but you will occasionally find brown ale (*bere neagră*). All beer is usually sold by the bottle, so a request for *una sticlă* will normally get you one of whatever's available.

Romania's best **wines** – and they *are* good – are the white *Grasa* from Cotnari, near Iaşi, and Tamaioasa, a luscious late-harvested Moldavian dessert wine, Fetească Neagră, the blackberryish reds from Dealu Mare, east of Ploieşti, and the sweet dessert wines from Murfatlar (notably Merlot and Cabernet Sauvignon, and white Muscat Ottonel). They can be obtained in the better restaurants without too much trouble; other restaurants may just offer you a choice of red or white. Sparkling wines from Alba Iulia and Panciu (north of Focşani) are very acceptable. Wine is rarely sold by the glass, but it does no harm to ask – *Serviţi vin la pahar?*

A FOOD AND DRINK GLOSSARY

Basic foods

Brînză	cheese	Piper	pepper	Supă	soup with one
Iaurt	yoghurt	Pîine	bread or Pâine		maincomponent
Lapte	milk	Sare	salt	Ciorbă	mixed soup, with
Oţet	vinegar	Sandvici	sandwiches		sour cream
Omleta	omelette	Ul tartina		Ulei	oil
Orez	rice	Smîntînă	sour cream	Unt	butter
Ouă	egg			Zahăr	sugar

Soups (supe)

Ciorbă de burtă	tripe soup	Supă de carne	consommé
Ciorbă de cartofi	potato soup	Supă de găină	chicken soup
Ciorbă de fasole	dried or green bean soup	Supă de galuşti	dumpling soup
Ciorbă de miel	lamb broth	Supă de roşii	tomato soup
Ciorbă perişoare	soup with meatballs	Supă de taitei	noodle soup
Ciorbă de peşte	fish soup	Supă de zarzavat	vegetable soup
Ciorbă ţaranească	soup with meat and mixed vegetables		

Salads (salate)

Salată de cartofi cu ceapa	potato and onion salad	Salată de roşii şi castraveţi	tomato and cucumber salad
Salată de fasole verde	green bean salad	Salată de sfeclă roşie	beetroot salad
Salată de icre de crap	carp roe salad	Salată verde	lettuce salad

Meat and poultry (carne şi pasăre)

Babic (Ghiudem)	smoked (goat's meat) sausage	Patricieni	sausages (skinless)
		Pui	chicken
Berbec/Oaie	mutton	Raţă (pe varză)	duck (with sauerkraut)
Biftec	steak	Rinichii	kidneys
Chiftele	fried meatballs	Salam	salami
Curcan	turkey	Slănină	bacon fat
Ficat	liver	Şniţel pané	Wiener schnitzel
Găină	hen	Şuncă	ham
Ghiveci cu carne	meat and vegetable hotpot	Tocană de carne/ de purcel	meat/pork stew
Gîscă	goose		
Miel	lamb	Vacă	beef
Mititei	spicy sausages	Varz acră cu costiţe afumate	sauerkraut with smoked pork chops
(Pastrama de) porc	(salted and smoked) pork		

Vegetables (legume)

Ardei (gras/iute)	(green/chilli) pepper	Lăptucă	lettuce
Cartofi	potatoes	Mazăre verde	peas
Ceapă (verde)	(spring) onion	Morcovi	carrots
Ciuperci	mushrooms	Roşii	tomatoes
Conopida	cauliflower	Sfeclă roşie	beetroot
Dovleci (cu floare)	marrows (courgettes/zucchini)	Spanac	spinach
		Usturoi	garlic
Fasole (albă grasă/verde)	(broad/string) beans	Varză	cabbage
Ghiveci	mixed fried vegetables, sometimes eaten cold	Vinete	aubergines (eggplant)
Gogoşari	red peppers		Continued over

Continued from over

Fish and seafood (*peşte*)

Cegă	sterlet	*Nisetru*	sturgeon
Chiftele de peşte	fish cakes	*Păstrăv*	trout
Crap	carp	*Scrumb*	herring
Icre negre	caviar	*Şalău*	pike/perch
Midii	mussels	*Ton*	tuna

Fruit (*fructe*)

Caise	apricots	*Pere*	pears
Căpşuni	strawberries	*Piersici*	peaches
Cireşi	cherries	*Prune (uscate)*	plums (prunes)
Mere	apples	*Struguri*	grapes
Pepene galben	melon	*Zmeure*	raspberries
Pepene verde	watermelon		

Desserts and sweets (*dulciuri*)

Bomboane	sweets (candy)	*Măr in foietaj*	baked, stuffed apple
Clătită (cu rom)	pancake (with rum)	*Papanasi*	cream doughnut
Cozonac	brioche	*Pasca*	Easter cake
Dulceaţă	jam (served in a glass)	*Plăcinta cu brînză*	cheese pie
Ecler	éclair	*Plăcinta cu mere*	apple pie
Gogoşi or *langoş*	doughnut	*Plăcinta cu vişine*	cherry pie
Halva	halva	*Prăjitură*	cake
Îngheţată	ice cream	*Rahat*	Turkish delight
Mascota	chocolate fudge cake	*Rulada*	sponge and jam roll
Miere	honey		

Drinks (*băuturi*)

Apă minerală	mineral water	*Vin roşu* (or *alb*)	red wine (or white)
Suc de fructe	fruit juice	*Şampanie*	sparkling wine
Cafea mare cu lapte	large white coffee	*Sticla*	bottle (of beer)
Cafea neagră	sweet black coffee	*Ţuiclă*	plum brandy
or *cafea naturală*		*Vodca*	vodka
O ceaşcă de ceai	a cup of tea	*Rom*	rum
Bere	beer		

Common terms

Aveţi?	Do you have?	*Noroc!*	cheers!
Aş/am vrea	I/we would like	*Pahar*	a glass
Anghemaht de	in a white sauce	*Piureu de*	mashed
Cu maioneză	with a mayonnaise sauce	*Poftă bună*	enjoy your meal
Cu mujdei de usturoi	in a garlic sauce	*Prăjiţi*	fried
Dejun	lunch	*Prînz, cină*	dinner
Fierţi	boiled	*Pulpă de... la tavă*	roast leg of
Friptură	roast	*Rasol*	poached
La grătar	grilled	*Tare/moale*	hard/soft boiled
Meniu or *listă*	menu	*Umpluţi*	stuffed
Micul dejun	breakfast		

Coca-Cola, Pepsi, and Romanian mineral water are omnipresent; other **soft drinks** are more or less drinkable nowadays, but only severe dehydration justifies resorting to the indigenous *sirop*.

BUYING YOUR OWN FOOD

Shopping for food is a dispiriting task, since most stores have a limited choice of dried and bottled foodstuffs and a few imported items; a few new supermarkets have a decent range of imported foods but these are relatively expensive. You should always check the sell-by dates on imported goods as they may have been dumped by the countries of origin. The basics are sardines, meat paste, pickled fruit and vegetables, pasta, jam, processed cheese and biscuits. Cheese, eggs and meat can be bought in the general foodstores (*alimentară*), while fruit and veg should be bought in the market (*piaţa*) – in smaller towns and villages you'll be expected to bring your own bag.

Most **bread** is white, and not unpleasant, but it's worth asking for wholemeal bread (*pîine graham* or *pîine diatetică*). Most, but not all, stores will sell a half-loaf to a solo traveller.

POST AND PHONES

Major **post offices** are open Monday to Saturday from 7am to 8pm, and on Sundays from 8am to noon; like the red-painted mail boxes, they are marked *Poşta*. **Stamps** (*timbru*) and pre-paid envelopes (*plic*) can be bought here; there may be long queues, but they're almost certainly not for stamps. Stamps are often huge and several are needed, so stick them on *before* writing your card.

   Sending mail home from Romania is relatively pricey – L2400 to overseas destinations – and takes about five days to Britain, two weeks to North America and Australasia. If you're sending important packages, you're probably better off using a **courier** service, such as DHL, which has offices in Bucharest, Braşov, Constanţa, Craiova and Timişoara.

Letters can be sent **poste restante** to main post offices in Romania: make sure they're addressed *Officiul Poştal no. 1, poşte restante*, followed by the name of the town, and that the recipient's last name is underlined. To collect letters, you'll have to show your passport and pay a small fee. Important messages should be sent by postcard, as letters from abroad can go missing if they look as if they might contain dollars. American Express also offer a poste restante service to their cardholders via their office in Bucharest.

PHONES

The **telephone service** is at last seeing some much-needed improvements, such as a new fibre-optic link from Arad to Constanţa (linking Hungary and Turkey), thanks to loans from the World Bank and European Bank. Private phones are still relatively uncommon, but as more people buy into the service and exchanges change over to digital connections, telephone numbers are being expanded (by adding a new first digit) to accommodate the demand – there is a wait of several years for connection.

   All towns and many villages have a telephone and telegraph office or **PTTR** (usually open weekdays 6.30am–10pm, sometimes seven days a week), where the staff will connect your call. You'll normally pay the three-minute minimum in advance, and the balance afterwards; calls are most expensive from 10am to 4pm and 7pm to 10pm, and cheapest from midnight to 6am. In

PHONING ROMANIA FROM ABROAD

Dial the international access code (given below)
+ 40 (country code) + area code (minus initial 0) + number

Australia ☎0011	Ireland ☎010	UK ☎00
Canada ☎011	New Zealand ☎00	USA ☎011

PHONING ABROAD FROM ROMANIA

Dial the country code (given below) + area code (minus initial 0) + number

Australia ☎0061	Ireland ☎00353	UK ☎0044
Canada ☎001	New Zealand ☎0064	USA ☎001

USEFUL ACCESS NUMBERS

BT Direct ☎01800/4444	Sprint ☎01800/0877
Canada Direct ☎01800/5000	WorldPhone (MCI) ☎01800/1800
USA Direct (AT&T) ☎01800/4288	

USEFUL TELEPHONE NUMBERS

☎930 directory enquiries for business numbers	☎955 police
☎931 & 932 directory enquiries for domestic	☎959 weather forecast
numbers (A–L and M–Z respectively)	☎961 ambulance/rescue (*salvarea*)
☎936 TAROM	☎962 emergency hospital
☎952 rail information	☎981 fire service
☎953 taxi	☎971 international operator

main cities there may also be a **Romtelecom** office, with card-phones, open till about 9pm. Phone-cards (*cartelă telefonică)* currently sell for L20,000; insert them with the gold lozenge foremost and facing upwards, and after a few seconds you should get a sign indicating that you can start dialling. Calls to Britain cost L6000 a minute, and to North America and Australasia L12,000, so the cards don't last long.

Local calls can be made from blue coinphones and cost L100 for three minutes; orange card-phones are increasingly common in towns with modern exchanges, used for both long-distance and also international calls.

International calls can be made from cardphones, from the PTTR/Romtelcom offices (with a wait of ten minutes or so, as a rule), or by dialling ☎971 for the international operator from domestic phones and the better hotels. Using hotel facilities inevitably means a steep service charge, so always ask the price beforehand. An alternative is to use a **direct access** number to your home telecom company, billing either your chargecard or the number you're calling. However, chargecard calls from Romania are peculiarly expensive – a third more than from neighbouring countries.

Faxes (*telefax*) are increasingly common now, easily found in the top hotels and in principal post offices. **Email** has yet to make much impact, although where internet cafés do exist, we've listed them in the text.

THE MEDIA

Romania's **newspapers** used to be housed together in the *Casa Scînteii*, north of central Bucharest, and although there is now a free press and indeed the building has been renamed the *Casa Presei Libere*, many newspaper offices remain there. There are supposedly 1600 titles nationwide, many of them local, and very few of any real worth. Papers pander to the national obsession with crime and, as is the case all across East-central Europe, there has been an explosion of soft (and not so soft) porn. Nationalist papers have a total circulation of around a million, while the biggest sellers are the sensationalist tabloid *Tineretul Liber* (Free Youth) and the most useful, *România Liberă* (Free Romania).

There are a few **English-language** publications, none easily found outside Bucharest, of which the most useful are the listings magazine *Bucharest – What, Where, When*, and *Nine O'Clock*, a daily news sheet available free in hotels. Here and there you'll also come across the official tourist mag *Holidays in Romania*, which occasionally runs interesting articles. Western newspapers can be bought in the classier hotels or you could try the British, American, French and German libraries in the main cities, where you can find newspapers a week or so old.

Television is inescapable, since it's rarely turned off in many homes and bars. Once restricted to two hours a day, with half of that devoted to Ceauşescu's feats, these days there is no shortage of programming. TV played a crucial role in the overthrow of Ceauşescu ("The people must seize the means of projection!" as Andrei Codrescu put it), and the nationwide state TV channel, plus the second channel received in a few major cities, helped Iliescu to retain power at election time. The success of the private ProTV helped bring about his defeat in 1996; in the opinion of many: the instant that his defeat was obvious, TVR changed sides, but its management was soon dismissed in any case. The number of private local TV stations (many only on cable) is increasing, as are satellite dishes picking up SKY, CNN and MTV.

There are plenty of private **radio** stations, most notably Radio Contact, but for news, many Romanians tune into foreign stations, notably the Romanian-language broadcasts of the BBC World Service and Voice of America. The World Service also broadcasts in English between approximately 8am and 5pm GMT on 17.64, 15.07 and 12.09MHz (17.01, 19.91 and 24.80m), and from 4 to 7am and from 5 to 10pm on 9.41, 6.20 and 6.18MHz (31.88, 48.43 and 48.54m). Reception quality varies greatly: generally, lower frequencies give better results early in the morning and late at night, higher ones in the middle of the day.

OPENING HOURS, SHOPS AND MONUMENTS

Opening hours in Romania are notoriously unreliable and weekends can be like the grave, with a surprising number of restaurants and cinemas closing mid-afternoon or not opening at all. Stores are generally open from 9 or 10am to 6 or 8pm on weekdays, but may close for several hours during the middle of the day. They are also liable to close at any time for deliveries or stock control (*inventar*).

Some shops have longer hours, with **department stores** (*magazin universal*) and some food stores opening from 8am to 8pm Monday to Saturday and from 8.30am to 1pm on Sunday. If you're trying to sort out flights, visas, or car rental, beware that most offices are closed by 4pm.

CHURCHES

Romania's abundance of **churches** testifies to its history of competing faiths. In **Transylvania** these became aligned in medieval times with the ethnic stratification of society, so that the rights of "four religions" and "three Nations" were recognized (but not those of Orthodoxy and its Romanian adherents – an order stigmatized as the "Seven Deadly Sins of Transylvania"). In **Moldavia and Wallachia** Orthodoxy, supported by the boyars and princes, had a monopoly, but the clergy and the Patriarchate consisted of Byzantine (and later Phanariot) Greeks more often than Romanians, and as late as the nineteenth century performed the liturgy and rites in incomprehensible Slavonic rather than the native tongue.

This religious mix, together with the frequency of invasions, accounts for the extraordinary diversity of church **architecture** in Romania. Churches range from the inspired wooden *biserici de lemn* in Maramureş villages to the austere fortified *Kirchenburgen* raised by the Saxons around Braşov and Sibiu. Having absorbed the Byzantine style of architecture in Moldavia and Wallachia, masons and architects ran riot with colour and mouldings (as at Curtea de Argeş) before producing wonderful ornamental stone facades – most notably at Iaşi's the Church of the Three Hierarchs, and in Wallachia, where the "Brîncoveanu style" flourished, with its porticoes

and stone carving derived from native woodwork motifs.

The **frescoes** so characteristic of medieval Orthodox churches achieved their ultimate sophistication in Maramureş, at the hands of largely unknown artists, and were boldly executed on the exterior walls of Suceviţa, Voroneţ and the other "painted monasteries" of Bucovina, in northern Moldavia, which are today recognized as some of Europe's greatest artistic treasures. The Orthodox Church maintains dozens of **monasteries** (many in fact nunneries), the most famous, after those in Bucovina, being Snagov, where Vlad the Impaler is buried, and Horez, Brîncoveanu's masterpiece.

Orthodox **services** (*slujbă* or *liturghie*) are impressive occasions, both on Sunday mornings and at the great festivals like Easter, and it's no problem for non-believers to attend. Orthodox churches are often left **open**, with old women selling tapers or praying fervently, while Roman Catholic churches are more likely to allow access only as far as a grille just inside the door, so that passers-by can say a quick prayer. Protestant churches are usually closed altogether outside services, but you can ask around for the caretaker.

CASTLES AND MUSEUMS

Romania's most spectacular **castles** are located in Transylvania, where you'll also find towns such as Sibiu and Sighişoara, built around an inner citadel or *cetate*. Bran and Hunedoara are both superb Gothic/Renaissance castles, while at Alba Iulia, Arad and Oradea stand three colossal Hapsburg fortresses laid out in the geometric style of the Swiss military architect Vauban. Castles are normally **open** from 9am to 5pm or 10am to 6pm daily, except on Mondays and national holidays.

Museums (*muzeu*) are open similar hours to castles (Tues–Sun 9am–5pm or 10am–6pm), though sometimes (particularly in Bucharest) they're also closed on Tuesdays. For visitors, museums can soon pall thanks to the lack of information in any language but Romanian, not to mention the uniform approach to national history. **Village museums** (mostly closed in the winter), however, are interesting even without the benefit of captions, containing peasant houses filled with artefacts, huge oil presses, watermills and other structures rescued from the the agrarian past, laid out as if in a real community.

Student reductions are usually only granted to groups of ten or more, but in any case, museum **admission charges** are not high, a few thousand lei.

FESTIVALS AND PUBLIC HOLIDAYS

Romanian festivals fall into four groups: those linked to the Orthodox religion, with its twelve Great Feasts and hosts of lesser festivals; those marking events such as marriage, birth and death; those marking stages in the agricultural cycle; and secular anniversaries. While the last are national holidays, and never change their date, other festivals are less predictable. The Orthodox Easter is a moveable feast and still reckoned according to the Julian calendar rather than the Gregorian calendar that's used in the West and for secular purposes in Romania. Rural festivals take place on a particular day of a month, the actual date varying from year to year, and they can also be advanced or delayed depending on the progress of the crops. Given the collapse of the tourist information system, the place to check dates is the cultural office in the county *prefectură*.

Festivals specific to particular places are listed at the appropriate point in the guide; the following is an overview.

WINTER FESTIVALS

Christmas (*Crăciun*) and **New Year** (*Revelion*) celebrations are spread over the period from December 24 to January 7, and preparations often begin as early as December 6 (St Nicholas' Day) while on 20 December, pigs are slaughtered for the forthcoming feasts. Groups of youths and children meet to prepare the festival costumes and masks, and to rehearse the *colinde* – allegorical songs wishing good health and prosperity for the coming year that are sung outside each household on Christmas Eve (*Ajun*), when the faithful exchange thin pastries called *turte*.

In **Moldavia and Bucovina**, processions follow the *Capră* (Goat), a costumed dancer whose mask has a moveable lower jaw which he clacks in time with the music (to represent the death pangs of the old year). The masked carnival on December 27 in the Maramureş town of **Sighet** has similar shamanistic origins.

On **New Year's Eve**, groups of *plugăraşi* pull a plough festooned with green leaves from house to house in rural areas, cutting a symbolic furrow in each yard while a *doină* calling for good health and fecundity is recited, accompanied in Transylvania by carolling, for example at **Arpaş** and **Şercaia** in Braşov county. In Tudora and the villages around Suceava, and in Maramureş, New Year's greetings are delivered by the *buhai*, a friction drum which imitates the bellowing of a bull when horse hair is drawn through the hole in a membrane. This accompanies the *Pluguşor*, a mime play featuring people masked as goats, little horses and bears. At dawn on New Year's Day the "little ploughmen" take over, sowing in the furrows ploughed the day before.

Although the official holidays end on January 2, villagers may keep celebrating through to Epiphany (*Bobotează*) on the 6th, when water is blessed in church and taken home in bottles for medicinal purposes, and **horse races** are staged in areas like the Wallachian plain and Dobrogea. The **Huţuls** and **Lipovani**, who follow the Julian calendar, celebrate Christmas on January 6. The final celebration in January is Three Hierarchs' Day on the 30th, celebrated with great pomp in **Iaşi**'s Trei Ierarhi Church, which is dedicated to the saintly trio.

A review of Gorj county's folk ensembles and miners' brass bands – the *Izvoare fermecate* or "Enchanted Water Springs" – is held on the third Sunday of **February** in **Tîrgu Jiu**, winter conditions permitting. **March** is the time of Lent, and though few Romanians are nowadays devout enough to observe the fast, some rural folk still bake twisted loaves – *colaci* – on March 9, Forty Saints' Day, and take them to the village church to be blessed and distributed as alms. On one weekend during the month (decided at fairly short notice) an early spring festival, the Kiss Fair, takes place at **Hălmagiu**, providing the opportunity for villagers from the Apuseni and Banat regions to socialize and trade crafts.

EASTER AND FERTILITY FESTIVALS

With the onset of spring in **April and May**, agricultural work begins in earnest, roughly coinciding with Easter, the holiest festival of the Christian year. Urbanization and collectivization have both affected the nature of **spring festivals**, so that **Reşiţa**'s *Alaiul primaverii* features firefighters and engineers as well as folklore ensembles in its parade of floats (first week in April). Village festivals have tended to conglomerate, so that perhaps a dozen smallish fetes have been replaced by a single large event drawing participants and visitors from across the region – for example, the *Florile Oltului* (Flowers of the Olt) at **Avrig** on the second Sunday of April, attended by dozens of communities around Sibiu, some of whom wear the traditional Saxon jewellery of vel-

vet and paste. Similarly, the Girl Fair at **Gurghiu**, on the second Sunday in May, is an occasion for villagers from the Gurghiul, Beica and Mureş valleys to make merry. For pomp and crowds on a larger scale, the Pageant of the Juni (see p.137) is held in Braşov on the first Sunday of May.

Though its exact dates vary, the Orthodox **Easter** (*Paşte*) also falls in April or May. From *Floriile*, Palm Sunday, through the "Week of Sufferings" (*Săptămîna patimilor*, during which, it's believed, souls will ascend directly to heaven), the devout attend church services, culminating in the resurrection celebration at midnight on Easter Saturday. The cry "Christ has risen" (*Hristos o-nviat*) and the reply "Truly he has risen" (*Adevărat c-o-nviat*) resound through the candle-lit churches, full to overflowing with worshippers. With the exception of Pentecost or **Whitsun** (*Rosalia*), fifty days after Easter Sunday, other Orthodox festivals are nowadays less widely observed.

In southern Romania, there's a traditional belief (still held by a minority) that groups of village mimes and dancers can work magic if all the rites were correctly observed, and to this end selected young men were initiated into the **ritual of Căluş**. This took place in secret, and was performed by a *vătaf* who had inherited the knowledge of *descîntece* (magic charms) and the dance steps from his predecessor. On **Whit Sunday**, an odd-numbered group of these *Căluşari* began their ritual dance from house to house, accompanied by a flag-bearer and a masked *Mut* (a mute who traditionally wore a red phallus beneath his robe and muttered sexual invocations), thus ensuring that each household was blessed with children and a bountiful harvest, and, if need be, exorcizing anyone possessed by the spirits of departed friends and family. *Căluş* rites are still enacted in some Oltenian villages, and the *Căluşari* meet for a two-day celebration of their dancing and musical prowess at **Slatina** sometime in May. There's a similar festival, the *Căluşarul Transilvanean*, in **Deva** during the second week of January, which doesn't have any particular magical significance, being nowhere near the heartland of *Căluş* culture, but is nevertheless impressive.

Meanwhile, the Roman Catholic Székely hold their Whitsun pilgrimage to Csíksomlyó (near Miercurea Ciuc) on a date determined by the Gregorian calendar. The Székely also hold their version of the Festival of the Plough at **Băile Jigodin**, near Miercurea Ciuc, on the third

Sunday of May. Once common practice, the ritual garlanding of the plough is now rare, although the *Tinjaua* or Festival of the First Ploughman (first Sunday of May) at **Hoteni**, in Maramureş, is similar. The age-old **pastoral rites and feasts** marking the sorting, milking and departure of the flocks to the hills are still widespread throughout Maramureş and the **Apuseni mountains** during late April or early May, depending on local tradition and climatic factors. The best-known *Sîmbra oilor* occur on the first or second Sunday of May, at the **Huta pass** into Oaş and on the ridge of **Măgura Priei**; but lingering snows can delay the smaller festivals, perhaps even until early July.

SUMMER FESTIVALS

The Cherry Fair at **Brîncoveneşti** on the first Sunday of **June** anticipates other harvest festivals later in the month, and the round of great **summer fairs** known as *Tîrg* or *Nedeias*. In the days before all-weather roads, these events provided the people of remote highland villages with an annual opportunity to acquire news of the outside world, and to arrange deals and marriages. On the second Sunday of June, folk from some thirty Banat settlements attend the *Nedeia of Tălcălşele* at **Avram Iancu**; and another village with the same name is the base for the famous Girl Fair of **Mount Găina** (see p.206), held on the Sunday before July 20. **Fundata**'s *Nedeia of the Mountains*, theoretically on the last Sunday of June (but sometimes not until September), is the traditional gathering for people of the Braşov, Argeş and Dîmboviţa regions; while the highlanders of Oltenia have their own equivalent in the great **Polovragi Fair** (on July 15 or 20).

There are **weddings** in the villages every Saturday throughout the summer, which continue through the weekend with music, drinking and dancing. Other summer festivals perpetuate Romania's old customs and folklore: the light-hearted Buying Back of the Wives at **Hodac**, and the funereal declamation of *boccas* during The King of the Fir Trees (see p.187) at **Tiha Bîrgăului** in the heart of fictional Dracula country (on the second and third Sundays of June). *Drăgaica*, the pagan pre-harvest celebration in

the fields on Midsummer Day, is only practised in a few districts of southern Wallachia today, but *Sînziene*, the feast of St John the Baptist on June 24, is celebrated in many places with bonfires. The diversity of folk costumes and music within a particular area can be appreciated at events like **Şomcuta Mare**'s pastoral *Stejarul* (The Oak Tree), or the larger Rarău Mountain festival at **Ilişeşti**, held respectively on the first and second Sundays of **July**.

August is probably the best month for **music**, with four major festivals. During the first week,the Songs of the Olt at **Călimăneşti** in Wallachia draws musicians and folklore ensembles from all over Oltenia. On the first Sunday people from Maramureş, Transylvania and Moldavia meet for the great *Horă* at the **Prislop Pass** to socialize, feast and dance in their finest costumes; a week later, the Festival of the Ceahlău Mountain is held at **Durău** near the shores of Lake Bicaz. The music of pan pipes and the bands of Gorj county (around Tîrgu Jiu) characterize another festival, At Tismana in a Garden, where you can also find a wide range of handicrafts (for which bartering may secure the best bargains). This is held on August 15, the **Feast of the Assumption** or Dormition of the Virgin Mary, when there are many church festivals and pilgrimages across the country, notably at **Moisei** in Maramureş.

Reaping preoccupies many villages during **September**, giving rise to **harvest festivals**, although the custom is gradually declining. The timing of these varies with the crop, and from year to year, but you can usually rely upon At the Vintage at **Odobeşti** in the eastern Carpathians being held on the last Sunday. In mid-September the remaining Saxons gather for the *Sachsentreffen* at **Biertan**. Earlier in the month, on the first Sunday, you can hear the pan-pipers of the northwest perform the Rhapsody of the Trişcaşi at **Leşu**, in Bistriţa-Năsăud county. Many of the musicians are shepherds, who also play alpine long horns and bagpipes, and compete with each other at The Vrancea Shepherd's Long Pipe, a festival held at **Odobeşti** on the third Sunday of **November**.Finally, **December 1** is the national day, celebrated above all in Alba Iulia, scene of the declaration of union between Transylvania and the rest of Romania.

SPORTS AND OUTDOOR PURSUITS

Although two thirds of Romania is either plains or hills and plateaux, the country's geography is dominated by mountains, which almost enclose the "Carpathian redoubt" of Transylvania, and merge with lesser ranges bordering Moldavia and Maramureş. The scenery is often beautiful, with pastoral valleys nestled between foothills ascending to wild crags or precipitous gorges. Much of it has escaped the ravages of hasty industrialization visible in lower lying regions, and some areas, like the Harghita mountains and the ranges north of Bistriţa and Maramureş, are still essentially wildernesses, inhabited by bears, wolves and birds of prey. Throughout the mountain areas there are opportunities to pursue outdoor activities – hiking, skiing, caving and even shooting rapids.

The Danube Delta is a totally different environment, unique for its topography – of which only one tenth is dry land – and as a wildlife habitat which attracts some three hundred species of bird during the spring and autumn migrations.

SKIING

Skiing is a popular sport in the mountains from November or December through until March, or even April, depending on conditions at the nine resorts. Foreign package operators favour Poiana Braşov for its superior slopes and facilities, but by going through local agencies or turning up on the spot you can also ski at Predeal, Buşteni and Sinaia, Borşa in Maramureş (for beginners), Păltiniş south of Sibiu, Semenic in southwestern Transylvania or Durău/Ceahlău on the edge of Moldavia. The majority of pistes are rated "medium" or "easy" (colour-coded red or blue), but each of the major resorts has at least one difficult (black) run, and the descents from Coştila and Caraiman to Buşteni are positively hazardous. Details of the slopes, chair-lifts and snowcover at each resort are contained in an ONT brochure.

HIKING

The **Carpathians** – a continuation of the Alps – are the most sinuous chain of mountains in Europe, in Romania forming a natural barrier between Transylvania and the old Regat provinces, interrupted by a few narrow passes or wide depressions. Though few of Romania's Carpathian peaks are higher than 2500m, and the majority between 1000m and 2000m, lack of altitude is more than compensated for by the variety of geological formations and rockscapes, with mighty gorges (*cheile*) at Turda and Bicaz, and spectacular valleys cut by the Olt and Prahova rivers. Bizarrely eroded **rock formations** characterize Mount Ceahlău and karstic areas such as the Padiş plateau and the "Valley of Hell" in the Apuseni mountains, while the Bucegi range is famous for the Babele Sphinx, and the sheer walls overhanging Buşteni in the Prahova valley.

Dozens of **hiking trails** – signposted with red triangles, blue stripes or other markings – are shown on *Hartă Turistică* maps. Several walks are detailed in the text where appropriate, while many individual ranges are minutely covered by booklets in the "Our Mountains" series – unfortunately only published in Romanian (*Munţi Nostri*) and German (*Unsere Berge*) and available mainly from second-hand bookstores. The **Bucegi massif** is perfect for short hikes within a limited time, for it offers dramatic crags, caves and waterfalls within a few hours' walk of the cable car, which ascends from the valley just an hour's train ride from Braşov or two from the capital. To the southwest, the Făgăraş, Retezat and Parîng mountains offer the chance of longer hikes crossing several ranges.

USEFUL HIKING TERMS

hartă	map	*poiana*	glade
potecă/traseu	path/route	*izvor*	spring
nerecomandabil iarna	unsafe during winter	*cascada*	waterfall
rofugiu (salvamont)	refuge (with first aid)	*telecabina*	cable-car
şau	col (caddlo)	*toloochi*	ski-drag
stînca	rock	*telescaun*	chair lift
colţ	cliff	*vîrf*	peak
aven	doline	*cale ferată îngustă*	narrow-gauge rail line

Some tour operators organize all-inclusive **walking holidays** in the Carpathians. Independent hikers should bring camping gear and food, since accommodation in mountain *cabanas* can't be guaranteed, and some huts don't serve meals. These **cabanas** (marked on hiking maps) are convivial places where you can learn much about the mountains; but many Romanians simply pitch camp by rivers, and providing you're not in a nature reserve, you can do the same.

CAVING AND CANOEING

Though a number of large mountain **caves** (*peş teri*) with magnificent stalactites are easily accessible – at Chişcău, Meziad, Scarişoara and Polovragi, for example – most of Romania's caves are known only to a dedicated band of pot-holers.

The science and practice of caving owes much to a Romanian, Emil Racoviţa, who founded the world's first speleological institute at Cluj University, near the karst zone of the **Apuseni mountains**. This region offers the greatest range of possibilities, from easy strolling passages to vertical shafts and flooded tunnels; there are tourist caves such as Chişcău and Meziad, big river caves such as Humpleu, Magura and Cetaţile Ponorului, and any number of crevices that should only be attempted by experts. The second main area is the southern Banat and the **Mehedinţi massif**, which has river caves such as Topolniţa, Cloşani and Comarnic.

Romanian enthusiasts continue to explore the deeper reaches of many caves, constantly yielding fresh surprises. Interested groups or individuals should write several months in advance to the **Racoviţa Institute** (Str. Clinicilor 5, 3400 Cluj, or Str. Frumoasă 11, 78114 Bucureşti) , stating their experience. An offer to contribute gear and a share of the costs should increase your chances of acceptance by a local club.

It's likely that the Racoviţa Institute can also put foreigners in touch with **canoeing** enthusiasts devoted to shooting the rapids: an exciting sport practised on rivers like the Vaser in Maramureş and the Bistriţa in Bucovina, which descend steeply from their highland sources. You'll need to bring all your own equipment, since there's little chance of renting or buying anything decent.

BIRD-WATCHING

The best place for seeing **birdlife** is without a doubt the Danube Delta in late May and early June. Millions of birds winter here, or stop over during the spring and autumn migrations to northern Europe, the Mediterranean, China, Siberia and parts of Africa – a unique concentration of different species, including Europe's largest colonies of pelicans. Agencies can arrange boat tours down the main Sulina channel of the Delta, and their Tulcea or Crişan offices may sometimes be wheedled into renting small boats, which are the only means to penetrate the backwaters, where most of the birds nest. Canoes, kayaks or rowing boats are best for exploration, since boats with motors scare the wildlife and get caught up in vegetation.

You may be able to negotiate with a local fisherman for a boat (*Pot să închiriez o barcă?*), bearing in mind that he'll probably act as rower and guide. Doing it this way lessens your freedom of movement and is likely to be fairly time-consuming.

FOOTBALL

Football's 1994 World Cup brought the Romanian soccer team to international attention but many have been aware of their strengths ever since **Steaua Bucharest**, Romania's leading club, won the **European Champions' Cup** in 1986, and reached the semifinals in 1988. Although Inter Milan allegedly offered to build a Fiat car plant in Romania in order to get their hands on Gheorghe Hagi, players have only been able to move freely to West European clubs since 1990: by 1992 nine of the national team were playing abroad, in teams ranging from Red Star Belgrade to Real Madrid. Clearly, this led to a rapid development both in their individual skills and in the national team's performance.

Romania qualified top of its group for the 1994 **World Cup** in the USA and played the game of the tournament to beat Argentina 3–2, finally losing in the quarterfinal to Sweden on penalties. Since then, the team manager, Anghel Iordanescu, has been promoted to major-general in the army, and the leading Romanian players have all figured in million-pound transfer deals.

Gheorghe Hagi was seen by many as the best player of the competition, although his nickname "the Maradona of the Carpathians" is due not to his footballing or handballing skills but to his insistence on wearing the number 10 shirt. Born in Constanţa, he played for the local side before transferring to Steaua on the orders of Ceauşescu's son Valentin, who effectively ran the team. After the revolution he moved to Real Madrid for a fee of £1.8m, and after the World Cup to Barcelona, Brescia, and now Galatasaray. Many players moved to English clubs for a while (the presence of striker **Ilie Dumitrescu** and midfielder **Gica Popescu** at Tottenham Hotspur in London was supposedly dependent on the interpreting skills of the Spurs player Ronnie Rosenthal, who is of Romanian–Jewish extraction), but most have now moved on, many to play in Spain. One of the best of the younger generation, defender **Dan Petrescu**, signed to **Chelsea** from Sheffield Wednesday in 1995 for a fee of £2.3 million.

The **domestic game** is dominated by Steaua Bucharest, who won the League in 1993, 1994, 1995 and 1996. Another Bucharest team, Dinamo, are their nearest rivals, trailed at a distance by Rapid Bucharest and Universitatea Craiova. As elsewhere in Eastern Europe, clubs have traditionally been linked to workplaces or trades: Steaua (Star) is the army team, Dinamo the police (and Securitate) team, and Rapid that of the rail workers.

Every town has its stadium (*stadion*), and you should have no problem catching a **game**. Matches are played on Saturdays from August to May, with a break from November to February and tickets for league games cost around 2000 lei. Many terms, such as *meci* (match), *gol*, and *ofsaid* have been borrowed from English, although *arbitru* comes from the French for referee.

POLICE, TROUBLE AND HARASSMENT

For visitors, Romania remains generally safe, despite an explosion of violent crime, usually blamed on Gypsies but in fact more to do with alcohol abuse and the collapse of police authority. However, robbery with violence is rare, and a few commonsense precautions should minimize the risk of your possessions being stolen.

You should watch out for **pickpockets**, in particular in Bucharest, where groups of Gypsies and the like hang around the Gara de Nord and the Calea Victoriei stores; wearing a moneybelt is advisable. Take care on overnight trains, shutting the door of your sleeper compartment as securely as you can (there are no locks). If your **passport** goes missing while in Bucharest, telephone your consulate immediately; anywhere else, contact the police, who'll issue a temporary visa. It's almost impossible to replace **travellers' cheques** in Romania, so these should be guarded fanatically. Thefts and other losses can be reported to the police (*Poliția*) who will issue the paperwork required for insurance claims back home, though only slowly and with painstaking bureaucratic thoroughness.

THE POLICE

The **police force** lost its moral authority by playing a very minor role in the revolution, while the army established its position as guardians of freedom; since then the police have been reformed to a certain extent, and are generally regarded as honest if ineffectual. However they continue to attract Western disapproval by abusing the rights of Gypsies, homosexuals and other citizens. What's more, there have been cases of self-styled "police" relieving tourists of their cash in Bucharest by flashing false ID, demanding to see your passport and refusing to return it until you've bought yourself off their trumped-up charges of blackmarketeering. In rural areas the police rarely emerge from their stations except for spot-checks on cars or to bum drinks in the bars. The **border police**, though, are notoriously corrupt – always keep your baggage with you when entering or leaving the country.

Unfortunately, the **Romanian Information Service** (the SRI, still generally known as the Securitate) is still on the scene, although no longer blackmailing people to report on their neighbours, friends and family. An obsession with anti-socialist activities long ago changed to a commitment to keeping the ruling elite in power, and this has not changed with the so-called revolution. Iliescu was even more adept than Ceaușescu at manipulating opinion and engineering provocations, and the SRI was kept busy. Environmental and human rights activists may still be harassed but the SRI don't normally concern themselves with tourists.

SPECIFIC OFFENCES

Foreigners are sometimes stopped and asked for **identification** (which should be carried at all times). However, this should be the extent of your dealings with the police, unless you have something stolen or break the law. Firstly, it's obviously safer not to become involved with the black market (see below). **Photography** is permitted everywhere except in areas designated by a sign (showing a crossed-out camera), usually near any barracks, no matter how unimportant; while **nudism** and topless bathing are forbidden except on a few beaches (although offenders are more likely to be cautioned than punished). **Camping wild** is not allowed in nature reserves and forests, and dropping litter in theory incurs a $40 fine. **Sleeping rough** in towns is risky and will attract the *poliția*'s displeasure unless you do so in a train station and claim to be waiting for a train departing in the small hours. Should you be arrested, identify yourself, be polite and stay cool;

try to avoid making a statement unless the officer speaks your language fluently; and demand to contact your consulate.

BRIBES AND THE BLACK MARKET

Bribery and corruption are rife in Romania, oiling the creaking machinery of everyday life. Bribes or tips (*ciubuc*) are the means to secure proper medical attention, a telephone, a parking space, luxuries, educational opportunities, promotions – the list is practically endless. Nor is money always involved; more frequently, what happens is a reciprocal exchange of favours. Romanians refer to *pile* or "files", meaning contacts who can smooth over rough edges and expedite matters. Naturally enough this ties in with the **black market**, which is omnipresent. This has less to do with supplying illicit goods than with meeting the shortcomings of the economy.

As a visitor, you're unlikely to come into contact with this system, and as a rule the safest policy is simply not to get involved. However, if ever you can't get a room or a seat on a plane, or if you're pulled over for speeding, it's worth remembering that even one dollar can work wonders.

SEXUAL HARASSMENT AND WOMEN IN ROMANIA

It's rare for Romanian men to subject women tourists to **sexual harassment**. Foreigners can be a different matter, since, amazing as it sounds, Turks and Greeks have taken to driving north from their homelands to engage in sex tourism – Bucharest even has a couple of strip clubs now.

As independent women travellers are rare, they're likely to be accorded some respect (if not excessive solicitude) – but also viewed with some amazement, particularly in rural areas. Most trouble is alcohol-fuelled, so it's best to avoid going alone to any but the classiest bars, especially on weekend evenings. Within earshot of other people, you should be able to scare away any local pest by shouting *lasați-ma in pace*! (Leave me alone!) or calling for the *Poliția*.

Romanian women carry a double burden of work and child care in a male-dominated society, and there seems little immediate prospect of this changing. Feminism, like the peace movement, was totally discredited by the hypocritical verbiage of the Communists, and above all by having Elena Ceaușescu in charge of the national women's committee.

ATTITUDES TO GAYS

The Communist regime was relentlessly homophobic. Sexual relations between consenting adults of the same sex were illegal; offenders were jailed or forced to submit to "voluntary treatment", including electric shocks, drugs or even castration, unless they agreed to become an informer for the Securitate, a bait for other victims.

Since then things have got slightly more complicated: the Iliescu government, trying to balance liberal Western opinion with more conservative public opinion, announced that homosexuality was to be legalized for men over 18, but in fact parliament voted merely to "condone" it, with seven-year prison terms still on the books for cases "causing public scandal" (for which simply being gay can be enough). The Constantinescu government, on the other hand, is committed to adhering to international norms such as the European Convention on Human Rights, and should soon introduce proper laws to legalize homosexuality. Nevertheless, there is at least one AIDS charity in Bucharest, the *Asociație Româna Anti-SIDA*, working for safe sex and a more enlightened attitude on all sides.

DIRECTORY

USEFUL THINGS TO BRING

An alarm clock, flashlight, water-bottle, film, batteries, needle and thread, ear plugs, razor blades, first-aid kit, any prescribed medication, contraceptives, tampons, contact-lens solution, multivitamin and mineral tablets, toilet paper, a supply of concentrated food for emergencies and morale boosting, high-factor sun block, and books to read.

ADDRESSES are written as Str. Eroilor 24, III/36 in the case of apartment buildings, ie Street (*Strada*) of Heroes, number 24, third floor, apartment 36. Some blocks have several entrances, in which case this is also given, eg *scara B*. Each district of Bucharest has a *sector* number, while in some towns each district (*cartier*) is named. In small villages, houses simply have a number and no street name. Streets, boulevards (*bulevardul*), avenues (*calea* or *şoseaua*) and squares (*piaţa*) are commonly named after national heroes like Stephen the Great – Ştefan cel Mare – or Michael the Brave – Mihai Viteazul – or the date of an important event such as December 1, 1918, when Transylvania was united with the Old Kingdom.

CHILDREN qualify for various reductions, depending on their age. Rail transport is free for under-fives, and half-price for under-tens. On TAROM flights, children under two pay only 10 percent, and up to the age of twelve, 50 percent, providing they share a seat with an adult. In hotels, children under ten may often share an adult's bed for free, or pay half of the adult cost for an extra bed in the room. In big coastal resorts and at Poiana Braşov there are kindergartens for the benefit of holidaymakers. A few train stations have a specially heated room for mothers with babies (*camera mama şi copilul*).

For travellers with children, the big problems are shortages of nappies (diapers) and baby food. Local milk is not to be trusted – bring supplies

with you. Mamaia and Poiana Braşov offer the best entertainments for kids, but most large towns have a puppet theatre (*Teatrul de Păpuşi*).

CIGARETTES Romanian cigarettes are generally unappealing. The cheapest, Mărăşeşti and Carpaţi, are of rough black tobacco; Snagov are milder and slightly more expensive. The most common Western brands are Hollywood, L&M and Monte Carlo. Kent is the most expensive brand (over $1 a pack); under Communism, for some reason, this had great status on the black market, although its uses as an "alternative currency" were overstated. Matches are called *chibrit*, while a light is *foc* and a lighter is a *brichetă*. On trains smoking is allowed only in corridors or vestibules; buses are smoke-free.

DEPARTURE TAX Where applicable, departure tax is included in the cost of air tickets.

ELECTRIC POWER Nominally delivered at 220 volts at 50Hz; plugs have two prongs 18mm apart.

FISHING Permits can be arranged through OJTs in provincial towns – the Danube Delta is an angler's paradise – and other bodies of water like Lake Bicaz and the Bistriţa River in the mountains between Moldavia and Transylvania are also rewarding.

LAUNDRIES are virtually unknown, although some exist under the trade name of Nufarul; for travellers it's usually a choice between washing yourself or paying a hotel to do it.

LEFT LUGGAGE Offices (*bagaje de mîne*) exist in most train stations; there may also be lockers, but it's best to avoid these, since the locks have a tendency to jam. Always allow plenty of time to reclaim your baggage, especially in Bucharest and Constanţa, which are the only places where you're likely to have to show your passport.

PHOTOGRAPHY is forbidden near military or government buildings. ASA100 print film is available (and can be developed in an hour in many places), but anything more specialized is best brought with you.

TIME is normally two hours ahead of the UK, seven ahead of New York and ten ahead of California: clocks go forward one hour for the summer at the same time as other European countries (from the last Sunday of March to the last Sunday of September).

TIPPING Not necessary, but it's appreciated if you round the bill up for good service.

TOILETS In public places these are generally awful. You should carry a supply of paper.

PART TWO

THE
GUIDE

CHAPTER ONE

BUCHAREST AND AROUND

BUCHAREST (*Bucureşti*), with a population of over two million, is the largest city between Berlin and Athens, but it's certainly not the most beautiful. At first sight the city is a chaotic jumble of traffic-choked streets, ugly concrete apartment blocks and grandiose but uncompleted Communist developments. Lying 64km from the Danube, Romania's southern border, but 600km from its northern frontier, it's also far removed from the country's more obvious attractions. And yet, it's Romania's centre of government and commerce and site of its main airport, so most visitors to the country will find themselves passing through Bucharest at some point.

Founded by the princes of Wallachia and dominated by their Turkish overlords, Bucharest only came into its own with Romanian independence in the late nineteenth century, when it was remodelled by French and French-trained architects. The city was dubbed the "Paris of the East", as much for its hectic and cosmopolitan social scene as for its architecture. The Romanian aristocracy were among the richest and most extravagant in Europe, but this lifestyle depended on the exploitation of the poor, and in Bucharest the two co-existed in what Ferdinand Lasalle described as "a savage hotchpotch", with beggars waiting outside the best restaurants and appalling slums within a few steps of the elegant boulevards. Under Communism, these extremes were reduced, and while Capitalism has brought back conspicuous consumption and a new poor, it bears no comparison to the prewar situation. However, despite the signs of Westernization and a new prosperity, with glossy shops full of designer clothes, and kiosks selling Coca-Cola and bananas at every corner, there is still little nightlife in Romania's capital.

The architecture of the old city, with its cosmopolitan air, was notoriously scarred by Ceauşescu's redevelopment project, which demolished an immense swathe of the historic centre and replaced it with a concrete jungle, the **Centru Civic**, including a huge new palace for the Communist leader, now known as the **Palace of Parliament**. The palace has become one of the city's prime tourist sites and is best viewed along the approach from Piaţa Unirii. The other site that can on its own justify a visit to the city lies to the north of the centre: the **Village Museum**, a wonderful collection of vernacular buildings collected from all regions of Romania. Between these two poles, in the centre of the city, the **National History Museum** lays out the story of Romania's development from prehistoric times to the 1920s. It's in much the same style as every other county museum, but this is the biggest and best in the country.

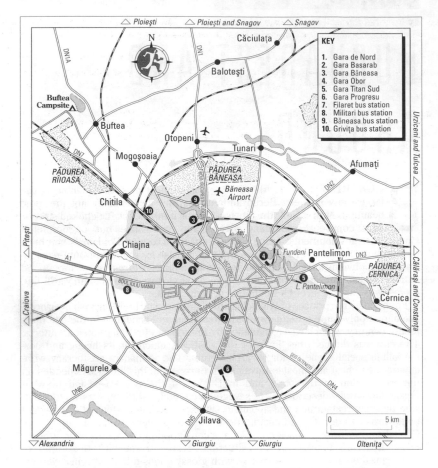

More than most European cities, Bucharest is an insider's city. Behind the congested arteries lies a tangle of backstreets where concrete is softened by abundant greenery and the inhabitants manage to rise above the bureaucratic obstructions and inadequacies of the city's infrastructure. The **people** are a cosmopolitan mixture: Romanians, Gypsies, Turks, Arabs, Africans and Pakistanis, now joined by thousands of Chinese who add yet another layer to the thriving underworld of traficanți, prostitutes and beggars.

Accommodation is more expensive in Bucharest than elsewhere, and you're more likely to be hassled, hustled and overcharged. Though power and water cuts are now rare, many hotels are overheated in summer and freezing in winter, when snowdrifts grip the city and the temperature plunges to -20°F (-4°C). Unless Bucharest is your only destination, it's as well to head for Transylvania or the coast as soon as possible. There are good train and road connections to the rest of the country, but local services to the towns and villages in the immediate vicinity are often limited or tortuous. However, there are some monasteries and mansions, notably at Snagov, which can be visited as day-trips.

Some history

According to legend, Bucharest was founded by a shepherd called **Bucur**, who built a settlement amid the Vlăsia forest. It was recorded as a nameless "citadel on the Dîmbovița" in 1368, and named as Bucharest in an edict from the time of Vlad the Impaler. Over the centuries, both Tîrgoviște and Bucharest have served as the Wallachian capital, but Bucharest finally secured its claim in 1659 – its location at the convergence of the trading routes to Istanbul outweighing the defensive advantages of Tîrgoviște's location in the Carpathian foothills.

As the boyars (nobles) moved into the city they built **palaces** and **churches** on the main streets radiating from the centre; these streets were surfaced with timber baulks and known as "bridges" (*pod*). Despite earthquakes and periodic attacks by Turks, Tatars, Austrians and Russians over the course of its history, the city has continued to grow and to modernize. New **boulevards** were driven through the existing street pattern in the 1890s, after the style of Haussmann's Paris, and they still form a ring road and the main north–south and east–west axes of the city. Most of the major buildings, such as the **Romanian Athenaeum** and the **Cercul Militar**, were designed by French or French-trained architects and built in the years before World War I. By 1918 the city's population had grown to 380,000 and roads such as Podul Mogoșoaiei, Podul de Pămînt and Podul Calacilor were widened, paved and renamed as the Calea Victoriei, Calea Plevnei and Calea Rahovei, in honour of the battles of the 1877–78 War of Independence from Turkey.

After World War II the city was ringed with ugly apartment buildings, first in areas such as "Red" Grivița, which the Allies had bombed flat (aiming for the rail yards), then expanding into the surrounding countryside; the population doubled from one to two million. Finally, in 1984, Ceaușescu set out to impose his megalomaniac vision on the city, demolishing most of the area south of the centre to create a new **Centru Civic** which remains unfinished and seems likely to scar the city for many years yet.

Arrival, information and city transport

While city transport, at least round the centre, is fairly adequate during the day, it is almost non-existent at night and street lighting throughout Bucharest leaves a lot to be desired. It is therefore best to avoid arriving in Bucharest late at night, unless you're willing to take a taxi to your hotel. Both of the city's **airports** are on the main road north of the city and are linked by express bus with the city centre; the **train station** is a little way out of the centre to the west, but is on the city's metro system. There are six **bus stations** in the city, all in the suburbs and mainly serving the local villages, so its unlikely that you'll arrive at any of them, but there are **private bus services** to major destinations throughout the country, which come and go from Calea Griviței, opposite the train station.

By air

International air passengers arrive at **Otopeni airport**, 16km north of the centre. You can buy your visa (if needed) on arrival and change money. There are several car rental companies with outlets here, including Hertz (☎01/212.01.22; daily 8am–8pm). If your flight does not include transfers to the city, you can either give in to the mob of taxi drivers ($25), or fight your way across the car park to find express bus #783 to Piaţa Unirii (Mon–Fri every 15min, Sat & Sun every 30min; journey time 30–40min; about $1). The ONT tourist office in the city centre can also arrange transfer by car for $20.

Internal flights (and those of Air Moldova, Ukrainian Airlines and DacAir) land at **Băneasa airport**, from where you can catch bus #131, #334 or #783 or tram #5 into the centre, or bus #205 to the Gara de Nord, until around 11.30pm; night bus #414 runs to Piaţa Unirii.

By train

Virtually all international and domestic services terminate at the **Gara de Nord**, a busy, squalid hive. Luggage can be stored at the *bagaj de mînă* on the concourse opposite platforms 4 and 5. A few trains, mostly locals, terminate at the **Gara Basarab** (700m northwest of the main station, or one metro stop towards Republica), **Gara Obor**, northeast of the centre (trolley buses #69 and #85) and **Gara Progresu**, on the southern outskirts (bus #116). **Gara Băneasa**, north of Piaţa Presei Libere, is used mainly by summer trains to the coast.

It's a thirty-minute walk from the Gara de Nord to the city centre; head right along Calea Griviţei to reach Calea Victoriei, the city's main north–south axis. Alternatively, you could take the metro to Piaţa Victoriei (one stop towards Dristor II), where you can change onto line M2 to reach Piaţa Universităţii, the nearest stop to the heart of the city, or catch a taxi, which shouldn't cost more than a couple of dollars. Buses and trams from the Gara de Nord run around the centre rather than straight through it.

By road

Arriving **by road** in your own vehicle is much the easiest option, although drivers should be wary of potholes, cyclists, drunks and wandering animals on the "highways" at night. Approaching from Transylvania on the DN1 you'll pass both airports before reaching the Şoseaua Kiseleff, an avenue which leads directly to the centre. The approach from Giurgiu (the point of entry from Bulgaria) on the DN5 is less inspiring, with a long run through high-rise suburbs until Bulevardul Dimitrie Cantemir finally reaches the Piaţa Unirii; likewise, the A1 motorway from Piteşti and the west brings you in through serried ranks of apartment blocks before reaching the Cotroceni Palace. The DN3 from the coast leads through the modern suburb of Pantelimon before reaching the older districts along Bulevardul Carol I.

Long-distance buses and private buses from towns such as Tîrgovişte or Rîmnicu Vîlcea will drop you at the *Hotel Nord* (semi-permanently closed for refurbishment), on Calea Griviţei by the Gara de Nord. Bucharest's six **bus stations** are all on the edge of town and primarily serve the local villages. The main ones are Filaret, on Piaţa Filaret (in the station built in 1869 for Bucharest's first rail line), which sends buses south and southeast towards Giurgiu and Olteniţa; Băneasa, on B-dul Ionescu de la Brad 1, serving Snagov, Fierbinţi and Ploieşti to the north; Militari, B-dul Păcii (Metro Păcii or bus #785) for points west, including Clejani and Potlogi; and Griviţa, Şos. Chitilei 221 (at the *Mezeş* terminal of tram #45), serving Tîrgovişte.

Information

Bucharest's **tourist office**, ONT, is 150m south of the Piaţa Romană metro station at B-dul Magheru 7 (Mon–Fri 8am–5pm, until 8pm for currency exchange, Sat 8am–3pm, Sun 8am–1pm; ☎01/613.07.59 or 614.51.60). The staff here will change money, rent cars and rooms and arrange "programmes" with alacrity.

Desks in the hotels *Intercontinental*, at B-dul Bălcescu 4, and *Bucureşti*, at Calea Victoriei 63–81 (Mon–Fri 8am–4pm, Sat 8am–2pm), also supply tourist information, but this may mean little more than providing you with a city **map**. The ONT maps are serviceable, but better ones are available from stalls on the north side of Bulevardul Carol I by the university, particularly the map by Editura Museion (1992). *Nine O'Clock*, the main English-language newspaper available free from major hotels and airline offices, and the new listings magazine *Bucureşti What, Where, When*, contain listings of weekend events, such as theatre and opera.

City transport

Public transport is a little chaotic, but has improved over recent years, with route maps now appearing on the new aluminium bus shelters; smaller stops give details of the frequency but not the routes of bus services. Most **bus** and **tram** routes avoid the central zone, apart from some express buses on the main axes. Now that the core **metro system** is open this isn't such a problem, but you may still find yourself walking a lot – no great hardship in this city of green, picturesque backwaters. Beyond the downtown thoroughfares, roads are still poor so that buses and trams seem set to rattle themselves to pieces, and trolley buses frequently slip from the wires and stall.

Buses and trams

There is a flat fare of about 15¢ on **trolley buses** (*troleibuz*), **trams** (*tramvai*), and most **buses** (*autobuz*), all of which run from 5am until midnight. You need to buy tickets in advance, for two rides or more, from street kiosks (5am–8pm), and punch them once aboard. It costs about double the standard fare to travel on the city's **express buses**, using magnetic tickets, also bought in advance. In addition private **minibuses** (*maxitaxis*) operate along the major arteries; these too charge about double the standard bus fare, the current rate being posted in the window.

KEY BUS ROUTES	
• North–South	along B-duls Magheru and Bălcescu: #781, #783 and #784.
• East–West	(north of the centre)
	along B-dul Dacia: #785 (Mon–Sat) and #133.
	along B-duls Regina Elisabeta and Carol I (via the university): #66 (Metro Obor), #69 (Gara Obor).
	from Gara de Nord to Strada Baicului (Gara Obor): #85.
• East–West	(south of the centre)
	along Splaiul Indepentei and B-dul Unirii: #104 (Opera–National Stadium), #123 (Gara de Nord–Vitan).
• East	From Piaţa Rosetti: #782 (to Granitul) and #63 (to Metro Obor).

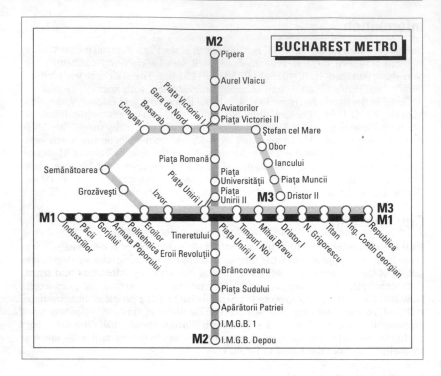

BUCHAREST METRO

The metro

The **metro** runs from 5am until 11pm, with magnetic tickets costing from about 20¢ for two rides to 90¢ for ten; there's a day ticket which is worth having if you're planning to make five or more metro trips. The first line, M1 (shown in yellow on maps), was built to serve the new working-class suburbs, and runs east–west; the second, M2 (blue), runs north–south through the centre, and the third, M3 (red), branches off M1 and loops north to link the Gara de Nord with Piaţa Victoriei and Dristor II. Although local maps indicate a change from M1 to M3 at the Gara de Nord, trains do in fact run through from Republica to Dristor II; this may change when the branch to Laromet finally opens.

With poor maps, signposting and lighting, it is not easy to find your way around the stations; announcements giving the name of the next stop once you are on the trains are helpful, if difficult to hear at times.

Taxis

Taxis are easy to find, although regular rises in the price of fuel lead to frequent protests and strikes. State-owned vehicles are generally the only ones with meters, so agree a fair price (in lei, as a rule) before getting into the more numerous private *taxis-particular*. For a short journey anywhere in the centre, a few dollars should suffice; you shouldn't pay more than $10 or so to travel right across the city, while the airport run starts at $25. Don't expect to get any change.

Accommodation

Most of Bucharest's **hotels** are optimistically aimed at foreign businessmen and the city's few budget places are in the worst area of town. To make matters worse, many of the least expensive hotels have either closed down for refits, or have been snapped up for their real-estate value and turned into offices. Of those that remain, many fail to come up to Western standards. Hotels are found in four main areas of the city, as listed below; most places are rather run-down (if not plain sleazy), but some retain Art Deco furnishings and an old-world feel. In addition, there's a limited selection of **private rooms** and **dormitory beds** available; you can contact these direct, or the tourist office can arrange bookings for you.

Hotels

The cheapest location is around the **Gara de Nord**, where the late-night ambience is much as you'd expect in this seedy area. Around the **Piaţa Revoluţiei and the university** you're in the true heart of the city, where many of the better hotels are. If you can afford to, this is the best place to stay. The area between the **Cişmigiu Gardens and Piaţa Unirii** contains the hotels of most architectural character; while the most pricey, privately run establishments lie out on the fringes of the inner city. In the no-man's-land to the **north beyond Piaţa Presei Libere** are three modern hotels (reached by bus #331 from Piaţa Lahovari), patronized by bus parties and those working at the nearby Exhibition Complex; the luxury *Sofitel* hotel, also serving business parties from the Exhibition Complex, is on the south side of Piaţa Presei Libere.

Around the Gara de Nord

Astoria, B-dul D. Golescu 27 (☎01/637.73.36, fax 638.26.90). A Stalinist pile owned by the CFR and newly renovated. Some rooms have cable TV and air-conditioning. It's the largest hotel in this area and is overpriced, so there should be space. Singles and doubles (all with bathrooms). ⑧.

Bucegi, Str. Witing 2 (☎01/637.52.25). Popular with the local underworld and not exactly spotless, but conveniently located, offering one- to four-bed rooms; some doubles have private bathrooms. There's also a restaurant. ②.

ACCOMMODATION PRICES

Hotels listed in this guide have been price-graded according to the scale below. Prices given are those charged for the cheapest **double room** available, which in the less expensive places usually comes without private bath or shower and without breakfast. Price codes are expressed in US dollars as the Romanian leu is not a stable currency, but you will generally pay for your room in lei.

Note that some hotels are currently closed for modernization, and others, now open, will no doubt follow in the near future. This is bound to result in higher rates when they reopen, so the prices quoted should be taken only as a guideline.

① $10 and under	④ $20–25	⑦ $40–50
② $10–15	⑤ $25–30	⑧ $50–65
③ $15–20	⑥ $30–40	⑨ $65 and over

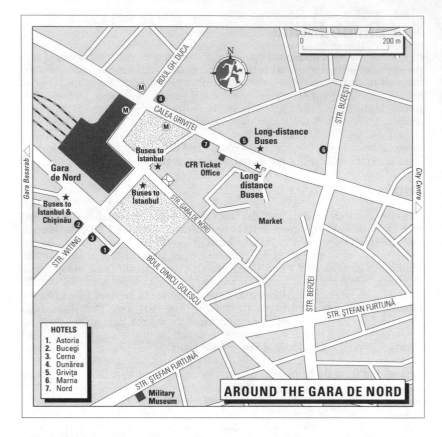

AROUND THE GARA DE NORD

HOTELS
1. Astoria
2. Bucegi
3. Cerna
4. Dunărea
5. Grivița
6. Marna
7. Nord

Cerna, B-dul D. Golescu 29 (☎01/637.40.87, fax 311.07.21). Small, clean and warm. Used by Turks in transit. Takeaway patisserie on the ground floor. Singles and doubles. ②.

Dunărea, Calea Griviței 140 (☎ & fax 01/222.98.20). Opposite the Gara de Nord, at the junction with B-dul Gh. Duca. Friendly, with singles, doubles and triples, some only with basins; some are nice, but most are noisy. ②.

Grivița, Calea Griviței 130 (☎01/650.23.27). Two hundred metres east of the Gara de Nord. One- to four-bed rooms; basic and run-down, but still usually full. ①.

Marna, Str. Buzești 3 (☎01/659.67.33). Just around the corner from the *Grivița*. Much improved by privatization, with a bar (for guests only) and rooms at a range of prices, but with trams rattling by, it's fairly noisy. ③.

Nord, Calea Griviței 143 (☎01/650.60.81). The only luxury hotel in this area, but semi-permanently closed for refurbishment.

Around Piața Revoluției and the university

Ambasador, B-dul Magheru 10 (☎01/615.90.80 or 614.61.50, fax 312.12.39). A vaguely Art Deco block built in the 1930s and situated opposite the tourist office. Now modernized – with air-conditioning sauna, gym, disco and cabaret – and at least some of the prostitutes have been cleared out. ⑨.

Athénée Palace, Str. Episcopei 1, on the northern side of Piața Revoluției (☎01/614.18.11 or 614.08.99). Now closed for restoration by the Hilton chain (at a cost of $21m), when it reopens, it will be one of the most expensive hotels in the city. It's already the most famous hotel in Romania, with a long history of intrigue and espionage (see p.67).

Banat, Piața Rosetti 5 (☎01/613.10.56, fax 312.65.47). Four hundred metres east of Piața Universității. Recently refurbished, but some rooms remain basic, with shared showers. Shame about the showgirls bar on the ground floor. ④.

București, Calea Victoriei 63–81 (☎01/312.70.70, fax 312.09.27). Sited near the Piața Revoluției, this is the country's best Romanian-managed hotel, albeit with heavy French investment. Restaurant and grill, sauna and swimming pools. Most of the prostitutes from the *Athénée Palace* seem to have moved in. ⑨.

Bulevard, B-dul Regina Elisabeta 1 (☎01/615.33.00, fax 312.39.23). A *fin-de-siècle* pile with Louis XIV decor. Fantastic marble and stucco in the bar and restaurant. Nightclub with cabaret. ⑥.

Capitol, Calea Victoriei 29 (☎01/615.80.30 or 613.94.40, fax 312.41.69). A fine turn-of-the-century building near the central post office. The hotel has its own beer hall as well as a good restaurant. No single rooms. ⑨.

Carpați, Str. Matei Millo 16 (☎01/615.76.90, fax 312.18.57). A friendly place, just north of the *Palas* hotel. Singles and doubles with bathrooms; being renovated in 1997. ⑦.

Continental, Calea Victoriei 56 (☎01/614.53.49 or 638.50.22, fax 312.01.34). Dating from 1877. Expensive, but more classy than the *București*. ⑨.

Dorobonați, Calea Dorobanților 1 (☎01/211.54.90, fax 312.01.51). A high-rise with almost three hundred rooms and slow lifts. Some rooms have air-conditioning. ⑨.

Intercontinental, B-dul Bălcescu 4 (☎01/210.73.30, fax 312.04.86). One of the city's main landmarks and still the businessman's and journalist's first choice. Some refurbishment since privatization, with sauna, gym, pool and casino. American breakfast included in the price of a room. ⑨.

Lido, B-dul Magheru 5 (☎01/614.49.30, fax 312.65.44). Built in 1930 and restored in 1995, this is now a luxury hotel with a sauna, gym, pool, jacuzzi and Chinese restaurant. ⑨.

Majestic, Str. Academiei 11 (☎01/210.27.25, fax 210.27.49). Magnificent building, renovated at last to live up to its name, with every conceivable comfort, as well as Western oddities such as a "no-smoking" floor and proper fire escape signs. Good location near the university. The main entrance is now by the *Odeon* theatre on Calea Victoriei. Singles, doubles, and suites. ⑤.

Minerva, Str. Gh. Manu 2 (☎01/650.60.10, fax 312.39.63). Furthest north of this group, housing Bucharest's longest-established Chinese restaurant. Satellite TV, air-conditioning and expensive mini-bars, with an efficient reception and room service. Reservations are necessary as it's usually full. ⑨.

Muntenia, Str. Academiei 21 (☎01/614.60.10). South of Piața Revoluției. Bar and travel agencies in the hotel. One- to four-bed rooms, some with showers. Pricey for a one-star place. ⑥.

Opera, Str. Brezoianu 37 (☎01/614.10.75, fax 312.52.91). Currently closed for refurbishment, but due to reopen in 1999. Located two blocks west of the Calea Victoriei, near the Cișmigiu Gardens. Singles, doubles and apartments, some with bathrooms.

Palas, Str. C. Mille 18 (☎01/615.37.10, fax 312.22.49). Just west of Calea Victoriei, one block south of the *Opera* hotel. Singles and doubles, some with bathrooms. ③.

Between the Cișmigiu Gardens and Piața Unirii

Central, Str. Brezoianu 13 (☎01/615.56.37, fax 615.56.34). Behind *McDonald's*, off the busy B-dul Regina Elisabeta. Faded atmosphere; overpriced doubles and triples. All with bathrooms and breakfast. ⑨.

Dîmbovița, Str. Schitu Măgureanu 6 (☎01/615.62.44 or 615.62.45). Cramped, old-fashioned place on a quiet side street by the seventeenth-century Church of Sf Ilie-Gorgan. Near the Centru Civic and Metro Izvor; some rooms overlook the Palace of Parliament. Beware of the low bathroom doors. Breakfast included in the price, but served in the nearby *Veneția* hotel. ②.

Hanul lui Manuc, Str. Iuliu Maniu 62 (☎01/613.14.15, fax 312.28.11). Simple, agreeable rooms in a famous old *caravanserai* just off Piața Unirii. Only two stars but worth every penny; reservations usually required. Restaurant and wine cellar. ⑧.

Universal, Str. Gabroveni 12 (☎01/614.85.33). On a quiet side street parallel to Str. Lipscani, to the west of B-dul Brătianu. Easily the least expensive hotel in the centre, if you can get in. It's only open July and August; the rest of the year it's used as student accommodation. ②.

Veneția, Piața Kogălniceanu 2 (☎01/615.91.48 or 615.91.49). Small, fairly clean, old-fashioned place with basic – and noisy – singles, doubles and triples, all with shared facilities. A few have balconies over the Cismigiu Gardens. Ten minutes' walk from the Palace of Parliament and the university. ③.

North and east of the centre

Casa Victor, Str. Cîmpia Turzii 44 (☎ & fax 01/222.94.36). A pleasant private hotel with just twelve rooms, in a quiet area north of the centre (metro Aviatorilor); the fine *Bolta Rece* restaurant (☎01/222.72.58) is just a block away. ⑨.

Erbas, Av. Alexandru Șerbănescu 27 (☎01/223.48.56, fax 223.45.27). Upmarket, with air-conditioning, cable TV and conference facilities, but convenient only for the airports. ⑨.

Flora, Str. Poligrafei 1 (☎01/222.39.00, fax 312.83.44). By the *Parc* and *Turist* hotels, now privatized and expensive; with pool, sauna, tennis and geriatric treatment centre. ⑥.

Helveția, Piața Charles de Gaulle 13 (☎01/223.05.66, fax 223.05.67). Bucharest's first privately built hotel – small, select, in a quiet area out north by the Aviatorilor metro. ⑨.

Lebăda, B-dul Biruinței 3 (☎01/624.30.10, fax 312.80.44). Inaugurated in 1987, in the former Pantelimon Monastery, later used as a TB sanatorium (and rumoured to be still infected with the bacillus); on an island in a lake, south of the suburb of Pantelimon (bus #782 to Granitul, then any bus east except #246 or #322). Facilities include tennis courts, bowling alley and pool. ⑨.

Parc, Str. Poligrafei 3 (☎01/222.90.85, fax 222.59.38). This is the only hotel in Bucharest that accepts ACR hotel coupons. Housed in an unattractive high-rise, but with plenty of facilities, including a sauna and pool (shared with the *Turist* hotel), hairdresser, coffee shop, bar and restaurant. ⑧.

Sofitel, B-dul Expoziției 2 (☎01/223.40.00, fax 222.46.50). Opened in 1994 and catering for conference members from the Exhibition Centre nearby. Luxury class, with the best fitness and leisure facilities in town, but fairly anonymous; you could be anywhere in the world. ⑨.

Triumf, Șos. Kisseleff 12 (☎01/222.31.72, fax 223.24.11). A huge red-brick building in the indigenous neo-Brîncovenesc style, set in parkland (with tennis courts) off Șoseaua Kisseleff. Lots of singles, as well as twin rooms, all with showers, and a top-class restaurant. ⑧.

Turist, Str. Poligrafei 5 (☎01/222.83.23, fax 222.46.19). More down-at-heel than the *Parc* hotel next door, but cheaper and with its own self-service restaurant. ④.

Camping

Camping is only feasible in summer, when the campsites are sure to be open and the weather is warm enough. In any case, the facilities are pretty run-down and the remoteness of the sites adds to their disadvantages. Previously, the main alternative to hotels was *Băneasa* campsite, situated out towards Otopeni airport, but this is currently being used to house Somali refugees. The other sites are even further from the city, in the villages of Buftea and Snagov.

In **Buftea** you can camp or take a chalet at the *plaja*, which is a 25-minute walk around the west side of the lake. The village is served by seven slow trains a day on the Bucharest–Ploiești line, by the busy *maxitaxi* #508 from the Gara de Nord, and by bus #460 from the Laromet tram terminus (tram #20 from Schitu Măgure-anu, west of the Cişmigiu Gardens, and #31 from the Gara de Nord).

Snagov is an excursion in its own right (see p.88), but it is harder to reach by public transport than Buftea, with just three buses from Băneasa bus station, and two local trains from the Gara de Nord on summer weekends only. The village has **two campsites** – the *Snagov Sat*, by the train station in the railway-owned CFR Complex, and the *Snagov Parc*, 5km along the turn-off on the DN1 at km35.

Private accommodation and dormitory beds

The ONT office on Bulevardul Magheru will give you a list of addresses for **private rooms**; if you phone ahead (☎01/614.07.59) and ask for *Relaţia Anglia* you may find someone who is prepared to make arrangements for you. Fortunately most high-rise suburban apartments are too cramped to have spare rooms, so you're likely to find yourself in an older house not far from the centre. Not all places include breakfast, so be sure to check before you commit yourself. Expect to pay $15 for a centrally located double room; for longer stays you'll pay less – around $50 a week, sometimes with meals included. You may also be approached at the Gara de Nord by locals offering a room, but you should exercise caution here.

Beds in student **hostels** (*cămin de studenţi*), available in the summer holidays, are often a cheaper alternative to the hotels, but they offer only the most basic of facilities. The most central is the **Nicolae Bălcescu Agronomical Institute**, near the Casă Presei Libere (bus #105 from the Gara de Nord, or trams #41 or #42), and the best is the **Villa Helga**, at Str. Salcimilor 2 (☎01/610.22.14), a new, independent youth hostel, with a communal lounge, cable TV, kitchen and free use of a washing machine.

The City

The heart of the city is the **Piaţa Revoluţiei**, site of the old Royal Palace and the scene of Ceauşescu's downfall. It lies halfway along Bucharest's historic north–south axis, the **Calea Victoriei**, which is still the main artery of city life. Buses heading north and south, however, use the unattractive boulevards east of Calea Victoriei; the main junction along them is the **Piaţa Universităţii**, scene of major events immediately after the 1989 revolution.

The majority of sights are within walking distance of these two Piaţas. Just to the south lies the historic centre of the city, with the remains of the original **citadel**. Beyond this, across the River Dîmboviţa, is the contrasting cityscape of Ceauşescu's **Centru Civic**, with its centrepiece, the monstrous **Palace of Parliament**, now perhaps the city's main tourist attraction. Just west of the centre are the **Cişmigiu Gardens'** a tranquil space and a popular place for assignations. For a taste of the old atmosphere of the city, you need to wander north and west of the gardens past the vine-covered facades, to suburbs where life retains a village-like slowness and intimacy, or head north from Piaţa Revoluţiei along Calea Victoriei to **Herăstrău Park**, the site of a superb collection of buildings brought here from all over Romania and assembled in an area known as the **Village Museum**.

BUCHAREST'S NEW STREET NAMES

If you have an old map or are trying to find a pre-revolutionary address, it is worth noting some of the street names that have changed since 1989.

Old name	New name
Aleea Trandafirilor	B–dul Constantin Prezan
B-dul Ana Ipătescu	B-dul Lascăr Catargiu
B-dul Anul 1848	B-dul Brătianu
B-dul Armata Poporului	B-dul Iuliu Maniu
B-dul Dimitrov	B-dul Ferdinand I
B–dul George Coşbuc	B–dul Regina Maria
B-dul Gheorghiu-Dej	B-dul Kogălniceanu, then B-dul Regina Elisabeta
B-dul Ilie Pintilie	B-dul Iancu de Hunedoara
B-dul Petru Groza	B-dul Eroilor Sanitari
B-dul Republicii (eastern end)	B-dul Carol I
B-dul Vacăreşti (northern part)	B-dul Mircea Vodă
B-dul Victorie Socialismului	B-dul Unirii
Calea Călărăşilor	Calea Copoşu
Casa Republicii	Casa Poporului, then Palatul Parlamentului
Str. Galaţi	Str. Vasile Lascăr
Str. Nuferilor	Str. General Berthelot
Str. A. Sahia	Str. J. L. Calderon
Str. 13 Decembrie	Str. Ion Câmpineanu
Str. Mărăşeşti	Str. Octavian Goga
Str. Oneşti	Str. Dem. Dobrescu
Str. Cosmonautilor	Str. George Enescu
Str. N. Beloiannis	Str. Tache Ionescu
Str. 30 Decembrie	Str. Iuliu Maniu
Str. T. Speranţă	B-dul Decebal
Str. D. Lupu (southern half)	Str. T. Arghezi
Piaţa Aviatorilor	Piaţa Charles de Gaulle
Piaţa Cosmonautilor	Piaţa Lahovari
Piaţa Scînteia	Piaţa Presei Libere
Piaţa Ilie Pintilie	Piaţa Sfinţii Voievozi
Piaţa Gheorghiu-Dej	Piaţa Revoluţiei

Piaţa Revoluţiei

The **Piaţa Revoluţiei** (Square of Revolution) is a large, irregular space towards the southern end of Calea Victoriei. The square was created in the 1930s to ensure a protective field of fire around the Royal Palace, in the event of revolution. While Romania's monarchy was overthrown by other means, the square fulfilled its destiny in 1989, when the Ceauşescus were forced to flee by crowds besieging Communist Party headquarters; two days of fighting left the buildings around the square burnt out or pockmarked with bullet holes – with the conspicuous exception of the Central Committee building, which was at the centre of the storm. With many of the grand edifices that surround it closed for restoration, the Piaţa Revoluţiei now has a melancholy air.

THE FALL OF THE CEAUŞESCUS

Romania's revolution was the most dramatic of the popular revolts that convulsed Eastern Europe in 1989. On the morning of December 21, 1989, a staged demonstration organized to show support for the **Ceauşescu** regime following days of rioting against it in Timişoara backfired. Eight minutes into Ceauşescu's speech from the balcony of the Central Committee building, part of the eighty-thousand-strong crowd began chanting "Ti-mi-şoa-ra, Ti-mi-şoa-ra", the leader's shock and fear were televised across Romania before transmissions ceased. From that moment it was clear that the end of the Ceauşescu regime was inevitable. Though the square was cleared by nightfall, larger crowds poured back next day, emboldened by news that the army was siding with the people in Timişoara and Bucharest. Strangely, the Ceauşescus remained inside the Central Committee building until midday, when they scrambled aboard a helicopter on the roof, beginning a flight that would end with their **execution** in a barracks in Tirgovişte, on Christmas Day.

The revolution was tainted by having been stage-managed by the National Salvation Front that took power in the name of the people. The National Salvation Front consisted of veteran Communists, one of whom later let slip to a journalist that plans to oust the Ceauşescus had been laid months before. Among the oddities of the "official" version of the events were Iliescu's speech on the Piaţa Revoluţiei at a time when "terrorist" snipers were causing mayhem in the square, and the battle for the Interior Ministry, during which both sides supposedly ceased firing after a mysterious phone call. Given the hundreds of genuine "martyrs of the revolution", the idea that it had been simply a ploy by Party bureaucrats to oust the Ceauşescus was shocking and potentially damaging to the new regime – so the secret police were ordered to mount an investigation, which duly concluded that while manipulation *had* occurred, the Russians, Americans and Hungarians were to blame.

The Royal Palace and National Art Museum

The most imposing of the buildings surrounding the Piaţa Revoluţiei is the former **Royal Palace**, on its northwestern corner. When the original single-storeyed dwelling burnt down in 1927, the then king, Carol II, decided to replace it with something far more impressive. The surrounding dwellings were razed in order to build a new palace, with discreet side entrances to facilitate visits by Carol's mistress, Magda Lupescu, and the shady financiers who formed the couple's clique. However, the resultant, sprawling brownstone edifice has no real claim to elegance and the palace was spurned as a residence by Romania's post-war rulers, Ceauşescu preferring a villa in the northern suburbs pending the completion of his own palace in the Centru Civic, and Iliescu and Constantinescu opting for the Cotroceni Palace, previously used by the Party youth organization, "The Pioneers".

Since 1950 the palace has housed the **National Art Museum** (Wed–Sun 10am–6pm) in its southern wing. This building was one of those most seriously damaged in 1989, when over a hundred paintings were said to have been destroyed by gunfire. Eight years later, it remains closed, other than for temporary exhibitions, due to lack of sponsorship for its restoration.

The rest of the square

The north side of the square is filled by the **Athénée Palace Hotel**, which, since it was built in 1912, has been one of the most prestigious hotels in Bucharest. The

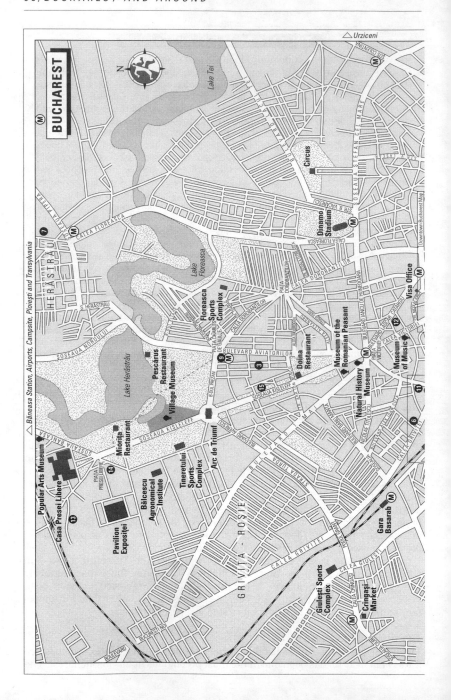

△Urziceni

BUCHAREST

Lake Tei

Circus

Dinamo Stadium

Lake Floreasca

Floreasca Sports Complex

S. HERASTRAU

CALEA FLOREASCA

HERASTRAU

SOSEAUA NORDULUI

Lake Herăstrău

Pescarus Restaurant

Village Museum

Museum of the Romanian Peasant

Natural History Museum

Doina Restaurant

Visa Office

BULEVARD AVIATORILOR

PIAŢA CHARLES DE GAULLE

SOSEAUA KISELEFF

Miorita Restaurant

SOSEAUA KISELEFF

Arc de Triumf

Museum of Music

Popular Arts Museum

Casa Presei Libere

PIAŢA PRESEI LIBERE

Pavilion Expoziţei

Băicescu Agronomical Institute

Tineretului Sports Complex

GRIVIŢA - ROŞIE

Gara Basarab

Giuleşti Sports Complex

Cringaşi Market

CALEA GIULEŞTI

CALEA GRIVIŢEI

BOULEVARD

BUCUREŞTI NO

Downtown Bucharest Map

△ Băneasa Station, Airports, Campsite, Ploieşti and Transylvania

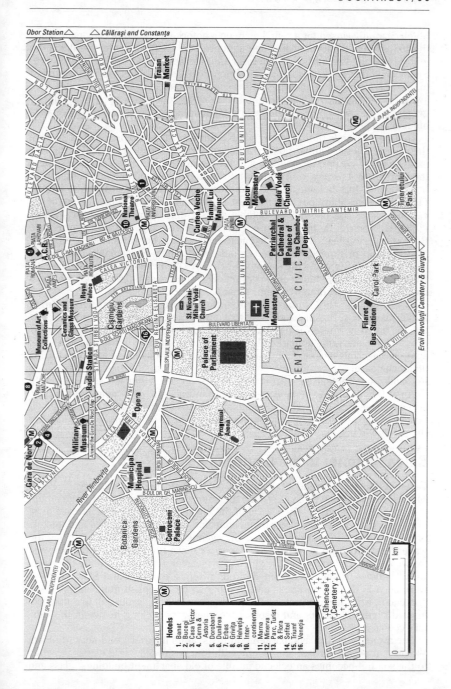

Obor Station △   △ Călăraşi and Constanţa

Traian Market

National Theatre

Curtea Veche

Hanul Lui Manuc

Bucur Monastery

Radu Vodă Church

BULEVARD DIMITRIE CANTEMIR

Patriarchal Cathedral & Palace of the Chamber of Deputies

Tineretului Park

A.C.R.

PIATA ROMANA

Royal Palace

Museum of Art Collections

Ceramics and Glass Museum

Cişmigiu Gardens

St. Nicolai-Mihai Vodă Church

CIVIC

Carol Park

Radio Station

Antim Monastery

Filaret Bus Station

BULEVARD LIBERTĂŢII

B-DUL UNIRII

Palace of Parliament

Military Museum

Opera

CENTRU

Progresul Arena

Gara de Nord

Municipal Hospital

B-DUL DR. GH. MARINESCU

River Dîmboviţa

Botanical Gardens

Cotroceni Palace

B-DUL IULIU MANU

Ghencea Cemetery

Eroii Revoluţii Cemetery & Giurgiu ▽

1 km

Hotels
1. Banat
2. Bucegi
3. Casa Victor
4. Cerna & Astoria
5. Dorobanţi
6. Dunărea
7. Erbas
8. Grivita
9. Helveţia
10. Inter-continental
11. Marna
12. Minerva
13. Parc, Turist & Flora
14. Sofitel
15. Triumf
16. Veneţia

hotel, currently closed for a refit, has been a notorious hotbed of espionage since the 1930s, when the liveried staff and almost all the characters who populated the lobby spied for Carol's police chief, for the Gestapo or for British Intelligence. Symbolic of that fevered, corrupt era, Bucharest's elite partied here through the night while police were shooting strikers in the "Red" Grivița district only a mile away. During the early 1950s the hotel was extensively refurbished as an "intelligence factory", with bugged rooms and tapped phones, to reinforce the reports of its informers and prostitutes.

To the east stands the classical-style **Romanian Athenaeum**, opened in 1888; the George Enescu Philharmonic Orchestra performs here in the hall of its rampantly *fin-de-siècle* interior beneath a dome decorated with lyres. To the south is the **University Library**, which was totally gutted in December 1989, but has now been rebuilt. Just behind this, at Str. Rosetti 8, is **Theodor Aman's House** (Tues–Sun 9am–5pm), possibly the best and certainly the most convenient of the various "memorial houses" of notable artists dotted around the city. Aman (1831–91) trained in Paris before returning to be the first director of the Bucharest Art College. A somewhat academic painter, he was a leading member of the group of Francophile intellectuals (with fellow Romanians, the painter Gheorghe Tattarescu and the sculptor Karl Storck) which dominated Bucharest's cultural life in the late nineteenth century. The house was built in 1868 to Aman's own designs and decorated by himself and Storck.

Southeast of the square stands the **former Communist Party Headquarters**, a Stalinist monolith that now houses government offices. The famous **balcony** where Ceaușescu delivered his last speech is surprisingly near ground level, and quite unmarked by bullet holes. Ironically, it was from the same spot, two decades earlier, that Ceaușescu had drawn cheers of approval for his denunciation of the Soviet invasion of Czechoslovakia, and made his vow that Romania would defend its own independence – casting himself as a "maverick Communist" whom Western leaders could embrace. It was a delusion that persisted almost until the end; as Romanians point out, the honorary knighthood bestowed on Ceaușescu by Buckingham Palace in 1978 was only revoked after the revolution began.

Calea Victoriei to the Centru Civic

Calea Victoriei (Avenue of Victory), on the site of the wood-paved Podul Mogoșoaiei, has been Bucharest's most fashionable street since boyars first built their residences along it. The arrival of the boyars encouraged Bucharest's most prestigious shops to open along the avenue and, after it was repaved and took its present name in 1918, strolling along the avenue became *de rigueur*, causing the writer Hector Bolitho to remark that "to drive down the Calea Victoriei between twelve and one o'clock will prove you a provincial or a stranger". Along the street were "huddles of low, open-fronted shops where Lyons silk and Shiraz carpets were piled in the half-darkness beside Siberian furs, English guns and Meissen porcelain", while lurking in the side streets were starving groups of unemployed, lupus-disfigured beggars and dispossessed peasants seeking justice in the capital's courts.

The avenue still displays marked contrasts: at its northern end near the Piața Victoriei, it seems verdant and sleepy with touches of old-world elegance, while to the south it becomes an eclectic jumble of old apartment buildings, glass and

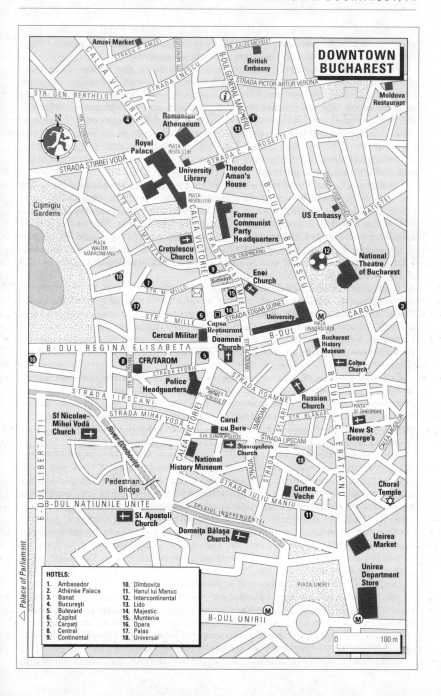

DOWNTOWN BUCHAREST

Amzei Market

STRADA P. AMZEI

STR. JULLES MICHELET

British Embassy

STRADA PICTOR ARTUR VERONA

STRADA ENESCU

B-DUL GENERAL MAGHERU

CALEA VICTORIEI

STR. GEN. BERTHELOT

STR. LUTERANA

Moldova Restaurant

Romanian Athenaeum

STRADA C. A. ROSETTI

Royal Palace

PIAŢA REVOLUŢIEI

STRADA ȘTIRBEI VODA

University Library

Theodor Aman's House

Cişmigiu Gardens

B-DUL N BALCESCU

STR. BATISTEI

PIAŢA WALTER MĂRĂCINEANU

Former Communist Party Headquarters

US Embassy

STR. CIMPINEANU

Cretulescu Church

PIAŢA REVOLUŢIEI

STR. ONCINPLEANU

National Theatre of Bucharest

Enei Church

STR. M. MILLO

Subway

STRADA EDGAR QUINET

STR. C. MILLE

University

CAROL I

Capsa Restaurant

Cercul Militar

Doamnei Church

Bucharest History Museum

B-DUL

PIAŢA UNIVERSITĂŢII

B-DUL REGINA ELISABETA

CFR/TAROM

STRADA EFORIE

STRADA DOAMNEI

Colţea Church

STRADA LIPSCANI

Police Headquarters

PASAGIU L VILLACROSSE

Russian Church

STR. BLANARI

STRADA MIHAI VODA

Sf Nicolae-Mihai Vodă Church

River Dimbovita

Carul cu Bere

STR. STAVROPOLEOS

STRADA LIPSCANI

PIAŢA SF. GHEORGHE

New St George's

CALEA VICTORIEI

Stavropoleos Church

B-DUL LIBERTĂŢII

National History Museum

Curtea Veche

Choral Temple

Pedestrian Bridge

STRADA IULIU MANIU

B-DUL NAŢIUNILE UNITE

SPLAIUL INDEPENDENŢEI

Sf. Apostoli Church

Unirea Market

Domniţa Bălaşa Church

Palace of Parliament

PIAŢA UNIRII

Unirea Department Store

B-DUL UNIRII

0   100 m

HOTELS:
1. Ambasador
2. Athénée Palace
3. Banat
4. Bucureşti
5. Bulevard
6. Capitol
7. Carpaţi
8. Central
9. Continental
10. Dîmboviţa
11. Hanul lui Manuc
12. Intercontinental
13. Lido
14. Majestic
15. Muntenia
16. Opera
17. Palas
18. Universal

steel facades, and shops selling cakes and Western *couture* – still the setting for a promenade around noon and in the early evening. To the east and west lie Piaţa Amzei and Piaţa Sf Voievozi, two areas with busy markets.

The **Creţulescu Church**, a short walk south along the avenue from Piaţa Revoluţiei, fronts a tangle of streets which wend west towards Cişmigiu Gardens. The church – high and narrow with mock arches, with bricks laid in saw-toothed patterns around the towers and elaborate carvings over the entrance – is built in the style created by Constantin Brîncoveanu, a seventeenth-century ruler of Wallachia who set out to forge a distinctive national genre of architecture. It was paid for in 1720 by the boyar Iordache Creţulescu and his wife Safta, Brîncoveanu's daughter. Sadly, little remains of its frescoes by Tattarescu, but the battered little church is currently being restored.

Further south, the Pasagiul Victoriei (Victory Passage) sneaks one block further east to the **Enei Church**, built in 1702; the church is also known as the *Dintr-o zi* or "(Made) In One Day" church. The cluster of shops and cinemas at the junction of Calea Victoriei and Bucharest's main east–west axis, Bulevardul Regina Elisabeta, is dominated by the imposing **Cercul Militar** (Army House, 1912). Just to the south, an alleyway slips off to the courtyard of the picturesque **Doamnei Church** – built in 1683 and now frequented by devout grandmothers and hordes of local cats.

Bucharest's **police headquarters,** further south along the Calea Victoriei, is now screened by a tall fence, after it was stormed by a mob in 1990. Iliescu used this attack as his pretext for calling in the miners to smash his student opponents. Directly opposite the headquarters, an inconspicuous portal leads into the **Pasagiul Villacrosse** (Villacrosse Passage) whose glass roof and gracefully curved arcade of shops gives an idea of why Bucharest once claimed to be the "Paris of the East".

East off the Calea, on Strada Stavropoleos, is the small **Stavropoleos Church** which gives the street its name. Built between 1724 and 1730 for the first Phanariot ruler, Nicolae Mavrocordat, the church has a gorgeous, almost arabesque, facade, with a columned portico carved with delicate tracery. On Strada Stavropoleos you'll also find *Carul cu Bere* (The Beer Cart), an ornately decorated tavern dating from 1875 (see "Eating and drinking" p.81).

The **National History Museum** (Wed–Sun 10am–4pm; Tues for treasury and lapidarium only) is housed in the former Post Office building of 1900, just north of the river, at Calea Victoriei 12. The modern lapidarium, in the courtyard, houses plaster casts from Trajan's Column covered with depictions of his Dacian campaigns, as well as Greek, Roman and medieval tombstones and carvings. A basement vault displays Romania's **national treasures**: a dazzling display of gold and jewellery, from prehistoric finds (see particularly the elaborate "Coţofeneşti helmet") to Queen Marie's crown and the casket said to hold her heart, to the sceptres of Ferdinand I and Carol II. The rest of the museum covers Romanian history from the earliest times to the 1920s, with some labels and summaries written in English. There is a fine collection of anthropomorphic figures moulded in clay by the Neolithic Cucuteni and Hamangia cultures (including the "Thinker", possibly the model for Rodin's statue), Bronze Age Thracian tools, Geto-Dacian coins, a replica of the Coţofeneşti helmet, Celtic weapons, Roman tools and glassware, and medieval clothing and manuscripts. The exhibits still refer in places to the *lupta de clasa* or class war; but the post-1920s section that formerly eulogized Communism in general and Ceauşescu in particular (with two rooms full of gifts presented to him on his sixtieth birthday) is now closed. Romanian museums still tend to serve the ruling ideology, and the recent rehabilitation of the wartime dictator, Antonescu, suggests that the reaction against Communism may go too far in the other direction.

From the National History Museum, it's a short walk to the **River Dîmbovița**. An old saying has it that whoever drinks the "sweet waters" of the Dîmbovița will never wish to be parted from Bucharest, to which one nineteenth-century traveller retorted that anyone who ever did "would be incapable of leaving the city for ever afterwards". Always prone to flooding, the Dîmbovița was canalized in the 1880s and now passes underground at Piața Unirii. The river marks the abrupt transition from the organic fabric of the old city to the arbitrarily imposed pattern of the Centru Civic.

The Centru Civic

In 1971 Ceaușescu visited North Korea and returned full of admiration for the grandiose avenues of Kim Il Sung's capital, Pyongyang. Thirteen years later, inspired by what he had seen in Pyongyang, Ceaușescu set out to remodel Bucharest as "the first socialist capital for the new socialist man", and to create a new administrative centre which was to be "a symbolic representation of the two decades of enlightenment we have just lived through". In truth, of course, this **Centru Civic** was meant to embody the state's authority and that of Ceaușescu himself.

Implementing this megalomaniac vision entailed the demolition of a quarter of Bucharest's historic centre (about five square kilometres), said to be slums damaged by the 1977 earthquake, but in fact containing 9000 largely undamaged nineteenth-century houses, whose 40,000 inhabitants were relocated in new developments on the outskirts of the city. There was worldwide condemnation of this vandalism, particularly since many old churches were to be swept away. Though some of the churches were in the end reprieved, they are now surrounded by huge modern apartment blocks and are torn from the urban context that gave them meaning.

The core of the Centru Civic was largely completed by 1989, just in time for the dictator's overthrow. This western end of the development now seems almost human – unlike the larger eastern extension, where a forest of frozen cranes in an undergrowth of rusting reinforcing rods mark the site of what was to have been a cultural centre; the area is referred to by the locals as "Hiroshima". The nearby National Library seems abandoned in this wasteland.

Bulevardul Unirii unites the two halves of the Centru Civic; at 4km long and 120m wide, the road is intentionally slightly larger than the Champs Elysées after which it was modelled. To the north of the complex, a banking district is slowly being developed.

The Palace of Parliament

Dominating the entire project from the western end of Bulevardul Unirii is the colossal **Palace of Parliament** (*Palatul Parliamentului*), the third largest building in the world – after the Pentagon and the Potala – measuring 270m by 240m, and 86m high. It epitomizes the megalomania that overtook Ceaușescu in the 1980s; here he intended to house ministries, Communist Party offices and the apartments of high functionaries. Built on the site of the former Spirei Hill, which was razed for this project, the sheer size of the building can only be grasped by comparison with the toy-like cars scuttling past below. It has twelve storeys, four underground levels (including a nuclear bunker), a 100m-long lobby and 1100 rooms. The interiors are lavishly decorated with marble and gold leaf, and there are 4500 chandeliers (11,000 were planned), the largest of which weighs 1.5 tonnes and cost 2.5 milllion lei, but the decoration was never finished due to the Ceauşescus' ever-changing whims; they were demanding patrons, allowing little more than a technical role to the architects – one staircase was rebuilt three times before they were satisfied.

This huge white elephant was officially known as the Casa Republicii, then as the Casa Poporului, but more generally as the Casa Nebunului (Madman's House) before taking on its present name. The new government spent a long time agonising about an acceptable use for it, and in 1994 it was finally decided to house the Senate and Parliament here; it is now also used for international conferences. You can visit (10am–4pm daily, except during major conferences) by showing your passport at the south door and paying about $5. The 45-minute tour takes you through ten of the most dazzling, most representative or simply the hugest of the halls. There's also a hall for temporary art shows on the north side of the building. Although Izvor is the nearest metro stop, approach along Piaţa Unirii gives you an impressive view of the building.

The surviving churches

Among the rows of new buildings that make up the Centru Civic are hidden the various tiny Orthodox churches reprieved from demolition. In Bucharest you'll frequently find churches in incongruous places – such as the courtyards of apartment buildings – where the city planners have built around them, but here the churches seem even more disregarded and incongruous than elsewhere. The most striking example of this is the **Sf Nicolai-Mihai Vodă Church**, built by Michael the Brave in 1591; to make way for the Centru Civic development, the church was moved 279m east on rails, to Str. Sapienţei 4, and dumped on what now appears to be a building site. The church's medieval cloisters and ancillary buildings were demolished. What's more, as it's now standing on a concrete platform, the church will probably collapse when the next earthquake comes. The largely seventeenth-century **Sf Apostoli Church** is nearby at Str. Sf Apostoli 33A, while just west of the Piaţa Unirii, at Calea Rahovei 3, is the eighteenth-century **Domniţa Bălaşa Church**; one of the most popular churches in the city, with an excellent choir, it was only saved from demolition by UNESCO funds.

On the southern side of Bulevardul Unirii, at Str. Justiţiei 64, is **Antim Monastery**, a surprisingly large, walled complex dating from 1715 with a high-domed church and a small chapel, but minus half its eastern wing. At the top of Dealul Mitropoliei stands the **Patriarchal Cathedral**, built in 1655–68, with a later campanile designed by Brîncoveanu and some older stone crosses with Slavonic inscriptions. Alongside are the **Patriarchal Palace** (built in 1875), and the former **Palace of the Chamber of Deputies** (1907). There are other churches on this side of Bulevardul Dimitrie Cantemir, including **Sf Spiridon Nou** (1768), at Calea Şerban Vodă 29, which holds Tattarescu paintings dating from 1858. Just east on Bulevardul Mărăşeşti, by the Dîmboviţa, is the **Bucur Monastery** (1743), in front of the **Radu Vodă Church** (also known as Holy Trinity or *Sf Treime*), founded in 1568, which was once the richest monastery in the country with 8342 properties.

South: parks and cemeteries

From Piaţa Unirii, in the heart of the Centru Civic, Bulevardul Dimitrie Cantemir runs south about 1km to the much older Calea Şerban Vodă. The two roads cover the site of Podul Şerban Vodă, destroyed by a fire in 1825. This was the route taken by all the merchants and Turkish officials heading for the Sublime Porte of Constantinople, the Sultan's Court, laden with gold and salt. The two roads meet at the north end of **Parcul Tineretului** (Youth Park) which contains a fairground and a lake, as well as the Uman crematorium, a strange rather Masonic chapel filled with caskets of ashes. To the west is the more formal **Parcul Carol**; it has a smaller lake and a "Giants' Grotto" and holds the graves of Gheorghiu-Dej and other Communist leaders. It also houses the **Museum of Technology** (Tues–Sun 9am–5pm), an oddball place intended to assert Romania's technological fecundity, particularly several "firsts", such as the metal-bodied aeroplane (1912) and the streamlined motor car (1923). However it's the names of British, French and German firms that dominate the collection.

On the west side of Parcul Tineretului, at the Eroii Revoluţii metro station and the junction of the highways to Olteniţa and Giurgiu, is the **Eroii Revoluţii Cemetery**; buried here are more than 250 **"Heroes of the Revolution"**, gunned down by "terrorists" in 1989. Saturday is a good day to visit. From here you can see the minaret of Bucharest's working mosque, at Str. C. Mănescu 4. Next to the Eroii Revoluţii Cemetery is the **Bellu Cemetery**, resting place of Romania's greatest writers, and opposite, on the Şoseaua Giurgiului, is the **Sephardic Jewish Cemetery** (shut on Saturdays) and the **Lutheran Cemetery**.

The Ceauşescus are buried in **Ghencea cemetery**, southwest of the city along Drumul Sării; you can get here by bus from Eroii Revoluţii metro station (#173, Mon–Fri only) and from Piaţa Unirii (#385; nearest stop at the junction of Drumul Sării and Calea 13 Septembrie). Originally buried under pseudonyms, the Ceauşescus' graves are now marked with their own names. Nicolae's grave is in the last alley on the left before the chapel; there are candles and flowers left by those who feel that life was easier and simpler under his dictatorship than under "democracy". Next door is a Military Cemetery, a surreal forest of propellor blades marking the graves of airmen, even those who didn't die in crashes.

Piaţa Unirii to Piaţa Universităţii

Piaţa Unirii (Square of Union), midway along Bulevardul Unirii in the Centru Civic, is an oversized expanse of concrete dominated by traffic. It is notable only as a key metro interchange, as the site of the city's main department store, the Unirea, and of its first McDonald's, and as the best place to view the Palace of Parliament. The sixth-floor café in the Unirea department store also offers good views of the city. If plans go ahead to pedestrianize the central area of the square around the fountains, this should improve matters.

Immediately to the east of Piaţa Unirii stands the large, domed hall of **Unirea market** (Mon–Sat 6am–8pm, Sun 6am–noon). The market is very popular and there are always huge queues for its fish, meat and dairy produce; buying fruit and vegetables from the stalls outside (which also trade on Sunday afternoons) is a less frustrating, if more expensive, business. You'll also find intriguing wooden, ceramic and enamel household items here. The market's fifth-floor café offers good views of the city.

In the backstreets to the east of the market are hidden the Jewish **Choral Temple**, Str. Sf Vineri 9, and the **Great Synagogue**, Str. Mămulari 3; the latter houses a **museum** of Jewish history (Wed & Sun 9.30am–1.30pm). There are still around four thousand Jews in Bucharest. The community is now reasserting its presence, but it is an ageing population and declining by about seven hundred a year.

The historic centre

Just north of Piaţa Unirii, Strada Iuliu Maniu leads west off Bulevardul I. C. Brătianu into the maze of streets and pleasantly decrepit houses which surround the oldest part of Bucharest. It was here that Prince Vlad Ţepeş ("Vlad the Impaler", otherwise known as Dracula – see p.384) built a **citadel** in the fifteenth century. The building was severely damaged during Ţepeş' attempt to regain the throne in 1476 (in which he succeeded, only to be murdered a few months later), and was further damaged by various earthquakes and fire over the following centuries; it was subsequently auctioned off as wasteland. Thus little remains of the ancient citadel – just some of the walls, arches and shattered columns of the **Curtea Veche** (Old Court), Str. Iuliu Maniu 31, which can only be viewed through the railings, and its adjoining **church**. Established by Mircea the Shepherd in 1546–58, this is the oldest church in Bucharest. It is a typical example of sixteenth-century Wallachian church architecture, with its horizontal bands of brick facing and rows of small niches beneath the cornice.

A few doors east from the Curtea Veche, at Str. Iuliu Mániu 62, an austere white wall with barred windows conceals Bucharest's most famous hostelry, **Manuc's Inn** (*Hanul lui Manuc*). It was built as a *caravanserai* in 1808 by a wealthy Armenian, Manuc-bey Mirzaian, and now houses a hotel (see p.64), a restaurant (see p.83) and a *cramă* or wine cellar (daily 7am–11pm).

It is a short walk north along Bulevardul I. C. Brătianu to **Strada Lipscani**, a narrow street named after the merchants from Leipzig who traded here in the eighteenth century, which holds a lively Gypsy street market (Mon–Sat), selling Turkish jeans or pirated cassettes. This area is a labyrinth of little shops and cafés, interspersed with arcades, such as the **Hanul cu tei** at no. 63 – a former *caravanserai* whose iron-doored lockups now contain a rich mixture of shops. Beware of pickpockets in this area.

Continuing north up Bulevardul I. C. Brătianu into Piaţa Universităţii, you will pass two ancient and much-loved churches on the right: **New St George's** (1575), the burial place of Constantin Brîncoveanu and now ringed by trams breaking the tranquil atmosphere, followed by the **Colţea Church** (1700–15), in front of the hospital of the same name and period. To the left, Strada Doamnei leads to the small, bulbous-domed **Russian Church**. The church, faced with yellow brick, Art Nouveau green tiling and pixie-faced nymphs, has a small interior, with frescoes, blackened with age and smoke, and icons whose haloes glow like golden horseshoes.

Around the Piaţa Universităţii

Piaţa Universităţii is a focus of city life and traffic, and a key site of the recent revolutions – there are memorials here to those killed at Christmas 1989 and in June 1990. The latter marks the date on which miners, under Iliescu's orders, drove out students who had been on hunger strike since April 30, causing the square to be nicknamed "Piaţa Tienanmen".

West of the square is **Bucharest University**. Occupying the first block on Bulevardul Republicii, its frontage is lined with statues of illustrious pedagogues and statesmen as well as a regular crop of bookstalls. Established in 1859 after the union of Wallachia and Moldavia, the university equipped the sons of bourgeois families to become lawyers and men of letters until the Communists took over in 1949. Technical skills and education for women were subsequently given top priority, but since the revolution, business studies and foreign languages have overtaken them in popularity. The university continues to have an excellent reputation.

Just north of the square, next to the *Intercontinental* hotel, is the **National Theatre of Bucharest (TNB)**, which resembles an Islamicized reworking of the Colosseum; it was a pet project of Elena Ceauşescu who had the facade rebuilt twice, and the roof once, before she was satisfied. Opposite is the **School of Architecture**, built in 1912–27 in the neo-Brîncovenesc style – ornate pillars, prominent, richly carved eaves and a multitude of arches – but now more notable for its rash of pro-monarchist graffiti.

Bucharest History Museum (Tues–Sun 9am–5pm), on the southwest corner of the Piaţa Universităţii, traces the city's evolution over the course of 150,000 years by means of old documents, coins, photographs and prints; there's also a poignant display about the 1989 revolution. The neo-Gothic building was built as the Suţu Palace in 1833–34; its superb porte-cochère was added later in the century.

West to the Botanic Gardens

West of the square, along Bulevardul Regina Elisabeta, are the **Cişmigiu Gardens**, which were bequeathed to the city in 1845 and laid out as a park. They originally belonged to a Turkish water inspector, and fittingly contain a serpentine lake upon which small rowing boats and pedalos glide, rented by couples seeking solitude among the swans and weeping willows (rental 9am–8pm in summer; about $1 per hour, and the same as a deposit, from a kiosk by the waterside). The gardens provide a tranquil space, with workers snoozing beneath the trees at lunchtimes in summer and pensioners meeting for games of chess.

The **Opera Romană**, a drab 1950s building containing a museum of operatic costumes, scores, photographs and posters, lies beyond the gardens at the western end of Bulevardul Regina Elisabeta. It is overshadowed by a huge, unfinished building similar to the Palace of Parliament, which was intended to house the National History, Army and Communist Party Museums, as well as Ceauşescu's tomb. As with the Palace of Parliament, it is now hard to know what to do with this unnamed building – it may yet house the National History Museum, or perhaps a new radio centre as rumour has it.

The **National Military Museum** (Tues–Sun 9am–5pm), displaced from its original site in 1988 by the Centru Civic development, is housed at Str. Ştefan Fortună 125 in a former army barracks. There are weapons, banners and uniforms galore, although Romania has rarely gone in for martial adventures; indeed, from 1958 it was the only Warsaw-Pact country without Soviet troops on its soil. Ceauşescu called vociferously for disarmament, announcing peace proposals and cuts in the defence budget. Post-Communist Romania has become more involved in international concerns, contributing a chemical-warfare unit to the Gulf War forces, a military hospital to the UN in Somalia, peace-keeping troops to Albania and the former Yugoslavia, and has attempted to enforce the UN blockade against Serbian shipping on the Danube.

North of the museum, towards the Gara de Nord, is a village-like neighbourhood of tiny street-corner churches and dimly lit workshops. Ivy and creepers cloak the houses – all outwardly run-down, but often concealing parquet-floored apartments with elegant antique furniture and other relics of prewar bourgeois life.

From the Opera Română, buses and trolley buses trundle south across the river along Bulevardul Eroilor Sanitari to the Cotroceni Palace and the Botanical Gardens, pass an area of lovely bourgeois villas, each one individually designed. The **Cotroceni Palace** was built as a monastery by Şerban Cantacuzino in 1679–82 and served as base for the Austrian army in 1737, the Russian army in 1806, and Tudor Vladimirescu's rebels in 1821. Damaged by many fires and earthquakes over the course of its history, the original building was demolished in 1863 and the Palace was rebuilt in 1893–95 to provide a home for the newly wed Prince Ferdinand and Princess Marie. Under Communism it served as the "Palace of the Pioneers" – the Soviet-bloc equivalent of the Scouts. A new south wing was added during restoration following the 1977 earthquake, and this is now the presidential residence. In 1984 the church was demolished. Tour groups enter the Palace by a small door in the north wall at Şos. Cotroceni 37 (10am and 3.30pm; advance booking necessary by phoning ☎01/221.12.00). Tours first pass through the remains of the monastery, where the Cantacuzino family gravestones are kept, then through the new rooms from the 1893-95 rebuild, decorated in an eclectic variety of Western styles.

On the other side of Şoseaua Cotroceni lie the university's **Botanical Gardens** (daily 7am–8pm), with the glasshouses and a museum of botany (Tues, Thurs & Sun 9am–1pm).

North to Piața Victoriei

Heading north from Piața Revoluției towards Piața Victoriei along the quieter, northern end of Calea Victoriei, you'll pass three museums of interest. At no. 107, in the former Ştirbey Palace (built in 1856), is the **Ceramics and Glass Museum**. The collection is small and varied – in rooms furnished with splendid mirrors, carpets, chandeliers and tiled stoves, you can see eighteenth- and nineteenth-century Turkish and Iranian tiles, European, Japanese and Chinese porcelain, and lovely Art Deco pieces, including a Tiffany lamp. The early nineteenth-century Ghica Palace at no. 111 houses the **Museum of Art Collections** (Wed–Sun 10am–6pm) – an assortment of paintings, furniture, icons on glass and other antiques "donated to" (confiscated by) the state. Temporary exhibitions and films are also shown here – check the posters outside for details. At no. 141, a superb clamshell-shaped porte-cochère shades the entrance of the **Museum of Music** (Wed–Sun 10am–5pm); its displays on the life of Romania's national composer, George Enescu, are not that gripping.

On the east side of **Piața Victoriei** stands the main government building, the **Palatul Victoria**, completed in 1944 but already showing a chilly Stalinist influence in its design. For some reason the ugly boulevards to the west house many expats; there are Western supermarkets and bars, and plenty of cash machines here. To the north, at Şos. Kiseleff 1, is the **Natural History Museum** (Tues–Thurs & Sun 10am–5pm, 6pm in summer, Fri & Sat 10am–4pm). Named after Grigore Antipa, the founder of Romanian icthyology and a pioneering conservationist before World War I, the museum's collection of 300,000 items includes a 4.5m-high skeleton of a dinosaur unearthed in Moldavia, and 82,000 butterflies and moths.

The northern suburbs

The Şoseaua Kiseleff, a long avenue lined with lime trees, extends north from the Piaţa Victoriei towards the Herăstrău Park and the Village Museum, the best of Romania's open-air museums of vernacular architecture, before heading out towards the airports and the main road to Transylvania. Modelled on the Parisian *chaussées* – though named after a Russian general – Şoseaua Kiseleff is a product of the Francophilia that swept Romania's educated classes during the nineteenth century; it even has its own Arc de Triumpf.

Just north of Piaţa Victoriei, at Şos. Kiseleff 3, is the Museum of the Romanian Peasant (*Muzeu Ţăranului Român*; Tues–Sun 10am–6pm), 1995's "European Museum of the Year". The premises were occupied by the Museum of Communist Party History until 1990, but they now house traditional textiles, carvings and ceramics in a setting which attempts to recreate an authentic Romanian village. A wooden church, typical of those found in Maramureş, stands at the rear of the museum. The Geological Museum opposite this at Şos. Kiseleff 2 (Mon–Fri 10am–4pm; by appointment only on ☎01/650.50.94) is an impressive exhibition which illustrates the great mineral riches of Romania; the highlight is the collection of luminescent rocks exhibited in an otherwise unlit basement room.

About 1km north along the avenue is the Arc de Triumpf, built in 1878 for an independence parade, and patched together in 1922 for another parade to celebrate Romania's participation on the winning side in World War I and the gains achieved at the Versailles peace conference. Originally made of wood, it was more fittingly rebuilt in stone in 1935–36, in the style of the Arc de Triomphe in Paris.

Immediately beyond the Arc de Triumf is Herăstrău Park, which is best reached by metro – the Aviatorilor stop is at its southeastern corner. Paths run past formal flower beds to the shore of Lake Herăstrău, one of the largest of a dozen lakes strung along the River Colentina. These lakes were created by Carol II to drain the unhealthy marshes that surrounded Bucharest and form a continuous line across the northern suburbs. Arched bridges lead via a small and fragrant Island of Roses to the *Miorita* bar and restaurant, from where rowing boats can be rented.

The residential area east of the park is one of Bucharest's most exclusive. It is where the Communist elite once lived, cordoned off from the masses they governed; the Ceauşescus lived in the Vila Primavera, at the east end of Bulevardul Primăverii. The area is still inhabited by technocrats, favoured artists and other members of the ruling elite.

The village museum

Undoubtedly one of the most worthwhile sights in Bucharest is the Village Museum (*Muzeul Satului*: Oct–March daily 9am–5pm; April–Sept Mon 9am–5pm & Tues–Sun 9am–8pm) at Şos. Kiseleff 28–30. Established in 1936, this fascinating collection of over three hundred houses and other structures from every region of Romania shows the extreme diversity of folk architecture. It is a

---

THE SKOPŢI

The **Skopţi** coachmen, who worked along the Şoseaua Kiseleff until the 1940s, were one of the curiosities – or grotesqueries – of Bucharest. Members of a dissident religious sect founded in Russia during the seventeenth century – and related to the Lipovani of the Danube Delta – the Skopţi ritually castrated themselves in the belief that "the generative organs are the seat of all iniquities", interpreting literally Christ's words on eunuchs in the Gospel of St Matthew. This was done after two years of normal married life – a period necessary to ensure the conception of future Skopţi. Driving *droshkys* pulled by black Orloff horses, the coachmen wore caftans sprouting two cords, which passengers tugged to indicate that the driver should turn left or right.

---

wonderful ensemble of wooden churches and peasant dwellings, including a bizarre subterranean house.

Perhaps the most interesting are the oaken houses from Maramureş with their rope-motif carvings and shingled roofing, and their beamed gateways carved with animals and hunting scenes, Adam and Eve and the Tree of Life, and suns and moons. Other highlights are the heavily thatched dwellings from Sălciua de Jos in Alba county; dug-out homes (with vegetables growing on the roof) from Drăghiceni and Castranova in Oltenia; and windmills from Tulcea county in the Delta. Mud-brick dwellings from the fertile plains ironically appear poorer than the homes of peasants in the less fertile highlands where timber and stone abound; while the importance of livestock to the Székely people of Harghita county can be seen by their barns, which are taller than their houses.

Piaţa Presei Libere

Şoseaua Kiseleff ends at **Piaţa Presei Libere** (Free Press Square), in front of **Casa Presei Libere** (Free Press House), a vast, white Stalinist building, which was once the centre of the state propaganda industry; little seems to have changed, as the "free" publishing industry is still largely corralled into this one building. Romania's new Commodities Exchange has also been set up here.

THE BĂNEASA BRIDGE

The bridge immediately north of the Băneasa station, where the DN1 crosses the Colentina River, was the scene of a crucial battle in August 1944. The success of the August 23 coup against Marshal Antonescu (see p.351) meant that Hitler's oil supplies were more than halved, and it is reckoned to have shortened the war in Europe by at least six months. However, at the time just 2800 Romanian troops faced between 20,000 and 30,000 Germans, mostly at Băneasa and Otopeni, but without orders due to the cutting of phone lines. King Mihai offered the Germans safe passage out of Romania, but they responded by bombing Bucharest. The bridge was held by a Romanian lieutenant and a handful of men until August 25 when Romanian reinforcements began to arrive from Craiova. Allied help finally came the following day when four hundred American planes bombed the German positions, and by August 27 Bucharest had been cleared of German forces (only to be occupied by the Red Army four days later).

Just beyond this, by the Băneasa train station on the Bucureşti–Ploieşti Highway, stand two rather eccentric buildings built for the Minovici family. One, built in 1905 in the style of a fortified manor house, contains the **Museum of Popular Arts** (Wed–Sun 9am–5pm), exhibiting woven blankets, Transylvanian blue pottery, painted Easter eggs, spinning wheels, musical instruments, furniture and beautiful peasant garments. The other, built in 1910 in a bizarre fusion of English Tudor and Italian Renaissance styles, is the **Museum of Old Western Arts** (Wed–Sun 9am–5pm), filled with hunting trophies and weapons, Flemish tapestries, Florentine furniture, and German and Swiss stained-glass windows.

Eating, drinking and nightlife

Between the wars Bucharest was famed for its bacchanals, its gourmet cuisine and its Gypsy music – but all this ended with the puritanical postwar regime of Communism. Although private enterprise is beginning to improve this situation, bad service and very restricted menus are still the norm in most restaurants, and the city is amazingly dull after dark.

Eating

The cheapest places to eat at midday are the **street stalls**, **pizzerias**, **kebab** and **burger bars** on the main avenues, around the Gara de Nord and in the Piaţa Universităţii underpass. Mostly, these are open Monday to Saturday from 9am till around 7pm – some near the station are open daily and around the clock. In the evenings the **restaurants** in the cheaper hotels are the most reliable economy option, although they may close early, around 8.30pm. The more expensive hotels provide standard international fare. The availability of **bistro food**, served in bar-style surroundings, is on the increase; these places offer steaks, salads and a selection of home-cooked food changing daily and chalked on blackboards.

For **snacks** check out the **patisseries**, which serve small portions of sticky confectionery with cola or coffee, or look for pavement stalls that dispense freshly baked *pateuri cu brînză* (cheese pastries), filled baguettes, bananas, biscuits and buns.

Food shops are now reasonably well stocked, and the **markets** (see "Listings" p.87) sell a fair variety of fruit and vegetables depending on the season. There are many new private shops and kiosks selling imported goods, especially alcohol, sweets and cigarettes; those around the Gara de Nord stay open until around 2am. The best **delicatessens** are UNIC, at B-dul G-ral Magheru 19, and Delicatesse Antoine, at Str. Mendeleev at the junction with Str. Tache Ionescu. There's a 24-hour shop selling general groceries at Calea Griviţei 142, opposite the Gara de Nord. The **supermarkets** with the best choice of imported foodstuffs are La Fourmi in the Unirea department store (Mon–Fri 9am–8.30pm, Sat 9am–7.30pm, Sun 10am–4pm) and also at B-dul 1 Mai (Mon–Sat 9.30am–8.30pm), Mega Image at Şos. N. Titulescu 15 (Mon–Sat 9am–9.30pm, Sun 9am–2.30pm) and Vox Maris at Str. Enescu 36 (Mon noon–9pm, Tues–Fri 9am–9pm, Sat 9am–7pm, Sun 9am–2pm).

Patisseries
Note that in Bucharest the cheaper patisseries often have only stand-up counters rather than seats.

Academiei, Str. Academiei 3. Convenient for the university and the main banks; lively, cheap and popular with students.

Bucureşti, Calea Victoriei, at the side of the *Hotel Bucureşti*. It serves delicious ice cream and cakes and is perhaps the nicest place in the city for treats. Daily 8am–8pm.

Casablanca, B-dul Magheru 25 (at Str. Tache Ionescu, two blocks north of the tourist office). Excellent croissants, cakes and Italian ice cream, with a range of coffees. No smoking. Open daily 8am–10pm.

Casata, B-dul Magheru 28. Just north of *McDonald's*, with good pastries but slow service.

Dunkin' Donuts, on Piaţa Unirii opposite *McDonald's*.

Foreign Languages Faculty Café, Str. Edgar Quinet. In the basement, at the rear of the university, it is a fashionable spot for students.

Lăpteria Enache, upstairs in the National Theatre, Piaţa Universităţii. A milk bar – or rather a drinking-yogurt bar – which also serves alcohol and has live jazz at weekends.

Nord, Str. Gara de Nord 6. The only place to sit in peace when your train is delayed.

Panipat, Str. Rosetti 15, Calea Victoriei 204, B-dul Bălcescu 24 (to midnight), B-dul Brătianu 44, Şos. Ştefan cel Mare 48 and Gara de Nord. Thoroughly modern franchise patisserie with good takeaway buns and pizzas and fashionably sulky staff. Daily 8am–10pm.

Sanda, B-dul Magheru 32. A friendly stand-up place, close to the *Casata*.

Scala, B-dul Bălcescu 36 (at Str. Rosetti). Huge choice of delicious pastries, especially baklava.

Burger bars and cafeterias

Bon Appétit, in *Hotel Ambasador*, B-dul Magheru 10. A better class of fast food.

Fraga & Nuris, Str. Piaţa Amzei 10. Outside the Piaţa Amzei market and across the road from the *Horoscop Bistro*, serving salads, burgers and omelettes. Open daily.

Horoscop Bistro. Outside the Piaţa Amzei market. Reasonable light meals, with a tiny terrace. Mon–Sat 7am–9pm.

Lacto Academiei, Str. Academiei 29. Right in the centre of town, serving lacto-vegetarian and meat-based dishes.

Lacto Marna, Strada Buzeşti 3. Cheap chicken and stuffed peppers.

McDonald's. At Piaţa Unirii, B-dul Magheru 24, B-dul Regina Elisabeta 23 (Sun–Fri to midnight, Sat to 1am), Şos. Olteniţei 29, and drive-ins on Şos. Mihai Bravu, beyond Otopeni, and by the Brîncoveanu, Dristor, Obor and Ing. Costin Georgian metros.

McMoni's, Piaţa Rosetti and B-dul Mărăşeşti 28. Pizza, burgers and sandwiches for under a dollar. Open 11am–11pm.

Sheriff's Fast Food, B-dul Brătianu. Occupying a whole block just north of Piaţa Unirii, this is the Romanian answer to *McDonald's*.

Zodiac, Calea Victoriei 116. A modern fast-food joint – roast chicken is a speciality.

Bistros, pizzerias and restaurants

In addition to those listed here, there are many other bistros, pizzerias and restaurants which come and go following current trends – at present there is a plethora of Italian restaurants. All the main hotels also have restaurants, serving a fairly dull international cuisine with a Romanian influence.

Bistro Atheneu, Str. Episcopiei 3 (☎01/613.49.00). Just north of the Atheneum concert hall, this small restaurant is one of the friendliest and cheapest in the city, with tasty continental food; popular with Romanians and expats and always busy. Daily 10am–midnight.

Brădet, Str. C. Davila 60 (☎01/638.60.14). Lebanese restaurant towards Cotroceni Palace, a haven for vegetarians thanks to its felafel and hummus. Service is slow.

Buongustaio, Calea Dorobanţilor 172 (☎01/230.01.57). A new restaurant with attractive modern decor, offering pizza, pasta and, alas, a variety show. Open noon–3am.

Carul cu Bere, Str. Stavropoleos 3 (☎01/613.75.60). Beer hall with splendid *neo-Tannhäuser* decor and draught beer, with a limited range of meals, notably *mititei* (grilled sausages) famed throughout Bucharest. The name means "Beer Cart" and it rivals *Manuc's Inn (Hanul lui Manuc)* as the premier hang-out for tourists and locals in Bucharest. Beware of the tendency to overcharge tourists. Open daily 10am–midnight with a Gypsy band and a folklore show Fri, Sat & Sun at 8.30pm. No smoking.

Casă Capşa, Calea Victoriei 36 (☎01/613.44.82). Restaurant established in 1852, with good traditional Romanian cuisine and an old salon atmosphere. Daily noon–midnight.

Casă Veche, Str. Enescu 15 (☎01/615.78.97). Not at all old, despite the name. Bar, café and patisserie all under one roof. Serves wood-oven-baked pizza. Major credit cards accepted. Daily 11am to early morning.

Cercul Militar, Calea Victoriei 27 (☎01/614.37.35). A wonderfully ornate restaurant with a well-placed terrace with fountain. Serves good Romanian food, mainly, it seems, to wedding parties.

Continental, corner of Cîmpineanu and Academiei (☎01/638.50.22). Classy hotel restaurant serving Romanian and international cuisine, with accompanying live music. Daily 6am to early morning.

Da Vinci, Str. I. Cîmpineanu 11 (☎01/312.24.94). In the Union business centre, Italian cuisine at $3–4 a dish; also serving good desserts. New and popular. Daily 11am–11pm.

Hanul lui Manuc, Str. Iuliu Maniu 62, entrance also on Piaţa Unirii (☎01/613.14.15). An old merchants' *caravanserai* with indoor and outdoor dining. Restaurant open Mon–Fri 7am–11pm, Sat & Sun 7am–midnight; patisserie, bar and wine cellar open daily 10am–midnight.

Hong Kong, Calea Griviţei 81 (☎01/659.50.25). Small, pleasant and inexpensive Chinese restaurant, 10–15 minutes' walk from the Gara de Nord. Daily noon–11pm.

Horoscop Pizzeria, B-dul Cantemir 2. Large pizzas of above-average quality with wine for around $5. Daily noon–midnight.

Moldova, Str. Icoanei 2, to the east of B-dul Magheru (☎01/611.37.82). A former Securitate haunt serving Moldavian cuisine, traditionally Romania's best.

Nan-Jing, Str. Gh. Manu 2, in the *Hotel Minerva* (☎01/650.60.10). Established since the 1960s, and still serving remarkably good Chinese food. Daily 7–10am and noon–midnight.

Pasagiul Victoriei, in the passage of the same name linking the Calea Victoriei and the Enei Church. Fairly slick and upmarket, specializing in caviar and other delicacies.

Pescarul, B-dul Bălcescu 9. Reasonable fish dishes and snacks, all at reasonable prices. Open Mon–Sat 10am–11pm; disco-bar until 2am.

Pescăruş, in Herăstrău Park, off B-dul Aviatorilor (☎01/679.46.40). Specializes in fish.

Pizza Atelierului, Str. Atelierului 24. Decent cheap pizza place, convenient for the Gara de Nord.

Pizza Hut, in Hotel Dorobanţi (☎01/210.84.21). Reliably the same as anywhere else in the world; no-smoking. Daily 11am-11pm.

Pizza Mini, Str. Lipscani. Situated next to the National Bank of Romania with a good range of pizzas. Also doubles as a bar. Daily 9.30am–7pm.

Pizzeria Julia, B-dul N. Titulescu 16. A wide choice of authentic pizzas, although one wonders what inspired the fiery *pizza serbeasca* ("Serbian pizza").

Premiera, Str. T. Arghezi 16 (☎01/312.43.97). Behind the *Intercontinental* hotel, this is Bucharest's longest-established private restaurant. Daily 10am–2am.

Quattro Stagioni, Str. Buzeşti 55, near Piaţa Victoriei (☎01/312.77.30). Italian food. Daily 11am–1am.

Sahib, Calea 13 Septembrie 127 (☎01/410.22.23). Bucharest's first genuine Indian restaurant, good and not too expensive. Daily noon–3pm & 6pm–midnight.

Tandoori, Str. Budai Deleanu 4, near Piaţa Victoriei (☎01/335.42.47). Excellent Indian food and good (English-speaking) service. Open 6am–midnight, closed Tues.

CASINOS

There's a rash of **casinos**, which pander unashamedly to the pretensions of Bucharest's new upwardly mobile businessmen, with overpriced drinks and under-clad hostesses. Some of them are in very beautiful historical buildings, and they often have genuinely good restaurants, open well into the early hours. The most attractive are the *Casino Palace* (☎01/659.34.42) at Calea Victoriei 133, incorporating the *Vernescu* restaurant in the Lenş-Vernescu palace at Calea Victoriei 133; *Victoria Casino* (☎01/312.95.16 or 312.18.01) and *Simfonia* restaurant at Calea Victoriei 174; and *Casino Bucur* (☎01/336.15.92) at Str. Poenaru Bordea 2, with a distinctly Middle Eastern restaurant.

Drinking

Bars have sprung up all over the city – some are rough and very basic, others quite flashy with videos and espresso machines. The larger hotels also have "night bars", often taking only hard currency and putting on tacky shows.

Bars

Bar Felix, Str. V. Lascăr 54. A trendy young hang-out in a quiet backstreet north of B-dul Dacia – crowded and noisy.

Berarie Turist, B-dul Magheru 43. Beer and pizza until 10pm, overlooking the traffic in Piaţa Romană.

Bulevard Bar, in the *Hotel Bulevard*, B-dul Carol I no. 1. Gorgeous *fin-de-siècle* decor, with upmarket prices and prostitutes hanging around.

Café Indigo, in the Cinematecă Str. Eforie 2. Live jazz at weekends, artsy crowd all week.

Club Champion, Şos. Kisseleff 32. Ten-pin bowling and pool. Open 24-hours a day, seven days a week.

Dubliner Irish Pub, B-dul N. Titulescu 18. The best of the expat hang-outs, just west of Piaţa Victoriei. Step inside and you really could be miles away. Daily noon–2am.

Green Hours, Calea Victoriei 120. The best jazz bar in town, open until 2am.

Kontact, Str. Berzei 60. A German pub, with DAB and Tuborg beers.

Lukan's Pub, B-dul Cantemir 13. Close to Unirii II metro, this is a "cook your own steak" house (with a self-service salad bar) in a lively bar-style atmosphere.

Miorita, Şos. Kiseleff 24. Trendy and lively, especially at weekends.

Sarpeletu Roşu, Str. Eminescu 119, corner of Str. V. Lascăr. The "Red Serpent" is a raucous place full of character, with dancing and singing to Gypsy music. Serves good home-made food. Open till 3am.

Sydney, Calea Victoriei 224. Has that world-famous Aussie hospitality, but uninspiring decor. Open every day, round the clock, and serving steaks and cooked breakfasts.

WEB Club, B-dul 1 Mai 12 (☎01/650.64.17, *http://webclub.kappa.ro* or *web@webclub.kappa.ro*). You can send and collect email here, as well as play pool and drink fancy cocktails.

Nightlife and entertainment

A fair number of the restaurants listed on p.82–83 feature **live acts** in the evenings; usually a quartet of Gypsies, or youths playing last year's pop hits for middle-aged couples to dance to sedately. If you want to find some better quality entertainment to accompany your meal, try one of the places specializing in Romanian cuisine, such as the *Hanul lui Manuc* and *Carul cu Bere*, which sometimes put on good Gypsy musicians or *doina* singers, the best of whom can move diners to open-mouthed amazement by their shrieks and laments.

Discos of dubious trendiness are bursting out all over Bucharest: try the *Vox Maris*, Str. Buzeşti; *Bavaria 2000*, Calea Griviţei 143; *Black & White*, B-dul M. Eliade 16; *Salsa You & Me*, Str. 11 Iunie 51; *Atlantic*, Str. Acadamiei 35; *Why Not*, Str. Turturelelor 11; *Disco Club Vogue*, Str. Enescu; or *Martin Club*, B-dul Iancu de Hunedoara 61. Romanians dance well and in couples; just jigging around in the Anglo-Saxon manner is seen as not really trying at all.

Finding **rock concerts** largely depends on pot luck or contacts as they are not advertised. Bucharest's *Students' Club* at Calea Plevnei 61 (☎01/615.15.58), behind the *Opera*, is one place to make enquiries; another is *Club-A*, the Young Architects' Club, at Str. Blănari 14, which often features drama, foreign films and **jazz**. These are both pretty well dormant over the summer holidays. There's more jazz at the *Café Indigo*, *Green Hours* and *Lăpteria Enache* (all listed above).

Classical music and drama

Most of the **theatres** and **concert halls** are closed through the summer. Information should be available through your hotel reception desk or from ONT. Bucharest's cultural forte is **classical music**, and several internationally acclaimed musicians have cut their teeth with the George Enescu Philharmonic Orchestra, which plays in the Romanian Athenaeum on Piaţa Revolutiei (☎01/615.81.42). A **festival** of piano music, named after the pianist Dinu Lipatti, is becoming established in early May. Concerts and operatic productions also take place at the Opera Română at B-dul Regina Elisabeta 70 (☎01/614.69.80), the Radio Studio at Str. Berthelot 62, the Opereta next to the National Theatre at B-dul Bălcescu 2 (☎01/614.11.87), and in the Palace of Parliament (☎01/615.97.10). Performances are lavish with fantastic sets and huge casts; tickets cost about $2 from the venues' box offices. **Outdoor concerts** are held in Cişmigiu Gardens and Tineretului Park during the summer.

Theatre productions which might just surmount linguistic barriers are the Tăndărică Puppet Theatre, Str. E. Grigorescu 24, the two music halls at Calea Victoriei 33 and 174, the Comedy Theatre at Str. Măndineşti 2 and the State Jewish Theatre, Str. I. Barasch 15. In the second week of November the **Ion Luca Caragiale Festival**, named after Romania's best-known playwright, brings to town the best of the year's drama from provincial theatres. The **circus** is at Aleea Circului 15 (Metro Ştefan cel Mare; ☎01/211.41.95), but is usually closed through the summer months.

Cinemas

Cinemas are plentiful, both in the centre and the suburbs, showing films from all over the world – although subtitled Hollywood films are the most popular fare. Tickets cost about $1 and there are posters listing what's on displayed all over town each week. The main city centre cinemas are on **Bulevardul Magheru**, **Bulevardul Regina Elisabeta** and **Calea Griviţei**. There are also open-air cinemas such as the Gloria on Bulevardul N. Grigorescu. The Cinematecă, at Str. Eforie 2 (☎01/613.04.83), shows a good selection of classic films from around the world, sometimes dubbed live by a single translator.

Listings

Airlines Bookings for TAROM internal flights from Băneasa airport are handled at Str. Buzeşti 61, just off Piaţa Victoriei (Mon–Fri 7am–7.30pm, Sat 7.30am–1.30pm; ☎01/659.41.85); for international flights from Otopeni go to Str. Brezoianu 10 (Mon–Fri 8am–7.30pm, Sat 8am–noon; information ☎01/615.04.99; reservations ☎01/615.27.47; business class ☎01/613.03.63). DacAir is at B-dul Carol I no. 16 (☎01/311.10.83) and Jaro at Băneasa Airport (☎01/212.22.73, fax 312.97.58). Most foreign airlines have their offices on B-dul Magheru, B-dul Bălcescu or Str. Batiştei: Air Moldova, Str. Batiştei 5 (☎01/312.12.58); Air Ukraine, Str. Batiştei 5 (☎01/311.14.08); Austrian Airlines, B-dul Bălcescu 7 (☎01/311.12.66); British Airways, Suite 215, Hotel Intercontinental, B-dul Bălcescu 4 (☎01/210.58.80, fax 312.29.90); Delta, Suite 601, B-dul D. Cantemir 1 (☎01/330.44.02); LOT, B-dul Magheru 41 (☎01/659.25.75); Lufthansa, B-dul Magheru 18 (☎01/650.40.74); Malév, Str. G. Enescu 3 (☎01/312.04.27); Swissair, B-dul Magheru 18 (☎01/312.02.39).

Airport information Otopeni ☎01/320.00.22; Băneasa ☎01/633.00.30, ext 165.

American Express, Marshall Turism, B-dul Magheru 43 (☎01/659.68.12, fax 223.12.03).

Banks and currency exchange As a rule, you're as well off using the exchange counters or Bancomats (ATM), now increasingly widespread. You'll find them at the BCR (Romanian Commercial Bank) head office at B-dul Carol I no. 14, and at its branches, Calea Victoriei 153 and Calea Dorobanţilor (opposite *Pizza Hut*); Bancorex has machines at B-dul Bălcescu 11 and Calea Victoriei 155 and Citybank at Str. Iancu de Hunedoara 8. The National Bank of Romania is at Str. Lipscani 25.

Bicycle repair Str. General Berthelot 10.

Books and newspapers Dacia at Calea Victoriei 45, Sala Dalles at B-dul Bălcescu, Luceafarul at B-dul Unirii 10, and Eminescu at B-dul Carol I no. 5, stock Romanian novels and poetry and books on native art and ethnography in English, French and German. Second-hand *anticvariat* bookshops are at B-dul Brătianu 14, Str. Iuliu Maniu 54, B-dul Magheru 2 and Calea Victoriei 45. There are lots of stalls on Piaţa Romană and in the Piaţa Universităţii underpass which occasionally have foreign books. The main English-language paper is called *Nine O'Clock* and on Fridays it lists weekend events, theatre and opera and is available free from major hotels and airline offices. You may also find the better *Times of Bucharest* in kiosks. *Bucureşti What, Where, When* is a glossy listings magazine, with lots of advertising for casinos and escort services. Foreign newspapers and magazines are available from the more upmarket hotels.

Car rental The cheapest companies are Budget (☎01/210.28.67, fax 210.29.95); Eurodollar (01/211.04.10, fax 211.43.66), and the Romanian companies JET Car (☎01/614.80.82/86) and Sebastian (☎01/330.60.09). Avis (☎01/210.43.44/45, fax 210.69.12) has the widest range of outlets. The Romanian tourist office, ONT, use Europcar (☎01/613.39.15).

Car repairs ACR has technical assistance centres at Calea Dorobanţilor 85 and Şos. Colentina 1 (☎01/635.41.40). Arthur Motor Cars, Str. Ştirbei Vodă 122 (☎01/615.52.75; 7.30am–8.30pm), and Automecanica, Str. Dreptăţii 1 (☎01/660.65.38; Mon–Thurs 8am–4pm, Fri 8am–2pm), are private companies that may be able to help with foreign cars.

Courier services DHL has an office at *Hotel Bucureşti*, Calea Victoriei 63–81 (☎01/312.26.61); TNT are at B-dul Magheru 16, Suites 4 and 35 (☎01/212.12.10, fax 210.59.00); and UPS are at Calea Rahovei 196 (☎01/336.20.39, fax 337.32.30).

Embassies and consulates Australia, c/o Liviu Buzila, Str. Dr E. Racota 16–18 Suite 1 (☎01/666.69.23); Britain, Str. J. Michelet 24 (Mon–Fri 9am–5pm; ☎01/312.03.03–05 or 615.35.71, fax 312.02.29); Canada, Str. N. Iorga 36 (☎01/222.98.45, fax 312.03.66); USA, Str. T. Arghezi 7 (☎01/312.40.40 or 210.40.42, fax 210.03.95).

Emergencies Ambulance ☎961; police ☎955; fire service ☎981.

Fuel Central filling stations are at Str. T. Arghezi (by the *Intercontinental* hotel), Splaiul Independenţei (near the Palace of Parliament), Calea Dorobanţilor, Str. I. Mincu and B-dul D. Golescu (at the Gara de Nord). There are others on all main routes out of the city, notably at

Băneasa and at Militari (the start of the Bucureşti–Piteşti motorway). Lead-free fuel is available at Str. Arghezi, Calea Dorobanţilor and Băneasa (all 24hr) and at the km36 services on the Piteşti motorway.

Football The most popular teams are the army team Steaua Bucureşti (B-dul Ghencea 35; tram #8 or #47, trolley bus #69), and the rail-workers' team Locomotiv-Rapid (Şos. Giuleşti 18; Metro Cringaşi). Less popular is Dinamo, once the Securitate team; the Dinamo stadium is at Şos. Ştefan cel Mare 9 (Metro Ştefan cel Mare).

Hospitals The Clinica Batiştei, Str. T. Arghezi 28 (☎649.70.30) opposite the US embassy, and the Spital Municipal, Splaiul Independenţei 169, are both used to dealing with foreigners, but for emergency treatment you should go to the Spital Clinic de Urgenţa, Calea Floreasca 8 (Metro Ştefan cel Mare; ☎01/679.43.10), or to the private Brimax International Medical Centre (☎01/410.15.65). Your embassy can recommend doctors speaking your language.

Libraries The British Council Library, Calea Dorobanţilor 14 (Mon–Fri 10am–5pm, Sat 10am-1pm, closed Aug), has week-old British newspapers. The US Cultural Centre at the south end of Str. Calderon (closed July & Aug) is similar.

Markets Fresh produce is sold in the Unirii, Amzei, Obor, Cringaşi, Traian and Matache (Ilie Pintilie) markets, as well as the Aviaţiei market just east of Băneasa airport; the Piaţa Amzei also has a colourful flower market. There is a huge Sunday morning flea market (*Tîrgul Vitan*) on Calea Vitan, fifteen minutes' walk south of the Dristor I metro station, alongside the Dimboviţa embankment.

Motoring information From Touring ACR, Str. Cihoski 2 (☎01/611.04.08 or 650.70.76; Mon–Fri 7.30am–7.30pm, Sat & Sun 8am–2.30pm), and its parent organization, the Auto Clubul Roman (ACR), Str. Tache Ionescu 25 (☎01/615.55.10), both near the Piaţa Romană. They both sell hotel coupons and provide an insurance and breakdown service for members of foreign affiliates.

Pharmacies There is at least one emergency pharmacy in each sector of the city. The most central is at B-dul Magheru 18 (☎01/659.61.15; daily 8am–8pm). In addition there are new private pharmacies, which may be better supplied, for instance at Calea Victoriei 14, 91 and 103, B-dul Bălcescu 10 and 35 and Calea Griviţei 206.

Photography Film can be bought in most hotels. In addition, Kodak on the east side of Piaţa Unirii and Fuji outside ONT on B-dul Magheru can now develop and print your snaps in an hour.

Police For most routine matters go to the most central police station, at B-dul Lascăr Catargiu 22 (entrance on Str. Daniel; ☎01/630.51.74). Traffic accidents (with damage) should be dealt with at Şos. Pantelimon 290 (☎01/627.30.35).

Post office The main post office is at Calea Victoriei 37 with poste restante hidden behind at Str. Matei Millo 10 (Mon–Fri 7.30am–8pm, Sat 7.30am–2pm). To receive mail here, make sure it is addressed c/o Officiul PTTR no. 1, Bucureşti.

Shopping Department stores: Unirea, Piaţa Unirii 1 (Mon 10am–6pm, Tues–Fri 7am–8pm, Sat 8am–2pm); Romarta, Calea Victoriei 60–68 and many other branches. For craftwork head out to the Village Museum; for Romanian music, try Muzica, Calea Victoriei 41 (Mon–Fri 9.30am–7pm, Sat 9.30am–2.30pm).

Sports facilities The Stadion Naţional, entrances at B-dul Muncii 43 and Str. Major Coravu (hosting many different sporting events); Progresul, Str. Dr. Staicovici 42, just west of the Palace of Parliament (tennis); and Floreasca, Str. Aviator Popa Marin 2 (tennis, basketball, ice skating).

Swimming pools In the Naţional and Dinamo stadia, as well as in hotels such as the *Bucureşti* and *Parc* – you can also swim in lakes Floreasca (Metro Aurel Vlaicu), Strauleşti (western terminus of trolley bus #97) and Băneasa (bus #131 or #205). The students' swimming place is at Ştrandul Tei, off B-dul Lacul Tei.

Train tickets Agenţie CFR, Str. Domniţa Anastasia 10 (Mon–Fri 7.30am–7.30pm, Sat 8am–noon; ☎01/613.26.42, sleepers 613.90.21) or Calea Griviţei 139 (Mon–Fri 7.30am–7.30pm, Sat 8am–noon; ☎01/650.72.47); to be sure of a seat in summer, you should book at least one and preferably two days in advance. International tickets must be bought at

Str. Domniţa Anastasia 10 (☎01/614.55.28 or 311.08.57), or two hours before departure at the Gara de Nord.

Travel agents Atlantic Tour, Calea Victoriei 202; Mondo Intertours, Str. Eminescu 45; Nouvelles Frontières SimpaTurism, Str. Puţu cu Plopi 18 (services in Romania) and Str. Calderon 1 (flights out of Romania); Paralela 45, B-dul Regina Elisabeta 7; and Wasteels, in the Gara de Nord. For bus tickets to Turkey and Greece try Oz Murat, B-dul D. Golescu 31 (☎01/637.70.72) or Double T Turism Transport by the Dîmboviţa at Calea Victoriei 2 (☎01/613.36.42). For tickets to Germany try Atlas Tour, Şos. Mihai Bravu 124, Suite D26 (☎01/222.89.71), Mihu Reisen (☎01/220.84.40), or Touring Europabus, B-dul A.I. Cuza 5A (☎01/210.08.12) and at Str. Sofia 26 (☎01/633.16.61).

Around Bucharest

Bucharest is surrounded by a ring of monasteries and fine country houses, most of which are popular destinations for weekend outings, but are generally hard to reach by public transport. If you don't have transport of your own, you may prefer to take one of the trips organized by ONT (see box below).

ONT EXCURSIONS

For visitors with ample funds and limited time, ONT (see p.31) can readily arrange **excursions from the capital**, usually half-day trips by bus or car. These eliminate the hassle of getting to places independently, but rather sanitize the experience, which in some cases may fall short of the image advertized (read the small print before parting with your dollars).

Their **city tour** (5hr, including the Village Museum and Cotroceni Palace) costs $31 per person (less for a bus party); a half-day trip to Căldăruşani monastery costs between $26 and $53 per person. Day-trips to Sinaia and Curtea de Argeş cost $65–129 and $76–158.

North to Snagov

If you travel to Snagov by road, you will pass through the area most notoriously affected by Ceauşescu's **systematization** programme (see box on p.90–91). Baloteşti, just north of Otopeni airport, consists of stark modern apartment buildings housing people displaced from villages such as Dimieni, which lay just east of the airport. Vlădiceasca and Cioflinceni, on the road east to Snagov from the DN1 (km28.1), were bulldozed in 1988, and the inhabitants resettled in Ghermăneşti, on the western outskirts of Snagov.

Four kilometres east of Baloteşti is **CĂCIULAŢI**, built as a planned estate village by the Ghica family, whose villa – now the property of the Romanian Academy – was occupied by the Securitate; over 300 bodies, unrecorded victims of the Communist police state, have recently been found buried in its run-down park. Seven **trains** a day from Bucharest (to Urziceni) stop here and at **GRECI**, another 10km east. A couple of kilometres south of Greci is the **Căldăruşani Monastery**, which is otherwise beyond the reach of public transport from Bucharest. This inconvenience didn't stop the world press from mobbing it when tennis stars Mariana Simionescu and Bjorn Borg were married here in 1980. The church where the wedding took place was built in 1638 by Matei Basarab and is noted for its school of icon painting, established in 1787. Among the many icons on display here are eight by the juvenile Grigorescu (see box on p.97) who studied at the school from 1854 to 1855.

SNAGOV, a small village 40km north of Bucharest, is the most popular weekend destination: a beautiful lake with watersports facilities and a reserve for water plants, such as Indian waterlily, arrowhead, and also oriental beech. In the centre is an island occupied by a **monastery** built in 1519. King Mihai and later Ceaușescu and other high functionaries had their weekend villas around the lake, and it was the scene of the summit which saw Yugoslavia's expulsion from the Warsaw Pact in 1948. Bălcescu and other revolutionaries of 1848 were held here, as was the Hungarian leader Imre Nagy following the Soviet invasion of 1956.

Launches motor over to the island, where monks have become resigned to visitors seeking the **tomb of Dracula**, sited in front of the church altar. Though lacking identifying inscriptions, it's likely that this is indeed the burial place of Vlad the Impaler: his murder is believed to have occurred in the forests nearby and the monks would have been predisposed to take the body, since both Vlad and his father had given money to the monastery. Also, the richly dressed corpse exhumed in 1935 had been decapitated, as had Vlad, whose head was supposedly dispatched, wrapped and perfumed, as a gift to the Sultan. You must be decently dressed to gain admittance here.

Although it's vaguely proposed to extend the metro all the way to Snagov, there are currently only three **buses** a day from the Băneasa bus station, and two **trains** from the Gara de Nord on summer weekends only (7.25am and 8.30am, returning at 6.10pm and 8.25pm – get off at the Snagov Plajă terminus, not Snagov Sat).

In addition to the *Hotel Măgurele* (☎01/780.22.80; ③) and private rooms and villas, there are two campsites close by (see p.65). Across the lake in **CIOLPANI**, there's the better *Hotel Pacea* (☎01/614.99.76; ⑤) and attached villa.

Mogoșoaia and Potlogi

The lovely palace at **MOGOȘOAIA**, 10km northwest of Bucharest along the DN1, and served by local trains (to Urziceni) and by bus #460/461 from Laromet (terminal of trams #20 and #31 and trolley bus #97), is perhaps Wallachia's most important non-religious monument. Designed by Constantin Brîncoveanu in 1698–1702, it is a two-storey building of red brick with a Venetian-style loggia overlooking a lake. After Brîncoveanu's execution the palace became an inn, then, after a fire destroyed the interior, a warehouse; it was restored, but then suffered serious earthquake damage. The palace itself is, in theory at least, the Museum of Brîncovenesc Art, but in fact it remains closed as the building remains unsafe. However, the atmospheric gardens are still open and the exterior of the palace is well worth seeing. Elizabeth Asquith, daughter of the British statesman, is buried here; her epitaph reads: "My soul has gained the freedom of the night".

A good forty kilometres west of the city (on the DJ401A, between the old DN7 and the newer motorway to Pitești) lies the small village of **POTLOGI**, site of another palace, built in 1698. This is one of the most beautiful of Brîncoveanu's buildings and well worth the slow, crowded bus ride (weekdays only) from the Militari terminal.

SYSTEMATIZATION

Systematization was Ceauşescu's policy to do away with up to half the country's villages and move the rural population into larger centres. The concept was first developed by Nikita Krushchev in the Soviet Union in 1951, to combat the movement of younger people to the towns by **amalgamating villages** to raise the standard of rural life. Similar plans were put forward in Hungary, and in 1967 Ceauşescu reorganized Romania's local government system and announced a scheme to do away with up to 6300 villages and replace them with 120 new towns and 558 agro-industrial centres.

His declared aim (based on an original idea in Marx and Engels' *Communist Manifesto*) was "to wipe out radically the major differences between towns and villages; to bring the working and living conditions of the working people in the countryside closer to those in the towns", by herding people together into apartment buildings so that "the community fully dominates and controls the individual", and thus produce Romania's "new socialist man". Thankfully the project was forgotten while Ceauşescu was preoccupied by other prestige projects such as the Danube–Black Sea Canal and Bucharest's Centru Civic, but he relaunched it in March 1988, when he was becoming obsessed with increasing exports and paying off the national debt.

Since collectivization Romania's agricultural output had declined steadily, and this on fertile land with one of the longest growing seasons in Europe. In 1985 the minuscule private sector produced 29 percent of the country's fruit, 14 percent of its meat and almost 20 percent of its milk. Ceauşescu was determined to **revolutionize agriculture** by increasing the growing area, while also further increasing centralization and reducing the scope and incentive for individual initiative. While the peasants had previously been able to support themselves with their own livestock, there was to be no accommodation for animals in the new blocks. To add insult to injury the peasants were to receive derisory compensation for their demolished homes and then be charged rent.

travel details

Trains

Bucharest to: Arad (7 daily; 8hr–11hr); Baia Mare (3 daily; 9hr 30min–12hr); Braşov (24 daily; 2hr 30min–4hr 45min); Cîmpulung (1 daily; 3hr); Cluj (7 daily; 7hr–11hr 15min); Constanţa (11–15 daily; 2hr 15min–5hr 30min); Craiova, via Caracal (18 daily; 2hr 15min–4hr 45min); Iaşi (7 daily; 5hr 15min–6hr 45min); Mangalia (4 daily, summer only; 3hr 30min–5hr 15min); Piteşti (11 daily; 1hr 30min–3hr); Ploieşti (51 daily; 45min–1hr 45min); Sibiu (8 daily; 4hr 45min–11hr 30min); Sighişoara (11 daily; 4hr–7hr 30min); Snagov (2 daily, summer weekends only; 1hr 15min); Suceava (7 daily; 5hr–6hr); Timişoara (8 daily; 6hr 30min–8hr 30min); Tîrgovişte (6 daily; 1hr 15min–2hr 15min); Tîrgu Mureş (2 daily; 8hr 15min); Tulcea (2 daily; 5hr 15min–6hr 45min).

Buses

Bucharest (Băneasa) to: Snagov (3 daily).

Bucharest (Hotel Nord) to: Călimăneşti (2 daily); Cîmpulung (3 a day, Mon–Fri); Focşani (1 daily); Galaţi (1 daily); Piteşti (5 daily); Rîmnicu Vîlcea (15 daily); Tîrgovişte (5 daily); Tulcea (1 daily).

Bucharest (Militari) to: Cleja (1 daily); Curtea de Argeş (1 daily); Horezu (1 daily); Pologi (4 daily).

The model development was to be the **Ilfov Agricultural Sector**, immediately north of Bucharest, where the first evictions and demolitions took place in August 1988; only two or three days' notice was given before shops were closed down and bus services stopped, forcing the people out of the designated villages. Entire villages were removed to blocks in Otopeni and Ghermăneşti, where up to ten families had to share one kitchen and the sewage system had not been completed. At the same time the villagers of Buda and Ordoreanu, just south of Bucharest on the Argeş River, were removed to **Bragadiru** to make way for a reservoir for the proposed Bucharest–Danube Canal. In other villages across the nation, ugly **concrete Civic Centre buildings** began to appear in the centres of the planned New Towns.

Repairs were banned in all the doomed villages and on all single-storey buildings, but these regulations were interpreted differently by the various counties (*judeţs*). In Maramureş, the authorities, aware that greater distances to the agricultural land would be a disadvantage, allowed repair work on outlying farms and also permitted attics to count as a second storey. In the Banat, efforts were made to attract migrants to houses left by emigrating Schwabs, although these should have been demolished.

There was widespread condemnation of this scheme which was set to uproot half of the rural populace; in August 1988 the Cluj academic **Doina Cornea**, one of the country's few open dissidents, wrote an open letter (published in the West) in protest, pointing out that the villages, with their unbroken folk culture, are the spiritual centre of Romanian life, and that to demolish them would be to "strike at the very soul of the people". She was soon placed under house arrest, but the campaign abroad gathered pace. Although the Hungarian view that the plan was an attack on their community was widely accepted, it does seem clear that Ceauşescu's aim was indeed a wholesale attack on the rural way of life.

Approximately eighteen villages had suffered major demolitions by the end of 1989, when the scheme was at once cancelled by the FSN; new buildings are going up all over the country, and those people uprooted by Ceauşescu's scheme are returning to the sites of their villages and starting all over again.

International trains

Bucharest to: Belgrade (2 daily; 12hr 30min–13hr 15min); Berlin (1 daily; 28hr 30min); Budapest (6 daily, 12hr–13hr); Dresden (1 daily; 26hr); Istanbul (1 daily; 17hr); Kiev (8 weekly; 28hr–31hr); Moscow (8 weekly; 44hr–46hr); Prague (2 daily; 22hr–23hr); Ruse (4 daily; 2hr–3hr); Sofia (3 daily; 9hr–10hr); Thessaloniki (1 daily; 23hr); Vienna (2 daily; 17hr 18hr); Warsaw (1 daily; 26hr).

Planes

Bucharest (Băneasa airport) to: Arad; Bacău; Baia Mare; Cluj; Constanţa; Craiova; Iaşi; Oradea; Satu Mare; Sibiu; Suceava; Timişoara; Tîrgu Mureş; Tulcea.

CHAPTER TWO

WALLACHIA

C enturies before the name Romania appeared on maps of Europe, foreign merchants and rulers had heard of **Wallachia**, the land of the Vlachs or Wallachs, known in Romanian as *Ţară Romaneasca* (land of the Romanians). A distant outpost of Christendom, it succumbed to the Turks in 1417 and was then largely forgotten until the nineteenth century. Occasional travellers reported on the region's backwardness and the corruption of its ruling boyars, but few predicted its sudden union with Moldavia in 1859 – the first step in the creation of modern Romania. Today, in the highlands and on the Bărăgan Steppe – where pagan rites such as the festivals of *Ariet* and *Căluş* are still practised – peasant life still largely follows the ancient pastoral cycle, but industrialization and collective farming have wrought huge changes on the plains around Ploieşti, Piteşti, Craiova and the Jiu valley, all places that now have little to recommend them. The region is largely comprised of flat and featureless agricultural land, and is in many ways the least interesting of Romania's three principal provinces, but as it is home to the nation's capital, Bucharest, many people will find themselves passing through en route to Transylvania or the coast.

The most rewarding part of Wallachia is its western half, known (after its chief river) as Oltenia, which stretches from Bucharest via Tîrgovişte and Curtea de Argeş to the Iron Gates on the Danube. The region's main transport routes run across the Danubian plains, and you'll find it hard to avoid the big industrialized centres of **Ploieşti**, **Piteşti** and **Craiova** if you're exploring in any depth. However, the foothills of the Carpathians are scenic and unspoilt, and the most attractive and historically interesting towns, such as **Sinaia** and **Curtea de Argeş**, are found here. **Tîrgovişte** and **Poienari** are associated with Vlad Ţepeş, better known as Dracula, who was once ruler of Wallachia even though modern myth links him with Transylvania. In addition, a string of **monasteries**, such as

ACCOMMODATION PRICES

Hotels listed in this guide have been price-graded according to the scale below. Prices given are those charged for the cheapest **double room** available, which in the less expensive places usually comes without private bath or shower and without breakfast. Price codes are expressed in US dollars as the Romanian leu is not a stable currency, but you will generally pay for your room in lei.

Note that some hotels are currently closed for modernization, and others, now open, will no doubt follow in the near future. This is bound to result in higher rates when they reopen, so the prices quoted should be taken only as a guideline.

① $10 and under ④ $20–25 ⑦ $40–50
② $10–15 ⑤ $25–30 ⑧$50–65
③ $15–20 ⑥ $30–40 ⑨ $65 and over

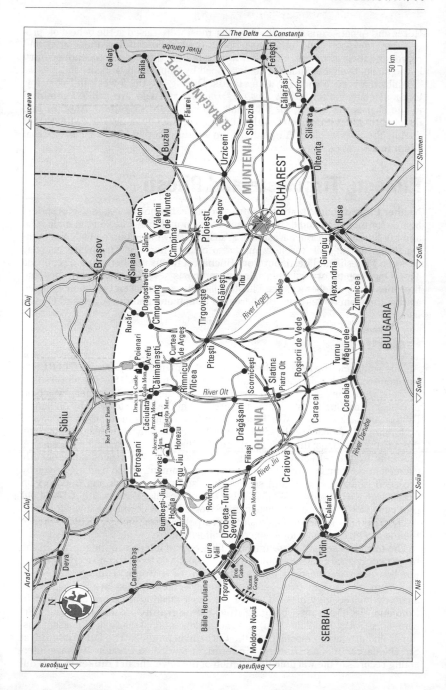

Horez and Arnota, runs along the foothills; most were raised at the behest of "progressive" despots (who otherwise spent their time fighting the Turks and repressing their own peasantry), but were rebuilt in the late seventeenth century in the distinctively Romanian style developed by Constantin Brîncoveanu.

Wallachia is renowned for its **festivals**. During the third week in February, folk musicians gather for the *Izvoare fermecate* at **Tîrgu Jiu**, while **Polovragi** to the east is the setting for a big fair between July 15 and 20. Another fair, devoted to pottery, coincides with the Songs of the Olt festival at **Calimăneşti** during the first week in August; and on August 15 pan-pipers congregate at **Tismana**.

Ploieşti, Tîrgovişte and Piteşti

Neither **Ploieşti** nor **Piteşti** is an attractive place, but both serve as useful springboards for more enticing destinations in the region. Ploieşti lies on the main road and rail line between Bucharest and Transylvania, with a couple of sites of interest to the north. Rail travellers may also change here for **Tîrgovişte**, midway between Ploieşti and Piteşti, but from Bucharest this is reached more directly via Titu. Once capital of Wallachia, Tîrgovişte boasts several ancient churches and the ruins of Vlad Ţepeş's court. Piteşti is likewise an important junction, situated astride the main routes from Bucharest to Cîmpulung and the Argeş and Olt valleys.

Ploieşti

An oily smell and the eerie night-time flare of vented gases proclaim **PLOIEŞTI** (pronounced "Ploy-esht") as Romania's biggest oil town. In 1857 the world's first oil wells were sunk here and in Petrolia, Ontario; the first ever refinery was built in Ploieşti, and Bucharest became the first city in the world to be lit by oil lamps. By the outbreak of World War I there were ten refineries in the town, all owned by foreign oil companies; these were wrecked in 1916 by British agents to deny them to the Germans; they were patched together only to be wrecked once more, this time by the retreating Germans in 1918. Royal Dutch Shell subsequently claimed huge damages from the Romanian government, which paid up, driven by the need to keep on the right side of the Paris peacemakers and thus to gain Transylvania as promised. While British companies like Vickers and ICI sold out profitably to Hitler's industrialists before World War II, it was the townsfolk who really paid the price when Allied aircraft carpet-bombed Ploieşti in 1944 – hence the town centre's almost total concrete uniformity.

The town has several museums, but little else of interest to the tourist. In the huge neoclassical Palace of Culture at Str. Catalin 1, the natural sciences museum has been transformed into a **Museum of Human Biology** (Tues–Fri 9am–5pm, Sat & Sun 9am–1pm), whose eye-catching displays on evolution, anatomy and ecology make it easily the most striking museum of its kind in Romania. In the same building the **Ethnography Museum** (Tues–Fri 8am–4pm, Sat & Sun 9am–1pm) has more conventional displays of peasant costumes and artefacts – mostly from the Carpathian foothills. The **Oil Museum**, at Str. Bagdascar 10, and **History Museum**, at Str. Toma Caragiu 10, have interesting records of the wartime destruction of the town; the **art museum**, at B-dul

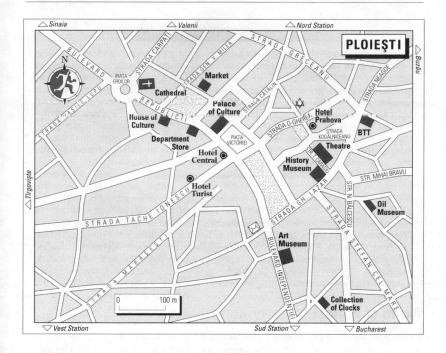

Independenţei 1, has paintings by Romania's foremost artists, including Aman and Grigorescu; and there's an engagingly varied collection of clocks at Str. Sinache 1.

The main reason to come to Ploieşti, however, is to take advantage of the excellent transport links to the more interesting parts of Wallachia. **Trains** to and from Transylvania use Ploieşti's Vest station, while those to and from Moldavia use Ploieşti Sud; trains from Bucharest may arrive at either. The two stations are linked by bus #2 and tram #103, both of which pass close to the centre of the town. There are two **bus stations**, the Nord on Strada Dragolina, fifteen minutes walk north of the centre and served by the occasional bus #4 (Mon–Fri), and the Sud on Strada Depoului, adjacent to the train station of the same name; however both are horrible and of little use except for reaching nearby villages. TAROM has an office at B-dul Republicii 17 (☎044/14.51.65) selling tickets for flights out of Bucharest's airports.

If you're stuck between connections and need a place to stay, there are three hotels in town. Ploieşti's newest **hotel** is the *Turist*, Str. Tache Ionescu 6 (☎ & fax 044/19.04.41; ⑤), slightly cheaper are the *Central*, Str. Tache Ionescu 2 (☎044/12.66.41, fax 12.25.59; ACR; ⑤), and the *Prahova*, a high-rise block at Str. Dobrogeanu-Gherea 11 (☎044/12.68.50, fax 12.63.02; ④). Without your own transport it's almost impossible to reach the **campsites** at Romăneşti (11km south on the DN1 towards Bucharest at km49), Pădurea Păuleşti (8km north on the DN1 to km68.5 and 3km east) and Paralela 45 (with rooms, 19km north on the DN1 at km79). The town now has a *McDonald's*, but otherwise there is no alternative to the hotel **restaurants**.

THE PLOIEŞTI PLOY

In 1940, it was feared that Germany would occupy Romania – as it had in World War I – to guarantee oil supplies from what was then Europe's second largest producer (after the Soviet Union). There was tacit support from the neutral Romanian government for Anglo–French plans to sabotage the oil wells, thus making a German invasion pointless. However, technical problems and bad luck meant that these plans never went ahead. Plan B, to stop the oil barges reaching Germany along the Danube by sinking barges in the Iron Gates gorge and blocking the navigable channel, was a greater fiasco: the Germans soon found out about the British barges making their way upstream from Galaţi, supposedly in secret, and forced the Romanian authorities to expel the crews, naval ratings ill-disguised as art students.

A third plan involved the RAF bombing the oil wells from its bases around Larissa in Greece. However, the 660km route would have taken the early Wellington bombers over Musala, the highest peak in southeastern Europe, to an altitude which would be at the extreme limits of their range. Following severe maintenance problems, the plan was abandoned. It wasn't long after this that the Allies were driven out of Greece, allowing the Axis to obtain a third of its aviation fuel from Romania. Between 1942 and 1944 there were heavy Allied raids on the town which succeeded in halving oil production, although the Allies suffered terrible losses.

North of Ploieşti

From Ploieşti, the DN1 and the DN1A head north towards Braşov, the gateway into Transylvania. The DN1 is the main route north, passing through **Cîmpina**, **Breaza**, Sinaia and Buşteni, and the rail line follows the road closely right through to Braşov. The DN1A, a much quieter and more relaxing route, runs along the **Teleajen valley** into the foothills of the Carpathian Curve; public transport along this route is poor, but it is well worth considering if you have your own transport.

Cîmpina and Breaza

Romania's oldest oil town, **CÎMPINA**, lies on the DN1, 32km north of Ploieşti, just before the mountains of the Prahova valley begin. Buses meet trains and take only five minutes to reach Bulevardul Carol I, the main road through town. Cîmpina is not a very attractive place, thanks to wartime bombing, and it has only one decent **hotel**, the *Muntenia*, at B-dul Carol I no. 61 (☎044/33.30.90, fax 33.30.92; ③), nevertheless the town has two tourist sights, both on the northern outskirts, that would make a stopoff worthwhile.

The **Nicolae Grigorescu Museum** (Tues–Sun 9am–5pm), at B-dul Carol I no. 166, is named after Romania's most prolific nineteenth-century painter who lived here towards the end of his life (see box). Further north, at no. 145, is **Haşdeu Castle** (Tues–Sun 9am–5pm), an odd cruciform structure with battlements and buttresses, built in 1894–96 by historian and linguist, Bogdan Petriceico Haşdeu (1838–1907). Haşdeu was director of the national archives for many years, one of the progenitors of the nationalist and anti-semitic philosophy that has infected Romanian politics throughout this century. He built the castle as a memorial for his daughter Iulia, to plans he claims were transmitted by her in seances. Iulia had graduated from elementary school at the age of eight and after high school went to study in Paris; she would have been the first woman to receive a doctorate from the Sorbonne, but died of tuberculosis in 1888, aged just nineteen. She left three volumes of plays and poetry, published after her death.

The small town of **BREAZA**, just a few kilometres north of Cîmpina on a loop road off the DN1, also offers the possibility of a quiet stopover. From the train station you have a long (25min), steep walk up the hill into town, and there are no buses or taxis to make the journey any easier. The town provides some excellent examples of the local architectural style – with many houses having carved wooden verandas – but Breaza's one real sight is the small Orthodox **church** of Sf Nicolae on the main road. Finished in 1777, the church's interior is totally covered in paintings; of special note is that of the Last Judgement in the porch. Just north of the church is the centre of town, with a supermarket, pizzeria, cofetaria (the *Britannia*) and the *Temperanţa* restaurant – possibly the only temperance restaurant in Romania (although there are a few women-only ones). Just north is the overpriced **hotel** *Aleea Nucilor* (☎044/34.09.99; ③) at Aleea Nucilor 1. The only alternative is the *Nistoreşti* tourist complex, 1km north of the train station on the DN1.

Continuing northwards from here takes you to Sinaia and Buşteni in the **Prahova valley** and on into Transylvania. The magnificent scenery and interesting hikes on this stretch of the approach to Braşov are described in the opening pages of the chapter on Transylvania (see p.126).

The Teleajen valley

The main place to stop along the DN1A route to Braşov is **VĂLENII DE MUNTE**, served by trains from Ploieşti 30km to the south; the town's train and bus station are just south of the *Ciucaş* **hotel** (☎ & fax 044/28.04.25; ③), in the ugly modern centre. To the north, at B-dul Iorga 90, a **museum** (Tues–Sun 9am–5pm) remembers the great historian Nicolae Iorga, who lived in this late seventeenth-century house from 1910 until his murder by the Iron Guard in 1940; ironically, Iorga had founded the National Democratic Party, a predecessor of the Guard. The **Vălenii monastery church**, founded in 1680, is opposite at Str. Berevoieşti 4.

NICOLAE GRIGORESCU

Romania's favourite painter was born in 1838 and came to Bucharest at the age of ten to train as a church painter; his earliest signed works, dating from 1853, are in the church of Sf Constantine and Helena in Baicoi (near Ploieşti). He worked in Căldăruşani (1854–55), in Zamfira (1856–58), and in Agapia (1858–60), where his work represents the high point of Romanian classicism. Here he met Kogălniceanu, who arranged a grant for him to study in Paris; he became a friend of Millet, joining the Barbizon group and beginning to paint *en plein air*. In 1869 he returned to Romania, where he painted society portraits, but also toured the Prahova, Dîmboviţa and Muscel counties painting local characters in a mobile studio in an adapted coach. In 1877–78 he accompanied the army in the War of Independence, producing, among others, major works of the battle of Griviţa. In 1881 he held his first solo exhibition, which was a great success, and from 1881–84 he lived in Paris. He kept a studio in Paris until 1894, although from 1890 he spent increasing amounts of his time in Cîmpina, with his companion Maria Danciu, where he died in 1907.

From Vălenii a minor road heads west for 11km to **SLĂNIC** (sometimes known as Slănic Prahova, to distinguish it from Slănic Moldova, to the north). Here, the *Muntele de Sare*, or "Salt Mountains" – a product of the salt mining which has taken place in the area since at least 1532 – stand between two lakes in which you can swim in summer. You can also visit the **museum** of the salt industry (Tues–Sun 8.30am–3.30pm) in the Casa Cămărășiei (former Salt Chancellery, built in 1800), and the adjacent Unirea mine (Tues–Sun 7.30am–3pm), displaying scenes from Romanian history carved in salt. Slănic lies at the end of a rail line from Ploieşti Sud via Ploieşti Vest; some of the eight daily trains do the distance in an hour and a quarter, but beware, others stop for 45 minutes in Plopeni. Slănic has three **hotels** (all ☎044/24.02.23; ③).

North of Vălenii a minor road forks east off the DN1A and about 7km along it another minor road forks north, running parallel to the DN1A, ending at the small village of **SLON**, 22km north of Vălenii. Five buses a day run from Ploieşti via Vălenii to this woodworking centre, which produces barrels, spindles, spoons and shingles; it is very much a working village, but you may be able to invite yourself into the workshops. The village's folk dance ensemble meets on Tuesday nights, and there's **accommodation** in private rooms here (①); ask in the shop or mayor's office for details.

The DN1A continues north along the Teleajen valley past Suzana nunnery (built in the eighteenth century and rebuilt in 1835–38 with icons by Tattarescu) to **CHEIA**, 35km north of Vălenii, at the foot of the Ciucaş mountains. Minibuses meet trains at Măneciu, 17km north of Vălenii, and head to this pleasantly relaxed resort. The Ciucaş is a compact range of weirdly eroded conglomerate outcrops and pillars, with fine open walking country all around; the *Ciucaş cabana*, between Mount Roşu and Mount Ciucaş, offers friendly but basic **accommodation**. From the Bratocea Pass the road leads downhill all the way past the *Babarunca cabana* into Săcele and Braşov. If you are looking to stay in Cheia, this tiny resort has a **hotel**, the *Cheia* (☎044/120; ②), **cabins** to rent, and a **campsite**. In addition, there is the *Muntele Roşu cabana* which lies on a side road, 7km north, at the foot of the mountains.

Tîrgovişte

TÎRGOVIŞTE, 50km west of Ploieşti on the DN72, was the capital of Wallachia for more than two centuries. Vlad Ţepeş, better known as Dracula, ruled from here in the fifteenth century. In recent times, the town has been best known as an industrial centre, producing equipment for the oil industry, but gained notoriety when Nicolae and Elena Ceauşescu were executed in its army barracks on Christmas Day, 1989.

The Town

From the train station, it's a pleasant fifteen-minute walk past the attractive villas of the tree-lined Bulevardul Castanilor to the centre of Tîrgovişte. The town's main attraction, the **Princely Court** (*Curtea Domneasca*; Tues–Sun 9am–5pm), is north of the centre on Strada Nicolae Bălcescu (also known as Calea Domneasca or Princely Avenue); now a mass of crumbling ramparts, with a few well-preserved sections, it was once the royal seat of Wallachia (1415–1659), from where more than forty voivodes exercised their rule. The Princely Court figured large in the life of **Vlad the Impaler** (or Dracula: see p.304), whose bust you'll

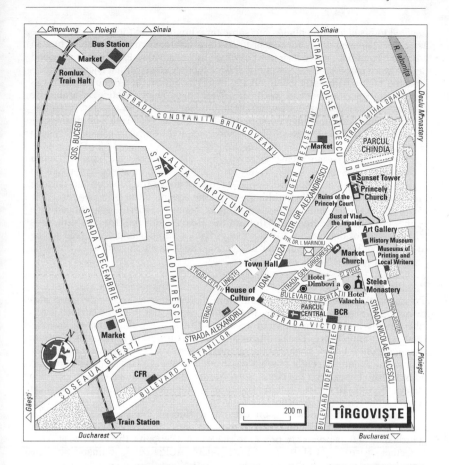

pass as you near the ruins. His early years were spent here, until he and his brother Radu were sent to Anatolia as hostages. Following the murder of his father and his eldest brother, Mircea, who was buried alive by Wallachia's boyars, Vlad returned to be enthroned here in 1456, and waited three years before taking his revenge. Invited with their families to feast at court on Easter Sunday, the boyars were half-drunk when guards suddenly grabbed them and impaled them forthwith upon stakes around town, sparing only the fittest who were marched off to labour on Vlad's castle at Poienari (see p.105). A **museum** of Vlad's life and times occupies the fifteenth-century **Sunset Tower** (*Turnul Chindiei*), although this has been closed for a long time pending repair. Nearby stands the sixteenth-century **Princely Church** where Vlad's successors used to attend services, sitting upstairs in a special section screened from the congregation.

South of the Princely Court, along Strada Nicolae Bălcescu, are the **Art Gallery** (Tues–Sun 9am–5pm) and **History Museum** (Tues–Sun 9am–5pm; summer 10am–6pm). The history museum was set up in the former Law Courts by Ceauşescu in 1986, and the first floor, now used for temporary art shows, was devoted to his achievements. At the same time he removed the heating from the art gallery, housed in the former prefecture, which, as a consequence, is now in a terrible condition; it exibits a few drawings by Pallady and Iosif Iser, and a good deal of more modern art. A few minutes walk further down Strada Nicolae Bălcescu is the **Stelea Monastery**; built in 1645 by Prince Basil the Wolf of Moldavia as part of a peace agreement with the Wallachian ruler, Matei Basarab, the monastery was closed under Communism but is once more in use and its Gothic arcading and Byzantine-influenced paintings are being restored. The **museums of printing and local writers** (Tues–Sun 9am–5pm) on Strada Justiţei are also worth a look.

Three kilometres northeast of town (bus #7) the graceful bulk of **Dealu Monastery** rises upon a hill. Built in 1501, it set the pattern for much of Wallachian church architecture – with its towers above the *pronaos* and cornice arcades separated by cable moulding – until the advent of the Brîncovenesc style at the end of the seventeenth century. Inside, beneath a marble slab topped by a bronze crown, lies **the head of Michael the Brave** – severed from his shoulders within a year of his conquest of Transylvania and Moldavia, putting paid to the unification of Romania for another 250 years. The inscription reads: "To him who first united our homeland, eternal glory."

Practicalities

Trains from Bucharest (via Titu), and from Ploieşti stop at Tîrgovişte **train station**. Bus #4 runs from the station to the town centre, but the road surface is terrible and it is far more pleasant to make the short walk along Bulevardul Castanilor to the centre. The new **bus station** is 1km west of town by the Romlux train halt, and is linked to the centre by most bus services, which run along Calea Cîmpulung. There are eight buses a day from Bucharest's Griviţa bus station and a few private buses from the city's *Hotel Nord*; the Găeşti–Sinaia bus service also passes through Tîrgovişte, linking the town to the main rail routes to Braşov (at Sinaia) and Piteşti (at Găeşti).

Tîrgovişte's two **hotels** are on the north side of the Parcul Central. The *Dîmboviţa*, at B-dul Libertăţii 1 (☎045/61.39.61 or 61.46.41; ①), is currently being refurbished and its prices are bound to rise when it reopens; the *Valahia*, at B-dul Libertăţii 7 (☎045/63.44.91, fax 01/312.59.92; ACR; ⑦), is uninspiring. The *Priseaca*, a **campsite** with chalets, is 7km out along the Cîmpulung road (bus #18).

Piteşti

About 100km northwest of Bucharest by road or rail, is **PITEŞTI**. Much of the town's architectural appeal has been wrecked by earthquakes and subsequent rebuildings and these days it is dominated by the Dacia factory – origin of most of Romania's cars – and the woodworking and petrochemical industries and their pollution. If you are planning to stop here en route to western Wallachia, come on Friday or Saturday, when it fulfils its traditional role as a market town for the country folk of the Argeş valley.

Bus #8 runs from the Sud station every eight minutes, dropping you near the hotels in the town centre. Strada Victoriei, just east of the hotels, is now a pedestrianized street, with the seventeenth-century **Princely Church** of Constantin

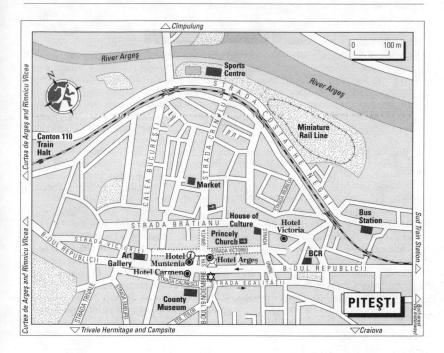

Şerban standing on a lonely patch of grass at its southern end. To the north, along the same street, are the **Naïf Art Collection** on Pasajul Victoriei, selling works by contemporary local artists, and the main **Art Gallery**, at B-dul Republicii 33 (the former town hall), housing a permanent display by more academic painters. A block west of the hotels, at Str. Calinescu 44, is the **County Museum**, housed in the turn-of-the-century prefecture building; it offers a standard review of the region's history. A synagogue survives nearby at B-dul Noiembrie 1. The seventeenth-century **Trivale Hermitage**, southwest of the centre in Trivale Park, is nothing special, but it's a lovely twenty minutes' traffic-free walk to it up Strada Trivale through fine oak woods. Alternatively, buses #2B, #5, #8 and #21 run up Strada Smeurei just to the east, leaving you in the midst of modern apartment blocks just above the hermitage. If you're in the mood for parks, the Parcul Ştrandului Argeş, on the bank of the Argeş at the end of Strada Rîurilor, is attractive, with a miniature rail line running round it (Fri, Sat & Sun 11am–7pm).

Practicalities

The main **train station** is Piteşti Sud – linked to the town centre by bus #8 – although trains serving Curtea de Argeş also call at the Canton 110 halt (no ticket office) and at Piteşti Nord, in the northern suburbs. Rail tickets are also available at the CFR bureau by the *Argeş* hotel. Piteşti's **bus station** is located on Strada Tîrgu din Vale, and runs services to Bucharest, Cîmpulung, Braşov, Craiova and Rîmnicu Vîlcea.

PITEŞTI PRISON

For many Romanians, the town of Piteşti is synonymous with its **prison**, scene under the early Stalinist regime of some of the most brutal psychiatric abuse anywhere in the Soviet bloc. In May 1948 there were mass arrests of dissident students, and from December 1949 about a thousand of them were brought here, to the so-called "Student Re-education Centre", for a programme aimed at "re-adjusting the students to Communist life" and eliminating the possibility of any new opposition developing. In fact it simply set out to destroy the personality of the individual: by starvation, isolation, and above all by forcing prisoners to torture each other, breaking down all distinctions between prisoner and torturer, and thus between individual and state. "United by the evil they have both perpetrated and endured, the victim and the torturer thus become a single person. In fact, there is no longer a victim, ultimately no longer a witness", as Paul Goma put it in his book *The Dogs of Death*. Sixteen students died during this atrocious "experiment".

The programme was extended to Gherla and other prisons and the Danube–Black Sea Canal labour camps, but security was looser here and the torture stopped when word got out. The experiment was abandoned in 1952, when the Stalinist leader Ana Pauker was purged; it was claimed that the authorities had not been involved, and in 1954, those running the Piteşti prison were tried secretly for murder and torture. The leader of the so-called "Organization of Prisoners with Communist Convictions", Eugen Ţurcanu was executed along with several of his henchmen, while others were sentenced to forced labour for life. Nevertheless, because of the guilt of all involved, both prisoners and guards, there followed a conspiracy of silence which only began to break in 1989.

Should you need to **stay the night** before pushing on up the Argeş valley all of the hotels are in the centre of town. The *Victoria* hotel (☎048/62.25.66; ③), a joint Romanian–Italian venture at the junction of Strada Unirii and Strada Brătianu, is the best bargain in town; the *Argeş* on the corner of Stradas Griviţa and Victoriei (☎048/62.54.50, fax 21.45.56; ②) and the *Muntenia* at Piaţa Munteniei 1 (☎048/62.54.50, fax 21.45.56; ④) are typical state hotels, tatty at the edges with indifferent staff and management; while the *Carmen*, at Str. Plevnei 1 (☎048/22.26.99, fax 21.52.97; ③), is a new, privately run establishment, more comfortable than the state hotels, but possibly too flash for some tastes. There are also chalets in the Trivale Park **campsite**. If you're looking for **places to eat**, you'll find little but fast food in Piteşti – Communist-style at the *Autoservire Cina* (6.30am–10pm) just west of the House of Culture on Strada Brătianu, and American-style at a *McDonald's* drive-in (6am–midnight) southeast of the Sud train station on Bulevardul Republicii.

Goleşti

The village of **GOLEŞTI**, 8km east of Piteşti on the Bucharest rail line, was the fiefdom of the Golescu family – one of the leading liberal families of nineteenth-century Wallachia. Their home – now at the heart of an open-air **Museum of Fruit and Vine Growing** (Tues–Sun 9am–5pm) – is in fact a *conac* or summer residence (winters would be spent in Bucharest or Paris), and is beautifully cool, with authentic furnishings and historical displays. The museum itself is behind the house and incorporates buildings from fruit- and wine-growing communities all over Romania. The oldest is the wooden church of Drăguteşti, built in 1814.

Over the gateway is the *foişor* or watchtower of Tudor Vladimirescu, leader of the 1821 peasant revolt who was captured here and taken to Tîrgovişte where he was killed. Beside this is a schoolhouse, with a sandbox which was used for practising writing. The village church, across the road from the museum's main gate, dates from 1646; you'll need to ask around in the village for the caretaker who will let you into the church if you want to look around.

Cîmpulung and beyond

CÎMPULUNG MUSCEL (as it is properly known), 55km north of Piteşti, is overshadowed by mountains to the north, and begrimed by pollution from its factories. However, the town, which dates back to pre-Roman times, has played an important role in Wallachia's history, including a stint as the region's first capital after the voivodate was forged around 1300. Most trains from Piteşti terminate at Cîmpulung station, two kilometres south of town, and are met by buses. About 500m north of the station on Strada Negru Vodă is Cîmpulung's main sight, the **Negru Vodă Monastery**, attributed to its namesake, Romania's legendary thirteenth-century Black Prince, but largely rebuilt following several earthquakes. The present building was completed in 1837 and incorporates stonework from the original; the infirmary chapel to its rear dates from 1718. The monastery's most striking feature is the massive seventeenth-century gate-tower, with its heavy beech gates and twelfth-century stone carving of a doe to the left as you enter; this was brought from a nearby Dominican monastery and is remarkably Western European in style.

Continuing north along Strada Negru Vodă, the town's main drag, brings you to Strada Republicii, which forms the southbound stretch of the centre's one way system (Strada Negru Vodă forms the northbound). The **Ethnographic Museum** (Tues–Sun 9am–5pm) is at Str. Republicii 5, in a fine seventeenth-century building. Beyond this is the town centre, with the wonderful neo-Brîncovenesc buildings on the west side of Strada Negru Vodă, and the town hall and the main hotel, the *Muscelul*, to the east. The fourteenth-century Roman Catholic **Bărătiei Church** is at Str. Negru Vodă 116, and Cîmpulung's **History Museum** (Tues–Sun 9am–5pm) at no. 119. This has more detailed coverage of local history than most Romanian museums, with special emphasis on medieval trade treaties with Braşov. There's also coverage of the Roman fort, or *castrum*, of Jidava, part of the *Limes Transalutanus* defensive line, which was destroyed by the Goths in 244 AD; the fort's remains, by the Pescăreasa rail halt, at km44.5 on the road south, have been preserved and can be visited. The museum's art section is housed on its first floor, with works by Grigorescu and Lucian, as well as a couple of sketches by Pallady, on exhibition.

Cîmpulung's main **hotel**, the *Muscelul* at Str. Negru Vodă 162 (☎048/81.24.00, fax 21.92.49; ⑥), is a standard modern block. A cheaper, cold-water alternative is the *Unic* on Piaţa Juramîntului, between Negru Vodă and Republicii (☎048/81.16.87; ①). A more basic option is the *Măgura*, 5km west in the tiny resort of Bughea de Sus, which can be reached by local buses. One of the oldest **agrotourism** programmes in the country centres on the village of **Lereşti**, 8km north of town. Homestays here (and in equally attractive villages such as Rucăr, Dîmbovicioara, Albeşti, Dragoslavele, and Bughea) can now be booked in Cîmpulung at the *filiala Antrec* (Mon–Fri 9am–5pm, Sat 10am–3pm; ☎

048/82.24.92), opposite the Bărătiei church. Fourteen buses a day go to Lereşti (also served by *maxitaxis*) from Cîmpulung's **bus terminal** – east of the town centre and across the river at Strada I.C. Frimu. The best place **to eat** is the *Hotel Muscelul*, the other options – the *Dolphins* pizza/burger joint at Negru Vodă 146 (open daily till midnight), and the *Intim* below the *Hotel Unic* – are considerably worse.

Beyond Cîmpulung

The scenery becomes increasingly dramatic on the road north from Cîmpulung into Transylvania. Eight kilometres beyond Cîmpulung, the Tîrgovişte road forks right just south of **Nămăeşti** (bus #4) – at the site of a rock church complete with an ancient and miraculous icon and cells hewn from sandstone by sixteenth-century monks – and heads on to the villages of **Dragoslavele** and **Rucăr** with their traditional wooden houses and verandas. Dragoslavele also has an eighteenth-century wooden church, and there's a **campsite** just beyond Rucăr, where home-stays are also available. From here, the road continues up in a series of hairpin bends towards the Bran (or Giuvala) Pass, encountering the **Bridge of the Dîmboviţa**, a spectacular passage between the Dîmboviciorei and Plaiu gorges to the north and the yet narrower Dîmboviţei gorges to the south (see p.140 for the continuation of the route beyond the Bran Pass).

Curtea de Argeş and Dracula's Castle

After the Old Courts of Bucharest and Tîrgovişte, Wallachia's Dracula trail continues west via the small town of **Curtea de Argeş**, another former princely capital, to the remains of **Dracula's Castle** at **Poienari**. Selling Dracula as hard as it can, the tourist industry concentrates its efforts on Bran castle in Transylvania, which has almost no connection to either the historical Dracula or Bram Stoker's fictional character. Yet the castle at Poienari is easily as impressive as that at Bran, and its location in the foothills of the Făgăraş mountains makes for a far more dramatic setting.

Curtea de Argeş

CURTEA DE ARGEŞ, Wallachia's second capital (after Cîmpulung and before Tîrgovişte), lies some 36km northwest of Piteşti, and is easily accessible by road or rail. It's just five minutes to the old town centre from the ornate Mughal-style **train station** and the **bus station** just to its south – turn left out of the stations and then right up Strada Castanilor. Not far north of the centre, enclosed by a wall of river boulders, is the **Court of Argeş** and the oldest church in Wallachia. The complex (Tues–Sun 9am–6pm) was rebuilt in the fourteenth century by Radu Negru, otherwise known as Basarab I, the founder of Wallachia. Its **Princely Church** was built in 1352 and decorated with frescoes in 1384; later restoration work has now been largely removed to reveal the original frescoes, which are fully in the Byzantine tradition but wonderfully alive and individual, reminiscent of Giotto rather than the frozen poses of the Greek masters. The town's **museum** (Tues–Sun 9am–6pm) is housed in a villa across the square.

A more impressive, but less authentic monument, the monastery or **Episcopal Church** (daily 8am–7pm), is sited a good kilometre north of the court along the main road, Calea Basarabilor, reached by bus #2 from the town centre. It resembles the creation of an inspired confectioner: a boxy structure enlivened by whorls, rosettes and fancy trimmings, rising into two twisted, octagonal belfries, each festooned with little spheres and the three-armed cross of Orthodoxy.

Manole's Well, in the park across the road, next to the restaurant of the same name, is a spring which is said to have been created by the death of **Manole**, the Master Builder of Curtea de Argeş. Legend has it that Manole was marooned on the rooftop of his creation, the Episcopal Church, when Neagoe Basarab, the ruler who had commissioned him to build it, ordered the scaffolding to be removed, in an attempt to ensure that the builder could not repeat his masterwork for anyone else. Manole tried to escape with the aid of wings made from roofing shingles – only to crash to his death on the ground below, whereupon a spring gushed forth immediately. The story is perhaps that of a crude form of justice, for legend also has it that Manole had immured his wife within the walls of the monastery – at the time it was believed that *stafia* or ghosts were needed to keep buildings from collapse.

The current Episcopal Church is not Manole's original creation of 1512–17 but a re-creation of 1875–85 by the Frenchman Lecomte de Noüy, who grafted on all the Venetian mosaics and Parisian woodwork; he wanted to do the same to the Princely Church, but the historian Nicolae Iorga managed to get legal backing to stop him doing so. The first kings of Romania and their queens are buried here, just inside the entrance, along with the church's founder, Neagoe Basarab.

Curtea de Argeş has some inexpensive **accommodation** on offer. The privatized *Cumpăna* hotel in the town centre at Str. Negru Vodă 36 (☎048/71.37.23; ②) is as cheap and cheerful as they come, and the *San Nicioară* campsite (☎048/71.37.26; ①) up the street of the same name, opposite the ruined seventeenth-century Potters' Church, is also worth trying – a chalet for two here costs a little less than a double at the *Cumpăna*, and tents and campervans are also welcome. The *Hotel Posada*, south of the monastery at B-dul Basarabilor 27 (☎048/71.18.00, fax 71.18.02; ③), is good value, and the only place in town with hot water. **Moving on by train**, your only option is one of the seven daily services to Piteşti; there's more choice at the **bus station**, with services to Bucharest, Cîmpulung, Braşov, Rîmnicu Vîlcea and Sibiu.

The real Dracula's Castle

Twenty-five kilometres north of Curtea de Argeş is **AREFU**, a long, ramshackle village just west of the valley road. It was to here, in 1457, that the survivors of Vlad the Impaler's massacre in Tîrgovişte (see p.98) were marched to begin work on his castle. This is the real **Dracula's Castle** – his only connection with the better-known one at Bran is that he may have attacked it once (see p.140). Situated on a crag north of the village, it can only be reached by climbing 1400 steps from the Poienari hydroelectric power station 4km north on the road from Arefu, which proves a powerful disincentive to most visitors. Struggle to the top and you'll find that the citadel is surprisingly small, one third having collapsed down the mountainside in 1888. Entering by a narrow wooden bridge, you'll find the remains of two towers within. The prism-shaped one was the old keep, Vlad's residential quarters, from where, according to one legend, the Impaler's wife flung herself out of the window, declaring that she "would rather have her body rot and be eaten by the fish of the Argeş" than be captured by the Turks, who were then besieging the castle. Legend has it that Vlad himself escaped over the mountains on horseback (fooling his pursuers by shoeing his mount backwards – or, according to some versions, by affixing horseshoes that left the impression of cow prints). Seven **buses** a day (two at weekends) head up the Argeş valley to Arefu; the **tourist agency** here offers **private rooms**, which can also be booked from Bucharest (☎ & fax 01/666.61.95; ③).

About 4km north of Poienari is **Lake Vidra**, where the road crosses a spectacular 165m-high dam just before the *Casa Argeşeana cabana*. Buses go all the way to the dam (*baraj*) only at 7.30am at weekends. However, unless you've the means to drive along the **Transfăgăraşan Highway** to Făgăraş in Transylvania (see p.142), or you're hiking around Bîlea in the **Făgăraş mountains** (see p.144), the lake is about as far north as you're likely to get.

The Olt valley

The **River Olt** runs south from its source in Transylvania through the "Red Tower Pass" below Sibiu, carving a stupendous 50km gorge through the Carpathians down into Wallachia, where it passes through the **Rîmnicu Vîlcea**, 34km west of Curtea de Argeş, and continues south to the Danube. From Wallachia the valley can best be approached by road from Piteşti and Curtea de Argeş or from Tîrgu Jiu further to the west. From Tîrgu Jiu the route is long but very scenic, while the one from the *autostradă* at Piteşti is very busy, as the closure of former Yugoslavia has made it the main truck route between Turkey and Western Europe. **Trains** from Piatra Olt, midway along the Piteşti–Craiova line, head along the valley to Podu Olt and Sibiu, with slower services stopping at the villages in between.

Rîmnicu Vîlcea

There are more interesting places further up the Olt valley but it's worth pausing in **RÎMNICU VÎLCEA**, west of Piteşti, to buy food, get local information and check out festival dates. Sprawling across successive terraces above the River Olt, it's a typically "systematized" town, with many modern apartment blocks but also many attractive old churches.

From the **train station**, it's a fairly short walk (10min) along Strada Cozia to Piaţa Mircea cel Bătrîn in the centre of town. To the south of the square lies the fruit and veg market (open daily) and to the north, opposite the *Alutus* hotel, is the sixteenth-century **Church of the Annunciation** (*Buna Vestire*), established in 1545–49 by Mircea the Shepherd and rebuilt in 1747 by the citizens of Sibiu. The main street, Calea lui Traian, runs along the western side of Piaţa Mircea cel Bătrîn; heading north along here you'll pass two old churches – **St Paraschiva**, built in 1557–87, and **All Saints**, built in 1762–64 in a post-Brîncovenesc style with distinctive oblique cable mouldings that make the towers seem twisted. Five minutes further north, at Calea lui Traian 159, is the **County Museum**, whose displays of local history stop at the 1920s. Behind All Saints, at the corner of Strada Antonescu and Strada Colonel Bădescu, is a modern villa housing the **art gallery**. Another five minutes north, at Str. Antonescu 53, is the **Bishopric** (*Episcopiei*), a wonderfully tranquil complex, with three small churches set in well-kept lawns. It dates from the sixteenth century, although the main church, with its Tattarescu paintings, was only built in 1856, after a fire destroyed the original. Further north, at Calea lui Traian 351, the **Citadel church** (1529) still stands amid the remains of its fortifications.

At the northern town limits (bus #7 [sic], or fifteen minutes walk south of Bujoreni station) is the excellent **Bujoreni open-air museum** (Tues–Sun 10am–6pm). The museum is centred on a *cula*, or fortified house, of 1802; the oldest building, built in 1785, is the church: note the candelabra, with wooden eggs hanging below wooden birds. The museum also has a perfectly furnished village school, complete with period books and maps.

Practicalities

Rîmnicu Vîlcea's **bus station** is south of the river, one block west of the Ostroveni train halt; it's a short walk to the centre along Strada Coşbuc and Strada Dacia; services cover all the surrounding villages and monasteries, and also Curtea de Argeş, Piteşti, Tîrgovişte, Cîmpulung, Braşov and Sibiu. At least half a dozen private companies offer buses to Bucharest, notably *1 Mai* (☎050/72.36.46), *Dacos* (☎050/73.97.49) and *Traian* (☎050/73.26.74). The main **hotel**, and the only one in the centre, is the *Alutus* on Strada G-ral Praporgescu (☎050/73.66.01, fax 73.77.60; ACR; ⑤). More restful alternatives are located on the slopes of the hills immediately west of the centre – the *Capela* (☎050/73.40.79; ⑤), at the top of Aleea Castanilor, has chalets and its rooms are marginally cheaper than at the *Alutus*; the *Gemina* (☎050/73.51.01; ③), at the top of Strada Colonel Bădescu, is basic but acceptable. The *Motel Riviera* (☎050/74.24.89, fax 74.26.38; ⑤) is a friendly private place 3km north; and on the southern outskirts there is the *Popas Ostroveni*, a basic campsite with chalets.

Călimăneşti–Căciulata

CĂLIMĂNEŞTI–CĂCIULATA marks the entrance to **the Olt defile**, a deep, sinuously twisting gorge of great beauty and the site of several monasteries, most notable of which are **Cozia** and **Turnul**. Although the river was notoriously wild and dangerous here, it has now been tamed, with a project, still underway, to build a series of dams; viaducts carry the road in places. While the main road runs along the Olt's west bank, a lesser road (as far as Cozia) and the rail line follow the other side of the defile.

CĂLIMĂNEŞTI, 15km north of Rîmnicu Vîlcea, is home to the renowned **Songs of the Olt folklore festival** and a **pottery fair**, both of which usually take place during the first week in August. The nearest **train station** to this spa town is actually in the neighbouring village of Jiblea just to the south, although the station itself takes Călimăneşti's name; **buses** run roughly hourly from the station into Călimăneşti, then on to its twin town of Căciulata and onwards as far as Cozia monastery. However, the station is only 1km from Călimăneşti, and it takes just ten minutes, walking beside the train tracks, then turning left along Strada Vlahuţă, to reach the dam which carries the main road across the Olt into Călimăneşti. This is an average sort of town with 1920s houses, bars forbidden to Gypsies, and the usual shops. The municipal park, **Ostrov island**, at the point where the Olt emerges from the mountains, is the site of a tiny **hermitage**, built in 1520–22 for Despina, wife of Neagoe Basarab, with painted frescoes dating from 1752–60 – the hideous green-faced women in the porch are no indication of the beautiful paintings inside.

The only **accommodation** in Călimăneşti itself is in the *Hotel Central* (☎050/75.09.91, fax 75.11.38; ③), a classic spa hotel at the northern end of the town at Calea lui Traian 398. The new *Pensiune Călimăneşti Varianta* (☎050/75.11.79; ④), at a filling station a kilometre south of the town, is worth considering, as is the *Seaca* campsite, on the main road north of the centre.

Immediately north of Călimăneşti is CĂCIULATA, a one-street spa town lined with villas; some claim to be too grotty to admit foreigners, but the *Merişorul* (☎050/75.10.76; ③) is friendly and clean, if smoky. The *Traian* (☎050/75.07.80, fax 75.01.64; ④) may also be able to find you villa accommodation. To the north of town the *Căciulata/Cozia/Olţul* complex of hotels (☎050/75.05.20, fax 75.11.38; ⑥), at Calea lui Traian 953–955, is far snobbier, and foreigners pay five times as much as Romanians even for car parking. There is also the *Ştrand* campsite immediately north of the *Traian* hotel.

Cozia, Turnul and beyond

One kilometre north of Căciulata (4km from the centre of Călimăneşti), is **Cozia Monastery**, the earliest example of Byzantine architecture in Wallachia; its architectural features include alternating bands of brick and stone, and fluted, false pillars. Cozia's foundation in 1388 was owing to the patronage of Dracula's grandfather, **Mircea the Old**, who is buried within the monastery. The church portico was added by Prince Constantin Brîncoveanu in the early eighteenth century, although it's not a particularly striking example of the Brîncovenesc style. The monastery houses a **museum of religious art**, and there's a fine view over the Olt valley and the mountains from its windows. Across the road is the minute *Bolniţa*, or **Infirmary Church**, built in 1542–43, with murals dating from the same period. Immediately south stands the *Hanul Cozia* motel (☎050/75.05.20; ②) where buses from the train station terminate; just to the north, the Olt is spanned by a dam, leading to the reconstructed Arutela *castrum* (built in 137 AD as part of the *Limes Alutanus*, the Romans' defensive line along the Olt).

About 2km north of Cozia Monastery, near the Mînăstirea Turnu train halt, is **Turnul Monastery**, based around rock cells hewn by hermits from Cozia at the end of the sixteenth century. From here it's a five- to six-hour walk up a steep trail marked by red stripes to the *Cozia cabana*, situated near the summit of the **Cozia massif**. Sheltered from northeasterly winds by the Făgăraş mountains, this has the mildest climate of all Romania's ranges, allowing oak, walnut and wild roses to grow at altitudes of up to 1300m.

Just to the north of here, the Lotru Valley heads west to the resort of **VOINEASA**, born as the construction base for a system of hydroelectric reservoirs, but now a self-styled mountain resort and a good base for walking. There are six one-star hotels (☎050/73.50.84, fax 71.99.63; ②), all run by the same management and fairly indistinguishable from each other; the *Poeniţa* is the smallest and the *Lotru* is the best bet for singles. Five **buses** a day run to Voineasa from Rîmnicu Vîlcea (one starting in Bucharest), and it's possible to continue westwards through the mountains, if you have your own transport, on an unsurfaced road all the way to Petroşani (see p.176).

Continuing north along the Olt valley, 17km beyond the Turnul monastery and just beyond the small village of Lotru, is the seventeenth-century **Corneţ Hermitage**, whose bizarre facade is decorated with a multitude of glazed ceramic plates, tiles and studs. Local **trains** stop both at Corneţ and at **VALEA MĂRULUI**, the start of the Făgăraş traverse hiking route. The road and rail routes head on towards the **Red Tower Pass** (*Pasul Turnu Roşu*). The pass itself, one of the few natural breaches in the Carpathians and site of many battles between Wallachian, Transylvanian, Hapsburg, Turkish and German forces over the past five centuries, is marked by the ruined medieval Spart Tower (*Turnul Spart*) and then by the fifteenth- and eighteenth-century castle of **BOIŢA**. Beyond lies Transylvania.

Tîrgu Jiu and around

Forewarned about **TÎRGU JIU** and the surrounding **Jiu valley**, visitors often decide to ignore them completely. Ranged along the valley, from Petroşani (see p.176) to Rovinari, are the **coal and lignite mines** that support all the country's other industries. For the most part, this is a bleak landscape, made grimmer by slag heaps, pylons and the mining towns themselves, while the sandbanks in the river are almost solid coal dust. Under Communism the miners were lauded as the aristocrats of the proletariat, but had to be placed under **martial law** in 1985, when Ceauşescu demanded ever higher output and docked pay by 50 percent when quotas weren't achieved. After the revolution of 1989, the **miners** were used as Iliescu's shock troops, being rushed on special trains to Bucharest to terrorize the opposition as required, and even to precipitate the resignation of prime minister Petre Roman himself.

Tîrgu Jiu is known for its great winter music gathering, the **Festival of Enchanted Water Springs** (*Izvoare Fermecate*), normally staged during the third week of February, but it's a pretty uninviting time of year for visitors to be here.

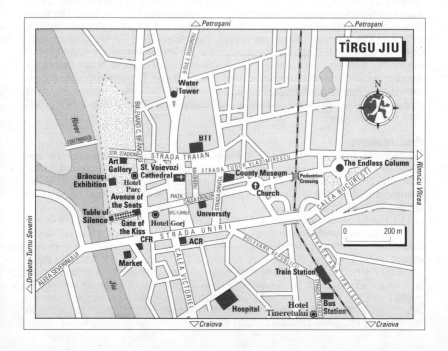

The Town

Although Tîrgu Jiu has no links with coal mining, it still suffered the gross "modernization" imposed by Ceauşescu on Romania's coal-mining centres. Nevertheless the town does hold some attractions, chiefly the monumental sculptures that **Constantin Brâncuşi** created in the late 1930s as a war memorial for the town of his boyhood. The most noticeable, at the eastern end of Calea Eroilor, is the *Coloană Infinita* (Endless Column), a vast totem-pole of rhomboidal blocks, whose rippling form is emulated on many of the verandas of the old wooden houses throughout the region. You'll find the other sculptures at the other end of the Calea Eroilor, which runs 1.7km west from the "Endless Column" to the park on the banks of the Jiu river – the *Poarta Sărutului* (Gate of the Kiss) at the entrance to the park opens onto the *Aleea Scaunilor* (Avenue of Seats), flanked by thirty stone chairs, which in turn leads to the *Masa Tăcerii* (Table of Silence), surrounded by twelve stools (representing the continuity of the months and the traditional number of seats at a funeral feast). Brâncuşi had originally proposed a series of twelve sculptures in Tîrgu Jiu, but completed only these four before he died. Just north of the "Table of Silence" is a villa housing a display of photographs of Brâncuşi's life and works, and to the north of this is the modern **art gallery** (Tues–Sun 9am–7pm), which has no works by the man himself but displays some excellent modern artists, as well as icons painted in the eighteenth, nineteenth and twentieth centuries.

Calea Eroilor cuts through the centre of this busy, dusty town, dominated by windswept concrete buildings; it is a surprisingly narrow street, and the vista east from the park to the "Endless Column" is blocked by a modern, and ugly, church. There are some striking architectural pieces amid the concrete, most notably around the pedestrianized Piaţa Victoriei where you will find the **neo-Brîncovenesc prefecture** and the tiny **Cathedral of St Voievozi**, built in 1749–64. The **County Museum** (Tues–Sun 9am–5pm) at Str. Griviţa 8, is unremarkable, offering the standard view of Romanian history, and, 3km north of the town centre on the main road to Petroşani, at B-dul Ecaterina Teodoroiu 270, is the birthplace of **Ecaterina Teodoroiu** (Wed–Sun 8am–4pm), Romania's answer to Joan of Arc; she was only 23 when she died in August 1917, fighting disguised as a man in the crucial battle of Mărăşeşti (see p.225).

Practicalities

There are bus services to Bucharest, Rîmnicu Vîlcea, Drobeta-Turnu Severin and Sibiu, as well as to the surrounding villages, from the town's **bus terminal**, at Str. Libertăţii 13. Tîrgu Jiu is on the Simeria–Petroşani–Craiova **train** line, with some trains continuing to Arad, Cluj, Deva and Bucharest. **Rail bookings** can be made at Bloc 2, Strada Unirii.

The *Hotel Gorj* at Calea Eroilor 6 (☎053/21.48.15, fax 21.48.22; ACR; ④) offers the best **accommodation** in town; it also houses the **tourist office** (Mon–Fri 8am–7pm). The *Parc* at B-dul Brâncuşi 40 (☎053/21.59.81, fax 21.11.67; ④) was owned by BTT, but has now been privatized and is much improved; there's still a *Hotel BTT* (☎053/21.64.69; ②) in the Debarcader quarter, north of the centre, as well as a BTT office on Str. Traian (☎053/21.24.56). There's also an overpriced youth hotel, the *Tineretului*, one block south of the bus station at Str. N. Titulescu 2/6 (☎053/24.46.82; ⑤), and a **motel with campsite** 10km east of the town on the DN67 at Drăgoeni (☎053/21.88.27; ①).

CONSTANTIN BRÂNCUŞI

One of the greatest sculptors of the twentieth century, **Constantin Brâncuşi** (pronounced "Brinkoosh") was born in 1876 in a peasant cottage at Hobiţa, some 28km west of Tîrgu Jiu. He came to town at the age of nine to work as an errand boy, and later learnt the techniques of the local wood carvers, who chiselled sinuous designs on rafters, verandas and wells in the region. Through the sponsorship of local boyars he was able to attend an art college in Craiova and went on to the National School of Fine Arts in Bucharest, before arriving at the École des Beaux Arts in Paris in 1904, with a government scholarship of L600. He stayed in France for over fifty years, helping create a revolution in sculpture with his strikingly strong and simple works. With a circle of friends that included Picasso, Gide and Pound, he was at the centre of the intellectual ferment of Paris at its height.

He worked briefly in Rodin's studio, then, in company with Amadeo Modigliani, discovered the primitive forms of African masks and sculptures, concentrating thereafter on stripping forms down to their fundamentals. In 1907 he claimed that "what is real is not the exterior form but the essence of things", a credo which he pursued for the rest of his career. In 1920 his *Prinţesa X* (Princess X) was removed by police from the Salon des Indépendents because it was considered obscenely phallic; it was bought by Fernand Léger and Blaise Cendrars, but Brâncuşi never exhibited in Paris again. A different sort of scandal followed in 1926 when Brâncuşi took his *Măiastra* (Magic Bird) with him to New York. US Customs classified it as "a piece of metal" and levied import duty of $10; Brâncuşi appealed against the decision, thereby starting a critical furore which made him a household name in America. During that same trip, the photographer Edward Steichen gave credibility to Brâncuşi's work by publicly announcing that he had bought one of the sculptor's bronze *Birds in Flight* for $600 – by 1967 it was worth $175,000. Brâncuşi died in 1957, with his series of sculptures for Tîrgu Jiu unfinished, and is buried in Montparnasse cemetery in Paris. You'll find examples of his work in Craiova and Bucharest as well as Tîrgu Jiu, and also in London, New York and Philadelphia; his last studio is preserved in Paris.

The best **restaurants** are the *Lider* (noon–midnight), serving standard Romanian dishes, and *Pizzeria Quattro Stagione* (10am–midnight), both on Calea Eroilor opposite the *Hotel Gorj*; also worth trying is *Simigerie* (8am–11pm), a decent little restaurant-bar on the west (older) side of Piaţa Victoriei.

East of Tîrgu Jiu

Away from the industry of the Jiu valley, there are plenty of tranquil villages where traditional customs and dress are still a part of everyday life. The area east of town has particularly impressive **cave formations** and important **monasteries**, notably those at Horezu. Even the more remote sights are well served by buses from both Tîrgu Jiu and Rîmnicu Vîlcea. There are also several mountain hikes north into Transylvania.

Polovragi and around

POLOVRAGI, 48km east of Tîrgu Jiu, dominated by the Căpăţînii mountains, is home to one of the great Wallachian **fairs**. An occasion for highlanders to dress up, dance and do deals in the old fashion, the *Nedeia* usually occurs on the Sunday between July 14 and 20. If your visit doesn't coincide with the fair, the main sights of interest are north of the village, where a forestry road runs into the mile-long **Olteţu gorges**, along which is the **Polovragi Monastery and cave**. The monastery, rebuilt by Brîncoveanu, is relatively small, but the later **Bolniţa Church** (1736) with its fine frescoes is definitely worth the trip. Further on, lurking behind the eastern rockface at the mouth of the gorge, is the Polovragi cave – once believed to be the abode of Zalmoxis, the Dacians' chief deity. Now fully illuminated and open for guided tours (daily 9am–5pm), it was first explored in 1860 by the French naturalist Lancelot, and is renowned for the stalactites in its "Candlesticks Gallery".

From Baia de Fier, 7km west of Polovragi, a road leads 3km north to a beautiful grotto in the smaller **Galbenul gorges** (daily 9am–5pm). Although only two passages out of the ten kilometres of convolutions of the so-called **Women's Cave** (*Peştera Muierii*) have been illuminated, it's an impressive sight; halfway in, multicoloured stone columns resemble petrified wood, while in the lower passage the skeletons of 183 cave bears have been discovered. The cave gets its name from the human skeletons – mainly those of women and children and dating from perhistoric times – found on its upper levels. From the cave and nearby cabana, a footpath leads up to the **Rînca tourist complex** (☎053/21.60.05; ②), 15km away in the Parîng mountains. The next settlement west, **NOVACI**, marks the start of the forestry road to Rînca and on to Sebeş (see p.163). There are two motels in Novaci, on Strada Tudor Vladimirescu.

Horezu and the monasteries

The small town of **HOREZU**, set amid apple and plum orchards, sweet chestnut trees and wild lilac, is 16km east of Polovragi, on the main road to Rîmnicu Vîlcea. It's the abode of numerous owls (*huhurezi*), hence the town's name (also given as 'Hurez' on some maps). Though wooden furniture and wrought-iron objects are also produced here, Horezu is best known for its **pottery**, especially the plates, which by tradition are given as keepsakes during the wakes held following a funeral. The *Cocoşul de Horezu* pottery fair, held on the first Sunday of June, is one of the year's biggest events in the area. Four kilometres south in **Măldăreşti** stand two *culas* or tower houses, built in the eighteenth and nineteenth centuries, when punitive raids by Turkish troops were still a possibility. **Accommodation** is available at the *Horez* motel (☎050/86.07.20; ②), or the *Stejarii* campsite (①), which also has chalets.

The real attraction lies a couple of miles to the northeast of town, near the little village of Romanii de Jos. **Horez Monastery** is the largest and finest of Wallachia's Brîncoveanu complexes, and is the site of the school which established the Brîncovenesc style. It is centred around the Great Church built in 1693, entered via a ten-pillared porchway and doors of carved pearwood. The colours of the church's interior frescoes, which include portraits of Brîncoveanu and his family, have been tarnished by the smoke from fires lit by Turkish slaves who camped here – those in the Nuns' Refectory give a better idea of their original colours. Outside the gates Brîncoveanu had the chapel of St Michael built for the people of the village. The monastic complex also includes Dionisie's fire-tower, built in 1753, with its finely carved columns and a stone balustrade, and, set apart to the north and west, the small hermitages of the Holy Apostles and of St Stephen, built in 1700 and 1703 respectively.

Six kilometres on towards Rîmnicu Vîlcea on the DN67, a left turn at Coşteşti leads another 6km north to **Bistriţa Monastery**, funded by the boyars of Craiova in the fifteenth century. As well as three churches, dating from the sixteenth and seventeenth centuries, there is a cave containing two more chapels, in one of which the relics of St Gregory the Decapolite were hidden during the Turkish wars; a nun will lead you to the cave along the precipitous cliffside path. The seventeenth-century **Arnota Monastery** stands on a hill, 4km north of Bistriţa beyond a large quarry; by financing the construction of this monastery, voivode Matei Basarab guaranteed himself a tasteful burial place within its church surrounded by his chattels and murals of his wife, of which only fragments remain. As is so often the case in this area, the porch is the work of Brîncoveanu.

West of Tîrgu Jiu

The small towns and villages to the west of Tîrgu Jiu are a complete contrast to the mining areas to the east and south. Buses run from Tîrgu Jiu along the DN67d, stopping close to most of the sites of interest.

HOBIŢA, 24km west of Tîrgu Jiu, is Brâncuşi's birthplace. It's a 3km walk south to the village from the main road at Peştişani. The main site of interest is the sculptor's childhood home, now a **museum house** (*Casa Museu*; Wed–Sun 9am–5pm), at about 100m turning left from the village crossroads. If it's closed, you can ask in the shop at the crossroads for the custodian of the museum to let you in. The birthplace is an attractive, traditional cottage, surrounded by plum and cherry trees, in which you'll learn relatively little about Brâncuşi, but it's worth seeing the ceramics and textiles displayed inside, and the intricate spiral motifs on the veranda posts. Another hundred metres along this road will bring you to the *Popas*, where you can sleep in *căsuţe* (summer only), by a ford which leads into a wood dotted with sub-Brâncuşi sculptures left by a 1981 summer-school group. Further south, at the edge of the same wood, but reached by the "main" road through the village, is the village cemetery, with a tiny wooden chapel; even if it's closed, it's possible to enter the chapel's roof space by a ladder from the open porch to admire the skill of the local carpenters.

TISMANA, another 10km west on the DN67d, harks back to the region's traditional pastoral ways. **Tismana Monastery**, 5km to the north of the village, is the oldest in Romania, founded in 1375; surrounded by a high wall during the reign of Matei Basarab, the monastery served as a meeting place for rebels during the 1821 rising led by Tudor Vladimirescu. Tismana is the setting for the annual **"At Tismana in a Garden" Festival** of music and crafts on August 15, where the most popular instrument is the *nai* or shepherd's pan-pipes. You'll find wooden utensils, sculptures, embroidered clothing and Oltenian rugs on sale during the festival, but the quality and range of goods has declined in recent years. Other festivals occur on March 25 and November 30. There are camping chalets and a motel in the village (②), and a tourist complex, *Hotel Tismana* (☎053/37.41.10; ③), just north of the monastery.

Buses for Călugăreni and Cloşani turn north off the main road about 12km west of Tismana, stopping after 5km in **PADEŞ**, where the 1821 peasant revolt, lead by Tudor Vladimirescu, began. Some village men still wear **folk costume** – narrow white homespun trousers piped with braid and voluminous cloaks – which resemble the uniforms worn by Vladimirescu's soldiers. Picturesque **karst formations** abound in the region, particularly around Cloşani and Ponoarele, 7km south of the main road just west of Baia de Aramă; here the **"Giant's Bridge"**, 25m wide by 50m long, was formed when the ceiling of a large cave collapsed.

Drobeta-Turnu Severin and the Danube

Drobeta-Turnu Severin lies in the far west of the region, on the north side of the **River Danube**, the country's natural border with Serbia. The river narrows below Moldova Veche before surging through the **Kazan gorge** towards Orşova, only to be tamed and harnessed by the dam at the **Iron Gates**, before reaching the town. Motorists driving down from Moldova Veche can see something of this magnificent panorama (the rail journey is less scenic); but if you're coming from Tîrgu Jiu, the real landscape feast doesn't start until you reach Drobeta-Turnu Severin. The shortest route from Tîrgu Jiu is via the badly surfaced DN67, usually crowded with trucks. By train, you'll have to travel down to the unappealing town of **FILIAŞI** to join the Craiova–Drobeta-Turnu Severin line. If you're stuck between trains, the only place to stay is the fairly basic, but very cheap, *Filiaşi* hotel (☎051/36.12.01; ①), at the far end of Strada Gării.

Drobeta-Turnu Severin

Dubbed the "town of roses" for its beautiful parks, **DROBETA-TURNU SEVERIN**'s modern appearance belies its origins as the Dacian settlement of *Drobeta*, more than two thousand years ago. Its Roman conquerors left more enduring landmarks, however, notably the **ruins of Trajan's bridge**, which Apollodorus of Damascus built to span the Danube at the order of the emperor in 103–105 AD. As the travel writer Patrick Leigh Fermor put it, "two great stumps

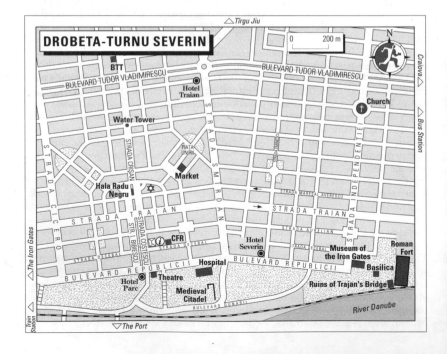

of his conglomerate masonry still cumbered the Romanian side", and these can be seen from the train or from the grounds of the excellent **Museum of the Iron Gates** (*Porţile de Fier*, Tues–Sun 9am–4pm) at the southern end of Strada Independenţei on the east side of town. Nearby, also within the museum precincts, are the remains of a Roman bath, and the foundations of the fourteenth-century **Metropolitan's Basilica** and of the Roman fort guarding Trajan's bridge. Inside the museum, an aquarium of various species from the Danube is the chief attraction, although the ethnographic, archeological and historical departments are also worth a look – the coverage of World War II has been recently reworked, although there's some way to go to bring things right up to date.

The remains of a **medieval citadel** stand between the museum and the town centre, a 15min walk west along Bulevardul Republicii, turning left just before the hospital. Further west along Bulevardul Republicii, Stradas Bibiescu and Costescu lead north from the *Parc* hotel past the prefecture to the Radu Negru Market, now a huge food shop (*alimentara*). Opposite is the amazingly dilapidated synagogue and the site for a new Orthodox cathedral, and beyond these, on Piaţa Unirii, is the lively market (open daily).

Practicalities

The main **bus terminal** is to the east of the centre, just off Bulevardul Vladimirescu (bus #9 every 30min), with services to Băile Herculane in the Banat and east to Tîrgu Jiu and Rîmnicu Vîlcea. Buses to the surrounding villages leave from Piaţa Unirii. The **train station** is just west of the town centre; train tickets can be booked at Str. Decebal 43.

BTT offers cheap dormitory **beds** in summer at Str. Crişan 25 (☎052/22.09.11; ①), but otherwise the cheapest **hotel** in town is the *Severin* at Str. Eminescu 1 (☎052/31.20.74; ④), followed by the *Traian*, B-dul Tudor Vladimirescu 74 (☎052/31.17.60, fax 31.17.49; ④) and the *Parc*, B-dul Republicii 2 (☎052/31.28.51–53, fax 31.69.68; ACR; ⑤). The *Vatra Haiducilor* ("Outlaws' Hearth") **campsite** is 3km north in the Crihala forest.

SC Mircioagă (☎052/36.26.78) operate **riverboats**, downriver to the island of **Ostrov Şimian** and upstream to **Moldova Veche**, offering spectacular views of the Kazan Gorge; you can book these through the **tourist office**, at Str. Decebal 41, and at the *Parc* hotel. However, there is a great temptation for the locals to sell all their spare fuel to Serbia on the black market and while this continues the availability of tours will be erratic.

The Iron Gates

The Iron Gates have a formidable reputation owing to the navigational hazards (eddies, whirlpools and rocks) on this stretch of the river, which formerly restricted safe passage during the two hundred days of the year when the river was in spate, and meant that boats had to take aboard a pilot at Moldova. The blasting of a channel in 1896 obviated these terrors, and the building of the **largest hydroelectric dam in Europe** (excluding the former Soviet Union) at Gura Văii, 8km upstream of Drobeta-Turnu Severin, finally tamed the river.

Conceived in 1956, the hydroelectric project was undertaken as a joint venture; Romania and Yugoslavia each built a 1000MW turbine plant and locks for shipping on their respective banks, linked by a slipway dam and an international road crossing, a task that took from 1960 until 1972 and raised the river level by 33m. Romantics have deplored the results, which, in the words of Leigh Fermor, "has turned 130 miles of the Danube into a vast pond which has swollen and blurred the course of the river beyond recognition", turning "beetling crags into mild hills". The damming has submerged two places worthy of footnotes in history – the island of **Ada Kaleh** and old **Orşova** – and has reduced the Danube's peak flow, so that the pollution of Central Europe is no longer flushed out to sea but gathers here, killing fish and flora.

Legend has it that the Argonauts discovered the olive tree on the island of **ADA KALEH**, an island which was famous at the beginning of this century for its Turkish community, complete with mosques, bazaars and fortresses. Their presence here at so late a date arose from a diplomatic oversight, for at the conference where the Ottoman withdrawal from the region was negotiated in 1878, Ada Kaleh was forgotten about, allowing it to remain Turkish territory until the Trianon Treaty officially made it part of Romania in 1920. Before Ada Kaleh's submersion in the Danube, Eugene of Savoy's citadel and the mosque were removed and reconstructed on the **island of Ostrov Şimian**, 5km east of Turnu Severin (served every 90min by buses to Ostrov Corbului), where there are also Dacian relics.

Before 1918, **ORŞOVA**, 23km upstream from Drobeta-Turnu Severin, was the frontier crossing into the Magyar-ruled Banat, and it was nearby that Kossuth buried the Crown of St Stephen on his way into exile after the failure of the 1848–49 revolt in Hungary. However, the town was flooded by the dam, and new Orşova, 3km east of its **train station**, has nothing of interest beyond a **hotel**, the *Dierna* (☎052/36.17.63 or 36.18.75; ④), at B-dul 1 Decembrie 1918 no. 18, on the main riverfront promenade. The **bus station** is up the steps behind the hotel, by a striking modern church and the market.

The Kazan gorge

Sixteen kilometres beyond Orşova, on both sides of the village of **DUBOVA**, the sheer cliffs of the **Kazan gorge** (*Cazanele Dunării*) fall 600m into the tortuous river. Rather than attempt to cut a path through the rock, the Romans built a road by boring holes in the cliff to hold beams upon which they laid planks, roofing over the road to discourage Dacian ambushes. The first proper road was created on the northern side of the gorge on the initiative of the nineteenth-century Hungarian statesman Count Széchenyi, but had not long been finished when the 1920 Trianon Treaty transferred it to Romania, whereupon it was neglected and finally submerged by the rising waters. Since the building of the dam, modern roads have been built on both sides of the river, and the dramatic landscape makes this an excursion not to be missed.

Moldova Veche and Moldova Nouă

The river continues west for 77km to the small port of **MOLDOVA VECHE**. Its old quarter is largely inhabited by Serbs; the high-rise blocks to the west are inhabited by Romanians brought in during the Communist period when the port was developed to serve the copper and molybdenum mines inland. Nowadays half the male population is working abroad, which has led to some excellent bars being set up with the earnings they send home. There is an unmarked **hotel** (③) on the riverbank, but nothing else of interest. The **bus station** is to the east of town on the road to Orşova. The new town, **MOLDOVA NOUĂ**, a mining community 4km inland from the port, is now in terminal decline and both its hotel and museum have closed.

Before Moldova Veche, within sight of the port, the river divides around an island near the isolated **rock of Babakai**. According to legend, the Turkish governor of Moldova marooned Zuleika, one of his seven wives, here because she had attempted to elope with a Hungarian noble. Admonished to "Repent of thy sin!" "*Ba-ba-kai*" and left to die, Zuleika was rescued by her lover, who later had the joy of taunting the mortally wounded governor with the news that Zuleika was alive and had become a Christian. Another legend refers to the caves near the ruined fortress of **Golubac**, just downstream on the Serbian bank of the river, where St George is said to have slain the dragon. Thereafter, its carcass has reputedly fed the swarms of bugs that infest the town of Golubac.

Southern Wallachia

In many respects **southern Wallachia** is tedious, uninviting terrain, for while the Subcarpathians provide varied scenery and picturesque villages, below them stretch miles of featureless plains, dusty or muddy according to season, with state farms lost amid vast fields of corn or sunflowers.

Craiova

Almost every locomotive on the tracks of Romania originally emerged from the Electroputere workshops of **CRAIOVA**, which also exports to Hungary, Bulgaria, China and even Britain. It is also a centre for the Romanian car industry, with the Oltcit works (now Rodae, a joint venture with the Korean Daewoo conglomerate) producing many of the country's cars. These industries are here because of the ready availability of oil, whose presence is attested to by the derricks surrounding what is now the chief city of Oltenia and capital of Dolj county. Craiova does have a longer history than it might appear from its industrialized heritage – **Michael the Brave** having begun his career here as deputy governor. Now it's a sprawling and polluted place, but you may find yourself breaking a journey to or from Bulgaria here, in which case you'll find a few attractions to while away the time.

From the train and bus stations it's a twenty-minute walk along Bulevardul Carol I (buses #1, #5, #12 and #29) to the main through road, Calca Bucureşti. The city centre lies beyond this road, hidden behind the university building, a monolith dating from 1890. Forking right off B-dul Carol I onto Strada Ştefan cel Mare will bring you directly to the *Hotel Jiul*, from where Calea Unirii leads south to the **Mihail Palace** at no. 10. Built in 1900–08 by a French architect for one of Romania's richest men, the palace was home to Nicolae Ceauşescu in the early 1950s when he was local party secretary, and since 1954 has housed Craiova's best museum – the **Art Gallery** (Tues–Sat 10am–5pm, Sun 9am–5pm). Two rooms to the left of the entrance house six works by Brâncuşi – some early pieces and versions of *Mlle Pogany* and *The Kiss*. There's also plenty of French decorative art, including Sèvres porcelain, and some Italian paintings, including works by Bassano and Bellotto. Upstairs you can see work by all of Romania's best-known artists, including a room of paintings by local lad Theodor Aman (1831–91) and two dozen by Grigorescu; also take a look at the mirrors and Murano chandeliers in the lecture room.

Continuing south, Calea Unirii becomes the pedestrianized axis of the modern city centre; immediately to the right on the main plaza, at Str. Popa Seacă 4, is the **Natural History Museum**, which gives a better than average overview of conservation nationwide. At the far end of the new centre, Strada Madona–Dudu heads to the right to the **History Museum** (Tues–Sun 10am–5pm), opposite the Madona–Dudu church, built in 1936 to house an icon of the Virgin. The museum displays the oldest archeological remains of Oltenia, medieval ornaments and frescoes, and Brîncovenesc art. Immediately to the south on Strada Matei Basarab is the cathedral of **Sf Dumitru-Băneasa**, built in 1652, but thoroughly transformed in 1889 by Lecomte de Noüy; now it's less gloomy than most Orthodox churches, with a gorgeous golden glow to its frescoes. Both this and the far larger Madona–Dudu church have good choirs. The **Ethnographic Museum** (Tues–Sun 10am–5pm) occupies the former governor's residence, or *Casa Banei*, at Str. Matei Basarab 14; built in 1699, it now houses a good collection of textiles, ceramics and agricultural implements.

Practicalities

The *Jiul*, Calea Bucureşti 1 (☎051/41.41.66, fax 41.24.62; ACR; ⑧), is the most comfortable **hotel**; it is a big modern building raised in 1969. The *Minerva* at Str. Kogălniceanu 1 (☎051/41.33.00; ④) is a splendidly atmospheric, but amazingly tatty, pile from 1902. The *Parc*, west of the centre at Str. Bibescu 16 (☎051/41.72.57, fax 41.86.23; ⑦), is basic and overpriced. The *Han Doctorul* (☎051/14.40.13; ②) is a motel with chalets at 7km along the DN6 – take bus #9 east. Alternatively you could pester BTT at Str. Olteţ 8 (☎051/11.73.96), in a pedestrianized area just west of the main square, for vacant college beds, particularly since both **campsites** are a long way out along the DN6 and hard to reach by public transport – the *Lunca Jiului* (Jiu Meadow) is to the west of town on the Bucovaţ road, beyond the Ethnographic Museum, and the *Terasa Baniei* (Governor's Terrace) is out to the east.

Craiova's main **bus station**, right beside the train station, serves destinations as far afield as Calafat, Cîmpulung, Tîrgu Jiu and Rîmnicu Vîlcea. The CFR and TAROM offices are at Calea Bucureşti 2 (in the arcade opposite the *Hotel Jiu*). There are two **train lines** between Craiova and Bucharest: one route crosses the southern plains by way of Caracal, Roşiori de Vede and Videle, there are stopping trains and several express trains, the latter taking about two and a quarter hours; the second goes further north, via Piteşti (see p.100) on a non-electrified line, making this route much slower with a journey time of about four hours. There are through trains from Craiova to Iaşi via Braşov, but it's far quicker if you change trains in Bucharest.

Calafat

The small town of **CALAFAT**, 70km south of Craiova by road and rail, is a major **border crossing into Bulgaria**. A neat orderly town on the banks of the Danube, with a tree-lined grid of streets, the town's main facilities are all close to hand. It's under ten minutes' walk straight ahead from the train station to the centre of town, marked by a war memorial; to the right is the market, and to the left is the *casa de cultură* (actually billiards and disco) and a couple of cafés and snack bars.

THE *RASCOALA*

Despite its rich soil, the southern plain has traditionally been one of Romania's poorest areas, as the boyars – and worse still, their estate managers – squeezed the peasants mercilessly with extortionate taxes on land. The amount of available land diminished as the peasant population, taxes and rural unemployment increased – building up to the explosive **1907 uprising**, the *rascoala*. Triggered near Vaslui in Moldavia where Jews, believed to prey upon peasants, were the first targets, the uprising raged southwards into Wallachia. Panic-stricken boyars flooded into Bucharest, demanding vengeance for the burning of their property – and the army obliged, quelling the ill-armed peasantry with cannon fire, and then executing "ringleaders" by the thousand. Though there's a **Museum of the Uprising** at Str. Dunării 54 (Tues–Sun 10am–5pm) in Roşiori de Vede (Teleorman county), the English translation of Liviu Rebreanu's novel *Uprising* is a more gripping exposition of the subject.

The *Hotel Calafat* (☎051/23.12.93; ③), on Strada 22 Decembrie, is near the port (*Vama*) and convenient for the ferries to Bulgaria; turn left a block before the war memorial for Strada 22 Decembrie and head towards the obvious dockside cranes. **Ferries** depart hourly to Vidin in Bulgaria (5.30am–midnight; 24hr in summer); fares are about $2 for pedestrians or $15 per car. Visas can be obtained from the Bulgarian embassy in Bucharest.

Scorniceşti

SCORNICEŞTI, the **birthplace of Nicolae Ceauşescu**, is on a minor road off the DN65 from Craiova to Bucharest, at km72. It was, fittingly, one of the first new towns created under Ceauşescu's systematization programme, and has thus been drowned in concrete. The actual birthplace is the only original building remaining in the whole town; and the only new edifice of any interest is the football stadium, one of Romania's largest. At Christmas 1989, the villagers danced on the grave of Ceauşescu's father, and a **museum**, that was until then a virtual shrine to the great *Conducator*, is now likely to be totally abandoned, rather than being reworked to give a fair analysis of the dynamics of power under Communism. You can get here by bus from Slatina, on the Craiova–Piteşti rail line.

Giurgiu

Virtually all traffic to Bulgaria from Bucharest passes through **GIURGIU**, 64km due south of the capital on the Danube. So-called *rapid* trains for Bulgaria take an hour and a half to crawl the 85km from Bucharest's Gara de Nord to Giurgiu Nord station just outside the town; slow trains run from Bucharest's Progresu station and continue from Giurgiu Nord to Giurgiu station, in the town next to the bus terminal. Giurgiu's 3km-long **Danube Bridge** (known as the "Friendship Bridge" under Communism) was built in 1954, to carry both road and rail traffic between Romania and Bulgaria. It's open 24 hours a day, and with the closure of the route through former Yugoslavia is now very congested. Visas are available at the crossing but it's cheaper to buy them in Bucharest or before you leave home.

The town has just two features of interest: Strada Gării leads from the bus station to the main square, to the right of which is the 22-metre-high *Turnul Ceasornicului*, built by the Turks as a fire-tower in the late eighteenth century, and converted to a clock-tower in 1839. Continuing right along Strada Mircea del Bătrin, past the cinema and post office, about 500m out on the edge of town some piles of stone rise by a small creek; these are claimed to be the most important military relics of Mircea the Old's reign.

With so much pollution from its notorious chemical works, there's really no reason **to stay** in Giurgiu, but if you don't want to arrive in Bucharest after dark, there are a few **hotels** in the town that are worth considering. The basic but pricey *Hotel Victoria* (☎046/21.21.69, fax 21.34.53; ③) is just five minutes from Giurgiu station at Str. Gării 1, hidden behind a block of flats to the right. For something more comfortable, try the *Vlaşca* at Str. Portului 12 (☎046/21.53.21, fax 21.34.53; ⑤). Better still are the *Steaua Dunării*, a vaguely post-modern pile (Str. Mihai Viteazul 1; ☎046/21.72.70, fax 21.34.53; ⑦), and *Giurgiu Vama*, (☎046/22.08.95, fax 21.34.53; ⑤), both in the eastern outskirts near the bridge; you'll also find a **campsite** nearby on the Danube meadow (*Lunca Dunării*); plenty of buses run out this way from the town centre.

travel details

Trains

Cîmpulung to: Bucharest (1 daily; 3hr); Goleşti (7 daily; 1hr–1hr 30min).

Craiova to: Bucharest, via Caracal (19 daily; 2hr 15min–4hr 30min) or Piteşti (3 daily; 4hr 15min–7hr 30min); Braşov (1 daily; 6hr 15min); Calafat (6 daily; 1hr 45min–2hr 30min); Drobeta-Turnu Severin (14 daily; 1hr 30min–3hr); Filiaşi (22 daily; 15min–1hr); Piatra Olt (13 daily; 45min–1hr 30min); Piteşti (6 daily; 2hr 30min–4hr 30min); Sibiu (3 daily; 4hr 15min–6hr 45min); Timişoara (11 daily; 4hr 45min–9hr); Tîrgu Jiu (5 daily; 2hr–3hr).

Curtea de Argeş to: Bucharest (1 daily; 3hr 45min); Piteşti (7 daily; 1hr).

Drobeta-Turnu Severin to: Băile Herculane (11 daily; 45min–1hr 15min); Caransebeş (10 daily; 2hr–3hr 30min); Craiova (14 daily; 1hr 15min–3hr); Orşova (11 daily; 30min–1hr); Timişoara (12 daily; 3hr–6hr).

Piatra Olt to: Călimăneşti (7 daily; 1hr 30min–3hr); Lotru (6 daily; 2hr–3hr 30min); Rîmnicu Vîlcea (10 daily; 1hr 15min–2hr

45min); Sibiu (5 daily; 3hr 30min–5hr 30min); Turnu Monastery (4 daily; 3hr–3hr 30min).

Piteşti to: Bucharest (11 daily; 1hr 45min–2hr 45min); Curtea de Argeş (7 daily; 45min–1hr); Titu (12 daily; 1hr–1hr 30min).

Ploieşti to: Braşov (27 daily; 1hr 45min–3hr 15min); Bucharest (50 daily; 45min–1hr 45min); Iaşi (6 daily; 4hr 30min–6hr); Slanic Prahova (8 daily; 1hr 15min–2hr); Suceava (9 daily; 5hr–6hr); Tîrgovişte (7 daily; 1hr 45min–2hr 30min); Văleni (11 daily; 1hr–1hr 30min).

Rîmnicu Vîlcea to: Călimăneşti (18 daily; 15–30min); Craiova (4 daily; 2hr–4hr); Lotru (14 daily; 30min–1hr); Piatra Olt (11–12 daily; 1hr 15min–2hr 45min); Podu Olt (6 daily; 1hr 30min–2hr 15min); Sibiu (7 daily; 2hr–3hr).

Tîrgovişte to: Bucharest (6 daily; 1hr 15min–2hr 15min); Ploieşti (7 daily; 1hr 30min–3hr); Titu (11 daily; 30–45min).

Tîrgu Jiu to: Filiaşi (9–10 daily; 1hr 15min–2hr); Petroşani (7–8 daily; 1hr–1hr 30min); Simeria (5 daily; 2hr 30min–4hr 30min); Subcetate (4 daily; 2hr 15min–3hr 30min).

Titu to: Tîrgovişte (11 daily; 30min–1hr).

Buses

Călimăneşti to: Bucharest (1 daily); Curtea de Argeş (1 daily); Polovragi (1 daily); Sibiu (3 daily); Tîrgu Jiu (1 daily); Voineasa (6 daily).

Cîmpulung to: Braşov (7 daily); Bucharest (Mon–Fri 3 daily); Craiova (Mon–Fri 1 daily); Curtea de Argeş (up to 4 daily); Lereşti (14 daily); Piteşti (up to 9 daily); Ploieşti (4 daily); Rîmnicu Vîlcea (up to 5 daily); Rucăr (up to 5 daily); Tîrgovişte (4 daily).

Craiova to: Calafat (1 daily); Cîmpulung via Piteşti (Mon–Fri 1 daily); Horezu (1 daily); Porţile de Fier (2 daily); Rîmnicu Vîlcea (2 daily); Tîrgu Jiu (Mon–Fri 2 daily).

Curtea de Argeş to: Arefu (up to 7 daily); Bucharest (1 daily); Braşov (2 daily); Cîmpulung (up to 4 daily); Piteşti (1 daily); Rîmnicu Vîlcea (up to 6 daily); Sibiu (1 daily); Vidra Dam (Sat & Sun 1 daily).

Drobeta-Turnu Severin to: Baia de Aramă (1 daily); Calafat (1 daily); Deva (5 daily); Orşova (4 daily); Rîmnicu Vîlcea (1 daily); Runcu (1 daily); Tîrgu Jiu (3 daily).

Piteşti to: Bucharest (5 daily); Braşov (2 daily); Cîmpulung (up to 9 daily); Craiova (Mon–Fri 1 daily); Curtea de Argeş (1 daily); Rîmnicu Vîlcea (3 daily); Tîrgovişte (1 daily).

Ploieşti to: Cîmpina (12 daily); Cîmpulung via Tîrgovişte (4 daily); Slon (5 daily); Slanic Prahova (up to 4 daily).

Rîmnicu Vîlcea to: Bistriţa (2 daily); Braşov (2 daily); Cîmpulung (2 daily); Craiova (2 daily); Curtea de Argeş (up to 6 daily); Deva (1 daily); Drobeta-Turnu Severin (1 daily); Horezu (14 daily); Piteşti (2 daily); Runcu (2 daily); Sibiu (2 daily); Tîrgovişte (1 daily); Tîrgu Jiu (3 daily); Voineasa (5 daily).

Tîrgovişte to: Braşov (2 daily); Bucharest (5 daily); Cîmpulung (4 daily); Piteşti (1 daily); Ploieşti (4 daily).

Tîrgu Jiu to: Baia de Aramă (7 daily); Baia de Fier (5 daily); Cloşani (3 daily); Craiova (Mon–Fri 2 daily); Deva (2 daily); Drobeta-Turnu Severin (3 daily); Lupeni (1 daily); Reşiţa (1 daily); Rîmnicu Vîlcea (3 daily); Sibiu (1 daily); Timişoara (1 daily); Tismana (7 daily).

Planes

Craiova to: Bucharest (1–2 daily).

International trains

Craiova to: Belgrade (2 daily; 10hr–11hr); Budapest (1 daily; 10hr 45min).

Drobeta-Turnu Severin to: Belgrade (2 daily; 8hr–9hr); Budapest (1 daily; 9hr).

Giurgiu Nord to: Istanbul (1 daily; 15hr 30min); Kiev (1 daily; 33hr); Moscow (1 daily; 48hr); Ruse (6 daily; 20min); Sofia (3 daily; 7hr 30min–8hr); Thessaloniki (1 daily; 21hr).

International buses

Craiova to: Istanbul (2 daily).

Piteşti to: Istanbul (5 daily).

Ploieşti to: Germany (3 daily); Istanbul (2 daily).

International ferries

Calafat to: Vidin, Bulgaria (roughly hourly).

CHAPTER THREE

TRANSYLVANIA

hanks to Bram Stoker and Hollywood, **Transylvania** (Latin for "beyond the forest") is famed abroad as the homeland of Dracula, a mountainous place where storms lash medieval hamlets, while wolves – or werewolves – howl from the surrounding woods. The fictitious image is accurate up to a point: the **scenery** is breathtakingly dramatic, especially in the Prahova valley, the Turda and Bicaz gorges and around the high passes; there are spooky Gothic citadels, around Braşov and at Sibiu, Sighişoara and Bran; and there was a Vlad, born in Sighişoara, who earned the grim nickname "The Impaler" and later became known as **Dracula** (see p.384).

But the Dracula image is just one element of Transylvania, whose 99,837 square kilometres take in alpine meadows and peaks, caves, dense forests sheltering bears and wild boars, and lowland valleys where buffalo cool off in the rivers. The **population** is an ethnic jigsaw of Romanians, Magyars, Germans, Gypsies, among others, formed over centuries of migration and colonization. Transylvania's history is still often disputed along nationalist lines, the feelings aroused running high in both Hungary and Romania and being routinely exploited by politicians.

Most Hungarians view *Erdély* (their name for Transylvania) as a land "stolen" by the Romanians, where some two million Magyars face continuing harassment and subjugation by a Romanian population that they claim arrived long after the Magyars had settled the area. Romanians assert the opposite: that Transylvania has always been rightfully theirs and that, for centuries, it was the Magyars who practised discrimination as colonialist overlords.

Since the Trianon Treaty of 1920, which placed Transylvania firmly within the Romanian state, the balance of power among the **ethnic groups** has shifted sharply in favour of the Romanian majority, with many peasants brought in from Moldavia and Wallachia to form a new industrial proletariat. The revolution of 1989 has allowed many of Transylvania's population, Germans in particular, to return to their ancestral homeland, leaving the Hungarians as the main minority group in the region. Meanwhile Transylvania's Gypsies (*Tigani*) still go their own way, eagerly participating in an economic free-for-all that they never really abandoned under Communism, and largely unconcerned by growing prejudice against them. The result is an intoxicating brew of different characters, customs and places that is best taken slowly. Many towns have Saxon and Hungarian names which are used alongside the Romanian ones and these are given in brackets in the text.

Although the same language is spoken on both sides of the Carpathians, there is a clear **cultural divide** between the provinces. Many people, mostly Transylvanians, will tell you that Transylvania is part of Central Europe, with a long tradition of culture, free enterprise, political decency and generally civilized behaviour, while the Regat or "Old Kingdom" of Wallachia and Moldavia is a primitive place, half Balkan and half Turkish, where everything is subject to corruption, inertia and maladministration, and nothing worthwhile ever gets done. There is some limited truth in this, and certainly if you find yourself suffering from culture shock in Bucharest the solution is to head for Transylvania.

Although modernization and population movements have eroded their sharp distinctions, Transylvania's historic towns still reflect the characteristics of the ethnic groups that once dominated them. Most striking of all are the *Stuhls*, the former seats of Saxon power, with their medieval streets, defensive towers and fortified churches. **Sighişoara**, the most picturesque, is the Saxons' greatest legacy and an ideal introduction to Transylvania, followed by the citadels and churches of **Braşov** and **Sibiu**, as well as smaller Saxon settlements like **Cisnǎdioara**, **Hǎrman** and **Prejmer**. The other highlight of this southeastern corner is the castle at **Bran**, which looks just how a vampire count's castle should look: a grim facade, perched high on a rock bluff, whose turrets and ramparts rise in tiers against a dramatic mountain background. Travelling west, routes towards the Banat and Hungary pass through southwestern Transylvania, a region of mountains and moorland peppered with the citadels of the Dacians, rulers of much of Romania before the Roman conquest. To the north and east, Transylvania has a more Hungarian flavour: cities such as **Cluj** and **Tîrgu Mureş** are strongly Magyar, while **Miercurea Ciuc** and **Sfîntu Gheorghe** are the cultural centres of the Székely, an ethnic group closely related to the Magyars.

The **Carpathian mountains** are never far away in Transylvania, and for anyone fond of walking this is one of the most beautiful, least exploited regions in Europe. **Hikes** to stunning places in the Fǎgǎraş, Apuseni and Retezat ranges can last several days, but it's perfectly feasible to make briefer yet equally dramatic forays into the Piatra Craiului or Bucegi mountains, or to one of Transylvania's many spectacular gorges.

When considering your itinerary, bear in mind the **festivals** which take place across Transylvania throughout the year. May and June offer the most choice, but during months with only one or two events there's usually something happening just over the mountains in Moldavia, Maramureş or the Banat. The really special events are detailed in the text.

ACCOMMODATION PRICES

Hotels listed in this guide have been price-graded according to the scale below. Prices given are those charged for the cheapest **double room** available, which in the less expensive places usually comes without private bath or shower and without breakfast. Price codes are expressed in US dollars as the Romanian leu is not a stable currency, but you will generally pay for your room in lei.

Note that some hotels are currently closed for modernization, and others, now open, will no doubt follow in the near future. This is bound to result in higher rates when they reopen, so the prices quoted should be taken only as a guideline.

① $10 and under	④ $20–25	⑦ $40–50
② $10–15	⑤ $25–30	⑧ $50–65
③ $15–20	⑥ $30–40	⑨ $65 and over

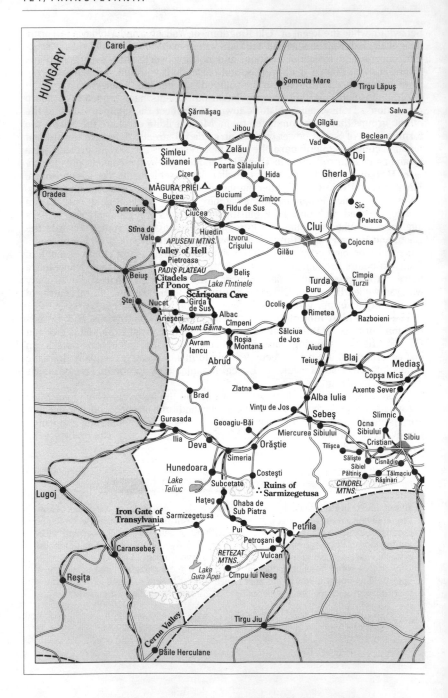

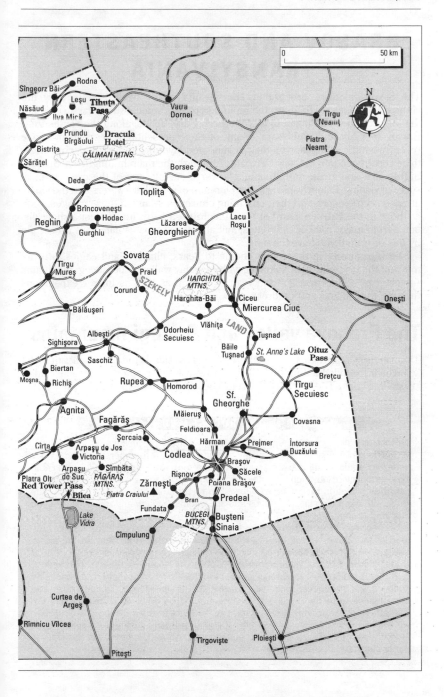

BRAŞOV AND SOUTHEASTERN TRANSYLVANIA

The Saxon colonists, brought to Transylvania in the twelfth century by the Hungarian monarchy to guard the mountain passes against the Tatars, settled in the fertile land to the north of the Southern Carpathians, along the routes from Braşov to Sibiu and Sighişoara. Many of their present-day descendants have recently left the **villages**, with their regimented layouts and **fortified churches**, to be repatriated into the new Germany. Although the main highlights at **Braşov**, **Sighişoara** and **Bran** are all definitely worth seeing, one of the greatest pleasures of visiting Transylvania is the exploration of quiet backwaters and the smaller Saxon settlements with their charming churches. Many of these villages, such as those in the **Burzen Land** or the **Marginimea Sibiului**, lie just a short distance from major road or rail routes, and all but the most isolated are accessible by bus or train if you have the time.

The **mountains** in this region, home to bears, chamois and eagles, provide much of the best **hiking** in Romania, with easy day walks in the Bucegi mountains (assisted by cable cars) and the Piatra Craiului, as well as longer expeditions through the Făgăraş and Cindrel ranges.

The Prahova valley and Bucegi mountains

Thousands of years ago, the site where Bucharest stands today lay beneath a vast sea which extended a hundred miles northwards to lap against a small island of crystalline rock. The remains of Cretaceous life forms which flourished in the

HIKING IN THE BUCEGI MOUNTAINS

The Romanian-language **maps** of the *Munţii Bucegi* are invaluable for anybody seriously contemplating hiking – they shouldn't be hard to understand if you refer to our vocabulary on p.47. Most walks in the region are easy day walks with cable cars as an alternative on the steeper sections. There are plenty of **mountain cabanas**, which in theory aren't allowed to turn hikers away, and if you're really stuck, the maps also locate refuges and sheepfolds (*refugiu* and *stînă*), where you may find shelter.

Snow covers **Mount Omu**, the highest point of the Bucegi (2505m), for two hundred or more days a year, but elsewhere retreats during April, leaving the meadows to a wealth of **wildflowers**. First come crocuses, snowdrops, sweet violets and ladies' gloves, followed by forget-me-nots, grape-ferns and marigolds, with violets, primroses, bellflowers, edelweiss and camomiles flourishing higher up, alongside junipers and rhododendrons. The forests shelter woodcock, hazel grouse and nightingales from the circling golden eagles, while other **wildlife** includes the Carpathian stag (around Bran), lynx, fox, rodents and wild boar. The last, like wolves and bears, are only a potential threat to humans during the winter (when food is scarce) or if their litters are endangered. Above the forest, on the cliffs to the north of the massif, you may well see chamois.

warm waters formed reefs that trapped grit as the sea level rose, holding it when the waters receded during the Neozoic period. The mountains that emerged were later shaped by glaciers which carved out the **Prahova valley**, while streams disappeared underground to form fantastic caves and other karstic phenomena. The valley is now traversed by the well-maintained **DN1** highway and the Bucharest–Braşov **rail line**: express services take just two and a half hours, stopping en route at Ploieşti (see p.94) and the resorts of **Sinaia**, in nothern Wallachia, and **Predeal**, in Transylvania proper. There are also plenty of slower trains which stop at the smaller towns and villages – change at either Sinaia or Predeal for a *personal* train to **Buşteni**, also served by some *accelerats*. A local bus links Sinaia and Buşteni roughly hourly.

From Sinaia to Predeal the River Prahova froths white beneath the gigantic **Bucegi mountains**, which overhang Buşteni with 600m of sheer escarpment, receding in grandiose slopes covered with fir, beech and rowan trees. These mountains are the real attraction of the area: the easiest walks are those above Sinaia and Predeal, with more challenging hikes above Buşteni. Even if you don't stop off to hike in the range (or ride up by cable car), the valley's upper reaches are unforgettable: sit on the west side of the train (the left, if heading north) for the best views.

Sinaia

SINAIA, 130km from Bucharest, has been dubbed the "Pearl of the Carpathians" for its magnificent mountain scenery and royal castle. Though technically in the province of Wallachia, it has much in common with the neighbouring Transylvanian towns and has been included in this chapter for convenience. Originally the preserve of a few hermits and shepherds, and later an exclusive aristocratic resort, it's nowadays full of holidaymakers here to walk or ski in the Bucegi mountain range.

The town's train station, a historical site in itself, is where the Iron Guard murdered the Liberal leader Ion Duca in 1933, only three weeks after he had taken office as prime minister. Steps lead up from the station to a small park, which contains a casino, a small museum describing the natural history of the Bucegi mountains, and two turn-of-the-century hotels, the *Palace* and the *Caraiman* – both fine neo-Brîncovenesc buildings. Beyond the park, Strada Mănastirii leads up to **Sinaia Monastery**, built by the boyar Michael Cantacuzino in 1690–95 on the site of an earlier hermitage, and so called because it contained a stone he had brought from Mount Sinai. The original church is not the one before you as you enter (built 1842–46), but hides through a passageway to the left.

Just behind the monastery, a road leads up to one of the most popular destinations in Romania, **Peleş Castle** (Wed–Sun 9am–3pm; $5). Set in a large **park**, which is landscaped in the English fashion, the castle outwardly resembles a Bavarian Schloss. It was built between 1875 and 1883 for Romania's imported Hohenzollern monarch, Carol I, and largely decorated by his eccentric wife Elisabeta (better known as the popular novelist Carmen Sylva, the "Romanian Sappho"), who once decreed that court life at Sinaia be conducted in folk costume. Peleş contains 106 rooms, richly decorated in ebony, mother of pearl, walnut and leather – all totally alien to the traditional styles of Romanian art. There are almost eight hundred stained-glass windows in the building whose rooms are stuffed solid with Persian carpets, Renaissance weapons, Murano chandeliers,

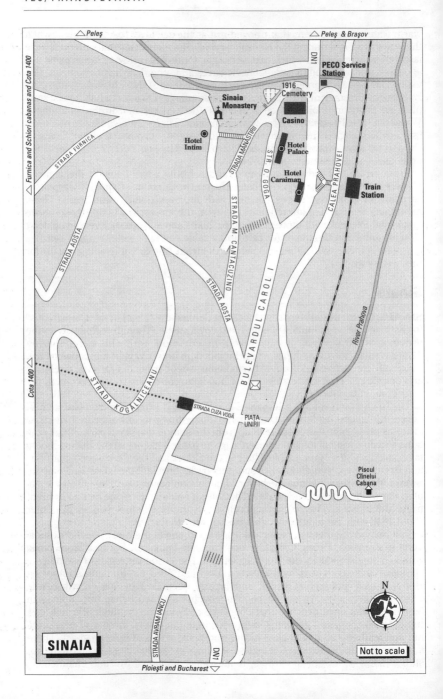

SINAIA

Not to scale

and copies of the Rembrandts and Canalettos which are now housed in Bucharest's National Art Museum. One Louis XIV room (with pre-Raphaelite paintings) houses Romania's first cinema. How a man of such reputedly austere tastes as Carol managed to live here is something of a mystery.

Following the monarchy's demise in 1947, Peleş was opened to the public, with a temporary interruption when the Ceauşescus appropriated it as a "state palace". The Ceauşescus actually preferred to stay in the **Pelişor Palace** (Little Peleş; Wed–Sun 8.30am–3.30pm; $3), a few hundred metres up the hill, built in 1899–1903 for Ferdinand and Marie, Carol I's heirs. Although its exterior is also in the German Renaissance style, the interior is Art Nouveau, with Viennese furniture and Tiffany and Lalique vases and is much more to the taste of Western visitors. **Foişor lodge**, a little above Pelişor, was the home of Prince Carol (later crowned Carol II) and Princess Helen from 1921; here Carol met the Jewish Magda Lupescu, who remained his mistress for thirty years and became the power behind the throne, outraging Romanian society, which tended towards anti-Semitism. Foişor park (Wed–Sun 9am–4pm) is open to the public, but the lodge, another former summer residence of the Ceauşescus, is still reserved for government entertaining.

Practicalities

Steps lead from Sinaia **train station** up to the town park, beyond which lies the main street, Bulevardul Carol I. Turn left along the boulevard for the town centre.

The town is well served with **hotels** and has one of the very best in Romania, the *Hotel Palace* (☎044/31.20.51; ⑥), at Str. Octavian Goga 8; this gem of a hotel, which actually stands in the park by the casino, was founded in 1911 and retains the Edwardian style and consistently good service that made it famous. The *Caraiman* (☎044/31.35.51, fax 37.46.33; ⑥), at B-dul Carol I no. 4, is also in the park; it was Sinaia's first hotel, built in 1880 and, like the *Palace*, it remains very classy, with large, comfortable rooms and helpful staff. In the town centre, at B-dul Carol I no. 24, is the *Montana* (☎044/31.27.51, fax 31.40.51; ⑥), a modern block, with sauna and pool, built for ski-package tourists who make it the liveliest place in town in season. To the west of the park, up Strada Furnica, there are some atmospheric hotels, starting with the *Intim* at no. 1 (☎044/31.17.54, ext 127; ②), which gives excellent views over and into the monastery; hot water is available only at limited times during the day, but otherwise this semi-privatized place gives good value. Further up the hill at no. 50, the *Furnica* (☎044/31.18.50, fax 31.18.53; ③) is a mock-Jacobean pile; facilities include cable TV and a disco.

Villas (②) can be booked through the tourist agencies, SC Montana at B-dul Carol I no. 22 (☎044/31.27.51, fax 31.40.51) and SC Sinarom (☎044/31.38.51, fax 11.09.82). There are **campsites** north and south of Sinaia, at Vadul Cerbului and Izvorul Rece, and you're rarely far from an inexpensive hikers' *cabana* – the *Piscu Cîinelui* and *Schiori* (☎044/31.47.51) *cabanas* are small but right on the outskirts of town. Someone at the station may offer you a private room (②), but be wary of making your arrangements this way.

The best **food and drink** is to be found in the restaurants of the *Palace*, *Montana* and *Furnica* hotels; otherwise there's the *Select* on Strada Octavian Goga, and various pizza joints, such as the *Carpaţi* opposite the *Hotel Montana* and the *Perla Bucegi* just north of it.

Ski gear can be bought or rented in the *Hotel Montana* and at the cable car terminal on Strada Cuza Vodă. **Car rental** is possible through Hertz at the *Palace* hotel (☎044/31.04.26).

Mountain walks from Sinaia

From the train station on Strada Cuza Vodă (behind the *Hotel Montana*), a cable car (Tues–Sun 8.30am–4pm; $2) whisks you aloft to an altitude of 1400 metres (**Cota 1400**) at the roadhead halfway up the hill, site of the *Alpin* hotel (☎044/31.32.51; ⑥) and numerous *cabanas*. From here another cable car (Tues–Sun 8.30am–4pm; $2) rises to **Cota 2000**, and a chair-lift (Wed–Mon 9am–5pm) will take you to **Cota 1950**, both near the *Miorița cabana*, on Mount Furnica. This is the start of the taxing *Papagul* ski run back down to Cota 1400. To the south, below Cota 1950 is the *Valea Dorului cabana*, from where there's a three-hour circular walk down the Dorului valley to the beautiful tarns of **La Lacuri**, following a path marked with yellow crosses and red stripes.

Heading north, another attractive and easy half-hour walk takes you from Mount Furnica to the half-built (but functional) *Piatra Arsă cabana* behind Mount Jepi Mari. Here, blue triangles indicate the route downwards to Bușteni (2hr maximum) via **La Scari**, a spectacular "stairway" hewn into rock, while another path (marked with blue stripes) drops westwards into the central depression of the Bucegi, reaching the *Peștera cabana* and monastery in about an hour (for routes north of *Peștera*, see "Mountain walks from Bușteni", p.132). Just west of *Peștera*, past the **Ialomișa cave** – a four-hundred-metre long grotto with a walkway in awful condition (bring a flashlight) – is an unmarked path leading up through the Batrîna valley past waterfalls, the "Gorge of the Bear" and two natural bridges. Half an hour to the south lies the *Padina cabana*, from where a very rough road leads south past more caves and gorges to a camping spot near **Lake Bolboci**, eventually emerging from the Izvorașu valley just south of Sinaia.

Bușteni

Ten kilometres up the valley from Sinaia is **BUȘTENI**, a small resort overshadowed by the sheer peaks of Caraiman (2384m) and Coștila (2498m), separated by the dark Alba valley, which boasts the highest conglomerate cliffs in Europe. Caraiman is identified by a huge cross, a memorial erected after World War I, and on Coștila there's a TV tower that looks like a space rocket. There's nothing much to Bușteni itself, but it's a good base for the excellent walking to be had in the surrounding mountains.

From the **train station**, which more or less defines the town centre, it's just a few metres south to the pleasant, privatized *Caraiman* **hotel** at B-dul Libertășii 89 (☎044/32.01.56; ①); further south, at Str. Telecabiniei 39, is the *Silva* (☎044/32.14.12, fax 32.09.50; ③), the most luxurious hotel in town. To the north of the main DN1 is BTT's *Hotel Tineretului* (☎044/32.01.38, fax 32.00.56; ①), at B-dul Libertășii 141, a youth hotel now open to all ages, with a lively disco and sports facilities. Across the tracks to the east, in the Zamora quarter, is the *Mini-Hotel Maximilian* (☎044/32.32.97; ①), at Str. Pescariei 8, most easily reached by car (take the first turning left south of Str. Telecabinei). It's also worth enquiring at the **tourist office** (☎044/32.00.27; Mon–Fri 9am–4pm, Sat 9am–noon), at Str. Libertășii 202, 150m north of the train station, about **private rooms** (①). The *Azuga* **campsite** is about 1km north along the main DN1, but is close to the train line and thus very noisy. The *Caminul Alpin cabana* at the top of Strada Valea Albă (☎044/32.01.67), just north of the station, is still run in the lax old state-owned manner, opening only when they can be bothered.

The best **restaurants** are in the *Silva* and *Caraiman* hotels; the *Cofetaria Roza* opposite the train station offers snack-sized pizzas as well as coffee and cakes.

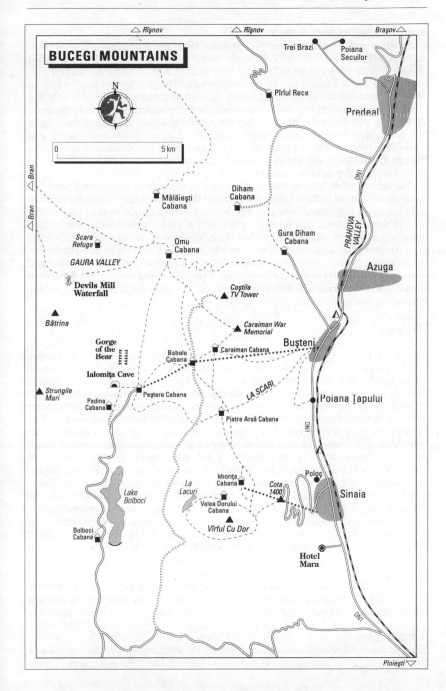

BUCEGI MOUNTAINS

N

0 — 5 km

△ Rîşnov △ Rîşnov Braşov△

Trei Brazi
Poiana Seculor

Pîrîul Rece

Predeal

△ Bran

△ Bran

△ Bran

Diham Cabana

Mălăieşti Cabana

Scara Refuge

Omu Cabana

GAURA VALLEY

Gura Diham Cabana

PRAHOVA VALLEY

Azuga

Devils Mill Waterfall

Coştila TV Tower

Bătrina

Caraiman War Memorial

Gorge of the Bear

Babolo Cabana

Caraiman Cabana

Buşteni

Ialomiţa Cave

Strungile Mari

Padina Cabana

Peştera Cabana

LA SCARI

Poiana Ţapului

DN1

Piatra Arsă Cabana

Lake Bolboci

La Lacuri

Miorița Cabana

Cota 1400

Poloç

Sinaia

Valea Dorului Cabana

Vîrful Cu Dor

Bolboci Cabana

Hotel Mara

DN1

Ploieşti ▽

Mountain walks from Buşteni

From the country's oldest paper mill and the *Hotel Silva* on Strada Telecabiniei, an easy path marked with red dots leads past a zoo to the **Urlătoarea waterfall** and back to the road at Poiana Şapului (2hr), while a harder footpath, marked with blue crosses, and a **cable car** (Wed–Mon) ascend the Jepi (dwarf pine) valley to the *Caraiman* and *Babele cabanas*. *Babele* offers a panoramic view, and is only five minutes' walk from an impressive skull-like rock formation, the **Babele Sphinx**. From here you can walk (1hr) or ride the cable car down to the *Peştera cabana* and monastery (see "Mountain walks from Sinaia" on p.130 for routes south and west of *Peştera*). North of *Babele*, a path marked by yellow stripes leads north to **Mount Omu** (4hr); alternatively, from *Peştera*, a blue-striped path takes you up the Ialomiša valley to Omu (1–2hr).

Though completely cloudless days are rare in the vicinity of **Mount Omu**, it is possible to see the Burzen Land, the ridge of the Piatra Craiului and, on particularly haze-free days, the Făgăraş range beyond – a mountain vista of rare splendour. From the *Omul* hut (closed in winter), a path marked with blue stripes descends a glacial valley past eroded rock "chimneys" to the *Mălăieşti* chalet (2–3hr); two other paths lead down **towards Bran** in about six hours – the route indicated by yellow triangles is easier going, while the path marked with red crosses drops down the superb Gaura valley past the **Cascada Moara Dracului** (Devil's Mill waterfall), a fitting approach to "Dracula's Castle" in the village below (see p.105).

Predeal

PREDEAL, sitting on the pass of the same name and marking the official border into Transylvania, is further from the more spectacular peaks that dominate Sinaia and Buşteni to the south, but a popular centre for skiing and easy strolls. There's a reasonable choice of **accommodation** in town, which can be booked through the accommodation agency (*Dispecerat Cazare*), which has offices in the train station and behind the post office at Str. Panduri 6 (☎068/45.50.42). The *Carmen*, a good private **hotel** just south of the station at B-dul Săulescu 121 (☎068/45.66.56, fax 45.54.26; ⑥), can also provide slightly cheaper rooms in villas. North of the station is the *Bulevard*, B-dul Săulescu 129 (☎068/45.60.22, fax 45.53.25; ②), a neo-Brîncovenesc pile with an attractive stair- and lift-well, probably the only really atmospheric place in town. Further north, on Strada Trei Brazi, are the *Cirus*, an old-style ski chalet (☎068/45.60.35; ③), and the *Orizont* (☎068/45.51.50, fax 45.54.72; ⑦), the resort's best modern hotel. Continuing east along Bulevardul Libertăšii you'll come to Cioplea, the area formerly patronized by the *nomenklatura* and Party members for their skiing holidays; the *Hotel Cioplea* at no. 102 (☎068/45.68.70, fax 45.68.71; ④) is very modern, with sauna and gym. The *Mama Maria* **restaurant** (closed Tues), on Strada Eminescu, is good, but serves traditional Romanian fare, not Italian.

Ski equipment can be rented at the *Orizont* and *Cioplea* hotels, or on the main DN1, at B-dul Săulescu 134 and at the Clăbucet-Sosire chair-lift terminal. There's a figure-of-eight cross-country ski track 2km south of town at the Rîşnov junction.

Around Predeal

The **Gîrbova** or **Baiului mountains** flanking the Prahova on the eastern edge of town are the site of numerous **ski runs** – a chair-lift (daily 9am–5pm) runs from

Clăbucet-Sosire, ten minutes south of the train station, to Clăbucet-Plecare. Most of the runs are graded "average", although the run southwards towards the *Gîrbova cabana* is the easiest and the *Sub Teleferic* run is the most difficult of all.

There is good **walking** in these hills, not as dramatic as in the Bucegi but with good views to the high peaks and cliffs. There are plenty of **cabanas** to aim for: *Gîrbova* and *Susai* are within a few kilometres of Clăbucet-Plecare, and there are others northwest of Predeal, in the foothills of the Bucegi massif, served by local buses. The latter include *Trei Brazi* (with a campsite nearby), *Pîriu Rece* and *Poiana Secuilor* – all within 2km walk of the bus terminals (the bus stops outside the *Pîriu Rece* site) – and *Diham*, higher up and further south with a slalom run nearby.

Braşov

The medieval Saxons, with an eye for trade and invasion routes, sited their largest settlements within a day's journey of the Carpathian passes. **BRAŞOV** (Kronstadt to the Saxons and Brassó to the Hungarians) was one of the best placed and grew prosperous and fortified as a result, and for many centuries the Saxons constituted an elite whose economic power long outlasted its feudal privileges. During the 1960s, the Communist regime attempted to create their own skilled working class in the city, and to this end they brought thousands of Moldavian villagers to Braşov, where they were drafted into the new factories and given modern housing. When the economy began collapsing in the 1980s, raised production quotas and cuts in pay at the Red Flag and Tractorul factories led to the **riots of November 15, 1987**, during which the Party offices were ransacked and a Militia officer was reportedly killed. Order was restored, but local pride in the rebellion survived, and in December 1989 there was again fighting here. Bullet holes remain as a memorial all over the facade of the university buildings at the east end of Strada Republicii, opposite the graves of some of those killed in the revolution. It seems that most of the casualties here were the victims of "friendly fire".

There are two parts to Braşov: the largely Baroque old town coiled beneath Mount Tîmpa and Mount Postăvaru, and the surrounding sprawl of apartments and factories. **Old Braşov** – whose Schei quarter, Black Church and medieval ramparts provide a backdrop for the town's colourful Pageant of the Juni (see box on p.137) – is well worth a day's exploration; and the town's proximity to the alpine resort of **Poiana Braşov**, the fortified Saxon churches of Hărman and Prejmer, and the so-called "Dracula's Castle" at Bran, make Braşov an excellent base.

The best **views** of the old town are from the forested heights of **Mount Tîmpa** (967m), accessible by cable car (Tues–Sun 10am–9pm) or by various paths which wind up to the summit.

Arrival and information

Braşov is Romania's second largest city and one of its most important rail junctions; served by long-distance **trains** from Bucharest and the coast, it is from here that most connections into Transylvania will be made. The train station is situated northeast of the old town, right in the heart of the concrete drabness of

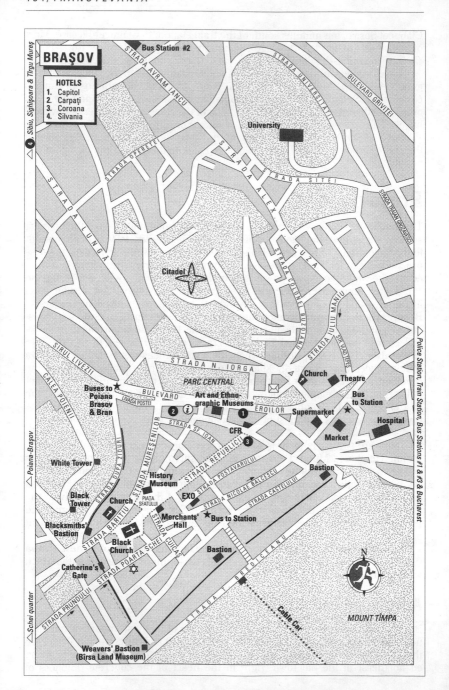

BRAŞOV

HOTELS
1. Capitol
2. Carpaţi
3. Coroana
4. Silvania

Bus Station #2

University

Citadel

STRADA AVRAM IANCU

STRADA OPERETE

STRADA ALEX

STRADA SITEI

STRADA UNIVERSITAŢII

BULEVARD GRIVITEI

STRADA TRAIAN GROZĂVESCU

STRADA A LUNGA

CUZA

STRADA COLONEL BUZOIANU

STRADA IULIU MANIU

STR VLAD TEPEŞ

STRADA VLAD TEPEŞ

STRADA N. IORGA

PARC CENTRAL

Church

Theatre

Bus to Station

Buses to Poiana Braşov & Bran

BULEVARD

LIVADA POSTEI

Art and Ethnographic Museums

EROILOR

Supermarket

Hospital

SIRUL LIVEZII

CALEA POIENII

STRADA SF. IOAN

CFR

Market

White Tower

STRADA DUPĂ ZIDURI

STRADA MUREŞENILOR

History Museum

STRADA REPUBLICII

STRADA POSTAVARULUI

Bastion

Black Tower

Church

PIAŢA SFATULUI

EXO

STRADA NICOLAE BĂLCESCU

STRADA CASTELULUI

Blacksmiths' Bastion

STRADA BARIŢIU

STRADA CLUCAŞ

Merchants' Hall

Bus to Station

Black Church

STRADA POARTA SCHEI

Bastion

Catherine's Gate

STRADA PRUNDULUI

STRADA T BREDICEANU

Cable Car

MOUNT TÎMPA

Weavers' Bastion
(Bîrsa Land Museum)

N

⊲ Sibiu, Sighişoara & Trgu Mureş

⊲ Poiana-Braşov

⊲ Schei quarter

Police Station, Train Station, Bus Stations #1 & #3 & Bucharest ⊳

Braşov's new suburbs. Bus #4 will take you down to Parc Central (also known as Titulescu), and on to the Schei quarter in the old town.

The town has three **bus stations**, with direct services from Budapest and connecting services to the villages north of Braşov calling at Autogară 1, by the train stations. Travelling from Piteşti, Curtea de Argeş and Rîmnicu Vîlcea, you'll arrive at Autogară 2, Str. Avram Iancu 114 (bus #12 to the centre, #10 to the train station), while services to the Székely Land use Autogară 3, 1km northeast of the main train station (trolley bus #1).

Braşov has a **tourist office** (Mon–Sat 7.30am–3.30pm; ☎068/14.11.96) at the rear of the lobby of the *Hotel Carpaţi*, near Parc Central, but it deals in little more than overpriced excursions to "Dracula's Castle" and the villages of Hărman and Prejmer.

Accommodation

The only reasonably priced places to stay are some way from town, with just a few bland and overpriced **hotels** in the centre. You might want to consider one of the thirteen tourist hotels at the nearby resort of Poiana Braşov (see p.139), but of those within reach of the town, the *Carpaţi*, (☎068/14.28.40, fax 15.04.27; ⑨), at B-dul Eroilor 9, is the best, a swanky place picketed by black-market moneychangers; while the *Stadion* (☎068/18.74.35; ②), at Str. Cocorului 12, is easily the best value (just 100m from the Autocamion bus terminal), with good, simple rooms, and tennis courts. The only hotel in town with real character is the *Coroana*, (☎068/14.43.30, fax 14.15.05; ⑧), at Str. Republicii 62. It also has a pleasant restaurant from where you can watch the city's main street. You should also consider the *Silvania* (☎068/41.55.56, fax 15.17.39; ⑥), a pleasant and comfy guesthouse at Str. Căprioarei 27, a dirt road north of the centre.

If you are looking to stay close to the centre, your best option may be one of the **private rooms** available through EXO, at Str. Postăvarului 6 (Mon–Sat 11am–8pm, Sun 11am–2pm; ☎068/14.45.91; ③) – these are likely to be in a modern apartment block, but will be fairly close to the town centre.

The *Dîrste* **campsite** (☎068/25.90.80) is about 7km from Braşov's centre, on the Bucharest highway, the DN1. Take trolley bus #3 or #6 from the centre or tram #101 from the train station to the Saturn/Autocamion terminus (also known as Roman or IABV) on Calea Bucureşti, and then bus #17 or #21 (for Săcele, every ten minutes) out along the main highway until it turns off; the campsite is ten minutes' walk further south along the DN1. The site has reasonable facilities with two-person chalets and permanent hot water, doubtless due to its former popularity with Securitate campers. You might prefer the small *Dîmbu Morii* **cabana** – another twenty minutes beyond the *Dîrste* campsite at km158, or a fifteen-minute walk to the north of the Timişu de Jos rail halt.

The Town

The bus from the train station will set you down either at **Parc Central**, on the edge of the old town, or on **Piaşa Sfatului**, at the heart of a Baroque townscape that is quintessentially Germanic. The hub of Braşov's social and commercial life is the pedestrianized **Strada Republicii** (*Purzengasse*) leading from the main square towards the new town and the train station. It's a popular place for a stroll at lunchtime and in the early evening – at its northeastern end are a department store, theatre and **market**, from where you can catch bus #4 back to the train station.

Piaţa Sfatului

Local legend has it that when the Pied Piper enticed the children from Hamelin in Germany, they vanished underground and emerged in Transylvania near the site of Braşov's main square, now called the **Piaša Sfatului** (Council Square). It is lined with sturdy merchants' houses, their red rooftiles tilted rakishly, presenting their shopfronts to the fifteenth-century Council House (*Rathaus* or *Casa Sfatului*), now the **History Museum** (Tues–Sun 10am–6pm), in the centre of the square. The exhibits tell the story of the Saxon guilds, who used to dominate Braşov and who met in the **Merchants' Hall** (1539–45) opposite. Built in the "Transylvanian Renaissance" style of the sixteenth century, this now contains craft shops, a wine cellar and the *Cerbul Carpatin* (Carpathian Stag) restaurant. Within sight of its terrace is the town's most famous landmark, the **Black Church** (*Biserica Neagră*; Mon–Sat 10am–3.30pm), whose towers stab upwards like a series of daggers. The church took almost a century (1385–1477) to complete and is so-called for its soot-blackened walls – the result of a great fire, started by the Austrian army, that swept through Braşov in 1689. Inside, however, the church is startlingly white, with Turkish carpets hung in isolated splashes of colour along the walls of the nave – a superb collection built up from the gifts of the local merchants returning from the east. The incongruity of having Islamic prayer rugs proudly displayed in a Lutheran church never seems to have bothered anyone. **Organ recitals** on the 4000-pipe instrument are held on Wednesdays at 6pm.

Dwarfed by the mighty Black Church, the Old Pharmacy is currently being restored to house the **Ethnographic Museum**; this features a collection of local costumes, and is presently housed next to the **Art Museum** at B-dul Eroilor 21 (both Tues–Sun 10am–6pm), which has a good selection of Grigorescu, Aman and Tattarescu canvases.

The fortifications

When the threat of Turkish expansion became evident in the fifteenth century, the inhabitants of Braşov began to fortify the town, assigning the defence of each bastion or rampart to a particular guild. A length of **fortress wall** runs along the foot of Mount Timpa, beneath a maze of paths and a cable car running up to the summit – fine views of the old town can be had from Strada Brediceanu, the semi-pedestrianized promenade past the lower cable car terminal.

Of the original seven **bastions**, the best preserved, with three tiers of wooden galleries and meal-rooms – in which the townsfolk stocked bread, meat and other provisions in case of siege – is that of the Weavers (*Bastionul Ţesătorilor*), on Strada Coşbuc. This now contains the **Museum of the Bîrsa Land Fortifications** (Tues–Sun 10am–4pm), where models, pictures and weaponry recall the bad old days when the surrounding region, known as the Bîrsa or Burzen Lands, was repeatedly attacked by Tatars, Turks and, on a couple of occasions, by Vlad Ţepeş. **Catherine's Gate** (*Poarta Ecaterinei*; which bears the city's coat of arms), the **Blacksmiths' Bastion** (*Bastionul Fierarilor*) and the **Black and the White Towers** on Calea Poienii (best seen from Strada Dupa Ziduri, squeezed between stream and walls) all managed to survive these onslaughts, but the inhabitants didn't always fare so well. When Ţepeş attacked Braşov in 1458–60 he burnt the suburbs and impaled hundreds of captives along the heights of St Jacob's Hill to the north of the city, to terrorize the townsfolk. Referring to allegations that Vlad dined off a holy icon surrounded by his suffering victims, his hagiographer Stoicescu writes that "being on campaign...the terrible Prince may not have had the time to take his meals otherwise".

The Schei quarter
During the heyday of Saxon rule, the Romanian-speaking population was compelled to live beyond the citadel walls, in the southwestern district of **Schei** (pronounced "Skei"). They could only enter the centre at certain times, and had to pay a toll at the gate for the privilege of selling their produce to their neighbours. The gate on the present Strada Poarta Schei was built in 1825 by Emperor Franz I, next to it is the splendid Catherine's Gate of 1559. Today Schei is a residential dead end, with the peace of its Baroque streets broken only by occasional buses and by children returning from school. The quarter's main sight is the **Church of St Nicholas**, on Piaša Unirii, which was the first Orthodox church to be built in Transylvania by the voivodes of Wallachia, between 1493 and 1564. On the left as you enter the churchyard is the first Romanian-language school (established 1761), now a museum exhibiting the first Romanian-language textbooks, printed in Braşov in 1581.

North of the centre
North of Bulevardul Eroilor and the Parc Central is a lowish hill crowned by the overgrown **citadel ruins**, with a touristy restaurant (the *Cetate*) hidden inside. To the west, Strada Lungă (Long Street) stretches for 3km to the thirteenth-century **Church of St Bartholomew**, a toothy Gothic edifice under the hill where Vlad impaled his victims. It stands at the junction of the DN13 to Sighişoara and Tîrgu Mureş and the DN1 to Sibiu; Autogară 2 and the Bartolomei station, for **local trains** to Zărneşti and Sibiu, are nearby.

THE PAGEANT OF THE JUNI

The **Pageant of the Juni** (*Sărbătoarea junilor*) is held on the first Sunday of May, traditionally the only day of the year that Romanians could freely enter the Saxon city. The name derives from the Latin for "young men", and on this day the town's youths dress up in costumes and, accompanied by brass bands, ride through town in groups named after famous regiments – the *Dorobanţi*, or the *Roşiori* – while the married men, or "Old Juni", bring up the rear.

The parade assembles in the morning on the **Piaţa Unirii** which forms the historic heart of Schei. It then marches to Piaţa Sfatului, returns to the Schei backstreets, and finally climbs a narrow valley to the **Gorges of Pietrele lui Solomon**. Here, spectators settle down to watch the Round Dances (*Horăs*), which for the participants are really a kind of endurance test. Some of the elaborate Juni costumes are 150 years old, while one of the *Roşiori* wears a shirt sewn with 44,000 spangles that weighs 9kg – the product of four months' work by the women of Braşov.

Eating, drinking and entertainment

Braşov has a better than average selection of places to **eat and drink**, with excellent **restaurants** in the main hotels, and quite a few others worthy of mention. Chief among these are the *Cerbul Carpatin*, in the Merchants' Hall on Piaša Sfatului, once reputed to be the best restaurant in Romania and still not bad, and the *Chinezesc*, also on the square, still possibly the finest Chinese restaurant in the country. Others worth seeking out are the *Panorama* on top of Mount Tîmpa (daily 9am–10pm) and the *Cetate* in the old citadel on Dealul Cetăšii, with kitsch medieval decorations, and great views in the early evening. There are **pizzerias** at Str. Bǎlcescu 2 and in the *Postăvarul* hotel. Preferable to the fast-food *Casablanca*, at the corner of B-dul 15 Noiembrie and Str. Castanilor, and *McDonald's*, at the edge of town on the Bucureşti highway, is the *Intim* at Str. Mureşenilor 4 – try the *mǎmǎligǎ* (polenta).

The **cafés** around Piaša Sfatului have the largest range of cakes and buns in town, while allowing you to watch the comings and goings on this lively square; the best are the *Cafea Orient* at Str. Republicii 2 and the *Casata* at Piaša Sfatului 13. The creamiest cakes in town are at the *Vatra Ardealului*, Str. Barišiu 14, and the best ices at *Mamma Mia*, Str. Mureşenilor 25. For **drinking**, try the *crama* (beer cellar), on Str. Republicii opposite the *Postăvarul*, or the *Crama Negustorilor* in the Hirscher House, Piaša Sfatului 15; the *Grenadier* and the *Scotch Club*, at the junction of Str Bǎlcescu and Str. Aleco Russo, are supposedly sophisticated drinking clubs, actually quite tacky and open to anyone who doesn't turn up in shorts and flip-flops.

Nightlife and entertainment

In Braşov, as in the rest of Romania, **nightlife** is basically whatever happens in the restaurants attached to the hotels – Gypsy music, singing or disco, depending on pot luck – although the restaurants in nearby Poiana Braşov lay on folklore events in season. Students tend to meet in the cafés around Piaša Sfatului or the *Casa Studenţilor* at B-dul Eroilor 29 (bring your passport, and student card if you have one).

Classical concerts are held at the Gh. Dima Philharmonic, Str. Mureşenilor 25; though tickets are inexpensive, they're usuallly sold out well in advance – you can try asking for tickets at the booking office at Str. Republicii 4. Tickets are also on sale here for the **theatre** on Piaša Teatrului, at the east end of Bulevardul Eroilor, and for the **puppet theatre** on Strada Ciucaş.

The **Springtime Jazz and Blues Festival** takes place in early May in the theatre, the **Golden Stag** light music festival takes over Piaša Sfatului in June, and the **Beer Festival** brings a range of near-identical lagers to town in October.

Nightlife of a different sort comes in the form of **bear-watching**. About a dozen bears come down every night to forage in the rubbish tip on Strada Rǎcǎdǎu, an area better known to the locals as Valea Cetǎšii, while the local dogs go crazy and the populace sleeps unconcernedly. After a night on the town, watching them from the security of the inside of a taxi is a popular activity.

Listings

Bike repairs Str. Bǎlcescu 55 and Calea Bucureşti 82.
Car rental Avis have a desk at the *Hotel Carpaţi* (☎068/14.28.40, ext 174).
Car repairs Romanian Automobile Club (ACR) are at Str. Iorga 13 and Str. Lungǎ 14.

Currency exchange BCR has a Bancomat outside the *Hotel Carpaţi*. There are private exchange offices at the junctions of Str. Republicii and B-dul Eroilor, and of Piaša Sfatului and Str. Mureşenilor, which will accept travellers' cheques. You can also change money at the CEC office (8am–3pm) in the police headquarters building on Str. Titulescu, or at the Banca Commerciala Romanǎ, Str. Republicii 45 (8.30am–noon).

Fuel If you're driving out of Braşov, the best places to fill up your tank are the fuel stations on the Fǎgǎraş and Hǎrman highways, and the 24hr Shell station at Saturn, on the DN1 towards Bucharest.

Laundry ID Group Self-Lavoir, Calea Bucureşti 73 (Mon–Fri 7.30am–7.30pm, Sat 7.30am–noon).

Pharmacy Aurofarm, Str. Republicii 27, open 24 hours.

Police The county (*judeţ*) police headquarters are on Str. Titulescu. This is also the place to go for visa extensions.

Post office Str. Iorga 1 (daily 7am–8pm). Poste restante service available.

Shopping Braşov's department store, at Str. Bǎlcescu 62, seems to have been left behind by events, and you'll probably find the second-hand store (*consignaţie*) along Str. Republicii more useful. A few English-language books can be found at Str. Republicii 29. The central market is near the theatre on Str. Bǎlcescu, and there's another behind the apartment blocks opposite the train station; both are food markets and are open daily. There are two decent modern supermarkets, the Bîrsa opposite the market on Str. Bǎlcescu, and the Premial at the south end of B-dul Grivišei, east of the university, as well as the older UNIC on Str. Mureşenilor.

Telephone office B-dul Eroilor 23 (daily 7am–9pm).

Travel agents Nouvelles Frontières–SimpaTurism at Piaša Sfatului 3 (☎068/15.32.44) is a Western-style travel agency, booking and confirming air tickets, selling holidays and renting cars; KronTour, Str. Barišiu 12, is similar. Train tickets can be booked at the CFR office, Str. Republicii 53 (Mon–Fri 7am–7.30pm). The tourist office (Mon–Sat 7.30am–3.30pm; ☎068/14.11.96) in the *Carpaţi* hotel will book you on excursions to "Dracula's Castle" at Bran ($28) and to the villages of Hǎrman and Prejmer ($20), but its prices are well over the odds.

Around Braşov

Braşov nestles right under the mountains and there are opportunities for hiking and skiing just a few kilometres from the city at **Poiana Braşov**. The most popular bus excursion is to the castle of **Bran**, and in spite of the crowds it's well worth a visit. Further to the south, the Bucegi mountains (see p.126) are in easy reach, and to the southwest the Fǎgǎraş range (see p.144), containing Romania's highest peaks, can be reached by train. Between these two ranges lies the very distinctive ridge of the **Piatra Craiului**, a single block of limestone that offers a marvellous, if tiring, day's walking. Hǎrman and Prejmer villages, with their remarkable moated fortress-churches, are a short train ride northeast of the city. They are described on p.146, along with the other Saxon villages to the west, but it's worth noting that they can be visited on organized tours from Braşov if you're pushed for time.

Poiana Braşov and Risnov

The resort of **POIANA BRAŞOV** is set at an altitude of 1000m, at the foot of the spectacular Mount Postǎvaru, 12km southwest of Braşov (bus #20 every half hour from Livada Postei, by the Parc Central). There is **skiing** here from December to March on a variety of runs: the *Intim* and *Drum Roşu* are the easy ones, the *Lupului* and *Sub Teleferic* the steepest. While it's considered a great place to learn to ski, with lots of keen English-speaking instructors, experienced skiers are likely to get bored. Lessons are organized by the **tourist office** in the *Complex Favorit*, which can also arrange guides for year-round **hiking**. **Skiing equipment** can be rented at the *Ciucaş, Şoimul, Teleferic* and *Sport* hotels.

The **hotels** are mostly filled by ski-package groups from Britain and elsewhere, but they may have space, especially outside the ski season. The best is the *Alpin* (☎068/26.23.43, fax 26.21.11; ④), closely followed by the *Sport* (☎068/26.23.13; ④), the oldest and most attractive hotel in the resort, now privately run. The other hotels are all of a slightly lower, but still perfectly acceptable, standard, with the *Poiana* (☎068/26.28.13; ④) offering tennis courts, the *Soimul* (☎068/26.23.43; ④), saunas and massage, and the *Telerific* and *Bradul* (☎068/2623.13; ④) discos and crèches. The **tourist office** may be able to find you cheaper **rooms** in a villa or at the *Cabana Junilor*, over a kilometre along the road back to Braşov; but the only truly budget places to stay are the two **cabanas** on the high slopes of Mount Cristianu (1960m), reached by the *Kanzel* cable car and gondola – phone ☎068/18.63.46 to reserve beds beforehand.

The resort's **restaurants** (10am–midnight) go in for "folk" architecture and local cuisine, as you'd expect with names like *Şura Dacilor* (Dacians' Grange) and *Coliba Haiducilor* (Outlaws' Hut); the *Coliba Haiducilor* has a farm which produces bread, milk and cheese daily.

The **discos** in the *Sport, Teleferic* and *Şoimul* run from 10pm to 4am. **Folkdancing** shows are laid on for groups at the *Mioriţa*. The *Capra Neagră* (Chamois) looks rustic but in fact is a **nightclub**, open until 1am, with the same tacky floorshows as in the Bucharest clubs; the *Favorit*, in the main complex, has a less exotic variety programme, as well as **bowling** and **dancing**.

A further 12km west of Poiana Braşov on the road to Bran, accessible by bus or train from Braşov, is **RÎŞNOV**, where a ruined **castle** crowns one of the fir-covered hills that surround the town. This was founded by the Teutonic Knights in the early thirteenth century, who were soon expelled from Transylvania, but what you see now are the remains of a fourteenth-century structure.

To get to Rîşnov's castle, head through the archway by the bus stop on Strada Republicii and up the steps from the courtyard of the Casă de Cultură. Just two hundred Saxons remain here in the village they call Rosenau; their church (founded in 1360), in the centre of the village, can be visited by asking at the *Pfarrhaus*, two doors along the Braşov road. There is also a good **campsite** on the far side of the castle, on the Poiana Braşov road.

Bran and around

The small town of **Bran** is probably the most popular tourist site in Romania. Its fourteenth-century castle, Bran Castle, is more popularly referred to on tourist maps and in local guides as "Dracula's Castle", although Vlad the Impaler never lived here. Nonetheless, the castle lives up to the gothic–fairytale image that Stoker's book evokes and it is well worth a trip.

Aside from the attractions of the castle, Bran is a good base for hikes into the Bucegi mountains to the east and onto the narrow ridge of the **Piatra Craiului**, the eastern extremity of the Făgăraş mountains, to the west. **Fundata**, 14km south of Bran, sits at the top of Bran Pass and is one of the highest villages in Romania. It is host to a lively annual **festival**, and lies at the start of some interesting hikes south into Wallachia.

Bran

Situated only 28km southwest of Braşov and easily reached by bus (from Livada Postei or Autogară 2, near the Bartolomei station), as well as on organized excursions, the small town of **BRAN** commands the entrance to the pass of the same name, formerly the main route into Wallachia. A castle was built here in 1377–82 to safeguard this vital route, and although what's now billed on every tourist brochure and itinerary as "**Dracula's Castle**" (Tues–Sun 9am–5pm) has only tenuous associations with Vlad the Impaler – it's likely he attacked it in 1460 during one of his raids on the Burzen Land – the hyperbole is forgivable as Bran does look like a vampire count's residence. Perched on a rocky bluff, it rises in tiers of towers and ramparts from the woods, against a glorious mountain backdrop. When Ceauşescu was in his most nationalistic phase, extolling Vlad as a true Romanian hero resisting the alien hordes, the Dracula link was played up for all it was worth here, with staff hiding in chests which they swung open menacingly, until an American tourist dropped dead of a heart attack.

The castle has now reopened after a long period of restoration and looks much as it would have done in the time of its most famous resident, **Queen Marie of Romania**. A granddaughter of Queen Victoria and married to Prince Ferdinand in 1893, Queen Marie soon rebelled against the confines of court life in Bucharest – riding unattended through the streets, pelting citizens with roses during the carnival, and appointing herself a colonel of the Red Hussars (*Roşiori*). Her popularity soared after she organized cholera camps in the Balkan war and appeared at the Paris peace conference in 1919, announcing that "Romania needs a face, and I have come to show mine". Marie called Bran a "pugnacious little fortress", but whether because of her spirit pervading the rooms or the profusion of flowers in the yard, it seems a welcoming place, at odds with its forbidding exterior. A warren of spiral stairs, ghostly nooks and secret chambers filled with elaborately carved four-poster beds and throne-like chairs overhangs the courtyard. Not surprisingly, it can get horribly crowded: the trick is to arrive on the dot as the castle opens – the bus parties will be arriving as you leave.

In the grounds are some fine examples of local architecture, including a fulling mill, and by the road south, a **museum** (Tues–Sun 9am–5pm) in the former *vama* or customs house; this predictably stresses the trade links from the earliest times between the Vlachs on either side of the Carpathians, and displays examples of foreign goods including an English clock and a Canadian travelling trunk.

Practicalities

Some **buses** from Braşov's Autogară 2 pass through Bran, but there is also a private service to Bran and Moeciu (12 daily Mon–Fri, 8 on Sat & Sun) from Livada Postei, by the Parc Central in the city. From Bran there are buses almost every hour (fewer on Sundays) north to Rîşnov and Braşov, and a few south to Piteşti and Cîmpulung.

There are few **hotels** in Bran; the best is the motel (✆Bran 16; ②). Across the road from the castle and beyond a tiny park and river, the *Castelul Bran* **cabana** offers double rooms and a varied menu, including large cheap brandies. In point of fact, the kitchen produces only sausages in the mornings, and chicken thereafter; so if you want a fancier meal or room, go to the costlier motel on the Braşov side of town. There's also a *Mini-Hotel* (②) at the fuel station further north on the Braşov road.

Private rooms (②) are big business here, with almost sixty local homes offering accommodation: book through Eurogites (see p.34) or Bran IMEX (Str. Dr. Stoian 395; ✆068/23.66.42, fax 15.25.98 in Bran, or 01/666.59.48 in Bucharest).

Hiking along the Piatra Craiului

Mountains dominate the skyline around Bran. To the east is the almost sheer wall of the **Bucegi range** – it takes about eight hours to climb the path from Bran to Mount Omu, where there's a *cabana* (see p.132). To the west, gentler slopes run up to the **Piatra Craiului**, a narrow ridge at the eastern extremity of the Făgăraş mountains. This 20km-long limestone ridge, punctured with karst caves along its eastern face, is known as the "Royal Rock" (*Király-kö* in Hungarian and *Königstein* in German). Carpathian bears, lynx and chamois live here, and the endemic Piatra Craiului pink grows on the northeastern side.

It is easiest to reach the Piatra from **ZĂRNEŞTI**, accessible from Braşov via Rîşnov by bus (Mon–Fri hourly from Autogară 2 in Braşov) and train (six a day), or by a 4km side road from Bran. It's a fairly mundane place, although what is supposedly a bicycle factory along the road to the east of town is in fact one of Romania's largest arms factories, with a notorious accident record. From here it's under three hours' walk up the Bîrsa Mare valley to the *Plaiul Foii cabana*, the main centre for **hiking** in this area. There's a day's hike from here to the *Curmătura cabana* or back to Zărneşti; the hike begins with a (3–4hr) climb (following red cross markings, and using fixed cables in places) to the main ridge, 1400m above, and continues north along the knife-edge ridge (following red dots), finally descending (following yellow stripes) to the right to the *Curmătura cabana* and to the left to Zărneşti. Although you can see Romanians hiking in bikinis near the *Curmătura*, the ridge route itself is quite demanding and you should really be properly equipped with boots, waterproofs and above all plenty of water. The ridge offers fantastic views both west towards the Făgăraş range and east towards the Bucegi, while the succession of peaks and parallel strata along the ridge itself are uniquely impressive.

Fourteen kilometres south of Bran is **FUNDATA**, one of the highest villages in Romania, situated at the top of the spectacular **Bran (or Giuvala) Pass** (1290m) and served only by occasional Braşov–Cîmpulung buses. The village itself is little more than a scattering of small farm houses with no discernible centre other than the shop on the main road, but it is host of the popular peasant festival – the **Mountain Festival** (*Nedeia Muntele*) – which takes place on the last Sunday of June and attracts crowds from Braşov, Dîmboviţa and Argeş counties. The underlying purpose of the festival is to transact business: exchanges of handicrafts, livestock and (formerly) of pledges of marriage. As Fundata straddles the border between Transylvania and Wallachia, the festival was important as a means of maintaining contacts between ethnic Romanians in the two provinces. Although the matchmaking aspect has disappeared, it remains a lively event with plenty of singing and dancing and a chance to see traditional costumes. On the far side of Bran pass, the road hairpins down to a ruined castle, on to the karstic Podul Dîmboviśei depression, and ultimately to Cîmpulung (p.103).

Făgăraş and around

FĂGĂRAŞ, 54km west of Braşov, has a reputation as a grim polluted place thanks to its chemical works, but it has its attractive aspects, and even some small-town charm in places. It's a useful base for the mountains to the south and the Saxon villages just to the north. Between 1366 and 1460, the town and the surrounding duchy of Amlaş were under Wallachian rule, and when Vlad the Impaler was dis-

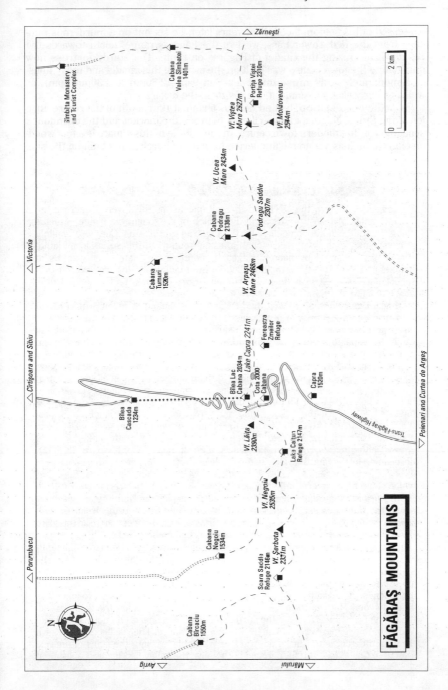

FĂGĂRAŞ MOUNTAINS

△ Zărneşti

Cabana
Valea Simbetei
1401m

Simbăta Monastery
and Tourist Complex

Portita Viştei
Refuge 2310m

Vf. Viştea
Mare 2527m

Vf. Moldoveanu
2544m

Vf. Ucea
Mare 2434m

Cabana
Podragu
2136m

Podragu Saddle
2307m

△ Victoria

Cabana
Turnuri
1520m

Vf. Arpaşu
Mare 2468m

△ Cîrţişoara and Sibiu

Lake Capra 2241m

Fereastra
Zmeilor
Refuge

Bîlea Lac
Cabana 2034m

Cota 2000
Cabana

Capra
1520m

Bîlea
Cascada
1234m

Trans-Făgăraş Highway

▽ Poienari and Curtea de Argeş

Vf. Lăiţa
2390m

Lake Căltun
Refuge 2147m

Vf. Negoiu
2535m

△ Porumbacu

Cabana
Negoiu
1534m

Scara Saddle
Refuge 2146m

Vf. Şerbota
2331m

Cabana
Bîrcaciu
1550m

▽ Avrig

▽ Mărului

2 km
0

N

possessed of his fiefdom a couple of years later, he set out on a murderous rampage from the Red Tower Pass, west of the Făgăraş range, north towards the Burzen Land, razing the citadel of Făgăraş en route. The sturdy **fortress** now dominating the town centre was built on the ashes of this citadel and today houses a moderately good **museum** (Tues–Sun 9am–12.30pm & 1.30pm–5pm), as well as a fairly classy restaurant, the *Cetate* in the cellars.

From the **train station**, behind the bus terminal 1km south of the centre, turn left along Stradă Negoiu, and you'll pass between the market and the abandoned synagogue to the modern town centre. In the middle of this square is a tiny wooden church, built as a fund-raising device for a new church being built on the site,

HIKING IN THE FĂGĂRAŞ MOUNTAINS

Northwest of Braşov, the DN1 and the rail line follow the River Olt across the Transylvanian plateau towards Sibiu. For much of the journey, a fringe of peaks along the southern horizon delineates the **Făgăraş mountains**. Composed mainly of crystalline schists with occasional limestone outcrops, this series of pyramid-shaped peaks linked by narrow ridges harbours more than seventy **lakes** at heights of 1800–2250m. Up to about 2000m the mountain sides are covered with spruce forests sheltering deer, Carpathian bears, chamois and other **wildlife**; above this line there may still be snow as late as June.

Most **hiking routes** are well marked and fairly simple to follow with a *Hartă Turistică Munţii Făgăraşului* map, which can be bought in Braşov, Bran, Făgăraş or Sibiu, or in the *cabana*s in the mountains. If you're planning to hike, it's useful, but rarely essential, to **reserve accommodation**. Always carry ample food and water, along with boots and waterproofs – the weather is very changeable on the ridge.

Almost invariably, the starting point is one of the settlements along the Olt valley, where routes lead from the train stations to the mountains. Almost all trains stop at **Ucea**, to disgorge both peasants on shopping trips and groups of hikers, who all clamber onto buses south to **Victoria**, dominated by its chemical works. From here a forestry track leads to the *Arpaş cabana*, and a route following red triangles leads past the *Turnuri cabana* (☎069/43.84.05) up to *Podragu cabana* (2136m; ☎069/43.84.05) in about nine or ten hours. The next day you can follow the **ridge path** marked with red stripes, either eastwards past Romania's highest peak, **Moldoveanu** (2544m), descending by the Simbăta valley to the *Complex Turistic Sîmbăta* (with a monastery, a *cabana* and a few Sunday buses to Făgăraş) or west to **Bîlea**; the *cabana*, *Bîlea Lac*, which stood here until recently, has burnt down, but will almost certainly be rebuilt. From *Bîlea lac* you can descend either by the Trans-Făgăraş Highway or by a cable car to the *Bîlea Cascada* (Waterfall) *cabana*, and from there to the *Vama Cucului cabana* (☎069/55.07.17), Cîrtişoara and the Cîrţa rail halt. In theory there are also two buses a day from *Bîlea Cascada* to Sibiu, but they cannot be relied on.

If you fancy a **longer hike**, you can continue westwards from Bîlea to climb (with the help of fixed chains) Romania's second highest peak, **Negoiu** (2535m); from the summit you can head down to the train stations at Porumbacu, Avrig or Racoviša. To the east, the hike to the Piatra Craiului (p.142) takes a couple of days; the approaches on the southern side are long and tedious, but it is possible to follow the Trans-Făgăraş Highway from Bîlea, or a forestry road from below the Podragu saddle, to the *Cumpăna cabana* at the northern end of the sixteen-kilometre-long **Lake Vidra**, or to two more *cabana*s on its southeastern shore. The road continues down through the gorges to Curtea de Argeş in Wallachia, passing the ruins of the real Dracula's Castle (see p.105), perched high above the valley just before Căpăşîneni.

and beyond this is the fortress. One block west is Piaša Republicii, the old town centre, with Orthodox and Lutheran churches to the north. This is the centre of social life in the town and you'll find three *cofetarie* and a cinema here. Immediately south, at the junction of Str. Eminescu and B-dul Unirii (the DN1), you'll see a couple of fine neo-Brîncovenesc buildings – the BCR bank and the high school – and there's a simple Gothic church immediately west on Bulevardul Unirii. An old custom of **ritual insults** still prevails in the modern town: on a certain day at the beginning of summer, townsfolk who bear grudges or grievances assemble on the hilltop overlooking town, and shout insults at their opponents, the aim being to vent their spleen, and hopefully become reconciled thereafter.

The *Progresul* **hotel**, at Piaša Republicii 15 (☎068/21.16.34; ①), is basic, inexpensive and welcoming enough; hot water is provided "as required", and there's a shared bathroom. For better facilities, head for the two private hotels on Stradă V. Alecsandri at the east end of the new town centre: the *Roata*, at no. 10 (☎068/21.24.15; ①) is warm and friendly, while the *Flora* at no. 12 (☎068/21.51.03; ②) seems over-priced, but both have en-suite facilities and non-stop hot water.

Wallachian rule gave rise to characteristic local art forms still evident in the villages surrounding Făgăraş, such as the **icons on glass** on display in the gallery at **Sîmbata Monastery**, 12km west and 15km south of the town, and which are still painted at Arpaşu, a further 15km along the DN1 towards Sibiu. The fifteenth-century church at **Vad**, reached by buses east to Şinca, also has a collection. To the north, buses to Agnita and Rupea (via Lovnic) pass through Saxon villages with fine fortified churches. Throughout the area, villagers still dress up in embroidered costumes for **New Year celebrations** – particularly at Şercaia, Arpaşu, Porumbacu de Jos and Porumbacu de Sus – and gather en masse together with Saxon dancers from Tilişca for the **Flowers of the Olt Festival** (*Florile Oltului*) at **Avrig** on the second Sunday of April.

Beyond Avrig the road forks: the DN1 heading to the right past the *Fîntîniţa Haiducului* (Outlaw's Spring) motel to Sibiu; the other branch veering south to Talmaciu and the Turnu Roşu (Red Tower) Pass and on into Wallachia. Travelling by train, you may need to change at Podu Olt for Piatra Olt in Wallachia; these services pass several of the monasteries in the Olt valley (see p.106).

Transylvania's Saxon Villages

Southern Transylvania was the heartland of the **Saxon community**, and although the Saxon people have almost all departed to Germany, the landscape is still dotted with the vestiges of their culture. In 1143 King Géza II of Hungary invited Germans to colonize strategic regions of Transylvania; most of the early settlers were from Flanders and the Mosel and Rhine lands, but with subsequent waves of immigration it was the appellation "Sachsen" that stuck. Their name for Transylvania was Siebenbürgen, derived from the original "seven towns" that divided the territory between them, of which Hermannstadt (**Sibiu** to the Romanians) became the most powerful. In between the towns hundreds of villages grew up, self-reliant God-fearing farming communities that developed a distinctive culture with a vernacular style of architecture. Although the Székely, immediately to the north, put low walls about their places of worship and the Moldavians raised higher ones about their monasteries, it was the Saxons who perfected this type of building; their Romanesque and early Gothic churches were initially strengthened to provide refuge from the Tatars, and then surrounded by high walls and towers to resist the militarily more sophisticated Turks. These **fortified churches**, some of which house warrens of store rooms to hold stocks of food sufficient to survive a siege, are some of the most individual and memorable religious buildings you'll find anywhere.

Alas for the Saxons, their citadels were no protection against the tide of history, which steadily eroded their influence from the eighteenth century on and put them in a difficult position during World War II. Although many bitterly resented Hitler's carving-up of Transylvania in 1940, which gave its northern half to Hungary, there were others who, relishing their new status as *Volksdeutsche*, embraced Nazism and joined the German army. As a collective punishment after the war, all fit Saxon men between the ages of seventeen and forty-five, and women between eighteen and thirty (30,000 in all) were deported to the Soviet Union for between three and seven years of slave labour; many did not return, and those who did found that much of their property had been confiscated.

Though road and rail routes diverge in places, it's fairly easy to reach settlements along the Olt valley in particular; however, there are many more in the side valleys which are well worth discovering and can only be reached by occasional buses, by car, bike or on foot. In summer many Saxons return from Germany to visit their home villages, but at other times you're likely to be the only visitor.

Hărman and Prejmer

Visiting the Saxon villages around Braşov on the eve of the World War II, the writer Elizabeth Kyle found churches prepared for siege as in the times of Sultan Süleyman and Vlad the Impaler. The village of **HĂRMAN** (Honigberg), 12km northeast of Braşov and served by trains and buses towards Sfîntu Gheorghe, still looks much as she described it: situated "in a wide and lovely valley, its houses arranged in tidy squares off the main street which sweeps up towards the grim fortress that closes the vista". Inside the fortified outer walls, wooden staircases lead to the rows of meal-rooms (*Speisesaal*) where each family stored a loaf from every baking and other essential supplies for use in times of siege. Here, Kyle encountered a Saxon Fräulein wearing a *Borten* – the high, brimless hats which denote maidenhood – who "flung open the door, and immediately a mingled stench of ancient cheeses, mouldering ham and damp flour rushed out to meet us. From the roof rows of hams were suspended on hooks. Those nearest us looked comparatively fresh, but the highest ones were green with age". Having been informed that "some of those hams have been hanging there two hundred years", Kyle enquired why. "Because, *Gott sei Dank*, they were not required," came the answer. "There was no siege."

At that time the number of Saxon "souls" in Hărman was 1500; now there are under 350, of whom perhaps seventy go to **church** on Sundays, usually at 9am. The church dates from the thirteenth century (with clear Cistercian influence), with later fortified walls and an ice-cellar with fifteenth-century frescoes. The tower was extended in the fifteenth century – note the one-handed clock, which tells the hour only. See also the mid-fourteenth-century pietà (with North Italian influence) on the north side of the choir.

PREJMER (Tartlau), 3km to the east, and off the main road, is also served by trains and buses to Sfîntu Gheorghe. The village was similarly well prepared for siege: a five-towered wall, 12m high, lined in the seventeenth century with four tiers of meal-rooms, surrounds the thirteenth-century church. The entrance tower is itself protected by another fortified enclosure, the Mayor's Courtyard, added in the sixteenth and seventeenth centuries, to which an arcaded corridor, the Bakers' Courtyard, was appended as a Baroque flourish in the less perilous times of the late seventeenth century. Prejmer's church is the easiest of the Saxon churches to visit, as it has official opening hours (Tues–Fri 9am–5pm, Sat 9am–3pm, Sun 11am–5pm) and a sort of concierge's lodge in the entrance passage; there is even a small **museum**, and some signs in English.

The land around Hărman was the first in the Braşov region to be collectivized (in 1950), and today Prejmer is the centre of a prosperous agricultural region, with a trout farm and textile factory. Note that the Ilieni **train** halt is closer to the centre than Prejmer station proper (and nowhere near the village of Ilieni); all local trains stop at both, and fast trains at neither.

The riverside villages

Further north, towards Sighişoara, along the River Olt, there are many more Saxon villages; the *personal* trains between Braşov and Sighişoara stop at most of the villages mentioned here. The train route passes through **Feldioara** (Marienburg), 21km from Braşov, where the Teutonic Knights built a citadel, now in ruins, near the rail line at the south end of the village; **Rotbav** (Rothbach), 3km on, and **Maieruş** (Nussbach), a further 4km, both have typical fortified churches; and Apaša, 6km towards Sighişoara, is just across the Olt from **Aita Mare** (Nagyajta), where there's a late Gothic fortified church used by a Unitarian congregation. Continuing north, the trains stop at Ormeniş, across the river from **Micloşoara** (Miklósvar), where the castle of the Kálnoky family, a rare example of the Italian Renaissance style, is being restored; and at **Racoş** (Alsórákos), where a castle, built for the Bethlen family in 1625, is also being restored. At Maieruş the road swings left across the wooded Perşani mountains, leaving the Burzenland for the Kokelgebiet or Tîrnave plateau; it rejoins the river and the rail line where they emerge from a defile at Rupea Station.

RUPEA (Reps), a small industrial town 4km from its train station, is dominated by a basalt hill crowned by the remains of three citadels, built between the thirteenth and seventeenth centuries. The hill is also known for its springs of sulphurous, salty water. The town is big enough to have a **hotel** (②), the *Rupea*, on Piaţa Republicii, a local **museum** (Tues–Sun 10am–5pm) at Piaša Republicii 191, and a bus station west of the centre. The bus from the train station to the town passes first through the village of **HOMOROD** (Hamruden), whose church dates from 1270 with fortified walls from the fifteenth century and a tower from the sixteenth, and three layers of paintings in the choir, all pre-Reformation. Now that almost all the Saxons have left, and the church is used only by a few Hungarians, it's getting very dilapidated, but restoration is planned with the help of German funds. A back road leads north from Homorod to **Caţa** (Katzendorf) and **Drăuşeni** (Draas), both also with fortified churches.

Beyond Rupea, the main road again diverges from the rail line and the river, passing further south, through **Buneşti** (Bodendorf), where the church's Speckturm (Bacon Tower) is still in use as a bacon store. Ten kilometres south of here, along an unmade road, is **VISCRI** (Deutsch-Weisskirch), one of the most impressive of all the Romanian citadels, set, gleaming white, upon a hill. The church is largely thirteenth-century Gothic, with fortified walls built in 1500 and an assortment of towers from the fifteenth, seventeenth and eighteenth centuries. From the tower there's a view of idyllic countryside and of the village, a classic Saxon *Strassendorf*, with a row of houses on either side of a single street and a brook running down the centre. The church key is available from Frau Dootz at no.141. The village has a profitable co-operative farm, and visitors can stay in the *Burghüterhäuschen*, the former church caretaker's cottage (②); water is fetched from the well. Twenty kilometres further north, back on the main road, lies **Saschiz** (Keisd), where a hilltop citadel looks down on the village's fortified church, whose main tower shows clear earthquake damage.

Rejoining the rail line in the Tîrnava Mare valley you pass **ALBEŞTI** (Weisskirch bei Schässburg), where a small museum commemorates the life of Hungary's national poet **Petöfi Sándor**, killed nearby in battle against the Russians in 1849. As foreseen in one of his own romantic poems, Petöfi's body was never found; most likely it was trampled beyond all recognition by the Cossacks' horses, but it is also conceivable that he ended up as a prisoner in Siberia, where it's claimed that his remains have been found.

Sighişoara

A forbidding silhouette of battlements and needle spires looms over **SIGHIŞOARA** (Schässburg to the Saxons and Segesvár to the Hungarians) as the sun descends behind the hills of the Tîrnava Mare valley, and it seems fitting that this was the birthplace of Vlad Ţepeş, "The Impaler" – the man known to so many as **Dracula**. Visually archaic even by Romanian standards, Sighişoara makes the perfect introduction to Transylvania: especially as the eastbound *Dacia*, *Traianus* and *Pannonia* express trains all stop here, and in daylight, enabling travellers to break the long journey between Budapest and Bucharest with an overnight stop.

The old town

The old town or **citadel** dominates the newer quarters from a rocky massif whose slopes support a jumble of ancient, leaning houses, their windows overlooking the steps leading up from Piaša Hermann Oberth to the main gateway. Above rises the mighty **Clock Tower**, where each day a different wooden figure emerges from the belfry on the stroke of midnight. The tower was raised in the thirteenth and fourteenth centuries when Sighişoara became a free town controlled by craft guilds, each of which had to finance the construction of a bastion and defend it during wartime. It has subsequently been rebuilt after earthquakes and a fire in 1676. Originally a Saxon town known as Castrum Sex (Fort Six, of the seven Siebenbürgen), Sighişoara grew rich on the proceeds of trade with Moldavia and Wallachia, as the Clock Tower's **museum** attests (Tues–Sun 9am–3.30pm). Most of the burghers were Magyar or Saxon, and the Romanians – or Vlachs as they were then called – became inferior citizens in Transylvanian towns following edicts passed in 1540. These excluded Vlachs from public office and forbade them to live in townhouses with chimneys or with windows overlooking the streets, and also prohibited them from wearing furs, embroidered dress, shoes or boots. To the right of the Clock Tower stands the Dominican or **Monastery Church**, also now Saxon, which has a stark, whitewashed interior hung with colourful carpets similar to those in the Black Church at Braşov, and an altar which resembles a wooden carpet-beater. The church was established in 1298, but was progressively rebuilt between 1484 and 1680. It is often closed but hosts occasional organ recitals.

The main Saxon church dominates the hill at the southern end of the citadel. It is appropriately named the **Church on the Hill** (*Bergkirche*), and is reached by the impressive covered wooden **Scholars' Stairs** that rise steeply at the southern end of Strada Şcolii; the stairs, consisting of 175 steps and 29 landings, date from the seventeenth century. Massively buttressed, the Church on the Hill has a surprisingly roomy interior that seems austere despite its array of frescoes. Founded in 1345 and finished in 1525, it is currently under restoration, due to be completed in 1999, and may only be open for one hour per day (noon–1pm) until then. Some lovely stone tombs lodged near the entrance are a harbinger of the **Saxon cemetery**, a melancholy, weed-choked mass of graves spilling over the hilltop beside the ruined citadel walls.

Of the citadel's original fourteen **towers**, named after the guilds responsible for their upkeep, nine survive, the most impressive being the hexagonal Shoemakers' Tower (*Turnul Cizmarilor*), the Tailors' Tower (*Turnul Croitorilor*) and the Tinsmiths' Tower (*Turnul Cositorarilor*), best viewed, with its fine wooden gallery, from the gateway of the Lutheran parish house (*Pfarrhaus*), below the Church on the Hill.

Vlad's birthplace

In 1431, or thereabouts, in a two-storey house, at Piaţa Muzeului 6, within the shadow of the old town's Clock Tower, a woman whose name is lost to posterity gave birth to a son called Vlad, who in later life earned the title of "The Impaler". Abroad, he's better known as **Dracula**, which can be translated as "Son of the Devil", or more accurately as "Son of the Dragon" – referring to his father, **Vlad Dracul**, whom the Holy Roman Emperor Sigismund of Hungary made a knight of the Order of the Dragon for his prowess against the Turks. When Vlad Jr was born, Vlad Dracul was merely the guard commander of the mountain passes into Wallachia, but in 1436 he secured the princely throne of Wallachia and moved his family to the court at Tîrgovişte. Young Vlad's privileged childhood there ended eight years later, when he and his brother Radu were sent by their father as hostages to the Turkish Sultan in Anatolia in an attempt to curry favour. There, they lived in daily fear of the silken cord with which the Ottomans strangled dignitaries – Radu sleeping his way into the favours of the Sultan while Vlad observed the Turks' use of terror, which he would later turn against them as the Impaler. Nowadays, Vlad's birthplace contains a **restaurant**, serving typical Romanian fare, and a small **museum** of medieval weapons (Tues–Sun 10am–3.30pm).

The lower town

The **lower town** is less picturesque than the citadel, but there's a nice ambience around the shabby centre, consisting of **Piaša Hermann Oberth** and **Strada 1 Decembrie**, where townsfolk gather to consume grilled sausages, *ţuică*, cola or watery beer, conversing in Romanian, Magyar and, occasionally, antiquated German. The number of hangouts is so small that it's easy to track down anything that's happening; any films will be screened at the Lumina cinema at the north end of Str. 1 Decembrie. In late July the streets are taken over for a week by an immensely popular **Medieval Arts Festival** and on national holidays, when people stream up to Dealul Gării (the hill above the train station) with bottles and food, a brass band may perform in the citadel's Piaša Cetăšii. Gypsies arrive by cart, their hats crowned with flowers, to *bashavav* (play the violin), tell fortunes and pick pockets.

The area between the citadel and the river was partially cleared before 1989 for redevelopment as a Civic Centre similar to the one in Bucharest, and the land is still in limbo. Taking the footbridge over the Tîrnave Mare river, you come to the Romanian **Orthodox Cathedral**, built in the Byzantine style in 1937. Its gleaming white, multifaceted facade is in striking contrast to the dark interior, where blue and orange hues dominate the small panels of the iconostasis. Close by is a group of Soviet war graves; note how, in the people's paradise, the graves of the "unknown heroes" are much smaller than that of the Major.

Practicalities

The **train station** is north of the centre, across the Tîrnave Mare river; outside, you'll see an antique locomotive which ran on the Sibiu–Agnita–Sighişoara narrow-gauge line from 1896 to 1965. Immediately to the east is the **bus station**, which serves neighbouring Saxon villages and, every hour or two, Tîrgu Mureş. Buses to Germany are run by *AtlasSib*, at Str. Morii 21 (☎065/77.37.95) and *Mihu Reisen* (☎065/77.19.30). Most other services are grouped on Strada 1 Decembrie, in the lower town, including a **tourist information** office at no. 10, which sells a good new town guide (Mon–Fri 9am–5pm, Sat 9am–2pm); the **post office** is on Piaţa Oberth.

Sighişoara's only central **hotel** is the *Steaua* at Str. 1 Decembrie 12 (☎065/77.15.94, fax 17.19.32; ④), next door to the tourist office; recently privatized, with some minor refurbishment, it's a pleasant and affordable stopover. The other hotels are all new private places: the best is the *Poeniţa* (☎065/77.27.39; ④), in a lovely location on the edge of town at Strada D. Cantemir 24, while the handiest for the station is the *Chic* (☎065/77.59.01, fax 16.41.49; ③) at Str. Libertăşii 44 – a simple place, with no en-suite facilities, but a pleasant small bar-restaurant. The *Hostel Bobby*, at the southern end of town at Str. Tache Ionescu 18 (☎065/77.22.32; ③), is open from June 15 to August 31; fridges and a washing machine are available, and there's a good restaurant opposite. You can find **private rooms** in the old town by asking in the restaurant in Dracula's birthplace or at the café around the corner. The *Dealul Gării* **campsite** (with *cabana*s and a restaurant; ☎065/77.10.46) is on the hilltop overlooking the train station: turn left from the train station to cross the tracks by a bridge and follow Strada Dealul Gării up the hill.

There are a few good **places to eat** in town, including the hotels, the restaurant in Vlad's birthplace, a snack bar at the north end of Strada Morii, and some pizzerias, the *Perla* (daily10am–11pm), on Piaša Oberth and the *Pizza 4 Amici* (noon–midnight), at Str. Morii 7. For **drinking**, try the *Crama* at Str. Morii 17, a little bar frequented by the locals; the best coffee and cakes are found along the road south of Piaša Oberth.

Sighişoara to Sibiu

The main approach to Sibiu is to follow the Tîrnave Mare river west from Sighişoara. From the train or the DN14, you'll see buffalo pulling wagons or wallowing in the water, watched by their drovers, and glimpse the towers of fortified Saxon churches in villages situated off the main road. The area south and west of Sighişoara is particularly good for leisurely exploration, its villages all accessible by bus from Sighişoara. The road south takes you to **AGNITA** (Agnethelm), 40km away. An old Saxon settlement with a grimly towered church and the **Museum of the Hîrtibaciu Valley** (Tues–Sat 8am–4pm) which displays Saxon measures, brands and newspapers, it also has a remarkably good hotel, the *Dacia* (☎069/51.09.00; ③). From here you can travel by bus or narrow-gauge train to Sibiu, passing **Hosman** (Holzmengen), whose fortified church stands against the backdrop of the Făgăraş mountains, or by bus to Făgăraş through the villages of **Dealu Frumos** (Schönberg) – supposedly the geographical centre of Romania – **Merghindeal** (Mergeln) and **Cincu** (Gross-Schenk), all of which have imposing fortified churches.

Following the route west, about 26km from Sighişoara along the main DN14, a turning to the left leads to the village of **BIERTAN** (Birthälm); if you are travelling by train, you'll need to get off at Mediaş where you can catch a local bus into Biertan itself. The village, set high on a hill within two and a half rings of walls linked by a splendid covered staircase, has the best known of all the Saxon fortified churches. Completed as late as 1516, and recently restored and added to UNESCO's World Heritage List, this was the seat of the Lutheran bishops until

THE BURGENVEREIN

The *Burgenverein* (literally Union of Castles) is a group dedicated to the preservation of the **fortified churches** and associated aspects of the Saxon culture; in addition to raising money among the Saxon diaspora in Germany it has set up a network of *Gästehäuser* or small **guesthouses** (①), so that those interested in seeing the churches can contribute financially to the cause, and vice versa. These generally charge for a bunk or a bed and a basic bathroom; breakfast may be available by arrangement, but you shouldn't rely on it. The coordinators, in Mediaş, are Kilian Dörr, Piaţa Castelului 2 (☎069/81.33.12), and Hugo Schneider, Str. Gh. Doja 23 (☎069/82.86.05); there are also local contacts, listed with the villages in question.

1867, and their fine gravestones can be seen inside the bishops' tower. Other notable features are the altarpiece (1483–1515), a classic polyptych, and the sacristy door (1515), with no less than seventeen locks, and a room where couples wanting to divorce were supposedly shut up for two weeks. Home-made cheese can be bought at the private dairy (*lăptărie*) hidden near the junction of the Richiş and Copşa Mare roads; good wine can be bought for next to nothing at the last house on the right on the Richiş road. The village is the site of the *Sachsentreffen* or Saxon Meeting, held annually in mid-September.

Mediaş

The only town between Sighişoara and Sibiu is **MEDIAŞ** (Mediasch), which despite the tanneries and chemical works feeding off the Tîrnava Mare valley's methane reserves, gets more prepossessing the further in you venture. Originally an Iron Age and then a Roman settlement, Mediaş was a predominantly Saxon town for many centuries, walled and with gate towers, two of which remain, on Strada Cloşca. After 1918 it began to develop an industrial and Romanian character, stemming from political changes after World War I and the construction here of Transylvania's first gas pipeline.

From the **train and bus stations** on Strada Unirii, opposite the synagogue at Str. Kogălniceanu 45, follow Strada Pompierilor and then Strada Roth to the right to the town centre, **Piaša Regele Ferdinand**, dominated by the **Evangelical Church**, its seventy-metre belltower slightly askew. Completed by 1500, this is a true citadel, surrounded by store rooms, high ramparts and towers (one of which, the Tailors' Tower, served as a jail for the Impaler in 1467). Inside there are Anatolian carpets, frescoes, a Crucifixion with a view of Vienna painted in 1474–79 and a superb Gothic altarpiece in the style of Roger van der Weyden. The *Schullerhaus*, on the square, at no. 25, was built in 1588 and once housed the Transylvanian Diet. For a limited insight into the history of the town, and a better wildlife display, visit the **town museum** in a former monastery at Str. Mihai Viteazul 46 (Tues–Sun 9am–5pm). Next door, the Roman Catholic church retains its late fifteenth-century Gothic chancel.

Mediaş's only **hotel** is the ugly *Central* (☎069/81.17.87, fax 82.17.22; ②), at the top of Strada Pompierilor. Bus services operate from the **bus station** to Agnita, Sibiu and Tîrgu Mureş, and to all the surrounding villages. Some especially picturesque villages with fortified churches, such as **Moşna** (*Meschen*), lie along the road to Agnita where you are safe to camp in the surrounding hills.

Copşa Mică and beyond

Filthy **COPŞA MICĂ**, 13km west of Mediaş, is probably Romania's most polluted town and if you're unlucky with connections you may have to change trains for
Sibiu here rather than in Mediaş. A plant producing carbon black (for dyes) was
established here in 1936 and consistently left everything – plants, laundry, people
– covered in soot until it was finally closed in 1993; white snow was seen for the
first time in 1994. The other industrial plant here, the SOMETRA lead smelter to
the west, is more deadly; for thirty years it has been spraying a cocktail of twenty heavy metals over the surrounding area (and up to 50km away). Production has
dropped by a third since 1990, which has helped to improve environmental matters, but has left five thousand men unemployed. Millions of dollars have been
spent on filters and pollution control, dust emissions have halved, and other types
of pollution are now just one or two percent of previous levels; even so it will be a
long time before the local people's health returns to normal – currently life
expectancy is nine years below the national average and instances of tuberculosis
and other lung diseases are two or three times higher than normal.

The villages beyond Copşa Mică – **Valea Viilor** (Wurmloch; 5km south of the
main road and rail routes), **Axente Sever** (Frauendorf) and **Agirbiciu** (Arbegen)
– all have good fortified churches. However, there is little worth stopping for en
route to Sibiu other than **OCNA SIBIULUI** (Salzburg), a bathing resort with
fizzy, salty water which bubbles up in four lakes formed in abandoned salt-work-
ings. Beyond the spa on the town's central Piaşa Traian is a solid walled
Romanesque church (Thurs 3–4pm), which, unusually, now has a Hungarian
Evangelical congregation. The nearest train stop to the spa is Băile Ocna Sibiului,
2km north of Ocna Sibiului station proper.

Sibiu

"I rubbed my eyes in amazement," wrote Walter Starkie of **SIBIU** in 1929. "The
town where I found myself did not seem to be in Transylvania, for it had no
Romanian or Hungarian characteristics: the narrow streets and old gabled houses made me think of Nuremberg." Nowadays the illusion is harder to sustain, in
a city surrounded by high-rise suburbs and virtually abandoned by the Saxons
themselves, but the old town is still a startling sight and home to some of
Romania's best museums.

Some history

Sibiu, known in German as Hermannstadt, grew to be the chief city of the
Transylvanian Saxons. Clannish, hard-working and thrifty, its merchants dominated trade between Transylvania and Wallachia by the Olt gorge route, and prospered, forming exclusive guilds under royal charter. The Saxons, industrious and
prosperous in medieval times, were envied by others and knew it. Their literature
and proverbs are marked by admonitions to beware of outsiders, while Sibiu's
plethora of fortifications testifies to their historical caution. Mindful of the
destruction of their first citadel by the Tatars in 1241, the townsfolk surrounded
themselves during the fifteenth century with fortified walls and forty towers; built
of brick since firearms were then transforming siege warfare, they were mighty
enough to repel the Turks three times. Behind these defences, the people of Sibiu
linked their buildings and streets with tunnels and gateways, and set heavily grat-
ed windows to cover the stairways and corners where they might ambush intrud-

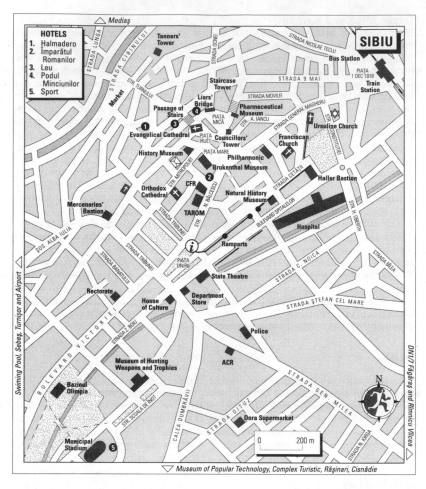

HOTELS
1. Halmadero
2. Împăratul Romanilor
3. Leu
4. Podul Minciunilor
5. Sport

Mediaş

SIBIU

Tanners' Tower

STRADA LUNGA

STRADA CIBINULUI

STRADA NICOLAE TECLU

Bus Station

PIAŢA 1 DEC 1918

Train Station

Market

STR. TURNULUI

Staircase Tower

STRADA 9 MAI

STRADA MOVILEI

Liars' Bridge

Passage of Stairs

Pharmaceutical Museum

PIAŢA MICĂ

STR. A. IANCU

STRADA GENERAL MAGHERU

Ursuline Church

STR. CONSTITUŢIEI

Evangelical Cathedral

PIAŢA HUET

Councillors' Tower

Franciscan Church

History Museum

PIAŢA MARE

Philharmonic

Brukenthal Museum

STR. MITROPOLIEI

CFR

STRADA CETĂŢII

Haller Bastion

Orthodox Cathedral

STR. N. BĂLCESCU

Natural History Museum

STRADA TRIBUNEI

TAROM

BULEVARD SPITALELOR

STR. H. OBERTH

Mercenaries' Bastion

SOS. ALBA IULIA

Hospital

STRADA TRIBUNEI

STRADA BANATULUI

Ramparts

PIAŢA UNIRII

STRADA C. NOICA

STRADA BILEA

Rectorate

State Theatre

House of Culture

Department Store

STRADA ŞTEFAN CEL MARE

BULEVARD VICTORIEI

STRADA Z. BOIU

Police

Museum of Hunting Weapons and Trophies

ACR

STRADA GEN. MILEA

Swimming Pool, Sebeş, Turnişor and Airport

Bazinul Olimpia

CALEA DUMBRĂVII

STR. SCOALA DE ÎNOT

STRADA OITUZ

Dora Supermarket

DN1/7 Făgăraş and Rîmnicu Vîlcea

Municipal Stadium

0   200 m

N

STRADA N. IORGA

▽ *Museum of Popular Technology, Complex Turistic, Răşinari, Cisnădie*

ers. Parts of the walls were demolished, and new gateways opened up, in the nineteenth century, but much remains.

Arrival and information

Sibiu's **bus terminal** and **train station** are on the northeast side of town. To reach the centre, cross Piaša 1 Decembrie 1918 (still generally known as Piaša Gǎrii) and follow Strada General Magheru up the hill. The **airport** is on the western edge of town, and linked to it by buses to and from the TAROM office at Str. Bǎlcescu 10 (buses leave from the centre an hour before each flight); alternatively you can take the Cristian bus (#20). There are three flights a week to and from Bucharest.

Sibiu's **tourist office** at the corner of Strada Bǎlcescu and Piaša Unirii has closed, but immediately behind it, at Str. Cetǎšii 1, is the Prima Ardeleana tourist agency (daily 8am–4pm; ☎069/41.17.88), which sells the good *Transpress* town map. In addition Sibiu has a telephone information service, *Infotel*, on ☎069/43.76.68 (some English spoken).

Accommodation

There is an increasingly wide range of **hotels** in Sibiu; the state hotels are much of a muchness, but the new generation of small private hotels span the range from cheap backpackers' places to bases for foreign businessmen. The *Hotel Leu*, at Str. Moş Ioan Roata 2 (☎069/21.83.92; ①), has tiny, basic, but clean rooms, with communal showers; but the real bargain-basement option is the *Sport*, at Str. Octavian Goga 2 (☎069/42.24.72; ①). By far and away the best place in town is the recently refurbished *Împăratul Romanilor*, at Str. Bălcescu 4 (☎069/21.65.00, fax 21.32.78; ⑥); the *Casa Moraru*, at Str. A. Vlahuşă 11A (☎069/21.62.91, fax 21.54.90; ⑨), is a similar, and new, private hotel with good facilities, including fitted hair dryers and alarm clocks in all the rooms, a sauna, a good restaurant and bar.

In addition, there are two **guesthouse** options – the *Halmadero*, at Str. Măsarilor 10 (☎069/21.25.09; ③), and the *Podul Minciunilor* (Liars' Bridge), at Str. Azilului 1 (☎069/21.72.59; ②) – the *Halmadero* has more spacious rooms, but the *Podul Minciunilor* is more centrally located. There is also a good quality **motel** and a **campsite** in the Dumbrava forest 4km to the south (☎069/21.40.22; trolley bus #T1 from the train station). In the same direction (bus #5) is the *Valea Aurie cabana* (☎069/42.43.04; ③), well run and with a good restaurant.

The Town

Sibiu is an attractive and lively town where many of the houses are painted sky blue, red, apricot or pea green, and cafés and restaurants do a busy trade along the length of the promenade. The town is split into a **historic centre** and a **new town**, and has many fine old **churches**, and the remains of the original **Saxon Bastions** which formed the town's fortifications.

The historic centre

The old town is centred around three squares – the **Piaša Mare** (*Grosser Ring*), the **Piaša Mică** (*Kleiner Ring*) and the **Piaša Huet** (*Huetplatz*). Strada G-ral Magheru leads south from the train station, to Piaša 1 Decembrie 1918, to Piaša Mare, the traditional hub of public life. The Catholic chapel in front of the train station contains a finely carved stone crucifix (1417). Heading along Strada Magheru, you will pass two other religious sites of interest, the **old synagogue** (which is still used in the summer by Sibiu's remaining two dozen Jews) and the **Ursuline church** at the corner with Strada Avram Iancu, dating from 1474–78. One block south, on Strada Şelarilor, is the **Franciscan church**, also built in the fifteenth century and rebuilt in the Baroque style after the roof collapsed in 1776.

Piaša Mare is surrounded by the renovated premises of sixteenth- and seventeenth-century merchants, whose acumen and thrift were proverbial. The eighteenth-century Brukenthal palace, at Piaša Mare 5, was the home of Samuel Brukenthal, the imperial governor of Transylvania. The palace was designed by a Viennese architect in a refined Late Baroque style and now houses Transylvania's finest museum, the **Brukenthal Museum** (Tues–Sun 10am–5pm), partly assembled by Brukenthal himself. As well as an extensive collection of Romanian and

Western art, the collection includes the best of Central European silverware, fifteenth- and sixteenth-century Transylvanian wooden religious sculptures and eighteenth-century Romanian icons which seem positively naive in comparison. Heading from here into Piaša Huet, you will pass near the **History Museum** (Tues–Sun 9am–5pm), at Str. Mitropoliei 2 (*Fleischergasse*), housed in the former Old City Hall (*Primăria Veche*), which was built in 1475 and remodelled in 1545; the courtyard is worth a look even if you choose not to go inside.

In the **Piaša Huet**, the **Evangelical Cathedral** (Mon–Fri 9am–1pm), a massive halled church, completed in 1520, dominates its neighbours, the Saxon Gymnasium (grammar school) and Theological Institute – confirming the town's pre-eminence as a centre of the Lutheran faith. The cathedral houses Romania's largest church organ and in summer there are recitals on Wednesday evenings. There is a superb altarpiece in the north transept (1512), a fresco of the Crucifixion on the north wall of the choir (1445), showing Italian and Flemish influences, and the **tomb of Mihnea the Bad**, Dracula's son, is held in the crypt. Mihnea was voivode of Wallachia for just one year before he was stabbed to death outside the cathedral after attending Mass in 1510; the building was still a Catholic place of worship at that time. There's also a fine collection of funerary plaques, including a well-tended memorial to the Hungarian dead of World War I. By the cathedral, an alley leads to the thirteenth-century **Passage of Stairs** (*Pasajul Scărilor* or *Saggasse*), which descends into the lower town overshadowed by arches and the medieval citadel wall.

Alternatively, head north into **Piaša Mică**, where a kind of miniature urban canyon runs down from the northwest corner under an elegant wrought-iron bridge. This **Iron Bridge** (*Podul de Fier*), dating from 1859, is nicknamed the **Liars' Bridge** (*Podul Minciunilor*), the story being that if someone tells a lie while standing on it the bridge will collapse. Ceaușescu managed to give a speech from it and survive, although he disliked the town and never returned.

On the far side of the bridge, at Piaša Mică 21, stands the arcaded **old market hall**, built in 1789, now hosting temporary art exhibitions. Also on the north side of the square are the **Pharmaceutical Museum** at no. 26 (Tues–Sun 10am–5pm) and the **Ethnology Museum**, at no. 11 (Tues–Sun 10am–5pm). To get back to Piaša Mare, cut through the gate below the **Councillors' Tower** (*Turnul Sfatului*); built in 1588, the tower has been "temporarily" closed to visitors for several years.

Alternatively, a passageway leads through the **Staircase Tower** (*Fingerlingstiege*) at Piaša Mică 24 into Strada Movilei, a street pock-marked with medieval windows, doorways and turrets. Down in the rambling lower town are the octagonal-based **Tanners' Tower**, northwest of the squares, on Strada Pulberăriei, reached via Strada Valea Mare and Strada Rimski-Korsakov, and a busy food **market** beside the river on Piaša Cibin.

The new town

In Saxon times Sibiu's promenade took place along *Heltauergasse*, now **Strada Bălcescu**, which heads south from Piaša Mare to Piaša Unirii, and this is still the heart of the modern city. At the northern end of the street is Sibiu's oldest hotel, the **Împăratul Romanilor** (Roman Emperor), still recognizable as the grand establishment once patronized by the likes of Liszt, Johann Strauss and Eminescu. The design of the hotel, which dates from 1773, was a reaction against the militaristic architecture which had previously dominated the town, which can be seen in the three rows of **ramparts and bastions** along the length of Strada Cetăšii to the southeast, where three mighty **towers** were once manned by contingents of the Carpenters', Potters' and Drapers' guilds. The **Haller Bastion** at the northern end of the street and the **Mercenaries' Bastion** further west on Strada Bastionului, which was the last to be built in 1627, also survive. To the east the **Carpenters' Tower** (*Pulverturm*) is slowly being restored to its earlier role as the town's theatre.

With the encouragement of governor Samuel Brukenthal, Sibiu developed as a centre of intellectual life, providing a haven during the nineteenth century for Romanians bent on raising their own people's cultural horizons: Gheorghe Lazăr and others opened a Romanian high school (*Liceu*), still functioning today; Ioan Slavici and George Coşbuc edited the *Tribuna* (at Str. Bălcescu 1), a magazine which campaigned for the rights of Romanians; and the first congress of **ASTRA** – "The Association for the Propagation of Romanian Culture in Transylvania" – was held in October 1861 at Str. Mitropoliei 20. Opposite is the early twentieth-century **Orthodox Cathedral**, which was based on the Aya Sofya in Istanbul and is embellished with all manner of neo-Byzantine flourishes and frescoes. Beyond the cathedral is the **ASTRA Park**, lined with busts of Romanian worthies. In 1905, ASTRA opened a library and museum overlooking the park in a fine building at Str. Lupaş 5; from here Str. Lupaş leads you east to Piaša Unirii.

The **Natural History Museum**, at Str. Cetăšii 1 (Tues–Sun 10am–5pm), is northeast of Piaša Unirii, on a turning left off the main Bulevard, just before the hospital; the museum occasionally has astronomy evenings on Thursdays. Two blocks southwest of Piaša Unirii, at Str. Şcoala de Înot 4, is the **Museum of Hunting Weapons and Trophies** (Tues–Sun 10am–5pm). The former home of a Hapsburg general, it still shelters his collection of weapons and stuffed animals and is worth a brief visit.

Outside the centre

Southwest of the centre along Calea Dumbrăvii (trolley bus #T1 from the train station), near the **Zoological Gardens** in the Dumbrava forest, is the excellent **Museum of Popular Technology** (May–mid-Oct Tues–Fri 10am–6pm, Sat & Sun 10am–8pm), a rival to the Village Museum in Bucharest as perhaps the best of Romania's open-air museums. The emphasis is on folk technology, with windmills and watermills from all over the country rebuilt here in working order. Under the Ceauşescu regime the museum faced constant political obstruction as it struggled to keep alive a pride in rural traditions when the government wanted to make country life indistinguishable from urban life – one village church actually had to be dismantled and buried for two years until it was permissible to re-erect it here.

Bus #8, from the bridge south of the train station at Bulevardul Spitalelor, takes you to **Turnişor**, where it will drop you outside the parish house (*Pfarrhaus*) at Str. Bielz 62 (*Kirchgasse*). To Romanians, Turnişor is simply a suburb of Sibiu, but to its German populace it's a distinct village, Neppendorf. Originally Saxon, its population was boosted in 1734–37 by an infusion of Austrian Protestants, expelled by their Catholic neighbours; these *Landlers* were traditionally less dour than the somewhat stolid Saxons. Although the two groups never mixed in other villages throughout the region, here the Saxons and *Landler* intermarried – yet they are still seated separately in the church, with *Landler* women on one side of the nave and Saxon women on the other. The **church** was never fortified – the villagers fled to Sibiu when the Turks came to burn their village in 1493 – but the interior is typical of Saxon village churches, with lovely paintings on the gallery, and one Turkish rug; ask at the *Pfarrhaus* for the key. There's also a brilliant **museum** in the north transept, mapping the history of the village, with lots of old photos and plenty of text (all in German). Today there are only about 200 Germans in Turnişor, compared to about 4000 before World War II.

Eating, drinking and entertainment

Places to eat cluster along Strada Bălcescu and around Piaşa Mare and Piaša Unirii, and the best are almost all in the main hotels. The **restaurant** in the *Împăratul Romanilor* hotel, with a glitzy courtyard and a sliding roof at the northern end of Strada Bălcescu, is noted for the quality of its Romanian cuisine and much frequented by local black marketeers. There are some passable places further down this lively street, all serving traditional Romanian fare of a similar standard – the *Mara* at no. 21, the *Unicum* at no. 38, the *Bufniţa* at no. 45, and the *Trandafirul Roşu* at no. 47. Near the station, the *Roşu Negru* on Piaša Oberth (Mon–Sat 7am–9pm) also serves decent, simple food, and is slightly cheaper than the restaurants on Strada Bălcescu. The *Continental* hotel contains an *expres* joint.

You could also try the **cafés** on Piaša Mare: the *Macul Roşu* at Piaša Mare 12 has real coffee and good cakes, served in an Art Deco interior; next door are the *Dunarea*, serving the best ices in town, and the *Pupa* deli, a good food shop selling imported goods; the *Intim*, also on the square, but with the address Str. Magheru 2, is another coffee and cake shop, with a no-smoking policy (Mon–Sat 8am–9pm). The best place for **breakfast** is the *Ceainăria Aroma* at Str. Bălcescu 1 (Mon–Sat 8am–9pm, Sun 9am-8pm), which even has toasted rye sandwiches. West of the centre, the *Cofetaria Universităţii* at the corner of Bulevardul Victoriei and Strada Banatului (Mon–Fri 7am–8pm, Sat & Sun 10am–8pm) has a good range of pastries and a lively student atmosphere.

There's a good selection of **bars** in the centre and the southern part of town, including *Sibiu Vechi*, at Str. Papiu Ilarian 3 (Mon–Thurs & Sun 10am–midnight, Fri & Sat noon–2am), often with good traditional music, and the *Crama Naţional*, a cheap and very cheerful cellar behind the old market hall on Piaša Mică (daily till 11pm, closed in summer). The *Restaurant Union*, at Piaša Mică 7, has live rock and blues music in its labyrinthine cellars on Saturday nights. South along Calea Dumbrăvii, at 79A, is the *Club Premier*, which has four billiard tables in action till 2am. The *Hard Rock Café* (*not* part of the international chain), further south, at Str. Arieşul 8A, just off the Cisnădie road, has good music until around 4am. The Tineretului **cinema**, at Str. Odobescu 4, sometimes doubles as a disco. **Classical concerts** are held in the House of Culture on Str. Şaguna and the adjacent Army House (*Cercul Militar*), as well as in the theatre; tickets are bought directly from the theatre and details of what's showing are displayed on posters around town.

A **Jazz Festival** is held in the spring (some time between March and July), and the **International Theatre Festival** is some time between March and June. The **pottery fair** is more reliably held on the first Sunday of September.

Listings

Bike repair Str. 9 Mai 43; Str. Aron Pumnul 16 (off Calea Dumbrăvii).

Books and maps ThauSib (Piaša Mică 3) and the Libraria Dacia Traiana (Piaša Mare 7) sell books on Transylvanian architecture and culture, and English-language books.

Car rental Avis at Hotel Continental (☎069/21.10.25 or 21.81.00 ext 31); you'll need to book a day in advance.

Car repair ACR, bloc 13, Str. Gen. V. Milea and Str. Ştrandului; Autoservice, opposite Autogară 2 on Şos. Alba Iulia; Concordia, Str. Cîmpului 13 (☎069/22.29.09).

Email PVD Net-Group, Str Bălcescu 5 (☎ & fax 069/21.67.71; *prdnet.logicnet.ro*), and Internet Verena, Str. Ocnei 11 (☎069/21.25.00).

Exchange Platinum, at Str. Cetăşii 1, and the Bancomat ATM in BCR, Str Bălcescu 11, both give good exchange rates. The IDM at Str. Papiu Ilarian 12 (off Str. Bălcescu) accepts credit cards and travellers' cheques, but at poor rates.

Hospital On B-dul Spitalelor, opposite the Haller Bastion.

Libraries The university rectorate at B-dul Victoriei 10 houses American, British, French and German libraries (Mon–Fri 8am–4pm, British section 10am–1pm & 2–5pm).

Pharmacy The private San Marco at Str. Nicolae Iorga 50, to the south in the Hipodrom II quarter, is open round the clock, while the Farmasib at Str. Bălcescu 53 is open daily (Mon–Fri 7am–9pm, Sat & Sun 8am–8pm).

Police Str. Revolušiei 4.

Post office Str. Mitropoliei 14.

Shopping Most stores and supermarkets are on Str. Bălcescu. The main department store, the Dumbrava, is on the far side of Piaša Unirii, opposite the *Continental*.

Sport Facilities are clustered around the open-air swmming pool, the Ştrand, on Şos. Alba Iulia, while there's an indoor Olympic-size swimming pool on B-dul Victoriei. Sibiu's football team, FC InterSibiu, play in the Municipal Stadium in the *Parc sub Arini*.

Travel agents CFR, Str. Bălcescu 6 (Mon–Fri 7am–7pm), handles train bookings; TAROM, is at Str. Bălcescu 10 (Mon–Fri 8am–7pm, Sat 8am–noon; ☎069/21.11.57).

Around Sibiu

Buses from the terminal by the train station serve many of the **old Saxon settlements** around Sibiu. Many of these villages have sizeable Romanian and Gypsy populations, now far outnumbering the Germans, but most have fortified churches and rows of houses presenting a solid wall to the street – hallmarks of their Saxon origins. "They have existed for seven hundred years, a mere handful, surrounded by races that have nothing in common with them, and yet they have not lost those customs that attach them to their fatherland", observed Walter Starkie in the 1920s. This remained largely true of the Saxon communities until 1989 – for example **Cisnădioara**, where the sight and feel of the place suggested Bavaria two hundred years ago – but the Saxons are disappearing fast, and it won't be long before their culture has vanished with them from the area.

The villages south of Sibiu lie in the foothills of the **Cindrel** (or Cibin) **mountains**, where enjoyable day walks and longer hikes can be taken from the small ski resort of **Păltiniş**. To the east and north of Sibiu, there are more Saxon villages with doughty fortress-churches, including Vurpăr (Burgberg), Şura Mare and Şura Mică (Gross-Scheuren and Klein-Scheuren), all accessible by bus, a pretty excursion through rolling hills and orchards.

Cisnădie and Cisnădioara

Two or three buses an hour leave Sibiu's bus station for **CISNĂDIE** (*Heltau*), 12km to the south. Cisnădie's modern outskirts quickly give way to the old Red Town (so called by the Turks both for the colour of its walls and the bloodshed attempting to breach them) – a long square leading to the largely Romanesque **church**, whose walls are lined with medieval meal-rooms. If you ask a warden, you may be taken up the massive thirteenth-century **tower**, fitted in 1795 with Transylvania's first lightning conductor; the climb takes you up a succession of lofty vaults linked by creaking ladders and narrow stairways to the four turrets, medieval symbols of civic status, which crown the tower. From the belfry the view of Cisnădie's angular courtyards and red rooftops is superb, while just visible in the distance below the Cindrel mountains is the conical rock crowned by a church that overlooks the village of Cisnădioara – legend has it that a tunnel links the two villages. On the way out, you can call in at the **Textile Museum** (Mon–Fri 8am–4pm), which has comprehensive coverage of the local household industry.

If you're keen to stay in Cisnădie, ask at the museum about **private rooms** (①–②), which can also be booked at the tourist offices in Sibiu and Bucharest. The *Disco-Bar Remember* (also known as the *Casa Blanca*; ☎069/56.12.75) to the right at the end of Str. Podului, at Str. Ţesătorilor 80, also has rooms.

From Cisnădie's centre, it's a four-kilometre walk west along Strada Măgurii and the valley road, lined with poplars and orchards, towards the striking seventy-metre-high rock that looms over **CISNĂDIOARA** (Michelsburg). The tiny **Romanesque church** built in 1223 on the summit of this rock frequently withstood Tatar attacks, villagers defending it by hurling down rocks which had previously been carried into the citadel by aspiring husbands – the custom was that no young man could marry until he had carried a heavy rock from the riverbed up the steep track, for the villagers were anxious to prevent weaklings from marrying in case they spoiled the hardy race. The church and adjoining **ethnographic museum** are supposedly open Tuesday to Sunday from 10am to 5pm, but you may have to ask around to find the curator.

Follow the river down through the village and you will pass a few shops and rows of neat, unmistakably German houses, now used as holiday homes by the new bourgeoisie of Sibiu (and a few foreigners). There's an official **campsite** here, but you should be wary of light-fingered Gypsies wandering over the hills from their camp near Răşinari. Alternatively there are bungalows at the *Bufet Pinul* at the edge of the village on the road to Răşinari, and a *Gästehaus* (advance bookings only, through Max Herzberg, DFDR, Str. Gen. Magheru 1–3, 2400 Sibiu; ☎069/21.54.17).

Răşinari and Păltiniş

RĂŞINARI lies 12km from Sibiu on the road to Păltiniş. It's a tight-packed Romanian village with a painted Orthodox church built in 1752, and an ethnographic museum (Tues–Sun 10am–5pm), showing the usual range of local costumes and pottery. However, it's more noteworthy for the large Gypsy encampment (*Ţara*) on its southern outskirts, and the village's annual **Pastoral Album Folklore Festival**, held on the third Sunday of April. **Trams** run from the Dumbrava forest (trolley bus #T1 from Sibiu station) to the north end of Răşinari, while an hourly *maxitaxi* leaves from opposite Sibiu's Olympic-size swimming pool, on B-dul Victoriei, and goes through to the southern end of Răşinari.

In addition to the road, a track petering out into a path (marked with red stripes) leads from Răşinari's outskirts over the mountains to the resort of Păltiniş in six to seven hours. About an hour before Păltiniş, near Mount Tomnaticu, a path marked with blue triangles turns right to the *Şanta* mountain *cabana*, a few kilometres east of the resort.

AMBIGUOUS PHILOSOPHERS

Răşinari was the birthplace not only of the anti-Semitic prime minister and poet Octavian Goga, but also, in 1911, of the philosopher **Emil Cioran**. In 1934 he published *Pe culmile disperarii* (*On the Heights of Despair*), setting out the nihilist antiphilosophy that the only valid thing to do with one's life is to end it. He continued, with a total lack of humour, to expound this view in a succession of books, but never quite managed to actually do away with himself, dying only in 1995. In the 1930s he supported the Iron Guard, but, after moving to Paris in 1937, became less extreme in his views.

Another philosopher, **Constantin Noica** (1908–87), spent the last years of his life in nearby Păltiniş. In the 1930s he was a supporter of the Legion of the Archangel Michael, better known as the Iron Guard, although he retreated to the mountains to translate detective stories; in 1949 he was arrested (supposedly for writing a study of Goethe) and exiled to Cîmpulung Muscel, and from 1958 to 1964 he was imprisoned (for writing to Cioran, and in effect for "Letters to a Distant Friend", which Cioran published as a reply in Paris) – this case contributed to the founding of Amnesty International in 1961. He made his name with "Romanian Philosophical Speech" in 1970, and "The Romanian Sense of Being" in 1978. In 1974 he settled in a one-room cabin in Păltiniş, where he was visited by a growing circle of disciples.

Noica remains an ambivalent figure. With a Platonic distrust of democracy and a fascination with "the Romanian soul" and with "pure" intellectual rigour, he preferred to criticize Western decadence rather than Ceauşescu's dictatorship, and his admirers included both prominent supporters and opponents of the regime. A romantic nationalist, he was opposed to materialist ideologies and saw culture as the only means of survival for a people's soul. Since 1989 his influence has been generally positive, but Romanian intellectual life in this century has been tainted by anti-Semitism, and he said little to help counter this.

PĂLTINIŞ (*Hohe Rinne*), at 1442m, is primarily a minor **ski resort**, but also attracts summer hikers. It was founded in 1894 by the *Siebenbürgischer Karpatenverein* (Transylvanian Carpathian Association), the now defunct body which opened up the Romanian Carpathians to tourism and built many of the original *cabana*s. Three or four **buses** a day (#22) come here from the grey TurSib kiosk at the corner of Strada 9 Mai, near the train station in Sibiu – where the Păltiniş travel agency has an office at Str. Tribuniei 3 (☎069/21.52.23) booking villa **accommodation** (①). You should phone directly to book a bed at the *Gasthaus zum Hans* (☎069/21.07.79; ①) or the *Casa Turistilor cabana* (☎069/21.60.01; ①).

The Cindrel and Lotrului mountains

Păltiniş makes a good starting point for walks into the **Cindrel and Lotrului mountains**. It's only two or three hours' walk north, predominantly downhill, through the **Cheile Cibinului** (Cibin gorges), past Lake Cibin, to the *Fîntînele cabana*, following the red dots beyond the *Casa Turistilor*. From here you can push on in a couple of hours either to **Sibiel** village (see p.163) following blue dots, or direct to Sibiel rail halt following blue crosses.

However, the route barely takes you above the tree-line, so if you are keen, it would be worth while trying some **longer hikes** of two or three days. One two-

---

RECYCLED BUSES

The tram line from Sibiu's Pădurea Dumbrava station to Răşinari closed when the vehicles finally wore out. It seemed to be totally derelict, but, surprisingly, re-opened in 1994. This was made possible by the provision of **cast-off trams** from Geneva, which now trundle to and fro, still bearing French-language adverts. Similarly, the **trolleybuses** of line #T1, which run from Sibiu's train station to its tram station, Pădurea Dumbrava, were donated by the city of Lausanne, and buses to Cisnădie still carry *Berliner Morgenpost* adverts. Similarly, many of the express buses to central Bucharest from Otopeni airport are Genevan cast-offs, while many of the airside buses are of German origin, as the handling agent has set up a joint venture with Lufthansa.

These are only the most obvious examples of a trend seen throughout Romania. Foreign ambulances are common too and the vast majority of **buses** running all over the country are east German cast-offs – the east German towns having acquired the west German cast-offs. Now a second wave of buses is arriving in Romania as the east German towns throw them out too and invest in their own new buses.

---

day route south, marked with red triangles, leads via the *Gîtu Berbecului cabana* (2–3hr) and a forestry road along the Sadu valley and the Negovanu Mare (2135m) in the Lotrului mountains to Voineasa in the Lotru valley. If you take this route you will need to camp, but the more popular route is to the west, into the Parîng mountains, east of **Petroşani** (see p.176), which has well-spaced *cabana* accommodation. This second route, indicated by red stripes, follows a mountain ridge to the *Cînaia* refuge (5–6hr) and then continues over open moorland (poorly marked with red stripes and red crosses – be careful not to lose your way) to the *Obîrsia Lotrului cabana* (another 9–10hr), at the junction of the north–south DN67C and the east–west DN7A, both unsurfaced and open only to forestry traffic. This is the gateway to the **Parîng mountains**, an alpine area with beautiful lakes; the red crosses continue up to the main ridge, from where red stripes lead you west to Petroşani.

The Mărginimea Sibiului and Sebeş

West of Sibiu, the DN1/7 and the rail line pass through the **Mărginimea Sibiului** (Borders of Sibiu) towards Sebeş. This area is fairly densely populated, mostly by Romanians rather than Saxons, with a lively folklore recorded in small ethnographic museums in most villages. There are many sheep-raising communities here and you'll see many flocks of sheep on the move, with donkeys carrying the shepherds' belongings. Although the shepherds are notoriously well off in this area and could easily afford four-wheel-drive vehicles, most prefer to keep to the old ways. *Personal* **trains** between Sibiu to **Sebeş** halt a short distance from several settlements en route.

The first of the accessible villages, reached from Sibiu by *personal* trains and bus #20 (hourly), is **CRISTIAN**, where a double wall protects the fourteenth-century Saxon church of Grossau, with its massive towers. Since 1752, the village has in fact been largely dominated by an Austrian Protestant population, who fled here to avoid Catholic oppression. The *Spack* (☎069/55.92.62; ③), just north of the train station at Str. II 9, is a good, clean hotel owned by a Saxon family.

The main road passes to the north of all of the villages after Cristian, and some of the train stations – notably those for Sălişte and Tilişca – are several kilometres north of the villages they serve, which makes using public transport slightly problematical here. ORLAT, with its medieval castle ruins, is about 6km south of Cristian, on a minor road off the main DN1/7 and is served by buses (to Gura Râului) as well as by the *personal* trains. About 4km west by road, and 3km from its train station, is SIBIEL, a sheep-raising community with a strong tradition of witchcraft. Perhaps understandably, witches and ghosts are more feared for their attacks on livestock than on people. The villagers blow horns to prevent witches (*strigoi*) from stealing their ewes' milk on St George's Day, but also credit witches with occasional good deeds, such as magically shutting the jaws of wolves intent on ravaging their flocks. In Sibiel you'll find lovely **paintings on glass** among the collection of peasant art in the local museum, next to the eighteenth-century Orthodox church; from here a footpath leads uphill past a ruined citadel to the *Fîntînele cabana* and through the Cibin gorges to Păltiniş in eight hours (see p.161).

Continuing north from Sibiel, the road meets the route east back to the main DN1/7 at SĂLIŞTE, famous for its peasant **choir**, which give concerts in the community centre here, and for its co-operative produced carpets and embroidered costumes, the latter worn during Sălişte's **Meeting of the Youth Festival** (December 24–31). From a distance, the village church could almost be Saxon, but it is in fact firmly Orthodox. Just beyond it, on Piaša Eroilor, is the **ethnographic museum**, which can only be visited by booking a day ahead (☎069/55.30.86). The Sălişte **motel** is 6km west of the village on the DN1/7. Costumes are more likely to appear during the course of everyday life at TILIŞCA, about 3km west of Sălişte. This is an older, less spoilt, settlement than Sălişte and can trace its origins back to a Dacian settlement on nearby Cătănaş Hill, site of an unremarkable ruined fort.

North of Sălişte, the main road takes a direct route west through the attractive village of **Apoldu de Sus** (Grosspold), also settled by Austrian *Landlers* in 1752, while the railway crawls through beautiful oakwoods, loops south around Apoldu de Sus, and passes through the Hungarian village of **Apoldu de Jos** (Kisapold). Road and rail are reunited at MIERCUREA SIBIULUI (Reussmarkt), a village whose name derives from the Romanian word for Wednesday, the traditional market day – there is still a market here on this day. In the centre of the village is a small, well-preserved thirteenth-century basilica, fortified like other Saxon churches during the fifteenth century. Trains and buses also stop 5km further on at BĂILE MIERCUREA, a modest spa resort with a tourist *cabana* and run-down campsite. A few cabins stand a few kilometres west, at the junction to CÎLNIC (Kelnek), 3km south of the DN1/7, where a massive keep, built around 1300, and a very simple Romanesque chapel of the same period, are enclosed within two rings of walls that resisted several Turkish sieges. Work is under way to restore the castle and open it to visitors; local trains halt at Cut, just northwest of the road junction.

Sebeş

The town of SEBEŞ grew up on the proceeds of the leather-working industry, trading mainly with Wallachia; as *Mühlbach* it was the capital of the *Unterwald*, the westernmost zone of Saxon settlement. In 1438 the Turkish army arrived, demanding that the town be surrendered. A number of inhabitants refused, barricading themselves in one of the towers of the **citadel**, which the Turks stormed and burned. The only survivor, a student aged sixteen, was then sold as a slave at Adrianople (now Edirne), but escaped twenty years later to write *Of the Religion, Manners and Infamies of the Turks* – a bestselling exposé of the bogey-men of fifteenth-century Europe; signing himself the "Nameless One of Sebeş"; he was in fact a Dominican monk who died in Rome in 1502. The **Student's Tower** (also known as the Tailors' Tower), at Str. Traian 6, is thus one of the main sights of Sebeş, together with a large **Evangelical Church**, perhaps the finest Gothic church in Transylvania. The original Romanesque basilica was built between 1240 and 1270, a disproportionately large and grand choir was added by 1382, followed by the upper part of the tower in 1664. The choir boasts the best Parleresque statues in Transylvania, as well as a large polychrome altar, dating from 1518. Just to the north stands the cemetery chapel, built in 1400 and now used by the Uniates. A **museum** (Tues–Fri 8am–4pm, Sat 9am–1pm) is housed on the north side of the square in the late fifteenth-century **House of the Voivodes**, where János Zápolyai died in 1540. The museum has material on the local guilds, paintings by the locally born Sava Henšia (1848–1904), and the usual ethnographic display.

The **train station** (Sebeş Alba) and **bus station** are to the east, in the new town. There is little incentive to linger, but should you wish to stay overnight, there's only the *Motel Dacia* (☎& fax 058/73.27.43; ①) just east on the DN1 (offer-ing a good view of the famous *Rîpa Roşie*, the red cliffs to the north of town), and the grotty **campsite** at Băile Miercurea, 16km east. If you are continuing west by road towards Arad and the border, you'll find several **new motels** (②).

SOUTHWESTERN TRANSYLVANIA

Heading west from Mediaş or Sibiu, you soon leave the Saxon part of Transylvania and move into an area where Hungarian influence is more apparent. However, while a Hungarian ruling class lived here for centuries, the peasantry has always been Romanian. Over the course of millennia, the stone-age tribes that once huddled around the caves and hot springs of the Carpathian foothills devel-oped into a cohesive society, whose evolution was largely determined by events in **the southwest** of the region. The stronghold of the Dacian kingdom lay in the centre of the region, in the hills south of **Orăştie**, and these were ultimately con-quered by Roman legions marching up from the Danube through the narrow passes known today as the Eastern Gate (*Poarta Orientală*) and the Iron Gate (*Poarta de Fier*) of Transylvania. The conquerors founded their new capital, **Roman Sarmizegetusa**, in the Haţeg depression, and the city became one of the earliest centres of Romanian culture in Transylvania; it's known for the *haţegana*, a quick dance, and some of Romania's oldest and most charming churches can be found here. To the north, Hungarian churches and castles dominate the main route along the Mureş valley to and from Hungary – **Hunedoara** is the site of the greatest medieval fortress in Romania. **Alba Iulia**, one of the most important towns of this Hungarian-influenced region, is today a centre of Romania's wine industry. By contrast, the smoggy mining towns at the feet of the **Retezat moun-tains**, in the far southwest of Transylvania, belie the beauty of the range, whose peaks feed dozens of alpine lakes, making this perhaps the most beautiful of the Carpathian ranges and deservedly popular with hikers.

Alba Iulia and around

The tension between the Hungarian and Romanian communities is symbolized in **ALBA IULIA**, 14km north of Sebeş, by the juxtaposition of the Roman Catholic and Orthodox cathedrals in the heart of its citadel. This hilltop was fortified by the Romans and then by the Romanians, before the Hungarian ruler, István I, occupied it and created the bishopric of Gyulafehérvár – the Magyar name for Alba Iulia – in the early part of the eleventh century, to consolidate his hold on Transylvania. Only after World War I did the Romanians take over the levers of power here and build their own cathedral.

The Town

Alba Iulia is dominated by its huge citadel, in effect the **upper town**, laid out in the shape of a star. It was here that the declaration of Romanian Unification was made in 1918 and the leaders of the 1784 peasant uprising executed; the citadel also holds the tomb of the Transylvanian warlord, Hunyadi, in the Catholic

Cathedral of St Michael. The **lower town**, east of the citadel, was partly cleared for "rationalization" in Ceauşescu's last years; it's been tidied up but remains less than attractive.

Between 1715 and 1738, twenty thousand serfs under the direction of the Italian architect Visconti built the Vauban-style **citadel**, which was named Karlsburg in honour of the reigning Hapsburg monarch. Imperial levies on the countryside did much to embitter the Romanian peasants, who turned on their (mainly Hungarian) landlords in the 1784 uprising led by Horea, Cloşca and Crişan. After the uprising had been crushed, Horea and Cloşca were tortured to death, a martyrdom commemorated by an obelisk standing before the richly carved Baroque main gateway (above which is Horea's death-cell). Crişan cheated the excecutioner by committing suicide. To the south of the gateway, the Trinity church is a modern wooden structure, in traditional Romanian style.

Within the citadel, the exhaustive **Museum of Unification** (Tues–Sun 10am–5pm) embodies the credo that Romania's history has been a long search for national unity. Exhibits glorify the Wallachian prince, **Michael the Brave**, who briefly united Wallachia, Transylvania and Moldavia under his crown in 1600. In a fit of pique, the Magyars later demolished his Coronation Church, so, unsurprisingly, the Romanians built a vast new **Orthodox Cathedral** in 1921, in which King Ferdinand and Queen Marie were crowned the next year. The neo-Brîncovenesc cloister through which you enter belies the medieval style of the cathedral, filled with neo-Byzantine frescoes, including portraits of Michael and his wife Stanca. In the ornate marble **Unification Hall** facing the museum, the Act of Unification between Romania and Transylvania was signed on December 1, 1918, as the Austro-Hungarian Empire commenced its death throes.

The Catholic **St Michael's Cathedral** on the south side of Strada Mihai Viteazu testifies to the Hungarian connection. The foundations of the eleventh-century church have been preserved, as has a superb *Maiestas* carving, now above a blind door in the south aisle. What we see now was mostly built between 1247 and 1256, in Romanesque style, with the Gothic choir added in the fourteenth and fifteenth centuries; of the later accretions, the most notable are the Renaissance Lászó and Váraday chapels, built in 1512 and 1524 respectively. The **tomb of Hunyadi**, the greatest of Transylvania's warlords (see p.346), is the middle one of the three to the right of the west door; a century after his death the tomb was vandalized by the Turks, still bitter at their defeats at his hands. Having been neglected for much of this century, the cathedral is currently under restoration, and this won't be finished before the end of the century. If the cathedral is closed, ask for the key at the Bishop's Palace, flanking the gate to the new town. To the south of the Catholic cathedral stands the former **Princely Palace**, where the Transylvanian Diets met between 1542 and 1690.

Practicalities

Everything of practical importance is found in the **lower town**. Alba Iulia's **bus and train stations** are 2km south of the centre on Str. Republicii (DN1), reached by bus #18 (pay on board). Strada Iaşilor, parallel to the DN1, makes a pleasant walk from the stations into town; turn left at the police station and post office for the citadel. **Accommodation** is limited and pricey. The *Parc* hotel, at Str. Primăverii 4, on the Parc Central (☎058/81.17.55, fax 81.21.30; ⑦) is the most modern in town but it is not particularly grand; VISA cards are accepted and

there's cable TV. Nearby at Piața Iuliu Maniu 22 is the *Transilvania*
(☎058/81.25.42, fax 81.11.95; ACR; ⑤), which only has twins; it also houses the
tourist office. The *Cetate*, in the new town to the west at Str. Unirii 3
(☎058/81.17.80, fax 83.15.01; ACR; ⑥), is slightly more expensive although a few
rooms only have communal showers, but credit cards are accepted here and
there are a few triple rooms. The only budget option is the *Motel Dîntre Sălcii* (③)
2km south of the bus and train stations on the DN1. The only alternative to the
hotel restaurants is the aptly named *Fast Food* by the *Parc* hotel.

Around Alba Iulia

Many of the small towns around Alba Iulia also bear witness to the centuries of
Hungarian rule. You may prefer to avoid the polluted atmosphere of Zlatna, but
Teiuș and **Aiud** have a pleasant ambience and are probably the best examples of
the Hungarian influence in this area; **Blaj** is of historical interest as the cradle of
Romanian Nationalism. The area is easily visited on public transport: there are
buses more or less hourly heading into the Apuseni highlands and good train
links to Teiuș, Blaj, and Aiud.

Teiuș

Fifteen kilometres north along the main DN1 from Alba Iulia, through the wine
country where white Fetească and sparkling Spumos are produced, is the small
town of **TEIUȘ** (Tövis), best known as a rail junction on the main Cluj–Sighișoara
line. Few travellers leave the station to make the fifteen-minute walk to the centre, although the town has a pleasant village-like atmosphere and there are several notable old **churches** that make the effort worthwhile. Most interesting of
these is the Roman Catholic church, built for János Hunyadi (Iancu de
Hunedoara) in 1449, and rebuilt in 1701–1704 in the same simple Gothic style. It
lies in a tranquil location just north of the town centre (Teiuș, like most Romanian
towns, has a systematized Centru Civic), signposted left off the road to Stremț
and Rîmeț. Coming from the station, you'll also pass an early seventeenth-century Uniate church, boasting fine Byzantine-style paintings.

Blaj

Twenty-five kilometres east of Teiuș on the DN14b to Sighișoara, the small town
of **BLAJ** stands at the junction for the rail branch to Sovata and Praid (see p.179)
and the main Sighișoara–Odorheiu Secuiesc line; the town itself lies about 1km
east of the train station. Blaj's main claim to fame is its historical status as the ark
of Romanian Nationalism. When Hungary revolted against the Hapsburgs in
1848, Magyar demands to reincorporate Transylvania within the "lands of
Stephen" provoked a famous Romanian response. Forty thousand Romanians,
mostly serfs, were summoned by the leader of the revolt, Avram Iancu, to Blaj,
headquarters of the **Uniate Church** (see box). They gathered on the **Field of
Liberty** (*Cîmpul Libertății*), east of the town, to demand equal political rights,
chanting "No decision about us, without us" (*"nimic despre noi fără noi"*). This
event is remembered by a semi-circle of statues in the Field of Liberty park, east
of the town centre.

From the north east corner of the Field of Liberty, a gap in the fence leads to a
small market and then up an alleyway to the corner of Piața 1848 and Strada Astra;
to the left is the **cathedral**, overshadowing the field. This was built in 1749–79,

THE UNIATE CHURCH

In 1596 the Austrian government persuaded the Orthodox Church in Galicia (now southern Poland and Ukraine) to accept the authority and protection of the Vatican, hoping to detach them from eastern, and above all Russian, influences and to tie them more firmly to the western fold. Thus was born the **Uniate Church**, also known as the Catholic Church of the Eastern Rite, or the Greco-Catholic Church. However, the new Church failed to attract most Romanian Orthodox believers, and was further marginalized when Romania's Orthodox Church gained autonomy in the 1920s; even so its leading figures exercised great influence. At the end of the eighteenth century the *Scuola Ardeleana* (Transylvanian School), a group of clerics and teachers in Blaj, played a key role in making Romanian a literary language, revitalizing Romanian culture and instilling a sense of nationhood into the Romanian people. The Uniate Church stood for independence of thought and self-reliance, as opposed to the more hierarchical and conformist Orthodox Church, so the Communist regime called its million-plus adherents "agents of imperialism" and forcibly merged them with the Orthodox Church, confiscating the Uniate church. Uniates remained a harassed and often imprisoned minority, with no status under the 1948 and subsequent constitutions (although these recognized the existence of fourteen other denominations or "cults"), until the overthrow of Communism.

The Uniates accept four key points of Catholic doctrine: the *Filioque* clause in the creed (according to which the Holy Spirit proceeds from the Father and the Son, as opposed to the Orthodox doctrine by which the Holy Spirit proceeds only from the Father); the use of wafers instead of bread in the mass; the doctrine of Purgatory (unknown in the East); and, above all, the supremacy of the pope. All the other points of difference – the marriage of priests, a bearded clergy, the cult of icons, different vestments, rituals and usages – remain identical to Orthodox practice.

In certain areas, such as Maramureş, there is now a considerable revival in the fortunes of the Uniate Church, although hopes that it can again revitalize the country as it did around 1800 under the *Scuola Ardeleana* appear misplaced. The Iliescu government also supported, and was supported by, the Orthodox Church, and the Uniates have found it a long hard struggle to even reclaim their buildings.

making it the first Baroque building in Transylvania – the church of Lugoj (Banat) was begun later, in 1759, but completed in 1766. It's a large echoing building, its east end shut off by a huge iconostasis, dating from 1760. Across the square in the bishop's palace at Str. Petru Pavel Aron 2, the **History Museum** has coverage of the 1848 gathering, and of the many intellectuals (notably Samuil Micu-Klein, Gheorghe Şincai and Petru Maior) who taught in the high school (*liceu*; and are remembered by plaques there) at the end of the eighteenth century, when they reinvigorated Romanian culture and led the fight against Hungarian chauvinism.

The only place to stay in town is its one hotel, the *Tîrnavele* (☎058/71.19.50; ⑤), at B-dul Republicii 1, right in the centre.

Aiud

Back on the DN1, 11km north of Teiuş, is **AIUD** (Nagyenyed), an attractive town despite the grim reputation of its prison, which was used to hold Soviet spies during World War II and former Iron Guardists after the Communist takeover. From the **train station** it's a fifteen-minute walk to the centre – head up Strada Coşbuc, just to the left of the station, and after the stadium turn right then left past the prison to the bus station on Strada Băilor. The town's centre has one of the oldest **fortresses** in Transylvania, dating back to 1302, and still boasting a full ring of walls and eight towers. It shelters two Hungarian churches and a **History Museum** (Tues–Sun 9am–5pm); there's a **Natural Sciences Museum** (Tues–Sun 10am–5pm) across the road in the Bethlen College. Behind the fortress, the turn-of-the-century **Industrial School** rises up like a huge Renaissance palace.

The town's only **hotel**, the *Mureşul*, is at Str. Transilvania 3 (☎058/86.18.20; ①), or there's a **campsite**, *Căprioara*, 5km south of town on the DN1.

Orăştie, Deva and Hunedoara

South of Alba Iulia, in the mountains between Timişoara and Sibiu, are a number of **Dacian citadels**, the most interesting of them accessible from **Orăştie**, a quiet town 38km southwest of Sebeş on the main road and rail line west towards Timişoara and Arad. There are also two striking medieval structures in this part of Transylvania: the ruined fortress on the Hill of the Djinn, overlooking **Deva**, and the huge, practically undamaged, Gothic castle, with a later Renaissance wing, of the Corvin family at **Hunedoara**. Deva lies east beyond Orăştie on the main road and rail lines, while Hunedoara is accessible by rail from the Simeria station on that same line, or by bus from Deva. The Dacian citadels, however, are further off the beaten track and you'll have to walk or hitch to reach them.

Orăştie and around

ORĂŞTIE is the jumping-off point for the Dacian citadels and a pleasant small town in which to break a journey through the Mureş valley. From the train station, 3km west of the town, trains are met by buses for the town centre (buses back are from stops along the DN1/7 and are not so reliable, so you'll need to allow a bit more leeway). Heading into town, buses turn right by several bank offices; get off here and follow Strada Armatei south to Piaţa Victoriei, dominated by a 1930s Orthodox cathedral, and the main street, Strada Bălcescu. The town **museum** (Tues–Sun 10am–5pm), at Piaţa Aurel Vlaicu 1, whose exhibits include Dacian relics, is off Strada Bălcescu to the right, as is the old **citadel**, with large German Evangelical and Hungarian Reformed churches crammed close together, and some interesting old stonework now being excavated.

There are two **hotels** in town, both on Str. Bălcescu – the *Dacia* at no. 5 (☎054/64.73.81; ②), with cold water but a good *cofetaria* next door for breakfast, and the *Mini-Hotel* (☎054/64.15.74; ③) at no. 36, a good private guesthouse which offers a sauna, table tennis and safe parking, as well as non-stop hot water. There are also half a dozen cabins attached to the *Poieniţa popas* restaurant, just over 1km west of town on the DN7.

Four buses a day head 11km north to the spa town of **GEOAGIU–BĂI** where there's the choice of the *Hotel Diana* (☎054/64.82.80, fax 64.81.95; ②) *cabana*s, villas or camping space.

Cetatea Costeşti and Sarmizegetusa

Cetatea Costeşti, the first of the **Dacian citadels**, is south of Orăştie along the Grădiştie valley. Six buses a day cover the 17km to the village of Costeşti, but from there you'll have to continue on foot for about 1km to the *Popas Salcîmul* campsite and *Costeşti cabana*, then a further 3km west to the citadel – cross the river at the bridge and turn right past the sign to the citadel, then left at the junction and sharp left at the farm to reach the three rows of earthworks grazed by cows and surrounded by birch and cherry trees.

The largest of the citadels, **Sarmizegetusa**, lies deeper into the mountains, about 8km from Costeşti – you'll have to walk or hitch if you don't have your own transport. Continue south along the valley road from Costeşti through the hamlet of **Grădiştea de Munte** and on a further 8km over the roughest stretch of the road. Sarmizegetusa, situated 1200m above sea level and covering an area of 3.5 hectares, was the Dacian capital from the first century BC to 106 AD. It requires some imagination now to conjure up a picture of the citadel from the weathered walls and stumps of pillars that remain, but it's clear that Sarmizegetusa was divided into two distinct quarters: the citadel, used as a refuge by people from the surrounding residential areas during times of war, and four religious sanctuaries where ritual sacrifices to Zamolxis, Gebeleizis and Bendis – the deities of the Earth, Heavens and Hunting – were performed. (Grădeştii mountain was considered sacred by the Dacians, who called it *Kogaion*.) The Romans, shrewd imperialists, rebuilt Sarmizegetusa after its capture in 106 AD, stationed a detachment of the IV Legion here and appropriated the shrines, rededicating them to Diana and other members of their pantheon. The Roman capital was southwest of here, near the modern town of Sarmizegetusa – and took its name from the Dacian citadel.

Deva

The county capital, **DEVA**, 30km west of Orăştie, is gathered around a citadel, built during the thirteenth century and transformed into one of Transylvania's strongest fortifications on the orders of the warlord, Hunyadi. The **citadel** crowns a volcanic hill in the shape of a truncated cone – supposedly the result of a stupendous battle between the djinns (spirits) of the Retezat mountains and of the plain, hence the fort's old nickname, the "citadel of the Djinn". Although the mason charged with building it reputedly immured his wife in its walls in order to guarantee his creation's indestructability, the citadel was destroyed in 1849, when the magazine blew up after a four-week siege by Hungarian rebels, leaving only the ramparts and barracks standing. The tough 184-metre climb to the citadel is rewarded with views over the Mureş valley – which enters a defile between the Metaliferi and Poiana Rusca mountains near Deva.

In the park at the bottom of the hill, the seventeenth-century *Magna Curia* palace of Voivode Gábor Bethlen, under whom Deva was briefly capital of Transylvania, now contains a **museum** (Tues–Sun 9am–5pm) exhibiting archeological finds from the Orăştie mountains. The adjacent building houses a natural history museum, and there's a tiny art gallery in the prefecture opposite, on the corner of Strada Avram Iancu. Head down Strada Avram Iancu to the Orthodox cathedral of Sf Nicolae, built in 1893. To the north on Strada Progesului is the Franciscan church, built by a group of Bulgarian Catholics who arrived here in 1710, fleeing Turkish persecution; the Bulgarians have now vanished and the church has been taken over by the local Hungarian Catholics.

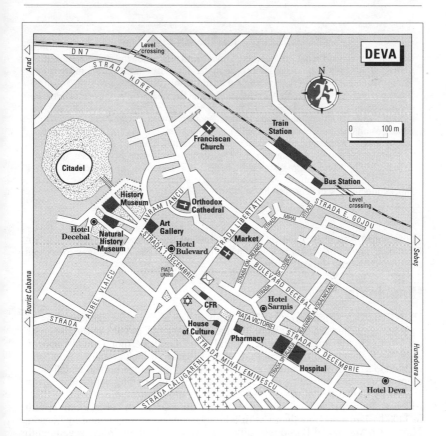

Practicalities

All **trains** on the main line from Arad stop at Deva, making it a good place to pick up services to Budapest or the further corners of Romania. From the well-run **bus station**, next to the train station, services leave every half-hour for Hunedoara (hourly at weekends), and for the Apuseni mountains. The town centre is just five minutes south along Strada Libertății.

If you're planning on stopping overnight, there are several **hotels** in town. The *Bulevard* (☎054/21.19.76; ⑤) is at Str. 1 Decembrie 16, on the semi-pedestrianized main street; it's somewhat tatty and poorly run. To the south of the citadel is the *Decebal* (☎054/21.24.93, fax 21.92.45; ④) at Str. 1 Decembrie 37A, a good modern hotel with dated decor. To the east of the centre stand the new *Deva* at Str. 22 Decembrie 110 (☎054/21.12.90, fax 21.58.73; ACR; ⑤) and the *Sarmis* on Piața Victoriei (☎054/21.47.31, fax 21.58.73; ACR; ⑤), both run by the same management and somewhat pretentious. In addition, Strada Aurel Vlaicu leads 5km south to the *Căprioara cabana*, a good base for walks in the Poiana Rusca hills.

The only **restaurants** are in the hotels: the *Castelo* pizzeria (7am–midnight) on the corner of Str. 1 Decembrie and Str. Aurel Vlaicu, is more of a snack bar.

THE FESTIVAL OF THE CĂLUŞARI

Around the second week of January, Deva hosts the colourful **Festival of the Căluşari** (*Căluşerul Transilvănean*), seen by few foreigners. Ensembles from Wallachia and southern Transylvania perform the intricate dances and rituals originally devised to ensure good harvests and dispel the *Rusalii* – the spirits of departed friends or relations, who, according to Romanian folklore, would take possession of the living should any of the taboos associated with the Week of Rusalii (following Whitsun) be violated. The only cure was exorcism by a group of *Căluşari*, led by a *vătaf* who knew the secrets of magic charms. The rite was also intended to promote fertility, and in the old days the dancers (all male) were accompanied by a mute who wore a huge red phallus beneath his robes and muttered lewd invocations. Under Communism such antics were discouraged and the mute carried a more innocuous wand covered in rabbit-fur.

There's also *Max Fast Food* in the front half of the former synagogue on Str. Libertăţii. The *Calul Balan* is a very basic beer hall on Str. Avram Iancu between the prefecture and the cathedral.

Hunedoara

HUNEDOARA (*Eisenmarkt*), 16km south of Deva, would be dismissed as an ugly, smoggy, inudstrial town were it not also the site of **Corvin Castle**, the greatest fortress in Romania. The travel writer, Patrick Leigh Fermor, found its appearance "so fantastic and theatrical that, at first glance, it looks totally unreal". It's moated to a depth of 30m and approached by a narrow bridge upheld by tall stone piers, terminating beneath a mighty barbican, its roof bristling with spikes, overlooked by multitudes of towers, "some square and some round and all of them frilled with machicolations". Founded during the fourteenth century and rebuilt in 1453 by Iancu de Hunedoara, with a Renaissance-style wing added by his son, Mátyás Corvinus, and Baroque additions by Gabriel Bethlen in the seventeenth century, it was extensively (and tastefully) restored between 1965 and 1970. Within, the castle is an extravaganza of galleries, spiral stairways and Gothic vaulting, with an impregnable donjon and a Knights' Hall with rose-coloured marble pillars.

The castle's **museum** relates the achievements of **Iancu de Hunedoara**, the warlord known as János Hunyadi in Hungary. Legend has it that Hunyadi was the illegitimate son of King Sigismund, who gave the castle to Hunyadi's nominal father, Voicu, a Romanian noble, in 1409. Hunyadi, the "White Knight", rose largely by his own efforts – winning victory after victory against the Turks, and devastatingly routing them beneath the walls of Belgrade in 1456. Appointed voivode of Transylvania in 1441, Hunyadi later became regent of Hungary and a kingmaker (responsible for the overthrow of Vlad Dracul and the coronation of the Impaler, see p.384), while his own son, Mátyás Corvinus, rose to be one of Hungary's greatest kings.

From the train and bus stations it's a twenty-minute walk south to the castle: turn right onto the main road, Bulevardul Republicii, heading into the town centre, and right onto Bulevardul Libertăţii until you reach a bridge on the right; cross over the bridge and follow the signs for the remaining five-minute walk to the castle.

Practicalities

Once you've seen the castle there's no reason to remain in Hunedoara except to break your journey. The *Hotel Rusca* at B-dul Dacia 10 (☎054/71.20.01; ③) is one of the country's best one-star **hotels**, conveniently situated five minutes south of the station, or there's the private *Termoreț* at Str. Ștefan cel Mare 1 (☎054/71.24.49; ④), well south of the centre near the market. The *Cinciș* motel with cabins stands on the shore of Lake Teliuc, 14km southwest of Hunedoara and served by buses to Toplița, Hășdău, Lunca Cernii and other villages in the Poiana Rusca hills.

Around Hațeg

Fifteen kilometres southeast of Hunedoara is **HAȚEG**, the gateway to Transylvania's greatest Roman remains and one of the most convenient approaches to the Retezat mountains. To reach the ruins at **Roman Sarmizegetusa** you should continue by bus towards Caransebeș, Reșița or Timișoara. In addition to the ruins, you'll find a number of interesting **Romanesque churches** in the area immediately around Hațeg, all of which are reasonably well served by local buses from the terminal at Str. Caragiale 14, off the Caransebeș road by the market. There's no real reason to stop here if you're heading on to Sarmizegetusa and the mountains, but if you do need **accommodation**, the only hotel in town is the small, private *Belvedere* (☎054/77.76.04; ②), at the Abator bus stop on Strada Progesului, the main road south.

The Romanesque churches

Northwest of Hațeg, and west of Silvașu de Jos off the Hunedoara road, is **Prislop Monastery** – at the head of the Silvașului valley in the foothills of the Poiana Ruscă mountains. Founded in 1400, this is one of the oldest monasteries in Romania, but it is remarkably little known and very tranquil. **CĂLAN**, on both the rail line and the DN66 north, seems, at first sight, to be little more than an ugly steel-making town; however, there is a more pleasant spa (dating from Roman times) across the river to the east, with the lovely twelfth-century frescoed **church of Streisîngeorgiu** on its southern fringe. A couple of kilometres south of Călan, a similar church at **STREI** dates from the thirteenth century and has fine fourteenth-century frescoes.

Four kilometres south of Hațeg is **SÎNTĂ MĂRIA-ORLEA**, site of another late thirteenth-century church, which marks the transition from the Romanesque to Gothic style and has a fine collection of fourteenth-century murals; from the tower there's a great view of the Retezat range. Twelve kilometres west of Hațeg, in **DENSUȘ**, a very strange little church has been cannibalized from the mausoleum of a fourth-century Roman army officer – most of what you see dates from the early thirteenth century, with frescoes from 1443. The south aisle is now open to the elements, but otherwise the interior is dark and gloomy, with a massive construction in the centre to support the tower's weight. Ask at no. 15 on the main road, east of the statue of the etymologist Ovid Densușianu, for someone to let you in.

Roman Sarmizegetusa and the Iron Gate of Transylvania

SARMIZEGETUSA, 17km southwest of Hațeg, is the site of one of the key Roman settlements. Having forced the Iron Gate (see below), the Roman legions led by Trajan marched northeast to subdue the Dacian citadels in the Orăştie mountains. Within a few years they had founded towns, most notably Colonia Ulpia Traiana, to which the name of the old Dacian capital, Sarmizegetusa, was later appended. Today, the town has a **motel** (☎054/77.73.60; ②) and **campsite** and serves as a starting point for the road to the Gura Zlata dam; but its fame still derives from the **Roman ruins** nearby, whose excavated portions are only part of the original town, which contained a citadel measuring some 700m long by 500m wide. You can see the remains of the forum, the palace of the Augustales where priests were trained, and the elliptical brick and stone amphitheatre where gladiatorial combats and theatrical spectacles were staged. The **museum** (Tues–Sun 10am–5pm) exhibits artefacts and stonework finds, and avoids mentioning the likelihood that most of the glorified "Roman" colonists believed to have interbred with the Dacians to create the ancestors of today's Romanians were actually of Greek or Semitic origin.

Even if you have no luck with onward buses it's only about 6km from Sarmizegetusa to Zeicani village at the entrance to the **Iron Gate of Transylvania** (*Poarta de Fier a Transilvanei*), a narrow pass 700m above sea level. A monumental mace erected near Zeicani commemorates the defeat of 80,000 Turks by 15,000 Transylvanians under the command of Hunyadi in 1442. Further up the pass, in 106 AD, the Dacians had their fateful clash with the Romans; as recorded by Roman scribes, this battle was a disaster for the Dacians – their forces were crushed, and their ruler Decebal committed suicide rather than be ignominiously paraded through the streets of Rome. The pass itself is 10km long, and accessible by road (DN68), but rail services aren't resumed until the mining village of Bouţari on the far side so you'll either have to hitch or walk across this stretch if you're travelling by train.

The Retezat mountains

Road and rail routes southeast from Haţeg skim the northern reaches of the **Retezat mountains**. Although access is slightly harder here than in the other Transylvanian mountain ranges, with longer walks in to the central peaks, the Retezat massif offers full recompense. Whereas in the Făgăraş or Piatra Craiului you find yourself for the most part following a ridge walk, with little opportunity to step aside and view the summits from a distance, here you'll find yourself surrounded by well-defined peaks, often reflected in clear alpine lakes. There is a large network of routes, so you'll meet fewer hikers and have a better chance of seeing **wildlife** such as chamois and eagles. The northwestern part of the massif is a scientific reserve; Ceauşescu treated this as a private hunting reservation, but it is now being properly managed again – entry is allowed only with express permission.

Approaches to the mountains

There are three main approaches to the Retezat – from Roman Sarmizegetusa by a 20km road to the Gura Apei dam on the west side of the massif, from various points along the Subcetate to Petroşani road and rail line to the northeast, and from the West Jiu valley to the south. The road to the Gura Apei dam starts from the village of **Rîu de Mori**, a two-hour walk east from Roman Sarmizegetusa or a

bus ride from Haţeg. From Rîu de Mori it's at least a three-hour walk south along the Rîul Mare valley to the **Gura Zlata cabana**, the point from which to strike out for the high peaks.

Another possible angle of attack is from the northeast, along tracks and roads leading from villages along the rail line between Subcetate and Petroşani. From **Ohaba de sub Piatră**, it's five and a half hours' walk up to the **Pietrele cabana**. Buses from Haţeg follow the route to the *cabana* as far as Sibişel and Nucşoara, with some even going as far as Cîrnic during the summer, but both the trail and *cabana* are popular and can get quite crowded. Some hikers therefore prefer to start from the campsite at **Pui**, further east along the main road, and trek for six and a half hours up a steep and winding, 23-kilometre-long mountain road to the **Baleia cabana** (see box on p.176 for hikes beyond these *cabana*s).

It's also possible to approach the mountains from the **mining towns of the West Jiu** to the east, but these are grim places surrounded by bleak mountains. The coalfields were first exploited during the eighteenth century and became an environmental disaster area under Ceauşescu: the accident record remains appalling, and the rivers are black with coal dust. The miners are relatively well paid, but their search for adequate compensation for their dire living and working

HIKING IN THE RETEZAT

FROM GURA ZLATA

The most popular hikes start from **Gura Zlata cabana**, south of Sarmizegetusa along the Rîul Mare valley. A succession of coloured symbols – red stripes, blue crosses, red spots, red stripes and then blue triangles – mark successive phases of the trail east from here to the Pietrele *cabana*, going by way of Lake Zănoaga, Lake Tăul Portii and the Bucura Saddle. This is a nine- to ten-hour hike, and it is forbidden to undertake it in winter. The road through Gura Zlata continues 12km south to the "Mouth of the Water", Lake Gura Apei, from whose western extremity well-equipped hikers can follow a trail west across the mountains to the Muntele Mic *cabana* in the vicinity of Caransebeş, or south to Băile Herculane; allow two days for each. Heading east along the reservoir and up the Lăpuşnic valley takes you to either Buta or the Bucura valley in four hours.

FROM CÎMPU LUI NEAG

Also leading to **Buta cabana** are two of the most popular trails from Cîmpu lui Neag in the south of the region. Red crosses mark the quickest route to the *cabana* (6–7hr), which runs through a forest of Douglas firs and up to the La Fete sheepfold, offering great views of the "karst cathedrals" en route. Red triangles indicate the longer trail (10–12hr) to the *cabana*, which goes via the strange formations of the Scocului Jiului gorge, and the plateau of Piatră lui Iorgovan, where you can sometimes spot chamois. A forestry road continues southwest over the watershed from the Jiu valley into the Cerna valley, and on towards **Băile Herculane**, a good two days' walk (see p.308); another path, marked with blue triangles, heads south to **Tismana** in roughly six hours (see p.113).

Buta lies in the **Little Retezat**, the limestone ridge south of the great glacial trough of the Lăpuşnic valley, which has an almost Mediterranean flora and fauna. However, the best hikes take you into the crystalline **Great Retezat** to the north, past serried peaks and alpine lakes. There are two trails into the Great Retezat from the Buta *cabana*; the first, marked by blue stripes, follows a switchback path to **Cabana Pietrele** (7hr), dropping into the Lăpuşnic valley, and leading up past the wonderful lakes of the Bucura valley before coming down from a pass of 2206m past the *Gentiana* club's hut; the second, marked by red stripes then blue triangles, follows a trail to the **Baleia cabana**, going by way of the Bărbat springs and the Ciumfu waterfall (9hr; forbidden during winter).

conditions allowed them to be manipulated into becoming Iliescu's stormtroopers.

Petroşani and beyond

The largest of the mining towns is **PETROŞANI**, served by trains between Simeria and Tîrgu Jiu. The only reason to stop here is to stock up on food before hiking in the Retezat mountains, unless you're particularly interested in the history of the mines, which is related in the **museum** (Tues–Sun 10am–5pm) at Strada Bălcescu 2. If you need to stay overnight, you've a choice of three **hotels**, all on Strada 1 Decembrie, across the footbridge from the train station and south towards the centre. All of the hotels only have hot water for a short time each day; the *Onix* at no. 73 (☎054/54.46.13; ⑦) is nothing special, given its price; the *Tulipan* at no. 88 (☎054/54.35.82; ④) is pretty basic; and the friendly staff at the

Petroşani at no. 110 (☎054/54.44.25, fax 54.53.83; ACR; ⑤) make this last hotel the best choice of the three. Five kilometres south of town is the *Gambrinus* motel while the *Rusu Cabana* lies to the east, near the chair lift into the Parîng mountains. There's a **restaurant** in the *Petroşani* and a pizzeria and supermarket opposite the *Tulipan*.

Most people heading for the Retezat mountains push straight on to the *cabana*s at Vulcan and Lupeni in the West Jiu valley; both of which can be reached by train from Petroşani. From Lupeni a few buses continue up the valley to CÎMPU LUI NEAG, where there is a very basic tourist chalet and motel (②) and from where there are some good hikes into the mountains (see box on p.176 for hikes from here). From Petroşani, the main road and railway follow the Jiu valley south to Tîrgu Jiu, cutting through a scenic cleft between the Vîlcan and Parîng mountains and passing **Lainici**, whose motel (②) stands near a fine nineteenth-century monastery. This stretch of railway, which goes through thirty tunnels, was built by political prisoners in the 1940s.

THE SZÉKELY LAND AND THE EASTERN CARPATHIANS

In the ethnic patchwork of Transylvania, the eastern Carpathians are traditionally the home of the **Székely** (pronounced "Saik-aihy"), a people closely related to the Magyars who speak a distinctive Hungarian dialect and cherish a special historical identity. For a long time it was believed that they were the descendants of Attila's Huns – who had entered the Carpathian basin in the fifth century, five hundred years before the Magyar conquest. There are traces of Central Asian shamanism in the Székely arts and crafts, and their ancient runic alphabet is similar to that of the Turkic nomads of western China. However, most modern historians and ethnographers believe that the Székely either attached themselves to the Magyars during the latter's long migration from the banks of the Don, or are simply the descendants of early Hungarians who pushed ever further into Transylvania, having been assigned the task of guarding the frontiers by King László in the twelfth century. Whatever the truth of their origins, the Székely feel closely akin to the Magyars who, in turn, regard them as somehow embodying the finest aspects of the ancient Magyar race, while also being rather primeval – noble savages, perhaps.

The Székely retained a nomadic, clan-based society for longer than their Magyar kindred, and were granted a large measure of autonomy by the Transylvanian voivodes. They were recognized as one of the three "Nations" of Transylvania during the Middle Ages: privileges that the Hapsburgs attempted to abolish, culminating in the massacre at Madéfalva (1764), which prompted many Székely to flee to Moldavia and Bucovina, where they founded new villages with names such as "God Help Us" and "God Receive Us". Today, their traditional costume is close to that of the Romanian peasants, the chief difference being that Székely men tuck their white shirts in while Romanians wear them untucked and belted.

For visitors, the chief attractions of the region are likely to be the **Székely culture** and the scenery. Religion plays an important part in Székely life, as shown by the prevalence of their **walled churches**, the fervour displayed at the

Whitsun pilgrimage to Miercurea Ciuc, and the continuing existence of Székely mystics. Traditional Székely **architecture** is well represented throughout the Székely Land (Székelyföld); it is epitomized by blue-painted houses with carved fences and gateways, incorporating a dovecote above, the best examples of which can be found in Corund. The **landscape** gets increasingly dramatic as you move through the Harghita mountains, particularly around the Tuşnad defile and St Anne's Lake to the south, and Lacu Roşu and the Bicaz gorges just before the borders of Moldavia.

Into the Székely Land

This section describes two interconnected routes which head into the Székely Land, starting in Sighişoara and in Braşov. **From Sighişoara** and Odorheiu Secuiesc, the region's western capital, you can either head east to Miercurea Ciuc, the capital of the southern Székely Land, or take a shorter loop to Tîrgu Mureş via Sovata. It is possible to make the approach **from Braşov** by rail; passing first through the showpiece Saxon villages of Hărman and Prejmer (see p.146), the route follows the Olt and Mureş valleys through Sfîntu Gheorghe, Miercurea Ciuc and Gheorgheni, looping around to Tîrgu Mureş or heading east through the Bicaz gorges into Moldavia.

Odorheiu Secuiesc and around

ODORHEIU SECUIESC (Székelyudvarhely) lies 48km east of Sighişoara at the end of the rail line. The town hosts the excellent *Seiche* **festival**, usually on the first Sunday in June; at other times, the main sights of interest are a few minutes south of the bus and train stations.

Turning left out of the bus station on Strada Tîrgului, or right out of the train station on Strada Bethlen, will bring you in a couple of minutes to Strada Horea, which leads south to the fifteenth- and sixteenth-century **citadel**; this now houses an agricultural college, but you can go inside to stroll along the walls. Beyond the citadel, Strada Cetăţii leads to the two squares, **Piaţa Libertăţii** and **Piaţa Márton Arón**, which make up the town centre. Three churches stand in a row here: to the west, the former Franciscan monastery (1712–79), reoccupied by Clarissite nuns since the revolution; on the island between the two squares the Reformed church (1781); and on the hill beyond, the Catholic church of Sf Miklós (1787–93), between the Jesuits' building of 1651 and the huge high school (*liceu*). Beyond the squares, at Str. Kossuth 29, the **museum** (Tues–Fri 9am–4.30pm, Sat & Sun 9am–1pm) has a fine ethnographic collection, with ceramics and Székely funerary posts (*kopjafálva*). The funerary posts, used only in Protestant areas, bear carvings of flowers or the tools of the deceased's trade; some say that the posts hark back to the days when a Magyar warrior was buried with his spear thrust into the grave. At the southern end of town, on the Sighişoara road, is the **Jesus chapel**, one of the oldest buildings in the area, built in the thirteenth century, with a coffered ceiling, a distinguishing feature of Hungarian churches, fitted in 1677.

Other than the *Tîrnava* **hotel**, near the Franciscan church at Piaţa Libertăţii 16 (☎065/21.39.63, fax 21.39.70; ⑤), there is a *Sport-Hotel* (☎065/21.33.77; ②) on Strada Parcului and a spartan **campsite** 3km north at Băile Seiche. The only **restaurant** in town is in the *Tîrnava* hotel.

The Palace of Parliament from B-dul Unirii, Bucharest

The Russian Church, Bucharest

View from the Intercontinental Hotel, Bucharest

Vlad Ţepeş' house, Sighişoara

Dawn from Cozia Cabana, Wallachia

Vineyards, the Danube Valley

The Village Museum, Bucharest

Countryside around Sighişoara

Bran Castle

Wooden church, Bucegi Mountains, Transylvania

Sibiu

Market at Sibiu

Magyar farmers, Transylvania

Around Odorheiu Secuiesc

The Unitarian village of **DÎRJIU** (Székelyderz), 17km southwest of the town, has a particularly fine fortified church with frescoes that date from 1419. As in the Saxon villages, ham and grain are still stored in the church, a tradition dating back to the time when there was the risk of siege. The key to the church is held next door. **MUGENI** (Bögöz) village, 9km west of Odorheiu by road and rail, has a fine fourteenth-century church with valuable frescoes and a coffered ceiling. Continuing west along these routes will bring you to the village of **CRISTURU SECUIESC** (Székelykeresztúr) whose excellent **museum** tells the story of the ceramic industry, established here since 1590. Through buses stop in the main square, but those that terminate here arrive at the bus terminal, which, like the train station, is ten minutes' walk to the east of the main square.

East of Odorheiu Secuiesc, en route to Miercurea Ciuc, are several little resorts with low-key accommodation which are good options for breaking your journey. Four kilometres beyond the town, a badly surfaced road turns north through Brădeşti towards Gheorgheni and the isolated *Harghita-Mădăraş cabana* in the mountains. Back on the DN13A, low-lying **BĂILE HOMOROD** has hot springs and a *cabana* used by Scouts and vacationing Trade Unionists, and both **CĂPÎLNIŢA** and **VLĂHIŢA** have campsites. About 13km beyond Vlăhiţa, at the *Cabana Brădet*, a turning to the north leads up to another resort, **HARGHITA BĂI** (*Hargita-fürdő*), in the beautiful **Harghita mountains**, which has the *Hotel Ozon* (②) and a *cabana*. There are two buses a day up here from Miercurea Ciuc rail station, or it's under an hour's walk from Brădet. These mountains are renowned for their abundant wildlife, including **bears**.

Corund, Praid and Sovata

CORUND (Korond), 25km north of Odorheiu, is famed for its green and brown **pottery**, as well as the cobalt blue introduced by the Germans in the eighteenth century. Corund pottery is for sale at every fair, tourist site and event across Transylvania, but for the best choice you should poke around in the town's backstreet workshops (you might also find some of the carved Székely beamgates painted the traditional red and green) or visit the colourful **market** held every year on the weekend closest to August 10.

For a complete change of atmosphere, push on to **PRAID** (Parajd), 12km to the north and served by local buses from both Odorheiu and Sovata and by the rail branch from Blaj. The **salt mine** at the northern end of the village is still active, and there's also an underground sanatorium for chest complaints. Praid is a popular holiday centre, with **accommodation** in private rooms (①) available from the **tourist office** by the bus stop, a fairly standard **motel** (②) just north, and a basic hotel (①) to the south.

Seven kilometres further north by road and rail is **SOVATA** (Szováta), with the spa of Sovata Băi 2km to the east. This is a **bathing resort**, surrounded by beautiful forests, on the shore of Lacul Ursu (Bear Lake), where a surface layer of fresh water, a metre deep, acts as an insulator keeping the lower, salt water at a constant temperature of 30°–40°C all the year round. The resort's most distinctive feature is the array of wooden buildings that line the main street, Strada Trandafirilor: huge, extravagantly balconied villas, many of which now operate as private hotels, and twee Hansel and Gretel churches.

Frequent local buses to the resort arrive at the **bus station** on Strada Trandafirilor. Of the **private hotels**, the best is *Piroska*, at Str. Trandafirilor 12, on the main road north (☎067/57.73.99, fax 57.87.98; ②). There is an excellent private hotel a few minutes off Strada Trandafirilor; turn left along the track just beyond the strikingly modernist Catholic chapel, which brings you in about ten minutes to the *Tivoli* hotel (☎067/57.84.93, fax 57.04.93; ⑤ half-board), surrounded by woods with deer foraging outside the windows. The track continues to Lacul Tineretului (the Lake of Youth), where you can rent pedalos from the kiosks serving snacks. A short walk north along Strada Trandafirilor brings you to the *Stîna de Vale* campsite, just beyond the edge of town.

Sfîntu Gheorghe and around

SFÎNTU GHEORGHE (Sepsi-Szentgyörgy), thirty kilometres northeast of Braşov, is a drab industrial town and a centre of the Romanian cigarette industry, but following Ceauşescu's demise it has become the heart of the Székely cultural revival. The highlight of the town is the **Székely National Museum** (Tues–Fri 9am–4pm, Sat 9am–1pm, Sun 9am–2pm) at Str. Kós Károly 10, south of the centre (take bus #1 to the central park and walk south along Strada Kós Károly). Built in 1910 to the design of **Kós Károly** (see box), the museum covers the archeology, history and ethnography of the area, focusing on the revolution of 1848–49 (see p.349) and the local figures, such as Kelemen Mikes and Arón Gábor, who played prominent roles in it.

The town centre lies to the north of the museum, focused on the **Piaţa Libertăţii**, with a technical college designed by Kós to the west and the **Arcaded House**, the oldest building in town, to the east. North of the square, beyond the *Bodoc* hotel, Strada Kossuth leads past the Romanian Information Service building and a Kós Károly house (no. 19) to the cobbled Strada Şoimului and the old town, with a fine sixteenth-century walled Reformat **church** at the top of Piaţa Kalvíny. In its cemetery, behind a Székely beamgate raised in 1981, you'll find stone versions of traditional wooden Székely graveposts, together with wooden pillars raised for each class leaving school.

Both **train** and **bus stations** are 2km east of the centre; follow Strada 1 Decembrie 1918 to get to Piaţa Libertăţii. The state **hotel**, the *Bodoc*, in the centre at Strada 1 Decembrie 1918 no. 1 (☎067/31.12.92, fax 31.12.91; ⑥), has partially reopened after earthquake damage. Far better value are two small private hotels, the *Korona* (☎067/32.51.64; ③) opposite the station, which sells good new **maps** of Sfîntu Gheorghe, and the *Consic* (☎067/32.69.84; ②) at B-dul Bălan 31 – bus #5 from the station, or walk north from the BTT office at the junction of B-dul Bălan and Str. 1 Decembrie 1918. This BTT branch (☎067/32.48.69, fax 32.49.36) is particularly active in **agrotourism**, arranging homestays in nearby spas and villages such as Zăbala and Covasna, and even has a hostel planned for Braşov. The only reasonable place **to eat** in town is the vegetarian *Restaurant Tribel* at Strada 1 Decembrie 1918 no. 2. There's a BCR Bancomat on Strada Iorga, on the way to the station.

Ilieni

The old road to Braşov runs down the right (west) bank of the Olt river to Hărman, passing through **ILIENI** (Illyefalva), 9km south of Sfîntu Gheorghe. Buses from Sfîntu Gheorghe to Doboli de Jos halt in the village where the whitewashed **church**, built in 1782–86 and beautifully restored in 1990, dominates the

<hr>

KÓS KÁROLY

Kós Károly (1883–1977) was the leading architect of the Hungarian "national romantic" school, which derived its inspiration from the village architecture of Transylvania and Finland. The Transylvanian style is reflected in the wooden roofs, gables and balconies of his buildings, while the Finnish influence appears in the stone bases and trapezoidal door frames. Fine examples of Kós's work can be seen in Sfîntu Gheorghe and Cluj (notably the Cock Church), as well as in Budapest.

After the separation of Transylvania from Hungary, Kós, a native of Timişoara, was one of the few Hungarian intellectuals to accept the new situation and to choose to remain in Cluj and to play a leading role in Hungarian society in Transylvania. While continuing to work as an architect, he also travelled around Transylvania, recording the most characteristic buildings (of all ethnic groups) in delightful linocuts; these were published in 1929 by the Transylvanian Artists' Guild (co-founded by Kós himself), with Kós's own text outlining the historical influences on Transylvanian architecture. In 1989 an English translation of the book was published by Szépirodalmi Könyvkiadó in Budapest, although the Hungarian edition is well worth having just for the linocuts.

<hr>

whole area from its hilltop. The Reformat priest has also created an ecumenical conference and youth centre at the bottom of the hill, with **accommodation** in the church's defensive towers, a model farm, meat and dairy processing plants, and a children's village in which adult couples live with groups of four orphans, staying together for up to twenty years.

Covasna and around

The rail line east from Sfîntu Gheorghe to Breţcu runs close to **COVASNA** (Kovászna), 30km away, although the DN11 passes well to the north. Known as the "spa of the thousand springs", the Fairies' Valley (*Valea Zînelor*), to the east of town, is always busy with track-suited strollers from the sanatorium, hotel and campsite along its length; from the valley there is easy access to the Vrancea and Penteleu mountains. Buses meet each train to take you the 2km to the modern centre of town, and most continue to the Voineşti hospital in the Valea Zînelor. For access to the mountains, the best place **to stay** is the *Hotel Bradul* (☎067/34.00.81, fax 34.00.30; ②), an excellent modern hotel opposite the hospital. The best value place in the town centre is the *Turist* (☎067/34.05.73; ①) at Str. Gării 2, a small, friendly place with limited facilities, which is close to a group of more modern tourist hotels.

Covasna's main attraction, another kilometre further up the valley, is an amazing inclined plane, built in 1886 as part of Romania's oldest narrow-gauge **forestry rail line**. You can still see waggons of timber from the nearby logging settlement of Comandău being lowered down the 1232-metre slope. At the bottom, the waggons continue by steam train to the main-line transfer sidings in Covasna. Little is now left of the complex 760mm rail system, interconnected by funiculars, which used to serve forestry operations in the mountains of the Carpathian Bend, from the Oituz pass southwards to the Ciucaş mountains, but if you're hiking in this region you will come across its remains.

Covasna's only other claim to fame is as the birthplace of **Sándor Körösi Csomas** (1784–1842), who walked to Central Asia in 1820, visited Tibet from 1827 to 1831, and compiled the first Tibetan–English dictionary; he became the librarian to the Asiatic Society in Calcutta and is now buried in Darjeeling.

Around Covasna

The village of **ZĂBALA** (Zabola), just north of Covasna on the Tîrgu Secuiesc road, boasts a sixteenth-century Székely walled church (at the junction of the road to Surcea) and an arboretum, while **GHELINȚA** (Gelence), on a side road further north, has a walled church dating from around 1300, with a fine fresco. **TÎRGU SECUIESC** (Kezdivásárhely), almost half an hour beyond Covasna and served by trains from Sfîntu Gheorghe, was a major trading centre in medieval times and the first Székely town to be granted a charter in 1427, hence its Romanian name meaning Székely Market. Today Tîrgu Secuiesc is something of a backwater, but of interest as a stronghold of Székely culture; Romanian is little spoken here. From the train and bus stations, at the south end of town, it's about a ten-minute walk along Strada Gării to the central Piața Gábor Arón, lined with sixteenth- and seventeenth-century artisans' houses, one of which (at Curtea 10) contains the **Museum of the Guilds** (Tues–Fri 9am–4pm, Sat 9am–1pm, Sun 9am–2pm). In addition to the history of the guilds (a vehicle for an exposition of Székely culture in general), there are temporary art shows, and a surprisingly good display of over 300 dolls in Magyar and other costumes. If you are looking for somewhere **to stay**, the *Hotel Sarmis* (☎067/36.37.98; ②) opposite the museum at Piața Gábor Arón 9, is small, but friendly, with shared bathrooms and limited hot water. The *Restaurant Bujdosó*, by the park at the southern end of Curtea 33, serves Székely specialities, such as goulash and kohlrabi.

From Tîrgu Secuiesc, and from the end of the rail line at Brețcu, you can continue by bus over the Oituz Pass to Onești in Moldavia, but be warned that three of the four trains from Sfîntu Gheorghe to Brețcu stop in Tîrgu Secuiesc for an hour.

Băile Tușnad and St Anne's Lake

To the north of Sfîntu Gheorghe, the River Olt has carved the beautiful **Tușnad defile**, at the far end of which is **BĂILE TUȘNAD** (Tusnádfürdó), a bathing resort set amid larch and fir woods, with three hotels and a bungalow-campsite, all easily spotted just south of the train station. To the south of the town, at Bixad village, a road leads east to **St Anne's Lake** (Lacu Sf Ana) where there's a *cabana* popular with students. Occupying a volcanic crater on Mount Ciumatu (2hr walk from the Tușnad spa, following blue dot markings), the lake is spectacularly twee and is the site of a fervent **festival** on St Anne's day (July 26). During the 1970s, one festival turned into a nationalist demonstration attended by 6000 Székely; the local Securitate kept this a secret from their superiors, and Ceaușescu reportedly learned of it only because his son Nicu heard the story from a hitchhiker whom he picked up in his Jaguar. Beyond, on the Tîrgu Secuiesc road, are rare peat bogs and the tiny spa of **BĂILE BĂLVÁNYOS**, where there is *cabana*-type accommodation and the *Hotel Carpați* (☎067/36.14.49; ③).

Miercurea Ciuc and around

The industrial city of **MIERCUREA CIUC** (Csíkszereda) is capital of Harghita county, in the southern Székely Land. Its city centre, with the windswept Piața

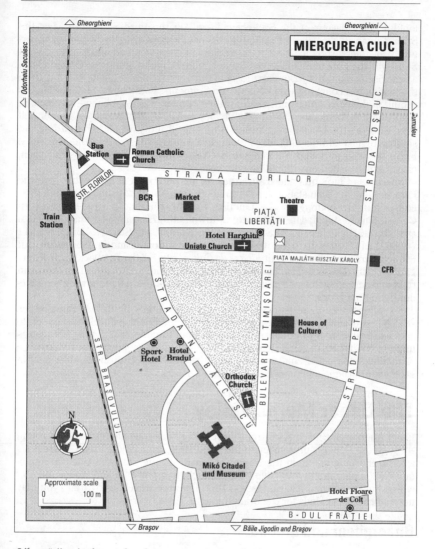

Libertăţii at its heart, has been extensively rebuilt in concrete and aside from the **Mikó citadel**, south of the centre at Str. Gh. Doja 2, there is little of architectural interest here. The citadel was built in 1611–21 and burnt down by the Turks in 1661; it was rebuilt in 1716 to the plans of the Austrian general Stefan Steinville, and now contains an excellent county **museum** (Tue–Sat 9am–5pm, Sun 9am–1pm), which provides information on Székely churches; on its south side is a deracinated row of beamgates overlooking the remains of the moat.

The city's only other attractions are its **Spring Festival** and the annual hallowed **Székely pilgrimage to Şumuleu**, and both are worth the trip if you are looking for a flavour of the Székely culture. On the third Sunday of May, the Spring Festival takes place at Băile Jigodin just south of town, providing an opportunity for the Székely to dress up in traditional costumes and make merry. Whit Sunday is the time of the hallowed Székely pilgrimage to Şumuleu (Csiksomlyó), a Franciscan monastery 2km northeast of the town (buses #21, #40, #41, #42 from the station forecourt towards Păuleni and Şoimeni). Founded in 1442 but largely rebuilt in the early nineteenth century, the complex was established by Iancu de Hunedoara in thanks for the Székely victory at Marasszentimre, commemorated ever since by the black-clad pilgrims who still fill the yard and church interior, singing hymns and queuing up to touch the wooden Madonna in the sanctuary. From the nearby hilltop you can see **Székely villages** dotted across the plain, either whitewashed or with old blue farmsteads.

Miercurea Ciuc's **bus** and **train stations** are both west of the centre, near the Odorheiu road; Ciceu station, one stop north (also bus #22 from the station forecourt, roughly hourly), is the junction for the rail line across the Eastern Carpathians to Adjud. The best **hotel** in town is the *Harghita*, on Piaţa Libertăţii (☎066/11.61.19, fax 11.31.81; ⑤); the *Bradul* at Str. N. Bălcescu 11 (☎066/11.14.93, fax 13.01.81; ①) has its own **restaurant** and is good value, but the real bargain is the excellent *Floare de Colţ,* at Str. Frătiei 7 (☎066/17.20.68, fax 11.25.33; ①). There is also a **campsite** in Băile Jigodin, 2km south on the main road and served by buses #10 and #11; you can walk there by following the blue-dot hiking markings.

Six kilometres northeast of Miercurea Ciuc, served by bus #20 to Bîrzava, lies **DELNIŢA** (Csíkdelne), where there is a fine walled Gothic church with fifteenth-and sixteenth-century murals and a cassette roof fitted in 1673. Three kilometres further, **NICOLEŞTI** (Csíkszentmiklós), also reached by buses from Miercurea Ciuc to Frumoasa and Lunca de Jos, has a lovely walled church on a hill, built in 1498 with Baroque additions dating from the 1770s.

The Upper Mureş valley

From Miercurea Ciuc, a semicircular route, by both road and rail, curves round through the Upper Mureş valley to the great Hungarian city of **Tîrgu Mureş**. It's a leisurely route taking in the tranquil Lacu Roşu, the untamed Căliman mountains and a plethora of attractive villages, including Gurghiu and Hodac, both of which hold renowned festivals (see p.187). If you're travelling by train, you may need to change at Deda for the branch line to Tîrgu Mureş.

Gheorgheni and around

Forty-five kilometres north of Miercurea Ciuc, just beyond the Izvoru Mureşului pass, lies **GHEORGHENI** (Gyergyószentmiklós), jumping-off point for **Lacu Roşu** (see below). The town's **tourist office** is on the south side of Piaţa Libertăţii, the central square, which is ringed with tatty buildings redolent of the era of Austro-Hungarian rule. To the north of the square, on Bulevardul Lacu Roşu, is the splendid *liceu* (high school), completed in 1915, and to the east Strada Márton Arón leads past the Catholic church to the **museum** (Tues–Sat 9am–4.30pm, Sun 9am–1pm) on Piaţa Petöfi. Housed in a former Armenian merchants' inn, and run by a dedicated young couple, the museum contains some fascinating artefacts of both the Székely and Magyar communities, including Székely fenceposts, bark salt-baskets and weatherboards carved with shamanistic motifs brought by the Magyars from Asia. In the garden is a derelict steam locomotive that used to work the narrow-gauge line towards Lacu Roşu. Just to the north of the museum is the church of the Armenian community. Armenians fled here in the seventeenth century to escape Turkish persecution; they are now almost wholly assimilated into the Hungarian population. The church's interior is standard Baroque, but if you would like to look inside, the key can be obtained opposite at Strada Biserica Armeana 4.

Trains arriving at Gheorgheni are met by buses to spare passengers the twenty-minute hike east into the town centre. Getting back to the station is not so easy and you'll probably end up having to walk. The **bus station** is immediately south of the train station, but you can also board eastbound buses on Bulevardul Lacu Roşu in the town centre; there are no buses on the DN13B west.

Gheorgheni's best **hotel** is the *Mureş* (☎066/16.19.04; ④), opposite the Trade Union House of Culture at Bulevardul Frăţiei 5. The cheaper *Szilagyi* hotel (☎066/16.25.91; ②), which has just four twin rooms, four triples and a quad, is on the south side of Piaţa Libertăţii, or try the *SportHotel Avîntul* (①) between the synagogue and a stadium on Str. Bălcescu (the Topliţa road). There's also a **campsite** 4km east of town on the Lacu Roşu road.

The Red Lake

Lacu Roşu (Gyilkos-tó), the **Red Lake**, lies in a small depression 25km east of Gheorgheni. It was formed in 1838 when a landslide dammed the River Bicaz and the tips of a few pines still protrude from the water, which is rich in trout. Surrounded by lovely scenery and blessed by a yearly average of 1800 hours of sunshine, this is an ideal stopover if you're crossing the Carpathians into Moldavia through the wild Bicaz gorges (p.232). It's a popular tourist spot and the target of bus parties from all over Romania. At km26, in the centre of the resort, a track crosses a bridge to the north and climbs to the simple *Bucur* **hotel** (☎066/16.29.49; ②). There's a **campsite**, with cabins, at the eastern end of the resort, although nobody seems to mind if you just pitch camp anywhere. The area has now been designated a national park, and boasts an Eco-Info-Center (Tues–Sun 10am–6pm) on the main road near the lake at the western end of the resort; this has some information on walks and is also leading the way in cleaning up the area and developing green tourism.

Lăzarea

Six kilometres north of Gheorgheni (one stop by train) on the DN12, is the village of **LĂZAREA** (Szárhegy), which is worth a stop to see **Lazăr Castle**, unusually situated just below the Franciscan monastery whose white tower is visible from the station. The fifteenth-century castle's fine Renaissance hall and frescoed facade are being gradually restored by artists who hold a summer camp here each year, sleeping in the monastery cloister. The **castle gallery** (Tues–Sun 9am–5pm) exhibits the work of artists attending the summer camp, and there is also now a well-stocked sculpture park, open all year. The office of *Operation Villages Roumains* (☎ & fax 066/16.14.64), the Belgian charity formed to combat Ceauşescu's systematization plans, can provide further information about their work as well as details of homestay schemes in the area.

Topliţa and the Căliman mountains

The train line continues north for a further 30km from Lăzarea to **TOPLIŢA** (Maroshévíz), a third-rate spa and logging town whose only real sights of interest are two wooden churches – the church of Sf Ilie, 1km north on the main road, built in 1847 and moved here in 1910, and the Doamnei Church 10km further on, dating from 1658. A road runs through the Eastern Carpathians from Topliţa into Moldavia, served by buses to the spa of Borsec, Poiana Largului and Tîrgu Neamţ. If you need to break your journey, the *Căliman* **hotel** at Str. Republicii 1 (☎065/14.29.43; ③), across the river from the station, is good value (although the bathroom boilers seem rather explosive) and has a good cheap **restaurant**, but the facilities at the *Bradul* campsite, up the hill to the right of the station, are pretty dire.

From Topliţa the road and rail routes head west along the Mureş valley, which is lined with various places to stay; notably the *Şoimilor cabana*, 2km west of the Stînceni Neagră train halt, 16km west of Topliţa; the *Doi Brazi* motel in Sălard, a further 9km west and 3km west of Lunca Bradului station; and a homestay in Androneasa (Str. Principală 160), a further 6km west of Sălard. The wild, unpopulated **Căliman mountains** rise steeply to the north of this narrow, rugged defile, in which retreating German soldiers made a vain attempt to ambush the Red Army in 1944; the Romanian army, having suddenly changed its loyalty from the Axis to the Allies, had denied them the Carpathian passes, so the battle was largely lost before it had begun. Today, the Căliman range is a paradise for hikers, where you can walk for days without meeting a soul. The best route in is probably from Răstoliţa, 30km west of Topliţa. There's plenty of construction traffic on the road up to Secu where a dam is being built, and from here paths head northeast to the volcanic peaks and the settlements in the huge crater beyond, leading ultimately to **Vatra Dornei**.

South to Tîrgu Mureş

Road and rail routes head southwest through Deda and on to Tîrgu Mureş. **BRÎNCOVENEŞTI**, 13km south of Deda and served by slow trains between Deda and Tîrgu Mureş, was founded on a Roman site and has a five-towered **castle** dating from the fourteenth century, once owned by Sava Armaşul, a lieutenant of Michael the Brave. However, the village is probably best known as the site of the first "Home for Irrecuperables", housing handicapped orphans judged too sick or traumatized to recover, which hit the headlines in the West after Ceauşescu's fall. On a lighter note, the village also hosts the **Cherry Fair** (Culesul cireşelor), which normally takes place here on the first Sunday of June, to celebrate the most important harvest of the year.

REGHIN (Szászrégen/Sächsisch Reen), 10km beyond Brîncoveneşti, is ringed by factories, which have done nothing for the town's appearance. Most notable of the factories are the violin factory and a brewery, one of Romania's best thanks to the pure water of the Gurghiu valley to the east of town. The main reason to stop here is to make bus connections to the villages of **Gurghiu** and **Hodac**, 21km east of town – this can be done immediately outside the train station, so there's little reason to venture into town. Despite industrialization, there's still evidence of the four main communities – Saxon, Hungarian, Romanian and Jewish – that made this so quintessentially a Transylvanian town.

GURGHIU and HODAC, 14km further east, are traditional shepherding communities. The shepherds here were easily manipulated by extreme nationalists in March 1990, who told them that Hungary was set to annexe Transylvania. The shepherds were bussed to Tîrgu Mureş, issued with axes, pitchforks and alcohol by the local priests and let loose on the offices of the Hungarian political party. Gurghiu is known for its **Girl Fair** (Tîrgul de fete) on the second Sunday of May, when splendid folk costumes are worn. At Hodac, 7km beyond Gurghiu, the second Sunday in June sees the **"Buying Back of the Wives" Festival** reaffirming the economic underpinnings of matrimony. To guard against a wasted journey, it's best to check when it's going on at the Cultural Inspectorate of the prefecture in Tîrgu Mureş (see below).

Tîrgu Mureş

TÎRGU MUREŞ is still at heart **Marosvásárhely**, one of the great Magyar cities of Transylvania, although the Magyar influence has been diluted by recent Romanian and Gypsy immigration. The city was briefly notorious as a centre of ethnic tension, with riots in March 1990, largely stirred up by the right-wing extremists of the *Vatra* with government connivance, in which at least three died, and the desecration of Jewish graves in May of the same year. It is more reputably known as a centre of learning – its university is small, but both the medical and drama schools are renowned nationally; under Communism both of these formerly Hungarian establishments ended up teaching entirely in Romanian and consequently admitting only Romanian students, but today the Hungarian language has equal status once more. The city suffers from heavy pollution generated at the Azomureş chemical plant, near the main road and rail line to the southwest of town – it's liable to be an unpleasant experience entering or leaving town along this route.

The Town

It's a twenty-minute walk north from the bus station to the city centre (bus #2, #4, #16, #17, #18 or #22) – turn right along Strada Gheorghe Doja and left past the train station, halfway to the centre, and on to Piaţa Victoriei at the southern end of Piaţa Trandafirilor, the city's focal point. **Piaţa Trandafirilor** is lined with fine Secession-style edifices, of which the most grandiose, at its southern end, are the adjacent prefecture and Palace of Culture. These fantastic buildings both date from 1913 and are typical of that era, when a self-consciously "Hungarian" style of architecture reflected Budapest's policy of Magyarizing Transylvania.

The prefecture's rooftops blaze with polychromatic tiling, while the **Palace of Culture**'s most stunning features are its internal decorations, including 50kg of gilding – the caretaker should show you around. The most spectacular room in the Palace is the **Hall of Mirrors**, with stained-glass windows illustrating local myths and a fine organ; concerts are often held here. Another hall, with special lotus-shaped chairs, is used for weddings. The **County History and Art Museums** (Tues–Fri 9am–4pm, Sat & Sun 9am–1pm), on the floor above, emphasizes the town's links with Moldavia, Michael the Brave and anti-Hapsburg fighters such as Avram Iancu. Among the portraits held in the museum, look out for the careworn face of **György Dózsa** (Gheorghe Doja in Romanian), a local

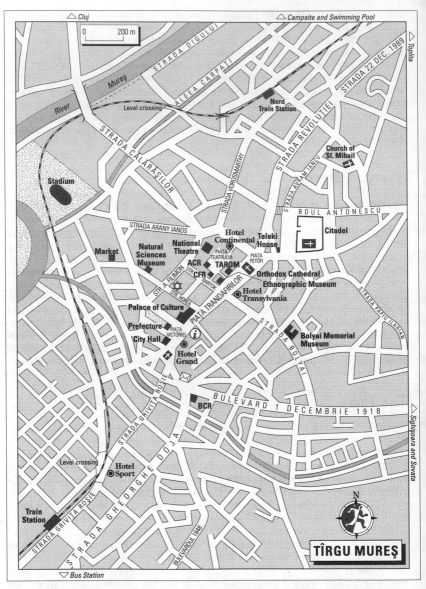

Székely mercenary in Archbishop Bákocz's crusade, who thrust himself to the forefront in 1514 when the peasants' crusade became a radical anti-feudal uprising. After the rebellion's suppression, the aristocrats led by János Zápolyai arranged a particularly ghastly execution at Timişoara for Dózsa and his followers (see p.303).

The **natural sciences section** of the museum is west of the Palace of Culture at Str. Horea 24. Heading along here from Piaţa Trandafirilor you'll pass the city's synagogue – all rose windows and domes – where Strada Horea crosses Strada Aurel Filimon. The colourful **ethnographic section** of the museum is two blocks north of the Palace of Culture at Piaţa Trandafirilor 11 in the Toldalagy House, a fine Baroque pile built in 1759–62. Behind, at the entrance to the modern plaza of Piaţa Teatrului, stands a tower raised in 1735, all that remains of the Minorite (Franciscan) monastery.

The neo-Byzantine **Orthodox Cathedral** (1925–34) marks the northern end of Piaţa Trandafirilor. It was the Romanians' riposte to the imperialistic Magyar administrative buildings, which dominate the southern end of the square, pushing aside the more modest Baroque church of the Jesuits on its east side; for good measure they followed up with a statue of Avram Iancu, on the cathedral's southern side.

Just north of the cathedral is Piaţa Bernady György, dominated by the walls of the **citadel**, inside which shelters the Protestant church, built for the Dominicans in 1430 and later used by the Transylvanian Diet. Two blocks east of the citadel, along Bulevardul Antonescu, Strada Şaguna heads north to the **wooden church** of Sf Mihail (1793–94). The church has a beautifully decorated interior, and a virtual shrine to the national poet, Eminescu, who slept in the porch in 1866 because there was no room at the inn.

Despite its long-standing role as a garrison town, Tîrgu Mureş also takes pride in its intellectual tradition; the mathematicians **Farkas Bolyai** (1775–1856) and his son **János** (1802–60), founders of non-Euclidean geometry, receive their due in the **Bolyai Memorial Museum** at Str. Bolyai 17 (Tues–Fri 10am–6pm, Sat & Sun 10am–1pm), east from Piaţa Trandafirilor. The museum also houses a hundred paintings by the Székely artist Nagy Imre (1893–1976, not to be confused with the Hungarian leader of 1956) as well as Tîrgu Mureş's greatest treasures, the Teleki and Bolyai libraries. The Teleki collection, consisting of 40,000 volumes, was built up by Count Samuel Teleki, Chancellor of Transylvania, in the eighteenth century, and with the later addition of the Bolyai collection, it now includes many ancient medical and scientific texts as well as the works of the philosophers of the French Enlightenment. It was opened to the public in 1802, since when another 80,000 volumes have been added.

Practicalities

Tîrgu Mureş is on a minor line between Razboieni and Deda and is served by several fast **trains** a day, with extra services running in the summer; however connections south are poor and if you're planning to head on in that direction, you're best off catching a bus to Sighişoara, 55km south, and making train connections there. TAROM flies a triangular route from Bucharest to Tîrgu Mureş and Sibiu, six times a week; buses to and from Tîrgu Mureş' airport run from TAROM's office in the centre of town. From the **bus station**, at Str. Gheorghe Doja 52, there are services to the major towns of Transylvania, as well as to Tîrgu Neamţ and Vatra Dornei in Moldavia, and a dozen buses a week to Budapest. The former **tourist office** at Piaţa Trandafirilor 31 is now a private travel agency, which will change travellers' cheques and Eurocheques, but may not be able to do much else for you; **plane** and **international bus tickets** can be booked at the TAROM office, at Piaţa Trandafirilor 6 (☎065/43.62.00). There's a Bancomat at BCR at the junction of Str. Gheorghe Doja and B-dul 1 Decembrie 1918.

Turning left out of the main train station, it takes under five minutes to reach the *Sport* **hotel** at Str. Grivița Roșie 31 (☎065/13.19.13; ①), most rooms are with shared bathrooms and the restaurant is poor, but it is easily the cheapest place to stay. The *Grand* (☎065/16.07.11, fax 13.02.89; ACR; ④) is opposite the City Hall at Piața Victoriei 27, the western end of Piața Trandafirilor. It has faded 1960s decor, but the rooms come with breakfast included, private bath and TV. The *Continental* at Piața Teatrului 6 (☎ & fax 16.09.99; ⑧), is the best hotel in town, with modern fittings, a casino and cable TV. There's camping at the *Ștrand* campsite at Aleea Carpați, on the River Mureș north of town (take bus #14 or walk from Tîrgu Mureș Nord train station), and at the *Stejeriș* motel (☎065/13.35.09), 7km along the Sighișoara road.

Piața Trandafirilor is the place to find **food**, either in the supermarket or in the several snack bars and restaurants that line the square, notably the *Mureșul*, a delightful time warp at no. 44, the *Vegetarian* (in fact serving meat) at no. 22 and the atmospheric *Trandafirul* at no. 14. All three serve a similar selection of traditional Romanian dishes. The *Panda*, at Piața Trandafirilor 14, is a stand-up salad bar.

CLUJ AND NORTHERN TRANSYLVANIA

Cluj is the great Hungarian capital of Transylvania and a natural gateway to the region, just six hours from Budapest by train. There is more buzz to café life than in other towns, maybe due to the thirty thousand students resident here, and shops also seem better stocked than elsewhere.

The area surrounding Cluj, particularly the **Transylvanian Heath** to the east, harbours some of the richest, most varied **folk music** in Europe. Weekends are the best time to investigate villages such as **Sic, Cojocna, Rimetea** and **Izvoru Crișului**, where almost every street has its own band and there are rich pickings to be had at spring and summer festivals. Cluj is also a natural base for visiting the **Apuseni massif**, immediately to the west, with wide green pastures, easy walking and caving opportunities, particularly on the **Padiș plateau**.

To the north of the Apuseni is **Sălaj county**, a rural backwater scattered with quaint wooden churches. Further east, the historic town of **Bistrița**, once centre of an isolated Saxon community (and today more widely known for its Dracula connections), still guards the routes into Maramureș and northern Moldavia.

Cluj-Napoca

With its cupolas, Baroque outcroppings and weathered *fin-de-siècle* backstreets, downtown **CLUJ** (Klausenburg to the Germans and Kolozsvár to the Hungarians) looks like the Hungarian provincial capital it once was. The town was originally founded by Germans in the twelfth century for the Hungarian King Geza, and the modern-day Hungarian population still regrets its decline, fondly recalling the Magyar *belle époque*, embodied in Cluj's café society and literary reputation which surpassed all other cities in the Balkans. Most Romanians think otherwise: for them, Kolozsvár was the city of the Hungarian landlords until its restoration to the

GHEORGHE FUNAR

Gheorghe Funar, the "Mad Mayor" of Cluj since 1992 and former leader of the Romanian National Unity Party, is notorious for his anti-Hungarian stance, and you'll see plenty of evidence of this around the city. In 1994 the central Piaţa Libertăţii was renamed **Piaţa Unirii**, as "Unification" implies the union of Transylvania with the rest of Romania, and thus its removal from Hungary. Similarly, the lettering on the statue of Matthias Corvinus, on Piaţa Unirii, which used to read *Hungariae Matthias Rex*, now reads only *Matthias Rex*, and is flanked by six Romanian flags. In 1994 an archeological dig (which has revealed nothing of importance) was begun in front of the statue, and would have provided a pretext for removing it altogether if the government had not intervened. Additionally Funar has raised an absurdly expensive statue of Avram Iancu, leader of the 1848 revolt against the Hungarians, and a monument to the Romanians imprisoned for protesting in the 1892 *Memorandum* against Hungarian chauvinism. He even objected to a Bartók concert because the words would be sung in Hungarian. Having again failed in the 1996 presidential election, he lost the leadership of the Romanian National Unity Party and is under investigation for corruption, his reputation further damaged by a scandal concerning two million Lei worth of calls to foreign sex lines from his private office.

national patrimony in 1920; they consider Ceauşescu's addition of Napoca to its name in 1974 as recognition that their Dacian forebears settled here 1850 years ago, long before the Magyars entered Transylvania. Cluj is also the birthplace of the Unitarian creed and its centre in Romania, further adding to the multi-ethnic, multi-faith cocktail.

Under Communism Cluj was industrialized and grew to over 300,000 inhabitants, but the city retained something of the langour and raffish undercurrents that had characterized it in former times, as well as a reputation for being anti-Ceauşescu. Now the city has a rabidly nationalist mayor, **Gheorghe Funar** (see box), who goes out of his way to offend the Magyars, still a third of the city's population, by banning all Hungarian-language signs and by constantly accusing Hungary of seeking to undermine Romania's government and regain Transylvania.

Arrival and information

From Cluj's **train station**, it takes about twenty minutes to walk into the centre down Strada Horea, past the Mughal-style synagogue built in 1886, across the Little Someş river, where the road becomes Strada Gheorghe Doja, and into the spacious **Piaţa Unirii**, the focus of the city's life. Across the road from the station, trolley buses #3, #4 and #9 stop on their loop route into the centre, going south on Strada Traian and returning along Strada Horea; there's a ticket kiosk at the stop. There are two **bus stations** – Autogară 1, 2km east of the centre along Bulevardul 22 Decembrie, for local services (trolley bus #6 from the tourist office); and Autogară 2, just across the tracks to the north of the train station, for all major destinations (bus #31 or #42). The city's **airport** is 5km east of the city, connected to the centre by bus #8, stopping at Piaţa Mihai Viteazul, node of the city's public transport system, just east of Str. Gheorghe Doja.

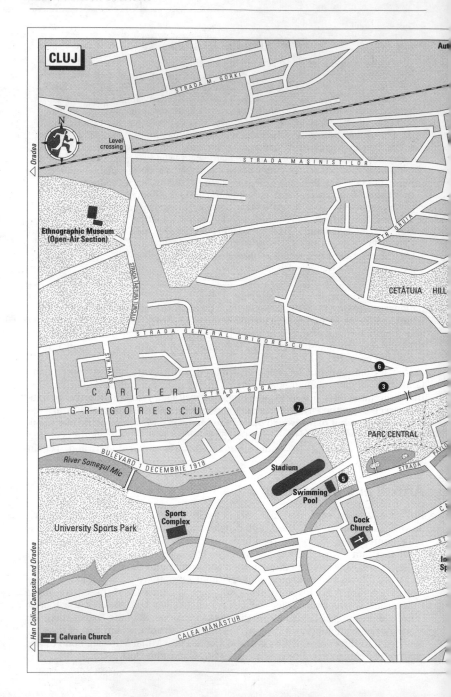

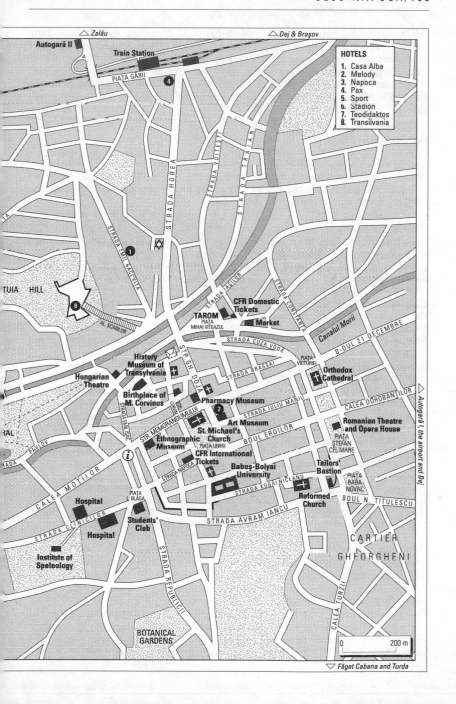

△ Zalău
△ Dej & Braşov

Autogară II
Train Station
PIAŢA GĂRII
④

HOTELS
1. Casa Alba
2. Melody
3. Napoca
4. Pax
5. Sport
6. Stadion
7. Teodidaktos
8. Transilvania

STRADA HOREA
STRADA VOITEŞTI
STRADA TRAIAN

①

TUIA HILL
⑧
AL. SCĂRILOR

STRADA IAŞILOR
STRADA CONSTANTA

CFR Domestic Tickets
TAROM
PIAŢA MIHAI VITEAZUL
Market
Canalul Morii
B-DUL 21 DECEMBRE

STRADA CUZA VODA
PIAŢA VICTORIEI
CALEA DOROBANŢILOR
△ Autogară I, the airport and Dej

History Museum of Transylvania
STR. GH. DOJA
STRADA BRASSAI
Orthodox Cathedral

Hungarian Theatre
Birthplace of M. Corvinus
②
Pharmacy Museum
STRADA IULIU MANIU

STRADA RĂIL ISAC
STR. MEMORANDUMULUI
Art Museum
Romanian Theatre and Opera House

PAVLOV
Ethnographic Museum
St. Michael's Church
BDUL EROILOR
PIAŢA UNIRII
PIAŢA STEFAN CEL MARE

ⓘ
CFR International Tickets
Babeş-Bolyai University
Tailors' Bastion
PIAŢA BABA NOVAC

STRADA NAPOCA
CALEA MOTILOR
PIAŢA L. BLAGA
STRADA KOGĂLNICEANU
Reformed Church
BDUL N. TITULESCU

Hospital
Students' Club
STRADA AVRAM IANCU
CARTIER

Hospital
GHEORGHENI

STRADA CLINICILOR
Institute of Speleology

STRADA REPUBLICII
CALEA TURZII

BOTANICAL GARDENS
0   200 m

▽ Fåget Cabana and Turda

The privatized **tourist office** (Mon–Fri 8am–8pm, Sat & Sun 9am–1pm; ☎064/19.69.55) is at Str. Şincai 2, left along Strada Memorandumului, the main road west from Piaţa Unirii (trolley bus #9 from the station); it's primarily concerned with booking holidays on the coast. An excellent map of Cluj (including public transport routes) is published in Budapest by *Top-o-Gráf/Freytag & Berndt* and can be found, among other places, in a cramped newspaper shop on the north side of Piaţa Unirii.

Accommodation

Cluj has a wide range of **hotel** accommodation with welcome city comforts, but prices do tend to be higher than in most other towns in Romania. Thanks to its large student population, the city can also offer plenty of cheaper rooms over the summer in the vacant student accommodation.

Hotels

Casa Albă, Str. Racoviţa 22 (☎ & fax 064/43.22.77). A very quiet and select stopover in a small villa, with secure parking. ⑨.

Continental, Str. Napoca 1 (☎064/19.54.05, fax 19.39.77). Once-grand establishment, still the most atmospheric hotel in the centre. Rooms with baths twice the price of those without. ACR; ④.

Liliacul, Calea Turzii 251A (☎064/43.81.29, fax 43.81.30). A new private hotel out of town on the DN1, at the turning to the campsite. Well appointed, with private bathrooms and cable TV. ⑤.

Melody, Piaţa Unirii 29 (☎064/19.74.65, fax 19.74.68). Also known as the *Central*, with friendly staff, reasonable rooms, and showgirls in the basement club. ③.

Napoca, Str. Octavian Goga 1 (☎064/18.07.15, fax 18.56.27). Good modern hotel with restaurant and MTV, across the river from the Parc Central (bus #27 from the station). ⑧.

Pax, Piaţa Gării 1 (☎064/13.61.01). Small, gloomy and overpriced, but handy for the train station. With only 12 rooms – no singles and none with private bathrooms – it fills up fast. ⑥.

Sport, Str. Coşbuc 15 (☎064/19.39.21, fax 19.58.59). Another modern building, and a grand hotel, with hairdresser and brasserie. Actually in the Parc Central itself (bus #30). ACR; ⑨.

Topaz Hotel, Str. Septimiu Albini 12 (☎064/41.40.76, fax 41.40.47). Not to be confused with the similar, but more expensive, *Hotel Topaz*, Str. Septimiu Albini 10 (☎064/41.40.21, fax 41.40.66; ⑥), this is a business-like new place east of the centre. ④.

Transilvania, Str. Călăraşilor 1 (☎064/43.20.71, fax 43.20.76). Originally named the *Belvedere* (until mayor Funar realized it was the Belvedere Treaty that gave Northern Transylvania to Hungary), this luxurious modern place has an indoor swimming pool, sauna, gym and covered parking and overlooks the town from Cetăţuia hill. Main access by foot (up dilapidated steps) or by taxi – nearest bus is #38, stopping not too far north at Str. Gruia. ACR; ⑨.

Camping, Cabanas and Hostels

The **Făget campsite** (open May–Oct; ☎064/19.62.27; ①) is 4km south along the DN1 and a further 1.5km off the main road towards Turda (turn off by the *Liliacul* hotel); bus #40A goes there from the south side of Piaţa Ştefan cel Mare every hour or two in season, or failing that take any of the frequent buses for Feleacu and Turda to the *Hotel Liliacul* and then walk the remaining 1.5km. The site's facilities include cabins, a restaurant and bar, and non-stop hot water; there's also plenty of space for tents and caravans. Next to the campsite is the *Silva*, a nice private bar with six two-bed cabins attached. There's also plenty of good woodland for camping wild.

About fifteen minutes' walk beyond the campsite is the *Făget* **cabana**; there are others at Cheile Baciului (trains or bus #42 west on the DN1F to Baciu), and Făget-Izvor (☎064/16.29.91), west on the DN1 towards Huedin and a kilometre to the left at the sign.

For **dormitory** accommodation over the summer vacation, try the *Do-re-mi*, Str. Braşov 2 (near the Turda road; bus #3 to Piaţa Ciprariu), so called because it's home to music students from mid-September to the end of June. English is spoken, and there are cooking facilities; booking is possible through West-Carp Tours, Str. Eremia Grigorescu 112A (☎064/18.34.62). In August, other self-styled "youth hostels" may operate in the *complexul studentesc Observator* at the south end of Strada Republicii (☎064/19.71.59, fax 19.62.63), or the Protestant (*Reformat*) Theological Institute, Piaţa Avram Iancu 13 (at Str. Cuza Vodă). The *Hostel Teodidaktos* at B-dul 1 Decembrie 1918 no. 30 (☎064/18.67.34; ②) is quiet and comfortable, with hot showers, washing machines and cooking facilities; group bookings are preferred and these should be made in advance.

The City

Unlike almost every other Romanian city of comparable size, Cluj has no Civic Centre; it has thus avoided a widespread demolition of its old central zone, which remains largely unspoilt within the line of the city walls. The walls themselves have now been almost entirely demolished, although the remains of a fifteenth-century **citadel** still surround the *Transilvania* hotel on Cetăţuia Hill, north of the river. Behind the hotel, the citadel's gatehouse, added in 1715, bears a plaque commemorating the execution of the nationalist writer Stefan Ludwig Roth, following the failure of the 1848 revolution. The Securitate used the hotel as its powerbase, and twelve people were supposedly gunned down on the steps in the 1989 revolution. The site of the massive cross, raised here by the Uniate Church, is the best place to view the city.

Piaţa Unirii

Piaţa Unirii, surrounded by shops and restaurants, is the centre of the city; it's dominated by **St Michael's Church**, which was founded in the mid-fourteenth century, when the Saxons ruled unchallenged over the city. Dwarfing the congregation in the nave, mighty pillars curve into austerely bare vaulting like the roof of a forest. To this great halled church, the Hungarian aristocracy later added the massive nineteenth-century belltower and a sacristy, whose door (dated 1528) encapsulates the Italian Renaissance style introduced under Mátyás Corvinus.

On the south side of the church, a clumsy but imposing equestrian **statue of Mátyás Corvinus** tramples the crescent banner of the Turks underfoot. His formidable Black Army kept the Kingdom of Hungary safe from lawlessness and foreign invasion for much of his reign (1458–90), but just 36 years later the nation was more or less wiped off the map at the battle of Mohács. A popular lament that justice departed with his death highlights Mátyás's political and military achievements; but the leader's reputation derives equally from his Renaissance attributes, for which his wife **Beatrix of Naples** should share the credit. By introducing him to the Renaissance culture of Italy and selecting foreign architects and craftsmen, and humanists like Bonfini to chronicle events and speeches, Beatrix was a catalyst for Hungary's own fifteenth-century Renaissance, and she personally commissioned many volumes in the Corvin library.

CARITAS

One of the most bizarre episodes of post-revolutionary Romanian life is centred on the **Caritas Bank**, which promised investors eight times their money in a hundred days, creating a true mania throughout Transylvania and making a boomtown of Cluj for a while. In reality this was a classic pyramid investment scheme, which relied on deposits doubling every month to maintain its payments, and thus could not possibly keep going for more than a limited period. Founded in early 1992, by October 1993 it had three million investors and had moved from its offices in central Cluj to take over the municipal sports centre. Trains to Cluj carried four times their usual load, packed with peasants bringing their life savings to invest, and trains out were even more congested as they took their new televisions and microwaves home three months later. The town enjoyed gold-rush prosperity, with many new shops and jobs, but it also suffered from an increase in crime.

Many similar schemes were set up elsewhere, but none enjoyed the success of Caritas, largely because its founder Ion Stoica had managed to use television to build an almost messianic image for himself, even claiming that he had been given the secret of success by God in order to help the poor. However, it was inevitable that things would fall apart; at the end of 1993 64 Caritas cashiers were arrested and accused of embezzling 17 billion lei, and early in 1994 returns were running three months behind schedule. Stoica moved to Bucharest to drum up new business and opened branches in Snagov, Craiova and Focşani, but then vanished before finally being arrested and sent to prison (not for fraud but for taking money from the local council), where he wrote a book and made lots more money.

There are many questions still to be answered, above all why the government allowed this patently fraudulent and probably illegal scheme to be set up in the first place and why it was allowed to continue for so long. There are many theories to do with laundering money made from drugs- or gun-running and Yugoslav sanctions-busting, fund-raising for Funar's PUNR (Romanian National Unionist Party), or a government scheme to build an artificial boom and boost the value of the leu by reducing the demand for dollars. This last does seem almost plausible, as the Iliescu government came up with equally ingenious schemes for reducing the demand for dollars, and with at least $1 billion invested Caritas was quite big enough to produce macro-economic effects in a country with exports (in 1993) of just $4.2 billion.

West of the church, at Piaţa Unirii 30, stands the **Art Museum** (Wed–Sun 10am–5pm), which, until the museum in Bucharest reopens, offers perhaps the best survey of Romanian art. The museum is housed in the Baroque Bánffy Palace, built in 1774–91 to the design of Johann Eberhardt Blaumann for the Magyar family of Bánffy; many of the items now in the museum were expropriated from the family and other members of the Magyar aristocracy. The collection is dominated by works of the largely French-influenced artists of the nineteenth and twentieth centuries, with pieces by Theodor Aman (1831–91) and Romania's best-known painter, Nicolae Grigorescu (1838–1907) – both of whom were influenced by the Barbizon group and the Impressionists – and Theodor Pallady (1871–1956), who spent several decades in Paris and was clearly inspired by Matisse. Surprisingly, there's nothing by Brâncuşi, and there's virtually no abstract or truly modern art.

On the northern side of the square, on the corner of Strada Gheorghe Doja, is the **Pharmacy Museum** (Mon–Fri 10am–4pm), in the Hintz House which served as Cluj's first apothecary, opening in 1573 and finally closing in 1948. Like the other pharmacy museums dotted across Eastern Europe, it displays ancient prescriptions and implements, as well as eighteenth-century aphrodisiac bottles.

The university area
The university area lies to the south of Piaţa Unirii, with Strada Napoca leading west to the **Students' Club** and the old library on Piaţa Blaga, and Strada Universităţii heading south past the Baroque church of the Piarist Order (1718–24) to the **Babeş-Bolyai University**. Since its foundation in 1872 the university has produced scholars of the calibre of Edmund Bordeaux Székely (translator of the Dead Sea Scrolls), but has also served as an instrument of cultural oppression. Long denied an education in their own language, the Romanians promptly banned teaching in Hungarian once they gained the upper hand in 1918, only to hurriedly evacuate students and staff when Hitler gave northern Transylvania back to Hungary in 1940.

After liberation, separate universities were created to provide education in the mother tongues of the two main communities, and for a while it seemed that inequality was a thing of the past. However, in 1959 the authorities decreed a shotgun merger, enforced by a little-known cadre called Nicolae Ceauşescu, which led to the suicide of the Bolyai's pro-rector, and, more predictably, a rapid decline in its Hungarian-language teaching. This, and a similar running-down of primary and secondary schooling, convinced many Magyars that the state was bent on "de-culturizing" them. In 1997 it was decided once more to demerge the universities. Outside the main door of the university stand three statues representing the **School of Transylvania** whose philological and historical researches fuelled the Romanian cultural resurgence of the nineteenth century and the resistance to Magyarization.

At Str. Republicii 42, just south of the university, are the **Botanical Gardens** (daily 9am–9pm), the largest in the country with more than 10,000 species. They include a museum, greenhouses with desert and tropical plants including Amazon waterlilies two metres across, and a small Japanese garden. The gardens attract 600,000 visitors a year, including newlyweds seeking the perfect backdrop for their photos.

East to Piaţa Ştefan cel Mare
Strada Kogălniceanu runs east from the university to the Reformed (Calvinist) church, founded in 1487 by Mátyás Corvinus, with a Renaissance chancel added in 1646. Outside the church stands a copy of the statue of St George and the Dragon from Prague's Hradčany castle, made in 1373 by the Cluj masters Martin and Gheorghe. Organ recitals are held in the church and at other times the key is available at Str. Kogălniceanu 21.

Just east of the church is the restored **Tailors' Bastion** on Piaţa Baba Novac, supposedly containing a branch of the museum, but always closed. The hole in the ground beyond this is to become a Uniate cathedral. North of the bastion is the elongated square of Piaţa Ştefan cel Mare and Piaţa Victoriei. Its southern end, Piaţa Ştefan cel Mare, is dominated by the neat yellow and white facade of the **Romanian National Theatre and Opera**, built in 1906 by the ubiquitous Viennese theatre architects Fellner and Helmer. To the north, the huge and startling **Orthodox Cathedral** dominates the smaller Piaţa Victoriei. Actually built in 1920, the cathedral looks as if it fell through a time warp from Justinian's

Constantinople. It was raised to celebrate the Romanians' triumph in Transylvania, and the neo-Byzantine stone facade hides a concrete structure. Inside, the frescoes, though religious in content, bear the ugly heavy-handedness characteristic of the 1950s, when Socialist Realism was the prescribed mode.

To the south of the cathedral is the notorious statue of Avram Iancu commissioned by Funar (see box on p.191). From here, the most direct route back to the centre is along the fine nineteenth-century Strada Iuliu Maniu, or the grander Bulevardul Eroilor, at the east end of which is Funar's *Memorandum* monument, known as the Guillotine.

North of Piaţa Unirii

From the northwest corner of Piaţa Unirii, Strada Matei Corvin leads to the small fifteenth-century mansion at no. 6, now an art college, where Hungary's greatest king was born in 1440. He was the son of Iancu de Hunedoara, and thus a Romanian (although myth makes his father the illegitimate son of the Hungarian King Sigismund), but nonetheless this was virtually a place of pilgrimage for Hungarians in Hapsburg days. Continuing north, Strada Corvin leads into Piaţa Muzeului where newly discovered Roman ruins are being excavated in the centre. Just to the left of the square, at Str. Daicovici 2, is the **History Museum of Transylvania** (Tues–Sun 10am–4pm). On the first floor, strange skulls and mammoth tusks are succeeded by arrow- and spearheads, charting progress from the Neolithic and Bronze Ages to the rise of the **Dacian civilization**, which reached its peak between the second century BC and the first century AD; a reconstruction of Sarmizegetusa, the Dacian's highland citadel, is included in models and pictures. On the floor above the story continues to World War I, but this is a fairly standard display, with information in Romanian alone.

West of Piaţa Unirii

The city's main east–west axis runs across the northern edge of Piaţa Unirii – to the east of the square as Bulevardul 21 Decembrie 1989 and westwards as Strada Memorandumului. Str. Memorandumului 21, the palace where the Transylvanian Diet met in 1790–91, now houses the main branch of the **Ethnographic Museum** (Tues–Sun 9am–5pm). It contains what is probably Romania's finest collection of

---

UNITARIANISM

The first **Unitarian church** was founded in Cluj in 1556 by the hitherto Calvinist minister Dávid Ferenc (1510–79), and by 1568 it was already accepted as one of the four official churches of Transylvania. Unitarianism had its origins among the Italian and Spanish humanists and some of the more extreme Anabaptists, and one of its Italian leaders, Faustus Socinus (1539–1604), came to Cluj in 1578, before moving on to Kraków in 1580. There are now around 75,000 Unitarians in Romania, almost all among the Hungarian community.

Unitarianism derives its name from its rejection of the doctrine of the Trinity, as well as other basic doctrines such as the divinity of Christ, his atonement for the sins of the world, and thus the possibility of salvation. However, its significance lies in its undogmatic approach – adherents are conspicuous for their devotion to reason in matters of religion, and to civil and religious liberty, and their exercise of tolerance to all sincere forms of religious faith.

traditional carpets and folk costumes – from the dark herringbone patterns of the Pădureni region to the bold yellow, black and red stripes typical of Maramureş costumes. While blouses and leggings might be predominantly black or white, women's apron-skirts, and the waistcoats worn by both sexes for special occasions, are brilliantly coloured. Peacock feathers serve in the Năsăud area as fans or plumes, and the love of complicated designs spills over onto cups, masks, distaffs (used as an application for marriage), and linked spoons (used as a charm against divorce). The museum also has an excellent **open-air section** (Tues–Sun 9am–4pm) to the northwest of town on the Hoia hill, with peasant houses and three wooden churches from the surrounding areas; the best way to get there is to take bus #27 from the station or #30 from Piaţa Unirii to Str. Haţeg (Cartier Grigorescu), and then head ten minutes north from there (thirty minutes walk from the centre).

Strada Memorandumului continues west from the museum to the tourist office and the splendidly towered prefecture, from where it continues west as Calea Moţilor. At no. 84 is the **Cock Church**, a beautiful Calvinist church built in 1913 by Kós Károly, who designed everything down to the light fittings, all with a cock motif symbolizing St Peter's threefold denial of Christ before cock crow. Ask for the key at the parish office behind the church. Further west is the **Mănăstur** quarter, the oldest part of Cluj, although you wouldn't know it from the serried ranks of 1980s apartment blocks – the best views are from the Calea Mănăstur flyover, where you can see ancient earthworks to the south and a relatively modern shrine and belfry atop them; behind these is the **Calvaria church**, built by the Magyars in the twelfth century and rebuilt by the Benedictines in 1466. It's a Gothic hall church, simple but surprisingly large, recently restored and with a new belfry.

Eating, drinking and entertainment

For traditional Romanian **food**, and occasionally music, try the *Dacia* at Str. Memorandumului 13, the *Humbertus* at B-dul 22 Decembrie, or the *Zahana* at B-dul Eroilor 10. The *Vărzărie*, at B-dul Eroilor 35, serves the local speciality, *varza clujeana* (cabbage), while the *Pescărul* at Strada Universităţii 3 specializes in fish dishes. The best of the hotel restaurants, serving typical Romanian fare, is the *Continental*, with its splendid decor. Of the rash of Italian and pseudo-Italian joints that's taking over the city, the best three are the *To Steki*, at Calea Moţilor 17, *Napoca Cincipe*, at Str. Napoca 15, and *Rex*, at Str. Bolyai, but it's the *Casa Blanca* pizza/burger restaurant at Piaţa Unirii 11 that is currently *the* place to hang out. *Panegrano* is a private chain of good bakeries with outlets on all the main streets.

There are two **bars** on Piaţa Unirii, the *Ursus* at no. 19 and the *Someş* at no. 30; both are pleasant places from which to watch the world go by. There are relatively few beer gardens (*gradinas*): try the *Decanat*, near the Hungarian Theatre at the corner of Str. Isac and Str. Bariţiu, or the *Boema* at Str. Iuliu Maniu 34, which serves grills in a nice setting, but with loud music. Studenty places can be found on Strada Napoca, including the *Vioreaua* at no. 13, the *Cin-Cin* at no. 7, which serves hot wine (*vin fiert*), and the *Trandafirul* coffee bar at no. 17; there's also the *Tineretului* at Str. Universităţii 3 and the "House of Culture" and the *Croco* student bar on Piaţa Blaga.

The best **clubs** are the *Negro*, at Str. Observatorului 34, and the *Bianco*, at Str. Universităţii 7. The *Diesel Jazz Bar*, in the cellars of Piaţa Unirii 17, is trendy, but with terrible service, and the *Music Pub* (Str. Horea 5), another cellar, patronized largely by Hungarian students, has somewhat alternative music and serves good large pizzas. The *Art Club*, at Piaţa Ştefan cel Mare 14, is where the actors hang out; **theatre** tickets can be bought next door at no. 14. Cluj also has a good range of cinemas, well advertised.

Listings

Airlines The TAROM booking office is at Piaţa Mihai Viteazul 11 (Mon–Fri 7am–7pm, Sat 9am–1pm; ☎064/19.49.87). Seats on DacAir flights can be booked at Air Tracia, B-dul Eroilor 6 (☎064/19.78.06).

Bicycle repair at Str. Voiteşti and Piaţa Mihai Viteazul.

Bookstore There are very few English-language books available, but try the university bookstore on Piaţa Unirii, which has good dictionaries and books on Romanian ethnography and arts and some English-language titles.

Car rental Avis, at the *Hotel Transilvania* (☎064/43.20.71 ext 493).

Car repair ACR, B-dul 21 Decembrie 131 (☎064/19.65.03); Gabism, Str. Alverna 24 (7am–10pm; ☎064/14.52.52).

Laundry Curătătorie Express, Str. Horia 14 (Mon–Thurs 8am–5pm, Fri 8am–3pm).

Libraries British library (Mon & Wed 2–7pm, Tues, Thurs & Fri 9am–2pm), Str. Avram Iancu 11; American library and German cultural centre, at Str. Universităţii 7.

Markets Piaţa Mihai Viteazul: a daily food market, and on Thursdays a craft market selling wood carvings and embroidery from the Apuseni highlands and the Transylvanian Heath.

Money There's a Bancomat cash machine inside Bancpost, by the post office on Str. Gheorghe Doja (Mon–Fri 8.30am–7pm, Sat 8.30–1pm).

Pharmacy The emergency rota is posted in the southeast corner of Piaţa Unirii.

Post office Str. Gheorghe Doja (Mon–Fri 7am–8pm, Sat 7am–1pm).

Shopping Cluj's main department store, the Central, is on Str. Gheorghe Doja opposite the post office. The Iza mini-supermarket at Str. Gheorghe Doja 34 and Flip deli on Piaţa Mihai Viteazul have a large range of imported goods. The Elvira mini-market, on Strada Universităţii (Mon–Sat 7am–midnight, Sun 8am–2pm), has a wide selection of alcohol.

Telephone office Directly behind the post office and also on the south side of Piaţa Unirii (daily 7am–10pm).

Train tickets Domestic rail tickets can be bought at the Agenţia CFR at Piaţa Mihai Viteazul 20 (Mon–Fri 7am–7pm) and international train tickets from Piaţa Unirii 9 (Mon–Fri 8am–7pm).

The Transylvanian Heath

On the whole, the **Transylvanian Heath** (Mezőség) surrounding Cluj is a dull region covered with huge prairie fields. The only reason to stop is to seek out the impromptu **musical events** in villages, houses and sleazy smalltown bars. Finding the best – or anything at all – depends on local tip-offs and a bit of luck; it's often easy to spot musicians since so many of them are Gypsies (occasionally descended from the wandering Lăutari tribe) and thus noticeably darker than other people. **Turda**, an industrialized town 30km south of Cluj, is a good base from which to visit the **Turda gorge** and to explore the Arieş valley and the Apuseni mountains which lie to its west.

Sic and the musical villages

One of the best places for music in this area is the village of **Sic**, 70km northeast of Cluj; road and rail routes head to nearby **Gherla**, from where buses will take you the remaining 20km southeast to Sic. The traditional **Transylvanian musical style** has three musicians – on violin, viola (*contra*) and double bass, sometimes with another violinist for a fuller sound – with ancient Magyar and Romanian melodies woven in with Gypsy riffs from Indian. The violin plays the melody while the *contra* – often merely three-stringed – provides a chordal accompaniment with the bass. Other excellent bands can be found in the villages of Pălatca (Magyarpalatka), Vaida-Cămăraş (Vajdakamarás), Cojocna (Kolozs), Suatu (Magyarszovát) and Soporu de Cîmpie (Mezőszopor), all off the Reghin road to the east of Cluj.

GHERLA (Neuschloss) has been a centre of Armenian settlement since 1672 and was once called Armenopolis; carved Armenian family crests are still visible over many doorways. The lurid green Baroque Armeno–Catholic cathedral, built between 1748 and 1804, stands on Piaţa Libertăţii opposite the town's one hotel, the *Coroana* (☎064/24.19.27; ②), which is straight ahead of you as you head into town from the station. To the right, just before the hotel, is the town museum, which houses its collection of Armenian manuscripts and **icons on glass** behind a superb gateway at Str. Mihai Viteazul 6. The tradition of painting icons on glass derives from fourteenth-century Venice, from where it spread through the mountains of the Tyrol and Bohemia to the Carpathians; but popular tradition ascribes it to an icon of the Virgin which reputedly shed tears in the Monastery of Nicula, just east of Gherla, in 1694. Immediately south of Gherla is the small spa of Băile Băiţa Gherla where basic cabins and rooms are available at Str. Clujului 26.

SIC (Szék), reached by bus (seven a day) from Gherla's bus station, spreads over several hills, with a number of churches and municipal buildings testifying to its former importance as a centre of salt mining. There's a high proportion of Magyars here and some Gypsies, their dwellings neatly thatched and painted blue. In defiance of Ceauşescu's breeding policies, villagers here produced only one child per family, so as not to divide their land holdings further; therefore the population is actually shrinking.

The village is considered to be a kind of repository of Hungarian folk culture. Certainly, the Magyars here wear **costumes**, the like of which have long disappeared into museums in Hungary – the men in narrow-brimmed, tall straw hats and blue waistcoats and the women in leather waistcoats and black headscarves embroidered with flowers, blouses and full red pleated skirts.

It's said that every street in Sic has its own band, typically of the traditional Transylvanian style. During the weekend **markets**, Gypsies inspire the villagers to wild **dances** with a stream of rough-edged music overlaying a pulsating bass rhythm.

Turda

TURDA (Torda) lies 30km south of Cluj along the main DN1. The modern Turda, with its 58,000 mainly Magyar inhabitants, produces chemicals and building materials, and is ringed by filthy factories. Beyond these is a surprisingly elegant centre, but the main reasons to come to the town are to visit the spectacular **Turda**

gorge, 8km to the west, and to explore the Arieş valley beyond in the foothills of the Apuseni mountains.

Turda was once one of the wealthiest towns in the country, as the grand stone houses lining its streets bear witness. On the broad main street, Piaţa Republicii, stand two Gothic churches: the lower one is Calvinist and dates from 1400, and the upper one is late fifteenth-century Roman Catholic, with a Baroque interior, which housed meetings of the Transylvanian Diet, including the promulgation of the 1568 **Edict of Turda**. This edict recognized the equality of four faiths – Calvinist, Lutheran, Roman Catholic and Unitarian – in Transylvania at a time when religious wars were all the rage in Europe. However, it merely tolerated Orthodoxy, the religion of the Vlachs, and contributed to the ethnic and religious discrimination against them. There is a long history of Christianity in Turda – fifth-century Christian tombs have been found among Roman remains, and these can be seen in the **museum** in the Voivodal Palace at B-dul Haşdeu 2, behind the Calvinist church.

Turda is well served by **buses** from Cluj (generally two an hour from Autogară 1, picking up at Piaţa Ştefan cel Mare), which drop off on Strada Gheorghe Lazăr, beyond the market to the east of Piaţa Republicii. **Trains** stop at the town of Cîmpia Turzii, 9km east, where Michael the Brave was murdered. Take bus #2 from the train station to Piaţa Republicii. There's just one **hotel** in town, the *Potaissa* at Piaţa Republicii 6 (☎064/31.16.91; ③), which also has the town's only **restaurant**. There are coffee shops around Piaţa Republicii.

The Turda gorge

The **Turda gorge** (Cheile Turzii) is a two-hour walk from town, following red and blue cross markings southwest along the DN75 (west from the main roundabout below Piaţa Republicii). Buses towards Corneşti will take you part of the way – get off at the unmarked turning 2km beyond Mihai Viteazu and continue north on foot for 5km. Either way you'll end up at the *cabana* and campsite just before the gorge itself. A footpath, marked with red stripes and crosses, heads north up the gorge, overshadowed by 300-metre-high cliffs containing caves formerly used as hideouts by outlaws. After about an hour the path ends at **Petreştii de Jos**, from where there are occasional buses back to Turda. These pass 1km north of the village of **Sănduleşti**, where there's a fourteenth-century stone Orthodox church, a rare thing in Transylvania, as the Orthodox Church was forbidden to build its churches in stone at that time.

The Apuseni mountains

The **Apuseni mountains**, southwest of Cluj, are bordered to the south by the Arieş valley and to the north by the Crişul Repede valley, giving a variety of access points into the range that are reasonably well served by public transport. From Turda, the **Arieş valley** runs west, between the Apuseni massif to the north, and various smaller ranges such as the Trascău and Metaliferi ("Metalbearing") mountains to the south. Both the DN75 and the narrow-gauge rail line to Abrud follow the valley as far as Cîmpeni, capital of the **Moţi highlanders**. Having successfully resisted the Roman conquest, the Moţi moved from the valleys into the hills in the eighteenth century when the Hapsburgs attempted to conscript them into the army, and they now live all year round at up to 1400m, some of the highest settlements in Romania, in scattered groups of high-roofed thatched cottages. Along the **Crişul Repede valley**, most fast trains stop only at Huedin, Ciucea and Aleşd, but *personal* services open up countless opportunities for exploration by stopping at every hamlet along the line.

A **national park**, first proposed in 1924, is at last being created in the Apuseni mountains – despite opposition from the forestry and other industries. This should protect a huge area of karst with its unique culture, but industries in the area such as uranium mining, which actually make large losses, still remain open as the government cannot afford to close them down due to the jobs at stake.

The Arieş valley

Travelling up the Arieş valley towards Abrud is frustrating if you're relying on the trains – they take five hours to complete the 93km journey, stopping at every station en route, and there are only two services a day each way. Taking the morning train from Turda and returning by the evening service just about makes day-trips possible, and there are enough buses for you not to be left stranded. The *cabana* at **BURU** has its own rail halt (14km west of Turda) and is also served by buses, making it less of a strain to catch the morning train.

The attractive village of **RIMETEA** (Torockó), 8km south of the Buru train station, was built by German miners; its population is now largely Hungarian and traditional dress is worn for the local festival on February 22; there's homestay accommodation at Strada Principală 144 (☎Rimetea 117). Another three stops west is **OCOLIŞ**, 2km south of the **Runcu gorge**, where there's a hike, marked with blue crosses, which runs through the gorge to the *Muntele Băişorii cabana* and ski resort. Three stops west, at **SĂLCIUA DE JOS**, festivals take place on April 4 and October 20, and accommodation is available in the priest's house at no. 235 (☎Sălciua de Jos 131) and in no. 125 (☎Sălciua de Jos 118); from here there's a day's walk south to the **Huda lui Papară cave and the Rîmeţ gorge** (on a goat track along the cliff or through the stream itself). From the fourteenth-century **monastery** of **RÎMEŢ**, at the far end of the gorge, there are three buses a day south to Teiuş and Alba Iulia (see p.167).

In **LUPŞA**, 70km west of Turda, a well-known **ethnographic museum** (daily 8am–noon, 2–6pm; best to call ☎Lupşa 10 in advance) stands below a stone church raised on its hillock in 1421 and now being restored. Across the river to the south, reached by a footbridge, or a new road bridge 1km west, is the village of **HĂDĂRĂU** which boasts a similar Gothic church, also now undergoing restoration. **Lupşa monastery** is 2km west of the village itself, along the main road and just before the Muşca train station. It has a lovely little church, with wooden roof and belfry, which dates back to 1429.

Cîmpeni and around

CÎMPENI (Topánfalva), at the western end of the Arieş valley, is the capital of the *Ţara Moţilor* and a possible base for forays in to the mountains. The town is well served by buses, and the bus station is just east of the centre; but if you arrive by **train**, you face a twenty-minute walk into town – turn left out of the station and then right along Strada Gării to reach a bridge by the market, which marks the centre of the town. The only **hotel** in town is the rather poor *Tulnic* at Piaţa Avram Iancu 1 (☎064/77.16.97; ②), with an even more dispiriting restaurant, and a half-built campsite. The town's **Avram Iancu Museum**, by the river on the corner of

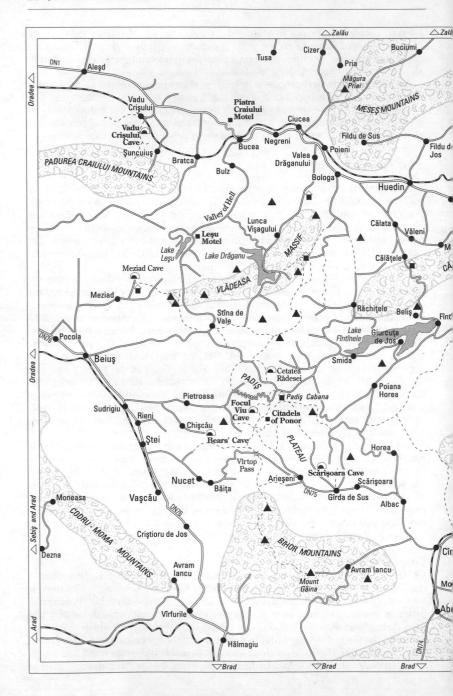

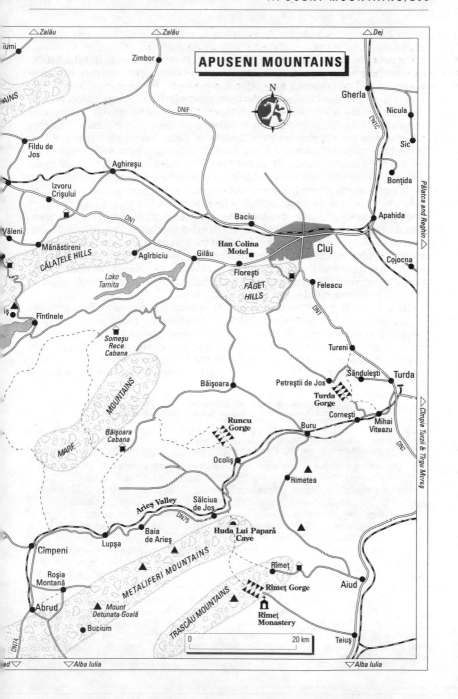

Strada Revoluției 1848, seems decrepit but is still functional, although opening times seem to be erratic.

The train line heads south from Cîmpeni to its penultimate stop, **ROȘIA MON-TANĂ**, where a subterranean curiosity lies a few kilometres to the east. Evidence suggests that Transylvania was a major source of gold for the ancient world – the Romans certainly used slaves to mine these mountains and 24 wax tablets recording details of the operation have been found. These can be seen in the **mining museum**, the highlight of which is a 400-metre section of the winding, ancient galleries, romantically dubbed the **Citadels of Gold**, but now overwhelmed by present-day mining operations. From here there's a one-hour walk (marked by red triangles) south to **ABRUD**, where the valley trains terminate. The old town, whose medieval buildings incorporate stones from earlier Roman structures and are liberally adorned with plaques commemorating the many notables who visited when Abrud was the Moți capital, is far more attractive than Cîmpeni; unfortunately the new – and only – hotel (④) lies amid the grim blocks of the new town, 2km southeast along Strada Republicii, the road to Zlatna. From Piața Eroilor there are buses to **BUCIUM**, 13km east and the commercial centre for some thirty small mining villages; it is also the starting point for an hour's climb to two basalt crags known as the **Detunata**. As in Slovakia and Silesia the miners here have a ceremonial "uniform", and the local folk costume combines elements of this with traditional highland wear.

GÎRDA DE SUS is 30km northwest of Cîmpeni. It is a pretty village with old houses and a part-wooden church built in 1792, with naive paintings inside; more notably, it is the starting point for several excellent hikes, the most popular of which, marked with blue stripes, begins near the **campsite** and leads north through the Ordîncușa gorges, past a mill and into a forest – a three-hour hike ending at the village of Ghețari. **GHEȚARI** is named after the **ice cave of**

THE GIRL FAIR OF MUNTELA GĂINA

The **Girl Fair** (*Tîrgul de fete*) of Muntela Găina takes place on the Sunday before July 20 on the flat top of Mount Găina, roughly 33km west of Cîmpeni, near the village of **AVRAM IANCU**. The fair is the region's largest festival, and was originally a means of allowing young men who were often away with the flocks for two-thirds of the year to meet young women from other communities and, if their parents were willing, to pursue matrimony. Naturally, prospective spouses made every effort to enhance their appeal, the girls being displayed in their finest attire, surrounded by linen, pottery and other items of dowry – even to the extent of carting along rented furniture. Nowadays this aspect of the fair has all but disappeared, but thousands still come for the music and spectacle.

A special bus service transports visitors from Cîmpeni to Avram Iancu, named after the leader of the 1848 revolt against the Hungarians who was born here in 1824. The village hosts a large and lively fair and some people never get beyond this, but the real action is on the hilltop, and you should really be there, camping, the night before to catch the local's dawn chorus on *tulnics* (alp horns). A rough forestry road takes an 8km loop to reach the hilltop, but you can find more direct routes on foot. The biggest names in popular traditional Romanian music appear here, with local dance ensembles, and plenty of food and drink; but there is little drunkenness and everyone behaves well, with unarmed Romanian Information Service troops in attendance.

Scǎrişoara (*Peştera gheţarul*; daily 9am–5pm), a few minutes' west of the village. The cave is filled with 70,000 cubic metres of ice, 15 metres thick, which has preserved evidence of climatic changes over the last 4000 years. At the back of the main chamber is the "church", so called because of its pillar formations, while the lower galleries, only discovered in 1950, are closed scientific reservations. From the cave it's a five-hour walk north to the karstic Padiş Plateau (see p.207). Local people are also creating new marked walking routes in the area between Albac and the Ice cave, taking in Horea's birthplace near the village of the same name.

The Padiş plateau

The **Padiş plateau** (Plateul Padiş) is in the heart of a classic karst area, with streams vanishing underground and reappearing unexpectedly, and dips and hollows everywhere, all promising access to the huge cave systems that lie beneath the plateau. It's a five-hour hike northwest of Scǎrişoara along a track marked with blue stripes to the *Padiş Cabana*, which lies at the crossroads of the plateau, the focal point of the Apuseni region and a paradise of caves, sinkholes and subterranean rivers. Motorists and cyclists can approach with care from the west via Pietroasa, or from the east via Rǎchiţele or Poiana Horea. There are buses from Huedin to Rǎchiţele and Poiana Horea (two or three a day, but no service at weekends), from where it's an easy day's hike to Padiş.

Hikes on the plateau

Of the various **trails** starting from the *Padiş cabana*, the most popular, marked with blue dots, is a three-hour hike south to the underground complex of **Cetǎţile Ponorului** (the "Citadels of Ponor"), where the Ponor stream flows through a series of sinkholes up to 150m deep. There's a good camping spot en route at Glavoi, a one-hour walk away. A trail marked by yellow dots leads back to *Padiş cabana* from the third hollow of the Ponor Citadels via the **Focu Viu** ice cave (from Focu Viu the route is marked with red stripes). Alternatively, you could head south from Ponor to Arieşeni in three hours (see p.294) following red trian-

---

KARST TOPOGRAPHY

Karst landscapes are formed by the action of rainwater on limestone. Rain picks up small amounts of carbon dioxide from the atmosphere as it falls, forming a weak carbonic acid which, when it falls on limestone rock, slowly dissolves it. Gradually, over millions of years, this causes hairline cracks in the limestone, which are steadily enlarged by running water. In its early stages, karst scenery is characterized by thin, narrow ridges and fissures; as these grow and deepen, the dry limestone is raked into wild, sharp-edged fragments and bleached white, like shards of bone.

In these landscapes rivers will often disappear down holes where the limestone is weakest, and flow for miles underground, suddenly bursting from rocks where the geology changes. If an underground river widens and forms a cavern, the drips of rainwater percolating through the soil above will deposit miniscule amounts of the calcium bicarbonate that the rain has dissolved from the limestone above. Over millions of years these deposits form stalactites and stalagmites which are often coloured by traces of other minerals such as iron and copper.

gles, or west from Focu Viu to Pietroasa in two-and-a-half hours (see p.293), following yellow dots and triangles.

North of the *Padiş cabana*, you can hike to **Cetatea Rădesei**; follow red stripes along a track to the forestry road and head north. Ten minutes beyond the Vărăşoaia pass, take another path (red dots) to the right to the citadel itself. Here you can follow the stream through a cave – slightly spooky but quite safe, although a flashlight helps – and follow the overground route back (marked by red dots) to see the various skylights from above.

Other hikes simply follow forestry roads, west to Pietroasa (marked by blue crosses), east to Răchiţele or Poiana Horea (unmarked), or northwest to **Stîna de Vale** (red stripes). This last route continues from Vărăşoaia, climbing to the Cumpănatelu saddle (1640m) and eventually turning right off the main ridge to descend through the forest to the resort (see p.293). Unlike most trails in the area, this six-hour walk is quite safe in winter.

Huedin and around

HUEDIN (Bánffyhunyad), to the north of the Apuseni range and 46km west of Cluj, is a small town with a largely systematized centre. The sixteenth-century Protestant church with its solid guard-tower survives, and inside there's a delightfully wonky coffered ceiling; ask at the parish office for the key. Huedin's one **hotel** is the modern but charmless *Vlădeasa* (☎064/25.15.90 after 3pm) and there's a good range of coffee shops (*cofetărie*).

However, the chief reason for stopping here is to pick up buses to settlements in the surrounding valleys, where traditional customs, architecture and crafts, both Romanian and Magyar, have so far escaped obliteration by the twentieth century. Huedin's **bus station** is five minutes west of the **train station** and from either its just five minutes, walk south to the centre of town. Most of the surrounding villages are served by two or three buses a day during the week, but the service is virtually nonexistent at weekends.

Villages around Huedin

A minor road heads 9km south to the village of **CĂLATA** (Nagykalota), where the Magyar population still wear their home-made **folk costumes**, and on to the nearby village of **CĂLĂŢELE** (Kiskalota), where you'll see carved wooden homesteads. Sixteen kilometres beyond is **BELIŞ** (Jósikafalva), where a resort (☎064/11.69.05), with camping and two identical hotels, the *Diana* and *Radu* (both ☎064/43.22.42), is being developed beside the artificial Lake Fîntînele.

MĂNĂSTIRENI (Magyargyerőmonostor) lies to the southeast of Huedin on a minor road south from the road out to Cluj. The village has a lovely thirteenth-century walled church whose gallery and pews were beautifully painted in the eighteenth century. Just west of here is **VĂLENI** (Magyarvalkó), where many of the houses have decorated mouldings. Its Gothic monastery church has a wonderful hilltop setting and a collection of typically Magyar carved wooden graveposts.

In the valleys to the north of Huedin there are half a dozen villages with striking **wooden churches** – examples of the Gothic-inspired wooden churches which once reared above peasant settlements from the Tisa to the Carpathians. The most spectacular, and the nearest to Huedin, towers over **FILDU DE SUS** (Felsőfüld), a small village reached by a 10km track west from Fildu de Jos (Alsófüld) on the Huedin–Zalău road. Built in 1727, the church was painted in

THE CULTURE OF THE KALOTASZEG

The area immediately west of Cluj is known to Hungarians as **Kalotaszeg** and, since the great Hungarian Millennium Exhibition of 1896, it has been revered as the place where authentic Magyar culture has survived uncorrupted. It's common to see local people selling handicrafts by the roadside – particularly to Hungarian tourists on pilgrimages to the wellsprings of Magyar culture.

The local **embroidery** is particularly famous, usually consisting of stylized leaves and flowers, in one bold colour (usually bright red) on a white background; the style is known as *irásos*, meaning "drawn" or "written", because the designs are drawn onto the cloth (traditionally with a mixture of milk and soot) before being stitched. The Calvinist churches of these villages are noted for their **coffered ceilings**, made up of square panels (often called "cassettes"), beautifully painted, along with the pew and galleries, in the eighteenth century in a naive style similar to the embroidery. The architects of the "national romantic" school, led by Károly Kós (see p.181), were strongly influenced by Transylvanian village architecture, as well as by that of the Finns, the Magyars' only relations.

The composers **Béla Bartók and Zoltán Kodály** put together fine collections of Transylvanian handicrafts, and Bartók's collection of carved furniture from Izvoru Crişului (Körösfő) can be seen in his home in Budapest. The composers' main project, however, was to collect the **folk music** of Transylvania. Starting in 1907, they managed to record and catalogue thousands of melodies, despite local suspicion of the "monster" (the apparatus for recording onto phonograph cylinders). Through the project, they discovered a rich vein of inspiration for their own compositions; Bartók declared that a genuine peasant melody was "quite as much a masterpiece in miniature as a Bach fugue or a Mozart sonata...a classic example of the expression of a musical thought in its most conceivably concise form, with the avoidance of all that is superfluous".

1860, with scenes of Daniel in the den with some wonderful grinning lions. The oldest of the wooden churches, erected during the sixteenth century, is at **ZIMBOR** (Magyarzsombor), a further 20km north along the Huedin–Zalău road. Later churches show developing flourishes including carved wooden gates, such as those at **SÎNMIHAIU ALMAŞULUI** (Almásszentmihály), 5km out of Zimbor. From here a minor road heads north to Jibou, passing through **HIDA** (Hídalmás) after 4km, and **RACÎŞ** (Almásrákos), a further 6km north, whose churches are distinguished by carved columns and old murals.

Ciucea and beyond

Twenty kilometres west of Huedin, by road and rail, is the village of **CIUCEA** (Csucsa). Midway along the route lies Bologa, whose fourteenth-century ruined castle can be seen from the road and railway. There is a two-day hike from Bologa to the Padiş plateau (see p.207) and a small private **hotel**, the *Romanţa* (☎064/25.15.85), where you could break your journey. At the east end of Ciucea village is a **museum** (Tues–Sun 10am–5pm) dedicated to the poet and politician **Octavian Goga** (see box on p.210). Goga bought the house of the Hungarian poet **Endre Ady**, who lived in the village until 1917, and had a sixteenth-century **wooden church** from Gălpîia brought here in order to preserve it. Later still Goga's own mausoleum was built in the grounds.

The Measurement of the Milk Festival

Like pastoral folk in Bulgaria, Spain and Greece, the Romanian highlanders entrust their sheep and goats to shepherds, who spend summer in the high pastures protecting the flocks from bears and wolves and making cheeses for the community's winter sustenance. In Romania, this has given rise to **Measurement of the Milk Festivals** (Măţurisul Laptelui), held by the villages around Ciucea and on the slopes of Măgura Priei, the highest ridge in the Mezeş range. At dawn on the first Sunday in May, the shepherds bring the flocks, which have spent a couple of days grazing on the new grass in the hills, to meet the villagers in a glade where the "measurement" takes place. The she-goats are milked by women and the ewes are milked by shepherds – the yield of each family's animals is measured to determine the quota of cheese that they will receive during that season. The ritual is accompanied by much feasting and dancing.

Măgura Priei is only a couple of kilometres north of the road east from Ciucea to Românaşi, but if you come by bus, you will approach from **PRIA**, to the north. The daily bus from Zalău to Ciucea will drop you at the turning to Pria, just north of Cizer, from where it's about 4km to the village. The only tourist **accommodation** between Bologa and Zalău is a campsite on the DN1F north of Românaşi.

South into the mountains

Two dramatically named valleys run south into the Apuseni mountains on either side of Ciucea, meeting at Stîna de Vale. To the east, the **Valea Drăganului** ("Devil's Valley") runs south from the train halt and tourist complex of the same name. A daily bus runs from Huedin as far as Lunca Vişagului, from where you can follow the forestry road south past a reservoir before following

<hr>

ENDRE ADY AND OCTAVIAN GOGA

Ady Endre, as he is known by the Magyars, was the great figure of early modernist poetry in Hungary. Born in 1877 in Érmindszent (now named Ady Endre) in Satu Mare county, he went to Paris in 1904, where he came into contact with Symbolist poetry, and returned to Hungary as a radical and exciting new poet. He stood against chauvinism and narrow-minded nationalism, but his poetry was not always properly focused. A notorious womanizer, he married in 1915, but died four years later, weakened by syphilis.

His near contemporary **Octavian Goga** was born in Răşinari, near Sibiu, in 1881, and studied at the Hungarian Lyceum in Sibiu and at Budapest University. However, while writing mainly for the Romanian literary magazine *Luceafărul*, he identified himself with the quest for Transylvanian independence from Hungary, and was imprisoned for his beliefs, then sentenced to death *in absentia* and further accused of raising legions from POWs in Russia to fight the Hapsburgs during World War I. In 1919 he married and travelled through Bolshevik Russia to Versailles under a false name to be Vice-President of the National Committee for the Union of the Romanians, lobbying successfully at the Versailles peace conference. For the 1937 elections, Iuliu Maniu made a pact with the Iron Guard to ensure his position as Prime Minister, but the king outmanoeuvred them by installing Goga as prime minister of a coalition government headed by the anti-semitic National League of Christian Defence; he lasted six chaotic weeks before the king dismissed him for insulting his mistress. Nevertheless his romantic poetry, "full of soil and peasant values", is still admired in Romania the track marked with blue crosses west to Stîna de Vale (see p.293). The road down the **Valea Iadului** ("Valley of Hell") turns off the DN1 at the Piatra Craiului train station, by the wooden church of Bucea, and just east of the *Piatra Craiului* motel. Civilization ends after 25km, at the *Leşu* motel, by the artificial lake of the same name; it's another 20km, past the Iadolina waterfall, to Stîna de Vale.

Local trains stop at ŞUNCUIUŞ (Vársonkolyos), 23km west of Ciucea and 10km south of the DN1. From here a track leads east to the **Peştera Vintului** ("Cave of the Wind"). The cave's 46km of passages are on four levels and have taken years to explore; access is still restricted to experienced cavers, but it's possible that part of the cave will soon be opened to the public.

From Şuncuiuş you can walk west along the river and the rail line to the next halt, *Peştera*, and the **Vadu Crişului** cave; ask at the *cabana* across the footbridge about visiting the cave 29km west of Ciucea. The cave is also accessible from Vadu Crişului (Rév), a village just south of the DN1, traditionally known for producing unglazed red and white pottery; it's a two-kilometre walk through the Crişul Repede gorge. Beyond Vadu Crişului, the road and the rail line run together across the plain to Oradea, the gateway to the Banat (see p.286).

Northern Transylvania

The two counties of Sălaj and Bistriţa-Năsăud, covering the swath of ranges from the Apuseni mountains to the Eastern Carpathians, are historically referred to as **Northern Transylvania**, the tract of territory which Hitler ordered to be handed over to his Hungarian allies. If you're travelling from Cluj to Maramureş, or eastwards over the Carpathians into Moldavia, road and rail routes are fast and direct, but it's well worth considering detours or stopovers in this little-visited region.

To the west, the chief attraction is the idyllic rural scenery of Sălaj county, with its many old wooden churches, rather more homely than the finest examples of the genre, found just to the north in Maramureş. Express trains into Maramureş run via Jibou to Baia Mare, just over two hours from Dej. The quickest road route north is the DN1C to Baia Mare. Trains from Cluj into Moldavia run via Năsăud and the Ilva valley to Vatra Dornei and past several of the Painted Monasteries (see p.252). The DN17 heads east from Dej to Bistriţa and through the Bîrgău valley to Vatra Dornei. Bistriţa and Năsăud, 22km apart, are linked by frequent buses, so it's easy to hop from one route to the other.

Dej

DEJ, 46km north of Cluj, lies at the junction of routes from Cluj to Maramureş and Bucovina. The town centre is a good kilometre to the right of the main station, Dej Călători (bus #2, #3 or #9); the bus station is almost as far on the other side of town – to reach the centre take the path left to the PECO station and head left to cross the Someş river. The town centres around Piaţa Bobîlna, where the **Reformed Church**, built in late Gothic style between 1453 and 1536, faces the **Municipal Museum** (Tues–Fri & Sun 10am–4pm, Sat 10am–1pm), featuring the usual local history and a room dedicated to the surrounding salt industry. The Baroque Franciscan church (1726–30) is down the alley at Piaţa Bobîlna 16.

THE VIENNA DIKTAT

On August 30, 1941, Hitler, needing Hungarian support in his new offensive against the Soviet Union, forced Romania to cede 43,492 square kilometres and 2.6 million people in northern Transylvania to Hungary in the **Vienna Diktat** (or "Belvedere Treaty"). The new border ran south of Cluj, Tîrgu Mureş and Sfîntu Gheorghe and then more or less followed the watershed of the Eastern Carpathians north to the border of what is now Ukrainian Transcarpathia. The border is still a living memory in these areas, and locals will be able to show you the earthworks that used to mark it.

Over 10,000 Romanians, mostly members of the educated classes, such as civil servants, teachers, lawyers and priests, were expelled in cattle trucks, some at just two hours' notice, and others after being subjected to mock executions. Atrocities were committed in the appropriated region by the Horthyist police, with 89 killed in the village of Treznea and 157 in Ip, both in Sălaj county, a pattern of atrocity that was repeated after the more extreme Sztójay Döme government took power in Budapest in March 1944 and the Hungarians, Hitler's last allies, retreated before the Red Army.

Dej has two **hotels**, the *Someş*, a decent enough 1970s tower block at Piaţa Mărăşeşti 1 (☎064/21.33.30, fax 43.22.39; ④), and the better *Parc-Rex*, by the river at Strada Aleco Russo 9 (☎064/21.37.99, fax 21.13.25; ⑤), which has good sized rooms with private bath and cable TV.

Zalău and around

You'll usually need to change trains at Jibou, 76km northwest of Dej, for the county capital, **ZALĂU**, 23km to the west. Zalău is in fact little more than a small country town with a large industrial fringe grafted on since World War II. There's nothing of interest in town beyond the county **museum** at Str. Pieţei 9 (Tues–Sun 10am–6pm), which has a good archeological display; the art section is not far south at Str. Doja 6.

Zalău has two **hotels**, just to the north of the museum: the *Porolissum*, on Piaţa Unirii (☎060/61.47.20, fax 61.64.31), and immediately behind it the much more welcoming *Meseş* (☎060/61.47.20). The **bus station** is about twenty minutes' walk north of the centre at Str. Mihai Viteazul 54, and the **train station** is a further fifteen minutes north, at the south end of the village of Crişeni; bus #1 links them both to the centre, taking about 15 minutes from the train station.

Around Zalău

The ruins of the Roman settlement, Porolissum, built to defend the northernmost limit of Roman Dacia, are 12km east of Zalău, immediately south of the village of Moigrad. The settlement's Praetorian Gate has been rebuilt, and you can still see the remains of the ramparts (*vallum*) that blocked the valley and the amphitheatre, as well as the ruins of an earlier Dacian citadel on the adjacent hill.

A couple of buses a day run south from Zalău to **BUCIUMI**, an old Romanian settlement noted for its local costumes and choral and flute music, which celebrates its festival on August 15, the Assumption of the Virgin. Rising to the west of Buciumi are the Meseş hills – rugged highlands that host the **Shepherds' Festival** (Măgura Priei) on the first Sunday of May.

Heading northwest from Zalău, you'll pass through Şarmăşag, from where you can reach the tiny village of **SIGHETU SILVANIEI** with its wooden church; from Şarmăşag station turn left and walk for about fifty minutes, then take the unmarked and unsurfaced road on the right. The church, built in about 1632, is small and simple, with a new basilica recently added. In addition, a village **fair** takes place here beneath Michael's Oak on the second Sunday of July. Southwest of Şarmăşag, towards Oradea, is **ŞIMLEU SILVANEI**, the main centre of western Sălaj, where there are the ruins of a fifteenth-century castle. Continuing south from here there are several remote villages in the foothills of the Plopiş massif – SÎRBI and TUSA have good wooden churches. Two stops north of Şarmăşag is **DERŞIDA**, which has a fine eighteenth-century wooden church. There's another one at **CORUND**, 8km southeast of the Supur train station, which also holds a fete on January 14 and 15. At the next stop, Aciş (which has a Romanesque church), the train line veers west to Carei, where you can pick up trains to Oradea as well as to Satu Mare and Baia Mare in Maramureş, while the main road continues northwards for 44km to Satu Mare.

Năsăud and the Someş Mare valley

Twenty-five kilometres east of Dej lies the small town of Beclean (Bethlen), at the junction of routes north into Maramureş. The road and rail routes to Vatra Dornei and Suceava in Moldavia also divide here, drivers heading southeast through Bistriţa while train routes run further north via Năsăud.

NĂSĂUD (Nussdorf) is at the heart of a region where villagers still wear their traditional embroidered waistcoats and blouses, and hats decorated with peacock feathers. A selection of these is on display in the **museum** in the former border guards' barracks at Strada Granicerilor 25. Just west, on the main Piaţa Libertăţii, the large Orthodox church still shows the signs of its Greek-Catholic origins in Hapsburg times. On the south side of the square, at Strada Ion Prodan 1, is the only **accommodation** in town, the *Hotel Sălăuţa* (☎063/36.26.01; ②), which has no hot water and only the most basic of facilities.

Just 5km south of town along the Bistriţa road is the birthplace of **Liviu Rebreanu** (1885–1944), whose novels *Ion, Uprising* and *The Forest of the Hanged* give a panoramic view of Romanian society before the First World War – the village is now named after its most eminent son.

The Someş Mare valley

Twenty kilometres east of Năsăud lies Ilva Mică, the junction of a minor branch line up the Someş Mare valley towards the Rodna mountains, which provides access to **Sîngeorz-Băi**, a good starting point for hikes north into the Rodna massif. Of this shabby spa's hotels and *cabana*s, the privatized *Vila Lotus* (☎063/37.07.97) is the best value. The line terminates at the mining town of Rodna Veche, 7km short of **ŞANŢ**; buses from Năsăud and Rodna Veche run here. This attractive village of wooden houses with open verandas and shingled roofs is noted for its elaborate wedding celebrations, usually held at weekends.

One of the best festivals in the region is held at **LEŞU**, eight minutes up the line from Ilva Mică towards Vatra Dornei; from the Leşu Ilvei train halt it's a further 4km walk east up the valley to the village. The village's **Rhapsody of the Trişcaşi Festival** is held on the first Sunday of September and brings together pipers from the counties of Bistriţa-Năsăud, Vîlcea and Maramureş, and is a great opportunity to hear pan-pipe music.

Bistriţa and the Bîrgău valley

BISTRIŢA (Bistritz), 40km southeast of Beclean, and the forested Bîrgău valley beyond, are the setting for much of Bram Stoker's *Dracula*; his Dracula's castle lies in the Bîrgău valley and it was in Bistriţa that Jonathan Harker received the first hints that something was amiss. Stoker never visited Romania, though he read widely about the terrain and accurately described the hills covered with orchards that surround the town.

The Town

Remains of Neolithic settlements have been found near Bistriţa, although the earliest records of the town coincide with the arrival of Saxon settlers, for whom this town was the capital of Saxon *Nösnerland*. Nowadays, Bistriţa's appearance is predominantly modern, and for evidence of its folk traditions you should pay a visit to the **museum** (Tues–Sun 10am–6pm) or, preferably, explore the neighbouring Bîrgău valley.

From the train and bus stations its about ten minutes' walk to the centre – head southeast on Strada Gării and then northeast on Strada Şincai to reach the main square, **Piaţa Centrală**, dominated by a great Saxon Evangelical **church**. Built in the Gothic style in the fourteenth century, the church was given Renaissance features in 1563, including a 76.5-metre tower, by Petrus Italus, who also introduced the Renaissance style to Moldavia. On the northwest side of Piaţa Centrală, the arcaded **Şugălete** buildings (occupied by merchants in the fifteenth century) give

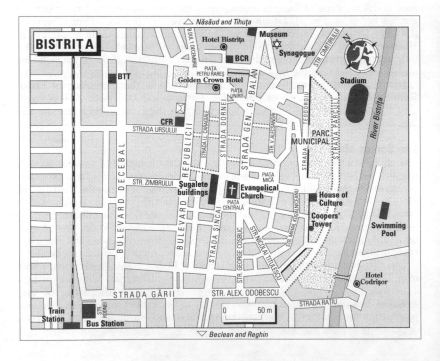

a partial impression of how the town must have looked in its medieval heyday. At Str. Dornei 5 you'll find the **Casa Argintarului**, a stone-framed Renaissance silversmith's house now housing an art college (Mon–Fri 8am–8pm), and continuing northeast, on Piața Unirii, is the Orthodox church, dating from 1280 (with fourteenth-century additions). Beyond it, in a former barracks at Str. Gen. Balăn 81, the **County Museum** (Tues–Sun 10am–6pm) has a collection of Thracian bronzeware, Celtic artefacts, products of the Saxon guilds, mills and presses. Like Brașov and Sibiu, Bistrița used to be heavily fortified, but successive fires during the nineteenth century have left only vestiges of the fourteenth-century citadel along Strada Kogălniceanu and Strada Teodoroiu, including the **Coopers' Tower** (*Turnul Dogarilor*) in the Municipal Park.

Practicalities

Trains from Beclean stop at Bistrița Nord, but you may have to make a connection at Sărățel, just southeast of Beclean on the Deda–Brașov line. There are several **hotels** in town, the most interesting to Dracula fans will be the *Coroana de Aur* (Golden Crown) at Piața Petru Rareș 4 (☎063/21.26.27, fax 23.26.67; ACR; ④), named after the inn where Jonathan Harker was warned not to travel on St George's Day: "Do you not know that tonight, when the clock strikes midnight, all the evil things in the world will have full sway?"; it exploits the connection still further by serving alcoholic blood-red "Elixir Dracula" to its guests. Slightly less costly options are the *Bistrița* opposite at Str. Petru Rareș 2 (☎063/23.11.54, fax 23.18.26; ④), one of Romania's cheapest three-star hotels, and the *Codrișor*, on Str. Onișor (☎063/23.12.06, fax 21.62.60; ④), has excellent service and is highly recommended. The only budget option is the *Apollo*, Str A Mureșanu 3 (☎063/21.35.24; ①). The Coroana **tourist agency**, at Piața Petru Rareș 7A (☎063/23.18.03, fax 21.62.60), can arrange "Jonathan Harker" meals ("I dined on what they call 'robber steak' – bits of bacon, onion and beef, seasoned with red pepper, and strung on stick and roasted over the fire, in the simple style of the London cat's-meat. The wine was Golden Mediasch, which produces a queer sting on the tongue, which is, however, not disagreeable."), excursions to, and reservations at, the *Dracula Hotel* (see p.216), and rural homestays. They will also be able to confirm the dates of **festivals** at Leșu and the Bîrgău villages, as well as the **International Folklore Festival** held in Bistrița itself in the second week of August. The CFR agency and post office are located right by the tourist office.

The Bîrgău valley

Buses leave Bistrița at 6.30am and 11am to head up the valley to Vatra Dornei in Moldavia (see p.260). Trains follow this route only as far as Prundu Bîrgăului, from where it's another 60km to Vatra Dornei, including the 1200-metre Tihuța Pass. Hitchhiking along this final stretch is not to be recommended since lifts may be few and wolves have been known to attack after dark; drivers, too, should bear in mind the possibility that snow might block the road at its highest point between October and mid-May.

The scenery of the Bîrgău valley is dramatic, with huge hills draped in forests of fir trees, and villages appearing as living monuments to a way of life unchanged for centuries; the ceramics, woodcarvings and folk dress displayed in the museum at **Livezele**, 8km from Bistrița (local bus #3), are part of everyday life in other villages further up the valley. In **Josenii Bîrgăului**, 8km beyond Livezele, black pottery is manufactured and old fulling mills and cottages remain in use. **Prundu Bîrgăului**,

6km east of Josenii, is the venue for the Raftsmen's Festival on March 28–29, when unmarried men crown their usual attire of sheepskin jackets with a small hat buried beneath a plume of peacock feathers. On St George's Day (April 23), it's customary for young men to light bonfires, over which unmarried girls jump – only one attempt is permitted, failure portending another year of maidenhood.

One kilometre on from Prundu Bîrgăului is **Tiha Bîrgăului**, which is occasional host to the interesting **Festival of Regele Brazilor** ("King of the Fir Trees"). This is an opportunity to hear the traditional songs, and the part-stereotyped, part-improvised lamentations (*bochet*) of relatives and friends of the deceased. The lamentations are an account of the deeds of the deceased in this life, which the peasants see as a necessary prelude to a continuing journey into another world, not much different from this one. If the festival runs at all, it is on the third Sunday of June; check at the tourist office in Bistriţa to confirm if the festival will take place.

Climbing steadily eastwards, the DN17 passes the village of Piatra Fîntînele and the **Dracula Hotel** (☎063/26.68.41, fax 26.61.19), which has one pseudo-medieval tower, and a cave-like tunnel in which they lay on spooky experiences. In the novel, Dracula's abode was located two days' journey from the "Borgo Pass" by Van Helsing's carriage, or one night's in the Count's calèche. In fact this hotel was built in 1983, to serve a few ski slopes. Just beyond lies the **Tihuţa pass**, which may be blocked by snow for a day or two between late October and mid-May. The surrounding mountains harbour more **bears** than in any other part of Europe, as well as red deer, boars and **wolves**, and the view from the pass of the green "crests" of Bucovina to the northeast and the volcanic Căliman mountains to the southeast is marvellous. The road descends past the picturesque village of Poiana Stampei to Vatra Dornei (see p.260).

travel details

Trains

Alba Iulia to: Arad (9 daily; 3–5hr); Cluj (9 daily; 1hr 30min–3hr); Sibiu (1 daily; 2hr); Timişoara (6 daily; 4hr–5hr); Tîrgu Mureş (1 daily; 2hr).

Bistriţa to: Bucharest (1 daily; 10hr); Cluj (3 daily; 3hr 30min).

Braşov to: Baia Mare (3 daily; 7hr–9hr); Bucharest (22 daily; 2hr 30min–4hr 30min); Cluj (6 daily; 4hr–5hr); Sibiu (9 daily; 2hr–4hr).

Cluj to: Baia Mare (1 daily; 3hr 30min); Braşov (7 daily; 4hr–6hr 30min); Bucharest (7 daily; 7hr–11hr 30min); Constanţa (1 summer only; 10hr); Iaşi (4 daily; 8hr–10hr); Oradea (12 daily; 2hr–3hr 30min); Sibiu (2 daily; 4hr); Sighişoara (15 daily; 3hr–4hr); Suceava (4 daily; 6hr–7hr); Tîrgu Mureş (3 daily; 2hr–3hr).

Deva to: Alba Iulia (13 daily; 1hr–2hr); Arad (20 daily; 2hr–3hr); Braşov (8 daily; 4hr–6hr); Cluj (5 daily; 2hr 30min–3hr); Sibiu (3 daily; 2hr 30min–3hr); Sighişoara (4 daily; 2hr–2hr 30min); Timişoara (7 daily; 3hr); Tîrgu Mureş (1 daily; 3hr 30min).

Făgăraş to: Braşov (12 daily; 1hr–2hr); Deva (3 daily; 4hr–5hr); Podu Olt (9 daily; 1hr–2hr); Sibiu (9 daily; 1hr 30min–2hr).

Hunedoara to: Bucharest (1 daily; 8hr 30min); Cluj (1 daily; 3hr); Simeria (14 daily; 30min).

Miercurea Ciuc to: Braşov (11 daily; 1hr 30min–2hr 30min); Dej (3 daily; 4hr–4hr 30min).

Sfîntu Gheorghe to: Baia Mare (1 daily; 8hr–9hr); Braşov (14 daily; 30min–1hr).

Sibiu to: Bucharest (8 daily; 5hr–11hr); Cluj (2 daily; 3hr–4hr); Iaşi (1 daily; 11hr).

Sighişoara to: Braşov (19 daily; 1hr 30min–3hr); Bucharest (13 daily; 4hr–8hr); Cluj (6 daily; 2hr 30min–3hr 30min).

Tîrgu Mureş to: Alba Iulia (2 daily; 2hr–3hr); Cluj (3 daily; 2hr–3hr); Timişoara (1 daily; 6hr 30min).

Buses

Abrud to: Alba Iulia (up to 7 daily); Arad (2 daily); Cîmpeni (12 daily); Cluj (2 daily); Oradea (2 daily); Sibiu (1 daily); Timişoara (1 daily).

Alba Iulia to: Cîmpeni (up to 6 daily); Oradea (2 daily); Sebeş (12 daily); Sibiu (1 daily); Tîrgu Mureş (1 daily).

Bistriţa to: Năsăud (20 daily); Tîrgu Mureş (up to 3 daily); Vatra Dornei (3 daily); Vişeu de Sus (1 daily).

Braşov Autogară 1 to: Piatra Neamţ (1 daily); Tîrgovişte (2 daily); Tîrgu Neamţ (1 daily). Autogară 2 to: Cîmpulung Muscel (7 daily); Curtea de Argeş (2 daily). Autogară 3 to: Băcau (4 daily); Iaşi (1 daily).

Cluj Autogară 1 to: Reghin (1 daily); Tîrgu Lăpuş (1 daily); Turda (up to 21 daily). Autogară 2 to Cîmpeni (4 daily); Sibiu (1 Mon-Sat), Tîrgu Mureş (1 daily), Zalău (4 daily).

Covasna to: Sfîntu Gheorghe (3 daily); Tîrgu Secuiesc (up to 6 daily).

Deva to: Brad (14 daily); Cîmpeni (2 daily); Haţeg (up to 4 daily); Hunedoara (up to 30 daily); Oradea (Mon–Sat 2 daily); Petroşani (3 daily); Reşiţa (Mon–Sat 1 daily); Rîmnicu Vîlcea (1 daily); Timişoara (Mon–Fri 2 daily); Tîrgu Jiu (2 daily).

Făgăraş to: Agnita (4 daily); Rupea (5 daily); Sîmbata (1, Sunday only).

Gherla to: Baia Mare (1 Mon-Fri), Bistriţa (1 daily), Sic (up to 7 daily); Tîrgu Lăpuş (1 daily); Tîrgu Mureş (1 daily).

Haţeg to: Deva (up to 4 daily); Hunedoara (up to 3 daily); Reşiţa (Mon–Sat 1 daily); Rîmnicu Vîlcea (Mon–Fri 2 daily); Tîrgu Jiu (2 daily).

Mediaş to: Agnita (3 daily); Făgăraş (1 daily); Sibiu (6 daily); Tîrgu Mureş (up to 9 daily).

Reghin to: Cluj (1 daily); Sighişoara (2 daily); Sovata (up to 2 daily); Tîrgu Mureş (up to 3 daily).

Sibiu to: Agnita (5 daily); Cisnădie (up to 32 daily); Cîmpeni (1 daily); Cluj (1 daily); Curtea de Argeş (1 daily); Mediaş (6 daily); Pitoçti (1 daily); Polovragi (1 daily); Rîmnicu Vîlcea (2 daily); Sighişoara (4 daily); Tîrgu Mureş (up to 3 daily).

Sighişoara to: Agnita (3 daily); Bistriţa (1 daily); Făgăraş (1 daily); Reghin (2 daily); Sibiu (4 daily); Tîrgu Mureş (up to 11 daily).

Sovata to: Miercurea Ciuc (up to 3 daily); Odorheiu Secuiesc (up to 8 daily); Praid (8 daily); Reghin (Mon–Sat 1 daily); Sighişoara (2 daily); Tîrgu Mureş (up to 10 daily).

Tîrgu Mureş to: Braşov (up to 2 daily), Bistriţa (up to 3 daily); Cluj (2 daily); Dej (1 daily); Mediaş (up to 9 daily); Miercurea Ciuc (up to 2 daily); Odorheiu Secuiesc (3 daily); Sfîntu Gheorghe (1 daily); Sovata (up to 10 daily); Tîrgu Neamţ (1 daily); Vatra Dornei (1 daily).

Tîrgu Secuiesc to: Bacău (1 daily); Miercurea Ciuc (1 daily); Sfîntu Gheorghe (3 daily).

Planes

Cluj to: Bucharest (Mon–Fri 2 daily, Sat 1 via Oradea).

Sibiu and **Tîrgu Mureş** to: Bucharest (1 daily, on a triangular route).

International trains

Braşov to: Berlin (1 daily; 26hr); Chişinău (3 a week; 15hr); Budapest (7 daily; 9hr–15hr); Dresden (1 daily; 23hr 30min); Munich (1 daily; 20hr); Prague (2 daily; 21hr); Vienna (2 daily; 15hr); Warsaw (1 daily; 23hr).

Cluj to: Budapest (3 daily; 6hr–8hr).

Deva to: Berlin (1 daily; 22hr); Budapest (4 daily; 6hr–7hr); Dresden (1 daily; 20hr); Munich (1 daily; 16hr); Prague (2 daily; 17hr); Vienna (2 daily; 11hr); Warsaw (1 daily; 18hr).

Miercurea Ciuc to: Budapest (1 daily; 13hr).

Sibiu to: Warsaw (1 daily; 21hr).

Tîrgu Mureş to: Budapest (1 daily; 10hr).

International buses

Braşov to: Budapest (2 weekly); Germany (daily); Istanbul (daily).

Cluj to: Budapest (6 weekly); Germany (daily); Istanbul (daily).

Deva to Budapest (1 daily); Germany (daily).

Gheorgheni to Budapest (4 weekly).

Miercurea Ciuc to Budapest (8 weekly).

Odorheiu Secuiesc to Budapest (12 weekly).

Reghin to Budapest (5 weekly).

Sfîntu Gheorghe to Budapest (11 weekly).

Sibiu to Germany (daily).

Sighişoara to Budapest (4 weekly).

Tîrgu Mureş to Budapest (12 weekly).

International planes

Cluj (DacAir) to: Budapest (Mon–Fri 1 daily); Munich (Mon, Wed & Fri 1 a day); Venice (Mon, Wed & Fri 1 a day).

CHAPTER FOUR

MOLDAVIA

This region, more than others in Romania, has experienced invasions, tumult, oppression and corruption, instilling in its people a fatalistic attitude. Throughout the centuries of Turkish domination, Moldavians burned lamps before the icons of a glorious past – embodied in the hero figure of Stephen the Great (Ştefan cel Mare) – and awaited its resurrection. It seemed to begin in the nineteenth century, with a flowering of art, liberal politics and land reform, but the wheel kept turning – through a bloody uprising and its suppression, Fascist and Communist terror, and a sham revolution, following which icon-burnishing remained as fashionable as ever.

Moldavia's complex **history** is best understood in relation to the cities of Iaşi and Suceava, the former capitals of the region, and you'll find more details under the individual city accounts. Moldavia used to be twice its present size, having at various times included Bessarabia (the land beyond the River Prut) and Northern Bucovina (on the edge of the Carpathians). Both territories were annexed by Stalin in 1940, severing cultural and family ties; these have revived since the fall of Communism, especially between Moldavia and the former Bessarabia – now the sovereign Republic of Moldova.

For travellers, Moldavia gets more interesting the further north you go, and the difficulty of some journeys can, perversely, add to the attraction of your final destination. This is particularly true of the jewels in the Moldavian crown, the **Painted Monasteries of Southern Bucovina**. Secluded in valleys near the Ukrainian border, their medieval frescoes of redemption and damnation blaze in polychromatic splendour at the misty, fir-clad hills – Voroneţ and Succviţa boast peerless examples of the Last Judgement and the Ladder of Virtue, Moldoviţa is famous for its fresco of the Siege of Constantinople, while Humor and Putna have a quieter charm. Though all are more or less accessible from the regional capital, **Suceava**, many visitors opt for ONT **tours** from Bucharest (see p.31), although it's far less expensive to make your own way to Suceava and book a tour there (see p.245).

As in Wallachia, most towns and cities have been marred by hideous concrete apartment blocks and factories, and only **Iaşi** holds any great appeal, having numerous churches and monasteries from its heyday as the Moldavian capital, and a charm that puts Bucharest to shame. In contrast to the new-town developments, the countryside looks fantastic, with picturesque **villages** dwarfed by the flanks of the Carpathians. Just over halfway to Suceava, Neamţ county contains Moldavia's largest **convents** – Agapia and Văratec – and the weirdly shaped **Ceahlău massif**, a paradise for hikers and climbers. While backwaters such as the Magyar-speaking **Csángó region** are worth investigating if you're seriously interested in rural life, the most approachable and rewarding aspect is local **festivals**. The main festivals are at Ilişeşti (July), Durău (August), Iaşi (October) and Odobeşti (November).

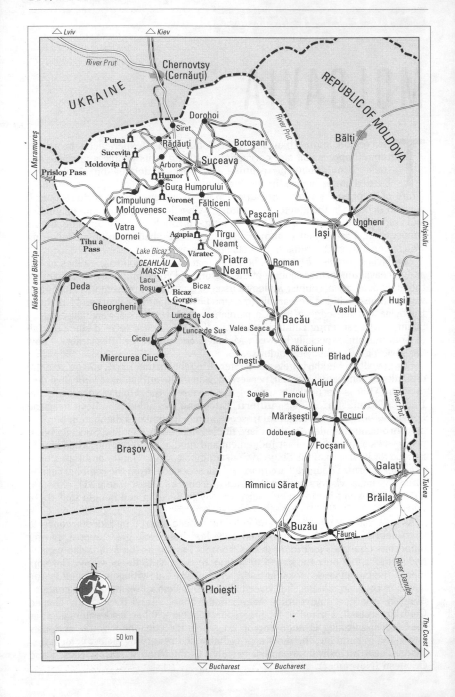

ACCOMMODATION PRICES

Hotels listed in this guide have been price-graded according to the scale below. Prices given are those charged for the cheapest **double room** available, which in the less expensive places usually comes without private bath or shower and without breakfast. Price codes are expressed in US dollars as the Romanian leu is not a stable currency, but you will generally pay for your room in lei.

Note that some hotels are currently closed for modernization, and others, now open, will no doubt follow in the near future. This is bound to result in higher rates when they reopen, so the prices quoted should be taken only as a guideline.

① $10 and under   ④ $20–25   ⑦ $40–50
② $10–15   ⑤ $25–30   ⑧ $50–65
③ $15–20   ⑥ $30–40   ⑨ $65 and over

Flights are the most convenient way of reaching Iaşi or Suceava from Bucharest. The main **train** line from Bucharest runs north to Suceava and Ukraine; with services to Brăila and Galaţi branching off at Buzău, and those to Iaşi at Mărăşeşti or Paşcani. Almost all services stop at Adjud, the junction for the Csángó region, and at Bacău, the springboard for Neamţ county. **Motorists** heading north along the DN2 should note that although the road is designated on maps as Euro-route 85, it's actually a country road where horse-drawn waggons without lights are a major hazard at night.

Most towns offer a choice of **accommodation**, while village homestay schemes are sprouting in tourist areas. As you would expect, the best time to visit is summer, when *cabanas* and campsites open in many rural areas, as do roadside **restaurants** catering to motorists.

Brăila and Galaţi

Lying well off the main route through Moldavia, close to the region's southeastern border and the Danube Delta, **Brăila** and **Galaţi** are seldom visited by tourists, and only then while en route to or from Tulcea, the Delta "capital". Both were once ports where the Orient and Occident colluded in exporting Romania's agricultural wealth; now they are backwaters and monuments to economic failure. Brăila's docks are almost moribund – though the town remains surprisingly nice – while Galaţi is blighted by bankrupt industries. Out of season, moving on to Tulcea entails an unenviable choice between an early morning bus from Brăila or one of the three ferries a week from Galaţi (Mon only in winter); in summer a daily hydrofoil makes the journey far easier. Both Brăila and Galaţi are linked to Bucharest by fast trains.

Brăila

Despite its reputation for being run by gangsters, **BRĂILA** seems a restful, pleasantly gone-to-seed Danubian town, laid out in concentric streets radiating from the port esplanade. Brăila was first recorded as Wallachia's principal harbour in the Spanish "Book of Knowledge" (*Libro de conoscimento*) of 1350, but there had almost certainly been a settlement there for many centuries before that. After three centuries of Turkish occupation, it resumed shipping the harvests of the Bărăgan Plain to the rest of Europe in the nineteenth century, creating huge fortunes for a few landlords who built elegant villas here. At that time, Brăila had the largest Gypsy population of any town in Europe; most were in domestic service (generally as slaves, before Gypsy slavery was abolished in 1855) or lived by entertaining the *gadjé*. The villas have long crumbled while the Gypsies remain; even so, the vestiges of wealth and splendour give the place a romantic, even Bohemian, feel.

Practicalities

From outside Brăila's **train station**, catch bus #4 or #10 (paying on board), or walk 1km down Strada Victoriei to B-dul A.I. Cuza; bear right as far as Strada Eminescu, the pedestrianized street which leads left to Piaţa Traian, centre of the old town. The **bus station** is about 200m left of the train station on Strada Siret. There's a Bancomat **cash machine** at BCR on Calea Călăraşilor. The Iris **pharmacy** is in the Centru Civic (open daily 7am–9pm).

Accommodation

Belvedere, Piaţa Independenţei 1 (☎ & fax 039/63.52.70). Behind the prefecture in the Centru Civic, overlooking the river. Modern and comfy, with a decent restaurant. ⑤.

Delta, Str. M. Eminescu 56 (☎039/61.16.10). Fairly cheery doubles with shared bathrooms and the only triples in town. Hot water may be supplied by 1998. ①.

Sport, Str. D. Boltineanu 4 (☎039/61.13.46). Nondescript building with basic facilities down the first turning to the right off Calea Galaţi, leading off Piaţa Traian. ③.

Tineretului, Calea Călăraşilor 56 (☎039/63.64.80, fax 61.12.63). Agreeable enough, if you can find it round the side of a white building with curved balconies, opposite the prefecture; BTT is next door. ④.

Traian, Piaţa Traian 4 (☎039/61.46.85, fax 61.28.35). Shabby high-rise building, a refit is imminent at time of writing. Plenty of singles. Avoid the basement bar, which poses as a nightclub and wildly overcharges on the grounds of having a few bored hookers and an empty stage. ACR; ③.

The Town

An attractive melange of Empire-style facades in pastel colours and sidewalks paved with Dobrogean granite, the old centre radiates from **Piaţa Traian**, a leafy expanse named after the Roman emperor Trajan. Trajan's bust is mounted on a tall plinth, admired by a sculpted peasant gesturing to his son as if to say, "This is your Daco–Roman heritage". Nearby stands the **Church of the Archangel Michael**, built as a mosque by the Turks, probably in the eighteenth century; its freestanding belfry was added later, with the bells and iconostasis both from Russia. The blue wrought-iron **clock-tower** adorned with the old town's ship emblem is regarded by locals as the highlight of the town's sights. Sepia photos of Brăila in its heyday appear in the **History Museum** (Tues–Sun 10am–6pm) on the corner of Piaţa Traian and Calea Galaţi.

Leading from Piaţa Traian, Strada Eminescu is the main shopping street, bedecked with colourful pots of flowers. From the far side of the square, another major axis, Calea Călăraşilor, leads to the **Centru Civic**, where broad steps flanked by abstract sculptures descend to the riverside Children's Beach from a **statue of Ecaterina Teodoriu**, the heroine of the battle of Mărăşeşti (see p.225), waving a sword. En route to the Centru Civic, you'll pass a large **Greek Orthodox church** built by the community that dominated the shipping business before World War II. A **synagogue** also survives at Str. Petru Maior 13, off Eminescu.

From beside the *Hotel Traian*, Strada Imperator Traian leads to the dismal **waterfront** with its mournful array of rusting freighters and patrol boats, solitary fishermen and drunks; when Ceaușescu visited here they even had to paint the grass green. The far shore is a thick curtain of poplars, full of birds and rodents; this is the Balta Brăilei, the huge island between the old and new arms of the Danube.

Eating, drinking and entertainment

The town's **market** is on Bulevardul A.I. Cuza and the **supermarket**, *FlexFoods*, is on Calea Călărașilor. If you are looking to **eat out**, the *Restaurant Lotca* (daily, 8am–10pm), on Strada Eminescu, is the best place in the centre of town; decorated with ships, it's named after a type of boat found in the Danube Delta, and, not surprisingly, it offers fish. Also worth trying is the *Hotel Belvedere* (7.30am–10pm; closed Mon), the best **restaurant** in town, on Piața Independenței. For breakfast, try the *Self Trading Company* café (daily, 7am–10pm) at Str. Eminescu 16. If you are looking for somewhere to drink, try either the upstairs bar in the *Traian* hotel or the basement of the *Lotca*. On Saturdays there's a **disco** (10pm–2am) in the *Cinema Bulevard*, at B-dul Independenței 57.

Galați

GALAȚI, 30km north of Brăila by road and rail, grew up as a port at the confluence of the River Danube and Moldavia's inland waterways, the Siret and the Prut. In Bram Stoker's *Dracula*, Jonathan Harker and Godalming come here to catch a steamer up the Siret and Bistrița rivers, heading for Dracula's castle at the Bîrgău Pass. In real life, Galați was associated with such figures as Alexandru Ioan Cuza – a local magistrate when he was unexpectedly elected Prince of Moldavia – and with the Victorian hero, Gordon of Khartoum, who served here as an obscure junior officer in 1872.

Probably your own reason for visiting here will be to make a connection for the ferry or hydrofoil to Tulcea. Badly bombed in 1944, Galați was largely rebuilt as a series of numbingly identical apartment buildings and swelled to its present size during the 1960s, when Romania's largest **steelworks** were constructed here. For Gheorghiu-Dej and Ceaușescu, this enterprise was the prerequisite for Romania's emergence as a fully industrialized nation, and a symbolic and concrete assertion of independence from the Warsaw Pact, which preferred Romania to remain a largely agricultural country. To finance the Sidex steelworks and other projects, Ceaușescu borrowed $12 billion from the West; when the products didn't sell, this could only be repaid by exporting vast quantities of food, leaving barely enough to feed the population. To make matters worse, the factory not only consumed energy and generated pollution with equal profligacy, but relied on imported iron ore to make the steel, this being the one mineral resource lacking in Romania. It was kept half-going by Iliescu simply because the political costs of closure were too high. It remains to be seen if Constantinescu will bite the bullet; by 1995 there were still 37,000 staff employed at the plant, which produced four million tonnes of steel, less than a third of the ouput of 1989.

Arrival and information

Galaţi's **train station** lies to the northeast of the town centre on Strada Domnească (bus #9 or #20). **Ferries** and **hydrofoils** depart from Gara Fluvială for Tulcea (Mon, Wed & Fri at 8.45am); both routes are very busy and you should try to book tickets a day ahead. From the train station it's less than ten minutes to the port – head left, passing the **bus station**, and walk straight ahead on Strada Dogăriei through a run-down neighbourhood to a T-junction, and then either left to the port or right to the town centre.

BTT is located at Str. Domnească 11, bloc P1, next to a permanently open pharmacy, and CFR at Str. Brăilei bloc BR2; there's a Bancomat at the new BCR building further west on Strada Brăilei at Strada Gen. Cernat.

Accommodation

In a town where your main objective is to leave, it makes sense to stay as close as possible to Gara Fluvială. The most convenient **hotels** are the *Dunărea*, at Str. Brăilei 101 (☎036/41.80.41, fax 46.10.50; ACR; ④), and the *Galaţi*, Str. Domnească 1 (☎036/46.05.21 or 46.00.40, fax 46.43.12; ⑦), at the junction of Strada Domnească and Strada Brăilei, right at the centre of the town. Neither are particularly preposessing. The best, and biggest, hotel in town is the *Faleza* (☎036/43.31.43, fax 46.13.88; ⑦), at Str. Roşiori 1 – turn west on Strada Brăilei and left at Romtelecom to reach it.

From Buzău to Bacău

The main routes northeast from Bucharest through Moldavia, the DN2 and the Bucharest–Suceava train line, are a miserable advertisement for the region, as one hideously modernized town succeeds another up the Siret valley, without even the sight of the Carpathians to lift your spirits until you're halfway to Suceava. There's little reason to stop anywhere along the way unless for a detour into the wine-growing or Csángó regions of the Subcarpathians.

That said, you might consider visiting **BUZĂU**, 128km from Bucharest on the southern border of Moldavia. On the last Sunday in June, it holds its kitsch *Drăgaica* **festival**, based on an ancient rite; once widespread in rural Romania, this Midsummer Day's custom required young girls wearing crowns and hoods to go singing and dancing into the fields to verify the readiness of the wheat for harvesting. In town, however, they can only go through the motions.

From the **train and bus stations**, it's a ten-minute walk along B-dul Gării and Strada Tudor Vladimirescu to the centre. The simplest stopover is at the *Bucegi* **hotel** (☎038/71.01.13; ②), opposite the stations at B-dul Gării 47; there are TVs and cold water in the rooms and hot communal showers. Opposite the imposing neo-Brîncovenesc town hall (*Palatul Comunal*), at Piaţa Daciei 2, is the *Hotel Pietroasa* (☎038/41.20.33, fax 71.09.42; ACR; ⑥), a modern block with basic facilities and a very average restaurant.

FOCŞANI, 70km further north, is an unattractive town, but has buses and trains to the **wine-growing regions** of Panciu and Odobeşti, and further into the hills of Vrancea county, just west of the main routes north. At **PANCIU** they make sparkling wines, while **ODOBEŞTI** produces the yellow wine that was Ceauşescu's favourite tipple. Odobeşti is also noted for its **festivals**; the grape harvest is celebrated in late September, and on the third Sunday of November the musically inclined shepherds of Vrancea county gather to entertain each other with performances on alpine horns and pan-pipes. The spa of **Soveja** is a base for visiting the hills to the west, with a museum, monastery (founded in 1645) and an open-air sculpture camp, as well as the *Zboina* and *Miorița* hotels (π & fax 037/63.60.21 ②).

In Romania, **MĂRĂŞEŞTI** rail junction, 20km north of Focşani, is remembered for a savage battle in the summer of 1917, when German forces advancing on Iaşi were halted by Romanian troops, determined to preserve the last unoccupied region of their country. On the southwestern edge of town, a giant **mausoleum** (Tues–Sun 8am–6pm) contains the remains of 7000 soldiers and, at its heart, the tomb of General Ieremia Grigorescu (1863–1919), who inspired his forces with the order "They shall not pass!" (*Pe aici nu se trece*); there's also a small **museum** (Tues–Sun 8am–6pm) next door. The mausoleum is the scene of **military parades** on public holidays and on August 6, the anniversary of the battle's climactic day. From the station it's a thirty-minute walk to the mausoleum, heading around to the left over the railway and DN2; drivers can simply stop by the truckstop south of km204 on the DN2. The town itself is moribund, and its sole hotel has closed.

The Csángó region

Csángó means "wanderer" in Hungarian, referring to those Székely who fled from religious persecution in Transylvania in the fifteenth century, to be joined in Moldavia by others escaping military conscription in the seventeenth and eighteenth centuries. Once there were some forty **Csángó villages** in Moldavia, a few as far east as the River Dnestr, but today their community has contracted into a hard core of about five thousand people living between Adjud and Bacău, and in the Ghimeş district at the upper end of the Trotuş (Tatros) valley. Most rural Csángó are fervently religious and fiercely conservative, retaining a distinctive folk costume and dialect; their music is harsher and sadder than that of their Magyar kinsfolk in Transylvania, although their dances are almost indistinguishable from those of their Romanian neighbours.

Mutual suspicions and long memories of the Ghimeş uprising of 1934 made this a sensitive area in Communist times. While allowing them to farm and raise sheep outside the collectives, the Party tried to dilute the Csángó and stifle their culture by settling Romanians in new industrial towns like Oneşti. Though things are a lot freer now, the upper valley is still rarely visited, and has almost no tourist infrastructure. Should you decide to spend any time here, come prepared to camp, with ample supplies.

Adjud is the junction on the main Bucharest–Suceava line for the branch line west to Oneşti, Ghimeş and Ciceu. Along this route are four major Csángó settlements. The first major stop is **ONEŞTI** (Onyest), formerly named "Gheorghiu Gheorghiu-Dej", after Ceauşescu's predecessor; dominated by the chemical industry, it is notable only as the birthplace of Nadia Comaneci. From here or **Tîrgu Ocna** (Aknavásar), a small spa 12km to the west which boasts the largest underground sanatorium in Europe, you can reach the larger spa of **SLĂNIC MOLDOVA** (Szlanikfürdő) which lies 20km southeast of Tîrgu Ocna and is known as the "Pearl of Moldavia". Of the spa's hotels, the *Perla* (π034/34.82.00, fax 34.81.57; ③) is the most modern, the *Venus* (π034/34.80.27, fax 34.87.17; ③) is the largest, and the *Flora* (π034/17.10.92; ②) is the cheapest.

GHIMEŞ (Ghimeş-Făget or Gyimesbükk), 62km west of Tîrgu Ocna, is the largest of four Csángó settlements in the Troţus valley, and is unusual for having a Gypsy population that is totally integrated into village life; it has a strong musical tradition and hosts a **winter fair** on January 20–21. Beyond Ghimes, near the head of the valley, Lunca de Jos (Gyimesközeplok) and Lunca de Sus (Gyimesfelsőlok) stand on the borders with Transylvania.

Bacău

BACĂU, 60km north of Adjud along the main rail and road routes to Suceava, is a large town with good hotels and transport services, but little else to recommend it. First industrialized in the mid-nineteenth century, it now has a huge chemical factory on the outskirts, and a modernized centre vastly out of scale with its backstreets. Aside from a neo-Byzantine church at the north end of the main street, Strada Bălcescu, and the neo-Brîncovenesc **Bacovia Theatre** further south, the only evidence that Bacău is more than a century old is the ruined **Princely Court**, southeast of the centre off Strada 9 Mai. Surrounded by apartment buildings, the enclosure contains the Church of the Virgin founded in 1491 by Stephen the Great's son, Alexandru, and a circular tower that's been completely rebuilt. The **Museum of History and Fine Arts** (Tues–Sun 10am–6pm) at Str. Şoimului 23, exhibits prehistoric and Dacian artefacts, and works by Theodor Aman, Nicolae Grigorescu and others; the **Natural Science Museum** (Tues–Sun 10am–6pm) is across the road.

Practicalities

To reach the centre from the **train station**, catch any bus marked *centru* or head east up Strada Eminescu, to the right of the department store (*magazin*) across the road, which eventually leads to a park opposite the *Hotel Moldova*, where the two central axes, Bălcescu and Unirii, converge. The **bus terminal** is ten minutes' walk east along Strada Unirii from the *Hotel Moldova*.

Most facilities in town are on Strada Bălcescu: from north to south there's an ACR tourist agency at no. 14, a CFR office at no. 12 (Mon–Fri 7.30am–8pm; ☎034/14.63.40), and a direct-dial phone office ar no. 10 (Romtelecom; daily 7am–10pm), while TAROM (Mon–Fri 8am–7pm, Sat 8am–noon; ☎034/11.14.62) has an office across the road at no. 1. The Pasajul Revoluţiei at the side of Romtelecom leads eventually to Str. 9 Mai, beyond which is the central **market**; there's a BCR Bancomat nearby on Strada 9 Mai. The town's emergency **hospital** (☎034/13.40.00), on the main road south, is the best equipped in the county.

Accommodation

Bistriţa, Str. Luminii 3 (☎034/13.35.44). Beige Stalinist low-rise. Rather gloomy, with shared bathrooms; some triples. ⑤.

Central, Str. N. Bălcescu 8 (☎034/13.48.37). Tucked away above the Bacovia Theatre, this old-fashioned place has a bar in a pseudo-Gothic hall that almost compensates for the spartan rooms and facilities (hot water *cu program*). ③.

Decebal, Str. Ioniţă Sandu Sturza 2 (☎034/14.62.11, fax 13.44.63). A concrete monster at the far end of Strada Bălcescu; has a video arcade in the foyer. ACR; ⑦.

Dumbrava, Str. Dumbrava Roşie 2 (☎034/14.38.38, fax 14.70.52). Head on 150m past the *Bistriţa* and turn right to find this decent 1960s place with a snazzy foyer and cable TV. ⑥.

Moldova, Str. N. Bălcescu 16 (☎034/14.63.22, fax 11.01.81). A high-rise building with a bizarre foyer which looks like something out of *Barbarella*. Its disco and bingo hall make this Bacău's main nightspot. ACR; ⑦.

Neamţ county

Neamţ county lies to the northwest of Bacău and is the only real attraction between Bucharest and the old Moldavian capitals of Iaşi and Suceava. Although its towns – **Piatra Neamţ** and **Tîrgu Neamţ** – are nothing special, they serve as jumping-off points for the historic monasteries of **Neamţ, Agapia** and **Văratec**, set in wooded foothills that turn gloriously red and gold in autumn. Further to the northwest rises the **Ceahlău massif**, whose magnificent views and bizarrely weathered outcrops make this one of the finest hiking spots in Romania.

Without a car, you're faced with the question of which town makes a better base for excursions. Tîrgu Neamţ is closer to the sights and runs a few more buses than Piatra Neamţ, but Piatra Neamţ offers a better choice of places to stay and eat. The two towns are 40km apart and are linked by hourly **buses**, all but two of which run via Bălţăteşti, the turn-off for Văratec and Agapia. On Sundays, there are fewer services to the monasteries and none to Durău.

Piatra Neamţ

Sixty kilometres northwest of Băcau by road and rail, where the River Bistriţa emerges into the Cracau basin, lies **PIATRA NEAMŢ**. Hemmed in by the Carpathian foothills, it is one of Romania's oldest settlements, inhabited by a string of Neolithic and Bronze Age cultures, and the Dacians, whose citadel has been excavated on a nearby hilltop. The town was first recorded in Roman times as Petrodava, and in 1453 under the name of Piatra lui Craciun ("Christmas Rock"); its present title may refer to the German (*Neamţ*) merchants who once traded here, or derive from the old Romanian word for an extended family or nation – *Neam*. As one of Moldavia's earliest industrial centres, the town later played a major role in the general strike of 1919, and was one of the few places where the Communists were able to sabotage production during World War II. That said, Piatra has little to attract visitors beyond a medieval church and a better-than-average collection of prehistoric relics in its museum.

The Town

Today, Piatra Neamţ features every style of Communist architecture from dismal low-rises to the pseudo-malls that mushroomed in the 1980s. What's left of the old town is clustered around **Piaţa Libertăţii**. The **Church of St John** originally formed part of a Princely Court, of which only vestiges remain. Erected by Stephen the Great in 1497–98, hard on the heels of his seminal church at Neamţ Monastery, it set a pattern for Moldavian church architecture thereafter. The upper part is girdled by niches outlined in coloured brick, probably intended to hold saintly images. Beside the door, a votive inscription by his son Bogdan the One-Eyed presages a host of tacky modern paintings of Stephen inside, where a dusty case of valuables justifies a small entry charge. A sturdy Gothic **belltower** with a witch's hat brim, constructed in 1499, stands on the north side of the church. On the western side of the belltower, in a building which combines folk

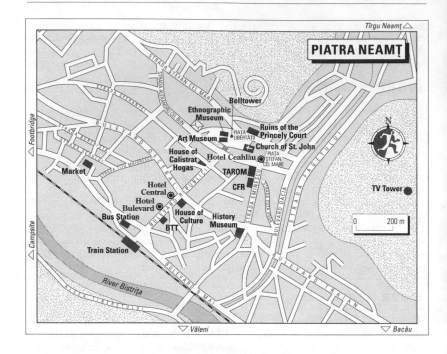

architecture with Art Nouveau, is the **Ethnographic Museum** (Tues–Sun 10am–6pm), and beside that is a Brîncoveanu-style mansion, with ceramic studs echoing those on the church, which houses the **Art Museum** (Tues–Sun 10am–6pm) showing work by local painters. On the northeastern side of the square, some vaulted **ruins of the Princely Court** have been laid bare by a shaft dug into the slope below the Petru Rareş Liceu, but it's hard to see much through the gate, which is kept locked; ask at the museums for entry.

Strada Ştefan cel Mare, dotted with several attractive old villas, heads west out of the square; Elena Cuza, the widow of the deposed leader, Alexandru Ioan Cuza (see p.349), lived at no. 55 until her death in 1909. The main thoroughfare south is Bulevardul Republicii; set back from the boulevard, one block south of the square, is the small **house of Calistrat Hogas** (Tues–Sun 10am–6pm), now a memorial museum to the writer (1847–1918), who praised the charms of Neamţ county when the town still consisted of Alpine-style chalets.

A small road heads east from Piaţa Libertăţii to Piaţa Ştefan cel Mare, from where Strada Eminescu heads south to the **History Museum** (Tues–Sun 10am–6pm) on the corner of B-dul Decebal and Strada Chimiei. The museum devotes its ground floor to ancient relics; the left-hand section features a lifesize replica of a Stone Age hut furnished with wolfskins and grindstones, and fertility charms and pottery created by the Cucuteni culture (c.3000–2000 BC). Across the corridor are a Bronze Age tomb, complete with skeleton, and a curious Iron Age figure dubbed the Scythian Rider (*Cavalier scit*). Upstairs, the Romanian aptitude for woodcarving is exemplified by a "knitted cable" throne and an exquisite door with the Moldavian crest entwined in foliage.

Practicalities

From the **train and bus stations** it's a ten-minute walk up the tree-lined Bulevardul Republicii to the centre. Piatra Neamţ's three **hotels** all have private bathrooms, and include breakfast, but they are pretty dismal just the same – the *Bulevard*, B-dul Republicii 38–40 (☎033/21.80.11, fax 21.81.11; ⑤), just 200m from the train station, is a drab 1950s shoebox; the *Central*, at Piaţa Petrodava 1 in the centre of town (☎033/21.64.12, fax 21.45.32; ACR; ⑥) is a gloomy high-rise flanked by damp houses, and the largest and best of this poor bunch, with decent rooms and views, is the *Ceahlău* at Piaţa Ştefan cel Mare 3 (☎033/21.99.90, fax 21.55.40; ACR; ⑧). There's a **campsite**, the *Bîtca Doamnei*, on Aleea Tineretului (☎033/21.12.16; ①), a wooded summer-only site with cabins. To get there, head west along Strada Bistriţei till you reach the footbridge (1km).

The best **restaurant** in town is the *Restaurant Cozla* (daily 7am–10pm) in the mall opposite the *Hotel Ceahlău*. For pizzas or burgers, try the *Rotisserie* (Mon–Sat 9am–9pm) on Strada Titu Maiorescu, just off B-dul Decebal. There are **bars** in the *Central* and *Ceahlău* hotels, and outside the station, while in summer local youths pack out the *Little Italy* **disco** near the campsite every night.

TAROM (Mon–Fri 7.30am–noon, 1.30–4pm) and CFR (Mon–Fri 7.30am–7.30pm) have offices at the northern end of Strada Eminescu. There's a BTT office (Mon–Fri 9am–4pm, Sat 10am–2pm; ☎ & fax 033/21.46.86) just north of the stations along Bulevardul Republicii, which offers summer homestays near the monasteries. You can **change money** in the *Hotel Ceahlău* (Mon–Fri 9am–5pm, Sat 9am–noon) or the Petrodava department store (Mon–Fri 8am–7pm, Sat 9am–1pm) around the corner from the *Hotel Central*. The **pharmacy** in the Mioriţa Complex, opposite the *Central*, is open round the clock.

Văratec and Agapia

The rolling countryside west of the road between Piatra and Tîrgu Neamţ provides an idyllic setting for Romania's largest convents: **Văratec**, with 280 nuns and **Agapia**, with 300. Each comprises a walled convent and a village, up the road from an agricultural village of the same name. The nuns live in cosy houses with pale blue, fretted eaves and glassed-in verandas; some were built for them by their families and are rented to tourists in summertime, the income going to the convent, which supports scores of nuns in their old age. Taking photos within the convents is not allowed.

You can get to the convents by bus from Piatra Neamţ; services normally wait thirty minutes before starting back, giving you time for a quick look at each convent. To visit both sites, it's quicker to walk between the two rather than return to town for another bus out. If you miss the last bus back and you don't fancy staying at Agapia or Văratec, walk or hitch the 5km back to the main road, and wait for one of the regular buses between Tîrgu Neamţ and Piatra Neamţ.

Văratec

Hedgerows line the narrow road winding through Văratec village to the pretty nuns' village and **Văratec Monastery**, its whitewashed walls and balconies enclosing a lovely garden shaded by cedars. The novices inhabit two-storey buildings named after saints, while the older nuns live in cottages, next to a **museum of icons** (Tues–Sun 10am–6pm), and an **embroidery school** established by Queen Marie in 1934. It's an odd but not unfitting site for the **grave of Veronica**

Micle, the poet loved by Eminescu, who couldn't afford to marry her after the death of her despised husband (see p.240).

Văratec was founded in the eighteenth century, around a church that no longer exists; the site of its altar is marked by a pond with a statue of an angel. The present **church**, built in 1808, is plain and simple, culminating in two bell-shaped domes and six chimneys. To cope with the harsh winters, the nuns have sensibly installed stoves in the narthex, which is barely separated from the nave by a pair of columns.

The *Hotel Filiorou*, a family-run bed-and-breakfast in Văratec, 1500m from the monastery, has pleasant **rooms** (①). In fine weather, it's a pleasant **walk from Văratec to Agapia**; the seven-kilometre trail through the woods takes one and a half hours, starting by house no. 219, back down the road from Văratec Monastery. Another trail, marked by blue dots, leads west **to Sihla hermitage** (2hr), built into the cliffs near the cave of St Teodora, and hidden by strange outcrops. A backroad (2 buses a day) connects Sihla to the **Sihistria and Secu hermitages**, and continues to the main road between Tîrgu Neamț and Ceahlău, 2km west of the turn-off for Neamț Monastery (see p.231).

Agapia

Agapia Monastery actually consists of two convents a couple of miles apart; most visitors are content to visit only the main complex of **Agapia din Vale** (Agapia in the Valley), at the end of a muddy village of houses with covered steps. The walls and gatetower aim to conceal rather than to protect; inside is a whitewashed enclosure around a cheerful garden. At prayer times, one of the nuns beats an insistent rhythm on a wooden *toaca*; another plays the pan-pipes, followed by a medley of bells, some deep and slow, others high and fast. The monastery **church** was built in 1644–47 by Prince Basil the Wolf's brother, Gavril Coci. Its helmet-shaped cupola, covered in green shingles, mimics that of the gatetower. After restoration, the interior was repainted in 1858–1860 by Nicolae Grigorescu, the country's foremost painter; he returned to stay at Agapia from 1901–02. Off to the right is a **museum** of icons and vestments from the seventeenth and eighteenth centuries (daily 10am–7pm). Downhill by the Topolnița stream stands a **wooden church** with three shingled domes and a modern gatetower.

The older **Agapia din Deal** (Agapia on the Hill) or Agapia Veche (Old Agapia) is a smaller, more tranquil convent, high up a wooded slope about half an hour's walk from Agapia din Vale; ten minutes out of Agapia din Vale turn right at the unmarked junction. Another trail from Agapia din Vale leads to Văratec (see below). The *Hanul Agapia* on the road to Agapia din Vale has **rooms** (②).

Tîrgu Neamț

TÎRGU NEAMȚ ("German Market") is smaller and duller than Piatra, making it a less attractive stopover. At its centre is a cluster of signposts to several museums in the vicinity – all of which are actually in Piatra Neamț, except for the **house of Veronica Micle** and the **Historical and Ethnographic Museum** (both Tues–Sun 10am–6pm), facing each other on Strada Ștefan cel Mare.

The town's saving grace is the Neamț **citadel** (Tues–Sun 10am–6pm), visible from the road to Neamț Monastery, but far more impressive at close quarters. The citadel a kilometre west along Strada Ștefan cel Mare and then ten minutes north up an asphalt path equipped like a motorway with street lights and crash barriers is Moldavia's finest ruined castle. Founded by Petru I Muşat in 1359, it was beefed up by Stephen just in time to withstand a siege by the Turkish sultan Mohammed II in 1496. Later, it was partly demolished on the orders of the Turks, but again saw service in 1691 in the war between Moldavia and Poland. The approach to the citadel is over a long curving wooden **bridge** raised on pillars high above a moat; the final stretch was originally designed to flip enemies down into an oubliette. Within the **bailey**, a warren of roofless chambers that used to be an arsenal, courthouse and baths, surrounds a deep well, ringed by battlements that survey the Neamţ valley for miles around.

Practicalities

Tîrgu's **bus station** is a few minutes from the centre on Strada Cuza Vodă and the **train station** is a further fifteen minutes east on the same road. There are just two **hotels** in town: the *Hanul Casa Arcaşului* (☎033/66.26.15; ④) is comfortable, but out of the way at the end of the road below the citadel, while the *Doina* (☎033/66.22.70, fax 66.06.20; ③) at the other end of Strada Ştefan cel Mare from the centre, behind the church, is more central. For places to **eat** other than the hotels, there's a pizza den and a *cofetărie* on Ştefan cel Mare, both usually closed, or the **market** off Bulevardul Eminescu; rather seedy **bars** operate round the clock near the bus station.

Neamţ Monastery

The twelfth-century **Neamţ Monastery**, 12km northwest of Tirgu Neamţ, is the oldest in Moldavia and is the region's chief centre of Orthodox culture; it is also the largest men's monastery in Romania, with seventy monks and dozens of seminary students. The original hermitage, founded by Petru I Muşat, was rebuilt in the early fifteenth century by Alexander the Good, with fortifications that protected Neamţ from the Turks and a printing house that spread its influence throughout Moldavia. The new church, founded here by Stephen the Great in 1497 to celebrate a victory over the Poles, became a prototype for Moldavian churches throughout the next century, and its school of miniaturists and illuminators led the field.

Outwardly, Neamţ resembles a fortress, with high stone walls and an octagonal corner tower (there used to be four). On the inside of the gatetower, a painted Eye of the Saviour sternly regards the monks' cells with their verandas wreathed in red and green ivy, and the seminary students in black tunics milling around the garden. The sweeping roof of Stephen's church overhangs blind arches inset with lozenges and glazed bricks, on a long and otherwise bare facade. Its trefoil windows barely illuminate the interior, where pilgrims kneel amid the smell of mothballs and candlewax. At the back of the compound is a smaller church dating from 1826, containing frescoes of the Nativity and the Resurrection.

Outside the monastery stands a large onion-domed **pavilion** for *Aghiastmatar*, the "Blessing of the water", to be taken home in bottles for use in times of illness. In prewar Bucharest, a similar ritual was performed beside the River Dîmboviţa, attended by the king, patriarch and other dignitaries. A wooden cross was cast into the icy river, and the faithful, dressed in white, dived in to retrieve it before the patriarch officially blessed the water.

The monstery can be reached daily by **buses** from Tîrgu Neamţ. You could also catch one of the frequent services along the main road and walk the remaining 4km to the monastery. Should need arise, there are **rooms** (②) and a summer **campsite** with huts (①) at the *Hanul Branişte*, 3km east of the turning to Neamţ monastery.

The Ceahlău massif

West of Tîrgu Neamţ, 60km beyond the turning to Neamţ monastery, lies the **Ceahlău massif**. Aptly designated on local maps as a *zona abrupt*, it rises above neighbouring ranges in eroded crags whose fantastic shapes were anthropomorphized in folk tales and inspired Eminescu's poem, *The Ghosts*. The Dacians believed that Ceahlău was the abode of their supreme deity, Zamolxis, and that the gods transformed the daughter of Decebal into the Dochia peak. The massif is composed of Cretaceous sediments – especially conglomerates, which form pillar-like outcrops – and covered with stratified belts of beech, fir and spruce, with dwarf pine and juniper above 1700m. Its **wildlife** includes chamois, capercaillie, bears and boars, and the majestic Carpathian stag. Ceahlău's isolation is emphasized by the huge, artificial **Lake Bicaz** (Lacul Izvoru Muntelei) that half-encircles its foothills. A hydroelectric **dam** (*baraj*), built in 1950, rises at the southern end, 3km from the village of **BICAZ**, which is accessible by bus and train from Piatra Neamţ. During summer, there are **boat trips** from the dam to the Pîrîul Mare landing stage below Ceahlău itself. Bicaz's **history museum** (Tues–Sun 10am–6pm) has a display on the building of the dam.

There's a good **campsite** with cabins midway between the dam and the village of Potoci. The *Hotel Bicaz* (☎033/67.11.22; ②) is a short distance along the road towards the dam from the centre of Bicaz, and the *Bicaz Baraj cabana* stands right below the dam. At the northern end of the reservoir, the route from Tîrgu Neamţ to Durău and Topliţa, and the mountain road north to Vatra Dornei, converge at **POIANA LARGULUI**, where it's feasible to **change buses** if you're prepared to wait a few hours. The local **campsite** is awful, but there's a decent new site, *Popas Petru Vodă*, at the Argel Pass, 12km uphill towards Tîrgu Neamţ.

Hiking above Durău

The main base for **hiking** in the massif is **DURĂU**, on its northeastern side, which can be reached by bus from Piatra Neamţ or Tîrgu Neamţ. Durău's major draw is the **Ceahlău Feast**, on the second Sunday in August, an opportunity for shepherds to parade their finery, which attracts many tourists. It also boasts a small **hermitage** built in 1830–35 and painted a century later by Nicolae Tonitza, who used local backgrounds for his biblical scenes. There are four **hotels** (all ☎033/67.80.78, fax 67.82.12; ⑤) in the town, all fairly indistinguishable, and two central **campsites**. The **tourist office** is in the *Hotel Durău*, at the end of the road. Mountain bikes can be rented at the *Bistriţa* hotel. From December to March, **skiing** replaces hiking as the main activity in the resort.

From the town it's a 45-minute walk to the *Fîntînele cabana*, on the steep red-striped trail starting at the end of the road. A longer route (marked by blue crosses, then red crosses and finally yellow triangles) also runs there via the **Duruitoarea cascade**, which falls a total of 25m in two stages.

From *Fîntînele*, the red-striped route (2hr) ascends within sight of the Panaghia rocks and Toaca peak to a plateau with glorious views and in a further two hours to the *Dochia cabana* (1750m). The route continues south via several massive **rock pillars** to Poiana Maicilor, where the red-striped route turns downstream to the *Izvoru Muntelui cabana* and the Bicaz road, while another trail marked with blue crosses runs on to Neagra village, on the road to the **Bicaz gorges**. Both routes take about two hours from Dochia.

Into Transylvania and north to Vatra Dornei

To the north and south of the massif, narrow valleys allow two routes **into Transylvania**. The northern one crosses a 1112-metre-high pass beyond the alpine spa of Borsec, before descending to Topliţa, in the upper Mureş valley. It's a scenic journey, and there are plenty of buses westwards from Borsec to Topliţa (see p.186). A better route runs through the **Bicaz gorges** (*Cheile Bicazului*), 25km upriver from Bicaz, past the lovely village of **BICAZ ARDELEAN**, which has a wooden church dating from 1829. Sheer limestone cliffs rise as high as 300m above the river, pressing so close around the "Neck of Hell" (*Gîtul Iadului*) that the road is hewn directly into the rockface. The *Cheile Bicazului cabana*, amid the gorges, marks the start of several **hiking** trails, and a longer one ascends from Lacu Roşu to the *Piatra Singuratică* (Lonely Rock) *cabana*. **Buses** from Piatra Neamţ, Tîrgu Neamţ and Bicaz travel this way en route to Gheorgheni (see p.184).

Alternatively, you can head north by bus from Tîrgu Neamţ to **Vatra Dornei** (see p.260). The 136-kilometre journey takes four hours following the River Bistriţa through a narrow, twisting valley hemmed in by fir-covered peaks. About 20km before Vatra Dornei, you'll see the well-signposted *Zugreni cabana*, across the river, from where a trail leads to the heart of the Rarău massif (see p.260).

Iaşi

IAŞI (pronounced "Yash"), in the northeast of the region, is the cultural capital of Moldavia and by far its nicest city – the only one where you're likely to want to stay a while. Its university, theatre and resident orchestra rival those of Bucharest – which was merely a crude market town when Iaşi became a princely seat – and give it an air of sophistication enhanced by a large contingent of foreign students. Cementing its place in the nation's heart, Romanians associate Iaşi with the poet, Eminescu, Moldavians esteem it as the burial place of St Paraschiva, and for several million smokers it's the home of *Carpaţi*, the country's cheapest brand of cigarettes.

Despite lying east of the main route northwards through Moldavia, Iaşi is accessible by direct **trains** from Bucharest, Cluj and several other major cities across the country, by **buses** from most towns in Moldavia and by daily **flights** from Bucharest.

Some history

Iaşi's ascendancy dates from the sixteenth century, when the Moldavian princes (*hospodars*) gave up the practice of maintaining courts in several towns, and settled permanently in Iaşi. This coincided with Moldavia's gradual decline into a Turkish satellite, ruled by despots who endowed Iaşi with churches and monasteries to trumpet their earthly glory and ensure their eternal salvation. **Basil the Wolf** (Vasile Lupu, 1634–53) promulgated a penal code whereby rapists were raped and arsonists burned alive; he also founded a printing press and school, which led to the flowering of Moldavian literature during the brief reign, in 1710–11, of the enlightened **Dimitrie Cantemir**.

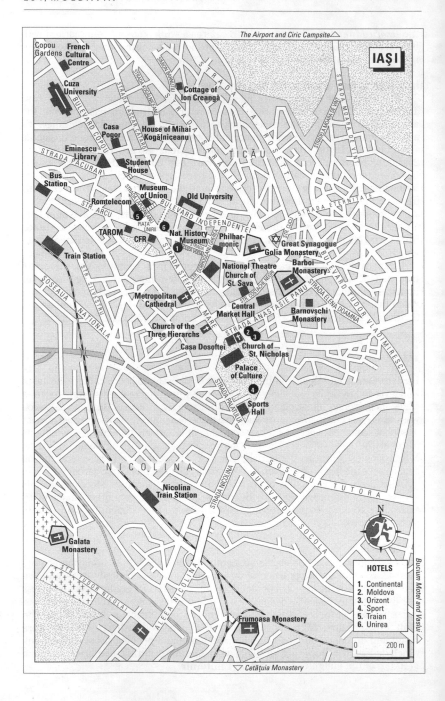

The Airport and Ciric Campsite △

IAȘI

Copou Gardens
French Cultural Centre
Cuza University
Cottage of Ion Creangă
Casa Pogor
House of Mihai Kogălniceanu
Eminescu Library
Student House
Bus Station
Museum of Union
Old University
Romtelecom
PIAȚA UNIRII
TAROM
CFR
Nat. History Museum
Philhar-monic
Great Synagogue
Golia Monastery
Barboi Monastery
Train Station
National Theatre
Church of St. Sava
Metropolitan Cathedral
Central Market Hall
Barnovschi Monastery
Church of the Three Hierarchs
Casa Dosoftei
Church of St. Nicholas
Palace of Culture
Sports Hall

TICĂU

NICOLINA

Nicolina Train Station

Galata Monastery

N

Frumoasa Monastery

▽ Cetățuia Monastery

Bucium Motel and Vaslui △

HOTELS
1. Continental
2. Moldova
3. Orizont
4. Sport
5. Traian
6. Unirea

0   200 m

After Cantemir's death, Moldavia fell under the control of Greek **Phanariots**, originally from the Phanar district of Constantinople, who administered the region on behalf of the Ottoman Empire, chose and deposed the nominally ruling princes (of whom there were 36 between 1711 and 1821), and eventually usurped the throne for themselves. The boyars adopted Turkish dress and competed to win the favour of the Phanariots, who alone could recommend their promotion to the sultan. As Ottoman power weakened, this dismal saga was interrupted by the surprise election of Prince **Alexandru Ioan Cuza**, who clinched the unification of Moldavia and Wallachia in 1859 with the diplomatic support of France. In the new Romania, Cuza founded universities at Iaşi and Bucharest, introduced compulsory schooling for both sexes, and secularized monastic property, which then accounted for a fifth of Moldavia. Finally, his emancipation of the serfs so enraged landowners and military circles that in 1866 they overthrew Cuza and restored the *status quo ante* – but kept the union.

The latter half of the nineteenth century was a fertile time for **intellectual life** in Iaşi, where the Junimea literary circle attracted such talents as the poet **Mihai Eminescu** and the writer **Ion Creangă**, who, like the historian, **Nicolae Iorga**, became national figures. Their Romanian nationalism was more romantic than chauvinist, but unwittingly paved the way for a deadlier version in the Greater Romania that was created to reward the Old Kingdom (*Regat*) for its sacrifices in **World War I**, when most of the country was occupied by the Germans, and the government was evacuated to Iaşi. With its borders enlarged to include Bessarabia and Bucovina, Moldavia inherited large minorities of non-Romanian-speaking Jews, Ukrainians and Gypsies, aggravating ethnic and class tensions in a region devastated by war.

During the 1920s, Iaşi became notorious for **anti-Semitism**, spearheaded by a professor whose League of Christian National Defence virtually closed the university to Jews, then over a third of the population, and later spawned the Iron Guard (see box below). Their chief scapegoat was **Magda Lupescu**, Carol II's locally born Jewish mistress, who was widely hated for amassing a fortune by shady speculations; in 1940, she fled abroad with Carol in a train stuffed with loot.

THE IRON GUARD AND ROMÂNIA MARE

Moldavia and Iaşi have long been associated with the far right of Romanian politics. The most ardent member of Iaşi's League of Christian National Defence was **Corneliu Codreanu**, who went on, in the early 1930s, to found the Legion of the Archangel St Michael, better known as the **Iron Guard**. Wearing green shirts with bags of Romanian soil around their necks, the Legionari chased away village bailiffs to the delight of the peasantry, and murdered politicians deemed to be insufficiently nationalistic, until Marshal Antonescu jailed its leaders and Codreanu was shot "trying to escape". His followers fled to Berlin; when allowed back home, they helped carry out the Nazis' genocidal "Final Solution" in Romania.

After the war, the Communists employed ex-Legionari as thugs against the socialists and the National Peasant Party, whom they regarded as their real enemies. Following the 1989 revolution, fascism has been making a comeback with the **România Mare** (Greater Romania) party of **Corneliu Vadim Tudor**, which ascribes all the nation's problems to a conspiracy of Jews, Magyars, Gypsies and everyone else who isn't a "pure" Romanian. Their headquarters in Iaşi is rather bizarrely shared with the Ecology Party.

Practicalities

Arriving at Iaşi's main **train station**, you can either catch tram #3, #9 or #ll, or walk to the central Piaţa Unirii in ten to fifteen minutes, past the ornamental tower up Strada Gării and right along Strada Arcu. TAROM flights are met by buses at the **airport**, which will drop you off in town, at TAROM's office at Str. Arcu 3; buses to the airport also leave from here, departing two hours before take-off time. The intercity **bus station** (☎032/14.65.87) is 300m along Şoseaua Arcu from the TAROM office, within walking distance of the town centre.

Accommodation

Iaşi has **hotels** to suit every taste and budget, although those on Piaţa Unirii are really the only convenient ones. You might find a bed in one of the many student dorms (*caminul de studenti*) located around the university on B-dul Copou, 1km northwest of the centre. **Camping Ciric** (☎032/17.35.20), by a lake, 2km north of town, is only open over summer, when hourly buses run there from Tîrgul Cocului, from outside the Golia Monastery. There are also cabins (②) here in a wooded setting, but the filthy toilets are a big deterrent.

Bucium Motel (☎032/14.07.12, fax 21.18.06). On the Vaslui road, 12km from town. Rooms and cabins, and own restaurant. Open all year. ②.

Continental, Str. Cuza Vodă 4 (☎032/21.18.46). Old-fashioned and a bit noisy, but not unpleasant. This is the smallest and least expensive downtown hotel and has rooms with and without private bathrooms. ②.

Moldova, Str. A. Panu 29 (☎032/14.22.25, fax 11.79.40). Comfortable but soulless tower amid the Centru Civic, with a restaurant, two bars, pool and gym. ⑥.

Orizont, Str. G. Ureche 27 (☎032/11.27.00, fax 21.50.37). Small hotel just south of the *Moldova*, modern and good value, with bar, coffee shop and restaurant. Breakfast included. ②.

Sport, Str. Sfîntu Lazar 76 (☎032/23.28.00). Five hundred metres downhill from the Palace of Culture. The cheapest place in town, no frills, no singles. ②.

Traian, Piaţa Unirii 1 (☎032/14.33.30, fax 21.28.62). Atmospheric establishment, designed by Eiffel in 1882, that's still quite elegant. All rooms with baths or showers; breakfast included. ACR; ③.

Unirea, Piaţa Unirii 2 (☎032/14.21.10, fax 21.28.64). High-rise 1960s building that's showing its age. All room have private baths. Breakfast included. ACR; ④.

The Town

Many of the sights of Iaşi can be found on the streets radiating from **Piaţa Unirii**. To the north, Strada Lăpuşneanu heads towards the university district of Copou and the residential district of Ţicău. Heading east, Strada Cuza Vodă leads towards ancient monasteries and synagogues, while Strada Ştefan cel Mare leads south towards the cathedral, the **Church of the Three Hierarchs**, easily the best known building in Iaşi, and the huge **Palace of Culture**, housing a range of museums. Beyond this lies the Nicolina quarter, where you'll find the hilltop monasteries.

North of Piaţa Unirii

Strada Lăpuşneanu heads northeast from Piaţa Unirii to Cuza's old house at no. 14, which now houses the **Museum of Union** (Tues–Sun 10am–5pm); among other exhibits here is a coffee set emblazoned with an imperial "N", symbolizing Napoleon III's support for unification. The rather comic tale of Cuza's downfall in 1866 is glossed over. Bursting into his bedroom, soldiers found Cuza making love to the King of Serbia's daughter-in-law; when pressed to sign a decree of abdication, he objected, "But I haven't got a pen". "We have thought of that", they said, producing a pen and ink; whereupon Cuza complained of the lack of a table. "I will offer myself", said a colonel, presenting his back to forestall further procrastination...and so Cuza signed and went into exile. He died in Heidelberg in 1873.

South along Strada Ştefan cel Mare

Iaşi's traditional interplay of civil and religious authority is symbolized by a parade of edifices along **Strada Ştefan cel Mare şi Sfânt**, where florid public buildings face grandiose churches. Midway along the street, the huge colonnaded **Metropolitan Cathedral**, built in 1761 and still the largest Orthodox church in Romania, dominates the neighbouring Metropolitan's Palace and Theological College, and dwarfs worshippers with its cavernous interior, painted by Tattarescu. In 1641 Basil the Wolf spent the country's entire budget for the following year and a half to acquire the **relics of St Paraschiva** of Epivat (c.980–1050), which were moved to the cathedral in 1889. Venerated as the patron saint of Moldavia, households, harvests, traders and travellers, St Paraschiva seems to be a conflation of four Orthodox martyrs of that name. In mid-October the cathedral overflows with thousands of worshippers who come to kneel before the blue and gold bier containing the relics. Immediately to the south stands the Old Metropolitan **Church of St George**, raised in 1761; the pillars of its porch are carved with symbolic animal reliefs, in the post-Brîncoveanu style of Wallachia.

Across the road and east of an elegant park, is the French-eclectic style **National Theatre**, built by the Viennese architects Fellner and Helmer in the 1890s with one of the most beautiful auditoriums in the country. The theatre is named after the company's founder, Vasile Alecsandri (1821–90) who, owing to a lack of plays in Romanian, had to write much of its initial repertory. He is duly honoured by a statue outside the theatre.

A few minutes further south along Strada Ştefan cel Mare from the Church of St George you arrive at the famous **Church of the Three Hierarchs** (*Trei Ierarhi*; daily 9am–noon & 3–7pm; you'll have to pay a small fee to enter), its exterior carved all over with chevrons, meanders and rosettes as intricate as lace. When it was completed in 1639 – perhaps by the Armenian master-builder, Ianache Etisi – Basil the Wolf had the exterior gilded, desiring it to surpass all other churches in splendour. Aside from its unique carvings, the church follows the classic Byzantine trilobate plan, with two octagonal drums mounted above the *naos* and *pronaos* in the Moldavian fashion. Over the following two centuries, the church was damaged by fire and six earthquakes, but was rebuilt by the French architect Lecomte de Noüy in 1882–87; the interior decor is wholly his and quite missable. The church houses the **sarcophagi** of Basil the Wolf, Dimitrie Cantemir and Alexandru Ioan Cuza. Since 1994 this has once more become a working monastery. The adjacent abbot's house, in which Basil the Wolf set up Moldavia's first printing press in 1644, contains a display of religious icons (Tues–Sun 10am–4pm).

From the Church of the Three Hierarchs, Strada Costache Negri heads east to the **Church of St Sava**, a contemporary, yet quite different building whose earth-coloured walls and red pantiles give it the look of an Andean village church. Its massive, squat bell tower is doubly impressive for being devoid of ornamentation.

The Palace of Culture and around

At the southern end of Ştefan cel Mare, an equestrian **statue of Stephen the Great** and a cross commemorating the martyrs of the revolution are overshadowed by the stupendous **Palace of Culture** – a neo-Gothic pile built between 1905 and 1926 as a government centre, which now houses four of the city's museums (Tues–Sun 10am–5pm). Its spired tower and pinnacled wings presage a vast lobby awash with mosaics, stained glass and armorial reliefs, dominated by a magnificent double staircase. You can admire the decor free of charge, but tickets are required for entry to the museums ($1).

The corridor on the left of the lobby leads to the **Museum of Science and Technology**, displaying music boxes, symphoniums and orchestrions; the curators might be persuaded to demonstrate the ingenious Popper's Bianca, a kind of projector, which anticipated the cinema. To the right of the lobby, the **Moldavian History Museum** is strong on local archeology. Upstairs, casts of antique statues line the way to an **Ethnographic Museum** whose collection includes woven skirts and embroidered waistcoats, six-foot-long Moldavian alpine horns, hollow trunks used as beehives, and oil-presses the size of trees. The **Museum of Art** has no fewer than two dozen paintings by Grigorescu, and a fine collection of post-1919 Colourist works, such as Pallady's *Nude on a Yellow Background*. Portraits of bearded boyars in Turkish fur hats, and scenes of Jewish life by Octav Băncila (1872–1944), give more local colour. The vaulted Hall of Voivodes (*Sala Voievozilor*), containing the portraits of dozens of rulers, is used for temporary art shows.

Two much-restored relics of Iaşi's past stand between the Palace and the Centru Civic. The arcaded seventeenth-century **Casa Dosoftei** is a fitting home for the dull **Museum of Old Moldavian Literature** (Tues–Sun 10am–5pm) – it once housed a press that spread the words of the cleric and scholar Metropolitan Dosoftei, a statue of whom sits outside. The Phanariot policy of using Iaşi's presses to spread Greek as the language of Orthodox ritual had the unintended result of displacing the ossified Old Slavonic tongue from this position, clearing the way for intellectuals to agitate for the use of their own language, Romanian. Next door is the **Courtly Church of St Nicholas**, the oldest bulding in Iaşi, erected by Stephen in 1491 but pulled down and rebuilt by Lecomte de Noüy in 1885–97; its svelte facade now masks a hermetic world of carved pews and gilded frescoes.

The Centru Civic and Golia Monastery

From the south end of Strada Ştefan cel Mare, Strada Anastasie Panu leads east through the **Centru Civic**. Due to the array of administrative buildings that already existed on Ştefan cel Mare, the architects of Iaşi's Centru Civic wisely focused on consumer aspirations instead, hence the modernistic **Central Market Hall** midway along Strada Anastasie Panu and the rounded **Scala complex** opposite. One block east, you can catch a glimpse, across the site of an unfinished department store, of the former **Barnovschi Monastery**, founded by Prince Barnovschi in 1627; the monastery is now reduced to a pale buff church with a shingled porch and onion-spire, flanked by a gatetower. The **Barboi Monastery**, at the far end of the main road, has fared better. Housed in a walled garden with a tall Byzantine gatetower, it still bears the name of its seventeenth-century founder, Urşu Barboi, although the monastery's Church of Peter and Paul, with an overhead gallery for the choir, was built in the 1840s by Dimitrie Sturza, who is buried in the pronaos.

North of the Centru Civic, protected by a thirty-metre-tall gatetower and rounded corner bastions, is the **Golia Monastery**, a peaceful haven in the heart of Iaşi, whose dozen monks enjoy a rose garden dotted with shrines. Founded in the 1560s by Chancellor Ion Golia, the monastery was rebuilt and fortified by Basil the Wolf, who began a new **Church of the Ascension** within the monastery's grounds, completed by his son Ştefăniţa in 1660. A striking mixture of Byzantine, Classical and Russian architecture, the church boasts of its associations with Tsarist Russia, having been visited by Peter the Great in 1711, and serving as the burial place for the **viscera of Prince Potemkin**, Catherine the Great's favourite. These were removed so that the rest of his body could be preserved and returned home after he died in 1791, after catching a fever in Iaşi and defying doctors' orders by wolfing huge meals, starting at breakfast with smoked goose and wine.

West along Bulevardul Independenţei
Bulevardul Independenţei, a drab thoroughfare linking the Golia monastery with Strada Lăpuşneanu, has a few sights worth noting. Between an apartment building and a clump of kiosks near the start of the boulevard, you can see the Star of David atop the **Great Synagogue** – a sad misnomer for this lowly domed edifice founded in 1671 and restored in the 1970s, shortly before most of its congregation left for Israel.

Midway along the boulevard, at no. 72, the **Natural History Museum** (Tues, Thurs & Sat 9am–3pm, Wed, Fri & Sun 9am–4pm) occupies the eighteenth-century Russet House, in whose Elephant Hall Cuza was elected Prince of Moldavia in 1859. At that time the house belonged to the Society of Physicians and Naturalists, who had opened their mineral, flora and fauna collections to the public in 1834, making this one of the first such museums in Romania. Opposite stands the **Old University**, a Baroque pile that was constructed between 1795 and 1806 as the Callamachi family palace, and given to the university in 1860; it is now the centrepiece of the University of Medicine and Pharmacology. On the university's west side rises the spooky **gatetower** of the Sf Spiridion Monastery of 1786, which now houses a hospital; the monastery's old **church** contains the tomb of its founder, Grigore II Ghica, whose head was sent giftwrapped to the Sultan, for harbouring treasonous thoughts.

The boulevard finally leads to the **Independence Monument**, a statuesque woman striding forth ahead of billowing drapery, sculpted by Gabriela and Gheorghe Adoc in 1980. From here you can head past a big **outdoor market** towards the university district or return to Piaţa Unirii via the shopping precinct behind the *Hotel Unirea*.

The university district
Copou, the university district, lies northwest of the centre, out along the boulevard of the same name, where trams (#1, #4, #8 and #13) rattle uphill with students hanging out of the doors. The foot of the hill is distinguished by a Stalinesque **Student House** to the right, with bas reliefs of musical youths, alongside a small park overlooked by crumbling **statues of Moldavian princes** (Dragoş, Alexander the Good, Basil the Wolf and Dimitrie Cantemir), and the

colonnaded **Eminescu Library** to the left; working here as a librarian, Eminescu could nip across the road for meetings of the Junimea literary society (1863–85) in the **Casa Pogor** just north of the Student House. Casa Pogor, which now houses the **Museum of Moldavian Literature**, belonged to Vasile Pogor, a co-founder of the Junimea society. Strangely, although mentioned in the museum itself, Pogor is not included in the canon of writers honoured by statues outside.

It's a few minutes' walk further uphill to **Cuza University**, an Empire-style edifice, built by Louis Blanc in the 1890s, which acts as an umbrella for twenty six faculties, and eight research institutes of the Romanian Academy. Just to the north are the tranquil **Copou Gardens**, where Eminescu meditated under a favourite lime tree, now squat and ugly and boxed in by a low hedge. The park, with its many ponds, has an Alley of Busts of the notables who once frequented the park, an obelisk to the dead of World War I, and an **exhibition centre** (Tues–Sun 10am–5pm) featuring a section on Eminescu (see box below).

Ţicău

Ţicău is a pretty, hilly, old residential quarter, east of the university area, where two memorial museums (Tues–Sun 10am–5pm) provide an excuse for a ramble. At no. 11 on the street that now bears his name, the **house of Mihail Kogălniceanu** commemorates the orator and journalist who was banned from lecturing for lambasting "oppression by an ignorant aristocracy", and who fled to Hapsburg Bucovina in 1848, but returned in the 1850s to help secure Cuza's election and serve as foreign minister. More entertaining is the **cottage of Ion Creangă** (*Bojdeuca*), at Str. Bărnuţiu 11, which displays first editions and prints of his works, including stills from films based on them. A defrocked priest and failed teacher, Creangă (1837–89) wrote *Recollections of Childhood* and fairy tales like the *Giants of Irunica*, finally achieving critical success just before he died.

The southern monasteries

A more ambitious way to stretch your legs is to visit the **monasteries** in the Nicolina district, south of the city centre, by the fetid stream of the same name. Catch bus #9 downhill past the Palace of Culture and out along Strada Nicolina; cresting the flyover, you'll see the Cetăţuia and Galata monasteries on separate

---

MIHAI EMINESCU

Mihai Eminescu, Romania's "national poet", was born in 1850 in Botoşani, east of Suceava, and schooled in Cernăuţi, the capital of Hapsburg Bucovina. At the age of sixteen, he gave his surname, Eminovici, the characteristic Romanian ending *-escu* and became a prompter for a troupe of actors, until his parents packed him off to study law in Vienna and Berlin. Returning to Iaşi in 1874, he found a job as a librarian, joined the Junimea literary society, and had a tortured affair with Veronica Micle, a poet and wife of the university rector. After the rector's demise, Eminescu decided that he was too poor to marry her and took an editorial job in Bucharest to escape his grief. Overwork led to a mental breakdown in 1883, and from then on, until his death of syphilis six years later, periods of madness alternated with lucid intervals. He is best remembered for *Luceafărul* (The Evening Star), a 96-stanza ballad of love, which unfortunately doesn't translate well into other languages.

hilltops to the east and west, and a modern Roman Catholic church with a prow-like spire in the valley, which is where you should alight. From here, either follow Şoseaua Tudor Nicolaie west up the hill and past a cemetery, to reach Galata Monastery; or cross the main road, and head east through apartment buildings and across the tracks to find Frumoasa Monastery and the trail south to Cetăţuia. If you're intending to visit all three, it's best to see Cetăţuia first and work your way back to the others, as the hike to Cetăţuia requires the most effort.

The **Galata Monastery** stands on Miroslavei hill and is entered by a fortified gate tower. To the right of the gateway, beside a newer building in use today, are the ruins of the original monks' quarters and a Turkish bath. The monastery's church was built in 1579–84 to a typically Moldavian plan, with an enclosed porch and narthex preceding the nave. Its founder, Prince Petru Şchiopul, is buried in the nave with his daughter, Despina.

Frumoasa Monastery, on a low hillock surrounded by ruined walls, was derelict for decades, but after restoration is close to living up to its name, meaning "beautiful", once more. Largely built by the ill-fated Grigore II Ghica in 1726–33, Frumoasa differs from the other monasteries thanks to the ponderous form of Neoclassicism in favour when the complex was reconstructed in the early nineteenth century. Its bell tower is capped by a black dome that vies for mastery of the skyline with two bell-shaped, brown cupolas atop the church.

Turn left out of the gate for Strada Cetăţuia, at the far end of which you'll find a truck park with a road climbing to the summit of a hill. This is also accessible by a path, which is quicker, but a hard slog. Here, the "Citadel" or **Cetăţuia Monastery** seems remote from Iaşi; on misty days, the city is blotted out, and all you can see are moors. Its high walls conceal a harmonious ensemble of white stone buildings with rakish black roofs, interspersed by dwarf pines and centred on a church that's similar to the Church of the Three Hierarchs in town, but less richly carved. Prince Gheorghe Duca and his wife, who founded the monastery in 1669–72, are buried in the nave.

Eating, drinking and entertainment

Easily the best **restaurants** in town are the private *Select Restaurant*, opposite the *Continental* hotel, which offers a wide range of tasty dishes (try the chicken stuffed with mushrooms – *pui umplut cu ciuperci*) and is not too expensive providing you watch what you drink; the Italian *Cucina Casalinga*, on Strada Costache Negri, which runs east from the Church of the Three Hierarchs; and the three *Metro* outlets, at Str. Gr Urcche 1, Str. Ştefan cel Mare 18 and Str. Silvestru 10, which serve upmarket pasta and pizza, accept credit cards and stay open till 1am. The *Traian, Unirea* and *Moldova* hotels have **restaurants** which stay open till 11pm (with bands after 8pm); the *Traian*'s is the probably the best, although they all have much the same menu. You'll find various joints dispensing pizza, spicy sausages (*mititei*) and other **snacks** in the vicinity of Piaţa Unirii, Strada Lăpuşneanu, and the university.

All the hotels have **bars**, and all of them are fairly seedy; the best are to be found in the *Unirea*, which has a café-bar with a terrace on the thirteenth floor, affording fine views of the city, and the *Moldova*, whose night bar (daily, 10pm–4am) offers a disco of sorts.

Entertainment

Lovers of classical music should try to attend a performance of the **Moldavian Philharmonic**, the country's second orchestra (after Bucharest). Tickets are available at the box office, behind the National Theatre at Strada Cuza Vodă 29, or from the ticket agency (*Agenţia Teatrală*) at Ştefan cel Mare 8, near Piaţa Unirii.

Iaşi's big annual event is the **St Paraschiva festival week** (*Sarbatorile Iaşului*) in mid-October, when people from all over Moldavia flood into town to pay homage to the saint buried in the Metropolitan Church. The exact date varies every year, but the main day is always a Friday. The **Festival of the Three Hierarchs** is celebrated on January 30. Traditional folklore festivals include the **Folk Music Festival** in mid-December, a **Festival of Winter Customs** on the first Sunday in January, and a week-long **Ceramics Fair** (*Tîrgul de Ceramica Cucuteni 5000*) towards the end of June.

Students frequent the **billiard hall** in the Scala complex on the corner of Strada A. Panu, opposite the Central Market Hall. Further up this side street is the *Dream Club* (Fri & Sat 7pm–4am, Sun 7.30pm–2am; $3), Iaşi's liveliest **disco**. Another trendy hang-out is the *Geletari Bar Arlechino* (8am–midnight; closed Tues), at the northern end of Strada Ştefan cel Mare, which serves Italian **ice cream** and imported alcohol.

Listings

Airlines TAROM has an office at Str. Arcu 3 (Mon–Fri 7am–7pm, Sat 7am–noon; ☎032/11.52.39).

Airport information ☎032/17.81.26.

Car repairs ACR has an office on Bulevardul Gării (☎032/13.01.77).

Exchange Cambio Exchange is on Strada C. Negru (Mon–Sat 9am–6pm, Sun 10am–1pm).

Fuel There are 24hr fuel stations on Şos. Păcurari and Şos. Bucium.

Hospital on the corner of Str. L. Catargi and Str. Berthelot (☎032/14.06.90).

Libraries The British Council library is at Str. Păcurari 4.

Photography You can buy film and get photos developed at the well-signposted Kodak outlet on Str. Ştefan cel Mare.

Post and telephone offices On Str. Lăpuşneanu (daily 7am–8pm).

Shopping The Galerile Anticvariat at Str. Lăpuşneanu 24 is a good place to browse for antique souvenirs and second-hand books in foreign languages. Foreign-language books are also good value at Casa Cartii, opposite the Three Hierarchs church. For food, try the Central Market Hall (Mon 7am–3pm; Tues–Fri 6am–8pm; Sat 7am–6pm) on Str. A. Panu, or the outdoor market on B-dul Independenţei, up the hill behind the *Hotel Unirea*.

Train tickets The CFR office is at Piaţa Unirii 9 (Mon–Fri 8am–8pm; ☎14.76.73); upstairs you can buy tickets for the overnight Prietenia to Chişinău in Republica Moldova, for which foreigners must already have a visa, obtainable from the Moldovan embassy in Bucharest.

Suceava and around

When confronted with the belching factories sprawling across the river, it's difficult to imagine **SUCEAVA**, 150km northwest of Iaşi, as an old princely capital. The city's heyday more or less coincided with the reign of **Stephen the Great** (1457–1504), who warred ceaselessly against Moldavia's invaders – principally the Turks – and won all but two of the thirty-six battles he fought. This record

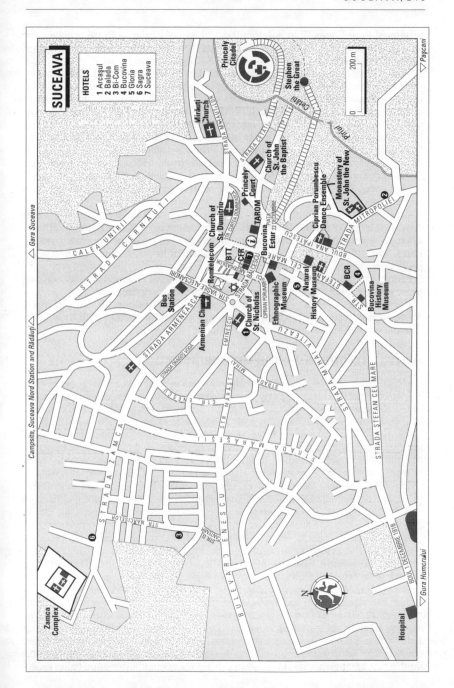

SUCEAVA

HOTELS
1 Arcaşul
2 Balada
3 Bi-Com
4 Bucovina
5 Gloria
6 Sagra
7 Suceava

prompted Pope Sixtus IV to dub him the "Athlete of Christ" – a rare accolade for a non-Catholic, which wasn't extended to Stephen's cousin Vlad the Impaler, even though he massacred 45,000 of the infidel during one year alone.

While Stephen's successors, **Bogdan the One-Eyed** and **Petru Rareş**, maintained the tradition of endowing a church or monastery after every victory, they proved less successful against the Turks and Tatars, who ravaged Suceava several times. Eclipsed when Iaşi became the Moldavian capital in 1565, Suceava missed its last chance of glory in 1600, when **Michael the Brave** (Mihai Viteazul) completed his campaign to unite Wallachia, Moldavia and Transylvania by marching unopposed into Suceava's Princely Citadel. In terms of national pride, Suceava's nadir was the long period from 1775 to 1918, when the **Hapsburgs** ruled northern Moldavia from Czernowitz (Cernăuţi), although Suceava was able to prosper as a trading centre between the highland and lowland areas.

Under Communism, this traditional trading role was deemed backward and remedied by hasty **industrialization** – the consequences of which now blight the town. Its wood-processing and tanning plants have poisoned the Suceava River for miles, while the "Suceava syndrome" of malformed babies has been linked to air **pollution** caused by the artificial fibres factory. Sadly, like many towns in Romania, Suceava can neither afford to scrap its noxious economic mainstays, nor more safely exploit the wealth of raw materials in the region.

For visitors, Suceava is primarily a base for **excursions to the Painted Monasteries** (see p.252), which are the only reason to spend much time here. The town's own sights can be covered in a day.

Arrival, information and accommodation

You'll probably arrive at one of the **train stations** in the industrial zone across the river to the north: the most likely is the **Gara Suceava**, in the Burdujeni district of the town, at Str. N. Iorga 7, linked to the centre by buses #2, #3, #26 and #30. The fast trains from Iaşi to Cluj and Timişoara call here, while services from Bucharest also call at **Suceava Nord**, at Str. Gării 1 in Itcani; catch bus #1 or #5 for the centre. The third station, **Suceava Vest**, connected to the centre by buses #12 and #13, chiefly handles freight trains and local services towards Vatra Dornei. Seats can be reserved a day in advance at CFR at Str. Bălcescu 8 (Mon–Fri 7am–8pm). Most **local buses** and trolley buses stop just east of the main square, Piaţa 22 Decembrie, between the Princely Court and the church of St John the Baptist. The **bus station** is just northwest of the centre, on Str. V. Alecsandri.

At the **airport**, eight kilometres from town, TAROM buses meet flights, dropping off in the centre at their office on Piaţa 22 Decembrie (☎030/21.46.86; Mon–Sat 7am–8pm); buses to the airport leave from outside the office an hour and a half before each flight. There are two flights to Bucharest on just three days a week (Mon, Wed & Thurs), which fly on a triangular route via Iaşi.

The Bucovina Turism **tourist agency** (formerly ONT; Mon–Fri 8am–3.30pm; ☎030/22.12.97) is also on Piaţa 22 Decembrie, but is only useful for changing money. Happily, an excellent substitute lies just across the square – Bucovina Estur (Mon–Fri 9am–8pm & Sat 9am–1pm; Mon–Fri 9am–5pm in winter; ☎ & fax 030/22.32.59 or 52.02.23), whose keen, English-speaking staff supply information on the city, arrange accommodation in private rooms, and offer good-value tailor-

---

TOURS TO THE PAINTED MONASTERIES

Given that everyone comes to Suceava to visit the **Painted Monasteries** (see p.252), and that public transport to them is limited, it's not surprising that many visitors opt for organized **tours**. The Bucovina Estur tourist agency will provide a car with a driver (who may not speak English, although guides are also available) for a $60 tour which covers **Putna, Sucevița, Moldovița, Humor** and **Voroneț;** the fee is for the car, not per person. You can also devise your own itinerary, based on a standard rate per kilometre (count on 250km) and a daily charge for the guide. Bucovina Estur's staff are knowledgeable and charming, and it is one of the cheapest and most reliable ways of making the tour. For $50 you can rent a small car without a driver, or take a taxi for the day

---

made tours of the monasteries, as well as changing money. They were planning to move to Strada Ciprian Porumbescu at the time of writing.

Accommodation

Suceava doesn't yet have the range of **hotels** you'd expect of a tourist centre. For solo travellers in particular, the best option may be a **private room** (⑤) in the centre, through the Bucovina Estur tourist agency; rooms are clean and warm and prices include three good meals a day. BTT, at Strada Meseriașilor 10 (Mon–Fri 8am–8pm; ☎030/21.52.35 or 21.43.89, fax 52.04.38), runs an agrotourism programme in neighbouring villages (②). Suceava's **campsite**, at Str. Cernăuți 1 (☎030/21.52.33; ①), has cabins and tent space; to get there, take any bus towards Suceava Nord station and get off at the Peco station before the rail bridge over the road.

Arcașul, Str. Mihai Viteazul 4 (☎030/21.09.44, fax 22.75.98). Best of the central hotels, with restaurant, bar and disco. Cheek-by-jowl with the fifteenth-century church of St Nicolae. ⑧.

Autogara, Str. V Alecsandri (☎030/21.60.89). Very basic rooms above the bus station, with occasional hot water. ②.

Balada, Str. Mitropoliei 3 (☎030/22.31.98, fax 52.00.87). Smart private hotel, the best in town, downhill from the Monastery of St John the New. Some rooms have double beds and balconies plus cable TV. Breakfast included. ⑧.

Bi-Com, Str. Narciselor 20 (☎030/21.68.81, fax 63.00.07). Another comfy private hotel, with its own hot-water supply, in a quiet suburb 15min walk from the centre, or bus #1 or #2 to Str. D Cantemir. ⑦.

Bucovina, B-dul A. Ipătescu 5 (☎030/21.70.48, fax 21.47.00). Typical 1970s high-rise on the edge of the centre. All rooms have private bath and cable TV; breakfast included. ACR; ⑧.

Gloria, Str. V Bumbac 4 (☎030/52.12.09, fax 21.54.08). Fairly unexciting, middle-of-the-range place, located behind the prefecture on Str. Bălcescu. Doubles only, some with kitchens and private bathrooms. ③.

Sagra, Str. Zamca (☎030/52.09.85, fax 21.59.19). Private hotel near the Zamca monastery (bus #29 or #30), modern and comfortable but hot water only at limited times. Ask about their cottages in the hills as well. ③.

Socim, Str. Jean Bart 24 (☎030/25.76.75, fax 52.26.62). The only convenient budget option, in an apartment block just a few hundred metres in front of Gara Suceava. Clean and decent, but hot water is only at scheduled times; light switches are hidden in the wardrobes. ①.

Suceava, Str. N. Bălcescu 4 (☎030/52.10.79, fax 21.47.00). Central, but not much else going for it. All rooms have private bathrooms, but hot water is only available at limited times. ⑤.

Tur-West, Str. Humorului (☎030/21.04.85). On the edge of town on the Gura Humorului road, a motel with small but nice rooms, safe parking, and a restaurant open till midnight. ④.

The Town

Most of Suceava's sights relate to its past as a princely capital, and are easily reached on foot. The Princely Citadel and the Zamca Monastery are a good twenty minutes' walk east and west from the centre respectively, but most other sites are a short walk from the city's main square, Piaţa 22 Decembrie.

The **Princely Court** (Curtea Domnească), which amounts to very little more than ruins, is just north of Piaţa 22 Decembrie. Just to its west is the **Church of St Dumitru**; built by Petru Rareş in 1534–35, it is typical of Moldavian churches of the period, with a double row of niche-bound saints on its facade, and coloured tiles ornamenting its drum. The freestanding bell tower, added in 1561, bears the Moldavian crest.

Five minutes' walk east along Strada Mirăuţilor from the Princely Court is **Mirăuţi Church**, the oldest in Suceava. Founded by Petru I Muşat, in about 1390, this was originally the Metropolitan cathedral, where the early princes of Moldavia were crowned. Its facade is decorated with blind arches and a saw-toothed cornice sandwiched between thick cable mouldings, while below the eaves are frescoes of saints, added at the end of the nineteenth century.

Continuing west from the Court along Strada Curtea Domnească will bring you to Suceava's **market**, which is busiest on Thursdays, when cartloads of peasants roll into town to sell their produce. Many wear traditional dress, such as fur-lined leather or sheepskin waistcoats (*pieptar*), wrap-around skirts (*catriniţă*) or white woollen pantaloons (*iţari*). Further examples – and finer embroideries and crafts rarely seen nowadays – are exhibited in an **Ethnographic Museum** at Str. Ciprian Porumbescu 5 (Tues–Sun 9am–5pm), one block west of Piaţa 22 Decembrie via Strada Bălcescu. The muesum is housed in a half-timbered building, the oldest civil edifice in Suceava county, which served as the court guesthouse during the seventeenth century.

The **Church of St John the Baptist**, built as his court chapel by Basil the Wolf in 1643, is just south of Piaţa 22 Decembrie, on the far side of the main Strada Ana Ipătescu. At weekends, visitors may encounter **funerals** where the deceased is laid out in an open coffin, amid candles and loaves of bread, while a horse-drawn hearse waits outside. Corteges often parade around Piaţa 22 Decembrie, as do wedding parties – sometimes one follows another. Further south along Strada Ana Ipătescu, the excellent **Ciprian Porumbescu Dance Ensemble**, a folk dance troupe, is based behind a modern facade beside the Invierea Domnului church, founded in 1552 by Petru Rareş's wife Elena.

Strada Ştefan cel Mare runs parallel to Strada Ana Ipătescu, south from Piaţa 22 Decembrie; the **Natural History Museum** (Tues–Sun 10am–6pm), at no. 23, is full of stuffed wildlife and the **Bucovina History Museum** (Tues–Sun 10am–8pm), at no. 33, begins with the usual array of Neolithic shards, and works stolidly on through medieval times and the independence struggles. There's better coverage of World War II here than in most Romanian museums, and the exhibits once devoted to Communism have been replaced by paintings – some portraits by local artists, and very minor works by Luchian and Pallady. The main attraction is a life-size **model of Stephen's throne room**, occupied by richly costumed figures of the monarch, his wife and boyars.

Midway between the Natural History Museum and the Bucovina History Museum, Strada Mitropoliei heads east to the **Monastery of St John the New** (*Mănăsteria Sf Ioan cel Nou*), which is readily identified by its colourful steeple,

PRINCE DRAGOŞ AND THE AUROCHS

Churches throughout Moldavia display the emblem of the medieval principality: an aurochs' head and a sun, moon and star. This symbolizes the legend of **Prince Dragoş**, who is said to have hunted a giant **aurochs** (the *zimbru* or European bison) all the way across the mountains from Poland, until he cornered it by a river and slew the beast after a fight lasting from dawn to dusk – hence the inclusion of the sun, moon and Morning Star in the emblem. Dragoş's favourite hunting dog, **Molda**, was killed in the fight, and the prince named the River Moldova in her honour, adopting the aurochs, the mightiest animal in the Carpathians, as his totem. The last wild aurochs in Romania was killed in 1852 near Borşa, although captive breeding populations survive.

striped with blue, black and yellow chevrons. Started by Prince Bogdan in 1514 and finished by his son Ştefaniţa in 1522, its monumental **Church of St George** was intended to replace the Mirăuţi Church as Suceava's Metropolitan cathedral, so no expense was spared. The facade was once covered with **frescoes** like the Painted Monasteries of Bucovina, but, sadly, only the *Tree of Jesse* and a fragment of the *Last Judgement* remain. The **relics of St John the New** rest here, to the right of the nave, and are taken on a grand procession through the city each year on June 24, the feast of St John the Baptist (the feast of *Sînziene*). St John the New's martyrdom is depicted on the wall of a small **chapel** near the church. Arrested for preaching in Turkish-occupied Moldavia, he was dragged through the streets of Cetăţii Alba behind a horse, and slashed to death by enraged Muslims. The monastery, which serves as the headquarters of the **Patriarchate of Suceava and Bucovina**, has a pavilion for the blessing of holy water, which is stored in 230-litre drums, for the faithful to take away in bottles.

The Princely Citadel

Suceava's most impressive monument is the **Princely Citadel** (Tues–Sun 10am–6pm), which overlooks the city from a hill to its east. Also known as the Throne Citadel of Moldavia (*Cetatea de Scaun a Moldovei*), the Princely Citadel was built by Petru I Muşat (1375–91), who moved the Moldavian capital from Siret to Suceava; it was subsequently strengthened in the fifteenth century by Alexander the Good. Stephen the Great added the moat, curtain walls and bastions that enabled it to defy the artillery of Mohammed II, conqueror of Constantinople, in 1476. Although blown up in 1675, much of the three-storey keep and the outlying chambers remain; from the ramparts, there's a fine view over the city and to the Mirăuţi Church across the valley.

To reach the citadel, which is a twenty-minute walk from the centre, head east from Piaţa 22 Decembrie through the park and across the bridge into the woods and follow the path uphill to the giant equestrian **statue of Stephen the Great**, unveiled in 1977; the bas-reliefs on the pedestal depict the battle of Vaslui against the Turks. From here, several paths lead up to the citadel.

The Zamca monastery

Another, more neglected, ruin, the Armenian monastery of Zamca, straddles a plateau on the northwest edge of town, 25 minutes' walk from the centre along Strada Armenească and also reached by buses #29 or #30. The Armenian diaspora had reached Moldavia by 1350, and Alexander the Good founded the Armenian bishopric of Suceava in 1401; in 1551 they fell foul of the Rareş family, leading to a pogrom, but in 1572 an Armenian actually became ruler of Moldavia. The Zamca monastery was founded in 1606, and later fortified with ramparts and a gatetower. Its churches combine Gothic and classical elements with oriental motifs, but are so derelict that you can't enter. Nowadays the moat is dry and the earthworks overgrown; much of the compound is planted with cabbages, belonging to a family squatting in the three-storey guesthouse (*clişarniţa*), where dignitaries were once accommodated. Though not much from a monumental standpoint, the site has a desolate grandeur, particularly at dusk.

Eating, drinking and entertainment

Aside from the **restaurants** in the *Suceava*, *Bucovina* and *Arcaşul* hotels, the choice of town-centre restaurants are the dark, old-fashioned *Naţional* (daily 7.30am–11pm) at Str. Bălcescu 3; the sleazy *Bucureşti* (daily 6am–8pm) on the corner of the main square; and the *Lacto-Vegetarian* restaurant on Strada Plăieşilor, an alley off the pedestrianized section of Strada Ştefan cel Mare, which does serve meat, but also has "fasting" (meatless) dishes. The *Corso*, 1km west of town at B-dul Enescu T90, near Str. Zorilor, is good and affordable, but hardly central; bus #2 heads out this way.

There are several **fast-food** outlets near the market; notably the *gospodina* at Str. Bălcescu 8 (7am–9pm), which serves ready-cooked dishes, salads and pastries. Further out, there's a genuine *Autoservire* opposite the Gara Suceava, and a 24-hour pizza place just up the road by the *Hotel Socim*; a few hundred metres away on Calea Unirii, the main Suceava–Dorohoi road, there's *Country Pizza* and *Betty's Icecream*, both are very good and very popular with the locals.

The only "nightlife" Suceava has to offer is a **disco** in the House of Culture (*Casa Culturii*) on the main square (Fri–Sun 7pm–2am), and the cinema at Str. Ştefan cel Mare 25. The **Ciprian Porumbescu Dance Ensemble** is often away on tour, but is sure to appear at the **folklore festival** at Ilişeşti, in July (see box opposite).

Listings

Car repairs ACR at Str. Bălcescu 8 (Mon–Fri 8am–4pm; ☎030/21.09.97).

Exchange There's a Bancomat cash machine at the BCR office on Str. Ştefan cel Mare (behind the *Bucovina* hotel).

Laundry Curătătorie Rapida Nufărul, at Str. Bălcescu 1, in the courtyard opposite Bancpost.

Pharmacies The 24hr pharmacy is at Str. Bălcescu 2.

Post and telephone offices Both on Str. Dimitrie Onciul, next to the synagogue.

Dragomirna Monastery

The nearest of the Bucovina monasteries to Suceava is the (unpainted) Dragomirna convent, 4km beyond the village of **Mitocul Dragomirnei**, 12km north of town. On weekdays, **buses** to the village leave at 6am, 11.50am and 3pm and on weekends at 8.30am and 3.20pm; in each case, the return journey to Suceava starts roughly half an hour after arrival. Rolling plains conceal the monastery from view until the last moment.

Massively walled like a fortress, the **Dragomirna Monastery** was founded in the early seventeenth century by Metropolitan Anastasie Crimca, who designed its **church**, which is dramatically proportioned at 42m high but only 9.6m wide. The church's white stone facade is encircled by a thick cable moulding, below a double row of pendentive arches; the trefoil windows reflect the influence of Polish Gothic architecture, with which Crimca was familiar. Its octagonal tower, resting on two star-shaped pedestals, is carved with meanders and rosettes, like the Church of the Three Hierarchs in Iaşi. The *pronaos* contains several pre-Christian tombs, brought here from the Black Sea coast, while Crimca himself is buried in the nave; his portrait is visible on the pillar to the left as you walk through. The star-vaulted nave is covered in dark blue, red and gold frescoes, including some with buildings in the background, which was uncommon in that period, with an iconostasis which comes from the demolished Socola Monastery.

The complex also contains a smaller church with an open porch in the Wallachian style, modernized living quarters for the seventy nuns who farm much of the land surrounding the monastery, and a **museum** harbouring seven of the surviving 26 illuminated manuscripts of the school of illuminators founded here by Crimca, who was himself a talented artist. The defensive **walls** and towers were added in 1627 by Prince Miron Barnovschi, owing to the threat of foreign invasions. These were so frequent that wooden village churches were sometimes mounted on wheels so that they could be towed away to safety.

The only **accommodation** available locally is for women, four of whom can stay at the convent at any given time. The lodgings are comfortable (but lacking

---

FESTIVALS AT ILIŞEŞTI

Many villages in northern Moldavia still hold **winter festivities** that mingle pagan and Christian rites. Preparations for Christmas begin in earnest on St Nicholas's Day (December 6), when people butcher pigs for the feast beside the roads – not a sight for the squeamish. Women get to work baking pies and the special *turte* pastries, which symbolize Christ's swaddling clothes, while the men rehearse songs and dances. On Christmas Eve (*Ajun*), boys go from house to house singing carols (*colinde*) that combine felicitations with risqué innuendoes, accompanied by an instrument which mimics the bellowing of a bull. After days of feasting and dancing, the climax of the festivities comes on the day of New Year's Eve, when a dancer, garbed in black and red, dons a goat's head mask with wooden jaws, which he clacks to the music of drums and flutes, and whips another dancer, dressed as a bear, through the streets. The bear symbolizes the forces of nature and dances until he drops (symbolizing winter, when everything dies off), only reviving when other dancers – dressed as lancers, Turks or "Little Horses" – appear. Then a brass band starts playing and everyone begins downing *ţuică* and dancing, setting the pattern for a binge that will last all night.

The easiest place to experience these festivities is the village of **Ilişeşti**,15km along the main road west from Suceava. The commune also hosts the **"From the Rarău Mountain" Folklore Festival** (*De sub montale Rarău*), on the second Sunday of July; ensembles from three counties – Bacău, Neamţ and Maramureş – participate, and it's a chance to enjoy a round dance (*horă*) and shepherds' dances, fiddles, flutes and alpine horns, and a panoply of costumes. Ilişeşti is easily reached by **bus** from Suceava. There's an old-style **motel-campsite** (☎Ilişeşti 4; ①) 6km west of the town on the Gura Humorului road.

hot water), and the ambience is tranquil. Would-be guests should book a week before, through the Bucovina Estur travel agent in Suceava.

Arbore and Solca

Though **Arbore and Solca** are often grouped together with the Painted Monasteries, neither of them has ever been more than a village church, and only Arbore has the external frescoes characteristic of the genre. Such quibbles aside, however, their kinship in form and spirit is undeniable. Getting there (and back) by **public transport** takes most of the day, and precludes carrying on to any of the other monasteries. Arbore lies about 35km northwest of Suceava and Solca a further 8km along the same road; buses leave Suceava for Arbore and Solca on weekdays only at 6.30am and 6.30pm.

Arbore

Opposite the cemetery on the road through **ARBORE** stands the village **church** built in 1503 by one of Stephen's generals, Luca Arbore, lord of the village. While its wooden stockade and stone bell tower are rustic enough, its frescoed walls and sweeping roof are as majestic as any monastic edifice. Like the Painted Monasteries, its murals, dating from 1541, follow iconic conventions inherited from Byzantium, which designated subjects for each wall, arranged in rows according to their hierarchical significance. This is obvious on the apses, where the angels and seraphim appear at the top; archangels and biblical saints below; then martyrs; and lastly a row of cultural propagators or military saints.

The images on the exposed northern side of the church have been obliterated by the weather, and the best-preserved **frescoes** are found on the relatively sheltered south and west walls. The south wall has eight rows of scenes from Genesis and the lives of the saints; red, yellow, pink and ochre counterpoint the prevailing green. The eaves and buttresses have protected half of the *Last Judgement* on the west wall, which consigns "heathens" awaiting hell to the top right-hand corner. In the courtyard lie two heavy, hollowed-out stone slabs used for mixing colours, after the walls had been rendered with charcoal and lamp-black. Arbore's tomb stands in its nave, but the church is not opened for tourism, only for services.

Solca

All the usual conventions for establishing a monastery were observed at **SOLCA** (see box), 8km up the valley, where the church, built between 1611 and 1615, was fortified like a monastery, due to its strategic location on the edge of the highlands. Though lacking any monks' quarters, it was meant to be garrisoned in times of crisis – there are cellars for storing gunpowder and holes in the wall for beams to support the archers' galleries. The **church** is tall and heavily buttressed, with the characteristically Moldavian octagonal belfry on a double star-shaped base, straddling a steep roof, newly retiled in red, purple, white and yellow – like that of the gate tower. In the courtyard there's a wooden cross in honour of the martyrs of the revolution, where funeral cakes are blessed and prayers are said at Easter. However, the beauty of the scene is marred by the foul smoke-stacks of Solca's **beer factory**, next door. Villagers once boasted of the product and of their pure spring water, but nowadays sadly acknowledge that the quality of both has declined.

MOLDAVIAN FORTIFIED MONASTERIES

Moldavian fortified monasteries were usually sited at the head of a valley to form a defensive bottleneck against the Turks or Tatars. The exact spot was decided by shooting arrows from a nearby hilltop; where the first one landed, a water source was dug and henceforth deemed holy; the second arrow determined the location of the altar; the third the belfry, and so on. After the monastery was finished, crosses were raised on the hill from where the arrows had been fired.

Should you feel like a day or two in the country, exploring the woods or **skiing** across country in wintertime, it's possible to stay with the Strugariu family, near the church at Str. Gheorghe Doja 30A (☎030/47.72.31; ①). Their house has warm **rooms** and hot water and hearty meals are included in the price; book a week in advance through the Bucovina Estur tourist agency in Suceava. The only alternative is the rather run-down *Hanul Solca* (☎030/47.75.08) on the road to the monastery and the only **restaurant** is the grubby facility in the Complex Commercial near the metal bridge (daily, 9am–10pm).

Rădăuți and Marginea

The dreary market town of **RĂDĂUȚI** (pronounced Ra-dah-*oots*) could be ignored but for its role in the local transport network, providing connections to Putna and the Painted Monasteries of Sucevița and Moldovița (see p.252). However, if you find yourself with a long wait between connections, there are a few sights of interest in the town centre.

The fourteenth-century **Bogdana Church** in the centre of town is the oldest stone church in Moldavia. It was built for Prince Bogdan, who forged the principality and made Rădăuți its capital. The tombs of Bogdan and of Stephen the Great's mother and grandmother lie in the nave. A few blocks northwest, on the corner of Strada Republicii, the **Ethnographic Museum** (Tues–Sun 9am–5pm), has a fine collection of local costumes and artefacts. The colours of the embroidered blouses remain fresh a century later thanks to the preparation of the textiles, which were washed up to twenty times. The museum also has a fine collection of the local **black pottery** and houses a studio which makes the painted ceramics of birds and flowers that are also typical of the region; items can be bought from their workshop.

On Thursdays and Fridays the town hosts a **bazaar** attended by peasants from the surrounding villages, and Ukrainians trying to earn money by selling their family heirlooms. To add to the mayhem, there's also a **car sparcs market** on Fridays that draws people from all over Moldavia, making this the worst time to try to change buses or get a room in town.

Rădăuți's **bus station** is 200m down the road from the *Hotel Nordic*. Accommodation is not available at the *Nordic*, but its **restaurant** is still open, and is the only one in town. If you need **accommodation**, the *Hotel Azur* (☎ & fax 030/46.47.18; ②) at Calea Cernăuți 29 has large plain rooms and good heating, although no restaurant or bar.

Marginea

If you're curious to see **black pottery** being made, there is a studio (Mon–Fri 9am–5pm) in **MARGINEA**, on the road between Rădăuți and Sucevița (see p.255); you'll find the studio off the main road opposite the metal sign in the form of a pot. Motorists should note that Marginea is also linked by side roads to Solca (see p.250) and Putna (see p.254). The latter route passes through Voitinel, which is notable for being entirely populated by **Gypsies** – the only such village in Suceava county; however the road's in terrible shape and you may prefer to go via Rădăuți. Should you need **accommodation**, the *Motel Vicovu* (☎ & fax 030/46.41.38; ③) between Voitinel and Gălănești will go to the trouble of warming up a room if you contact them in advance. It also has a **restaurant** (daily 10am–9pm).

The Painted Monasteries of Southern Bucovina

The **Painted Monasteries of Southern Bucovina**, in the northwest corner of Moldavia, are rightfully acclaimed as masterpieces of art and architecture, steeped in history and perfectly in harmony with their surroundings. Founded in the fifteenth and sixteenth centuries, they were citadels of Orthodoxy in an era overshadowed by the threat of infidel invaders. **Metropolitan Roşca** is credited with the idea of covering the churches' outer walls with paintings of biblical events and apocrypha, for the benefit of the illiterate faithful. These **frescoes**, billboards from the late medieval world, are essentially Byzantine, but infused with the vitality of the local folk art and mythology. Though little is known about the artists – who guarded their trade secrets by working in seclusion – their skills were such that the paintings are still fresh after 450 years' exposure. Remarkably, the layer of colour is only 0.25mm thick, in contrast to Italian frescoes, where the paint is absorbed deep into the plaster.

Perhaps the best of these frescoes are to be found at **Voroneț**, whose *Last Judgement* surpasses any of the other examples of this subject, and **Sucevița**, with its unique *Ladder of Virtue* and splendid *Tree of Jesse*. **Moldovița** has a better all-round collection, though, and **Humor** has the most tranquil atmosphere of them all. If you are making a trip to see the painted monasteries, it is worth including a visit to **Putna Monastery** and the churches at Arbore and Solca (see p.250). The organized tours of the painted monasteries, departing from Suceava (see box on p.245), include Putna Monastery in their itineraries, but you will need your own transport to reach Arbore and Solca.

The monasteries are scattered across a region divided by the imposing hills, or "crests" (*obcinie*), which branch off the Carpathians, and by the legacy of history. When the Hapsburgs annexed northern Moldavia in 1774, they called their new acquisition "Bucovina", a Romanianized version of their description of this beech-covered land (*Büchenwald*). Bucovina remained under Hapsburg rule until the end of World War I, when it was returned to Romania, only to be split in half in 1940 – the northern half being occupied by the Soviet Union and incorporated into the Ukraine, of which it is still a part today. Thus, Romanians speak of **Southern Bucovina** to describe what is actually the far north of Moldavia – implying that Bucovina might be reunited one day. Names aside, the scenery is wonderful, with misty valleys and rivers spilling down from rocky shoulders heaving up beneath a cloak of beech and fir. The woods are at their loveliest in May and autumn.

Visiting the monasteries

Without a car, visiting the monasteries is a time-consuming business, so many tourists opt for **excursions** run by agencies in Suceava (see box on p.245), which enable you to see all four Painted Monasteries plus Putna in a long day. Otherwise, **getting there** involves striking out by train from Suceava or by bus from Rădăuţi, about 40km north of Suceava, and staying overnight at each location. The routings make it hard to get from one monastery to another without backtracking, although this can be avoided by **hiking** across the hills at certain points. **Accommodation** is less of a problem as there are plenty of hotels and campsites – but the choice of **food** is limited, so you'd be wise to stock up in Suceava.

Though the monasteries have no set **visiting hours**, you can assume they'll be open daily from 9am to 5pm (8pm in summer). The museums are closed on Mondays. There is a modest **admission charge** ($1), plus a surcharge ($3) for cameras or videos. As working convents or monasteries, they prohibit smoking, and will turn away visitors whose **dress** offends Orthodox sensibilities.

Putna

Putna Monastery lacks the external murals of the Painted Monasteries, but as the first of the great religious monuments of Southern Bucovina and the burial place of Stephen the Great it's a good place to start, with the advantage of being accessible by train from Suceava via Rădăuţi. The slow ride past meandering rivers and fir-clad hills whets your appetite for **PUTNA** village – a wonderful jigsaw of wooden houses with carved gables and shingled roofs. Head uphill from the station to reach the main road, and bear left for the monastery, which is at the end of a tree-lined drive, 1km further on.

In 1466, Stephen chose the site of **Putna Monastery** by firing an arrow from the steep hill that now bears a white cross (see box on p.251). The monastery was rebuilt by Stephen after it burnt down in 1480, ravaged by war in the seventeenth century and repaired in the eighteenth, only to be damaged by an earthquake and restored again in 1902. Its walls and belltower were plainly intended for defence; in these less troubled times, they emphasize Putna's status as a patriotic reliquary, with a statue of Eminescu inside the entrance to identify the national poet with Moldavia's national hero.

The **church** is plain and strong, its facade defined by cable mouldings, blind arcades and trefoil windows, while the interior follows the usual configuration of three chambers: the sanctuary, containing the altar and iconostasis at its eastern end; the nave (or *naos*); and the narthex (or *pronaos*), just inside the porch – although at Putna the porch has also been enclosed to form an exonarthex. Prince Bogdan the One-Eyed, the wife of Petru Rareş, and Stephen's daughter and nephew are buried in the narthex, which is separated from the nave by two thick cable-moulded columns. Here, a graceful arch and a hanging votive lamp distinguish the **tomb of Stephen the Great** (right) from those of his two wives (both called Maria). Unusually for an Orthodox church, the interior is unpainted, but illuminated by stained-glass windows.

Outside stand three **bells**, the largest of which, cast in 1484, was only used to herald events such as royal deaths, and was last rung in 1918. When rung, the bell was heard as far away as Suceava. Hidden from the Communists for almost fifty years, it only came to light after the 1989 revolution. The middle bell traditionally served for everyday use, while the end one was the gift of an archimandrite who repaired its sixteenth-century precursor. At the rear of the yard stands a fifteenth-century tower, originally used as a treasury; the monks' cells along the wall date from 1856. Antique embroidery, silver psalters and illuminated manuscripts are exhibited in a small **museum** (Tues–Sun 10am–5pm).

Uphill and slightly to the east of the monastery, there's a curious hollowed-out rock with a door and window, reputedly once the **cell of Daniil the Hermit** – a monk who was indirectly responsible for the foundation of Suceviţa Monastery. The **wooden church** back along the main road is supposed to have been raised by Dragoş, and moved to its present location by Stephen.

Practicalities

Basic double and quadruple **rooms** are available at the *Motel Putna* (☎Putna 104; ①), near the wooden church, which is open year round and charges by the bed. There is also a summer **campsite** with huts and a **restaurant**, closer to the monastery. There are no **bus** services through Putna, so travelling on to the Painted Monasteries entails catching a train to Rădăuţi or Suceava, and then a bus from there. Alternatively, you could **hike to Suceviţa Monastery** in about three hours. Pick up the route (marked by blue crosses) from Putna station and follow the main valley for about an hour. Ignore the turn-off to the left near a hut and a bridge, but take the next turning on the right, cross another bridge and carry on round to the left, which will bring you out at a forestry hut, Canton Silvic 13. From here, stick to the forestry track up to another forestry hut, Strulinoasa Sud, which deteriorates into a pony trail as it approaches the watershed, but improves once it descends into an open valley. You should reach the monastery about an hour and half after crossing the watershed.

Suceviţa

Suceviţa Monastery – the last and grandest of the monastic complexes to be built – owes nothing to Stephen or his heirs; it is a monument to the feudal prince Iremia Movilă, his brother and successor Simion, and his widow, Elisabeta, who poisoned Simion so that her own sons might inherit the throne. The family first founded the village church in 1581, followed by the monastery church in 1584, and its walls, towers and belfry in stages thereafter. Massively built, the fortified church's whitewashed walls and steep grey roofs give an air of grandeur; its **frescoes** – painted in 1596 by two brothers – offset brilliant reds and blues by an undercoat of emerald green.

Entering the monastery, you're confronted by a glorious *Ladder of Virtue* covering the northern wall, which has been somewhat protected from erosion by the building's colossal eaves. Flights of angels assist the righteous to paradise, while sinners fall through the rungs into the arms of a grinning demon. The message is reiterated in the *Last Judgement* beneath the porch – reputedly left unfinished because the artist fell to his death from the scaffolding – where angels sound the last trump and smite heathens with swords, while Turks and Jews can be seen lamenting, and the Devil gloats in the bottom right-hand corner. Outside the porch, you'll see the two-headed Beast of the Apocalypse, and angels pouring rivers of fire and treading the grapes of wrath. The iron ox-collar hanging by the doorway is beaten to summon the monks to prayer.

The *Tree of Jesse* on the south wall symbolizes the continuity between the Old and the New Testament, being a literal depiction of the prophecy in Isaiah that the Messiah will spring "from the stem of Jesse". This lush composition on a dark blue background amounts to a biblical Who's Who, with an ancestral tree of prophets culminating in the Holy Family. *The Veil* represents Mary as a Byzantine empress, beneath a red veil held by angels, while the *Hymn to the Virgin* is illustrated with Italianate buildings and people in oriental dress. Alongside is a frieze of ancient philosophers clad in Byzantine cloaks; Plato bears a coffin and a pile of bones on his head, in tribute to his meditations on life and death. As usual, the hierarchy of angels, prophets, apostles and martyrs covers the curved apse at the eastern end.

Inside the narthex, the lives of the saints end with them being burnt, boiled, dismembered or decapitated – a gory catalogue relieved by rams, suns and other zodiacal symbols. As usual, the frescoes in the nave are blackened by candle-smoke, but you can still discern a votive picture of Elisabeta and her children on the wall to the right. Ironically, her ambitions for them came to nought as she died in a Sultan's harem – "by God's will", a chronicler noted sanctimoniously. Iremia and Simion are buried nearby.

By climbing the **hill** behind the village church's graveyard, you can see the complex as a whole, and appreciate its magnificent setting at the foot of the surrounding hills, carpeted with firs and lush pastures.

Practicalities

Sucevița lies midway between Rădăuți, 17km to the east, and Moldovița Monastery, to the west beyond the Ciumîrna Pass. From Rădăuți there are four buses daily. If time is short, get the mid-morning bus to Sucevița, visit the monastery, and then catch the Cîmpulung-bound service that passes through around 3.45pm and runs over the mountains to Vatra Moldoviței, enabling you to visit two monasteries in one day. This is a very scenic route, with a viewpoint at the pass over the low, parallel *Obcinele Bucoviniei* ridges.

Rooms are available at the run-down *Hanul Sucevița* (☎Sucevița 141; ①), 300m towards Rădăuți from the monastery – which also has a **restaurant** (daily noon–9pm) and a summer **campsite** with huts – or 3km uphill in the direction of Moldovița, where the private *Popasul Turistic Bucovina* (☎Sucevița 165) offers better huts (①) and fifteen rooms (all with bathrooms; ②). This has constant hot water, some centrally heated rooms, and an excellent restaurant.

Moldovița

Approaching from Sucevița over the Ciumîrna Pass, you'll come upon the monastery shortly before the village of Vatra Moldoviței. **Moldovița Monastery** is a smaller complex than Sucevița but equally well defended, its ivy-clad walls enclosing white stone buildings with lustrous black shingled roofs. The monastery was founded in 1532 by Stephen's illegitimate son, Petru Rareș, during whose reign the Turks finally compelled Moldavia to pay tribute and acknowledge Ottoman suzerainity. The monastery's **frescoes** were painted by Toma of Suceava in 1537, at a time when Petru Rareș still hoped to resist, despite the inexorability of the Turkish advance since the fall of Constantinople in 1453.

To raise morale, the Turkish siege was conflated with an earlier, failed attempt by the Persians in 626. A delightfully revisionist *Siege of Constantinople* along the bottom of the south wall depicts Christians routing the infidel with arrows and cannons and miraculous icons being paraded around the ramparts. Illustrated above this is the *Hymn to the Virgin* composed by Metropolitan Sergius in thanksgiving for her intervention, while further along is a lovely *Tree of Jesse*, with dozens of figures entwined in foliage. All the compositions are set on an intense blue background.

The open porch contains a fine *Last Judgement*, showing a crowd of dignitaries growing agitated as a demon drags one of their number, said to be Herod, towards the fires below, where Satan sits on a scaly creature – defaced with oddly formal nineteenth-century German graffiti. Within the church, saints and martyrs are decapitated en masse around the narthex (where Bishop Efrem is buried) and the nave, whose doorway bears an expressive *Mary with Jesus*. Also notice the mural of Petru Rareș, with his wife and sons, presenting the monastery to Jesus, on the right as you enter the nave (*naos*).

Nuns' cells line one side of the compound, while in the northwest corner rises an imposing two-storey *clisarnița*, a guesthouse for passing dignitaries, with a circular tower. Built in 1612, this contains a **museum** of monastic treasures (Tues–Sun 10am–6pm) including a silver-chased Evangelistry presented by

Catherine the Great and the wooden throne of Petru Rareş, a bust of whom has been erected outside.

Practicalities

The village of **VATRA MOLDOVIŢEI** can be reached by **bus** from Cîmpulung as well as from Rădăuţi and Suceviţa. It is possible to catch a **train** from Vama (on the Suceava–Gura Humorului–Cîmpulung line), up a branch line that runs along Vatra Moldoviţei's main street – but the only train arriving at a reasonable hour leaves Vama at 3pm; departures from Vatra Moldoviţei are at noon and 6pm. The closest **accommodation** to the monastery is the *Motel Mărul de Aur* (☎ & fax 030/33.62.01; ②)) at the turn-off for Suceviţa, which has basic rooms (hot water 6–9pm only) above a pretty rough bar. Some villagers rent **rooms** on request; ask the nuns about this.

Gura Humorului, Voroneţ and Humor

The last two Painted Monasteries lie a few kilometres either side of **GURA HUMORULUI**, a small logging town accessible by bus or train from Suceava and Cîmpulung, which has just enough facilities to make a tolerable base. The bus and train stations are adjacent to each other ten minutes' walk to the west of the town centre.You should check on the times of **buses to Voroneţ and Humor** as soon as you arrive. With the current timetables it's hard to visit both monasteries in the same day, unless you catch the 7am bus to Voroneţ and then catch a bus to Humor in the afternoon as there's no early bus to Humor. It's possible to make the 8km round trip to **Voroneţ** on foot in half a day; from Gura Humorului's bus station, head left along the main road, Strada Ştefan cel Mare, to the turn-off for Voronet 750m away.

To reach the centre of Gura Humorului, turn right out of the bus station onto Strada Ştefan cel Mare: bear right at the fork by Piaţa Republicii and head up the side street opposite the Catholic church. Private **rooms** (☎030/23.88.63; ④)) are advertised on the corner of Strada Ştefan cel Mare and the Voroneţ road, or you may prefer to press on to the *Voroneţ cabana*, which is open over the summer, near the bridge 1km down the village road. Private rooms are also available in Humor and Voroneţ. The best **restaurant** in Gura Humorului is the *Select*, on the corner of Strada 9 Mai, east of the centre by the post office; downstairs is a mini-market, the only place to buy imported foods. The *Popas Bucur* **restaurant**, at the eastern town limits, also provides good Romanian meals.

CFR (Mon–Fri 8am–3pm) is near the **market**, before the road forks at Piaţa Republicii. The road to Humor leads north from the square.

Voroneţ Monastery

There are four buses a day from Gura Humorului to Voroneţ, but on a fine day it's no hardship to walk the 4km; the turning is clearly signposted, and there's no chance of going astray on the valley road. At the fork, take the right-hand route to the monastery, entered by a gate near the cemetery. There are two convenient places to eat nearby.

Ion Neculce's chronicle records that Stephen founded **Voroneţ Monastery** in 1488 to fulfil a pledge to the hermit Daniil, who had previously assured the despondent *hospodar* that, should he undertake a campaign against the Turks, he would be successful. The Turks were duly forced back across the Danube, and Voroneţ was erected in three months; chronologically, it comes between Putna and Neamţ monasteries. Its superb **frescoes** – added at the behest of Metropolitan Roşca in 1547–50 – have led to Voroneţ being dubbed the "Oriental Sistine Chapel", and put "Voroneţ blue" into the lexicon of art alongside Titian red and Veronese green. Obtained from lapis lazuli, this colour appears at its most intense on a rainy day, just before sunset.

The church was designed to be entered via a door in the southern wall, with a closed exonarthex replacing the usual open porch, thus creating an unbroken surface along the western wall. Here is painted a magnificent *Last Judgement*, probably the finest single composition among the Painted Monasteries. Fish-tailed bulls, unicorns and other zodiacal symbols form a frieze below the eaves, beneath which Christ sits in majesty above a chair symbolizing the "Toll Gates of the Air", where the deceased are judged and prayers for their souls counted. On either side are those in limbo, the Turks and Tatars destined for perdition. Beneath them, devils and angels push sinners into the flames, while two angels sound the last trump on alpine horns. In response, graves open and wild animals come bearing the limbs they have devoured – all except the deer (a symbol of innocence) and the elephant (no threat in Romania). Amusingly, there's a crush of righteous souls at the gates of the Garden of Eden.

Weather has damaged the frescoes along the north-facing wall, but you can still distinguish Adam and Eve, the first childbirth, the discovery of fire and the invention of ploughing and writing. Also notice *Adam's Deed*, illustrating the myth that Adam made a compact with Satan. The south wall is covered by three compositions: comic-strip scenes from the lives of St Nicholas and St John on the buttress; a *Tree of Jesse*; and a register of saints and philosophers where Plato is depicted with a coffin-load of bones.

Inside, the walls and ceiling of the exonarthex are painted with martyrdoms and miracles. The second row from the bottom on the left depicts Elijah in his "chariot of fire", intent on zapping devils with his God-given powers. According to local folklore, God promptly had second thoughts and restricted Elijah's activities to his name-day. On the right-hand sides of the gloomy narthex and star-vaulted sanctuary are the **tomb of Daniil** the hermit, and a fresco of Stephen, his wife Maria Voichita and their son Bogdan presenting the monastery to Christ. After 1786, the monastery was dissolved and the surrounding monks' cells disappeared; aside from its church, only the **belltower** remains.

There are plenty of **private rooms** available here, with competitive prices at the bottom end, and full Western comforts at the top; if you want to rent one, don't make arrangements through anyone who approaches you on the streets, but ask at the monastery or at Bucovina Estur in Suceava.

Humor Monastery

In another valley 6km north of town, the wooden village of **MĂNĂSTIREA HUMOR** straggles towards its namesake, the sixteenth-century **Humor Monastery**. Unlike the other complexes, Humor is protected by a wooden stockade rather than a stone rampart, and lacks a spire over the *naos* – indicating that it was founded by the boyar, Teodor Bubuiog, Chancellor of Petru Rareş, who is buried here with his wife Anastasia. The **frescoes** were painted by Toma of Suceava; the prevailing hues are reddish brown (from oriental madder pigment), but rich blues and greens also appear.

The *Last Judgement* on the wall beneath the unusual open porch is similar to that at Voroneţ, with the significant difference that the Devil is portrayed as the Scarlet

Woman, though this patch is now so faint that you can't tell. Such misogyny had its counterpart in the peasant conception of hell – said to be a cavern upheld by seven old women who had surpassed Satan in wickedness during their lifetimes. Since the women are mortal, the legend goes, the Devil (*Dracul*) must constantly search the world for replacements – and he never fails to find them. The *Tree of Jesse* along the northern wall has been virtually effaced by weathering, but restorers are busy touching up the *Hymn to the Virgin* on the south front. As at Voroneţ, this depicts her miraculous intervention at the siege of Constantinople by the Persians – although the enemy has been changed into Turks for propaganda purposes. Morale may have been stiffened, but neither murals nor the stone watchtower added by Basil the Wolf could save Humor from marauding Turks, and the monastery was eventually declared derelict in the eighteenth century. It is now a small convent – the villagers use another church, on a nearby hillock.

The only nearby accommodation is in **homestays** such as *La Maison du Bucovine* (☎030/172; ②), around the left of the stockade; or the *Palma* campsite, to the left of a school along the road from the monastery. French is spoken at both places, but no English.

There are seven buses a day from Gura Humorului, but **hitching** is common practice as the bus service can be erratic. Two buses continue north up the Humor valley to the long, strung-out village of **POIANA MICULUI**, from which there are three **trails to Suceviţa**; the easiest one (marked by blue stripes) follows a forestry track and takes about five hours.

Cîmpulung Moldovenesc and Vatra Dornei

Cîmpulung Moldovenesc and **Vatra Dornei**, to the west of the Painted Monasteries, are chiefly of interest as bases for **hiking** in the Rarău and Giumalău massifs, and as way-stations en route to Transylvania or Maramureş; Vatra Dornei also serves as a springboard for reaching several **festivals** just across the Carpathians. There's less reason to come out of season – particularly once the snow arrives, a month or two earlier than in the lowlands. Both towns are situated along the main train line from Suceava to Cluj.

Cîmpulung and the Rarău massif

CÎMPULUNG MOLDOVENESC ("Moldavian settlement in the long field") is a logging town with a modern centre and some old wooden houses in the backstreets. Being strung out along the valley, it has two **train stations** – don't alight at Cîmpulung Est unless you want to hike straight off up Rarău. To reach the centre, bear left from Cîmpulung Moldovenesc station, then right, and left along Calea Transilvanei, the main street, which becomes Calea Bucovinei.

The **Museum of Wooden Art** (Tues–Sun 9am–5pm) on the corner at Calea Transilvanei 10 displays alpine horns, fiddles, looms, sledges and throne-like chairs, all beautifully carved. It stands beside a pseudo-medieval **church** with a multi-coloured mosaic roof, behind which you'll find the market with a small **Ukrainian bazaar**, and the bus station. Cîmpulung also boasts the late Professor Tugui's vast **collection of wooden spoons**, at Str. Gheorghe Popovici 3 – a kitsch delight.

Four **buses** daily run to Rădăuți via Vatra Moldoviței (for Moldovița monastery) and Sucevița monastery; there are also daily services to Iași and Piatra Neamț. The CFR agency is by the synagogue, opposite the *Zimbrul*. Out-of-season **accommodation** is limited to this clean, warm hotel (☎030/31.24.41, fax 31.18.90; ⑤), at Calea Bucovinei 1–3, or the smaller, private *Hotel Minion* (☎ & fax 030/31.15.81; ⑥), 300m north from the post office at Strada D. Cantemir 26B, which has smallish rooms with decent bathrooms and cable TV. The BTT complex (☎030/31.10.49, fax 31.12.50; ACR; ②), at Strada Pinului 37, has a restaurant, bar and bowling alley; hot water is laid on when groups are in residence. To the west of town, Strada Gramăda leads south beyond the hospital to the ski slopes and the new *Hotel Alpin* and the *Schiorilor cabana* (☎030/31.16.81), together high above the town. Just below them is the *Pensuinea Belvedere* at Str. Căprioarei 47 (☎030/31.36.03; ②). **Private rooms** are available from Agenția George (☎030/31.29.63, fax 52.29.22) at Calea Bucovinei 13, immediately east of the *Zimbrul*. The best **restaurant** is at the *Minion* hotel, while the *Brasserie Select* on Strada Porumbescu, diagonally opposite the church, is the place for drinking.

The **tourist office** (Mon–Fri 7am–3pm) is in the lobby of the high-rise *Hotel Zimbrul*, across the square from the CFR office (Mon–Fri 8am–3pm), while a hundred metres or so further on, there's an old-fashioned PTTR **telephone office** (Mon–Fri 7am–9pm) on the corner of Strada Dimitrie Cantemir. Agenția George (☎030/31.29.63, fax 52.29.22), at Calea Bucovinei 13, arranges **car rental** – don't miss the impressively kitsch bronze **statue of Dragoș and the aurochs**, locked in mortal combat, on the square across the road.

The Rarău massif

The **Rarău massif** to the south of Cîmpulung is said to be unlucky owing to an ancient curse. Nonetheless, it remains a popular **hiking** spot, with its dense spruce forests harbouring lynx, bears, roebuck and other **wildlife**. Most visitors base themselves at the *Rarău cabana*, 14km and three to fours hours' walk up the road from Cîmpulung Est station. From here, a four-hour trail marked by red triangles leads past the **Pietrele Doamnei** ("Princess's Rocks"), three huge Mesozoic limestone towers, to reach the ancient **Slatioara Secular forest** of fifty-metre-high firs and spruces. Another route (red-striped) runs southwest from *Rarău* to the *Giumalău cabana* (3–4hr), from where you can hike on to Vatra Dornei via the Obcina Mică peak (5–6hr). None of these trails is feasible in winter.

The road **to Vatra Dornei** crosses the Mestecăniș Pass (1099m), by way of two villages with Ukrainian-style **wooden churches**, to enter the Bistrița valley at the Iacobeni pass. The *Mestecăniș cabana* is here, 8km east of the large village of Iacobeni, where trains usually halt after emerging from a tunnel below the pass.

Vatra Dornei and beyond

The logging town of **VATRA DORNEI** has been a spa since Hapsburg times, and has dabbled in skiing and other outdoor activities since the 1970s. Across the river from Vatra Dornei Băi station (just west of the less useful Vatra Dornei station proper), you can spot the ochre and white Baroque **casino**, once popular with visitors but now derelict. Behind this is the spa's park, alive with squirrels, with a mineral spring housed in a mock-Gothic chapel. Turning left at the casino and keeping parallel to the river on Strada Republicii, you'll come to a junction: to the right is Strada Unirii (the Piatra Neamţ road), with a small **Museum of Natural Science and Hunting** (Tues–Sun 10am–6pm) at no. 3, while to the left, on Strada Oborului, are the **market** and **bus station**.

A long **hiking** trail (21–22hr) to the Rotunda Pass in the Rodna mountains (marked by blue stripes) begins at Vatra Dornei Băi station, runs left along Str. Eminescu past a derelict Moorish-style synagogue, and leaves town past a self-styled motel, actually a **bar** full of hunting trophies, and a campsite, where cabins are available in summer. Another hiking trail, rather shorter at about thirteen hours and with rather more dramatic scenery and a choice of mountain *cabanas*, heads east from the Băi station to Giumalău, Rarău and Cîmpulung Moldovenesc (blue then red stripes). There are some **skiing** opportunities in the area, with a **chair-lift** (*telescaun*); Tues–Sun 9am–4pm, open until 6pm during the summer) from Strada Negreştilor, behind the *Hotel Bradul*, ascending to the 1300-metre-high Dealul Negrii, a popular **skiing** spot to the southwest of town; there's also an Olympic cross-country ski centre near the campsite.

The *Dorna* (☎030/37.18.54; ②), at Str. Eminescu 15, near the post office and museum, is the only hotel in the town itself. Most **accommodation** is across the river in the overblown concrete complex at Str. Republicii 5, west of the casino; this comprises the *Călimani* (☎030/37.39.21, fax 37.11.50; ⑦), which has a limited supply of hot water, but also has four air-conditioned rooms; the *Bradul* (same ☎ & fax; ⑥), which is very similar, but generally tattier; the *Intus* (☎030/37.10.21, fax 37.10.25; ③), which is the cheapest of the three, but is in good condition; and the smaller *Rarău* (☎ & fax 030/37.37.09; ①). The *Intus* hotel houses the *Baza de Tratament* spa, offering **balneological therapy** involving turf mud and various mineral waters. The *Hotel Baza de Instruire Informatica* (☎ & fax 030/37.21.28 or 37.35.34; ②) at Str. Coşbuc 6, is a computing college which also offers very inexpensive rooms. **Private accommodation** can be booked through BVT (☎030/37.37.09).

Of the three hotel **restaurants**, the *Rarău's* is the liveliest. The *Western Restaurant* in the building that resembles the casino, further along Strada Oborului, is really a **disco** (10pm–3am), while the self-styled motel at the top of the hill behind the park is a **bar** full of hunting trophies. **Spa treatments** are bookable at Dorna Turism, opposite *Hotel Rarău*, which can also arrange **horse-riding** excursions.

On to Maramureş and Transylvania

From Vatra Dornei, you can head south towards **Neamţ county**, northwest into **Maramureş**, or west into **Transylvania**. Seven buses a day follow the scenic Bistriţa valley down to Poiana Largului, at the northern end of Lake Bicaz, in the vicinity of the Ceahlău massif (see p.232); three of them carry on to Piatra or to Tîrgu Neamţ.

The route to Maramureş heads up the valley past such lovely villages as **CIO-CANEŞTI**, where the houses are perched on hillocks, and **BOTOS**, which has a new **wooden church** in the Ukrainian style: very broad and square, with one large and four small cupolas. There's a **hotel** (②) with cabins north of **CÎRLIBA-BA**, 8km before the road forks towards the Rotunda Pass into Transylvania, and the **Prislop Pass** into Maramureş, where the **Horă at Prislop Festival** occurs on the second Sunday in August. One bus daily (at 1.30pm) crosses the mountains to Vişeu in Maramureş, while four others run as far as Cîrlibaba, from where you could probably hitch over the pass.

Of the three routes into Transylvania, the most dramatic is via the **Tihuţa Pass** – otherwise known as the Bîrgău Pass, where Bram Stoker located Dracula's castle. Three buses a day from Vatra Dornei run through the pass en route to Bistriţa. Travelling **by train**, you'll take a more northerly route via Ilva Mică; the Leşu Ilvei halt, one stop before Ilva Mică, is within walking distance of Leşu (see p.213). The third route, only possible if you're driving, crosses the 1271-metre-high **Rotunda Pass**, which is prone to blizzards.

travel details

Trains

Adjud to: Braşov (2 daily; 4hr 45min); Ciceu (4 daily; 2hr 45min–4hr); Galaţi (6 daily; 2hr 30min–6hr 15min); Ghimeş (9 daily; 1hr 45min–2hr 45min); Miercurea Ciuc (2 daily; 3hr); Suceava (10 daily; 2hr 30min–4hr 15min); Tîrgu Mureş (1 daily; 6hr 30min).

Bacău to: Bicaz (5 daily; 1hr 30min–2hr 15min); Iaşi (6 daily; 1hr 45min–3hr 30min); Piatra Neamţ (9 daily; 1hr–1hr 30min); Suceava (13 daily; 1hr 45min–3hr).

Galaţi to: Braşov (2 daily; 4hr–4hr 30min); Constanţa (2 daily; 4hr–5hr 45min); Iaşi (1 daily; 3hr 45min); Mărăşeşti (8 daily; 2hr–3hr); Oradea (1 daily; 16hr); Suceava (2 daily; 6hr–10hr 30min); Tîrgu Mureş (1 daily; 9hr).

Gura Humorului to: Cîmpulung Moldovenesc (9 daily; 45min); Suceava (9 daily; 45min–1hr 30min); Vatra Dornei (7 daily; 2hr).

Iaşi to: Braşov (2 daily; 7hr–7hr 30min); Bucharest (9 daily; 5hr 15min–7hr); Cluj (5 daily; 7hr 30min–9hr); Constanţa (2 daily; 7hr); Craiova (1 daily; 14hr 15min); Suceava (6 daily; 1hr 45min–3hr); Timişoara (4 daily; 13hr–16hr).

Mărăşeşti to: Iaşi (3 daily; 4hr–5hr); Panciu (3 daily; 30min); Suceava (8–9 daily; 3hr–4hr).

Paşcani to: Bacău (19 daily; 1hr–2hr); Iaşi (14 daily; 1hr–1hr 30min); Suceava (20 daily; 45min–1hr 15min); Tîrgu Neamţ (5 daily; 45min).

Piatra Neamţ to: Bacău (9 daily; 1hr–1hr 30min); Bicaz (5 daily; 25–45min).

Suceava to: Bucharest (10 daily; 5hr–6hr 30min); Cîmpulung Moldovenesc (10 daily; 1hr

15min–2hr 15min); Cluj (5 daily; 6hr–7hr); Iaşi (5 daily; 1hr 45min–2hr 45min); Putna (6 daily; 2hr 15min–2hr 30min); Rădăuţi (7 daily; 1hr 15min–1hr 30min); Timişoara (4 daily; 11hr 30min–13hr 15min); Vama (9 daily; 1hr–1hr 45min); Vatra Dornei (8 daily; 2hr 15min–3hr 15min).

Vama to: Moldoviţa (3 daily; 45min).

Vatra Dornei to: Beclean (7 daily; 2hr 30min–4hr); Iaşi (4 daily; 4hr 30min–5hr); Suceava (8 daily; 2hr 15min–3hr 30min).

Buses

Bacău to: Adjud (1 daily); Braşov (up to 6 daily); Comăneşti (7 daily); Iaşi (up to 4 daily); Oneşti (3 daily); Piatra Neamţ (Mon–Fri 1 daily); Sfîntu Gheorghe (1 daily); Tîrgu Neamţ (1 daily); Vatra Dornei (1 daily).

Brăila to: Constanţa (1 daily); Focşani (2 daily); Tulcea (2 daily).

Galaţi to: Focşani (3 daily); Iaşi (1 daily).

Gura Humorului to: Arbore (1 daily); Humor Monastery (8 daily); Piatra Neamţ (2 daily); Rădăuţi (2 daily); Solca (3 daily); Suceava (14 daily); Vatra Dornei (5 daily); Voroneţ Monastery (4 daily).

Iaşi to: Bacău (up to 4 daily); Braşov (1 daily); Comăneşti (1 daily); Cîmpulung Moldovenesc (1 daily); Galaţi (1 daily); Gura Humorului (daily); Oneşti (2 daily); Piatra Neamţ (3 daily); Rădăuţi (1 daily); Tîrgu Neamţ (2 daily); Tulcea (1 daily); Vatra Dornei (1 daily).

Piatra Neamţ to: Agapia (up to 2 daily); Bacău (Mon–Fri 1 daily); Braşov (2 daily);

Cîmpulung Moldovenesc (1 daily); Comăneşti (1 daily); Durău (Mon–Sat 1 daily); Galaţi (1 daily); Gheorgheni (up to 2 daily); Gura Humorului (2 daily); Iaşi (3 daily); Oneşti (1 daily); Suceava (2 daily); Tîrgu Neamţ (11 daily); Toplita (1 daily); Vatra Dornei (2 daily).

Suceava to: Cîmpulung Moldovenesc (up to 8 daily); Gura Humorului (14 daily); Piatra Neamţ (2 daily); Rădăuţi (up to 8 daily); Solca (up to 3 daily); Tîrgu Neamţ (2 daily); Vatra Dornei (4 daily).

Tîrgu Neamţ to: Agapia (up to 6 daily); Bacău (1 daily); Braşov (1 daily); Cîmpulung Moldovenesc (1 daily); Durău (2 daily); Gura Humorului (1 daily); Iaşi (2 daily); Neamţ Monastery (6 daily); Piatra Neamţ (14 daily); Rădăuţi (2 daily); Sihistria (2 daily); Suceava (2 daily); Tîrgu Mureş (1 daily); Văratec (3 daily); Vatra Dornei (1 daily).

Vatra Dornei to: Bacău (1 daily); Bistriţa (3 daily); Cîrlibaba (5 daily); Gura Humorului (5 daily); Iaşi (1 daily); Piatra Neamţ (2 daily); Poiana Largului (7 daily); Suceava (4 daily); Tîrgu Neamţ (1 daily); Vişeu (1 daily).

Planes

Iaşi and **Suceava** to: Bucharest (2 daily, on a triangular route).

International trains

Iaşi (Nicolina) to: Chişinău (3 daily; 5hr 30min–6hr 30min); Kiev (1 daily; 21hr); Moscow (1 daily; 36hr 30min).

Suceava Nord to: Cernăuţi (1 daily; 5hr 30min); Kiev (1 daily; 23hr 30min); Moscow (1 daily; 39hr); Sofia (1 daily; 17hr).

International Buses

Bacău to: Budapest (1 Thurs); Chişinău, Moldova (1 daily).

Galaţi to: Athens (1 Thurs & Sat)

Iaşi to: Bălţi, Moldova (2 daily); Chişinău, Moldova (5 daily); Istanbul (1 daily).

Piatra Neamţ to: Istanbul (1 daily).

Suceava to Cernăuţi, Ukraine (8 daily); Chişinău, Moldova (1 daily); Kolomea, Ukraine (1 daily); Preşov, Slovakia (1 weekly); Przemysl, Poland (Mon–Sat 1 daily).

CHAPTER FIVE

MARAMUREŞ

omania has been described as a country with one foot in the industrial
future and the other in the Middle Ages – still an accurate enough charac-
terization of its northwestern counties. Within 30km of heavily industrialized Baia Mare, thickly forested mountains and rough roads maintain
scores of villages in a state of almost medieval isolation, amid a landscape of
rounded hills with clumps of oak and beech and scattered flocks of sheep. One
nineteenth-century traveller compared it to an arcadian vision of England pervaded with "a feeling of remoteness", and since **Maramureş**, unlike other
regions, was never conquered by the Romans, some features of life appear to have
changed little since Dacian times.

This is certainly true of many of the **villages**, which are the main reason for visiting the area. The majority of buildings are made of wood by skilled craftsmen,
and the inhabitants produce virtually everything that they wear, use and eat – and
if not, do without. Nowhere else in Europe do **folk costumes** persist so strongly,
the men wearing tiny *clop* straw hats, and the women weaving boldly striped *catri-
niţa* aprons, with cloth from the water-powered fulling mills (*piuă*), and embroi-
dering intricate designs on the wide-sleeved cotton blouses worn by both sexes –
most conspicuously during markets and **festivals**, when the villages seem ablaze
with colour. On Sunday afternoons people promenade and there may be a public
dance, either in the street or on a purpose-built wooden platform. Just as old people wear the medieval rawhide galoshes (*opinchi*) or archaic felt boots bound with
thongs, so villagers have retained their traditional **religion** (a mixture of pagan
beliefs and the Uniate rite), their myths and codes of behaviour. Large families,
personal integrity and skilled work are all esteemed; the Church and community
exert powerful sanctions against transgressors, and men are wont to react to perceived slights on their honour by drawing knives.

Most interesting of all, perhaps, is the marvellous **woodwork** of Maramureş:
carvings decorate the eaves, doorways and windows of houses lining each village's main street. Each family occupies a compound with its livestock, fenced
with timber, brush or latticework, and entered via a beamed gateway (*poarta*), the
size of which indicates the family's status and prosperity. Many gateways are elaborately carved with symbols such as the "tree of life", sun, rope and snake, and
there seems to be no slackening in productivity. The most elaborate structures
are the *biserici de lemn* or **wooden churches**, mostly built during the eighteenth
century when this Gothic-inspired architecture reached its height. Originally
founded upon huge blocks of wood rather than stone, they rear up into fairytale
spires or crouch beneath humpbacked roofs, and are generally sited on the highest ground in the village to escape seasonal mud.

The historic county of Maramureş lies to the north of the Gutîi pass; in 1968
this was merged with Someş county to form present-day Maramureş, whose capital, **Baia Mare**, lies to the south of the Gutîi and Igniş mountains. Baia Mare is

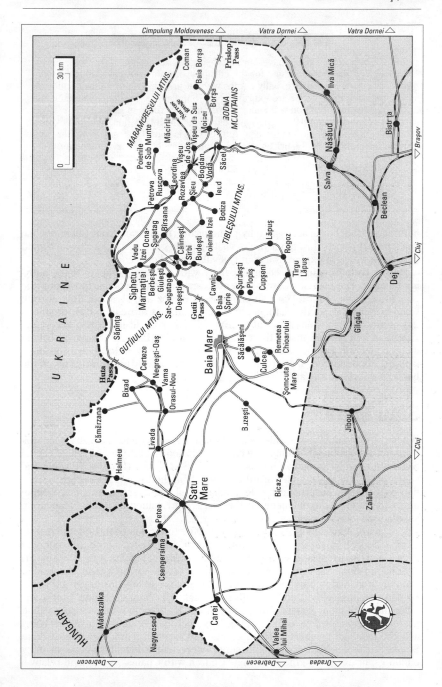

ACCOMMODATION PRICES

Hotels listed in this guide have been price-graded according to the scale below. Prices given are those charged for the cheapest **double room** available, which in the less expensive places usually comes without private bath or shower and without breakfast. Price codes are expressed in US dollars as the Romanian leu is not a stable currency, but you will generally pay for your room in lei.

Note that some hotels are currently closed for modernization, and others, now open, will no doubt follow in the near future. This is bound to result in higher rates when they reopen, so the prices quoted should be taken only as a guideline.

① $10 and under ④ $20–25 ⑦ $40–50
② $10–15 ⑤ $25–30 ⑧ $50–65
③ $15–20 ⑥ $30–40 ⑨ $65 and over

---

nothing special, but is accessible by plane or overnight train from Bucharest, so you'll probably pass through if you're visiting the region, and it does make a good base from which to explore the county's villages and churches.

Public transport in the region is patchy, with only limited buses to the outlying villages. The best solution is to rent a car; otherwise, it's worth making the effort to see the beautiful church paintings at **Rogoz** and **Deseşti**, the towering wooden church at **Şurdeşti**, the frescoes and icons of **Călineşti** and **Budeşti** and the quirky "Merry Cemetery" at **Săpînţa**. Further afield in the Iza valley, the visions of hell painted inside the church at **Poienile Izei** are the most striking images you will see in Maramureş, while the frescoes at **Ieud** are the most famous. Maramureş also offers hiking in the peaceful **Rodna mountains** on the borders with Moldavia and Ukraine.

Satu Mare

When the diplomats at Versailles signed the Treaty of Trianon they drew an arbitrary line across the old Hungarian county of Szabolcs-Szatmár and left its capital Szatmárnémeti in Romanian hands. Renamed **SATU MARE** ("Big Village") and shorn of its traditional links with the Great Plain, the town lost its original function as a trading post along the River Someş, shipping salt from Ocna Dejului downstream to Vásárosnamény on the Tisza, but retained a sizeable Hungarian population.

The centre of town is Piaţa Libertăţii with a fire tower, raised in 1904 and resembling a Turkish minaret, peering over its north side. There's little to detain you here. The **Historical and Ethnographic Museum** at Piaţa Lucaciu 21 (Tues–Fri & Sun 9am–5pm, Sat 9am–2pm), on the corner of Bulevardul Traian, the road in from the train and bus stations, has the usual mixture of folk costumes and Daco-Roman remains, while the **Art Gallery** at Piaţa Libertăţii 21 (same hours) features the work of local artist Aurel Popp (1879–1960), who produced sun-bathed post-Impressionist views of Baie Sprie, and much darker images of World War I and the death of capitalism. Heading one block north from the square, along Strada Ştefan cel Mare, lined with some interesting if tatty turn-of-the-century buildings, brings you to the Reformat "Church with Chains", a long and relative-

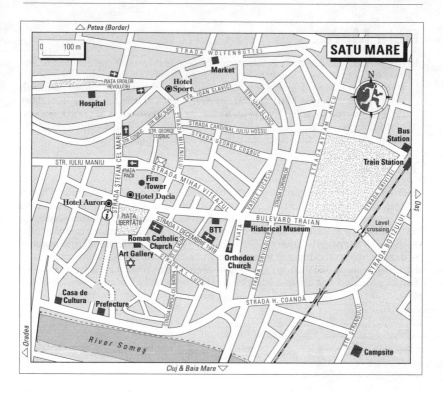

ly low Baroque church built at the turn of the nineteenth century in the middle of Strada Mihai Viteazul.

Practicalities

Satu Mare's main **hotels** are both on Piaţa Libertăţii; the best is the Secession-style *Dacia* (☎061/76.17.72, fax 71.57.74; ACR; ⑤), although the modern *Aurora* (☎061/71.49.46, fax 71.41.99; ⑤) is friendly and functional enough. There are **tourist agencies** in both. The only alternative is the *Sport* at Str. Mileniului 25 (☎061/71.29.59, fax 71.16.04; ④), far better than you might expect from the name, with TV and non-stop hot water and a decent bar and restaurant. The BTT office at Calea Traian 7 (☎061/73.79.15, fax 71.70.69) sells a good range of maps and can book you a rural **homestay**. Satu Mare's **campsite** is fifteen minutes' walk south-east of the centre by the River Someş on Strada Ştrandului; if you're driving, there's another one 5km east in Păuleşti. The *Amelia* motel (☎061/73.23.98; ②) lies 14km south in Mădăraş. In addition to the **restaurants** in the hotels, the town's Swabian (German) minority boasts a *Bierkeller* at Piaţa Lucaciu 9 (Mon–Fri 9am–5pm, Sun 9am–2pm).

Both **bus** and **train stations** are 1km east of the centre on Strada Griviţei, a con-tinuation of Bulevardul Traian, which runs out of the centre from Piaţa Libertăţii. TAROM has an office at Piaţa 25 Octombrie 9 (☎061/71.78.59), selling tickets for flights to Bucharest; bus #9 runs between the airport and Piaţa Libertăţii.

Baia Mare

BAIA MARE ("Big Mine"), is Romania's largest non-ferrous metals centre, and suffers badly from pollution, with lead levels high enough to produce headaches in some vistors. Mining mania has waxed and waned here since the fourteenth century when, under its Magyar name of Nagybánya, it was the Hungarian monarchs' chief source of gold. The main reason for staying here is to prepare for forays into the surrounding countryside, but it's an attractive town with a variety of museums to pass the time, including the excellent **Village Museum**.

The Town

From the train station, 2km west of the centre, take trolley bus #50, various buses or a *maxitaxi* to Piaţa Libertăţii, the centre of the **old town**. The thick-walled Casa Elisabeta at Piaţa Libertăţii 18, was the **house of Iancu de Hunedoara**, fifteenth-century Regent of Hungary. To the south of the square rises the fifty-metre-high **Stephen's Tower**, built between 1446 and 1468 and all that remains of a twin-naved cathedral that burnt down in 1769; the adjacent Baroque pile, built by the Jesuits in 1717–20, subsequently became the town's cathedral. The **Art Gallery**, behind this at Str. 1 Mai 8, exhibits eighteenth- and nineteenth-century

paintings on wood and glass, and a number of canvases by artists of the **Nagybánya School** (see box below), which transformed Hungarian art. Much of the work is now in Budapest, however, and the stuff here is attributed to the "Baia Mare School" – a sly piece of Romanian revisionism.

The **Reformat church** of 1809 at the junction of Strada Monetăriei and Strada Podul Viilor, just north of Piaţa Libertăţii, is a landmark that appears in many works of the Nagybánya School. Nearby, at Str. Monetăriei 1, the **County Museum** has a large exhibition of mining and minting, but has been closed for some time due to lack of funds. However, it is worth seeing the Mint Tower (*Bastionul Monetăriei*), incorporated in the museum building, as well as the medieval Strada Monetăriei itself. If you are keen to learn more about the region's mines, visit the **Museum of Mineralogy** at B-dul Traian 8, to the southwest of town heading out to the stations; it displays an amazing collection of crystals found in local mines.

Strada Dr Vasile Lucaciu, running east from Piaţa Libertăţii, has some interesting old buildings whose cellars are entered from the street. The turn-of-the-century Orthodox Cathedral stands five minutes' walk along here at the junction of Strada Olarilor; head south along Strada Olarilor, which follows the line of the old city walls, to reach Piaţa Izvoarelor, where the fifteenth-century Butchers' Bastion (*Bastionul Măcelarilor*) overlooks the market place in which outlaw Pintea Viteazul was shot in 1703.

THE NAGYBÁNYA SCHOOL

Simon Hollósy (1857–1918), born of Armenian stock in the village of Sighet, trained in Munich, where he was influenced by the refined naturalism of Jules Bastien-Lepage, and in 1886 set up his own school there. From 1896 he brought his students to a summer school in Baia Mare, where he painted *en plein air* for the first time. Unusually, an artists' community grew up in conjunction with the summer school – it's thought that some of the artists were deliberately distancing themselves from the celebrations in Budapest marking the millennium of Magyar settlement in Hungary. A shared commission to illustrate the poems of József Kiss and the resultant work, with its touches of Art Nouveau, was well received in artistic circles. An exhibition in 1897 of the school's paintings was seen as marking the start of a new era in Hungarian art and the school became known as the "Hungarian Barbizon", although the area's motifs and colours were more similar to those of Provence.

In 1902 Hollósy suffered a creative crisis, and the leadership of the school was taken over by **Károly Ferenczy**; tuition fees were abolished, and the embittered and jealous Hollósy left to set up a rival school in Técső, now the Ukrainian town of Tyachiv, just downstream of Sighet. Ferenczy suffered a similar crisis in 1910, and did little work thereafter. Of the second generation of artists, the most gifted was Cavnic-born Jenő Maticska (1885–1906). After his untimely death, Béla Czóbel, Csába Vilmos Perlrott, Sándor Ziffer and others revolted against creeping stagnation; their 1906 exhibition, influenced by German Expressionism and by Cézanne and Matisse, again marked the start of a new era in Hungarian art. After World War I the school was opened to both Hungarian and Romanian students – up to 150 a year – but interest in it faded away in the 1930s and the school closed its doors.

Other renowned artists associated with the school include Eugen Pascu (1895–1948), Tibor Boromisza (1880–1960), János Krizsán (1886–1948) and his wife Antónia Csikos (1887–1987).

Baia Mare's main tourist attraction is its **Village Museum** (Tues–Sun 10am–5pm), which is ten minutes' walk north of the town on Florilor hill. The museum contains over a hundred examples of peasant houses, watermills and other buildings from the surrounding region, and a fine, if simple, wooden church, which was raised in 1630 in the village of Chechiş, just south of Baia Mare. It is an extremely eye-catching collection, and if you don't have time to visit the villages themselves, this museum is the next best thing. The **Ethnographic Museum** (Tues–Sun 10am–5pm) and the **zoo** (same hours) stand nearby on Strada Dealul Florilor.

Practicalities

The **train** and **bus stations** lie 2km west of the town on Strada Gării; the TAROM office is at B-dul Bucureşti 5 (☎062/41.16.24), and the Agenţia CFR is at Str. Victoriei 57 (☎062/42.16.13). Baia Mare's **tourist office** (Mon–Fri 10am–6pm, Sat 10am–4pm) lies to the west of Piaţa Libertăţii at Str. Culturii 1; it sells a good map of the region, which is essential if you are planning on touring the villages. For information on festivals, contact the Cultural Inspectorate in the prefecture at Str. Gheorghe Şincai 46 (☎062/41.20.42); for tickets for the city's drama and puppet theatres, try the **theatrical ticket agency** at Piaţa Libertăţii 12.

To **rent a car**, you'll have to book in advance with Avis in Bucharest or Cluj. For **car repairs**, the ACR yard is at Str. 8 Martie 1, east of town at the turning north to the Firiza dam, and there are other garages along B-dul Independenţei, west towards Satu Mare. Baia Mare boasts a **laundry** with self-service washing machines, possibly the only one in Romania; it lies just north of the train station at B-dul Decebal 4. The glossy new mirror-glass BCR building at B-dul Unirii 15 will doubtless soon offer a Bancomat.

Accommodation

Baia Mare has a good selection of **hotels**, and the BTT office at B-dul Traian 8 (☎062/41.21.62) may also be able to arrange **homestays**, as can private agencies such as Ar-Thema at Str. Şincai 33 (☎062/43.71.95) and Mara at B-dul Unirii 5 (☎062/41.67.41). In addition there is a **cabana**, the *Apa Sărata* ("Salty Water"), 7km west of town on the Satu Mare road, reached by city buses #6, #7, #13 and #29. The nearest **campsite** is the *Motel-Camping Caprioara* at Firiza dam, 10km north of town and served by bus #8.

Bucureşti, Str. Culturii 3 (☎062/41.63.01). A run-down hotel, with a dingy foyer, but appropriately priced; rooms with or without showers. ①.

Carpaţi, Str. Minerva 16 (☎062/41.48.12, fax 41.54.61). Privatized and definitely the best place to stay in town; but be warned – the mini-bar costs a fortune. Plenty of single rooms. ⑧.

Laguna, Str. 22 Decembrie 13 (☎062/41.60.79). New private place with fourteen twin rooms and a decent restaurant. ④.

Mara, B-dul Unirii 11 (☎062/43.66.60, fax 43.11.00). Has a foyer fit for a luxury hotel but distinctly ordinary rooms. ACR; ⑤.

Maramureş, Str. Şincai 37a (☎062/41.65.55). The most modern hotel in town, frequented by businessmen and foreign groups. ④.

Minerul, Piaţa Libertăţii 7 (☎062/41.60.56). Excellent central location; fairly basic but pleasant. ②.

Minion, Str Malinului 22a (☎062/41.70.56). Small private hotel aimed mainly at foreigners. There's a swimming pool and sauna, but it's all rather tacky in style. ⑦.

Sport, B-dul Unirii 14a, but actually one block west on Strada Transilvaniei (☎062/43.49.00). A classic sport hotel intended for visiting teams. Plenty of space unless there's a big tournament on. ①.

Eating and Drinking

The best **restaurants** are the *Select* at Str. Progesului 54, behind the *Mara* hotel, and the *Carpaţi* hotel's restaurant. The *Şoricelul*, just north of the centre at Str. Petöffi Sandor 84, and the *Dealul Florilor*, just east of the Village Museum, are also very good. Other possibilities include the *Bulevard* at B-dul Bucureşti 26a, the *Săsar* at Str. D. Cantemir 1, the *Restaurant-Crama Veche* at Piaţa Libertăţii 18 and the *Dunărea* at the corner of Piaţa Libertăţii and 1 Mai. Fast food is available at the wonderfully named *FastFood Tearoom McDollar* on B-dul Independenţei, by the CFR agency, the *Café-Bar Universităţii* at Str. Victoriei 132 and the *Pizza-Bar Calipso* at B-dul Bucureşti 8, as well as at various branches of *Springtime*, *Autumn Time* and *Wintertime*. There's a good range of food shops on Bulevarduls Traian and Unirii. For **drinking**, try the traditional *Butoiasul cu Bere* at Str. Şincai 13 or the trendy *Café Dali* on the south side of Piaţa Revoluţiei.

Southern Maramureş

Beyond Baia Mare, the going gets harder: many of the villages are well off the main roads and awkward to reach without private **transport** – you'll have to rely on the overcrowded buses that run once a day to most villages. Private cars are scarce, so if you decide to hitch be prepared for intermittent lifts or short rides in the back of carts or vans. Cycling is a great way to get the most out of a visit to Maramureş, and mountain bikes are required on some of the back roads. There are **hotels** in Borşa, Ocna Şugatag and Sighet, and **homestay schemes** in some villages, but otherwise come prepared to camp wild, with plenty of food supplies. If you get really stuck in a village, ask the priest (*popă* or *preot*) for advice, and try to repay any hospitality with gifts (tea and coffee are ideal).

Codrul, Chioarul and Lăpuş

Maramureş proper lies to the north of Baia Mare, beyond the Gutîi pass; the area to the south of the town was part of Someş county until it was dismembered in the 1968 reforms. The southwestern corner of the present Maramureş county, beyond the Someş River, is known as **Codrul**; the area immediately south of Baia Mare is **Chioarul**; and further east is **Lăpuş**. Folk costumes here are similar to those of Maramureş, although the tall straw hats are unique to this region, and here too there are fine wooden churches.

The most accessible village in Codrul is **BUZEŞTI**, 30km west of Baia Mare, with a wooden church built in 1739, the bulbous steeple of which, now in poor condition, bears witness to the penetration of Baroque influences into this area, while the four corner pinnacles echo the Gothic towers of both Transylvania and Hungary. Much more remote, in the far western extremity of the county (though served by three buses a day from Baia Mare), is **BICAZ**, whose Orthodox church and wall paintings both date from the early eighteenth century. As in Buzeşti, a new church has been built here and the old one is decaying, although repairs are planned.

Many of the villages of Chioarul have old churches, but perhaps the most inter-esting is at SĂCĂLĂŞENI, only 10km south of Baia Mare. Rebuilt at the end of the seventeenth century, the church originally dates from 1442, with a carved doorway and paintings from 1865. CULCEA, just to the southwest, has an early eighteenth-century church with plastered walls; 6km further south is REMETEA CHIOARULUI, which also has a fine church, dating from 1800; the village is bet-ter known as the starting point for walks south through the gorge of the Lăpuş River to the Chioarului citadel. Ten kilometres further south of Remetea, on the DN1C, is ŞOMCUTA MARE, where choirs and bands assemble for the *Stejarul festival* on the first or third Sunday of July. Five buses a day run from Baia Mare to Şomcuta Mare, via Săcălăşeni and Remetea.

The centre of the Lăpuş area is the small town of TÎRGU LĂPUŞ, where the *Hotel Minion* (☎062/41.70.56) incorporates a mini-brewery. It can be reached by hourly buses from Baia Mare, and also from Gîlgău, Dej and Cluj, passing the wooden church of Drăghia (1706). Buses from the station, five minutes' walk east of the centre, allow you to visit the surrounding villages, many of which boast fine wooden churches. The best examples are the two in ROGOZ, 5km east of Tîrgu Lăpuş, a prosperous village with a growing population; local cus-tom forbids divorce and abortion, so there are five or six children per family. A large modern church has been built here, but the old churches are well main-tained. The Uniate church, built around 1695 in Suciu de Sus and moved here

WOODEN CHURCHES

There is a strong tradition of building **wooden churches** right across Eastern Europe, from Karelia and northern Russia all the way to the Adriatic, but in terms of both quality and quantity the richest examples are in Maramureş. From 1278 the Orthodox Romanians were forbidden by their Catholic Hungarian overlords to build churches in stone, and so used wood to ape Gothic developments.

In general, the walls are built of blockwork (squared-off logs laid horizontally) with intricate joints, cantilevered out in places to form brackets or consoles sup-porting the eaves. However, here Western techniques such as raftering and timber-framing allow the high roofs and steeples that are characteristic of the area, rather than the tent roofs or stepped cupolas used to the north. Following the **standard Orthodox ground-plan**, the main roof covers narthex and *naos* and a lower one the sanctuary; the *naos* usually has a barrel vault, while the narthex has a low planked ceiling under the tower, its weight transmitted by rafters to the walls; thus there are no pillars, although there is a wall between narthex and *naos*. The roof is always shingled and in many cases is in fact double, allowing clerestory windows high in the nave walls, while the lower roof can be extended at the west end to form a porch (exonarthex or *pridvor*).

Most of the Maramureş churches were rebuilt after the last Tatar raid in 1717, acquiring large porches and tall towers, often with four corner-pinnacles, clearly derived from the masonry architecture of the Transylvanian cities. Inside, almost every church now has a choir gallery above the west part of the *naos*, always a later addition, as shown by the way it is superimposed on the **wall paintings**. These extraordinary works of art were produced by local artists in the eighteenth and early nineteenth centuries, combining the icon tradition with pagan motifs and top-ical propaganda. They broadly follow the standard Orthodox layout, with the *Incarnation* and *Eucharist* in the sanctuary (for the priest's edification), the Last in 1893, stands within the grounds of the Orthodox church, built of elm some time between 1661 and 1701. The latter is unique thanks to its naturalistic horse-head consoles, which support the roof at the west end, and for its asymmetric roof, with a larger overhang to the north to shelter a table where paupers were fed by the parish. Some of the paintings by Radu Munteanu were painted over in the 1830s, but even so this remains one of the most beautifully painted churches: look out for a *Last Judgement*, to the left inside the door, and the *Creation* and the *Good Samaritan*, on the naos ceiling. There are four buses a day from Baia Mare, heading for Băiuţ or Grosii Tibleşului, as well as local services from Tîrgu Lăpuş. Băiuţ buses also pass through **LĂPUŞ**, 7km east of Rogoz, which boasts a village museum and the wooden Church of the Dormition built in 1672, whose walls are carved and painted. The oldest murals are those in the pronaos, dating from the early eighteenth century, and the icons include the first works of Radu Munteanu; unusually for this area the church has a veranda along its south side, an apse expanded to the full width of the church, and a table for feeding the old folk. **CUPŞENI**, 11km north of Rogoz (three buses a day from Tîrgu Lăpuş), is one of the most idyllic villages in the region and home of some of its best carpenters. Here, the upper church, built in 1600, has a fine tower, but badly damaged paintings, and the tiny lower church, moved here from Peteritea in 1847 by the Uniates, was beautifully painted in 1848 by Radu Munteanu.

Judgement and moralistic parables such as the *Wise and Foolish Virgins* in the narthex (where the women stand), and the *Passion* in the *naos*; however the treatment of the latter changed in the nineteenth century as the Uniate Church gained in strength, with more emphasis on the *Ascension* and the *Evangelists*.

Sixteenth-century icons (such as those found in Budeşti) show a northern Moldavian influence; the seventeenth-century Moisei school was the first to show the imprint of the Renaissance, and from the late eighteenth century, Baroque influences were added. The first of the major painters was **Alexandru Ponehalski**, who worked from the 1750s to the 1770s in Călineşti and Budeşti, in a naïve post-Byzantine style with blocks of colour in black outlines. From 1767 to the 1780s, **Radu Munteanu** worked around his native Lăpuş and in Botiza, Glod and Deseşti, painting in a freer and more imaginative manner. In the first decade of the nineteenth century, **Toader Hodor** and **Ion Plohod** worked in Bîrsana, Corneşti, Văleni, Năneşti and Rozavlea, in a far more Baroque style.

Since 1989 there has been a **renaissance of the Uniate or Greco-Catholic faith**, repressed under Communism and forcibly merged with the Romanian Orthodox Church: many parishes have reverted to Greco-Catholicism, reclaiming their churches, while in other villages one church is now Orthodox and the other Uniate. In addition many villages have started to build large new churches; because services are so long, it's not possible to cope with demand by having several services on a Sunday, and thus most of the women and children have to remain outside the small wooden churches, following proceedings inside either by pressing an ear to the wall or by a small loudspeaker. The appearance of the new churches will make it more and more likely that you'll find the wooden churches locked up, even on a Sunday – it's never hard to find the key-holder, but the fabric of the buildings will doubtless start to deteriorate. Remember that people **dress conservatively** here, and shorts are not appropriate, particularly for visiting churches.

Şurdeşti and Plopiş

From **BAIA SPRIE**, a small mining town noted for its autumn **Chestnut Carnival**, you can detour off the main road to reach some classic Maramureş villages, on the fringes of the Chioar district. The town lies 10km from Baia Mare along the Sighet road (served by city bus #8) and has a small private hotel, the *Giesswein*, at Str. Ignişului 2c (☎062/46.22.19).

The magnificent Uniate **wooden church** at **ŞURDEŞTI**, 10km south of Baia Sprie, stands just beyond the village on a hill overlooking a stream. Built in 1724 or 1738, the church is clad in thousands of oak shingles, and boasts a 45-metre-high tower, three times the length of the church itself, the tallest wooden structure in Europe until the new monastery at Bîrsana (see p.280) topped it; you can climb up into the tower and roof space from the porch. Inside the church, which someone from the painted house near the stream will unlock for you, there are remarkable wall paintings dating from 1810, and also interesting late eighteenth-century icons.

PLOPIŞ, a kilometre or so south across the fields, has a similar, though slightly smaller, church, built between 1798 and 1805, which likewise features four corner turrets on its spire, a feature of many wooden churches here and in the Erdehát region of Hungary. If you continue north along the minor road, it eventually leads through the mining town of Cavnic, over the **Neteda Pass** (1039m) and down to **Budeşti** (see p.277); there are seven buses a day from Baia Mare to Cavnic via Şurdeşti, of which one continues to Budeşti and Sighet; otherwise you'll have to hitch a ride in a mine vehicle, simply a Portakabin on a truck chassis.

From the Gutîi Pass to Berbeşti

Continuing from Baia Sprie, the main DN18 passes a turning to the Mogoşa ski complex, a couple of kilometres east (*Şuior* and *Mogoşa cabanas*; ☎062/46.08.00, fax 46.27.71), and zigzags up to the 987-metre-high **Gutîi Pass** before descending past the splendidly carved houses and gateways of **MARA**, into the valley of the same name.

The wooden church at **DESEŞTI**, 3km beyond Mara, is hidden among some trees to the left, above the road and the trackbed of a disused forestry rail line now used as a cycle track. Built in 1770, the church has a fine example of the "double roof" or clerestory style which enabled the builders to construct windows high up inside the nave to increase the illumination. Nevertheless, it's dark inside and even with candles you'll find it hard to pick out the marvellous **wall paintings**. Executed by Radu Munteanu in 1780, the paintings seem more primitive yet less stylized than the frescoes in the Moldavian monasteries which were painted some two hundred years earlier. Boldly coloured in red, yellow and white, the figures of saints and martyrs are contrasted with shady-looking groups of Jews, Turks, Germans, Tatars and Franks. The frescoes also include folk-style geometric and floral motifs, while the inscriptions are in the Cyrillic alphabet – Old Church Slavonic remained the liturgical language of Romanian Orthodoxy until the nineteenth century. Alas, the spire has been clad in sheet metal since a lightning strike.

The next church, also dating from 1770, is in the village of **HĂRNICEŞTI** and houses some fine icons; in 1942 the apse was widened, and in 1952 the porch was

Săliște, Transylvania

Horse hauling logs in the Carpathians

The Painted Monastery of Voroneţ

Taking a break, Southern Maramureş

Statue of Mátyás Corvinus, Cluj-Napoca

Measurement of the Milk Festival, Transylvania

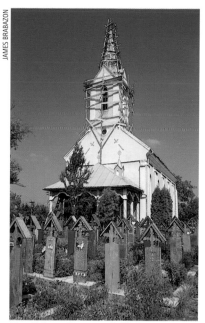

The "Merry Cemetery", Săpînta, Maramureş

The Painted Monastery of Humor

Mamaia beach, the Black Sea Coast

Saxon couple, the Banat

The Danube Delta

added, so that now the tower seems disproportionately short. While here, you may like to see the village's museum house, supposedly the only nineteenth-century home of a noble family remaining in Maramureş. The church stands just north of the junction of a back road east towards Ocna Şugatag and Budeşti; two buses a day from Baia Mare to Ocna Şugatag take this road via **HOTENI**, 3km east of Hărniceşti, known for its *Tînjaua* **festival**, held on the first or second Sunday of May. As in many of the villages of the Mara valley, this is a celebration of the First Ploughman, a fertility rite that dates back at least to Roman times.

Continuing along the main road towards Sighet will bring you to **SAT-ŞUGATAG**, with another fine church beside the road, built in 1642, and now in need of some repair. The graveyard contains beautiful stout wooden crosses and the village itself boasts some quite picturesque cottages. A minor road leads off to Ocna Şugatag, Călineşti, Sîrbi and Budeşti, with another right turn 2km north leading to **MĂNĂSTIREA GIULEŞTI**, a tiny village with a tiny church, founded in 1653 and now shared by Orthodox and Uniate congregations; it boasts fine paintings from 1653 and 1783, as well as late eighteenth-century icons by Alexandru Ponehalski.

The main road continues northwards to **GIULEŞTI** proper, which has a stone church and, like many of these villages, an ancient **watermill** (*moară*). Its two mill wheels are driven by water sluiced off a fast-flowing stream, the drive shafts running into a building where the miller can control the wheel with a kind of tension brake. The two millstones grind wheat and corn, with the miller traditionally taking one cupful of each hopper-load. Everything is made of wood, down to the little channels siphoning off water to lubricate the spindles of the wheels, and it doubles as a fulling mill, the wheel turning a spindle driving levers which lift wooden mallets and let them drop onto the cloth.

Further north, on the edge of **BERBEŞTI**, a carved wooden crucifix (*troiţa*), at least 300 years old, stands beside the road adorned with four mourning figures and symbols of the sun and moon. Similar wayside crosses can be found in Moldavia, sometimes inscribed *Doamne, apara-ma de dracul* ("Lord, protect me from the devil"), for traditionally travel was considered a hazardous undertaking. Tuesday was an unlucky day on which no journeys were made nor important work begun, and it was believed that after sundown ghosts and vampires (*strigoi*) roamed, seeking victims. From Berbeşti, the DN18 continues to Vadu Izei, the mouth of the Iza valley (see p.280), and Sighet (see overleaf).

The Cosău valley

At Fereşti, 2km south of Berbeşti, a minor road turns off to the right and leads up the Cosău valley to several picturesque villages – perhaps the most interesting of all from an ethnographic point of view – which can also be approached from the south by crossing the Neteda Pass (see p.274); from the west, using the road via Hoteni; or from Bîrsana, to the east.

Across the river from Fereşti is **CORNEŞTI**, where there's an early eighteenth-century church and another **watermill**, which also serves as a laundry. Women beat clothes with carved wooden laundry bats beside the river, often improvising songs and verses as they work. There's a distinctive local technique called singing "with knots", in which the voice is modulated by tapping the glottis while the singer doesn't breathe for lengthy periods. Certain instruments are peculiar to Maramureş, for example the *cetera*, a fiddle with a half-size bridge, producing a

MARAMUREŞ FUNERALS

The **cult of the dead**, central to Romanian culture, is particularly well developed in Maramureş, where the rituals to be observed after a death are fixed and elaborate; if anything is omitted, it is believed that the soul will return as a ghost or even a vampire. There are three phases, the separation from the world of the living, preparation for the journey, and entry into the other world. A dying person asks forgiveness of his family and neighbours, who must obey his last wishes. Black flags are hung outside the house where the deceased lies for three days, a period during which the church bells are rung thrice daily, neighbours pay their respects and women (but not men) lament the deceased in improvised rhymed couplets like those shouted at weddings, dances and other social events.

When the priest arrives at the house on the third day, the wailing and lamenting reach a climax before he blesses a bucketful of water, extinguishes a candle in it, and consecrates the house with a cross left etched on the wall for a year. The coffin is carried by six married male relatives or friends, stopping for prayers (the priest being paid for each stop) at crossroads, bridges and any other feature along the way, and then at the church for absolution. The funeral itself is relatively swift, with everyone present throwing soil into the grave and being given a small loaf with a candle and a red-painted egg, as at Easter; these must also be given to passers-by, including tourists, who would give great offence if they refused. The knot-shaped loaves or *colaci* bear the inscription NI KA ("Jesus Christ is victorious"), which is stamped in the dough by a widow or some other "clean woman" using a special seal called a *pecetar*. The seal's handle, usually wooden, is often elaborately carved with motifs such as the *axis mundi* ("Endless Column"), the tree of life, wolf's teeth or a crucifix.

Three days later there is another *pomană* or memorial meal, when bread is again given to church officials and all present; after nine days, nine widows spend the day fasting and praying around the deceased's shirt; six weeks and six months after the funeral the absolution is repeated, with another meal, as the dead must be given food and drink, and after a year a feast is given for all the family's dead. Mourning lasts for one year, during which time the close family may not attend weddings or dances and women wear black. As elsewhere in Romania, *şergare* (embroidered napkins) are hung over icons in the church or over plates on house walls in memory of the dead. The Uniates also remember their dead on All Souls' Day, which is not an Orthodox festival.

Marriage is seen as essential in Maramureş, so much so that if a person of marriageable age (in fact from eight years old, the age of first confession) dies unmarried a **Marriage of the Dead** (*nunta mortului*) is held. A black flag is carried, and the deceased and a bridesmaid or flag-carrier (best man) are in wedding costume, although everyone else dresses in mourning garb. In the case of a man, there is a stand-in bride, while for a woman the bride's crown is used symbolically.

very penetrating note, the *zongoră*, a guitar, often with three strings, used to mark the rhythm, and the *dobă*, a kind of drum.

Continuing south you come to three villages about 4km apart, with two **wooden churches** apiece. At **CĂLINEŞTI**, the beautiful *Susani* (upper) or Bǎndreni church, just north of the junction, was built and painted in the 1780s. Its companion, the *Josani* (lower) or Caieni church, built in 1663, is very special, one of the loveliest in Maramureş, with its huge nineteenth-century porch and internal paintings by Ponehalski from 1754. It's best reached by a path across the fields next to house no. 385, on the road east to Bîrsana. **SÎRBI** has two small and unassuming wooden churches – the *Susani* to the north, built in 1667, with icons by Radu Munteanu, and the *Josani*, to the south, built in 1703 – and some fine water mills.

Next is **BUDEŞTI**, a large village 4km to the south, but one of the least spoiled in Maramureş. The Josani church stands in the centre of the village by a memorial to the dead of the 1989 revolution; the church was built in 1643 and contains frescoes, icons on wood by Ponehalski, and the chain-mail coat of the outlaw Pintea the Brave. The upper church dates from 1586 and has particularly fine paintings from the 1760s, also by Ponehalski. The building has been gradually extended westwards, so that the tower is now almost central. From here there is a particularly fine walk through idyllic countryside to Hoteni (see p.275) via **BREB**, a small village with a hideous new church and a particularly lovely and tranquil wooden one dating from 1531 hidden away in the valley. Budeşti can be reached by four **buses** a day from Sighet, taking the high road via **OCNA ŞUGATAG**, a former salt-mining centre (also known as Ocna Maramureşului) that is now a small spa, with a **hotel** (☎Ocna Şugatag 178; ③), lots of cheap homestays, and the *Băi Noi cabana* and **campsite** (to the north), as well as a few shops and a weekly **market** on Thursdays.

VADU IZEI doesn't have a wooden church, but standing at the junction of the roads along the Iza and Mara valleys it is nevertheless well placed for tourism and takes advantage of this with a well-developed rural **homestay** scheme (②). Prices include a bed, plenty of food, and non-stop plum brandy (*horincă*). The scheme also operates in Botiza and Ieud, but you need to book here at the Agro-Tur office (☎062/33.01.71), opposite the *Casa de Cultură*. Local attractions include fishing, walking, riding, cycling along the old forestry railway, and the *Maramuzical* **festival** of folk fiddle-playing in mid-July. Vadu Izei is also known as the workplace of Gheorghe Borodi (1917–91), who carved monumental **gateways** erected by Maramureş families as symbols of nobility; as most Maramureş families claimed to be *nemeşi* or nobles, there's no shortage of gateways. The village is also convenient for Sighet, reached by bus #1 every half-hour.

Sighetu Marmaţiei and beyond

SIGHET, as it's generally known, stands just a few kilometres from the Ukrainian border and has the air of a frontier town, with churches of almost every denomination. When the territory to the north – now the easternmost province of Czechoslovakia – was called Ruthenia, Sighet was a famous smuggling centre. Today it is a peaceful modern town with 44,000 inhabitants, where you can see residents of the surrounding villages in local costume, especially on the first Monday of the month, when the livestock market takes place. The town is famed for its **winter carnival** when many of the participants wear extraordinary shamanistic costumes and masks; unfortunately few foreign visitors are around to witness this on December 27.

The Town

From the train and bus stations it's five minutes' walk south down Strada Iuliu Maniu to the **Reformat church**, perhaps the oddest building in town – a fourteenth century structure rebuilt on a rather strange ground plan. The town centre extends to the east of here and comprises two one-way streets, both of which change their names, and several squares between them, so it can be hard to make sense of addresses.

Immediately east of the Reformat church is the **Curtea Veche**, the Baroque county hall of 1690–93, now housing restaurants and shops. Piaţa Libertăţii lies just beyond here, with the **Roman Catholic church**, built by the Piarist order in 1734 on its northern side. On the east side of the square is the **Maramureş Ethnographic Museum,** which exhibits pottery, woodcarvings, masks and wall rugs (*scoarte*). Its **Natural Sciences** section is at Piaţa Libertăţii 15 on the west side of the Roman Catholic church, and is mainly stuffed with hunting trophies. If the **Art Gallery**, further west at Str. Mihalyi de Apşa 17, is shut, you can enquire here or at the Ethnographic Museum for someone to take you.

On Strada Barnuţiu, to the south of the Ethnographic Museum, stands the former **prison**, now marked with plaques listing the 51 prominent figures who died here in the purges of the early 1950s. The prison now calls itself the International Centre for Study of Totalitarianism, and opened as a museum in 1997. Turning right one block down Strada Barnuţiu brings you to an overgrown monument to the 38,000 Maramureş Jews rounded up by the Hungarian gendarmerie and deported in 1944. The community's nineteenth-century synagogue survives, and can be found on the far side of Piaţa Libertăţii at Strada Basarabia 10; while the childhood home of **Elie Wiesel**, who survived Auschwitz and won the Nobel Peace Prize for his work in helping to understand and remember the Holocaust, stands one block east on the corner of Strada Mihai Viteazul and Strada Dragoş Vodă. It's a plain house and as yet it's not open to visitors.

The **Village Museum** is situated on Dobăieş hill on the town's eastern outskirts; it's a thirty-minute walk, or take bus #1 to the bridge and School no. 5, then

---

THE PRISON OF THE MINISTERS

Sighet prison operated from 1898 until 1974, and in that time achieved a notoriety gained by few others. Its nadir was in the early 1950s, when it held many of the political prisoners (former government ministers, generals, academics and bishops) brought here so that they could be "protected" by the Red Army or rapidly spirited away into the Soviet Union if the Communist regime was threatened. The prison's 72 cells held 180 members of the pre-war establishment, at least two thirds of them aged over sixty; they were appallingly treated and not surprisingly many died. The most important figure to die in Sighet was **Iuliu Maniu**, regarded as the greatest living Romanian when he was arrested in 1947 and now seen as a secular martyr – the only uncorrupt politician of the pre-war period, organiser of the 1944 coup, and notably reluctant to pursue revenge against Transylvania's Hungarians after the war.

The leading Hungarian victim was **Arón Márton**, Roman Catholic bishop of Alba Iulia, who opposed the persecution of the Jews in 1944 and of the Uniates in 1949, and was imprisoned from 1950 to 1955, surviving until 1980. Others who died in Sighet included two of the three members of the Brătianu family imprisoned here – Dinu, president of the National Liberal Party and Finance Minister 1933–34, and Gheorghe, professor and second-division politician; Ion Mahalache, founder of the Peasant Party and Maniu's deputy in the merged National Peasants' Party, who died in 1963 in Rîmnicu Sărat prison; and Mihail Manoilescu, theoretician of Romanian fascism, and Foreign Minister in 1940. Their graves can be seen in a field just off the main road to the west of town.

walk northeast for five minutes up Strada Muzeului. Here you can see dozens of houses, farm buildings and churches collected from the Iza valley – an essential sight if you're intending to give the real thing a miss.

Practicalities

The **train station** is just north of the centre at Str. Iuliu Maniu 1 and the **bus terminal** stands opposite. Trains go through to Vișeu de Jos and on to Salva and Beclean, the junctions for trains to Suceava, Cluj and Brașov. There are good bus connections to the surrounding villages, usually departing at about 4pm.

You'll find a **tourist office**, which sells the odd map, on Piața Libertății, opposite the *Tisa* **hotel** at no. 8 (☎062/31.26.45, fax 31.54.84; ⑤), one of Romania's more pleasant and friendly hotels, though with no single rooms. The *Ardealul*, by the station at Str. Iuliu Maniu 91 (☎062/31.23.72; ①), has only six rooms, three of them triples, and all very basic with no hot water. To the west of town, Strada Eminescu leads in ten minutes to the Grădina Morii park where a footbridge leads over the river by the grubby chalet-style *Marmația* hotel to Solovan hill, where you can easily camp wild. The *Perla Sigheteana* motel (③) is due to open in 1998 on the edge of town at Str. Avram Iancu 11, the road to Oaș; it'll be easily the best place in Sighet, with pool, sauna and gym.

There's not much choice for **food**, other than the hotels and the *Curtea Veche* at Str. Mihalyi de Apșa 2. *Interbijoux*, at Str. Mihaly de Apșa 13, is in fact a lively pizzeria, while *Bar Europa*, at Str. Bogdan Vodă 11, is outrageously expensive and seedy.

Săpînța

SĂPÎNȚA, 16km northwest of Sighet, is served by twelve buses a day. This village has achieved a star on every tourist map, largely thanks to the work of the woodcarver Stan Ion Pătraș (1909–77). Its **Merry Cemetery** (*Cimitir vesel*) features beautifully worked, colourfully painted headboards carved with portraits of the deceased or scenes from their lives, chosen by relatives and inscribed with witty limericks composed by Pătraș as he saw fit. Some are terse – "who sought money to amass, could not Death escape, alas!" – while a surprising number recall violent deaths, like that of the villager killed by a "bloody Hungarian" during the last war, or a mother's final message to her son: "Griga, may you pardoned be, even though you did stab me". Pătraș left two apprentices, Turda Toader and Vasile Stan, to continue the funerary masterwork. The village is also known for the traditional *cergi* or woollen blankets and is now lined with handicraft stalls and rather too accustomed to busloads of tourists making a stop for half an hour and then rushing on.

The Oaș depression

Beyond Săpînța, the road turns south towards Satu Mare, winding up to the **Huta Pass** (587m) to enter the **Oaș** depression. The shepherds of this region assemble on the first or second Sunday of May for the **festival of Sîmbra Oilor**, when the milk yield of each family's sheep is measured. Whether this process – known as *Ruptul Sterpelor* – occurs in May (as here) or early July (as it does further south), the participants dress for the occasion in waist-length sheepskin jackets (*cojoc*) covered in embroidery and tassels, or fluffy woollen overcoats called *guba*, and heartily consume fiery Maramureș *horincă* (plum brandy) and sweet whey cheese.

Oaș is sometimes billed as undiscovered Maramureș, but most of the local men now work or trade abroad, so that the roads are lined with new bungalows and imported Audis, and **traditional costume** is little worn except in the remotest villages such as Cămărzana, and at festivals such as the *Sîmbra Oilor*. It's less likely to be visible at the **festival** on September 1 at **NEGREŞTI**, the largest settlement in the region, which is definitely part of the modern world. Here, the **Oaş Museum** (Tues–Sun 9am–3pm), at Strada Victoriei 17, just north of the centre, has a good display on local ethnography, and a small open-air display of half a dozen blue-painted houses and a wooden church on Strada Livezilor, to the south beyond the bridge. In addition to local buses, the village can be reached by trains on the Satu Mare–Bixad line: get off at the Negreşti halt, rather than at the station, which is a couple of kilometres west of town.

Accommodation is available in Negreşti at the *Oşanul* hotel at Str. Victoriei 89 (✆062/85.11.62, fax 85.11.63; ④), which has only double rooms, and the new private *Rebeca*, opposite the museum at Str. Victoriei 75 (✆85.10.43, fax 85.02.50; ②). The other hotels in Oaş are the *Valea-Măriei* (✆062/85.07.50; ②), 5km north of Vama, and the *Călineşti* (✆062/85.14.00; ②) in Călineşti-Oaş by a reservoir 15km west of Negreşti. The only places serving food are the hotel **restaurants**.

The Iza valley

Some of the loveliest villages and wooden churches in Maramureş are situated in the **Iza valley**, which extends for roughly 60km from Sighet to the Rodna mountains, which form the frontier with Moldavia. Most of the villages along the Iza and in the side valleys are served by a daily bus service from Sighet, and there are several buses to Vişeu and Borşa, most following the DJ186 along the Iza valley, some following the DN18 along the Rona and Vişeu valleys.

Bîrsana and Rozavlea

The church at **BÎRSANA**, 19km southeast of Sighet, is small and neat and perfectly positioned atop a hillock in the middle of the village. The florid paintings, among the best in Maramureş, were done in 1720, soon after the church's construction, and in 1806 by Hodor Toador and Ion Plohod, with icons on wood by Hodor Toador – the narthex is adorned with saints and processional images, while the *naos* is painted with Old and New Testament scenes, each in its own decorative medallion. Look in particular for the images of angels covered in eyes. A brand new nunnery is now being built at the east end of the village, with a wooden church whose steeple, at 56 metres, is even higher than that at Şurdeşti; unusually it also has a pentagonal *pridvor* and two apses.

Being a border region, Maramureş remained vulnerable to attacks by nomadic tribes until the eighteenth century, and the wooden church at **ROZAVLEA**, 20km further along the valley, was one of many rebuilt after the last Tatar invasion in 1717 and painted by Ion Plohod. Its magnificent double roof was recently restored and looks a little new, but will doubtless weather nicely.

Botiza and Poienile Izei

BOTIZA, 13km south of Rozavlea, is one of the best centres for **agrotourism** in this area, with two competing networks. The better is the Asociaţia Agroturistică Botiza, based near the church at no. 742 (✆062/33.49.91, ext 10); rooms can also be booked through Agro-Tur in Vadu Izei or Ar-Thema in Baia Mare. Craftwork, notably carpets and woodcarving, is big here, and you can see examples at the AAB office as above. The wooden church, beautifully located on a hillside, with a view down the valley to the peaks of Ukraine, was built at the turn of the eighteenth century in Vişeu de Jos and moved here 200 years later. Several mineral springs are located along the road to Poienile Izei, notably a sulphurous well at a ruined spa by the bridge about a kilometre from the village centre.

An execrable side track leads 6km into the hills to the village of **POIENILE IZEI** ("The Meadows of the Iza"). Anyone in the house above the new church will unlock the old wooden church for visitors. Inside, it is filled with **nightmarish paintings**, its walls red with the fires of Hell, wherein dozens of sinners have their vulnerable white bodies tortured by demons (*draci*) with goat-like heads and clawed feet. A woman is being pressed with a hot iron, a man is hung from a butcher's hook by his tongue, while others are furrowed by sharp ploughs or casually sawn in two. Beneath it all processions of sinners are driven into the mouth of Hell – an enormous bird's head with fiery nostrils.

These pictures constitute an **illustrated rule book** too terrifying to disobey, whose message is still understood by the villagers. A huge pair of bellows is used to inflict punishment for farting in church, while the woman being ironed had burnt the priest's robes while pressing them. Women violating traditional morality face torments in the afterlife: adultresses are courted by loathsome demons and a woman who aborted children is forced to eat them. These Hell scenes presumably formed the nasty part of a huge *Day of Judgement* in the narthex, which has half disappeared. Opposite are paintings of gardens and distant cityscapes in a sort of Gothic Book of Hours style, seemingly executed in 1793–4. Murals in the nave are badly damaged and soot-blackened, but from the balcony you can recognize Adam and Eve, the Fall, and episodes from the lives of Christ and John the Baptist.

Ieud and beyond

Back in the Iza valley, a turn-off about 6km east along the valley road at Gura Ieudului leads upstream to the village of **IEUD**, 3km south. Lanes fenced with lattices run between the houses, clustered within their courtyards, and during summer the air is pervaded by the scent of lady's mantle, a plant mixed with elder and wormwood to make "face water", which was also used for baths to invigorate weak children. Divorce is virtually unknown in this religious and traditional village; thus about fifty of Ieud's women are "heroine mothers", having borne fourteen children each, and nigh on half the population of 5000 is of school age. It was Ieud artisans, supervised by the master carpenter Ion Ţiplea, who restored Manuc's Inn in Bucharest, and the tradition of woodworking has been maintained since the superb Orthodox **Church on the Hill** was first raised here in 1364. Supposedly the oldest church in Maramureş (though largely rebuilt in the eighteenth century), with a double roof and tiny windows, it housed the Ieud Codex (now in the Romanian Academy in Bucharest), the earliest known document in the Romanian language. It has perhaps the best-known paintings of any Maramureş church, executed by Alexandru Ponehalski in 1782; look out for Abraham, Isaac and Jacob welcoming people in their arms, in the *pronaos*. Ask opposite the *bufet* or *Textile-Incaltimente* shop for the church key, and don't miss the ingenious removable ratchet used to open the bolt in the main door. Ieud's

Uniate **lower church**, the Val or Şes church, was built in 1718 and has an immensely high roofline and, unusually, no porch; there are few wall paintings left, but the icons on glass and iconostasis are valuable. **Homestay** accommodation is available in the village: if you haven't booked it in Vadu Izei, ask for Gavrila Chindris at no. 665 (☎Ieud 51).

BOGDAN VODĂ, 1km further along the valley road from Gura Ieudului, formerly known as Cuhea, is one of the valley's main villages, standing on the road leading to Moldavia and with long-standing ties to that region. The local voivode, Bogdan, left from here to march over the mountains, supposedly to hunt bison (see p.346), but ended up founding the Moldavian state in 1359 – the influence of Stephen and other Moldavian rulers seems to have imparted a semi-Byzantine style to the frescoes inside Bogdan Vodă's church. The building materials used in 1722 were typical of eastern Maramureş, however: thick fir beams rather than the stone used at Putna and other Moldavian monasteries, or the oak of western Maramureş. You can also see the ruins of a fourteenth-century stone church and princely residence. From here a rough road leads to Vişeu de Jos in the next valley north (see below), while the main road continues east to **DRAGOMIREŞTI**, whose original village church stands in Bucharest's Village Museum. The next village you come to is **SĂLIŞTEA DE SUS**, 4km east of Dragomireşti, which boasts two old wooden churches, one built in 1680 and the other in 1722 and painted by Radu Munteanu in 1775. The road passes a *cabana* at the Iza rail halt and ends at **SĂCEL**, known for its unglazed red ceramics, from where the DN17C heads north to Moisei or south to Salva and Bistriţa.

The Vişeu valley and the Rodna mountains

The River Vişeu is fed by numerous sources in the wooded highlands above the **Vişeu valley** and surrounded by mountains that merge with the "crests" of Bucovina and the higher peaks of Chornohora in Ukraine. From Sighet the DN18 leads east through **RONA DE JOS**, where there's a wooden church built in 1665 and painted by Ion Plohod in 1817, and on to Rona de Sus, after which a minor road heads south for 3km to the tiny spa of **COŞTIUI**, which has a motel and *căsuţe*. Buses are rare on this road, but all trains running between Sighet and Salva stop at the traditional village of **PETROVA** and at **LEORDINA**, which are not especially scenic. A rough road starts 2km east of Leordina and follows the Ruscova River into an enclave of Huţul or Ruthenian people centred on the villages of **REPEDEA** and **POIENILE DE SUB MUNTE**. Speaking a dialect of Ukrainian mixed with many Romanian words, these people are the archetypal inhabitants of the Carpathians. Most **trains** from Sighet turn southwards at **VIŞEU DE JOS**, passing through Săcel en route to Beclean; trains no longer run up the branch line from Vişeu de Jos to the alpine resort of Borşa, but there's a good bus connection as far as Vişeu de Sus, and less frequent buses on to Borşa.

VIŞEU DE SUS is a large settlement, but has few services and no accommodation other than beds at the school's grotty boarding house, the *Internat* (☎Vişeu 60590; ①). Across the river to the north the market stands on the edge of the Zipser quarter; this community of German foresters has largely evaporated since 1989, but it's still worth calling in at the *Zipserverein*'s bar behind Strada 9 Mai 29, or at their library at no. 21. Moving on towards Borşa, catch one of the **buses** from the dusty yard a couple of hundred metres beyond the shops. Early birds can catch the **logging train** up the steep **Vaser valley**, leaving between 6 and 7am. Hauled by a vintage steam engine, it carries lumberjacks (*butinarii*) up to their camps near the Ukrainian border, and at about 3pm begins the journey back down from Coman. Bears and deer drink from the river, unperturbed by the trains and loggers, while in the mountain forests live stags, elusive lynxes, and wolves. The Vaser River, rich in trout and umber, descends rapidly through the fifty-kilometre-long valley, and its whirling waters have begun to attract **kayaking** enthusiasts to logging settlements like **MĂCIRLĂU**, start of a very rugged trail over the Jupania ridge of the Maramureş mountains to the mining centre of Baia Borşa, just to the north of Borşa.

The long thin village of **MOISEI**, 12km beyond Vişeu de Sus, lies beneath the foothills of the Rodna massif, whose peaks are often still snowy while fruit is ripening in the village's orchards. Though today it seems bucolic, within living memory Moisei suffered a tragedy that's become a symbol of atrocity and martyred innocence in Romania; in October 1944, retreating Hungarian troops machine-gunned twenty-nine villagers and set Moisei ablaze – a massacre commemorated by a circle of twelve stone figures by Vida Geza with faces modelled on two of the victims and on the masks that are worn during festivals in Maramureş. The memorial stands at the eastern end of the village, opposite a small museum at km141.

Today, Moisei's peaceful existence is exemplified by its womenfolk – spinning wool as they walk down the lane, or working in the fields with their babies nearby, hung in cradles from trees. A couple of kilometres along a side valley south of the village stands a **monastery**, scene of a major pilgrimage on August 15, the Feast of the Assumption; there's a wooden church here, dating from 1672.

Most of the valley's amenities lie in **BORŞA**, 5km east of Moisei, including two **hotels**, the *Iezer* at Str. Decebal 2 (☎062/34.34.30, fax 34.24.42; ③), and *Perla Maramureşului* at Str. Victoriei 37 (☎062/34.25.39; ①), just east opposite the hospital. The *Perla* houses the best **restaurant** in town. Naturally, there's a wooden church, rebuilt in 1718 and hidden away north of Strada Libertăţii 171 west of the centre. **Buses** arrive at a sordid terminal further west, opposite Str. Libertăţii 119; four a day run here from the Iza valley to Baia Mare, and one each from Bistriţa and Vatra Dornei. Pre-1939 travellers describe Borşa, overshadowed by Pietrosul, as a centre of Jewish merchants, living from forestry and trade with Moldavia by the road over the Prislop Pass. It's roughly 10km from Borşa to the **Borşa Complex ski resort** with the *Cascada* (☎062/34.34.66; ⑤) and the much better *Stibina* (both ☎062/34.34.66; ⑤) hotels. Here too a new wooden church has been built in traditional style, except for its massive stone plinth. A hairpin road heads up from the resort to the Prislop Pass – 2km away as the crow flies, but closer to 10km by road on this tightly twisting route.

Hiking in the Rodna Mountains

The Rodnas are one of Romania's best **hiking** areas, largely because you are sure to have them virtually to yourself. The easiest way into the mountains is either by the chair-lift from the Borşa Complex (you may have to wait until a dozen or so people have gathered) or from the 1416-metre **Prislop Pass**; from the Prislop Pass you can head either north into the Maramureş mountains, wild and largely unvisited, although scarred by mining and forestry, or south into the Rodnas. Following red triangles, then blue stripes, it should take you two hours at most to reach the main crest at the Gărgălău saddle, from where you can follow red stripes east to the Rotunda Pass and ultimately to Vatra Dornei (see p.260), or west into the highest part of the massif. The route west will get you to La Cruce in four and a half hours, from where you can turn right to follow blue stripes up to the automatic weather station on the summit of **Mount Pietrosul** (2303m), ninety minutes away. There are great views in all directions, particularly deep into Ukraine to the north. Borşa is 1600m below, and it takes another two and a half hours to get back there.

Apart from camping, the only place to sleep in the mountains is the *Puzdrele* **cabana** – two to three hours' trek from the hamlet of Poiana Borşa, following the route marked by blue triangles, which continues to the main ridge in another couple of hours. With a map, you can hike on south and down towards the Someş Mare valley and Năsăud (see p.213) in two days, camping wild en route.

Travelling on from Maramureş

Just before the Prislop Pass, 12km east of Borşa and linking Maramureş with **Moldavia**, you'll see a monument marking the site where the last Tatar raid was finally driven off in 1717. At the pass, close to the bar, the **Hora at Prislop festival** takes place every year on the nearest Sunday to August 1, attracting thousands of participants and spectators. Although not a major part of the displays here, the Round Dance or *Hora* still has the power to draw onlookers into the rhythmically stepping, swaying and stamping circles. The *Hora* used to serve as a sanction in village society – local miscreants seeking to enter the circle were shamed when the dancing immediately ceased, and only resumed when they withdrew.

On the far side of the pass, the road runs down the lovely Bistriţa valley to Cîmpulung Moldovenesc (see p.259), from where you can reach Suceava and several of the Painted Monasteries by rail. Two buses run per day from Vişeu to Vatra Dornei; you can change either there or at Iacobeni for trains to Cîmpulung Moldovenesc. Travelling **to Transylvania**, four trains a day link Vişeu de Jos with Salva, 61km to the south and a junction on the busier line from Cluj to Vatra Dornei and Suceava.

travel details

Trains

Baia Mare to: Beclean (1 daily; 3hr); Braşov (3 daily; 7hr–9hr); Bucharest (3 daily; 10hr–12hr); Cluj (2 daily; 3hr 30min–5hr 30min); Dej (6 daily; 2hr–3hr 30min); Jibou (8 daily; 45min–1hr 30min); Satu Mare (9 daily; 45min–1hr 30min); Timişoara (1 daily; 6hr 30min).

Satu Mare to: Baia Mare (9 daily; 1hr–1hr 30min); Bucharest (1 daily; 11hr); Negreşti–Oaş (4 daily; 1hr 30min–1hr 45min); Oradea (7 daily; 2hr–3hr 30min).

Sighet to: Bucharest (1 daily; 12hr 45min); Salva (3 daily; 3hr 15min–4hr, summer 3hr); Timişoara (1 daily; 12hr 15min); Vişeu de Jos (6 daily; 1hr 30min–2hr 30min).

Vişeu de Jos to: Beclean (3 daily; 2hr 30min); Bucharest (1 daily; 11hr 15min); Sighet (6 daily; 1hr 45min–2hr 30min, summer 1hr 30min).

Buses

Baia Mare to: Sighet (7 daily); Borşa (5 daily); Bicaz (3 daily); Cluj (up to 2 daily); Negreşti–Oaş (4 daily); Ocna Sugatag (2 daily); Oradea (1 daily); Poienile de sub Munte (1 daily); Şomcuta Mare (5 daily); Tîrgu Lăpuş (up to 14 daily); Zalău (2 daily)

Borşa to: Baia Mare (1 daily); Bistriţa (1 daily); Sighet (3 daily).

Satu Mare to: Negreşti–Oaş (up to 2 daily); Oradea (1 daily); Sighet (3 daily); Şimleu Silvanei (1 daily).

Sighet to: Baia Mare (7 daily); Borşa (3 daily); Botiza (Mon–Fri 1 daily); Budeşti (Mon–Fri 5 daily); Ieud (Mon–Fri 1 daily); Negreşti–Oaş (4 daily); Oradea (1 daily); Poienile de sub Munte (1 daily); Satu Mare (3 daily).

Tîrgu Lăpuş to: Baia Mare (up to 14 daily), Cluj (1 daily); Gîlgău (up to 5 daily); Oradea (1 daily).

Vişeu to: Baia Mare (3 daily); Bistriţa (1 daily); Sighet (up to 4 daily); Vatra Dornei (1 daily).

Planes

Baia Mare and **Satu Mare** to: Bucharest (2 daily, on a triangular route).

International trains

Baia Mare to: Budapest (1 daily; 8hr).

Carei to: Budapest (2 daily; 5hr–6hr 30min); Mátészalka (4 daily; 1hr 30min–2hr).

Satu Mare to: Budapest (1 daily; 7hr).

Valea lui Mihai to: Budapest (2 daily; 4hr 15min–4hr 45min); Debrecen (4 daily; 1hr–1hr 30min).

International Buses

Baia Mare to: Budapest (2 weekly).

Satu Mare to: Budapest (Mon–Fri 1 daily); Debrecen (1 daily; Tues, Thurs & Sat); Nyíregyháza (Mon–Sat 1 daily).

CHAPTER SIX

THE BANAT

The **Banat** (Bánság in Hungarian) is the historical term for the western marches of Romania between the Timiş and Mureş rivers, but it has come to include also the Crişana, or the county of Oradea, on the Crişul Repede River. It has much in common with Hungary's Great Plain and ex-Yugoslavia's Vojvodina region, with its featureless scenery, great rivers, historical sites and an intermingling of different ethnic groups. The frontiers were finally settled according to the principle of national self-determination at the Versailles conference of 1918–20, to which each country's delegates brought reams of demographic maps and statistics to support their claims. During the Communist era, policies towards ethnic minorities were generous in Hungary and Yugoslavia, and comparatively fair in Romania until the 1960s, when an increasingly hard line began to cause a haemorrhaging of the population, particularly of ethnic Magyars. In both 1988 and 1989 around 80,000 left, as liberalization gained pace in Hungary but things went downhill fast in Romania. The Schwab Germans, who originally settled in this area when the marshes were drained and colonized after the expulsion of the Turks, have now almost all emigrated to Germany. Nevertheless many villages of Slovaks, Serbs, Magyars and other minority groups remain here.

From the visitor's point of view, the cities of **Oradea**, **Arad** and **Timişoara** are the region's most important attractions – partly on their own merits, but also because each town dominates a route between Transylvania and Hungary or Serbia, and provides access to most other places of interest in the region. When you're tired of such sights and café life as the cities have to offer, you'll find the western ranges of the **Apuseni mountains** with their **stalactite caves**, **wooden churches** and village **festivals** within easy reach, while Belgrade, Debrecen, Szeged, Cluj, Sibiu and other major cities are only a few hours away.

Oradea and around

Situated on the banks of the Crişul Repede River, with a population of 200,000, **ORADEA** is close to the site of Biharea – the capital of a Vlach voivode, Menumorut, who resisted Hungarian claims on the region during the tenth century – and bears the stamp of its subsequent rulers. Founded around a monastery, the medieval town of Nagyvárad (as the Magyars still call it) prospered during the reign of **Mátyás Corvinus**, who was raised at the Bishop's court here, and later acquired a mammoth Vauban-style citadel and the wealth of stately neoclassical, Baroque and Secession piles which constitute Oradea's most characteristic feature.

Oradea is the capital of **Bihor county**, known as the "Land of Hot Waters" for its profusion of thermal springs, which have been exploited to create **spas**, of which **Băile Felix**, 8km from the city, is the most developed.

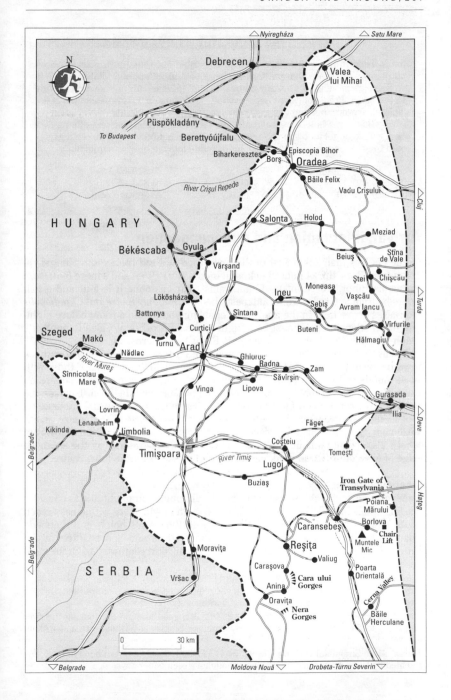

Hotels listed in this guide have been price-graded according to the scale below. Prices given are those charged for the cheapest **double room** available, which in the less expensive places usually comes without private bath or shower and without breakfast. Price codes are expressed in US dollars as the Romanian leu is not a stable currency, but you will generally pay for your room in lei.

Note that some hotels are currently closed for modernization, and others, now open, will no doubt follow in the near future. This is bound to result in higher rates when they reopen, so the prices quoted should be taken only as a guideline.

① $10 and under   ④ $20–25   ⑦ $40–50
② $10–15   ⑤ $25–30   ⑧ $50–65
③ $15–20   ⑥ $30–40   ⑨ $65 and over

Arrival, information and accommodation

Oradea is less than 20km east of the main road and rail routes into Hungary – 16km from Bors, the 24-hour checkpoint on the DN1 (E60) and a mere 6km from Episcopia Bihor, where international trains clear customs. It is four and a half hours by train to Oradea from Budapest; the *Partium*, *Ady Endre* and *Claudiopolis* expresses arrive here in the afternoon, enabling you to find a room before nightfall. International tickets must be bought at the CFR office at Calea Republicii 2 (Mon–Fri 7am–7pm) or at the Episcopia Bihor border crossing.

Trams #1 and #4 run south from the **train station** along Calea Republicii towards the town centre (those with red numbers run to the station and those with black numbers from it), pass the Crişul department store in a small square on Calea Republicii and continue southeast along Strada Gen. Magheru. To reach the town centre proper, get off the tram at the department store stop and continue on foot along Calea Republicii. The **bus terminal**, southeast of the centre at Str. Războieni 81, is immediately adjacent to the Oradea Est train halt (bus #13) from where it's a twenty minute walk into town, while the **airport** is on the southern edge of town on the Arad road; flights are met by buses for the town centre.

Accommodation

Oradea has a reasonable selection of hotels, although you might like to consider the spa hotels in Băile Felix and Băile 1 Mai, both of which are within easy reach of the town. Otherwise, the only alternative to the town's hotels is the outside chance of a **dormitory bed** from the County Youth and Sport Office, at Str. Vulcan 11. The nearest **campsite** is in Băile 1 Mai, 8km southwest of Oradea and reached by bus #15.

Astoria, Str. Teatrului 1 (☎059/13.60.94 or 13.14.95, fax 16.37.09). A pleasant Secession buiding with clean rooms, but nothing special; if you're prepared to take a room without a private shower, then they are probably good value. ① without shower, ③ with.

Crişul Repede, Str. Libertăţii 8 (☎059/13.25.09). In a good location overlooking the river and close to the central squares, but fairly ordinary. Singles and twins, with and without showers. ②.

Dacia, Aleea Ştrandului (☎059/41.86.56, fax 41.12.80). The only modern hotel in town, frequented by businessmen and tour groups, though it's seen better days. ⑨.

Parc, Calea Republicii 5 (☎059/41.16.99, fax 41.84.10). Friendly place on the city's main pedestrianized street. Rooms for one, two, three or four people, with shared facilities. Price includes breakfast. ②.

Transilvania, Str. Teatrului 2 (☎059/13.60.94, fax 16.37.09). Closed for renovation, but due to reopen in 1998. Traditionally good value.

Vulturul Negru, Str. Independenței 1 (☎059/13.54.17). The least expensive of Oradea's hotels, in a highly atmospheric building straight out of the pages of a cold-war thriller – the first stop in Romania for generations of backpackers. Single, twin and triple rooms, with shared showers. ①.

The City

The city's most famous sights are in the north of town, just west of the train station, on Strada Șirul Canonicilor. Countless serfs toiled from 1752 to 1780 to build what is the largest Baroque building in Romania, the Roman Catholic **Cathedral**, decorated with gold leaf and marble, with a huge organ (see posters for details of concerts). Their labour was also doubtless exploited to build the vast U-shaped **Bishop's Palace** in the same leafy park; built by Franz Anton Hillebrandt in 1762–77, it was modelled on Lucas von Hildebrandt's Belvedere Palace in Vienna. The palace is now the **Museum of the Crișana** (Tues, Thurs & Sat 10am–3pm, Wed, Fri & Sun 10am–6pm), with a fairly standard history display, and a good selection of nineteenth- and twentieth-century art. The museum has a famous collection of 14,000 decorated eggs from Bihor and Bucovina, but you'll only be able to see it if you're here at Easter.

Heading south towards the river, Calea Republicii becomes a pedestrianized promenade, lined with shops, *cofetărie*, cinemas and many ostentatious Secession buildings. It eventually opens onto **Piața Regele Ferdinand**, dominated by the State Theatre, opened in 1900 – a typically pompous design by the Viennese duo, Helmer and Fellner.

Just to the east are two **memorial houses**, of little interest to the average visitor. One, in the tiny Traian Park (Mon, Wed & Fri 10am–3pm, Tues, Thurs & Sun 10am–2pm), commemorates the Magyar poet **Endre Ady** (see p.210), who lived in Oradea for four years and, unusually for his era, opposed Hungarian chauvinism towards the Romanians; the other, at Str. Vulcan 16, remembers **Iosif Vulcan**, who lived here between 1880 and 1906 and edited the literary magazine *Familia*, in which Mihai Eminescu made his debut in 1866.

Piața Unirii and around

Apart from the nondescript Catholic church half-blocking the north side of **Piața Unirii**, most of the buildings around this square on the southern bank of the river were designed to maximize the impact of the waterfront. The former **City Hall** is a monumental restatement of well-worn classical themes to which the architects added a fun touch: chimes that play the March of Avram Iancu every hour. Given that the Austro-Hungarians were still in control when the building was raised in 1902–03, it seems odd that they allowed this commemoration of Iancu, a Romanian revolutionary whose agitation inspired the protest on the "Field of Liberty" at Blaj in 1848 (see p.167), and who then took to the hills with a guerrilla band, harassing Magyar troops and landlords and urging the serfs to revolt. The **City Library**, a more spectacular piece of architecture from 1905, stands just south of City Hall.

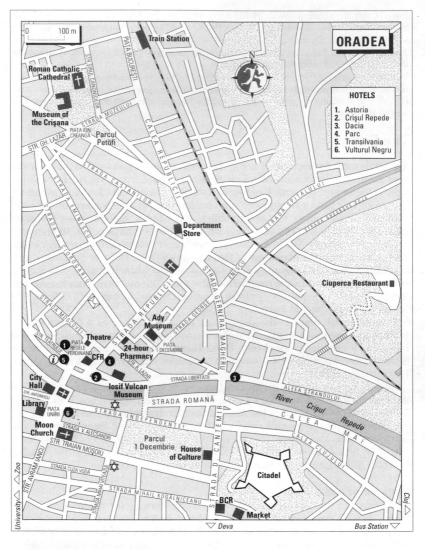

Facing these across Piaţa Unirii is an ornate Secession-style edifice of 1908 with the splendid name of the **Vulturul Negru** or "Black Eagle". Running through it is an arcade with a stained-glass roof, connecting three neighbouring streets. Part of the complex is occupied by a hotel that could have sprung from the pages of a Graham Greene thriller – an ill-lit labyrinth of rooms and corridors inhabited by brooding staff and a furtive clientele. To the south of the hotel, Oradea's main Orthodox church, built in 1792, marks the stylistic transition from

Baroque to Neoclassical; it is better known as the **Moon Church** after the large sphere mounted beneath its clock, which rotates to indicate the lunar phases over a period of 28 days. There are also no fewer than three imposing **synagogues** nearby: on Strada Independenţei opposite the *Vulturul Negru*; just east of Piaţa Unirii, at Strada Mihai Viteazul 2; and just west on Piaţa Rahovei. Oradea was a great centre of Jewish settlement. In December 1927, Codreanu's League of the Archangel Michael, soon to become the Iron Guard, held a congress here having been brought in special free trains – they wrecked four synagogues before leaving.

To the east of Piaţa Unirii, the imposing bulk of Oradea's **citadel** rises, a Renaissance stronghold enlarged during the eighteenth century by Italian disciples of the Swiss military architect Vauban. Pentagonal in shape, with bastions guarding each corner, the citadel used to be additionally protected by a moat filled with warm water from the River Peţea, which runs around the southern edge of the town. Although the external walls seem very dilapidated, the citadel is now the traffic police headquarters, and is busy with people seeking driving tests and number plates.

Heading south from Piaţa Unirii, Strada Avram Iancu becomes Calea Armatei Romăne, with a **Military Museum** (Tues–Sun 10am–4pm) on the left at no. 22 and the university on the right: the third gateway into this attractive leafy campus leads to a **wooden church**, built in Letca in 1760 and moved here in 1991 to serve as the theological faculty's chapel. With its new porch and radiators, it no longer has the authentic atmosphere of a village church, but it is usually open and you can climb up into the tower. Returning north, Strada Matei Basarab leads left to the **zoo** (daily 8am–8pm), which has monkeys, yaks, lions, llamas and various varieties of pheasant, as well as native Romanian animals such as wolves, goats, owls and squirrels.

Eating, drinking and entertainment

The best hotel restaurants are those in the *Dacia* and *Transilvania*, but there's a fair choice of other places. Strada Republicii and the streets leading off it have plenty of **cafés**, including the *Minerva* at Str. Republicii 10, and **restaurants** such as the *Oradea*, at Str. Vulcan 1, with average food and service under extraordinary *fin-de-siècle* ceilings, and *Olivery* at Str. Moscovei 12, a quiet place, serving decent breakfast, lunch and dinner; there's also a Chinese, *Tian Tang*, opposite the *Parc* hotel. For **fast food**, try the *Raşid* at Str. Republicii 11, the adjacent *Globus* hamburger joint, or the self-styled *Enjoy Delicious Fish and Chips* at Calea Averescu 33.

The downstairs bar in the *Astoria* hotel is the smart place to go **drinking** (there's a rougher bar upstairs), while there are several other bars, such as the *Atlantic*, along Strada Vulcan, and an appealing subterranean bar in the university.

For buying your own food, there are two **supermarkets** – the Promesc, under the *Parc* hotel, and the UNIC, on the corner of Strada Eminescu – and a private **bakery** at Str. Mihai Viteazul 5, selling hot fresh bread.

The town's **Philharmonic Orchestra**, housed at Piaţa 1 Decembrie 10 (tickets from Str. Republicii 6), is well regarded, while children might enjoy performances at the **Puppet Theatre**, Str. Alecsandri 9, part of the *Vulturul Negru* arcade.

Listings

Airport information TAROM has an office at Piaţa Regele Ferdinand 2 (Mon–Fri 7am–8pm, Sat 11am–2pm; ☎059/13.19.18); buses leave here for the airport seventy minutes before each flight. DacAir and TAROM have flights to Bucharest (Mon–Fri); tickets can be bought at Air Transilvania at Piaţa Independenţei 47 (☎059/47.90.16) and at the airport (☎059/41.60.82).

Car rental is available through Avis, c/o BanatAir (☎059/41.04.50), and from Hertz at Remtours, Str. Mihai Viteazul 2 (☎059/13.28.88).

Exchange There's a Bancomat cash machine at BCR on Str. D. Cantemir, immediately south of the citadel.

Pharmacies There are 24-hour pharmacies at Calea Republicii 33 and Strada Progresului bloc C 30–31.

Tourist agencies The Lucon, at Str. Moşoiu 1, offers day-trips to Hungary. The CIG, at Str. Moscovei 8, arranges day-trips to Uzhgorod and Mukachevo in Ukraine, as well as deals to Hungary, Poland and Istanbul. They may be able to fix you up with excursions to Stîna de Vale, the Bears' Cave at Chişcău and various folklore events in the Apuseni mountains.

The spas

The spa towns of Băile Felix and Băile 1 Mai are within easy reach of Oradea. Băile Felix is the larger of the two with a larger range of places to stay, but Băile 1 Mai is closer and has a good campsite. Treatments include healing mud-baths, either in sapropelic fossil gunge or the local peat bog, and dips in pools fed by the warm and slightly radioactive River Peţea, in which the **thermal lotus** (*Nymphaea lotus var. thermalis*), otherwise found only in the Nile Delta, has survived since the Tertiary Period.

BĂILE FELIX, just 8km southwest of Oradea along the DN76, offers a **thermal pool** (8am–6pm) surrounded by mock-rustic buildings and a park containing a wooden church, and a dozen modern hotels. It's served by tram #4 from Oradea's train station or bus #12 from the Moon Church to the Nufarul terminal, and then bus #14; or by trains (twelve a day) for Felix or Ceica. The best of the spa's **hotels** is the *Internaţional* (☎059/26.10.55, fax 47.00.02; ⑤), followed by the *Lotus* (☎059/13.43.55; ④), but there's also inexpensive accommodation at the *Muncel* (☎059/26.14.60, fax 13.43.73; ②) by the Beiuş turning. One-star hotels include the *Someş* (☎059/26.12.48; ②). Many of Băile Felix's hotels are home to the students of Oradea's Evangelical College, the first to be founded in Eastern Europe, but there is usually plenty of space during the summer holidays. **BĂILE 1 MAI** (Întîi Mai), is a similar but less developed spa, reached by bus #15 from Nufarul, turning off the DN76 just before Băile Felix; there is a **campsite** (with *căsuţe*) here, but no hotels.

The western flanks of the Apuseni mountains

Villages, festivals and hiking in the **Apuseni mountains** are generally described in the chapter on Transylvania (see p.202); what follows is a quick rundown of attractions along the mountains' **western approaches**, starting from Oradea. Most attractions lie close to the DN76, but trains to Beiuş and Vaşcău now take a very roundabout route, following the main Arad line through **SALONTA**, birthplace of the Hungarian poet Arany János (1817–82), who is remembered in a museum (Tues–Sun 10am–4pm) in the seventeenth-century tower on the main square.

Beiuş and around

The small town of **BEIUŞ**, 55km from Oradea, has Baptist, Greek Catholic, Roman Catholic and Orthodox churches cheek-by-jowl in the centre. However, its main attraction is as a jumping-off point for the impressive stalactite **caves of Meziad and Chişcău**. Minibus excursions are organized for around $20 per person by the Iadolina **tourist agency** (Mon–Fri 8am–3.30pm; ☎059/21.16.01, fax 21.25.59) in the *Crişul Negru* **hotel** at Str. Ioan Ciordaş 2 (☎059/21.18.09; ④), just north of the central Piaţa Vulcan. If you're killing time, the folk art and ceramics in the town's **Ethnographic Museum** (Tues–Sun 10am–5pm) are worth seeing.

Buses run twice daily (Mon–Sat) from the bus station, by the train station on the southern edge of town, to the village of **MEZIAD**, 10km northeast of Beiuş. The famous **Meziad cave**, with its huge entrance arch, is a further 3km beyond the village. The cave was first explored in 1859 and in the 1960s a road was built to it, enabling 25,000 visitors a year to come here until the even more spectacular cave at Chişcău (see overleaf) opened in 1980. Guides shepherd parties around the cave, commenting on the stalactites and other features of this warren, whose total length is almost 5km; the hour-long tours take place as soon as there are enough people grouped together, between 9am and 6pm every day.

There are also bus services (Mon–Sat 2 daily) between Beiuş and **CHIŞCĂU** ("Keesh-cow"), where local quarry workers accidentally discovered a cave in 1975. The cave contained dozens of Neolithic ursine skeletons, from which it takes its name, the **Bears' Cave** (*Peştera Urşilor*). Unlike other caves in Romania, this one is atmospherically lit, making the one-hour guided tour (Tues–Sun 10am–6pm) an experience not to be missed. The rock formations of the 488-metre-long upper gallery – shaped like castles, wraiths and beasts – are accompanied by the sound of water crashing into subterranean pools; the lower gallery is closed.

In summer, buses run from Beiuş to **STÎNA DE VALE**, a modest alpine resort at 1100m, where a one-star **hotel**, the *Iadolina* (☎059/21.16.01, fax 21.25.59), **cabins** and a **campsite** serve the hiking fraternity in summer. From here, it's about five hours' walk to the *Padiş Cabana* (see p.207), taking a path marked with red stripes which runs via the Poieni peak, the Cumpănăţelu saddle and the Vărăşoaia clearing. Experienced walkers might prefer the more challenging trail to Meziad (6–8hr, marked by blue triangles; not recommended in winter or bad weather). With many twists and turns around karstic features, this follows the ridge above the Iad valley, surmounting the Piatra Tisei peak before descending to the *Meziad Cabana* below. There's a long **ski season** here, with the resort's three pistes usually open from November to April, and lessons available for beginners.

Into the mountains

Buses run from Beiuş to **PIETROASA**, a picturesque village on the upper reaches of the Crişul Pietros River. Water-powered saw-mills still operate here and the older residents wear traditional Bihor costume. Each year, on a Sunday in August, the villagers troop 8km north up the Aleu valley for the **festival** of *Bulciugul de Valea Aleu*. The forest road, which leads up to the **Padiş plateau** near the "Citadels of Ponor" (see p.207), can be covered on foot or by car – there are no bus services beyond Pietroasa – and the hiking trail to the *Padiş cabana*, marked with blue crosses, follows the road for the most part, with a path diverging south after about 5km (marked by yellow triangles) to the Focul Viu cave, near Ponor.

DR PERTU GROZA

A delegate at the Assembly of Alba Iulia in 1918, **Groza** (1884–1958) was an important politician before and after World War II. With the Communist Party banned since 1924, it was he who in 1933 founded the agrarian party (based in Deva) known as the Ploughmen's Front, which was actually a front for the Communists; as a prosperous lawyer and landowner, Groza was well camouflaged. He was imposed as prime minister of the coalition government in 1945 – after Communist *agents provocateurs* had gunned down Communist demonstrators to discredit the democratic parties then leading the government – and it was his job to organize elections in 1946 to establish the Communists in power. Unfortunately the people voted overwhelmingly against them, so after three days' delay, totally false results were issued, and in mid-1947 the remaining leaders of the democratic parties were arrested.

Groza tried to moderate the nationalism of the Communist Party leader Gheorghiu-Dej; however on December 30, 1947 he visited King Mihai with Gheorghiu-Dej to force the king's abdication. Groza showed the Dowager Queen Marie his pistol, joking that he wouldn't let the king do to him what he'd done to Antonescu. As an internationalist Groza sought reconciliation with Hungary, and his dismissal in 1952, along with Ana Pauker's Hungarian acolyte Vasile Luka, was a harbinger of the regime's crackdown on Romania's Magyar minority.

About 3km south of the turning to Pietroasa is **RIENI**, worth a look for its **wooden church**, just west of the village, by the train halt. Built in 1753, the church is now slightly run-down, with lots of woodpecker damage, but is interesting for its doorway and its spire, typical of this area. However, the best part of the journey to Scarisoara comes once you leave the DN76 and the rail line beyond the small industrial town of Ştei and head eastwards on the DN75. **ŞTEI**, known as Dr Petru Groza under Communism, offers accommodation at the *Bihorul* hotel (☎059/23.06.38; ③) at Str. Cuza Vodă 13, near the train and bus stations. The village of **BĂIŢA**, 10km east along the DN75, has several caves nearby and holds a lively **fair** on the last Sunday in September. On the far side of the 1160-metre Vîrtop Pass lie **ARIEŞENI** and **GÎRDA DE SUS**, southern entry points to Padiş (see p.207).

The branch line from Oradea terminates at **VAŞCĂU**, but the DN76 continues through the mountains for 32km until it joins the Arad–Brad road and rail line at the village of **VÎRFURILE**. En route, just south of Criştioru de Jos, a rough track leaves the main road and leads 30km east to the village of **Avram Iancu** below **Mount Găina**, where the famous Girl Fair occurs every year (see p.206). There are several more festivals in the villages around Vîrfurile, but these are easier to approach from Arad (see p.294).

Arad and around

ARAD is a fine city of impressive buildings dominated by its eighteenth-century **citadel**. It is a major rail junction, so connections are good for both international destinations as well as for routes through Romania, with many of the nearby **villages** in the foothills of the Apuseni mountains reachable via branch lines.

The main street, **Bulevardul Revoluţiei**, is lined with the city's most impressive buildings; of particular note are the **City Hall** (1876) at no. 75, the **State**

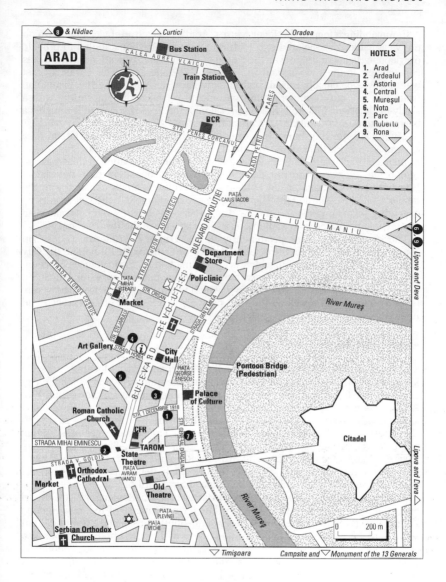

Theatre (1874) at no. 103, closing off its southern end, and the massive turn-of-the-century **Roman Catholic church** nearby, with a domed entrance hall. Behind the theatre is a series of squares including Piaţa Avram Iancu, just off which, at Strada Gh. Lazăr 2, is the **Old Theatre**, built in 1817 and now in need of extensive renovation, where Eminescu and many famous actors worked. The main **market** lies west of Piaţa Avram Iancu next to the Baroque Romanian Orthodox cathedral (1865).

Commanding a loop of the River Mureş, Arad's huge **citadel** faces the town on the west bank. A six-pointed star with ramparts and bastions angled to provide overlapping fields of fire, it was the "state of the art" in fortifications when it was constructed, in the style of Vauban, between 1762 and 1783. The Turks, against whom it was ostensibly raised, had already been pushed out of the Pannonian basin in 1718, but its underground casements provided the Hapsburgs with a ready-made prison following the suppression of the 1848 revolution. It remains a barracks to this day, and can only be admired from a distance.

After 1718 the Hapsburgs had drained the marshy southern Banat, an area known as the Partium, and colonized it with Swabians, Slovaks, Serbs and Romanians, excluding Magyars so as to facilitate the assimilation of this strategic region into their empire. But despite this, Arad's population rose up against Hapsburg rule several times in 1848–49. The revolt was finally crushed with the help of Tsarist Russia, and the Hapsburgs made an example of the ringleaders by executing thirteen generals, mostly Hungarian, outside the fortress walls – an event commemorated by a monument at the entrance to the town's campsite.

The executions feature prominently in the **History Museum** (Tues–Sun 10am–6pm) housed within the eclectic **Palace of Culture** (1913) behind the City Hall on Piaţa George Enescu, which is also home to a Natural Sciences Museum (same times) and to Arad's Philharmonic Orchestra. In the library building at Str. Stejarului 2, you'll find the **Art Gallery**, which features furniture from the seventeenth century on, as well as the odd painting by the likes of Grigorescu and Aman.

Practicalities

The **train and bus stations**, both handling international and local services, lie in the north of the city on Calea Aurel Vlaicu; take tram #1, #2 or #3 for the city centre. Some trains between Timişoara and Cluj halt in the southern suburb of Arad Nou – trams #3 and #5 to the centre.

Arad's **airport** is in the western suburbs, with two flights to and from Bucharest on weekdays and one on Saturday via Timişoara; buses meet flights and drop you off outside the TAROM office (Mon–Fri 7am–8pm, Sat 9am–2pm; ☎057/21.15.67) at the southern end of B-dul Revoluţiei at Str. Unirii 1 and leave from there for the airport an hour before each departure. CFR (Mon–Fri 8am–8pm; ☎057/23.71.11) also has an office at Str. Unirii 1.

Car rental is available through Avis at Banat Air, B-dul Revoluţiei 91 (Mon–Fri 8am–4pm; ☎057/28.21.70, fax 28.01.48). The former **tourist office**, now Agenţia Zarandul, at B-dul Revoluţiei 76 (Mon–Fri 8am–5pm) can sell you a few maps, but you'll probably get as much help from the foyers of the larger hotels. There's also an ACR office at Str. 1 Decembrie 1918 no. 2; their workshop is at Str. Poetului 54 (☎057/27.77.77). Pharmacies have a rota for weekend service, which is advertized in the window of each pharmacy. There are **Bancomats** (ATM machines) at the BCR just to the south of the train station at Str Peneş Corcanul 14 and the Bancpost on Calea Aurel Vlaicu.

Accommodation

Arad has some good **hotels**, with the best of the new private hotels on the outskirts of town. If you're looking for budget accommodation, you'll need to head for the *Subcetate* **campsite**, with cabins, just south of the citadel at Piaţa 13

Martiri 13 (buses #25, #26 and #27; ☎057/28.52.56; ②). In addition there's the small family-owned site, *Camping Voinicul* (☎057/26.66.52), on Strada Digului, south of the road to Lipova (trams #5, #7 and #13 to Strada Voinicilor). There are also two motels within reach of the city – *Sălaşul de la Răscruce* motel (②) is situated 7km west of town along the Nădlac road, the other (☎057/46.00.26; ②) is in **VINGA**, 20km south of Arad on the road to Timişoara.

Arad, B-dul Decebal 9 (☎057/28.08.94, fax 28.06.91). Reasonable hotel situated in the former Securitate headquarters – you can see the cells in the basement if you ask. ⑤.

Ardealul, B-dul Revoluţiei 98 (☎057/28.08.40, fax 28.18.45). The most interesting hotel in Arad, this former coaching inn incorporates a large hall (now a cinema) where Brahms, Liszt, Johann Strauss and Casals all performed. It has rooms with two, three and four beds, but no singles. ③.

Astoria, B-dul Revoluţiei 79 (☎057/28.17.00, fax 28.10.94). A slick place aimed at foreign tourists and businessmen. The main restaurant (open till midnight) is good, especially for breakfast, but the twelfth-floor "panoramic restaurant" is little more than a night bar, open till 4am. ⑨.

Central, Str. Horia 8 (☎057/25.66.36, fax 25.66.29). Privatization seems to be paying off here, with decent service and, at last, friendly staff. ⑧.

Motel Neta, Str. Iuliu Maniu 282 (☎057/26.78.24). At the eastern city limits, a private place with good-sized rooms but without TV or en-suite showers; secure parking is probably its main advantage. ④.

Mureşul, Str. V. Alecsandri 4(☎057/28.05.03 or 28.07.66). On a side street off B-dul Revoluţiei, with single, twin and triple rooms that are rather overpriced considering there are no private bathrooms. Breakfast at the *Astoria* is included in the price. ⑤.

Parc, Str. Gen. Dragalina 25 (☎057/28.08.20, fax 28.07.25). Comfortable and largely indistinguishable from the *Astoria*. The single, twin and triple rooms are much cheaper if you don't want a TV. Hairdressing and massage services available. ④.

Pensione Roua, Str. Şiriei 11 (☎057/25.94.71). Across the DN7 from the *Neta*, and rather more comfortable. ⑤.

Roberto, Str. Scrişoarei 5 (☎057/28.90.14). In a dull but safe area just off the road from the border and two stops north of the train station, with large and comfortable rooms. ④.

Eating and drinking

Of the hotel **restaurants**, the *Astoria*'s has the best reputation, but you'll find plenty of other options on Bulevardul Revoluţiei. Some of the more interesting places are the *Casata Vernieri* at no. 84, which serves good real pizza, Romanian dishes and expensive pastries; the *Coroana* at no. 44, for pizza, spaghetti and pancakes; and the *Internaţional* at no. 34, with good-value set menus. At no. 51 there's the *Libelula*, a pricey but busy 24-hour café-bar. Just south of the station on Calea Aurel Vlaicu is *Big Belly's Fast Food*, serving burgers, pizza, and pancakes until 2am; there are also some decent bars to the south of the station on Calea Vlaicu.

The **markets** in Piaţa Catedralei and Piaţa Mihai Viteazu sell bread, cheese and seasonal fruit and veg, while imported foodstuffs can be found at the Mini-Maxi Plus deli (Mon–Fri 7am–10pm, Sat 8am–6pm) at B-dul Revoluţiei 80 and at an unnamed supermarket at no. 26.

Moving on into Hungary and Germany

Like Oradea, 117km to the north, Arad lies just inside the border from Hungary. The crossing at Nădlac on the E68, 40km away, is now mainly used by trucks; cars and buses are encouraged to use a new, quieter route off the DN7 (E68) to Turnu, 17km from Arad, to Battonya in Hungary. Travelling **by train**, you'll cross over from Curtici, 12km to the north of Arad, to Lőkösháza, just inside Hungary; eight services a day leave Arad for Budapest, four of them during the day. All international **bus services** to Budapest and most of those to Germany run from the train station forecourt. Tickets can usually be bought on the bus, but you may need to buy your ticket to Germany in advance from one of the following companies: AtlasSib Reisen (Str. 30 Decembrie sc. C, ap. 5; ☎057/25.27.27); Touring (☎057/25.44.73); Andronik Reisen (Str. Revoluţiei 104; ☎057/22.21.05); or Armin Meyer (in Fîntinele; ☎057/45.61.75). For services to Istanbul call Oz Murat (☎057/24.70.12).

West of Arad

The area to the west of the Arad–Timişoara route is the quintessence of the Banat, once marshy plains drained after the expulsion of the Turks and settled with a patchwork of diverse ethnic groups, some of whom remain. Perhaps the largest town is **SÎNNICOLAU MARE** (Nagyszentmiklós), where you can visit the birthplace of the Hungarian composer **Béla Bartók** (1881–1945). The town is just as well known for the Nagyszentmiklós Hoard, the largest known find of ancient gold; 23 ten-kilogramme vessels, probably made in the late eighth or ninth century and buried at the time of the Magyar invasion of 896, were found here in 1799 and removed to Vienna, where they still reside in the Imperial collection. The town is about two hours by train from Arad or Timişoara, and you can stay at the *Victoria* hotel, Str. Republicii 10 (☎056/23.12.20; ②).

Germans remember this area for the poet Lenau, born in 1802 in the Schwab village now known as **LENAUHEIM** (Csatád to its Hungarian populace); he died in an asylum near Vienna in 1850. There's a small museum in the centre commemorating his life, but little else. You can get here by diesel railcar from Lovrin, on the Timişoara–Sînnicolau Mare line, a relic of the dense network of branch lines built by the colonizing Hapsburgs in this area.

Northeast of Arad

From Arad, it's possible to reach a number of villages noted for their **festivals**, either by road, or by branch rail lines. The formerly Schwab village of **SÎNTANA**, 7km east of the Arad–Oradea highway, hosts a festival in late May called *Sărbătoarea Iorgovanului*. By train, it's a 35-minute journey by train from Arad towards Oradea or Brad, then a fifteen-minute walk to the centre. Although the festival is nowadays an excuse for dancing, music and dressing up in traditional costumes, it originated as a parish fair, like the one on February 1 at **PÎNCOTA**, 15km east and another thirty minutes by train towards Ineu and Brad. The castle at **INEU**, 20km beyond Pincota, appears almost as abandoned as the orphans it houses; 18km beyond lies the village of **BÎRSA**, noted for its pottery and its fete, *Sărbătoarea Druştelor*, on the first Sunday in April.

Continuing towards Brad, you'll come to **VÎRFURILE** at the junction with the DN76 from Oradea. Just west, a minor road runs 6km north to the small village of **AVRAM IANCU** (not to be confused with the other village of the same name just over the mountains), where people from thirty mountain villages gather for the mountain **festival** *Tăcaşele*, on the second Sunday of June. Besides being an occasion for trading and socializing, this large **fair** provides a chance for musicians to play together, and the *Nedeia* is an excellent time to hear *cetera* (fiddles), *nai* (pan-pipes) and *buciume* or *tulnic* (alpine horns). The connection between new life and stirring lust probably underlies a good many spring festivals, and it is one that the delightfully named **Kiss Fair** (*Tîrgul Sărutului*) at **HĂLMAGIU** acknowledges. Traditionally, the event allows young men and women to cast around for a spouse while their elders discuss the fecundity of livestock and crops. The village lies two stops beyond Vîrfurile on the line to Brad; the festival takes place in March, but the exact date varies from year to year – check with Arad's tourist office. Continuing towards Transylvania, trains now terminate at **BRAD**, but fourteen buses a day plug the 32km gap to Deva; there are also daily services to Cluj, Oradea and Timişoara. A small **History and Ethnography Museum** (Tues–Sun 9am–5pm) stands on Strada Cloşca.

Accommodation is thin on the ground in this area. In **INEU** there's the *Moara cu Noroc* hotel (☎057/51.11.08; ①) at Strada Republicii 21, but the hotel in Sebiş has closed; the *Buteni* motel (☎Buteni 351) is about two kilometres east of the village of the same name, and about 6km south of Sebiş; and there's another motel and campsite at **DEZNA**, 12km northeast of Sebiş. This road continues to **MONEASA**, a spa in the Codru-Moma mountains, where the best hotel is the two-star *Moneasa* (☎057/43.91.51; ③) and homestays can be booked through the dispecerat de cazare (☎057/43.92.13); three buses a day go to Arad, as well as locals to Sebiş station. Near the bus station in **BRAD** the *Hotel Piaţa* (☎054/65.14.43; ①) is one of the cheapest and most basic in the country (there are no showers, hot or cold).

From Arad to Timişoara

In 1934 Patrick Leigh Fermor walked from Arad into Transylvania, staying with Magyar aristocrats whose dusty mansions and diminished bands of retainers spoke eloquently of the decline in their fortunes since the Trianon Treaty. Nowadays you're more likely to make the journey by road or train – but be warned that rapid services stop at few places of interest. Passing through **SÎMBĂTENI**, 17km east, you'll see huge Gypsy palaces with colonnaded and pedimented fronts, built with the proceeds of sanction-busting trade with former Yugoslavia. **GHIOROC**, just off the DN7, 22km from Arad, but reached by trams as well as local trains from the city, is basically a jumping-off point for the Zărand Mountains; there's a chalet 500m away, from which you can make the three-hour **hike** (marked with blue stripes) to the *Căsoia cabana*.

Radna and Lipova

RADNA, 35km from Arad, is the first major stop on the DN7 towards Transylvania. Here, Leigh Fermor played skittles with a Franciscan monk, communicating only in Latin, until "we were both in a muck-sweat when the bell for vespers put an end to play". The great **Abbey of Maria-Radna** is now a hospital, but the echoing church is open, and the corridor to its left, lined with sacred hearts and images of bloody crashes in which Mary supposedly helped make things less bloody, opens onto the abbey's courtyard. The Abbey is an old pilgrimage site, where many churches were built only to be destroyed by the Turks. The Baroque edifice of the current church was begun in 1756, but only consecrated in 1820; behind it, steps lead up to shrines and the "Stations of the Cross" in the oak woods.

Radna station, served by slow trains from both Arad and Timişoara, is actually nearer to **LIPOVA**, a rather more attractive town on the south bank of the Mureş. The town's hotel, the *Pletl* (☎057/56.13.77; ②), stands just north of the lovely fifteenth-century Orthodox **Church of the Annunciation**. Wth its classical facade and a rather eccentric spire, the church is the main sight in town; these features belie the interior, which dates from 1338 and contains the most important **murals** in the Banat – in a pure Byzantine style, though painted in the early fifteenth century. Fragments of old murals are also visible on the exterior of the north wall. The church served as a mosque from 1552 to 1718, and was then rebuilt in 1732 in the Baroque style. Ask at the parish house, immediately north, for access. The town's **museum** (Tues–Sun 9am–5pm), newly renovated, is on the main street at Str. Bălcescu 21, with casts of Trajan's Column over the door.

The spa of Lipova Băi (☎057/56.19.50) lies four kilometres south of Lipova and can be reached by eight buses a day from Radna station; it's really just a large campsite with villas and bungalows for rent. There's also the *Bistro* campsite, west of Radna on the DN7, just beyond a new service station.

The Mureş defile

Just a couple of kilometres beyond Lipova lies the ruined castle of Şoimoş. Built in the thirteenth century, and beefed up by Iancu de Hunedoara and his son Mátyás Corvinus in the fifteenth century, it guards the entry to the **Mureş defile** between the Zărand and Poiana Ruscă mountains. At the narrowest point of the defile is **SĂVÎRSIN**, which hosts fairs on January 30 and November 27; the *Săvîrşin* hotel (☎057/55.71.64 or 55.73.22) offers simple stopovers. Slow trains make half a dozen more halts before Ilia, notably at **ZAM** and **GURASA-DA**. Zam marks the frontier of Transylvania with an eighteenth-century castle, while Gurasada's highlights include a bamboo grove and a late thirteenth-century church, whose frescoes depicting women sinning and then suffering hint at the misogyny of the eighteenth-century artists, Nicolae of Piteşti and Ion of Deva. You might be tempted to linger at the junction of **ILIA** either by the ruined castle of Gábor Bethlen or to see the fairs on July 1 and March 25, but there's little real reason to stop. If you want to break the journey, there's a hotel (①) on the main road to the east of the centre, and in **LESNIC**, 10km east, there are several homestays (contact Dorinel Ilea, no. 174; phone ahead on ☎054/62.31.60). From here, the railway and the DN7 continue eastward towards Deva, Cluj and Sibiu, a route described more or less in reverse order in the Transylvania chapter. Alternatively, you can head southwest across the Poiana Ruscă range towards Lugoj, using the DN68A or the secondary railway (three fast and five slow trains daily).

Timişoara

TIMIŞOARA has long been the most prosperous and advanced of the cities of the Banat, and still boasts Romania's premier technical university. It claims to have been one of the first places in the world to have horse-drawn trams (1869), as well as the first in "Romania" to have a public water supply (the same year), and the first in Europe to have electric streetlighting (1884), but these days it's best known as the

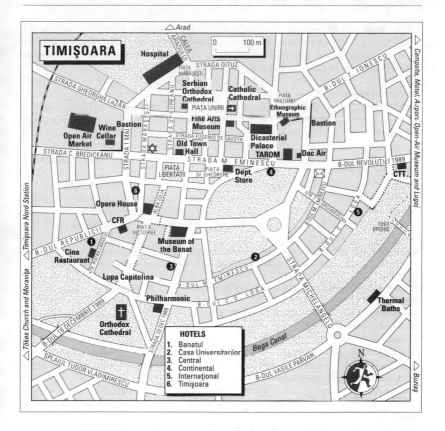

TIMIŞOARA

△Arad

0   100 m

Hospital

STRADA GHEORGHE LAZĂR

PIAŢA MĂRĂŞEŞTI
STRADA OITUZ

Serbian Orthodox Cathedral
Catholic Cathedral
PIAŢA UNIRII

PIAŢA BRATIANU
Ethnographic Museum

B-DUL I. IONESCU

Open Air Market
Wine Cellar
Bastion

STRADA C. BREDICEANU

STRADA EUGENIO DE SAVOYA
Fine Arts Museum
Old Town Hall
Dicasterial Palace
Bastion

STRADA M. EMINESCU
TAROM
Dac Air
B-DUL REVOLUŢIEI 1989
CTT

Timişoara Nord Station

PIAŢA LIBERTĂŢII
PIAŢA SF. GHEORGHE
Dept. Store
❹

Opera House
❻

CFR
PIAŢA VICTORIEI
❺
FOOT-BRIDGE

B-DUL REPUBLICII
Cina Restaurant
❶

Museum of the Banat
❸

Lupa Capitolina
B-DUL M. EMINESCU
❷

Tőkés Church and Moraviţa

Philharmonic
B-DUL C.D. LOGA

Thermal Baths

Orthodox Cathedral

STRADA MICHELANGELO
Bega Canal

B-DUL 16 DECEMBRIE 1989

STRADA 20 DEC 1989

SPLAIUL TUDOR VLADIMIRESCU

B-DUL VASILE PARVAN

HOTELS
1. Banatul
2. Casa Universitarilor
3. Central
4. Continental
5. Internaţional
6. Timişoara

N

△ Buziaş

Campsite, Motel, Airport, Open-Air Museum and Lugoj

birthplace of the 1989 revolution, and still sees itself as the only true guardian of the revolution's spirit, swiftly hijacked by the neo-Communists of Bucharest.

Close to the borders with Serbia and Hungary, and with the only Romanian airport besides Bucharest's operating scheduled international flights, Timişoara is a major hub for travel.

Arrival, information and acommodation

From Timişoara's main **train station**, Timişoara Nord, it's a fifteen-minute walk east to the centre along Bulevardul Republicii (trolley buses #11 and #14). The **bus station** is across the canal from the train station and one block west, at Str. Reşiţa 54, next to the largest of Timişoara's markets.

The **airport**, with international and domestic services, is east of the city. TAROM flights are met by buses which drop passengers outside TAROM's office at B-dul Revoluţei 1989 no. 3; buses also leave from here for the airport an hour before the departure of every flight. Other airlines should also transfer you to the airport; if not you'll have to rely on a taxi or bus #26.

The **tourist office** at Str. Piatra Craiului 3 has been privatized and is now the Cardinal's Exchange exchange bureau (Mon–Fri 8am–4pm, Sat 9am–noon); the staff are friendly and may still have a stock of pre-1989 town plans to give away. There's another branch, at B-dul Republicii 6.

Accommodation

There are plenty of rather soulless state **hotels** in the centre of Timişoara, all badly managed and reliant on the city supply for hot water; when this closes down for maintenance in the summer you get no hot water and no discount. Fortunately there are private hotels on the edge of town which have their own boilers and give better service; these are listed below. There's also a good **campsite** (☎056/20.89.25) with tent space (①) and cabins (②), open all year, on Aleea Pădurea Verde, 4km out in the Green Forest; some cabins have hot water, but as a rule hotels offer better value. The simplest way to get here is by trolley bus #11, which terminates just beyond the 24-hour PECO filling stations on Calea Dorobanţilor (the DN6), opposite the campsite; bus #26, from the airport, also passes by.

Banatul, B-dul Republicii 5 (☎056/19.19.03, fax 19.01.30). Currently excellent value, and convenient for the train station, although there have been some security worries with several thefts. ①.

Casa Universitarilor, B-dul Eminescu 11 (☎056/19.45.07). A quiet tasteful place; reservations needed. ⑤.

Central, Str. Lenau 6 (☎056/19.00.91, fax 19.00.96). A dull modern building, but the staff are welcoming. No singles. ④.

Continental, B-dul Revoluţiei 1989 no. 2 (☎056/13.41.44, fax 13.04.81). The former Securitate hotel, used by business men and tour groups. ⑦.

Eurohotel, Str. Mehadia 5 (☎056/20.12.51, fax 22.14.44). A high-standard hotel in an area of unmade roads; all rooms with double beds. ⑨.

International, B-dul C.D. Loga 44 (☎056/19.01.93, fax 19.01.94). Built as a villa for Ceauşescu, this was converted to an upmarket hotel in 1990; much of it is now used as office space. ⑨.

Monte Carlo, Calea Dorobanţilor 92 (☎056/19.00.76, fax 20.99.10). Comfortable place on the edge of town, used by foreign truckers. ④.

Nord, B-dul Gen. Dragalina 47 (☎056/19.75.04). Opposite the train station, this is a typical station hotel – rather tatty and currently overpriced. ④.

Perla, Str. Oltul 11 (☎056/19.52.02, fax 19.52.03) and Str. Turgheniev 9 (☎056/19.52.03, fax 19.94.27). Both very modern and chic. ⑧.

Timişoara, Str. Mărăşeşti 1 (☎056/19.88.56, fax 19.94.50). A good-quality hotel and reasonably priced. The old facade, overlooking Piaţa Victoriei, hides modern, new wings, a bar, casino and exchange facilities. No singles. ACR; ⑧.

The City

The city now called Timişoara originally grew up around a Magyar fortress called *Castrum Temesiensis* in the marshes between the Timiş and Bega rivers; from the fourteenth century onwards it functioned as the capital of the Banat – hence the old name for the region, the *Banat of Temesvár*. As a stronghold it played a crucial role during the 1514 uprising and Hunyadi's campaigns against the Turks, who in 1552 conquered the town, from where they ruled the surrounding area until 1716. The Hapsburgs who ejected them proved to be relatively benign masters over the next two centuries, the period when *Temeschwar*, as they called it, acquired many of its current features. To drain the marshes they dug the Bega Canal, which now separates the old town, to the north, from the newer quarters.

Piaţa Libertăţii and south to the canal

The city centre is a network of carefully planned streets and squares radiating from **Piaţa Libertăţii**, which boasts a substantial Baroque pile on its north side; originally built as the **Town Hall** in 1734 and now used as the university's music faculty, it stands on the site of the Turkish baths. The square was the setting for the particularly gruesome **execution of György Dózsa** (Gheorghe Doja), leader of the peasant uprising that swept across Hungary and Transylvania in 1514; an iron throne and crown for the "King of the Serfs" were both heated until red-hot, then Dózsa was seated and "crowned" before his body was torn asunder by pincers. Some of his followers were starved, compelled to watch his torture and then force-fed parts of the charred corpse, before themselves being executed, while others were hanged above the gates of Oradea, Alba Iulia and Buda as a deterrent.

To the south of Piaţa Libertăţii lie the Opera House and the **Museum of the Banat** (Tues–Sun 10am–4.30pm), occupying the fourteenth-century castle raised of the Hungarian monarch Charles Robert, extended by Hunyadi in the fifteenth century. Warlords and rebels figure prominently in the large historical section; the museum also has a large natural history section. The **Romanian Orthodox Cathedral** (1936–46), constructed after the signing of the Treaty of Trianon, stands near the river at the southern end of Piaţa Victoriei. The cathedral, whose architectural style blends neo-Byzantine and Moldavian elements, houses a fine collection of eighteenth-century Banat icons in its basement, but it is best known as the site where many of the protesters killed in the 1989 uprising were gunned down; there are memorials and candles to the victims outside.

Piata Unirii

Two blocks north and east of Piaţa Libertăţii is **Piaţa Unirii**, a splendid traffic-free showpiece of Baroque urban design, with a Trinity or plague column raised in 1740, and the former prefecture of 1754. The **Museum of Fine Arts** at no. 1 on the square, displaying work by minor Italian, German and Flemish masters, is overshadowed by the monumental Roman Catholic and Serbian Orthodox cathedrals. The **Roman Catholic Cathedral**, which stands along the eastern side of the square, was built between 1736 and 1754 to the design of the younger Fischer von Erlach and is a fine example of the Viennese Baroque style.

To the east of Piaţa Unirii, at the far end of Strada Eugeniu de Savoya, the huge but dull **Dicasterial Palace**, a complex of 450 rooms built for the Hapsburg bureaucracy of the nineteenth century, is worth a look for its sheer bulk. One block west, on the corner with Strada Augustin Pacha, a plaque marks the house in which Cuza apparently spent his last two nights in Romania on his way to exile – as the Banat was not part of Romania until 1918, he was presumably under the impression that he was already in exile.

In 1868 the municipality purchased the redundant citadel from the Hapsburg government, and demolished all but two sections, loosely known as the **Bastions**, to the west and east of Piaţa Unirii. The western section contains a wine cellar called *Timişoara 700*, in honour of the city's 700th anniversary in 1969, and to the east, the entrance at Str. Hector 2 admits you to a beer and wine bar; just west is the **Ethnographic Museum** at Str. Popa Şapcă 4 (Tues–Sun 9am–5pm), where varied folk costumes and coloured charts illustrate the region's ethnic diversity, but in an anodyne fashion – there's no mention of the 40,000 Serbs exiled to the Dobrogea in 1951, which radically altered the Banat's ethnic make-up. The museum also has an **open-air section** about 5km east of the town, where old Banat homesteads and workshops have been reassembled in the **Pădurea Verde** (Green Forest) – take bus #26 east along the DN6.

Eating, drinking and entertainment

Timişoara has a good selection of **restaurants**, fast-food places, cafés and food markets, especially along Bulevardul 16 Decembrie 1989 and around Piaţa Libertăţii. The *Bulevard*, on the corner of Piaţa Victoriei and Bulevardul Republicii,

LÁSZLO TÖKES AND THE REVLOUTION OF 1989

Despite doubts about the authenticity of the events of **December 1989** in Bucharest (see p.67), Timişoara's popular uprising is still regarded as the catalyst of the revolution. The spark was lit to the southwest of the centre, when crowds gathered to prevent the internal exile of the Reformat pastor **Lászlo Tökes**.

Pastor Lászlo Tökes comes from a distinguished dynasty of Reformed (Calvinist) churchmen. Born in 1952, he followed his father into the priesthood, but was soon in trouble for teaching Hungarian culture and history to his parishioners in Dej; after two years without a job, he was posted to Timişoara in 1986. Here he became increasingly outspoken in his criticism of the government and the church authorities, while stressing that he spoke not only for Hungarians but also for the equally oppressed Romanians. In particular he protested against the systematization programme, denouncing it on Hungarian television in July 1989. This led to an increasingly vicious campaign against him by the local Securitate, who spread slanderous rumours about him, smashed his windows and harassed his family and friends, culminating in the murder in September 1989 of one of the church elders.

Lászlo Papp, Bishop of Oradea, a government placeman, agreed that he should be transferred to the tiny village of Mineu, north of Zalău, but he refused to leave his parish and resisted legal moves to evict him. Being officially deemed unemployed, he lost his ration book, but his parishioners brought him food despite continuing harassment. Eventually he was removed to Mineu on December 17, and stayed there until the 22nd; the fact that it took so long for a police state to shift him, and that the eviction was so clearly signalled and then delayed for a day or two, is cited as evidence that plotters against Ceauşescu were deliberately trying to incite an uprising. After the removal of Tökes, **riots** erupted on the streets of Timişoara, culminating in Ceauşescu's order for the army to open fire on protesters.

The new National Salvation Front tried to co-opt Tökes onto its council, along with other dissidents, but he soon asserted his independence; appropriately, in March 1990 he took over the job of Bishop Papp, who fled to France. Romanian nationalists have always accused him of being an agent of the Hungarian government and of the CIA, and he continues to be a hard-liner, pushing for autonomy for the Magyar-dominated areas.

There is now a **plaque** on the plain apartment building at Str. Timotei Ciprariu 1 (left off B-dul 16 Decembrie 1989), where the eviction took place – Tökes's church was on the first floor and its stained-glass windows can just about be seen from the street.

opposite the Opera House, is one of Timişoara's more established restaurants, serving traditional Romanian dishes, and there's a busy beer garden here, too. **Patisseries** are popular with the locals – the best are *Violeta* at Piaţa Victoriei 6, *Trandafirul* at Str. Eminescu 5 and the *Cofetaria Unirea* on Piaţa Unirii.

The city's main entertainment venue, the **Opera House** on Piaţa Victoriei, also houses two **theatres** that stage plays in German and Hungarian. The **Banat Philharmonic** gives occasional concerts at B-dul C.D. Loga 2, and **dances** often take place in the *Continentul*, *Timişoara* and *Central* hotels' restaurants. If you are around in early May, be sure to check out the *Timişoara Muzicală* **festival**.

Listings

Airline office TAROM has an office at B-dul Revoluţiei 1989 no. 3 (Mon–Fri 7am–6pm, Sat 7am–1pm; ☎056/19.01.50); DacAir is at Str. Popa Sapca 1 (Mon–Fri 9am–8pm, Sat 9am–1pm; ☎056/22.15.55, fax 22.15.56), and Austrian Airlines have a desk in the *Hotel Internaţional* (☎056/19.03.20, airport 19.03.97).

Car rental Avis has a desk in the TAROM office at B-dul Revoluţiei 1989 no. 3 (☎056/20.32.33, airport 20.32.34); Europcar, B-dul Republicii 6 (Mon–Fri 8am–4pm, Sat 9am–noon), Hertz, Str. Hector 31 (☎056/13.33.33).

Car repairs ACR, at the *Timiş* motel, Calea Dorobanţilor 94 (☎056/11.23.45); Autoservice on the Lugoj road or at Intrarea Doinei 2, off Calea Aradului.

Exchange As well as Cardinal's Exchange, at B-dul Republicii 6 (Mon–Fri 8am–6pm, Sat 9am–1pm), there's a Bancpost cash machine in the central post office, and another at BCR on Calea Aradului.

Fuel There are 24-hour PECO fuel stations on Calea Dorobanţilor (DN6) out towards the Green Forest.

Hospital Str. Gheorghe Dima.

International buses Services to Germany are run by: Touring – tickets from BTT at B-dul Revoluţiei 1989 no. 26 (☎056/19.88.88, fax 19.40.40), Priamus, B-dul 16 Decembrie 1989 (☎057/19.29.92, fax 19.02.02) and the Banatul agency in the *Timişoara* hotel. There are also services running to Istanbul (Oz Murat; ☎056/19.78.68) and Athens (Bocheris Express Travel; ☎ & fax 13.62.83). There is a weekly service to Budapest (Sat) and daily services to Békéscaba and Szeged in Hungary.

Newspapers British papers can be read at the British Council library at Str. Paris 1.

Post office B-dul Revoluţiei 1989 no. 2.

Pharmacy There is no 24-hour pharmacy in Timişoara, but *Farmacia no. 2*, on the corner of B-dul 16 Decembrie 1989 and Str. Măciesilor, has long opening hours (Mon–Fri 8am–11pm, Sat & Sun 9am–11pm).

Shopping The Comtimaliment supermarket (Mon–Fri 7am–9pm, Sat 7am–8pm, Sun 7am–11am) is opposite the *Banatul* hotel. A couple of bookshops stock a few English-language editions: Eminescu on the corner of B-dul 16 Decembrie 1989 and Str. Măciesilor and the Libraria Universităţii on the corner of Str. Eminescu and Str. Pacha.

Train tickets CFR's office (Mon–Fri 8am–8pm; ☎056/19.18.89) has the postal address Piaţa Victoriei 2, but they're actually on B-dul Republicii. You can buy domestic and international tickets here.

The Timiş valley

The main rail line and the DN6 follow the River Timiş southwest from Timişoara towards Băile Herculane and Wallachia, passing through the small Hapsburg towns of **Lugoj** and **Caransebeş**. From Caransebeş, there is easy access into the **mountains**, either west into the Semenic massif, or east to Muntele Mic, Ţarcu, Godeanu and, ultimately, to the Retezat range to the east.

Lugoj

LUGOJ, 63km from Timişoara, is a peaceful place to stop over and is notable as the birthplace of several Romanian musicians, including the opera singer Traian Grozăvescu (1895–1927), and the composers Tiberiu Brediceanu (1877–1968) and Ion Vidu (1836–1931). Its non-Romanian sons are less likely to be remembered by plaques, but Béla Ferenc Blasko (1882–1956) immortalized his birthplace's Hungarian name when he became Béla Lugosi, Hollywood's most famous Dracula and its nearest thing yet to a genuinely Transylvanian Count. From the **train station**, the pedestrianized Strada Andrei Mocioni leads east to the River Timiş in five minutes, passing the hotels and shops and ending at the town's **museum** (Tues–Sun 9am–4pm), on the junction with Strada Bălcescu; the museum has displays of weapons, ceramics and local costumes. Continue east across the Iron Bridge to the **Uniate Cathedral** on Piaţa Republicii, which has some fine neo-Byzantine paintings. Nearby, on Piaţa Victoriei, is the Orthodox **Church of the Assumption**, a hall-church built in 1759–66 by the younger Fischer von Erlach, which is one of the most important Baroque buildings of the Banat. The fifteenth-century tower of the church of St Nicholas still stands next door.

There are two **hotels** in the town, both on Strada Mocioni – the *Timiş* at no. 20 (☎056/31.50.45, fax 31.27.40; ②), a block east of the train station, has a good old-style bar and *gradina*, and the *Dacia* at no. 7 (☎056/31.28.40, fax 31.27.40; ②) has a good restaurant. Both have a wide range of rooms, but only the *Dacia* offers singles. In addition there is a new hotel, the *Făget* (⑤), 3km out along the road to Făget and Deva (the DN68A) and served by buses #2 and #7 (peak hours only). It is state-owned, but built for foreign businessmen with plans for a swimming pool, tennis courts and horse-riding.

Caransebeş and the Muntele Mic

CARANSEBEŞ lies beneath the mountains at the confluence of the Timiş and Sebeş rivers, around which Gypsies of the Zlatari tribe used to pan for gold. Having served as the Banat's judicial centre during the Middle Ages and commanding communications through the Eastern Gate, Caransebeş inevitably became a Hapsburg garrison town – hence the outcrops of *belle époque* buildings among the prefabricated structures of the socialist era. There's little to occupy you here today, but you may well be passing through or need to stay the night if you're heading for the mountains.

Most **trains** arrive at the main station well north of town, from where it's a twenty-minute walk into the centre; some local services also stop 2km further south at the Caransebeş halt, west of the centre. The **bus terminal** is on Splaiul Sebeşului, south of the Sebeş river. For the town centre, cross the bridge and turn right at the spiky neo-Gothic synagogue. The bus from the main train station runs along Strada Bălcescu (DN6), and terminates just before the bridge over the Sebeş river.

The Schwabs' **Roman Catholic church** is on the pedestrianized Strada Mihai Viteazul; the Orthodox diocese wishes to build its cathedral in front of this, but unfortunately the (not particularly impressive) foundations of what is claimed to be a Franciscan monastery are in the way. Beyond is the leafy **Piaţa Dragolina**, where the statues of two lions flank a memorial to local-born General Ion Dragolina, who died at the head of his troops in the Jiu Valley in 1916. On the far side of the square is the **County Museum of Ethnography and the Border Regiment**, housed in the eighteenth-century barracks; there are ambitious plans for the museum, but at the moment you can only see a temporary display in four rooms.

The town's only **hotel** is the *Tibiscum*, on Strada Baba Novac, midway between the train station and the centre (☎055/51.12.55; ④); with a TV and fridge in every room, a restaurant, bar and disco, and hot water available morning and evenings, it's a better than average hotel for such a small town. To reach it, take the steps to the west from the south end of the rail bridge. A cheaper alternative is one of the five rooms at the *Twerasco* bar (☎055/51.29.65; ②) next to the post office at Strada Primăriei 6.

Borlova and the Muntele Mic

BORLOVA, 13km from Caransebeş, is noted for its embroideries and peasant weddings, and holds a "Measurement of the Milk" **festival**, around April 23 every year, but most visitors pass straight through en route to the **Muntele Mic** (Little Mountain) resort. You can hitch a ride to the resort on the staff bus or make the ten-kilometre walk from Borlova, followed by a chair-lift ride. Thanks to the heavy snowfalls in the area, you can **ski** here from late autumn until late spring; there are also good **hiking** trails for the summer months. The resort's one **hotel** is the *Sebeş* (☎055/51.23.35, fax 51.17.69; ③), with a selection of less expensive villas and chalets. You can walk north to the Muntele Mic itself in an hour or south to the weather station (2190m) atop Mount Ţarcu in three hours. Outside the winter months, suitably equipped hikers can take trails from here heading eastwards towards Lake Gura Apei and the Retezat mountains in four hours (following red stripes), or southwards to Godeanu and the Cerna valley in six hours (red dots) – be prepared for an overnight expedition (a tent is essential). From Muntele Mic, there's also a route (following blue stripes) to Poiana Mărului, to the east, from where three buses a day head back to Caransebeş via Oţelu Roşu.

The Cerna valley

Most trains from Caransebeş run north to Timişoara, or south to Orşova and Turnu Severin on the Danube (see p.114), but there are also branch services west to Reşiţa and east to Bouţari. Continuing south by road or rail, you pass through the **Poarta Orientalis** or Eastern Gate of Transylvania before reaching Băile Herculane and its spa at the bottom of the **Cerna valley**. The middle and upper reaches of the valley itself are still much as Patrick Leigh Fermor described them when he travelled through the region in the 1930s: "a wilderness of green moss and grey creepers with ivy-clad water-mills rotting along the banks and streams tumbling through the shadows [illuminated by] shafts of lemon-coloured light." Among the butterflies and birds that proliferate here you might see rollers, which the Romanians call *Dumbrăveancă*, "one who loves oak-woods".

Băile Herculane and around

BĂILE HERCULANE gets its name from the Roman legend that Hercules cured the wounds inflicted by the Hydra by bathing here, and the nine springs with their varied mineral content and temperature (38–60°C) are used to treat a wide range of disorders. During the nineteenth century, royal patronage made Herkulesbad one of Europe's most fashionable watering-holes. The **museum**, in the casino building behind the bandstand, displays photographs and other mementoes of this period. Today, several ugly modern hotels have sprung up among the elegant buildings, but the resort remains busy and surprisingly affordable.

Other than wallowing in the renowned **Apollo Baths**, Băile Herculane's chief attraction is its surroundings – statuesque limestone peaks clothed in lush vegetation and riddled with caves. You can bath in the **Seven Hot Springs** (*Şapte Izvoare Calde*) about 35 minutes' walk upstream, just beyond the Cerna rapids, while another two hours' hiking will bring you to the white **Gisella's Cross** from where there are magnificent views. From here, an unmarked path leads you in thirty minutes to a forest of black pines, dotted with boulders, and a spectacular 300-metre precipice. Other paths provide access to the vaporous **Steam Cave** on Ciorci hill (1hr 30min), the **Outlaws' Cave** where Stone Age tribes once sheltered (30min), and the **Mount Domogled nature reserve** which has trees and flowers of Mediterranean origin and more than 1300 varieties of butterfly (4hr).

It's roughly 40km from Băile Herculane to the watershed of the Cerna River, on a forestry road that continues to Cîmpuşel and the Jiu valley. A path marked with red stripes runs parallel along the ridge to the north to Piatra lui Iorgovan in the **Retezat mountains** – allow one or two days; see p.174.

Practicalities

Băile Herculane's lovely turn-of-the-century **train station** is 5km from the spa – bus #1 runs every half-hour to the central Piaţa Hercules. If you're arriving by **bus**, you'll be dropped at a dusty yard over a kilometre short of the centre. Eleven hotels offer a good range of **accommodation** both in the centre and in the modern satellite spa of **PECINIŞCA**, 2km towards the train station. In the old spa area, the best value hotels are the *Apollo* (☎055/56.06.88; ②) and the *Decebal* (☎055/56.04.54; ②) on Piaţa Hercules, and the *Cerna* (☎055/56.04.36; ②), by the church and casino; all are fairly basic, with hot water available for limited periods each day. The private *Belvedere* (☎055/56.18.86; ④) on Strada N. Stoica Haţeg is one of the more upmarket hotels, but excellent value too; all rooms have private bathrooms, TV and nonstop hot water. Just below the bus station is a group of big modern hotels, such as the *Herculane* and *Domogled* (both ☎055/56.08.19, fax 56.08.18; ②). There are four **campsites**: the *Plopii Fara Sat* at the train station, the *Pecinişca* and *Flora* along the road into town, and one at the Seven Hot Springs; all are very crowded in season.

Reşiţa and the Semenic range

People have been beating iron into shape around REŞIŢA, 40km from Caransebeş, since Dacian times. The foundry can trace its history back to 1771 and steam locomotives have been manufactured here since 1872; if you're entering town on the Timişoara road, Bulevardul Revoluţiei din Decembrie, you'll pass a rusting **collection of locomotives** outside the Reşiţa Nouă train halt. The iron works, and the ropeway across town, are still active, but the town has a depressed feeling, with many beggars on the streets. The county **History Museum** has moved to a new building at Str. Republicii 10, but is unable to open fully due to lack of funds, while the bus service to Văliug, starting point for excursions into the Semenic mountains, has ceased to operate. A private bus may run on summer weekends, but otherwise you'll have to hitch or take a taxi. The town's **bus station** is on Strada Traian Lalescu – to reach it head east from Piaţa 1 Decembrie, under the ropeway, over the footbridge and past the theatre and post office.

Local steelworkers take pride of place in the **Spring Parade** (*Alaiul Primăverii*), normally held during the first week in April; the town also hosts the **Bîrzava Song Festival** some time in August. At other times you may as well continue straight on to the mountains. If you do need a **hotel**, the *Semenic*, a standard high-rise, stands on the central Piaţa 1 Decembrie 1918 (☎055/41.34.80; ACR; ⑤), and the *Bistra*, currently being refurbished to three-star standard, is at Str. N. Bălcescu 5 (☎055/21.38.71; ⑤) – head north on B-dul Revoluţiei din Decembrie, parallel to the river, and it's to the left. However, if you're considering attending either of the festivals, it's cheaper to stay outside town at Semenic or Crivaia (see below) or at one of the three **cabanas**, the *Constructorul, Splendid* or *Turist*, 13km east on Lake Secu. If you're planning to do some hiking, Reşiţa is the last chance to stock up on food. There's a good **market** just east of the Sud train station, and the Comtimalimenta **supermarket** (Mon–Fri 7am–8.30pm, Sat 7am–6pm & Sun 7am–noon). The ACR, CFR and TAROM offices are all on Piaţa 1 Decembrie.

Into the Semenic mountains

From Văliug, 12km southeast of Reşiţa, one road leads 3km south to **CRIVAIA**, a good base for hikes, where there are **bungalows** and a **campsite**, while another leads up to **SEMENIC**, also accessible by chair lift from Văliug, which has chalet-style **accommodation** and two hotels, the *Central* (☎ & fax 055/43.36.24; ③) and *Gozna* (☎055/43.30.39; ③). **Skiing** is possible here from November to April – pistes are graded from "very easy" to "difficult".

Although the massif is lower and less rugged than others in the Carpathians, it still offers the chance of good **hiking**. One of the most popular treks is west from Semenic through Crivaia to the Comarnic Cave and on to the **Caraşului Gorges** (10–11 hours; blue stripe markings). Situated just before the eastern entrance to the gorges, the **Comarnic Cave** is the Banat's largest grotto, with a spectacular array of rock "veils" and calcite crystals distributed around its four hundred metres of galleries on two levels (guided tours daily until 3pm). The gorges themselves are extremely wild and muddy and harbour several more caves, of which Popovăţ (also open for tours) to the south is the most impressive. If you don't fancy hiking here from Semenic or Crivaia, the gorges can also be entered near **CARAŞOVA**, a village 16km south of Reşiţa on the main road. However, they may be impassable in part thanks to occasional flooding, in which case you should follow the blue stripes onwards from Comarnic to the hamlet of **PROLAZ**, and pick up the route through the gorges there.

Oraviţa and on to Moldova Nouă

From Reşiţa, the DN58 continues south to the coal-mining towns of Anina and Steierdorf, from where the DN57B leads east to Băile Herculane and west to

ORAVIŢA, the historic centre of the former Caras county, close by the border with Serbia. Oraviţa is a curiously long, thin town, stretching east from the bus and train stations. It is home to Romania's oldest **theatre**, at Str. Eminescu 18, between the end of the one-way system and the police station – some 3km east from the train station. Built between 1789 and 1817, the theatre no longer stages plays, but houses the town **museum** (Mon–Fri 8am–5pm), commemorating the German community that brought the Industrial Revolution to this corner of the Austro-Hungarian Empire, as well as the surprising number of local writers, as well as Eminescu who came here as prompter with a theatre company in 1868. There's a **hotel** (③) by the filling station on the main road north out of town and a **chalet** another couple of kilometres east.

Oraviţa is virtually the end of the rail line's penetration into the *Banat Romanesc*, the southwesternmost corner of Romania. Buses continue to Moldova Nouă (see p.117), including at least five a day owned by private companies, whose services are cheaper and slightly more comfortable than the state-run ones.

travel details

Trains

Arad to: Baia Mare (1 daily; 5hr 45min); Brad (4 daily; 3hr 30min–5hr); Braşov (5 daily; 6hr–7hr 45min); Bucharest (6 daily; 8hr 30min–10hr 15min); Deva (9 daily; 1hr 45min–3hr 15min); Hălmagiu (3 daily; 4hr); Oradea (5 daily; 2hr–3hr); Satu Mare (1 daily; 4hr 30min); Sebiş (6 daily; 1hr 45min–2hr 30min); Sibiu (3 daily; 4hr 15min–7hr); Sighişoara (3 daily; 4hr 15min); Sîntana (16 daily; 20–40min); Timişoara (10 daily; 50min–1hr 15min); Vîrfurile (3 daily; 3hr 45min).

Caransebeş to: Băile Herculane (11 daily; 1hr 15min–1hr 45min); Bucharest (8 daily; 6hr–9hr 30min); Drobeta–Turnu Severin (8 daily; 2hr–3hr); Lugoj (12 daily; 30min–1hr); Orşova (11 daily; 1hr 30min–2hr 15min); Reşiţa (8 daily; 50min–1hr 30min); Timişoara (12 daily; 1hr 15min–2hr 30min).

Oradea to: Arad (5 daily; 1hr 45min–2hr 45min); Baia Mare (1 daily; 3hr 30min); Beiuş (2 daily; 4hr 45min); Bucharest (2 daily; 11hr–11hr 15min); Ciucea (9 daily; 1hr 15min–2hr 45min); Cluj (8 daily; 2hr 30min–4hr 30min); Ştei (2 daily; 5hr); Iaşi (1 daily; 11hr 45min); Satu Mare (5 daily; 1hr 45min–3hr 15min); Suceava (1 daily; 9hr 30min); Timişoara (5 daily; 3hr–4hr 15min); Tîrgu Mureş (1 daily; 4hr 45min).

Timişoara to: Bucharest (8 daily; 7hr–14hr 30min); Buziaş (7 daily; 45min–1hr); Caransebeş (12 daily; 1hr 15min–2hr 45min); Lugoj (15 daily; 45min–1hr 30min); Oraviţa (2 daily; 2hr 45min–3hr 45min); Reşiţa (4 daily; 2hr–2hr 45min); Sînnicolau Mare (4 daily; 2hr).

Buses

Arad to: Abrud (1-2 daily); Cîmpeni (2 daily); Moneasa (3 daily); Satu Mare (2 daily); Ştei (Mon-Fri 1 daily); Timişoara (1 daily).

Băile Herculane to: Drobeta-Turnu Severin (Mon–Fri 3 daily); Orşova (Mon–Fri 1 daily).

Caransebeş to: Borlova (7 daily).

Oraviţa to: Băile Hecrculane (2 daily); Caransebeş (1 daily); Moldova Nouă (7 daily); Reşiţa (up to 4 daily); Timişoara (7 daily).

Oradea to: Alba Iulia (2 daily); Arieşeni (4 daily); Baia Mare (1 daily); Deva (Mon–Sat 2 daily); Sighet (1 daily);Tîrgu Lăpuş (1 daily).

Reşiţa to: Deva (Mon–Sat 1 daily); Lugoj (up to 3 daily); Moldova Noua (4 daily); Timişoara (1 daily); Tîrgu Jiu (1 daily).

Timişoara to: Abrud (1 daily); Anina (1 daily); Brad (2 daily); Cîmpeni (1 daily); Lipova (2 daily); Moldova Noua (3 daily); Moneasa (1 daily); Reşiţa (1 daily); Tîrgu Jiu (1 daily).

Planes

Arad to: Bucharest (1 daily; 1hr).

Caransebeş to: Bucharest (1 daily; 50min).

Oradea to: Bucharest (3 daily; 1hr).

Timişoara to: Bucharest (3 daily; 1hr)

International trains

Arad to: Berlin (1 daily; 21hr); Budapest (4 daily; 4hr 30min–5hr 15min); Munich (1 daily; 14hr); Prague (2 daily; 15hr); Vienna (2 daily; 9hr–10hr); Warsaw (1 daily; 19hr).

Curtici: as for Arad, plus a local service to Békéscsaba, Hungary (2 daily; 1hr).

Oradea to: Budapest (4 daily; 5hr 30min).

Timişoara to: Belgrade (1 daily; 4hr 45min); Budapest (1 daily; 5hr 15min).

International buses

Arad to: Békéscaba and Szeged, Hungary (Tues–Sat 1 daily); Budapest (up to 6 daily); Istanbul (1 daily).

Oradea to: Budapest (up to 6 daily); Kecskemét, Hungary (1 daily).

Timişoara to: Békéscaba, Hungary (1 daily); Belgrade, Serbia (3 daily); Budapest (1 Sat only); Istanbul (1 daily); Novi Sad, Serbia (1 daily); Szeged, Hungary (1 daily).

International planes

Arad to: Verona and Rome (BusinessJet; Mon, Wed & Fri).

Timişoara to: Budapest (Mon–Fri 2 daily); Chicago (Fri); Düsseldorf (Mon & Sat, and Jaro; Sat); Frankfurt (Mon & Fri); Munich (Mon, Wed & Fri); New York (Wed); Rome (Mon, Tues & Sat); Venice (Mon, Wed & Fri); Verona (Mon, Wed & Fri); Vienna (Austrian Airlines; Sun–Fri).

CHAPTER SEVEN

THE DELTA AND THE COAST

I n theory, the **Danube Delta** and Romania's **Black Sea coast** have a lot going for them. The Delta, a vast area of reeds and shifting land, provides a unique habitat for over three hundred species of bird (many of them found nowhere else in Europe), as well as a host of other creatures. The coast is blessed with abundant sunshine, warm water and sandy beaches, and when you've had enough of that, there are numerous Roman remains plus the occasional mosque to visit.

Don't come expecting an effortless trip to an unspoilt paradise, however. Although the **Delta wildlife** is as rich as you could wish, it's mostly found away from the main arms (*braţi*) of the river – in particular, the one flowing from the Delta capital of **Tulcea** down to **Crişan**, where most tour groups are taken. To really appreciate the diversity of birdlife, you'll have to pay one of the fishermen to row you into the backwaters and lakes; negotiations can be time-consuming, so if you're seriously bent on bird-watching, be prepared to spend at least a week here. Real enthusiasts should bring their own canoes.

Much of the coast has been ravaged by industry or tourism, or both, and it can get so overcrowded between June and September that the only way to avoid hassles over transport, rooms and meals is to book a package holiday from home to **Mamaia**, **Neptun**, **Venus** or one of the other resorts (see Basics). There's a more relaxed atmosphere about the coastal city of **Constanţa**, though, which

---

ACCOMMODATION PRICES

Hotels listed in this guide have been price-graded according to the scale below. Prices given are those charged for the cheapest **double room** available, which in the less expensive places usually comes without private bath or shower and without breakfast. Price codes are expressed in US dollars as the Romanian leu is not a stable currency, but you will generally pay for your room in lei.

Note that some hotels are currently closed for modernization, and others, now open, will no doubt follow in the near future. This is bound to result in higher rates when they reopen, so the prices quoted should be taken only as a guideline.

① $10 and under	④ $20–25	⑦ $40–50
② $10–15	⑤ $25–30	⑧ $50–65
③ $15–20	⑥ $30–40	⑨ $65 and over

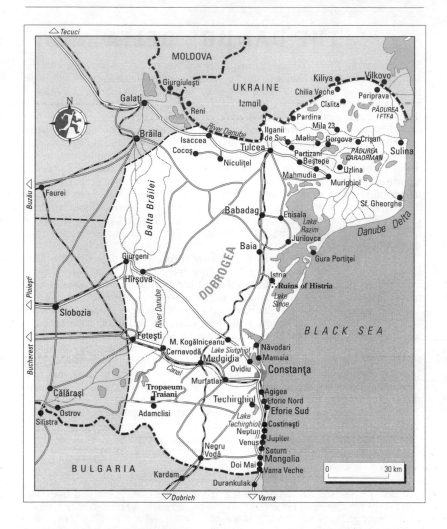

boasts lots of sights in the old quarter around the seaport, originally established by the ancient Greeks.

Transport to both the Delta and the coast is fairly simple. Both Constanţa and Tulcea are linked by **plane** to Bucharest, and there may also be charter flights in summer from European cities (including London) to Constanţa. **Train** services between Bucharest and Constanţa are fairly fast and frequent, but very overcrowded in season, when many services are extended to Mangalia, also served by additional trains from regional centres. Book well in advance (the return journey, too, if possible), changing at Medgidia for the Delta if there's no direct service to Babadag or Tulcea. Driving will be eventually be made easier by a new toll motorway between Bucharest and Constanţa, but little of it is likely to be open before the year 2000.

THE DANUBE DELTA

Every year the River Danube dumps forty million tonnes of alluvium into the **Danube Delta** (Delta Dunării), the youngest, least stable landscape in Europe. Near the regional capital, **Tulcea**, the river splits into three branches (named after their respective ports, Chilia, Sulina and Sfîntu Gheorghe), dividing the delta into large areas of reeds and marsh, over 4000 square kilometres in all, half of which are flooded in spring and autumn. Only five percent remains permanently above the water: these are the **grinduri** – tongues of accumulated silt supporting oak trees, willows and poplars twined round with climbing plants – as distinct from the **plaur**, or floating reed islands, which amount to some 700 square kilometres. Over time the distinction is a fine one, since flooding continually splits, merges and often destroys these patches of land, making any detailed map of the delta outdated almost as soon as it's drawn. Although fishing communities have lived here for centuries, it's an inhospitable environment for humans: a Siberian wind howls all winter long, while in summer the area is inundated with mosquitoes.

Yet it's a paradise for wildlife, particularly **birds**, which pass through from China, India and Mongolia during the spring and autumn migrations, or come from Siberia to winter here or from Africa to breed in summer. Besides herons, glossy ibises, cormorants, golden eagles, avocets, shelduck and other Mediterranean breeds, the Delta is visited by reed buntings, white-tailed eagles and various European songbirds; whooper swans, plovers, arctic grebes, cranes and half-snipes from Siberia; saker falcons from Mongolia; egrets, mute swans, cormorants and mandarin ducks from China; and its remoter lakes support Europe's largest pelican colonies. The best time to see birds is from May to early June, the latter being the wettest month of the year. In addition to birds, the Delta is home to otters, mink, muskrat, foxes, boars, wolves, polecats and other **animals**, which live on the abundant small game and fish.

The Delta is by no means an untouched environment, however: in the mid-1980s it was on the brink of ecological disaster, when intensive use of fertilizers a long way upstream increased the levels of nitrogen and phosphates in the Delta,

---

THE LIPOVANI

Formerly dispersed all over the Delta, the **Lipovani**, descendants of the Old Believers who left Russia in around 1772 to avoid religious persecution, are now only found at Periprava, Mila 23, Mahmudia, Letea, and at two villages on Lake Razim, Jurilovca and Sarichioi. Until early this century they were easy to recognize by their on-shore garb of tall hats and black cloaks; now the costume has been abandoned they can still be identified by their blond hair, beards and blue eyes.

Adapting to their watery environment, the Lipovani became skilled **fishermen** and gardeners, speaking a Russian dialect among themselves but equally fluent in Romanian. Since you're likely to rely on Lipovani boatmen to guide you through the confusing side channels (*gîrla*), be prepared for their fundamentalist abhorrence of the "Devil's weed", tobacco. However, any contact with them will like as not involve the partaking of **vodka**, their consumption of which is legendary. Normally, a single glass circulates incessantly, each drinker knocking back the contents before replenishing it and passing it on.

DELTA TOURS

The Delta is rightly seen as one of the greatest assets of Romania's tourist industry, and there is a widespread awareness of the need to protect it. The entire area was declared a **Biosphere Reserve** in 1990, with over 500 square kilometres strictly protected, and in 1991 it was named a World Heritage Site. Private tour companies (notably ATBAD in Tulcea) are now moving into the area, mostly offering **packages** in floating hotels in the heart of the Delta.

Most **tours** stick to the main axes, from which most of the wildlife has been scared off. Litoral's two-day trip from Constanţa – including a visit to Tulcea, a hydrofoil ride to Maliuc, lodgings at the hotel there, and a short exploration of the backwaters by smaller boat – is reasonable value at $88. However, beware that some so-called Delta tours, such as those organized by ONT from Bucharest, include very little time actually on the water. BTT (see below) operates its own base at Lacul Roşu, south of Sulina, reached by boat from its pontoon by Tulcea's Art Museum (June–Oct every 5 days; $25 return); huts cost $16 a night for two.

If you want to travel **independently** around the Delta, you can make all the necessary arrangements in Tulcea. Eurodelta offers a day-trip taking the backwaters to Crişan and returning by the main arm for $25, as well as overnight trips for $50 plus accommodation; Navitur does a similar day-trip for $13-plus, depending on numbers. Note that all the offices listed below are open similar hours, roughly Monday to Friday from 8am to 4pm.

ATBAD, Str. Babadag 11, Tulcea (☎040/51.44.14, fax 51.76.25).

BTT, Strada Kogălniceanu, almost opposite the Danube Delta museum, Tulcea (Mon–Fri 8am–4pm; ☎040/51.24.96).

Danubius, B-dul Ferdinand 36, Constanţa (☎041/61.58.36, fax 61.80.10), and in the *Hotel Europolis*, Tulcea (☎ & fax 040/51.78.36).

Eurodelta, Str. Isaccei 1 (☎040/51.66.04, fax 51.50.32).

Litoral, *Hotel Palace*, Str. R. Opreanu 5, Constanţa (☎041/61.77.84), and *Hotel Bucureşti*, Mamaia (☎041/83.11.52, fax 83.12.76).

Navitur, Str. Isaccei 4, Tulcea (☎040/51.88.94, fax 51.89.53).

causing a significant growth in the algal population, which in turn led to eutrophication (water deoxygenation) and a drop in fish stocks. Fish catches, previously over 10,000 tonnes a year, dropped dramatically as a result. Since then the situation has been gradually improving, and the annual catch is now up to 6000 tonnes. Bream, zander and roach don't seem to be affected by the green algal water, although stocks of sturgeon, the most lucrative fish of all, have largely vanished.

Tulcea

TULCEA has been tagged the "Threshold of the Delta" ever since ancient Greek traders established a **port** here – it was recorded by Herodotus, and later by Ovid, who used the town's Roman name, Aegyssus. Its maritime significance was slight until the closing stages of the period of Ottoman domination (1420–1878), when other powers suddenly perceived it as commercially and strategically

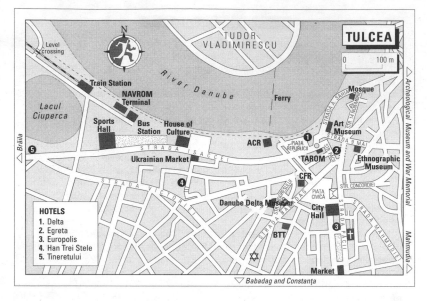

important. Tulcea then entered a cycle of rapid development and calamitous slumps. Nowadays the outskirts of the town are heavily industrialized and the port is too shallow for large modern freighters, but it's still the chief access point for passenger vessels entering the Delta – though without the decent restaurants and transport links you might expect. Tulcea is busiest in August and December, when its two annual **festivals** take place: the International Folk Festival of the Danubian Countries and a winter carnival.

The Town

The town is clustered around the south (right) bank of a bend in the Danube. To the northeast of **Piaţa Republicii**, on the corner of Strada Sahia and Strada 9 Mai, is the **Art Museum** (Tues–Sun 9am–5pm), built by Ismail Pasha in 1870; its fine collection of paintings includes Impressionistic female nudes by Pallady, Iosif Iser's and Theodor Aman's fanciful "Turkish" scenes, and Delta landscapes by Sirbu and Stavrov, as well as contemporary sculpture. You'll also see Igolesco's *Balchik*, painted at a time when Romania ruled the southern Dobrogea (regained by Bulgaria in 1940). The village of Balchik (Balčik) was a thriving artistic community, so loved by Queen Marie that, although she had to be buried with her husband in Curtea de Argeş, she asked for her heart to be buried in Balchik. When the southern Dobrogea was handed over to Bulgaria, the queen's heart was brought back to Romania in a casket that now rests in the National History Museum in Bucharest.

Strada 14 Noiembrie heads north from Piaţa Republicii to the nineteenth-century **Azizie Mosque**, a very ordinary-looking building, resembling a school with a minaret. Having been fairly inconspicuous under Communism, the local Turkish women are now much more visible, dressed in bright colours and baggy trousers. Beyond the mosque, Strada Gloriei runs through a pretty area of small white houses with gardens, ending at the **Parcul Monumentului Independenţei**, where you'll find the town's **Roman remains**, an **obelisk** to the dead of the 1877–78 war, and the **Archeological Museum** (Tues–Sun 10am–5pm), which is noted for its collection of Roman, Greek, Byzantine and medieval coins.

Back in the centre, the **Ethnographic Museum** at Str. 9 Mai 2 (Tues–Sun 10am–4pm) has displays on the varied groups inhabiting the Delta and the Tulcea region. On the far side of the systematized Piaţa Civică is the **Museum of the Danube Delta**, Str. Progresului 32 (Tues–Sun 9am–5pm); equipped with multilingual guides and captions, it focuses on the Delta as an ecosystem, and houses an excellent **aquarium** of fish from the region. Up the hill at Str. Babadag 7, the **synagogue** is barely in use these days, with a congregation of just half a dozen old folk .

Practicalities

Tulcea's **train station** is on the western edge of town, and it's an easy walk from there along the waterfront to Piaţa Republicii, passing the **bus station** and NAVROM **ferry terminal** and office on the way. Tulcea is linked to Bucharest and Constanţa by train, but it's a slow journey down to the junction at Medgidia. Unless you're heading for Constanţa, it's better to use the hydrofoil link with Galaţi to the northwest, where you can pick up express train services (see p.223). Buses leave for Focşani at 9.45am and for Brăila at 1.30pm, but it's a slow haul, with a ferry crossing over the Danube.

There's no official tourist office but the main hotels may be able to help with tourist **information**. The **Biosphere Reserve Administration** (ARBDD), currently at Str. Tabarei 32 (☎040/55.09.50), is due to move to a new visitor centre just east of the bus station. The **Danube Delta Research Institute** has a more specialized information centre at Str. Babadag 165 (☎040/52.45.50). Most **travel agencies** in town are only concerned with Delta trips, but those in the NAVROM ticket hall also sell tickets for **boats to Izmail**, in the Ukraine (about $10 for a day-trip, but you need to get a Ukrainian visa in advance). You'll find **TAROM** (Mon–Fri 11am–5pm; ☎040/51.12.27) at Str. Isaccei 1, opposite the *Delta* hotel.

Accommodation in Tulcea is fairly limited. There are just three main hotels: the *Delta* at Str. Isaccei 2 (☎040/51.47.20 or 51.62.60; ⑧); the *Egreta* at Str. Păcii 1 (☎040/51.71.03, fax 51.71.05; ⑦); and the *Europolis* (formerly the *Tulcea*) at Str. Păcii 20 (☎040/51.24.43, fax 51.66.49; ⑤) – all relatively pricey and characterless. Budget options include the *Han Trei Stele* at Str. Carpaţi 16, behind the Ukrainian market (☎040/51.67.64; ①), which is small and pleasantly chaotic, with nonstop hot water; and the *Tineretului*, upstairs at Str. Isaccei 24 in Ciuperci Park (☎040/55.07.30; ②). This is the polluted end of town, thanks to the smoke belching from the steel and aluminium plants just to the west. A more attractive choice is a night on a *ponton dormitor* or **floating hotel** moored alongside the promenade, such as the one belonging to Navitur (☎040/51.88.94, fax 51.89.53; ①), whose offices are opposite the *Delta* hotel at Str. Isaccei 4. Facilities are basic but the atmosphere compensates.

The main **market**, good for buying snacks and provisions for trips into the Delta, is just south of the centre down Strada Păcii, beyond St George's, one of the town's several barn-like churches built under Turkish occupation. The Ukrainian market, just south of Strada Isaccei (halfway to the station), is largely a venue for trading in imported goods, although you'll find some food here, too.

Upstream from Tulcea

Upstream of Tulcea the Danube is up to a kilometre wide, with a **floodplain** of almost 100 square kilometres that is still unaffected by dykes and is inundated every spring as nature intended. The area near Rotundu, 25km west of Tulcea, is especially rich in plankton and fish, and although it's a closed reserve there are plenty of birds, such as swans, little bittern and white-tailed eagles (Romania's largest raptor) to be seen in the neighbourhood. Three kilometres south of the

---

DELTA PRACTICALITIES

To enter the **Danube Delta Biosphere Reserve (RBDD)** you need a **permit**, which gains you access to everywhere except the strictly protected reserves. If you're taking a tour this will be handled by the tour company; independent travellers can get permits from the reserve administration in Tulcea for a basic price of less than a dollar, with supplementary charges for boating and fishing. Operators of organized groups have to pay about twenty times as much, and are limited to seven fixed routes. In addition to the three main arms (*brați*) of the Danube, these are from: Tulcea via the **Canal Mila 35** and Gîrla Şontea to the villages of Pardina and Mila 23, and via the **Canal Litcov** to Crişan (both parallel to the Sulina arm); from Mila 23 to Lacul Trei Iezere and Chilia Veche; from Mila 23 to Letea via the **Canal Magearu**; from Crişan southeast to Caraorman, Lacul Roşu and Sulina; from the Sfîntu Gheorghe arm to Lacul Razim via the **Canal Dranov**; and from Jurilovca to Gura Portiței. If you're planning to explore beyond these main routes, take a compass and a detailed **map**, such as the green CTT map (available in Tulcea),which has English text and shows the strictly protected zones.

Camping is prohibited except in designated areas in the villages. DeltaRom, which owns the **hotels** in Maliuc and Sulina, also owns the *Delta* hotel in Tulcea, so it's a good idea to ask here about reservations. Before you set off, buy **essential supplies** like bread, canned food, fruit and cheese in the market in Tulcea; candles, a big container for drinking water, and plenty of mosquito repellent are also vital.

Predictably, there's a certain amount of hassle and confusion involved in buying **tickets** from NAVROM's office on the waterfront (Mon–Sat 8am–8pm, Sun 8am–3pm), since they're only sold three hours before sailings to allow for connecting services from Galați. In summer NAVROM operates **daily services** along each main arm of the Delta, leaving Tulcea at 1.30pm for Periprava, Sulina and Sfîntu Gheorghe. In summer hydrofoils also connect Galați with Tulcea, continuing to Sulina at 9.30am and returning at 1pm. In winter, boats head downstream on Monday, Wednesday and Friday (with extra services to Sulina and Chilia on Sat), returning the next day. As a rule, services to Sulina sail from pontoon no. 1 (the westernmost) or no. 3, those to Periprava and Ismail from no. 2, and those to Sfîntu Gheorghe from no. 4. The hydrofoils are swift, businesslike vessels (with a 10kg luggage limit, in theory), but the ferries are far more fun: lumbering vessels crammed with people and piled high with dinghies, rods and camping gear, and greeted at every jetty stop along their route by crowds of kids selling melons and fish. **Fares** are heavily subsidized for Delta residents, but for everyone else they're very pricey: the trip from Tulcea to Sulina costs around $4 by ferry or $7 by hydrofoil.

main road the village of **NICULIŢEL** boasts a church dating from c.1300, which, according to legend, was found buried by a shepherd, a clear echo of Turkish restrictions on the height of churches, which led to them being built half-underground in places. **Accommodation** is available with Gicu Constantin (Str. Gurgoaia 746; ☎51.61.66; ②), who also acts as a guide here and in the Delta. Inland from here is a beautiful open forest, typical of the Dobrogean steppes rather than of the Delta, which was created a nature reserve in 1927 by the botanist King Ferdinand, thanks to its rare species of peonies; bird life includes buzzards, nightingales, ortolan buntings, tawny pipits and woodpeckers. Three famous **monasteries** are nearby, at Cocoş (1833, much visited due to the relics of four martyrs held there), Chilic-Dere (1840, where there's a wooden windmill), and Saun, just north of the main road.

Into the Delta

The following sections cover each arm of the Delta in turn, starting from Tulcea, and then the Lake Razim region. If you just want to take a trip down to the sea and back, **Sfîntu Gheorghe** is a preferable target to **Sulina**, as it's less built up, with more private rooms and places to camp; and above all you can take a quick look at the Delta on foot without having to cross the Danube or hike too far. Note that some of the **telephone numbers** given in this section can only be reached via the operator.

Tulcea to Periprava

The **Chilia arm** of the river (Braţul Chilia), which branches off upstream from Tulcea and marks the border with Ukraine, carries 58 percent of the Danube's water, but very little tourist traffic. For travellers, there are major drawbacks to this route: boats will only carry you to Periprava (100km from Tulcea but still 30km from the Black Sea), where there's a total lack of tourist accommodation and the prospects of finding smaller boats heading into the interior are poor. What's more, Periprava lies at the centre of the area worst affected by Ceauşescu's project to drain the Delta and turn it into agricultural land. One way to see a little of this route is to travel as far as **Ceatalchioi**, 20km from Tulcea, then walk 10km to **Tudor Vladimirescu**, where an hourly **ferry** crosses the river back to Tulcea, docking opposite the ACR office. Small settlements such as these are involved in the gathering of **reeds** (*stuf*), which are used to build Delta houses and to obtain cellulose, a material used in diverse industries. The cutting, which stimulates the reeds to grow up to 2.5m in two months, can only be done by hand, a task performed by thousands of prisoners during the Stalinist era, including Uniate priests, ex-*Legionari*, former captains of industry, and purged *Securisti*. Reeds still cover a quarter of a million hectares in the Delta, but their export only brings in half the income provided by tourism in the area. The reeds stifle most of the other plants around them but provide a warm, windfree shelter for countless small birds, rodents and amphibia.

Not far beyond Ceatalchioi (due north as the river flows), boats pass **Izmail**, the main Ukrainian city in the Delta, whose bloody recapture from the Turks in 1790 is described in Byron's *Don Juan*. You can get there by daily boats from Tulcea, though be warned that this is not the easiest place to enter Ukraine: you

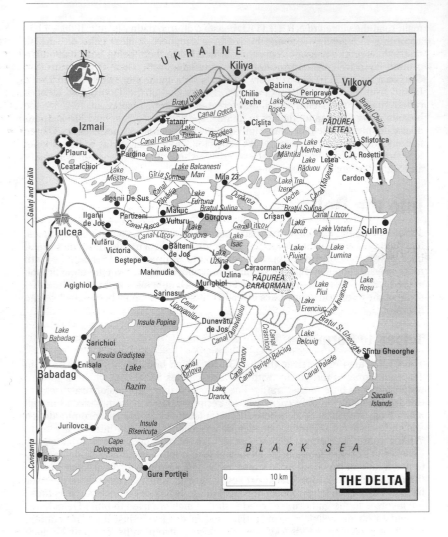

need a visa in advance from the embassy in Bucharest and border officials may demand extra payment.

Chilia Veche to Periprava

In the days when Bessarabia was part of Moldavia, **CHILIA VECHE** was merely a suburb of Chilia (now Ukrainian Kiliya) across the river. Chilia's moment of fame came in 1476 when its fort repelled a Turkish invasion; at that time it was just 5km from the coast – today it's 40km away. The hamlet of **CÎSLIŢA**, 8km south, lies at the end of a picturesque track, unusable for much of the year, which runs through an old forest frequented by **foxes** and **wild boar**.

Lake Roşca, roughly 10km south of **Babina** on the Cernovca tributary between Chilia Veche and Periprava, is one of the larger strictly protected reserves, harbouring geese, egrets, storks and Europe's largest **white pelican colony**. The dykes around Babina and Cernovca polders have been opened to allow the natural flood cycle to resume and rehabilitation is under way. Immediately to the east of the polders is the largely Lipovani village of **PERIPRAVA**, where passenger boats terminate. South of here lies the strictly protected **Pădurea Letea, a forest of oaks** tangled with lianas, now a haven for falcons, owls, white-tailed eagles, boar and wildcats, as well as snakes. Surrounding the forest are **sand dunes** inhabited by tortoises, lizards and 1800 species of insects. The Delta's leading ecotourism project is based in the villages at the southern edge of the forest, best reached from Crişan (see p.321).

Tulcea to Sulina

Between 1862 and 1902 the **Sulina arm** (Braţul Sulina) was shortened from 84km to 63km by the digging of long straight sections. Constant dredging and groynes running 10km out to sea still enable 7000-tonne freighters to take this route from Tulcea, and the additional tourist traffic makes this the busiest and least serene of the Danube's branches. However, it has the advantages of a tourist infrastructure and several settlements where there's a fair chance of renting boats to visit a variety of wildlife habitats. The journey from Tulcea to Sulina takes an hour and a half by hydrofoil or five hours by ferry, but there's not much point in staying on until the end – Sulina is a very dismal seaport and there are a couple of much better destinations en route. Travellers who come equipped to explore the Delta by **canoe** face turbulence from the wakes of passing ships on the main waterway, but **beyond Ilganii de Sus** you can escape into calmer backwaters leading to the inland lakes.

Maliuc

Beyond the river's fork, 12km from Tulcea, there's a **cabana** with accommodation for forty people at **ILGANII DE SUS**, opposite the fishing village of Partizani; accommodation is also available in private *cabanas*. It's worth asking around to rent a boat to visit two lakes further to the north, **Meşter** and **Lunga**. **MALIUC**, on the left bank of the river 12km further on, is a larger place, home to a **Museum of the Reed Industry** and a research station experimenting with different types of reed. There's also a **campsite** and the *Salcia* **hotel** (Maliuc ☎991; ④). Fishermen here might be prevailed upon to row you to see the pelicans and marsh terns nesting on **Lake Furtuna**.

The reeds in this area provide a home for fast-breeding great crested grebes; the solitary and less successful red-necked grebes; bearded reedlings, which nest in piles of cut reeds; and herons and little egrets, which favour nests in the overhanging willow trees. From Lake Meşter or the Păpădia channel, canoeists can try following the Gîrla Şontea to reach the original Dunărea Veche branch of the river near Mila 23 (see p.322), although be warned that submerged roots and aquatic plants may block the way. Nearby **Lake Gorgova** is rich in carp and catfish and hosts a large colony of glossy ibis.

Crişan, Mila 23 and around

CRIŞAN is the main tourist centre on the Sulina arm, a fishing settlement that straggles along the shoreline for 7km. Passenger boats stop on the south bank almost opposite the **monument** at Mila 13 (marking the distance from the sea in nautical miles), unveiled by Carol I in 1894 to inaugurate the new short-cut sections. On the north bank, before Mila 14, is an **EcoInfoCentre**, a good source of information on all areas of the Biosphere Reserve with an excellent viewing tower. Here, too, are the *Lebăda* **hotel** (☎040/54.37.78, fax 51.77.09; ④) and a **campsite** with bungalows but no running water; it's quite feasible to camp wild around here. **Boats** meet the ferry to take you across to the north bank, and the same boats continue (summer daily, otherwise Mon & Fri only) on to **Mila 23**, 10km north on the "old" branch of the Danube; this is the starting point for excursions to most of the surrounding lakes. Mila 23 is a large village of reed cottages (rebuilt after a flood in the 1960s), where the men fish and women tend the gardens of vegetables, plums, pears, grapes and quinces, and look after the poultry, pigs and beehives. Golden orioles – which nest high in deciduous trees – and bladder-frogs are widespread around here, while the **pelicans** have been driven north to Lake Merhei and south to Lake Iacob.

To the south of Crişan, it's an easy walk along the dyke to the southern end of Lake Iacob, where you might spot white-tailed eagles and pelicans. Further south, beyond the Crişan Canal, the forest of **Pădurea Caraorman** is now a strict reserve (protecting **wildlife** such as owls, white-tailed eagles, falcons, wildcats, boars and wolves). This is the best area of dunes in the Delta, striped with unusual linear forests of ancient oaks, poplar, ash and willow. To get there, catch the boat that connects with ferries at Crişan (June–Oct daily; otherwise Wed & Sun only) to take passengers to the predominantly Ukrainian village of **CARAORMAN**, where homestays are available.

The Delta's main **ecotourism** project is to the north of Crişan, on the south side of the Pădurea Letea, based in three very different villages. Although you may get a room on the spot, it's best to check with the ABRDD in Tulcea before setting out. **LETEA** is a village of 450 Lipovani/Ukrainian fisherfolk, where there's a rangers' house and bird-watching tower, while **ROSETTI** is home to 300 Romanian cattle breeders, holds an annual festival in early May and boasts the last windmill in the Delta. **SFISTOFCA** is an even smaller village of Lipovani fisherfolk. The Letea forest, just north of Rosetti and Letea, is strictly off-limits, but the Sfistofca forest, to the south, is almost as good, a maze of trees up to two hundred years old, tangled with lianas and orchids.

From any of the three villages you can make a trip to **Popina island**, just to the east, which is next in line for ecological rehabilitation. The island's northern half has been used for grazing cattle, while the southern half was a huge fish polder. Fish-farming began in the Delta in 1961, and grew to cover almost 50,000 hectares; it's totally unprofitable and survives only by cross-subsidy by conventional capture fishery, so that only fifteen percent or so of the wholesale fish price is left for the fishermen.

Sulina

Ever since it was recorded as a port by a Byzantine scribe in 950, **SULINA** has depended on shipping. Genoese vessels used to call here during the fourteenth century, while throughout the period of Ottoman power it was less a trading port than a nest of pirates who preyed on shipping in the Black Sea. From 1865, Sulina was the headquarters of the International Danube Commission, established by the great powers in 1856 to regulate free passage along the waterway, and in 1900 it became a free port. Its cosmopolitan heyday is described in the novel *Europolis* by Jean Bart (port captain for many years), as well as in Jules Verne's *Danube Pilot*. Within a decade, however, larger vessels and worldwide recession had emptied the port, so that by 1940 John Lehmann found "a hopeless, sinking feeling" in a place where "people get stranded, feel themselves abandoned by civilization, take to drink, and waste into a half-animal existence". The state has tried to sustain Sulina, an economically futile endeavour: expensive annual dredging is required to enable even small-capacity ships to enter, while larger freighters can now bypass the Delta altogether by taking the Danube–Black Sea Canal. Ceauşescu's solution was to establish a dump here in 1987 for imported industrial waste; however dioxins leaked out and polluted the Bulgarian coast, and radioactive leaks were spotted by the Mir space station, forcing a clean-up that undoubtedly cost far more than the $2 million earned.

Unless you like shabby bars and decaying waterfronts there's nothing to draw you except for the **Old Lighthouse**, built in 1802, and the **cemeteries** between the town and the sea, which provide an evocative record of all the nationalities who lived and died here in the days of the free port. Greeks dominated business, but there was also a large British contingent, now resident in the Anglican cemetery. If you get stranded here, try the *Sulina* **hotel** (☎040/54.30.17; ⑤), near the dock, or the *Europolis* (③), about 200m to the right as you disembark. The older, cheaper, *Farul* is in the no-man's-land of the free port, east from the dock.

Tulcea to Sfîntu Gheorghe

The Delta's oldest, most winding arm, the Braţul Sfîntu Gheorghe, is the least used by freighters and fishing boats; nevertheless it carries a fair amount of tourist traffic and, unlike other parts of the Delta, some of its settlements can be reached by bus from Tulcea. If you plan to visit these too, it's easier to go to direct to Sfîntu Gheorghe by boat to Murighiol, and then by bus back to Tulcea, stopping off along the way.

SFÎNTU GHEORGHE, 75km downriver from Murighiol, has depended on fishing since the fourteenth century. The most prized catch here is **sturgeon**, whose eggs, *icre neagre* or black caviar, draw thousands of Romanian tourists on shopping trips. Despite the onslaught of visitors, this remains a small village of just a thousand people, with one food shop, and running water available only in the mornings and evenings. **Private rooms** (①) are available, though there's no booking service as yet. The only other option is to camp wild, which is officially forbidden; if you do decide to risk it, watch out for snakes. Entertainment is provided at weekends by a band in the square and a floating disco-bar.

From Sfîntu Gheorghe, you can take **boat trips** into the Ivancea Canal, either north to Lacu Roşu, or out to the Sacalin islands at the river's mouth, which are now inhabited by sandwich terns, goosanders, red-breasted geese, and goldeneyes. This is one of the oldest parts of the Delta and a strictly protected reserve, so boats are not allowed to moor.

Returning towards Tulcea, the main settlement en route is **MURIGHIOL** (still shown on some maps as Independenţa). Six buses a day come here from Tulcea, on a circular route via either Mahmudia or Sarinasuf. A bus in each direction continues 5km east from Murighiol to **Dunavăţ** and can drop you at the turning to the gleaming white oasis of the *Pelican* **hotel** (Murighiol ☎17; ④) and **campsite** (with chalets); otherwise, get off at the shell of Dunavăţ's planned Centru Civic and walk 3km, turning left just before the last house in the village.

Murighiol has its natural attractions – namely black-winged stilts, red- and black-necked grebe, Kentish plover, avocets, and red-crested pochards, and Romania's only colony of Mediterranean gulls, all nesting around the late-freezing salt lakes nearby. From here, it should be possible to rent a boat and travel through the backwaters to **UZLINA**. Just south of this fishing village is the scientific centre of the Biosphere Reserve and the Cousteau Foundation, and an **EcoInfoCenter** in what was Ceauşescu's lodge, all set in a poplar plantation. North of Uzlina, the Isac and Uzlina lakes are home to a protected **pelican colony**, which you can see from a respectful distance. Heading downstream, the new channel is edged by high levees, but the meanders of the old channel are tree-lined and populated by deer, boar, foxes, water snakes, black ibis and egrets. **Lake Belciug**, roughly halfway back towards Sfîntu Gheorghe, is one of those least affected by algal blooms and deoxygenation, and retains the submerged vegetation once typical of the Delta, as well as a colony of glossy ibis.

Continuing west by bus, it's 10km from Murighiol to **MAHMUDIA**, where vestiges of the Roman-Byzantine citadel of **Salsovia** stand, on a low flat hill by the river; the Roman Emperor Constantine had his co-ruler Licinus killed here around 324 AD, thereby gaining absolute power. The fishponds and marshes around the village provide plenty of opportunities for watching waders and other birds, notably all three types of marsh tern in the breeding season.

Returning to Tulcea, buses allow you to stop in **BEŞTEPE**, whose five hills give a wonderful **panoramic view** of the Delta, and at **VICTORIA**, 12km before Tulcea, where you may be able to find a fisherman willing to row you across the river and into the water lily-smothered Litcov Canal.

Around Lake Razim

South of the Delta proper, **Lake Razim** is separated from the Black Sea by two long, tongue-like *grinds*. It's a good spot for bird-watchers, particularly in November and December, when the western shoreline is invaded by a million white-fronted and red-breasted geese from arctic Russia, which stay here, or around Istria further to the south, until the reed beds freeze. In the north of the lake, Popina island is now a closed reserve, hosting a colony of ruddy shelduck and a species of venomous spider. Like other parts of the Delta, however, Razim has been adversely affected by development: the western shores were empoldered in 1969 for fish farming, and in 1974 a sluice at Gura Portiţei cut the lake off from the sea, causing it to fill with freshwater, which has led to frequent algal blooms, deoxygenation, and a steady decline in fish yields and biodiversity. **Carp**, which move up into the shallows to spawn, account for the bulk of the catch; the Chinese variety, introduced during Romania's honeymoon with the People's Republic in the 1960s, has supplanted the indigenous species due to its greater voracity and resistance to low oxygen levels.

Babadag

From Tulcea, the DN22 and the rail line head south through the eroded Paleozoic hills of the Dealurile Tulcei to **BABADAG**, a town of 9000 people. From the **train station** it's fifteen minutes' walk down Strada Rahovei and Strada Stejarului to the **Mosque of Ali Ghazi** at Str. Geamiei 14, the oldest mosque in Romania, dating from 1522. There's a visible Turkish minority here, present since 1263, but the mosque is now disused. Babadag's facilities make it a useful base for exploring the west shore of Lake Razim; buses to Enisala and Jurilovca leave from behind the mosque. If you need to stay, continue north for ten minutes to the end of the town's one-way system, where you'll find the *Dumbrava* **hotel** (☎040/56.13.02; ②); the alternative is the *Doi Iepuraşi* **cabana and campsite**, in thick forest 6km south of town along the DN22, near the Codru rail halt. The town has some good, if seedy, **bars**, including the *Taj Mahal* and the *Crama Expres* on the main street, but the only decent place to eat is the restaurant in the *Dumbrava*.

Enisala, Jurilovca and Gura Portiţei

A quiet village of reed cottages, **ENISALA** lies 8km east of Babadag. About 1km away, overlooking the lake, is the **ruined Heracleia citadel**, built by Genoese merchants during the thirteenth century on the site of an earlier Byzantine fortress. This area is one of Europe's prime bird-watching sites, thanks to a mix of habitats: a vast area of reedbeds along the shoreline, stretching back to open land and the Babadag forest. You're likely to spot white-fronted and red-breasted geese, terns, waders, pelicans, herons and warblers.

The tiny fishing village of **JURILOVCA** (still shown on some maps as Unirea), 17km further down the coast, merits more attention, and there's accommodation at the *Albatros* **hotel** (②). The small **Ethnographic Museum** bears witness to the village's population of Romanians, Lipovani and a few Muslim Turks and Tatars: unlike Transylvania, the Delta has never really been noted for ethnic rivalry, since all groups are relatively recent colonists.

Around 5km east of Jurilovca, on Cape Doloşman, are the remains of the second- to sixth-century Greek citadel of Arganum, which faces **Bisericuţa Island**, itself the site of some medieval ruins. From Jurilovca you can take motorboat trips out to **GURA PORTIŢEI**, which consists of a few Lipovani reed huts, plus a **campsite** and a **restaurant** (noted for its fish broth), on a spit of land between Lake Razim and the sea. Before 1989 this was one of the few places where it was possible to escape the Securitate for a week or two, and it remains a popular holiday spot for the non-conformist intelligentsia, as well as the starting point for excursions to the **Periteaşca-Leahova reserve**, just north, where 20,000 red-breasted geese (half the world population) spend the winter. Heading back onto the main DN22, the next village south of Jurilovca is **BAIA**, better known as **Hamangia**, site of Romania's most famous Neolithic finds.

Istria

Heading south from Babadag towards Mamaia, you'll pass through **ISTRIA**. Eight kilometres east of the village, on the shores of Lake Sinoe, is the **ruined Greek city of Histria** with its shattered temples to diverse deities. The ruins (Tues–Sun 9am–5pm) cover a fairly small area, despite the fact that this was the most important of the ancient Greek settlements along the coast until the seventh century, when the port was smothered in silt and the town abandoned. Today this strictly protected zone is one of Europe's best areas for bird-watching, with all sorts of water birds making an appearance, peaking at 244 species in the winter months. Like Lake Razim, Lake Sinoe was open to the sea until 1960, since when there has been an increase in algal blooms and a decrease in biodiversity.

In the vicinity of the ruins you'll find a **campsite** with chalets; there's another site just south along the road to Năvodari at **NUNTAŞI**. Two buses a day run from Constanţa to Istria village, and one to Nuntaşi; the Istria rail halt is on the DN22, too far west to be of use.

THE COAST

Romania's **Black Sea coast** (the *litoral*) holds the promise of white beaches, dazzling water and an average of ten to twelve hours of sunshine a day between May and October. Under Communism this was countered by the logistical nightmare of one and a half million people flocking to the resorts during the season, but now that Poles, Czechs, Slovaks and East Germans can go elsewhere for sun and sea, the number of visitors has halved. Travelling from the Delta, your first stop on the coast will almost certainly be **Constanţa**, a relaxed seaport-cum-riviera town, dotted with Turkish, Byzantine and Roman remains, which has always seemed to keep a discreet distance from the resorts.

To get the best out of resorts like **Mamaia**, **Neptun**, **Venus**, **Saturn** or **Mangalia**, there's really no sensible alternative to **package tours** – you'll find the main operators listed in Basics. Though there are significant differences in price and standards, any tour will guarantee you a room and minimize extraneous hassles, and it tends to work out cheaper than doing the same trip independently. However, if you don't come on a tour, travel agencies in just about any town on the coast offer rooms in bungalows or basic hotels, while CTT can book rooms for students at its **Costineşti International Youth Camp**. The only resort you should actively avoid is **Năvodari**, which has been irredeemably ruined by industrial developments. If you're looking for somewhere as yet "undeveloped", try **Doi Mai** and **Vama Veche**, just a few miles from the Bulgarian border, or **Gura Portiţei** in the Delta (see p.325).

The Dobrogea and the Danube–Black Sea Canal

The overland approaches to Constanţa cross one part or another of the bleak northern **Dobrogea**, a poor area where donkeys still haul metal-wheeled carts. While there's no reason to break your journey here, the changes wrought over the last forty years certainly merit some explanation. Driving on the DN2A, you'll cross the Danube at **Giurgeni** and see orchards and fields planted on what used to be pestilential marshland; but this transformation is nothing compared to the great works further to the south, starting at Cernavodă, where the rail line crosses the Danube on what was, at 4088m, Europe's longest bridge when it opened in 1895. A road bridge was added in 1987, linking the DN3A and the DN22C to provide the most direct road route to Constanţa, parallel to the rail line and the **Danube–Black Sea Canal**.

Cernavodă and the canal

CERNAVODĂ, whose name rather ominously translates as "Black Water", was chosen in the late 1970s to be the site of Romania's first **nuclear power station**. Ceauşescu was personally involved in the scheme from the start: returning from a trip to Canada in 1985, where he'd inspected a CANDU reactor similar to the model chosen for Cernavodă, he immediately criticized managers for using too much concrete. Since then, problems with welding have meant that only one of the five reactors has so far come into service, in 1996.

Cernavodă is also the western entrance to the **Danube–Black Sea Canal**. Opened to shipping in 1984, the canal put Cernavodă a mere 60km from the Black Sea, rather than 400km via the Delta which, in any case, is impassable for larger freighters. The new canal route offers obvious savings in fuel and time, but realizing a profit on such a huge investment depends on European economic revival, and particularly on an end to the conflict in former Yugoslavia and on the success of the new Rhein–Main and Nürnberg–Regensburg canals. Charlemagne's vision of a 3000-kilometre-long waterway linking Rotterdam with the Black Sea finally came to fruition in 1993, although environmental protests in Bavaria and soaring costs had stalled the final stage of the project for ten years.

Along the canal

Most trains through the Dobrogea stop at the town of **MEDGIDIA** (junction for Tulcea and Negru Vodă, the crossing-point to Bulgaria) on the canal, 24km east of Cernavodă, while slow trains also halt at the canal-side town of **BASARABI** and its eastern suburb of **MURFATLAR**, which gives its name to the surrounding wine-growing region. There's a wine research station there, but the excursions put on by Constanța's tourist agencies (see p.330) visit the Complex Unirii factory, to the west of Basarabi. Tours start with a visit to the **museum**, containing displays of ancient amphorae, reliefs of Dionysos and a few photos of the modern processes, before moving on to sample the produce. Three million bottles a year are produced here, seventy percent white, although the full fruity reds are more distinctive. The nearest place to stay is the campsite at **VALU LUI TRAIAN**, on the rail line 4km east of Murfatlar.

Adamclisi and Ostrov

If you're interested in ancient monuments you might consider detouring south from Cernavodă or Medgidia to visit the Roman remains near **ADAMCLISI**. Just north of the DN3 and the village of Adamclisi rises an arresting marble structure,

---

THE CANAL OF DEATH

Work on the **Danube–Black Sea Canal** started in 1949, when the Party launched this "hero project", and soon writers like Petru Dumitriu (who made his name with a book on the canal, *Dustless Highway*) were waxing lyrical about the transformation of humble peasants into class-conscious proletarians through the camaraderie of the construction site. But as Dumitriu acknowledged after his defection in 1960, the *Canalul Mortii*, as it came to be known, claimed the lives of over 100,000 workers, the bulk of whom were actually there under duress. **Forced labour** was permitted from 1950, and six-month sentences were doled out without trial by the Ministry of the Interior; those affected included Uniate priests and tens of thousands of peasants who resisted collectivization. From 1952 these were joined by relatives of prisoners, war criminals and those who had tried to flee abroad.

In 1953, after years of untold suffering, it was realized that that the chosen route (through the 84-metre-high Canara Hills towards Năvodari, north of Constanța) was plain crazy and the project was abandoned. Work on a new route resumed in 1973, and the canal was successfully pushed eastwards to join the sea at Agigea, south of Constanța. However it carries less than ten percent of the predicted traffic and may well come to be remembered as another of Ceaușescu's follies.

a reconstruction of the **Tropaeum Traiani** (Tues–Sun 10am–6pm). The original was erected here in 109 AD to celebrate Trajan's conquest of the Dacians, and every facet reflects unabashed militarism, not least the dedication to Mars Ultor. The trophy-statue – an armoured, faceless warrior – gazes over the plateau from a height of 30m, on a hexagonal plinth rising from a base 32m in diameter. Carved around the side of the base are 49 bas-reliefs or **metopes** (there were originally 54), portraying the Roman campaign. Each of the six groups of metopes comprises a marching scene, a battle, and a tableau representing victory over the enemy, an arrangement identical to the one that underlies scenes XXXVI–XLII of Trajan's Column in Rome, created to mark the same triumph over the Dacians. (There's a copy of Trajan's Column in Bucharest's National History Museum). Around the statue are **ruins** of buildings once inhabited by the legionary garrison or serving religious or funerary purposes. Unfortunately, there's no tourist accommodation in the vicinity; public **buses** do run from Cernavodă and Medgidia (heading for Băneasa and Ostrov), but it's much more convenient to take a bus tour from the coast.

Into Bulgaria

Sixty kilometres west of Adamclisi along the DN3 is the small border town of **OSTROV**, where you can cross over to the Bulgarian town of **Silistra**. Ostrov has a **campsite** with chalets, near the jetty for ferries to Călăraşi on the north bank of the Danube. Although the **Vama Veche crossing** (see p.339) is more suitable if you're driving down the coast to Varna, it's also possible to enter Bulgaria from **NEGRU VODĂ** at the south end of the DN38, a crossing that's used by buses from Constanţa and three local trains a day from Medgidia. All three crossings are open 24 hours a day. Note that you can't get a Bulgarian visa at the border; if you do need a visa, make sure you get it either before leaving home or in Bucharest (see p.15).

Constanţa

Most visitors first encounter the Black Sea coast at **CONSTANŢA**, a busy riviera town and Romania's principal port. Its ancient precursor, Tomis, was supposedly founded by survivors of a battle with the Argonauts, following the capture of the Golden Fleece; centuries later the great Latin poet Ovid was exiled here for nine years until his death in 17 AD. These days the town is an attractive mix of Greco-Roman remains, Turkish mosques and crisp modern boulevards, swept and watered daily by Gypsy women. However, since 1989 Constanţa has gained notoriety as the world's child AIDS capital, while also increasingly falling under the sway of Gypsy and Turkish racketeers. Port traffic plummeted in 1992, with the collapse of COMECON and the imposition of sanctions on Yugoslavia, but the economy is now more export-oriented and the port is booming once more, as is the shipbuilding industry.

Arrival, information and tours

Constanţa is served by **Mihail Kogălniceanu airport**, 25km northwest of town, from where it's a half-hour journey into the centre by TAROM bus (or any bus on the DN2A between Constanţa and Hîrşova). The **train station** and Autogară Sud,

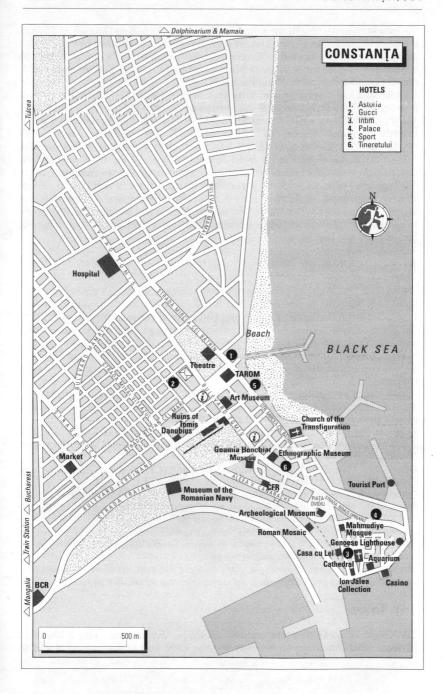

△ Dolphinarium & Mamaia

CONSTANȚA

HOTELS
1. Asturia
2. Gucci
3. Intim
4. Palace
5. Sport
6. Tineretului

N

Hospital

Beach

BLACK SEA

Theatre

TAROM

Art Museum

Ruins of
Tomis
Danubius

Church of the
Transfiguration

Market

Geamia Hunchiar
Mosque

Ethnographic Museum

Museum of the
Romanian Navy

CFR

Tourist Port

Archeological Museum

PIATA
OVIDIU

Roman Mosaic

Mahmudiye
Mosque

Casa cu Lei

Genoese Lighthouse

Cathedral

Aquarium

Ion Jalea
Collection

Casino

BCR

0   500 m

the **bus station** serving destinations south of town (including Dobrich and Varna in Bulgaria, and Istanbul), are 2km west of the centre. Take trolley bus #40 or #43 along Bulevardul Ferdinand to the centre, where both services swing north: #40 continues to the southern fringe of Mamaia, while #43 passes the Autogară Nord, serving destinations north along the coast

Constanța has several **tourist agencies**, with the state ONT Litoral now supposedly split into Danubius at B-dul Ferdinand 36 (☎041/61.58.36, fax 61.80.10) and Piața Ovidiu 11 (☎041/61.90.39, fax 61.90.41), and the Agenția de Turism Intern at B-dul Tomis 46 (☎041/61.71.27, fax 61.14.29) and no.69 (☎041/61.57.77). However ONT still has a branch at B-dul Tomis 78 (Mon–Fri 8am–7pm), as does Litoral in the *Hotel Palace* (☎041/61.77.84). ONT will only sell you air tickets, but the others are keen to sign visitors up for **excursions**, some of which are worth considering, particularly if you're keen to visit the Tropaeum Traiani monument at Adamclisi (see p.327) and the ruins of Histria. Both Danubius and Litoral offer trips to Adamclisi, Histria and Murfatlar, plus one- or two-day trips to the Delta, while Danubius also do longer jaunts to Bucharest, Sinaia, Bran and Bucovina.

Accommodation

There's not a great choice of **hotels** in Constanța itself, so at peak times you might have to find a room in one of the beach resorts to the north or south of town. Danubius, B-dul Ferdinand 36, may find you **private rooms**. Otherwise, CTT, B-dul Tomis 22 (☎041/61.52.62), might be able to arrange **dormitory beds** during summer, along with holidays at the International Youth Camp in Costinești. The closest **campsites** are on the outskirts of Mamaia and Eforie Nord. If you're hoping for a bungalow there, or a room in any of the other resorts, ask at the tourist offices.

Astoria, Str. Mircea cel Bătrîn 102 (☎041/61.60.64, fax 61.51.94). An oldish state hotel (once the party hotel, now popular with performers at the nearby theatre), but clean and nicely painted. Some four-bed rooms, all with bath (but there's no hot water after 10pm). ⑤.

Intim, Str. N Titulescu 9 (☎041/61.78.14, fax 61.82.85). An old hotel, once the *Hotel d'Angleterre*, where Eminescu stayed in 1882. Nice decor, but no facilities beyond the restaurant and bar, and only 16 rooms. ⑧.

Oriana, Șos. Mangaliei 86, at Str. Amurgului (☎041/68.14.25). A private guesthouse with constant hot water and restaurant-bar, but no other facilities. ④.

Palace, Str. R Opreanu 5 (☎041/61.46.96, fax 61.75.32). A fine period building with a beautifully cool and quiet marble foyer; it has some two-star rooms hidden away, which offer the best value in the city centre, plus a few triple rooms. ④.

Sport, Str. Cuza Vodă 2 (☎041/61.75.58). Nicely renovated, with cable TV and constant hot water, but only theoretically a sport hotel at this price. There's a restaurant and a bar with a pleasant terrace overlooking the sea. ⑧.

Tineretului, B-dul Tomis 24 (☎041/61.35.90, fax 61.12.90). Remarkably well-equipped for a youth hotel, with a travel agency, shop and currency exchange facilities. ⑥.

The Town

The oldest area of Constanța, centred on **Piața Ovidiu**, stands on a headland between what is now the tourist port and the huge area of the modern docks to the south and west. Here you'll find museums and mosques, as well as the casino and other relics of the city's nineteenth-century glory days. To the north, beyond the remains of the walls of ancient Tomis, is the modern **commercial area**, along bulevards Ferdinand and Tomis, where you'll find the tourist and airline offices and most shops, as well as the art museum. Further north, nearing the resort of Mamaia, are various sights that should appeal to children, including a funfair, dolphinarium and planetarium, as well as the city football stadium and other sports facilities.

Around bulevards Ferdinand and Tomis

The pivotal point of the new town is the junction of **Bulevardul Ferdinand and Bulevardul Tomis**. Here, under a mural depicting the Dobrogea's archeological sites, you'll find an archeological park displaying sections of ancient walls, serried amphorae and other **ruins of Tomis**. Whether or not the Argonauts were the first to come here, Tomis was settled by Greeks from Miletus in the sixth century BC as an annexe to Histria, which it later superseded before being incorporated within the Roman empire as Pontus Sinister at the beginning of the Christian era. The most prominent remains are those of the defensive wall created in the third and fourth centuries and the Butchers' Tower, raised in the sixth century by Byzantine colonists who revived the city and renamed it Tomis to honour Constantine.

South of the archeological park, Strada Traian overlooks the commercial *portul maritim*, and provides an appropriate setting for the **Museum of the Romanian Navy** at no. 53 (Tues–Sun 9am–5pm). The name is slightly misleading, since the museum includes models of Greek triremes that sailed long before "Romania" existed, and photographs recording the unexpected visit of the battleship *Potemkin*, whose mutinous sailors disembarked at Constanța in July 1905 and scattered. Little is said about the role of Romania's own navy during the last war, when it supported the occupation of Odessa and aided the Nazi fleet.

Back on Bulevardul Tomis, north of Bulevardul Ferdinand, the **Art Museum** at no. 84 (Wed–Sun 9am–5pm) has the usual sampling of Aman and Grigorescu, as well as painters of the Dobrogean landscape, such as Iosif Iser, Ștefan Dumitrescu and Francisc Șirato. South of here, at no. 32, you'll find the **Ethnographic Museum** (daily 9am–5pm), which has a fine display of colourful Dobrogean rugs and folk costumes. The museum stands almost opposite the **Geamia Hunchiar**, a small mosque built in in 1869, surmounting a tangle of dingy coffee houses, kebab and pizza joints. A couple of blocks east, at Str. Mircea cel Bătrîn 36, is the **Church of the Transfiguration**, dating from 1865 when the Greek community at last got permission from the Ottoman rulers for a church, and brought a monk from Athos to decorate it.

Piața Ovidiu

Piața Ovidiu, at the southern end of Bulevardul Tomis, is the central square of the old quarter. A statue of Ovid gazes mournfully down, as he might well have done when he was exiled here from Rome by Emperor Augustus in 8 AD (probably for intriguing at court and writing *The Art of Love*). Marooned in backwater Tomis, where he found the natives uncouth and the winters appalling, Ovid spent his last years unsuccessfully petitioning emperors for his return, and composing his melancholy *Tristia*:

Rain cannot pit it, sunlight fails in burning
This snow. One drift succeeds another here.
The north wind hardens it, making it eternal;
It spreads in drifts through all the bitter year.

On the southern side of the square, Constanţa's **Archeological and National History Museum** (Tues–Sun 9am–5pm, summer until 8pm) has an excellent collection, notably its statues of deities, displayed in the hall just left of the entrance. A menhir of a Hamangia-culture Earth Goddess, complete with battle-axes, occupies the first room, while in the lower section you'll find Fortuna and Pontos, the protectors of Tomis; an Aedicula carved with the chillingly lovely Nemesis twins, goddesses of Revenge and Universal Equilibrium; and other statues, including the extraordinary **Glykon Serpent**. Though considered to have been carved during the second century like the others, the Glykon statue is unique, being about the size of a squatting toddler, with an antelope's head, human hair and ears, and a gracefully coiled serpentine body ending in a lion's tail.

Outside the museum you can see a display of funerary inscriptions, and to its rear a modern structure encloses a fine **Roman mosaic**, more than 600 metres square. It was discovered 5m below street level in 1959, and may have once graced a third- to fourth-century commercial building, or even the upper hall of the Roman baths, whose outer walls, their archways sealed, can be seen from Aleea Canarache.

South of Piaţa Ovidiu

From **Piaţa Ovidiu**, it's a short walk south to the **Mahmudiye Mosque** (daily except Fri 9.30am–5.30pm), whose fifty-metre-high minaret spikes the skyline and offers a great view of the town and harbour. Built in 1910, the first reinforced-concrete building in Romania, it's the seat of the Mufti, the spiritual head of Romania's 55,000 Muslims (Turks and Tatars by origin), who live along the coast of the Dobrogea. South from the mosque along Strada Muzeelor are the fancy **Orthodox Cathedral** of SS Peter and Paul, an early (1884) neo-Byzantine design by Ion Mincu, and, at the street's end, opposite more ruins of ancient Tomis, the **Ion Jalea collection of sculptures** bequeathed by the artist (May–Oct daily 8am–8pm; Nov–April Wed–Sun 9am–5pm). Jalea, born in Tulcea in 1887, generally produced conventional and academic sculptures for the state, being forced to produce monumental equestrian work such as that of Mircea the Old in Tulcea's main square.

On the **waterfront**, the former **Casino** stands on a jutting promenade. Originally erected as a pavilion for Queen Elisabeta (Carmen Sylva) in 1904, it is now a restaurant. During a visit in 1914 by the Russian Imperial family, it was the venue for a disastrous gala performance of mystical allegories by little girls, which ended in smashed scenery and broken limbs. Despite a *Te Deum* in the cathedral and an amicable pip-spitting contest between the two parties, the Russians sailed away less than a day later, Grand Duchess Olga having refused the proposed marriage to Prince Carol, and thus sealed her fate: the Bolsheviks killed her along with the rest of her family.

The tanks of the **Aquarium** (daily 9am–4pm; to 8pm in summer), opposite the Casino, contain 4500 species of aquatic life from the Dobrogean lakes, the Delta and the Black Sea. Just beyond, you can see the so-called **Genoese Lighthouse**, erected in 1860 in memory of the thirteenth- and fourteenth-century mariners who tried to revive the port.

The beach and Lake Tăbăcăriei

Visitors with children or a low tolerance for museums often head straight for the **beach** behind the art museum, spread beneath a terraced cliff north of the *port turistic*. Another popular spot is the park at **Lake Tăbăcăriei**, between Constanța and Mamaia: trolley bus #40 runs along Bulevardul Mamaia, to the east of the park, and #43 heads up Bulevardul Alexandru Lapuşneanu, to its west, both starting from the train station. The #40 passes a more than usually depressing **dolphinarium** (daily 9am–7pm) and a **planetarium** (same hours) at the southeastern corner of the park; from the nearby Tăbăcăriei Wharf a **miniature train** carries children around the lake. **Luna Park**, north of the lake, has various rides and games, including bowling, and there is an **ice-skating** rink on the edge of the Pioneers' Park here, also the site of Constanța's football stadium.

Eating and drinking

Most hotels in Constanța have **restaurants** on the premises, but, for once, there are plenty of other places to choose from in town. In the backstreets of the old town, especially around the Hunchiar mosque, you'll find various seedy yet appealing **bars**; the *Cazino* also has an excellent terrace, great for a beer at sundown.

Astoria, Str. Mircea cel Bătrîn 102, on Piața Ovidiu. The only decent place to eat around the square.

Casa cu Lei, Str. N Titulescu 1 (☎041/61.80.50). The most stylish restaurant in town, in a beautiful historic house; international cuisine.

Cazino, B-dul Carpați 2 (☎041/61.74.16). Great view over the Black Sea, especially from the terrace; decent international cuisine, slightly perfunctory service.

Club Royal, Str. Mircea cel Bătrîn 5. A French-oriented restaurant, although mainly aimed at the local nouveaux riches (smugglers, gangsters etc).

La Strada, B-dul Tomis, opposite the Ethnographic Museum. A "genuine" Italian café, filled with video games.

Les Barons, corner of b-duls Ferdinand and Tomis. French cuisine, though not as classy as at the *Coq Simpa*. Credit cards accepted. Daily 9.30am–midnight.

Pescăruşul Arginţiu, Str. V Alecsandri 7. Half fish restaurant, half kebab and felafel joint.

Restaurant au Coq Simpa, Str. Ştefan cel Mare 19, opposite the post office (☎041/61.47.97). An excellent genuine French restaurant; credit cards accepted. Daily 11am–midnight.

Terasa Coloanelor, Str. Traian, just east of the Museum of the Romanian Navy. A beer garden serving up the usual grilled sausages.

Listings

Air tickets TAROM is at Str. Ştefan cel Mare 15 (☎041/61.40.66). DacAir tickets (to Istanbul; Mon, Wed & Fri) are available through ONT at B-dul Tomis 78.

Car rental Avis c/o TAROM (☎041/66.26.32); Hertz c/o Trans-Atlantis, B-dul Tomis 106 (☎ & fax 041/61.93.54).

Exchange Bancorex, on the north side of Piața Ovidiu, and BCR, at the south end of B-dul 1 Decembrie 1918, have cash machines. Marshall Tourism, Str. C. Brătescu 26 (☎041/66.59.96), is the agent for American Express.

Market Piața Griviței, just north of Str. Ştefan cel Mare, one block west of Str. Duca.

Pharmacy Urgenţa, at the corner of B-dul Tomis and B-dul Ferdinand.

Ships to Istanbul Avrasya carries cars and passengers from Constanţa to Istanbul on Monday and Friday afternoons (reduced service in winter). Tickets, from $40 one-way for a reclining seat, are sold by Danubius, B-dul Ferdinand 36 (☎041/61.58.36, fax 61.80.10). Turkish visas are available from the consulate at B-dul Ferdinand 82 (Mon–Fri 9am–noon).

Shopping Str. Ştefan cel Mare is the main shopping street – especially the pedestrianized stretch from Str. Rascoala to Str. Duca – with the Tomis department store opposite a big bookshop. The Russell supermarket (Mon–Sat 8am–8pm, Sun 8am–4pm) is on B-dul Tomis at Str. Brătescu, opposite the theatre. There's a decent photographic shop at B-dul Tomis 67.

Theatre At Str. Mircea cel Bătrîn 97, putting on the usual plays and music events. Buy tickets at the agency at B-dul Tomis 97.

Train tickets CFR, Aleea Vasile Canarache 4 (Mon–Fri 7am–7pm, Sat 7am–1pm), overlooking the new port. You need to book several days in advance in summer.

Travel agencies Nouvelles Frontières–Simpa Turism, Str. Rascoalei 9 (☎041/66.04.68, fax 66.44.03); Marshall Tourism, Str. C. Brătescu 26 (☎041/66.59.96).

Mamaia and around

MAMAIA, 6km north of Constanţa, is Romania's best-known coastal resort, and the place where the majority of package tourists end up. The **beach** of fine, almost white sand, fringed with wild pear trees, is Mamaia's greatest asset, especially since its gentle gradient and the absence of currents and strong tides make it particularly safe for children. Legend has it that the gods created the beach to reunite a kidnapped princess with her daughter, who was abandoned on the sea shore wailing "Mamaia, Mamaia!"; but the name could equally be derived from *mamakioi*, meaning "village of butter" in Turkish.

Ranged along a narrow spit of land between the Black Sea and Lake Siutghiol, most of Mamaia's 55 **hotels** are within 100m of the beach. In summer trolley bus #41 runs here directly from Constanţa's train station; out of season you'll have to change from the #40 to the #47 at the Pescarie terminal, one stop south of the thirteen-storey *Parc* hotel (☎041/83.17.20, fax 83.11.98; ④), which marks the beginning of the resort. From here the main street curves away around the shore of the lake, packed with tennis and basketball courts, restaurants and discos, passing clusters of mainly two-star hotels as well as a couple of one-star establishments, the *Pescăruş* (☎041/83.16.73; ③) and *Delfin* (☎041/83.16.40; ③).

North of the main watersports area, just beyond the casino, are three good privatized hotels: the excellent-value three-star *Condor* (☎041/83.11.42, fax 83.19.06; ②); the *Albatros* (☎041/83.13.81, fax 83.13.46; ④), which is open all year, offering rooms with bath and cable TV; and the nine-room *Pensiune Victoria* (☎041/83.11.53; ③), right on the beach and also open all year. Continuing north, you pass the *Rex* (☎041/83.15.95, fax 83.16.90; ⑨), Mamaia's best hotel, Club Med's exclusive *Thalassa* complex, and most of the hotels used by British package companies. The resort ends with a few newer three-star places (by a small naturist enclosure), and then a **campsite**, the *Turist*; from here it's about 5km straight up the road (or take bus #23) to the equally crowded *Hanul Piraţilor* site. If you do arrive without a room reservation, the **accommodation office** in the south wing of the *Bucureşti* hotel, in the middle of the resort (☎041/83.11.40, fax 83.12.76), is your best bet; they accept ACR vouchers. There's another branch in the *Aurora* (☎041/83.10.67, fax 83.12.80), which organizes accommodation in eighteen hotels.

Mamaia has ample **sporting facilities**. Unless your package includes all activities and equipment, you'll pay the following dollar-equivalent rates, stan-

HOTEL PRICES ON THE BLACK SEA COAST

In all the resorts along the Black Sea coast, the traditional rigid **pricing structure** has begun to fragment, but most of the hotels in each resort are still owned by one state holding company, with all their hotels in each category charging the same. Two-star hotels generally charge the equivalent of $15–20 a night in season for a double room (④), and three-star hotels $45–60 (⑤); there are very few one- or four-star establishments. **Private hotels** tend to cost slightly more than state hotels, but are usually worth it. You should check which meals are included, and also bear in mind that prices in July and August are up to twenty percent higher than in June and September; at other times most hotels are closed – the cheapest hotels tend to be the last to open and the first to close.

Few hotels are used to the concept of people turning up independently and it may take them a while to work out what to charge (probably around twenty per-cent over the group rate); foreigners can find themselves paying twice the rate charged to Romanians. Each resort has a *dispecerat cazare* or **accommodation office**, responsible for allocating lone arrivals: sometimes there are bargains to be had and this is usually the only way to get a self-catering villa.

dard along the coast: waterskiing costs $20 an hour, yachting $10, and surf-board rental $3 an hour or $11 for five hours. You'll pay $2 for fifty minutes on a tennis court, with an additional charge of $1.50 per hour for racquet and balls.

As for **nightlife**, the trendiest place to be is the pricey *Enigma*, at the *Turist* campsite, ten minutes' walk north beyond the trolley bus terminal. Alternatives consist of glitzy cabaret most nights at the *Melody* and *Orient* nightclubs near the casino, folklore displays at the *Orient* and *Hanul Piraţilor* at the north end of the resort, and nightly discos in hotels such as the *Perla*, *Select* and *Delta*, all at Mamaia's southern end.

Ovid's Island and beyond

From Mamaia, regular motorboat trips run to **Ovid's Island**, where there's a suit-ably rustic restaurant, the *Insula Ovidiu*, at the northern end of **Lake Siutghiol**. Also known as Lacul Mamaia, the lake was formed when a river's outlet silted up, and for many centuries it was a watering hole for herds of sheep and cows brought down from the Carpathians – hence the origin of the name Siutghiol, meaning "Lake of Milk" in Turkish.

Further north looms **NĂVODARI**. The beach here must have been lovely once, but with characteristic concern for the environment, a gigantic, reeking superphosphates plant has been constructed nearby, its pipelines running through the **campsite** which, unbelievably, has been designated a children's resort. Buses #22 and #23 run to Năvodari, beyond which a minor road heads north past Lake Nuntaşi and its **campsite** to the Greek ruins at Histria.

Agigea to Vama Veche

Just south of Constanţa, the road and rail line cross the new Danube–Black Sea Canal where it meets the coast at the **Agigea port complex**. Beyond this, the array of resorts extending to **Mangalia** is another facet of Romania's progress over the last twenty years – modern complexes created where only scrubland or run-down villages existed before. Except for the fact that most are situated along a clifftop overlooking the beach, they are fairly similar to their prototype, Mamaia, to the north. You can reach them from Constanţa by **local buses** or by **trains** along the rail line to Mangalia, although be warned that all transport is crowded in summer.

Around Lake Techirghiol

Trains and buses #10, #11 and #12 run 14km south from Constanţa to **EFORIE NORD**. Founded in 1899 by Bucharest's Eforia hospital as a spa for convalescent patients, Eforie Nord extends along a clifftop 15–20m above the beach. The resort is, however, best known for the therapeutic **black mud** scooped from the shores of **Lake Techirghiol**, whose mineral-saturated waters got the lake its name, derived from *tekir*, Turkish for "salt" or "bitter". **Baths** by the lake (a few minutes' walk south of the train station) specialize in treating rheumatic disorders and the after-effects of polio; while on the lake's single-sex nudist beaches people plaster themselves with mud, wait until it cracks (happily exposing themselves to passing trains), and then jostle good humouredly beneath the showers.

The resort itself basically comprises two parallel streets, Bulevardul Tudor Vladimirescu, running along the clifftop, and Bulevardul Republicii, where you'll find the bus stops, shops and offices. As a spa, Eforie Nord has some inexpensive **hotels** that are more likely to be open out of season than elsewhere, as well as the rather faceless blocks built for mass tourism. The *Decebal* (☎041/74.29.77; ⑥) is the station hotel, but far better than that implies, offering twin rooms all with hot water and TV, while the *Traian* (☎041/74.18.08, fax 74.26.01; ④), next door at Str. Traian 1, holds 232 basic twins. The twin rooms at the large *Hefaistos*, Str. 23 August 6 (☎041/74.29.46, fax 74.12.61; ③), have hot showers and are excellent value for money, and the hotel is open longer than many others, from April until October. Just south of the centre at Str. Republicii 9 is the *Europa* (☎041/74.29.90, fax 74.18.41; ⑤), now privatized and in the process of being revamped; you can **rent cars** here.

Of the two **campsites**, the nicer is the *Meduza*, just inland at the northern end of Bulevardul Vladimirescu; the *Şincai*, along Strada 23 August towards Techirghiol, is much more run-down. There are plenty of **restaurants** in town, of which the *Nunta Zamfirei*, at the northern end of town, is famous for its folklore show, presented in the format of a village wedding. Other eating and drinking places are clustered in the centre, near the bus stop.

Although there's nowhere to stay, it's a nice trip 2km around the lake to **TECHIRGHIOL** (terminus of bus #11), where there are three hundred Muslim families (Turks and Tatars by origin) among the village's population. Bizarrely, there's a wooden church here, transplanted from Vişeu in Maramureş.

Compared to its northern neighbour, **EFORIE SUD** (which has in theory retaken its original name of Carmen Silva, in honour of Carol I's queen) seems like a town that's died – many of the hotels are closed and the **accommodation office** (☎041/74.82.31, fax 74.88.89) isn't particularly helpful. The five identical hotel blocks along Strada Faleză are the most reliable (all open late June to Sept only; all ③): the *Gloria* at no. 2 (☎041/74.29.72), *Excelsior* at no. 4 (☎041/74.16.54), *Capitol* at no. 6 (☎041/74.29.82, fax 74.18.89), *Riviera* at no. 8 (☎041/74.15.33, fax 74.18.89), and *Ancora* at no. 10 (☎041/74.29.38, fax 74.18.89).

The large *Cosmos* **campsite**, at the southern end of the resort, near the sea, is squalid, and there is also a selection of rather unappealing hotels and villas along Strada Negru Vodă and Strada Dr Cantacuzino, squeezed between the train station (by Lake Techirghiol) and the sea. The only possibilities for eating, outside of the hotels, are the snack bars along the promenade.

South to Mangalia

Bus #10 from Constanţa terminates in Tuzla, 3km south of Eforie Sud; bus #12 continues on to Mangalia every thirty minutes, following the main road for the most part, which means that the resorts between here and Mangalia are best reached by train. Even express trains slow to a crawl between Constanţa and Mangalia, taking an hour to cover 43km. From mid-June to mid-September extra services are laid on, providing an almost continuous service along the coast, with reservations required only west of Constanţa.

The 8km of beach immediately north of Mangalia are now lined with the modern hotels of the new resorts, all given mythological names, that have grown up in the last three decades. The stretch of cliffs to their north is broken only by the former fishing village of **COSTINEŞTI**, now the site of Romania's principal **International Youth Camp**, with a fine sandy beach sheltered to the north by Cape Tuzla. This is run by the Compania de Turism pentru Tineret (Youth Tourism Company), and until 1989 only young people booked through CTT (or BTT as it then was) could stay here. Things have now changed and the **accommodation**, in *căsuţe* and villas, is open to all. It's best to book before coming; if you haven't, arrive early and head across the car park from Costineşti Tabără train station to the accommodation office (*birou cazare*). Alternatively you could try the **hotels** to the south of the beach, of which the *Forum* (✆041/74.28.55, fax 74.29.77; ④) is a friendly modern place. A jazz festival is held at the end of August or in early September, and there's plenty of other entertainment all summer long.

Eight kilometres further south is **NEPTUN**; fast trains stop only at the *halta*, at a level crossing by the *Hotel Doina*, and resorts to the south must be reached by bus #15, which follows the coast from here to Mangalia. Neptun was built in 1960 between the Comorova forest and the sea, ensuring a lush setting for the artificial lakes and dispersed villas that make this the most desirable of the Black Sea resorts. Shopping centres, discos, sports facilities and hotels here are a cut above the Romanian average, as is also the case in the satellite resort of **OLIMP**, just north; originally an enclave for the Communist *nomenklatura*, this is still frequented by the country's elite as well as Western package tourists.

Most **rooms** are still assigned to those on packages, however, so if you're hoping to find a room in high season it may be best to go through the accommodation office (✆041/73.18.45, fax 63.90.02) opposite Neptun's *Hotel Decebal*. The best hotel is the *Neptun* (✆ & fax 041/73.10.20; ⑤), which boasts a covered pool and a disco, and there are three other three-star places, including the *Doina* (✆041/73.18.18; ⑤), open all year thanks to its treatment centre, which has fifty single rooms as well as 250 twins. There are twenty two-star hotels (④), and just four one-star places, including the *Sibiu* (✆041/73.14.22; ③). In Olimp there are three large, identical three-star hotels (all ⑤) – the *Amfiteatru* (✆ & fax 041/73.14.28), the *Belvedere* (✆ & fax 041/73.12.56) and the *Panoramic* (✆ & fax 041/73.13.56) – and just seven two-star joints (④), which all have triple rooms as well as twins. There's a **campsite** at the north end of Olimp, and another tiny site with bungalows at the south end of Neptun, by the Autoservice yard; it's easy to camp wild near the station. Eating out, try the *Calul Bălan*, right at the southern end of Neptun, or the *Insula* (specializing in fish), on the lake behind the *Neptun* hotel. In summer you can **rent cars** at Olimp's *Hotel Belvedere*.

The four resorts to the south are more uniform, and the hotels are mainly state-owned two-star places, although a few have been privatized. The first, immediately abutting Neptun, is **JUPITER**, which rubs shoulders with the forest and has a gently sloping beach with fine sand. Centred on the artificial Lake Tismana, this draws a younger crowd than most of the resorts, many of whom take up the 2000 places available at the *Zodiac* and *Liliacul* **campsites**. **Rooms** can be arranged day or night at the accommodation office (☎041/73.11.84) at the southern end of the resort, next to the *Delta* restaurant. Nightlife focuses on the *Paradis* disco-bar, at the northern end of the beach, and the *Zodiac* holiday village to the west.

Imagine Mayan architects called upon to design Palm Beach and you'll get some idea of the pyramidal complexes that are the most striking feature of **AURORA**, the most recent resort, set on the cape of the same name southeast of Jupiter. Small and elegantly designed compared to the other resorts, Aurora has seven two-star **hotels** named after jewels, all charging standard prices (④) and all very popular with students out of season; of the seven, the *Granat* (☎ & fax 041/73.12.93), *Opal* (☎ & fax 041/73.13.74) and *Topaz* (☎041/73.12.92) all have a few cheaper rooms with shared showers.

There's a barely perceptible gap before **VENUS**, which is broadly similar to Jupiter, but more downmarket, with no fewer than sixteen one-star hotels. It has several man-made semicircular beaches, a disco and two main **bars**, the *Calipso* and *Auto-Night-Club*. There are ten private **hotels**, including the three-star *Dana*, near the main road to the west of the resort (☎041/73.15.03, fax 73.14.65; ⑥), which has a lovely terrace bar in the garden. The *Felicia* has a pool and is sited right by the sea (☎041/73.16.07, fax 73.10.14; ⑤), next door to the one-star *Silvia* (☎041/73.11.88; ③), one of the liveliest places to stay, with a 24-hour bar and shop and plans for refurbishment. Venus also has an accommodation office (☎041/73.16.74), should you need help finding a room. At the south end of the resort are a **campsite** and a sulphurous **spa** and, just inland, **stables** where you can hire horses to explore the forest, inhabited by roe deer, grouse and pheasants.

A reed-fringed lake lies between Venus and **SATURN**, a high-rise resort with lots of low-rent **hotels**, a large but run-down **campsite** and two **holiday villages**, the *Dunărea* and *Delta*. You can play tennis, minigolf or bowls, or dine to music at the *Balada*, *Prahova* or *Mercur* restaurants. As in Venus, CFR shares premises with the post office. All the hotels here are state-owned and booking should be made through the accommodation office (☎041/75.19.83, fax 75.55.59).

Mangalia and beyond

The modern suburbs of **MANGALIA** are close to swallowing up Saturn, and in fact Mangalia's **train station** is nearer to Saturn than to the centre of town. As with Constanța, Mangalia's appearance of modernity belies its ancient origin – the Greeks founded their city of Callatis here during the sixth century BC, when population pressure impelled them to colonize the Black Sea coast.

Heading south from the station and turning left at the first roundabout, you'll reach the *Mangalia* hotel (☎041/75.20.52, fax 75.35.10; ⑥), a decent enough place with a disco and casino. Behind, in Parc Stadionului, are the **ruins of Callatis**, which include sarcophagi and the vestiges of a Christian basilica, and beyond, at Şos. Constanţei 19 (the road from the roundabout to the centre), is the **Archeological Museum** (Tues–Sun 9am–5pm). Just south of the small town centre on Strada Oituz stands the **Sultan Esmahan Mosque**, built in 1590 and surrounded by a Muslim graveyard. There are medicinal baths on the town's south-western outskirts, beside Lake Mangalia, utilizing radioactive sulphurous hot springs to treat various muscular and neurological afflictions.

If you're planning to stay, head for the promenade (Strada Teilor) between the *Mangalia* and the harbour, where there are three near-identical **hotels** to choose from: the *Zenit* (☎041/75.16.45; ④), *Astra* (☎041/75.16.13; ④) and *Orion* (☎041/75.11.56; ④). At Strada Teilor 6, just south in the town centre, rises the four-star *President* (☎041/75.58.61, fax 75.56.95; ⑨), which relies more on business conferences than on the bikini brigade and is easily the best place to stay. Mangalia's **campsite** is north of town – from the train station turn left, then right after five minutes at the *Saturn* sign.

Doi Mai and Vama Veche

The laid-back villages of **DOI MAI** and **VAMA VECHE**, traditionally the haunts of artists, intellectuals and non-conformists, lie less than 20km south along the coast from Mangalia; bus #14 runs to both roughly every ninety minutes. Neither village has a hotel, but almost every house provides **private accommodation**, or you can **camp** in the dunes. Doi Mai (Second of May) has two **restaurants** and a food store but its beach (which does have free showers) is crammed between a naval dockyard and an anti-aircraft battery. There are plans to develop diving here, as this is the only place in Romania where marine turtles (loggerheads) can be seen, as well as dolphins and sea horses.

Under Communism Vama Veche (Old Customs Post), just short of the border with Bulgaria, was closed to all but staff of Cluj University or those who could claim some vague affiliation with it; it became a haven for non-conformists, who could escape the surveillance of the Securitate here. There was always some skinny-dipping, but now wearing clothes is the exception rather than the rule on the beach. There are no facilities at all, other than a bar/canteen, though if you want anything more than a snack you'll have to order it a day in advance.

travel details

Trains

Constanţa to: Braşov (2–4 daily; 5hr–5hr 45min, summer 6hr 15min);Bucharest (11–19 daily; 2hr 15min–4hr 45min); Galaţi (2 daily; 3hr 50min–6hr); Mangalia (5–16 daily; 1hr–1hr 25min);Medgidia (16–21 daily; 24–55min); Suceava (1 daily; 8hr); Tulcea (2 daily; 4hr–4hr 30min).

Medgidia to: Babadag (6 daily; 1hr 50min–2hr 20min); Bucharest (9–11 daily; 2hr 15min–4hr); Istria (5 daily; 1hr–1hr 15min); Mangalia (2–8 daily; 1hr 50min–2hr 30min, summer 1hr 45min); Negru Vodă (3 daily; 1hr 15min–1hr 25min); Tulcea (6 daily; 2hr 30min–3hr 15min).

Tulcea to: Bucharest (2 daily; 5hr 15min–6hr 50min); Constanţa (4 daily; 4hr–4hr 30min); Medgidia (6 daily; 2hr 35min–3hr 15min).

Buses

Constanţa to: Brăila (1 daily), Hîrşova (4 daily), Istria (2 daily), Mahmudia (1 daily), Tulcea (5 daily).

Tulcea to: Brăila (2 daily); Bucharest (1 daily); Constanţa (5 daily); Focşani (1 daily); Mahmudia (14 daily); Murighiol (6 daily); Niculiţel (1 daily).

Ferries

Tulcea to: Galaţi (daily in summer, 3 per week in winter; 3hr 15min); Periprava (daily in summer, 3 per week in winter; 5hr 30min); Sf. Gheorghe (daily in summer, 3 per week in winter; 5hr); Sulina (daily in summer, 3 per week in winter; 4hr); Izmail (not a scheduled service but operates roughly daily).

Hydrofoils

All services run daily in summer.

Tulcea to: Galaţi (1hr 30min); Periprava (2hr 30min); Sf. Gheorghe (2hr); Sulina (1hr 30min).

Planes

Constanţa to: Bucharest (1 daily; 45min).

Tulcea to: Bucharest (2 daily, Tues & Fri only; 45min).

International trains

Constanţa to: Budapest (1 daily; 16hr); Chişinău (3 per week, summer only; 13hr 45min).

International buses

Constanţa to: Athens (Tues, Thurs & Sat, 1 daily); Chişinău, Moldova (Thurs & Sat, 1 daily); Istanbul (1 daily); Varna, Bulgaria (4 weekly).

International ferry

Constanţa to: Istanbul (2 weekly in summer, 1 weekly in winter; 16hr).

International flights

Constanţa to Istanbul (DacAir; Wed, Fri, Sun).

THE HISTORICAL FRAMEWORK

Although inhabited since prehistoric times, Romania only achieved statehood during the nineteenth century, and Transylvania, one third of its present territory, was acquired as recently as 1920. Hence, much of Romania's history is that of its disparate parts – Dobrogea, the Banat, Bessarabia, Maramureş and, above all, the principalities of Moldavia, Wallachia and Transylvania.

ORIGINS: GREEKS, DACIANS & ROMANS (4000 BC–271 AD)

Despite the discovery of bones, weapons and implements within Carpathian caves, very little is known about the nomadic hunter-gatherers of the early **Stone Age**. With the recession of the glaciers, humans seem to have established their first settlements in Dobrogea, where the excavation of a Neolithic village at Habaşeşti and the discovery of numerous statues suggest that the tribes – known to archeologists as the **Hamangia Culture** – probably had a matriarchal society, worshipping fertility goddesses and the great Earth Mother.

Other cultures followed in the Bronze and Iron Ages, followed by the Celts of the **Hallstadt and La Tène cultures** who arrived from Asia in the last millennium BC; meanwhile during the sixth and seventh centuries BC, **Greek traders** established ports along the

Black Sea coast, the ruins of which can still be seen at Istria (Histria), Constanţa (Tomis), Mangalia (Callatis) and other sites. Commerce flourished between the Black Sea and Aegean ports, but the interior remained basically unknown to the Greeks until 512 BC, when the Persian emperor Darius attempted to expel the Scythians, another Asiatic people newly settled along the Danube. In 335 BC Alexander the Great crossed the Danube, defeating the Getae but failing to subdue them; in 292 BC his successor Lysimachus was captured by the Getic ruler Dromichaetes, only to be lectured on the value of peace and sent home.

The chronicler Herodotus had reported in the sixth century BC that of the numerous and disunited tribes of **Thracians** who inhabited the mountains on both sides of the Danube, the "bravest and most righteous" were those subsequently known as the "Geto-Dacians". The term Thracians is now taken as an umbrella term for the mix of original East Balkan tribes and incoming central European tribes then inhabiting this area, including the Getae on the Danube, the Dacians to their north, the Thracians proper to the south, and the Illyrians in present-day Albania.

Over the centuries these related tribes gradually coalesced and were brought under a centralized authority, so that by the first century BC a single leader, Burebista (82–44 BC), ruled a short-lived **Dacian empire**, occupying the territory of modern-day Romania and far more. It's assumed that, besides believing in a traditional mother goddess, the Getae and Dacians practised sun worship to a certain extent, and accorded semi-divine status to their chieftains, who ruled as priest-kings. Agriculture – and pastoralism in the highlands – provided the basis for the Dacian society, at the apex of which was the religious and political capital, **Sarmizegetusa**, located in the Orăştie mountains. Digs have revealed Dacian settlements from the Black Sea to Slovakia, and the sheer size of the kingdom contributed to its fragmentation after Burebista's demise.

A ROMAN COLONY

Before **Decebal** (87–106 AD) managed to reunite the kingdom, the lower reaches of the Danube had already been conquered by the **Romans**, who then began to expand northwards. The Dacians resisted, but were defeated during the course of two campaigns (in 101–2 AD and 105–6 AD) by the Emperor Trajan (98–117 AD). Although the Apuseni mountains and Maramureş were never subdued, most regions fell under Roman hegemony, maintained by the building of roads linking the garrison posts and trading towns. Besides the capital, Ulpa Traiana, important Roman towns included Apulum (Alba Iulia), Napoca (Cluj), Drobeta (Turnu Severin) and Porolissum (Zalău). For the **colonization of Dacia** (so rich and important a colony that it was known as Dacia Felix or Happy Dacia), settlers were brought from imperial territories as far afield as Greece and Spain and – on the evidence of shrines to Isis and Mithras – from Egypt and Persia. Later, the adoption of Christianity as the official religion led to its acceptance in Dacia, at least superficially; and in Hadrian's time the region was divided into two provinces to make its administration easier. With increasing incursions by nomadic Asian tribes such as the Goths in the third century, however, the defence of Dacia became too costly, and in 271 AD Emperor Aurelian ordered the withdrawal of Roman legions and administrators from the region.

THE AGE OF MIGRATIONS & DACO-ROMAN CONTINUITY

The Romans' departure was immediately followed by the arrival of other nomadic peoples sweeping out of Asia and on into western Europe during the **Age of Migrations**, including the Huns (4th and 5th centuries), Avars (6th century), Slavs (7th century) and Bulgars (7th century, along the coast en route to Bulgaria). The low-lying regions were greatly exposed to these invasions, whereas high mountains protected the region later to be called Transylvania. Excavations there have yielded coins bearing Roman inscriptions ranging from the time of Aurelian to the beginning of the fifth century, suggesting that the settlements continued to trade with the empire despite the Roman withdrawal – one of the arguments used to buttress the "Continuity Theory".

First propounded by Dimitrie Cantemir (see below), and elaborated later in the eighteenth century to draw together the Moldavian and Wallachian peoples, and later the Transylvanians, the **Daco-Roman Continuity Theory** holds that the Romanian people are

descended from the Roman settlers and the indigenous Dacians, who interbred and formed a hybrid culture. Since the poorer colonists (as opposed to rich ones, officials and troops) were likely to have remained following the imperial withdrawal, this process of formation continued for longer than the relatively brief period of Roman occupation (about 160 years) would suggest, and thus had a lasting impact on the culture of the population. Documentary evidence for this is, not surprisingly, practically non-existent, but Romanian philologists point to numerous words in their language derived from Latin; in particular, terms referring to pastoral activities (the mainstay of the Dacian lifestyle) and Christian worship. While some Romanians boast loudly about their Roman heritage, however, many of the imperial settlers would have been not free Romans but former slaves and soldiers, many of them Greeks and Arabs.

The theory would be of academic interest only were it not entwined with the dispute, now centuries old, between the Magyars and Romanians over the **occupation of Transylvania**. By claiming this racial and cultural continuity, and their uninterrupted residence within the Carpathian redoubt, Romanians assert their original, rightful ownership of Transylvania, and dismiss their rivals as usurpers. Conversely, the Magyars (who had first passed through around 896 as just another Asiatic horde before settling in the Pannonian basin, now Hungary) claim that their occupation of the "land beyond the forest" (from about 997 to the thirteenth century) met little resistance, and that the indigenous people were of Slavic stock, notably Cumans (or Kipchaks) owing their loyalty to the Bulgars, who had managed to forge an empire that by 812 included all of Romania. As the Bulgars extended their empire west to the Adriatic, they were driven south from Transylvania by the Magyars, and from Wallachia and Moldavia by the Pechenegs, who came from Asia in the eleventh century. According to some Magyar historians, **Vlachs** (Romanians) are first mentioned in Transylvania around 1222 as groups of nomadic pastoralists crossing the Carpathians, having wandered over the course of centuries from their original "homeland" in Macedonia and Illyria. This, together with other evidence (such as the Slavic rather than Latin derivation of the names of places and rivers), undermines the Romanian claim to prior occupation – or so some Hungarian scholars argue.

THE MEDIEVAL PRINCIPALITIES

TRANSYLVANIA

Whatever the indigenous population's identity, István I (Saint Stephen) and later monarchs of the Árpád dynasty such as Geza II gradually extended **Hungarian rule over Transylvania**, using foreigners to bolster their own settlements around the Mureş and Someş rivers, which allowed the region's mineral wealth to be shipped west. Besides subduing local Cumans, Bulgars and Vlachs, the colonists had to withstand frequent invasions by the "Golden Horde" of the **Tatars** (or Mongols), nomadic warriors who devastated much of Eastern Europe in 1241–42 and continued to reek havoc over the next five centuries.

While the Teutonic Knights invited to colonize the Bîrsa Land (around Braşov) in 1211 were evicted in 1225 for defying Andrew II, other groups of Germans – subsequently known as **Saxons** – built up powerful market towns like Hermannstadt (Sibiu) and Kronstadt (Braşov), which were granted self-government as "seats" (sedes or Stühle). Another ethnic group, the **Székely**, acted as the vanguard of colonization, moving during the thirteenth century from their settlements in the Bihor region to the eastern marches, where they too were allowed relative autonomy.

Unlike the Székely, who originally held land in common and enjoyed "noble" status, the Hungarians in Transylvania were either classed as plebs liable to all manner of dues and taxes, or as members of the tax-exempt nobility. This group dominated **the feudal system**, being represented alongside the Saxon and Székely "nations" (*Natio*) on the Diet which advised the principality's military and civil leader, the **Voivode** (vodă or voevod), who acted for the Hungarian king. Under the Árpád dynasty, Diets included *knezes* drawn from the Romanian-speaking Vlachs who, even then, may have constituted the majority of Transylvania's population. From the mid-fourteenth century onwards, however, Vlachs faced increasing **discrimination**, being gradually excluded from areas inhabited by Saxons or Magyars, and barred from public office. Besides the mistrust sown by

Bogdan Vodă's rebellion in Maramureş (see below), **religion** played an important part in this process. Whereas the Vlachs were Orthodox (barring a few apostate nobles), the other communities adhered to the Catholic church, which sought to undermine Orthodoxy throughout the Balkans. Over time, these divisions of class, race and religion coalesced into a kind of medieval apartheid system, which was to bedevil Transylvania's inhabitants for centuries to come.

WALLACHIA AND DOBROGEA

On the far side of the Carpathians, fully fledged principalities emerged somewhat later. Chronicles attribute the foundation of **Wallachia** (Vlahia or the Ţara Românească) to Negru Vodă (the Black Prince), who made Cîmpulung its first capital in 1290; but some confusion exists as to whether they refer to his son Radu Negru (1310–52), usually credited as the first of the Basarab dynasty, who beat off the Hungarians at the battle of Posada in 1330. The shift in Wallachia's capitals over the centuries – from Cîmpulung in the highlands down to Curtea de Argeş and Tîrgovişte in the foothills and then Bucharest on the plain – expressed a cautious move from the safety of the mountains to the financial opportunities of the trade routes with Turkey. Oppression, anarchy and piety were commonplace: the tithes and labour (*robot*) squeezed from the enserfed masses allowed the landowning **boyars** to pursue their favourite occupations – endowing Orthodox churches and engineering coups against the ruling voivodes. In centuries to come, the average duration of their reigns was to drop to less than three years.

Important trade routes linking Poland with the Black Sea passed through Wallachia, but commerce was entirely in the hands of Germans, Poles, Greeks and Jews. Though lavishly endowed, Wallachia's **Orthodox church** was subordinated to the Bulgarian and Byzantine patriarchates, writing its scriptures and conducting its rituals in Old Slavonic rather than the vernacular tongue. This was in part a legacy of Bulgar rule during the eighth and ninth centuries, but also reflected the policy of Wallachia's rulers, who tended to look south across the Danube for allies against the powerful kingdom of Hungary. These allies themselves faced a dangerous threat in the expansionist

Ottoman Turks, and were soon to be wiped from the map for centuries.

MOLDAVIA AND BESSARABIA

Attempts to enforce Hungarian rule in Maramureş provoked some of the indigenous population to follow **Bogdan Vodă** over the Carpathians in 1359. Their settlements around the headwaters of the Moldova were the cradle of a new principality, **Moldavia**; but the process of occupying the hills and steppes beyond the Carpathians had begun centuries earlier, more or less spontaneously. Groups of Romanian-speaking pastoralists and farmers gradually crossed the River Prut, moving on to the Dnestr where they encountered Ukrainians who called them "Volokhi". The Moldavian capital gradually shifted eastwards from Rădăuţi to Suceava, and then southwards to Iaşi when safety permitted. **Alexander the Good** (Alexandru cel Bun) may have gained his honorary title by ousting Turks from the eastern marches, though it could well have been bestowed by the Basarab family whom he made feudal lords of the region subsequently known as **Bessarabia**; or retrospectively by Moldavia's peasantry who suffered during the prolonged, violent anarchy that followed Alexandru's death. Besides Tatar invasions and rebellious boyars, Moldavia faced the threat of ambitious neighbouring powers – the kingdoms of Hungary and Poland on the western and northern borders, and the growing menace of the Turks to the south.

OTTOMANS, NATIONES AND PHANARIOTS

From the mid-fourteenth century onwards, the fate of the Balkan countries was determined by the **Ottoman empire** of the Seljuk Turks, which spread inexorably northwards, inflicting a shattering defeat on Serbia at Kosovo in 1389, crossing the Danube for the first time in 1390, and finally subjugating Bulgaria in 1393. Preoccupied with digesting these gains, the Turks were briefly halted by **Mircea the Old** (Mircea cel Bătrîn; 1386–1418) at the battle of Rovine in 1394. Appeals to the Pope and the Holy Roman Emperor Sigismund, King of Hungary and Bohemia, led to the dispatch of a crusading army, which through its own folly was crushed at Nicopolis on the Danube in 1396.

This and subsequent Christian defeats left the Turks entrenched along the lower Danube, compelling Mircea to acknowledge Ottoman suzerainty in 1417. By surrendering the fertile **Dobrogea** region and paying tribute, outright occupation was avoided and Wallachia's ruling class retained their positions; but henceforth both rulers and ruled were confronted with the alternatives of submission or resistance to an overwhelming force.

Even before the fall of Constantinople in 1453, Wallachia, Moldavia and Transylvania had become Christendom's front line of **resistance to the Turks**, and indeed, with Russia, the only Orthodox Christian state remaining free. Throughout the fifteenth century, the principalities' history is overshadowed by this struggle and the names of their military leaders are prominent. The Transylvanian voivode **Iancu de Hunedoara** (János Hunyadi) defeated the Turks near Alba Iulia and Sibiu in 1441–42, before becoming regent of Hungary in 1446 and leading multinational armies to victory at Niş and Belgrade, where he died of a fever in 1456. Iancu's son **Mátyás Corvinus** (1458–90, also known as Hunyadi Mátyás or Matei Corvin) became Hungary's great Renaissance king and continued to resist the Turks. Conflicting Polish and Hungarian ambitions periodically caused fighting between the principalities, whose rulers were as likely to betray each other as to collaborate, while the Sultans' willingness to accept tribute and appeasement allowed sporadic truces, and a particularly peaceful interlude under Neagoe Basarab of Wallachia (1512–21). The Ottomans were dislodged from southern Bessarabia by **Stephen the Great** (Ştefan cel Mare) of Moldavia and temporarily checked by the fortresses of Chilia and Cetatea Alba (now deep in Ukraine), but their resurgence under Bajazid II, and peace treaties signed by the Turks with Poland, Hungary and Venice in the 1470s and 1480s, presaged the demise of Moldavian independence, as was apparent to Stephen by the end of his embattled reign (1457–1504). Due to Wallachia's greater vulnerablity, its rulers generally preferred to pay off the Turks rather than resist them; **Vlad Ţepeş** (Vlad the Impaler – see p.384) being a notable exception from 1456 until his death in 1476.

In **Transylvania**, the least exposed region, the **Bobîlna peasant uprising** of 1437–38, under Antal Budai Nagy, rocked the feudal order. To safeguard their privileges, the Magyar nobility concluded a pact known as the **Union of Three Nations** with the Saxon and Székely leaders, whereby each of these three ethnic communities or *Nationes* agreed to recognize and defend the rights of the others. As a consequence, the Vlachs were relegated to the position of "those who do not possess the right of citizenship...but are merely tolerated by grace", and a spate of decrees followed, effectively prohibiting them from holding public office or residing in the Saxon and Magyar towns. The increasing exploitation of the Magyar peasantry led to another uprising under György Dózsa in 1514, savagely repressed by voivode **János Zápolyai** (1510–40), who imposed the onerous Werbőczy Code or Tripartium in 1517. This feudal version of apartheid was reinforced during the sixteenth century when Transylvania became a stronghold of the **religious reformation**. While the *Nationes* averted sectarian strife by decreeing equal rights in 1556 for the four religions (Calvinist, Lutheran, Catholic and Unitarian) to which their members subscribed, both the Edict of Turda (1568) and the Diet of 1571 merely tolerated the existence of Orthodoxy, the religion of the Vlach population.

The crushing defeat of Hungary by Suleyman the Magnificent at **Mohács** (1526) and the Turkish occupation of Buda (1541) exacerbated the **isolation of the principalities**. Although the Hapsburg dynasty of Austria laid claim to what was left of Hungary after Mohács, Zápolyai managed to play them off against the Ottomans, and thus maintain a precarious autonomy for Transylvania, even gaining control of Hungary east of the River Tisza (the Partium) in 1538; and successors such as István Báthori (1571–81, who was elected King of Poland from 1575 and drove back Ivan the Terrible), and Zsigmond Báthori (1581–97) were able to maintain this independence. In **Moldavia**, however, **Petru Rareş** could only hold his throne (1527–38 and 1541–56) by breathtaking duplicity and improvisations, while his successors plumbed even further depths.

SHORT-LIVED UNIFICATION

Understandably, Romanian historiography has scant regard for such figures, and prefers to highlight the achievements of **Michael the Brave** (Mihai Viteazul, often known in Wallachia as Mihai Bravul). Crowned ruler of Wallachia by the boyars in 1593, his triumph against the Turks in 1595 was followed by the overthrow of Andrew Báthori in Transylvania in 1599 and a lightning campaign across the Carpathians in 1600 to secure him the Moldavian throne. This opportunist and short-lived **union of the principalities** under one crown – which fragmented immediately following his murder in 1601 – has subsequently been presented as a triumph of Romanian nationalism, and evidence suggests that the Vlachs in Transylvania welcomed Michael as a liberator. However, although he improved the status of the Vlach nobles and the Orthodox church in Transylvania, he did nothing for the serfs, and the *Nationes* kept their privileges.

Between 1604 and 1657 Transylvania attained genuine independence from the Hapsburgs and Ottomans, although the region was rarely at peace. István Bocskai (1604–06) pushed its border westwards, and "Crazy" Gábor Báthori (1608–13) promoted himself to prince and pursued a vendetta against the Saxon towns until overthrown by **Gábor Bethlen**, whose encouragement of cultural and economic development and resistance to the tide of counter-Reformation made his reign (1613–29) a golden age by most standards.

From the 1630s onwards, **Moldavia and Wallachia** avoided direct occupation as Turkish *pashaliks* by accepting Ottoman "advisers". These Greek families – the Ghicas, Cantacuzinos, Rosettis, Ducas and others – originated from the Phanar district of Constantinople, and hence became known collectively as the **Phanariots**. In Moldavia, they encouraged the Orthodox church to abandon **Old Slavonic** as the language of the scriptures and ritual in favour of Greek; but this policy had the unintended result of stimulating a move towards the Romanian language, using books printed at Govora and Iaşi. This presaged a minor cultural renaissance – particularly in the field of architecture – during a period of relative stability provided by the reigns of **Matei Basarab** (1633–54), **Şerban Cantacuzino** (1678–88), **Constantin Brîncoveanu** (1688–1714) in Wallachia and **Dimitrie Cantemir** (1710–11) in Moldavia. After brutally terminating the reigns of the last two, the Turks dispensed with native rulers, and began appointing **Phanariot princes** instead. These were purely concerned with plundering the principalities to pay the huge bribes necessary to remain in good standing at court, and enrich themselves before relinquishing what was essentially a franchise to make money, and returning home. Their rapaciousness and more than seventy changes of ruler in Moldavia and Wallachia between 1711 and 1821 beggared both regions, and gave rise to the proverb that "madmen rejoice when the rulers change".

THE STRUGGLE FOR INDEPENDENCE & UNIFICATION

From 1683, when the siege of Vienna was broken, the alliance of Christian powers known as the "Holy League" succeeded in **driving the Turks out of Hungary**, Croatia and Slavonia; in 1686 Budapest was retaken, in 1687 the second battle of Mohács reversed the result of the first encounter, in 1688 Belgrade was retaken, and in 1691 the battle of Slankamen established the frontier along the line of the Danube and Sava rivers, and thus **Hapsburg control of Transylvania**. In 1697 the great general Prince Eugen of Savoy took command of the Hapsburg forces, and in the Treaty of Karlowitz of 1699 the Turks accepted their claims to all of Transylvania except for the Banat of Temesvár. The Turks attempted a comeback in 1714, but were finally driven from Hungary and the Banat in 1718. Thereafter, the **decline of Ottoman power** in the Balkans continued, and while nationalist movements struggled to free their countries during the nineteenth century, the main European powers became increasingly preoccupied with the **"Eastern question"** – which of them should inherit the Ottomans' influence? Foreign interests were generally entangled with local ones, so that the principalities' internal conflicts between the old nobility, the bourgeoisie and the peasantry could have repercussions on an international level, and vice versa.

This first became apparent in **Transylvania**, where Hapsburg recognition of the privileged "three Nations and four religions" – as established by the Leopoldine Diploma of 1691 – was followed by attempts to undermine this status quo, principally directed against the Hungarian nobility. As Catholics and imperialists, the Hapsburg monarchy persuaded the Orthodox clergy in Transylvania to accept papal authority, and promised that Vlachs who joined the

Uniate Church (see p.168) would be granted equality with the *Nationes*. Although the Diet's opposition ensured the retraction of this promise in 1701, Bishop Ioan Inocenţiu Micu and the intellectuals of the "Transylvanian School" (Şcoala Ardealana) agitated for equal rights and articulated the Vlachs' growing consciousness of being **Romanians**. By far the largest ethnic group, they now began to assert their "original claim" on Transylvania and solidarity with their kinsfolk across the Carpathians. The future Joseph II toured Transylvania incognito and begged his mother, the Empress Maria Teresa (1740–80), to protect the Romanians from discrimination. In 1781 he issued an edict of religious toleration before dissolving the monasteries and embarking upon the abolition of serfdom. All this came too late, however, to prevent the great peasant rebellion led by **Horea, Crişan** and **Cloşca** in 1784–85. Its crushing only stimulated efforts to attain liberation by constitutional means – such as the famous Supplex Libellus Valachorum petition of 1791, which was approved by the emperor but predictably rejected by the Transylvanian Diet.

The gradual development of liberal and nationalist movements in **Moldavia and Wallachia** stemmed from a variety of causes. The ideals of the Romantic movement and the French Revolution gained hold among the intelligentsia and many young boyars, while the success of Serbian and Greek independence movements and the emergence of capitalist structures in the principalities showed that Turkish dominance and feudalism were in decline. A rebellion in support of the Greek independence struggle organized by the Phanariot Alexandre Ypsilanti attracted little following within Moldavia, but the example inspired a major uprising against Phanariot rule in Wallachia in 1821, led by **Tudor Vladimirescu**. Although defeated, this uprising persuaded the Turks that it was high time for the **end of Phanariot rule**, and power was restored to native boyars in 1822.

THE RISE OF RUSSIA AND WORLD WAR I

As the power of the Ottomans declined, that of **Tsarist Russia** grew. Fired by imperialist and Pan-Slavist ideals and fear of Hapsburg encroachment (manifest in 1774, when Austria annexed the region henceforth known as

Bucovina), Russia presented itself in 1779 as the guardian of the Ottomans' Christian subjects, and expanded its territories towards the Balkans as well as into the Caucasus and Central Asia. In 1792 Russian forces reached the River Dnestr; one Russo–Turkish war led to the annexation of Bessarabia in 1812, and another to the Treaty of Adrianople (1829), by which Moldavia and Wallachia became Russian protectorates. The Tsarist governor **General Kiseleff** was in no sense a revolutionary, but he introduced liberal reforms and assemblies in both principalities under the terms of the Règlement Organique, which remained in force after the Russians withdrew in 1834, having selected two rulers. Of these, Michael Sturdza in Moldavia was the more despotic but also the more energetic, levying heavy taxes to construct roads, dykes, hospitals and schools.

Given the boyars' dominance of the assemblies, economic development took precedence over the political and social reforms demanded by sections of the liberal bourgeoisie, particularly the growing number of Romanians who had studied in France. The **democratic movement** which emerged in both principalities – led by **Nicolae Golescu, Ion Brătianu, Nicolae Bălcescu and Mihail Kogălniceanu** – campaigned against the Règlement and for the unification of Moldavia and Wallachia, which was anticipated by the removal of customs barriers between the two in 1846. This movement briefly came to power in 1848, the **Year of Revolutions**, which heightened nationalist consciousness in the principalities and among the Romanians of Transylvania (see below).

Russia, now claiming to be "the gendarme of Europe", intervened militarily to restore the status quo ante; likewise, the build up to the Crimean War saw Russia occupying Moldavia and Wallachia and fighting the Turks along the Danube. The Congress of Paris, ending the war in 1856, reaffirmed Turkish rule, although with increased autonomy for the boyars, while Russia was obliged to return part of Bessarabia to Moldavia. Thus the nationalist cause was thwarted until January 1859, when the assemblies of Moldavia and Wallachia were persuaded to elect a single ruler, **Alexandru Ioan Cuza**, thereby circumventing the restrictions imposed to prevent their **unification**. French support enabled the United Principalities (renamed Rumania in 1862) to weather Hapsburg hostility, and the government embarked on a series of reforms, the most important of which were the **abolition of serfdom** and the expropriation of the huge monastic estates. Although the peasants were still bound to pay for the land "given" to them (and, as a result, fell into greater debt than before), these measures enraged the landowning classes and other conservative elements, who forced Cuza's abdication in 1866 and selected the German Prince Karl of Hohenzollern to rule as Prince Carol I. In 1877 yet another Russo–Turkish war broke out, and Carol personally led a Romanian army into Bulgaria to help the Russians, suffering huge losses in taking Pleven and the Shipka Pass. Rumania declared its **independence** on May 9, 1877; the Treaty of Berlin, ending the war in 1878, forced Turkey to recognize this and to cede Northern Dobrogea to Rumania, and Carol became a fully fledged king in 1881, with an iron crown made from a gun captured at Pleven.

Events in **Transylvania** followed a different course during the nineteenth century. There, popular support for the 1848 revolution split along nationalist lines. Whereas the abolition of serfdom was universally welcomed by the peasantry, the Romanian population opposed the Diet's unification of Transylvania with Hungary, which Magyars of all classes greeted with enthusiasm; the Saxons were lukewarm on both issues. Following protest meetings at Blaj, **Avram Iancu** formed Romanian guerrilla bands to oppose the Hungarians; belated attempts by Kossuth and Bălcescu to compromise on the issue of Romanian rights came too late to create a united front against the Tsarist armies which invaded Transylvania on behalf of the Hapsburgs. As in Hungary, the Hapsburgs introduced martial law and widespread repression in the aftermath of the revolution.

As a result of the Ausgleich or Compromise of 1867 which established the Dual Monarchy of the Austro-Hungarian Empire, the Transylvanian Diet was abolished and the region became part of "Greater Hungary", ruled directly from Budapest. The governments of **Kalman Tisza** (1875–90) and his successors pursued a policy of **"Magyarization"** in Transylvania, as in Slovakia and elsewhere, although Bucovina and Maramureş remained under Austrian rule and avoided the worst of this. Laws passed in 1879 and 1883 made

Hungarian the official language, and a barrage of laws relating to education and the press were passed in an effort to undermine Romanian culture. The cultural association **ASTRA**, founded in 1861, acted in its defence until the establishment of the **National Party** in 1881, which maintained close links with kindred parties across the Carpathians.

The influence of foreign capitalism increased enormously around the turn of the century, as Rumania's mineral wealth – particularly its oil – inspired competition among the great powers. While liberal and conservative politicians engaged in ritualistic parliamentary squabbles, however, nothing was done about the worsening impoverishment of the people. Peasant grievances exploded in the **răscoala** of 1907 – a nationwide uprising which was savagely crushed (with at least 10,000 deaths) and then followed by a series of limited, ineffectual agrarian reforms.

Rumania's acquisition of territory south of the Danube in 1878 was one of the many bones of contention underlying the **Balkan Wars** that embroiled Rumania, Bulgaria, Serbia, Macedonia and Greece. Rumania sat out the first Balkan War (1912–13), but joined the alliance against Bulgaria in 1913 and gained the southern part of Dobrogea. King Carol had signed a secret pact with the Central Powers; however he died in 1914 and was succeeded by his nephew Ferdinand, married to Princess Marie, granddaughter of both Queen Victoria and Tsar Alexander II. Thus when Rumania entered **World War I** in August 1916, it joined the Triple Entente and attacked the Austro-Hungarian forces in Transylvania. After brief advances, the tide turned against Rumania, as Bulgarian and German forces crossed the Danube and captured all of Wallachia (including Bucharest) and much of Moldavia; desperate defence at Mărăşti, Mărăşeşti and the Oituz Pass, aided by French, Russian and even British advisors, finally averted total collapse, but the demise of Russia forced Rumania to sign an onerous peace treaty in May 1918. By October, however, the collapse of the Central Powers on the Western Front reversed this situation entirely. The Austro-Hungarian empire rapidly fragmented as its subject races established their own states with the support of the Entente and President Woodrow Wilson: Rumanian armies advanced into Transylvania, and then on into

Hungary to overthrow the short-lived Communist régime of Béla Kun in August 1919. On December 1, 1918 the Romanian assembly of Alba Iulia declared **Transylvania's union with Rumania** to scenes of wild acclaim. The Romanian population of Bessarabia, set free by the Russian Revolution, had already declared their union with Rumania in March 1918, followed in November by Bucovina.

Despite furious opposition, above all from the Hungarians, this was subsequently upheld by the Entente powers and the **Treaty of Trianon** in 1920, as a reward both for fighting on the "right side" (the winning side) in the war and for being such a firm bulwark against Bolshevism. Rumania doubled both in population and territory, while Hungary lost half of its population and two thirds of its territory, the source of great resentment ever since. The "successor states" of Romania, Czechoslovakia and Yugoslavia formed the "Little Entente", defensive alliances against Hungarian revanchism, cemented by a Franco–Romanian treaty in 1926.

"GREATER ROMANIA" (1921–44)

The country's enlarged territory was dignified by the adoption of the name **Greater Romania**, but the lives of the mass of the population hardly improved. The expropriation of Hungarian estates in Transylvania affected not only the nobility, but smallholders as well; Hungarian employees, no matter how lowly, of the railways, the post office, or any government body were dismissed on a huge scale and Romanian immigrants were brought in from Moldavia and Wallachia to replace them. Equally the many peasants who expected to benefit from the **agrarian reform** of 1921 were rapidly disillusioned when speculators and boyars appropriated much of the land by financial manipulation.

Romania was governed by the **National Liberal Party**, favoured by King Ferdinand, but soon standing for little except holding on to power for its own sake: it pursued nationalist and populist policies, damaging the economy by discriminating against foreign investors. On Ferdinand's death in 1927, they were dismissed and replaced by the National Peasant Party, which in 1928 won the only remotely fair election in this period. Despite its parliamentary majority and its genuinely reforming and honest policies, the National Peasant government, led by **Iuliu Maniu**, pursued conservative policies, constrained by a collapse in the price of Romanian grain following the world economic crisis of 1929, vested interests and entrenched corruption.

However, it was a bizarre moral issue that led to the government's fall: in 1930, after a three-year regency, **Carol II** took the throne and at once broke a promise to put aside his divorced Jewish mistress, Magda Lupescu. The puritan Maniu resigned and the government fell apart. Carol exploited the constitution of 1923, giving the king the right to dissolve parliament and call elections at will; a totally corrupt system soon developed whereby the government would fix elections by every means possible, only to be dismissed and replaced by the opposition when the king had tired of them. Between 1930 and 1940 there were no less than twenty-five separate governments, leading to the collapse of the political parties themselves. Strikes in the oil and rail industries in 1933 were put down by armed force; Carol set up his own "youth movement", and soon began routine phone-tapping by the Siguranța, the Securitate's predecessor.

THE IRON GUARD AND WORLD WAR II

A **fascist movement** also established itself, particularly in Bessarabia, which had a long tradition of anti-Semitism. The main fascist party, which inherited much of the National Peasant Party's rural support, was the Legion of the Archangel Michael, founded in 1927; its green-shirted paramilitary wing, the **Iron Guard**, extolled the soil, death and a mystical form of Orthodoxy, fought street battles against Jews and followers of other political parties, and murdered four current or former prime ministers. In 1937 the anti-Semitic National League of Christian Defence was installed in power by the king, but the prime minister, the poet Octavian Goga (see p.210), at once insulted Lupescu and was dismissed in February 1938, after just six weeks in power. This at last provoked Carol to ban all political parties (other than his own National Renaissance Front) and set up a royal dictatorship (soon to be endorsed by a fixed plebiscite); the Legionary leader **Corneliu Codreanu** was killed in November "while trying to escape".

Carol did not want to be driven into the _ of Hitler, desperately seeking closer economic ties with the West. However it was too late; in February 1939 Germany demanded a monopoly of Romanian exports in return for a guarantee of its borders, and in March agreed an oil-for-arms deal. In April, Carol obtained feeble guarantees from Britain and France, but in August the equilibrium was shattered by the Nazi–Soviet Non-Aggression Pact. In June 1940 a Soviet ultimatum led to the annexation of Bessarabia and northern Bucovina, and, two months later, Hitler forced Carol to cede Northern Transylvania to Germany's ally, Hungary, and southern Dobrogea to Bulgaria. On September 6, unable to maintain his position after giving away such huge portions of Romanian territory, Carol fled with Lupescu and his spoils, leaving his son **Mihai**, then nineteen years old, to take over the throne.

Mihai accepted the formation of a Legionary government, led by Codreanu's successor Horia Sima and by **Marshal Ion Antonescu**, who styled himself Conducator ("leader", equivalent to Führer) but had little influence over local legionary groups who unleashed an orgy of violence against Jews and liberals. To ensure himself a stable and productive ally, Hitler forced Antonescu to curb the Iron Guard; he began to disarm it, provoking an armed uprising (and the savage butchery of 124 Jews in Bucharest) in January 1941, only suppressed by the army after a fierce struggle.

Romania entered **World War II** in June 1941, joining the Nazi invasion of Russia, with the objective of regaining Bessarabia and northern Bucovina. Romanian troops took Odessa and joined in the attacks on Sevastopol and Stalingrad, taking heavy casualties. Jews and Gypsies in Bessarabia, Bucovina and the Hungarian-controlled area of Transylvania were rounded up and deported for slave labour and then to extermination camps. By 1943, however, the Red Army was advancing fast, and Antonescu began to look for a way to abandon Hitler and change sides. Opposition to the war mounted as the Russians drew nearer, and on August 23, 1944, a **royal/military coup** overthrew the Antonescu regime just as they crossed the border – a date commemorated until 1989 as Liberation Day, although it took until October 25 to clear the Germans from the country.

THE HOLOCAUST IN ROMANIA

...had the third greatest **Jewish** ...urope after Poland and the Soviet ... lived in Bessarabia, Bucovina and ...orthern Moldavia, notably around Do... ...n June 1940 Bessarabia and northern Bucovina were ceded to the Soviet Union, as demanded by Hitler, and at least fifty Jews were killed in Dorohoi by retreating Romanian troops. On June 22, 1941, Romania declared war on the Soviet Union, but action did not commence on this front until July 3, so the troops filled the interval by carrying out an awful pogrom in Iaşi, killing about 8000 Jews, leading the Germans to comment, "we always act scientifically....We use surgeons, not butchers". As the army advanced (with units of the German Einsatzgruppe D following), there were many more massacres; at least 33,000 Jews died in Bessarabia and Bucovina between June 22 and September 1, 1941.

Deportations to Transnistria, the conquered territory beyond the River Dnestr, began in earnest on September 16; around 150,000 Jews were taken, of whom 18,000 to 22,000 died in transit. Up to 90,000 more died from starvation, disease and general mistreatment. Between November 21 and 29, 1941, all 48,000 Jews held in the Bogdanovka camp in southern Transnistria were killed; another 18,000 were killed in the Dumanovka camp.

In July 1942, the Germans began to press hard for the Jews of Wallachia, Moldavia and southern Transylvania to be deported to the camps, following 120,000 taken to Auschwitz from Hungarian-controlled Northern Transylvania. This was agreed but then refused after lobbying by neutral diplomats and the Papal Nuncio, although it was probably due to the fact that the Jews were still vital to the functioning of the economy. In November

1942 it was agreed that Romanian Jews in Germany should be sent to the German death camps.

By November 1942, when the Allies launched their attack at El Alamein and the Operation Torch landings in North Africa, and it was likely that Stalingrad would be held by the Soviets, Romania was thinking of changing sides. The **World Jewish Congress** (in Geneva) proposed a **plan** to save 70,000 Romanian Jews, and possibly 1.3 million more in Eastern Europe, by paying the Romanian government twelve shillings per head to allow them to leave by ship for Palestine. This was blocked by opposition from anti-Semites in the US State Department and from Britain, worried about the reaction of Arabs to further Jewish immigration to Palestine, as well as by the practical problems inherent in sending money to a Nazi ally. Thirteen boats did leave, with 13,000 refugees, but two sank (with 1,163 on board) and others were stopped by Turkey, under pressure from both Britain and Germany.

In 1944, Antonescu, negotiating secretly in Stockholm for an exit from the war, began a **limited repatriation** from the camps of Transnistria, bringing back 1500 in December 1943 and 1846 orphans by March 1944. He warned the Germans not to kill Jews as they retreated; nevertheless a final thousand Jews were killed in Tiraspol jail. On March 20, 1944, the Red Army reached the Dnestr, and the worst of the nightmare ended. In Antonescu's trial in May 1946 it was said, "if the Jews of Romania are still alive, they owe it to Marshal Antonescu", who claimed to have saved about 275,000 Jews by his policy of keeping them for extermination at home. Overall between 264,900 and 470,000 Romanian Jews, and 36,000 Gypsies, died in the war; 428,000 Jews survived or returned alive.

THE PEOPLE'S REPUBLIC (1944–65)

While the Romanian army subordinated itself to Soviet command to help drive the Nazis out of Transylvania, Hungary and Czechoslovakia, the struggle to determine the state of **postwar Romania** was already under way. The Yalta agreement put Romania firmly within the Soviet sphere, but the Western powers maintained observers in Bucharest, requiring a veneer of democratic process. The first government

formed by King Mihai was a broad coalition, with Communists only playing a minor role, but gradually, due largely to the presence of the Red Army and veiled threats of annexation, the Communists and their fellow-travellers, such as the Ploughmen's Front, increased their influence. In March 1945, a new coalition was installed under the premiership of **Dr Petru Groza** (leader of the Ploughmen's Front); again this included politicians from the prewar parties as a sop to conservative opinion and the West, but the key posts were occupied by

Communists. The land reform of 1945 benefited millions of peasants at the expense of the Saxons and Swabians of Transylvania and the Banat, who had become the biggest landowners since the dispossession of the Magyars, while women were enfranchised for the first time in 1946, their votes supposedly contributing to the election of another ostensibly "balanced" government. In fact, while virtually every device ever used to rig an election was brought into play, it seems that the Communists and their allies only received about 20 percent of the votes: nevertheless it was announced that they had received almost 80 percent, and the takeover steamed on regardless.

Like Groza's first administration, this included leading capitalists and former Guardists, whom the Communists initially wooed, since their first aim was to eliminate the left and centre parties. The leadership of the National Peasant Party played into their hands by secretly meeting US officials, enabling them to be disposed of on espionage charges in 1947, while other parties were forcibly merged with the Communists. On December 30, 1947, **King Mihai was forced to abdicate** and Romania was declared a **People's Republic**.

Antonescu and up to 60,000 others were executed after highly irregular trials in 1946 and 1947. Eighty thousand arrests followed in an effort to overcome peasant resistance to **collectivization** (a reversal of the earlier agrarian reform), with many more in 1948 in the campaign to "liquidate" the Uniate Church. The **nationalization** of industries, banks and utilities in June 1948 placed the main economic levers in Communist hands; thereafter the bourgeoisie was assailed on all fronts, and the Party openly declared its intention to reshape society by applying Stalinist policies. While key sectors of the proletariat were favoured to secure their loyalty, **police terror** was used against real or potential opponents, with victims incarcerated in prisons like Jilava (an underground complex south of Bucharest) and Piteşti, or conscripted for reed-cutting in the Delta or work on the Danube–Black Sea Canal, the "Canal Mortii" which claimed over 100,000 lives before being abandoned in 1953.

The Communist Party itself was split by bitter conflicts between its "Muscovite" wing (those who had spent the war in Moscow, led by Ana Pauker and Vasile Luca) and the "nationalists", themselves split between the "prison-Communists" and the "secretariat-Communists" who had remained free and in hiding. In 1952 the prison-Communists emerged on top, under **Gheorghe Gheorghiu-Dej**, General Secretary of the party's Central Committee since 1948, who had retained Stalin's confidence largely because the secretariat group were too ideologically flexible, while Pauker and her group were simply too Jewish. She and 192,000 other members were purged from the Party, and Lucreţiu Pătrăşcanu (Minster of Justice 1944–48) was executed in 1954 after a show trial. Stalin had died in 1953, but Gheorghiu-Dej took great exception to reformist trends in the USSR, and stuck grimly to the Stalinist true faith. Disagreeing with the role of "breadbasket" assigned to the country by the Eastern bloc trade organization, COMECON, he followed a Stalinist policy of developing heavy industry, claiming the impossible growth rate of 13 percent per year.

The USSR, having annexed Bessarabia once more, had given parts of it to Ukraine and created the puppet **Republic of Moldova** from the rest. Therefore Gheorghiu-Dej's increasing refusal to follow the Moscow line was a great success domestically, tapping into a vein of popular nationalism that was exploited more systematically by Ceauşescu, his successor. By arresting the leadership of the left-wing Hungarian People's Alliance and establishing an "Autonomous Hungarian Region" in the Székely Land in 1952, Gheorghiu-Dej simultaneously decapitated the Magyar political organization in Transylvania while erecting a facade of minority rights.

In March 1965 Gheorghiu-Dej died, and was soon succeeded by **Nicolae Ceauşescu**, until then a little-known party hack, who was able by 1969 to outmanoeuvre his rivals in the collective leadership and establish undisputed power.

"YEARS OF LIGHT": THE CEAUŞESCU ERA

There seems little doubt that for the first few years of his rule, Ceauşescu was **genuinely popular**, and might even have been able to win an election: he encouraged a cultural thaw, put food and consumer goods into the shops, denounced security police excesses (blaming them on Gheorghiu-Dej), and above all denounced the Warsaw Pact invasion of

Czechoslovakia in 1968. His **independent foreign policy** gained Romania the reputation of being the "maverick" state of the Eastern bloc, maintaining links with Albania, China and Israel after the USSR and its satellites had severed relations, building links with West Germany, criticizing the invasion of Afghanistan in 1979, and defying the Soviet boycott by sending a team to the Los Angeles Olympics in 1984. Rewards included state visits to Britain and the USA, admittance to the GATT, IMF and World Bank, and trade deals with the EC and USA.

However, he soon reverted to tried and tested methods of control as the shops emptied again and his **economic failure** became obvious. Ceauşescu stuck throughout to the Stalinist belief in heavy industry, and during the 1970s the country's **industrialization programme** absorbed 30 percent of GNP, and \$10,200m in foreign loans. Because quality was always inadequate, little could be exported, but Ceauşescu became obsessed in the 1980s with the need to repay Western loans. Living standards plummeted as all but a minimal amount of food was exported, and the population was obliged to work harder and harder for less and less. Amazingly, all the foreign debt was repaid by 1989, although there was no prospect of any improvement in living standards thereafter.

Ceauşescu was convinced that the key to industrial growth lay in **building a larger workforce**, and therefore as early as 1966 he banned abortions and contraception for any married woman under 40 with less than four children (in 1972 the limits were raised to 45 and five). It was only in the 1980s, when developing paranoia and his personality cult put him increasingly out of touch with ordinary people, that he introduced the "**Baby Police**" and compulsory gynecological examinations, to ensure that women were not trying to avoid their "patriotic duty". Unmarried people and married couples without children were penalized by higher taxes. Ceauşescu also **discriminated against the minorities**, trying to persuade them to assimilate with the Romanian populace; it became increasingly hard to get an education or to buy books in Hungarian or German, or to communicate with relatives abroad, while families were pressured to give their children Romanian names.

The two million-plus Magyars (including the Székely and Csángós) bore the brunt of this chauvinism, causing a notable worsening of diplomatic relations with Hungary. Neither this nor criticism of the treatment of the Gypsy population worried Ceauşescu, but he tried to keep on the right side of the German and Israeli governments, which purchased exit visas for ethnic Germans and Jews in Romania for substantial sums in hard currencies.

There were other equally appalling **abuses of human rights**, all of which got worse through the 1980s: the **systematization** programme for rural redevelopment, censorship, the "typewriter law" (requiring that every machine be registered with the police) and constant repression by the **Securitate** or secret police, which produced an atmosphere of ubiquitous fear and distrust even between members of the same family, as up to one in four of the population was rumoured to be an informer, and virtually every home was supposed to be bugged. Increasingly, key posts were allocated to relatives of the Ceauşescus, while all other senior figures were rotated every few years between jobs and between Bucharest and the provinces, to prevent anyone building up an independent powerbase and being able to challenge for power.

In the **1980s** everything went downhill rapidly, as the truth about the country's economic collapse was hidden from Ceauşescu by his subordinates. Food, fuel, lightbulbs, everything was in short supply, but Ceauşescu and Elena pushed on with megalomaniac projects such as the Palace of the People in Bucharest, the Danube–Black Sea Canal (again) and the village systematization programme. Just as Gheorghiu-Dej had rejected Moscow's policy changes after Stalin's death, so too Ceauşescu made plain his opposition to *glasnost*, and it began to be rumoured that Gorbachev would be glad to be rid of the increasingly erratic Romanian leader.

In 1986 strikes, rapidly quelled, began to erupt in protest at ration cuts and increases in work quotas, and in November 1987 food and heating shortages and the introduction of a seven-day week at the Red Flag and Tractor factories in Braşov led to **riots**. Silviu Brucan, ambassador to the United Nations and United States from 1956–62, and others then issued a statement to the Western press warning that "the cup of privation is now full and the workers no longer accept that they can be treated like obedient servants". Again in March 1989 they wrote an open letter to Ceauşescu, urging an end to systematization and human rights abuses. Ceauşescu's response was to confine them to their homes and to rush food and Securitate to the cities. At the Party congress of November 1989 he rejected any change in economic or social policies and was re-elected unanimously, as usual.

THE REVOLUTION

By **December 1989** the situation in Romania was so desperate that it seemed impossible for Ceauşescu not to bow to the **wave of change** that had swept over the whole of Eastern Europe: yet he refused even to acknowledge its existence, beyond being convinced that Gorbachev and Bush were conspiring to remove him from power. Indeed most observers felt that change would not come until Ceauşescu had died, an event expected sooner rather than later.

However, the people of Romania were aware of events in the other countries of East-Central Europe, thanks to the BBC and Radio Free Europe. The people of **Timişoara** could receive Hungarian and Yugoslav television and radio as well, and it was here that the forces of change finally broke loose. A turbulent priest of the Hungarian Calvinist church, **Lászlo Tökes**, had become such a thorn in the establishment's side that he was to be forcibly removed from Timişoara to a tiny village in the back of beyond; the order for his transfer had been given in March but he had refused to leave his congregation. Tökes was due to be evicted on December 15; his congregation massed outside the church to prevent this, but he was nevertheless removed in the early hours of the 17th.

Both Hungarians and Romanians were already protesting on the streets, and this now turned into a **riot.** Ceauşescu ordered that this should be halted by any means necessary; protestors were met with bullets, and for a while the streets were cleared. However, from Monday, December 18, the factories around town went on strike and by December 20 the centre of town was filled with up to 100,000 protestors, **demanding Ceauşescu's resignation**, while the army chose to withdraw rather than launch a massacre.

Nicolae Ceauşescu, feeling that the crisis had been contained, went as planned to Iran on the 18th, to sign an arms deal, and unwisely left Elena in charge: she insisted on further savage and counterproductive action. When Ceauşescu returned from Iran on the evening of the 20th he ordered a crackdown on the "hooligan elements" in Timişoara, thinking that he could still manipulate the usual knee-jerk nationalist reactions (blaming all disturbances on Hungarian interference). However, the young soldiers in Timişoara, finding that they were faced with Romanians as well as Hungarians, refused to shoot.

Ceauşescu also called for a massive show of support by supposedly tame crowds in **Bucharest** the next day, December 21. Over 100,000 people were brought from their workplaces to Piaţa Republicii (now Piaţa Revoluţiei) to hear him speak, although he was soon interrupted by shouts of "Timişoara!" and the singing of "Romanians Awake". Television screens went blank, but not before the whole nation had seen the look of incredulity and confusion on his face as he realized that his regime was finished. The police and Securitate opened fire but were unable to clear the crowds from the city centre, partly because the Minister of Defence, **General Vasile Milea**, ordered the army not to shoot. On the morning of December 22, Ceauşescu had Milea shot, but this merely precipitated the defection of many army units to the side of the protestors. By noon the crowds had broken into the Party's Central Committee building, and the **Ceauşescus fled by helicopter** from the roof.

It's fairly clear what happened to them, but much less clear what was going on behind the scenes. They flew to their villa at Snagov and then on to a military airfield near Titu, before hijacking a car and finally being arrested in Tîrgovişte. They were held in the military barracks there, and when the news of their capture proved insufficient to stop loyal Securitate units firing on the crowds, they were tried and **executed on Christmas Day**. The "trial" was a farce, with no doubt of the outcome, but most Romanians felt it was justified and necessary to end the fighting.

Meanwhile, in Bucharest and in other cities such as Braşov, Cluj, Arad and Sibiu where there had been demonstrations and street fighting, army and police units were changing sides; it's unclear at what point their leadership had decided to abandon Ceauşescu, but evidence suggests that it was earlier rather than later. Nor is

ILIESCU AND THE NEW REGIME

Born in 1930 to Communist parents, **Ion Iliescu** spent World War II in internment, and then studied in Moscow at the same time as Gorbachev: rumours about their relationship later did him no harm at all, although there's no evidence that they met. Returning to Romania, he made his way up the party ladder, joining the Central Committee in 1964; already he was seen as the newly appointed Ceauşescu's heir apparent. In 1971 he accompanied him to China and North Korea; Ceauşescu came home full of enthusiasm both for the Cultural Revolution and for the totalitarian architecture of Pyongyang, but Iliescu disagreed and was sent to an unimportant job in Timişoara.

Although this was later presented as a break both with Ceauşescu and with Communist ideology, too, it's clear that he continued to be on friendly terms with the President, and in 1979 he returned as director of the National Water Council and a member of the Political Executive Council (Politburo). It's claimed that from 1982 Iliescu, General Militaru and Virgil Magureanu were plotting against Ceauşescu, and in 1984 there was supposedly a coup attempt. In that same year Iliescu was again demoted after disagreeing with the boss about the Danube–Black Sea Canal, being dropped from the Political Executive Council and the Party's Central Committee (after 19 years' service) and appointed director of the state Technical Publishing House.

It's odd that from now on he was consistently spoken of as the only possible candidate to **succeed Ceauşescu**; yet he was never a dissident and did nothing to put himself forward beyond building private links with the party and military hierarchies. It's said that in 1989 the generals required a seasoned politician at the helm, rather than a group of poets and intellectuals, before they would support the revolution.

Iliescu, with his affable smile and his aura of competence and experience, presented himself as **a figure of stability and continuity**, while also benefiting electorally from the gratitude due to the overthrower of Ceauşescu. He disowned Marxism, but for a long time showed no understanding of anything but authoritarianism, using standard phrases about "fascist elements" and "foreign agents", and continuing at first to call people "comrade". He kept power by employing familiar methods of manipulation mixed with strong-arm tactics, which usually worked domestically while losing support abroad.

Around two thirds of the **Securitate**'s manpower were taken on again by the new SRI, and under Iliescu it continued to operate in much the same way as before 1989, with opposition leaders (especially defectors from the FSN) being bugged and harassed. Around 40 percent of the successful private companies in Bucharest are run by former Securitate members. Up to a third of the population are supposed to have been Securitate informers (files have not been opened, but around 400,000 seems a more likely figure), and a sixth of the population were members of the Party. As a result of such general guilt there is much less stigma attached to people's past records than elsewhere in East-Central Europe.

Nevertheless there's a strong feeling that those at the top not only got away with murder, but in fact profited to a ridiculous extent from the new dispensation. Only twenty-five Communist officials were jailed for offences committed prior to the revolution, and the last of these were released in 1994. There were no trials for offences committed during the revolution itself, and there has still been no explanation of events. Under Constantinescu, elected in autumn 1996, there has been some investigation of abuses committed under the previous regime, most notably the arrest of the Jiu miners' leader Miron Cosma. Iliescu himself is still around, as senator and party leader, and is more obstructive than strictly necessary for the leader of the opposition

it clear at what point the **National Salvation Front** (Frontul Salvării Naţionale or FSN), which emerged to take power from December 22, had been formed: there are many conflicting accounts, but it seems certain that a coup of some kind had been prepared before the disturbances in Timişoara. The FSN was supposedly formed in the Central Committee building on the afternoon of December 22 by a group of people who had gathered there independently, but clearly many of them were already in contact. The key figures were Party members who had been side-lined by Ceauşescu, and **Ion Iliescu** was soon named as president; his prime minister was **Petre Roman**, an up-and-coming member of the younger generation of Communists.

It seems that around a thousand people died in the revolution and the "terrorist" phase that lasted until January 18; although, initially, both the new government and the Hungarian media published inflated death tolls of 10,000 or more.

FREE ROMANIA

It did not take long after the Ceaușescus' execution for the **FSN to consolidate its power**; almost at once it reversed its pledge not to run as a party in the elections due in May 1990. It was soon evident that revolutionary idealists were being elbowed aside by the former governing élite, who had no intention of leaving office. Supporters of other parties demanded the **removal of ex-Communists** from the government and began regular protests in Bucharest; these were disrupted by miners from the Jiu Valley, bribed and duped by the government to act as their enforcers.

From April 22, Bucharest's Piața Universității was occupied by **students** protesting against the ex-Communists and demanding an end to state control of TV. They began a hunger strike on April 30, and on June 13 the police cleared the square of the *golani* or hooligans, as they proudly called themselves. The police were in turn attacked, perhaps by provocateurs, and the next day **10,000 miners** arrived in town on special trains. They were greeted by Iliescu and taken by plainclothes agents to set upon the *golani* who had returned to the square and to ransack university, newspaper and opposition party offices. They terrorized the city until June 16, leaving at least seven dead and 296 injured. The reaction abroad was dismay, with the US suspending non-humanitarian aid and boycotting Iliescu's inauguration as president. At home, the nation went into shock, and remained cowed for the next year while the economy collapsed.

In the meantime, on May 20, the FSN had easily won **Romania's first free elections**, garnering 66.5 percent of the vote, while Iliescu won 85 percent of the vote for president. The actual voting was deemed fair enough by international observers, even though a million more votes were cast than were on the register, supposedly "due to the enthusiasm of the people for democracy". However the FSN's domination of the airwaves had won them the election well before the actual voting. Most urban intellectuals soon took to referring to December 1989 as the "so-called revolution", and it was increasingly taken for granted that nothing much had changed in the political life of the country.

Economic reform got under way slowly, but some adjustment was unavoidable as the country was rocked by the inevitable opening to Western imports and by the world recession. **Food rationing** had been ended as soon as the FSN took power, together with systematization, the registration of typewriters, and the bans on abortion, contraception and contacts with foreigners, and the new government took care to empty the warehouses and fill the shops with food. Food subsidies were cut in November 1990, and the state-controlled **prices rose** steadily from then on. Imports rose by 48 percent in 1990, and exports fell by 42 percent (due in part to agricultural produce being kept for home consumers), while **inflation** rose from 65 percent in 1990 to almost 300 percent in 1993.

In September 1991, the **miners**, although still better paid than most Romanians, went on strike for more pay and then rampaged again through Bucharest. The prime minister, Roman, was forced to resign, and was replaced by another technocrat, **Teodor Stolojan**, who continued with broadly reformist policies. Local election losses in February 1992 fuelled the fears of conservatives within the FSN, leading to their leaving the party to form the Democratic Front of National Salvation (renamed the Party of Social Democracy of Romania in 1993), led by Iliescu. Roman's wing became the Democratic Party or PD (FSN), and later merged with the Social-Democratic Party as the Social-Democratic Union. The PDSR government was kept in power by minority parties, and opposed by a coalition known as the Democratic Convention.

A **second general election** was held in September 1992, after the adoption of a new constitution; Romania is now a **presidential democracy**, in which the prime minister has little autonomy. Iliescu won 61 percent of the vote for the presidency, but his party won just 28 percent; the Democratic Convention had 20 percent, Roman's FSN 10 percent, and the main Romanian nationalist party and the Hungarian Democratic Union of Romania each took 7.5 percent. The opposition refused to form a government, so Iliescu selected **Nicolae Văcăroiu**, formerly head of taxation in the Finance Ministry, to lead another government of technocrats kept in power by the PDSR and an unholy alliance of neo-Communists and extreme nationalists. The government survived a succes-

THE KING

Many people now look to **the King** for an escape from the vile intrigues of the "democratic" politicians. **Mihai** was born in 1921 and reigned from 1927 to 1930 and from 1940 to 1947; he earned his people's respect by his role in the coup of August 23, 1944, when he dismissed Marshal Antonescu and had him locked in a safe, and by his attempts to maintain democratic government afterwards. His **abdication** was precipitated, in part, by attending the wedding of Britain's present Queen Elizabeth and Prince Philip in November 1947, meeting Princess Anne of Bourbon-Parma, and returning home engaged to be married to her. Faced with the prospect of a continuing dynasty, the Communists were forced to drive him out. He and his wife lived as market gardeners in England until 1956, when Mihai became a test pilot and then a broker in Switzerland.

After 1989 he tried several times to visit the royal graves in Curtea de Argeş, and the government's repeated refusal to allow this was an indication of its sense of illegitimacy. In April 1990 he was refused a visa, and although at Christmas 1990 he was allowed in (travelling on a Danish diplomatic passport), he was stopped on the motorway and deported twelve hours after arriving at Otopeni. At Easter in 1992 he was permitted a visit, which drew large crowds, but was not allowed back; in October 1994 he again arrived at Otopeni but was put straight back onto the plane. The situation changed totally with the election of Constantinescu; in February 1997 Mihai, bearing a new diplomatic passport, was greeted by government ministers as he and Anne arrived for a five-day visit. He has since lobbied for Romanian entry into NATO, and backed the economic reforms. He wants to return permanently, but is unlikely to get his home at Peleş back.

Under Iliescu royalist graffiti was widespread, and in opinion polls up to 20 percent of the population wanted Mihai's return. The present government is republican, and only the PNT–CD (National Peasants' Party–Christian Democratic) even favours a referendum on the subject. Mihai's heir is his nephew Prince Paul, an art dealer based in the USA, but it's Mihai's daughter Princess Margarita who is most visible and popular, and even Iliescu went out of his way to be photographed with her.

sion of parliamentary votes of confidence and strikes by miners, rail workers and other key groups, managing for the most part to avoid inflationary wage rises. The **need for aid and a fear of international isolation** kept the government on a reformist course, although key reformers periodically resigned, frustrated by the struggle against the conservatives. In February 1993, an agreement was reached for association with the European Union; in October, Romania became the last Eastern Bloc state to join the Council of Europe; and in January 1994 it was the first to sign the Partnership for Peace. The granting of Most Favoured Nation status by the USA in November 1993 led to huge cuts in tariffs, although the nascent private sector was slow to take advantage of the export opportunities. Although there had still been no mass privatization of state industries, the private sector now contributed 3.6m jobs and 30 percent of official economic activity.

Particularly welcome (and rewarded by substantial loan support from the World Bank and IMF) was Iliescu's support from mid-1994 for the

tight fiscal policies of the National Bank's governor Mugur Isarescu, which halved inflation to 6 percent per month and allowed the leu to actually rise slightly against the dollar. The official exchange rate matched the black market rate, and businesses were able to obtain as much hard currency as they required for imports and investment, having previously only been able to get a third of their needs through official channels. In January 1995 taxes were cut to the lowest levels in Central or Eastern Europe.

Iliescu's support for economic reform did not extend to **land reform**, although Văcăroiu and his government saw returning land to the people as the best way to revitalize agriculture. The president urged the courts not to issue property deeds, but even so 72 percent of the total area farmed (nine million hectares) is now divided between six million private owners. Parliament refused to allow foreigners to buy land, and this was at times interpreted as including any company with foreign investors; this was very swiftly corrected by the Constantinescu government.

Nevertheless it seemed that the corner had been turned: industrial output in 1994 was about 10 percent higher than in 1993, and exports in the first half of 1994 were 38 percent higher than in the first half of 1993. Unemployment stabilized at 11 percent, and inflation fell to 62 percent in 1994 and 28 percent at the end of 1995, while from mid-1994 real incomes at last began to rise. Iliescu then let the economy boom for eighteen months, with real wages rising 16 percent in 1995, but it wasn't enough to win him the **autumn 1996 general elections**; public opinion turned sharply against the government due to a series of scandals. An education bill that required history, geography and civics to be taught in the Romanian language even in Hungarian-language schools led to a campaign of civic disobedience by the Democratic Union of Hungarians in Romania, the largest opposition party, and the European parliament condemned the bill in 1995. In 1996 Iliescu agreed a Basic Treaty with Hungary which met most international concerns, but in turn enraged his nationalist supporters. As the elections drew near, Iliescu became less dependent on the support of the nationalists, and was able to expel them from the government.

POST-ILIESCU ROMANIA

The 1996 election was won by the Democratic Convention of Romania (CDR), a coalition of fifteen small parties, itself in coalition with Petre Roman's SDU grouping; they won 200 of the 341 deputies' seats and 87 of the 143 senators' seats. **Emil Constantinescu**, a professor of geology and formerly rector of Bucharest University, was elected president after a run-off against Iliescu, and appointed the youthful mayor of Bucharest, **Victor Ciorbea**, as prime minister. They head a government that is genuinely liberal-democratic and Western-oriented; their priorities are accelerated privatization, the slashing of the budget deficit and elimination of almost all price controls, introduction of a transparent tax system, and an attack on corruption. Before the elections they had drawn up a Gingrich-esque "Contract with Romania", promising radical reforms with increased social protection; in the event they found the economy had been abused even more seriously than expected by Iliescu's attempts at re-election, and the result has been the most radical "shock therapy" campaign anywhere in East-Central Europe. In January 1997 fuel prices were doubled, the cost of electricity rose five times, telephone charges doubled, and rail fares rose by eighty percent, as subsidies were removed, so that **real wages fell by twenty percent** in January alone; fuel prices rose by half again in February. Social spending (ten percent of GDP) will cushion the impact to a certain extent, and it's expected that the government will have a year or so to begin to turn the economy around before losing public support; certainly Roman (now speaker of the Senate) will not hesitate to make capital if he sees the tide turning against the reforms. The economy, which grew by over four percent in 1996, is likely to shrink by two percent in 1997, and inflation (39 percent in 1996) is likely to reach 110–140 percent at the end of 1997, before returning, if all goes well, to 30 percent at the end of 1998. Unemployment fell to a record low of just six percent at the time of the elections, but is expected to be ten percent or more by the end of 1997. Some help will come from the ending of the Yugoslav civil war and trade embargo (which cost Romania nigh on $7 billion), economic growth in the former Soviet Union, and Romania's accession in 1997 to CEFTA, the Central European Free Trade Area. The IMF and World Bank view the government's programme favourably, and are supporting it with $630m in loans. A further boost will come from mass privatization, to increase private enterprise's share of the economy from little more than half to a proportion which will produce real economic growth.

The treaty with Hungary is being followed by a similar settlement with Ukraine, which is crucial to convincing the West that Romania is actually one of the most stable countries in Eastern Europe. Constantinescu's foreign policy is entirely based on **integration with the West**, and he made early entry into NATO a touchstone of his success. There was massive popular support (76 percent in favour of NATO entry, even more for EU entry, the highest levels in any ex-Communist state), but also general belief that there would only be one chance of entry. Inevitably, at 1997's Madrid summit, NATO decided that Romania was not ready to join, but fortunately President Clinton at once went in person to Bucharest to encourage Romania to try again soon.

The new government's first main challenge came, not surprisingly, from the Jiu valley miners (80 percent of whom voted for Iliescu); their pay is still double the national average, but 42 of them die each year in accidents underground. A strike in June 1997 ended with a 23 percent payrise, but the government refused to release their leader Miron Cosma, arrested for his role in Petre Roman's overthrow. At least a quarter of the miners are surplus to requirements, and at some point the government will have to break their political power; thus far, however, Constantinescu has been happy to enjoy his political honeymoon, with the war on corruption being especially popular.

CHRONOLOGY OF MONUMENTS

pre-4000 BC	Tribes roam the valleys and plains.	Remains of bones and weapons found at Băile Herculane.
4000 BC	Earliest settlements on the Dobrogea.	Hăbăşeşti Neolithic village, "Hamangia Culture" carvings include **goddess figures** and the "**Hamangia Thinker**".
3000 BC	Copper-working in Transylvania.	Axes, adzes etc. exhibited in Cluj History Museum.
C7–C6 BC	Coast colonized by **Greek** trading ports (ruled by Roman and Byzantine empires from C1 AD onwards).	Walls dating from foundation of **Histria** (675 BC), **Tomis** and **Callatis** (C6 BC) overlaid with **Roman and Byzantine** remains, including a fine mosaic floor at Constanţa.
C3 BC–C1 AD	**Dacians** inhabit area of present day Romania; ruled by Burebista in C1 BC, and Decebal (87–106 AD).	**Goldwork** (C3 BC). Excavations of many earthworks, citadels and sanctuaries, including **Sarmizegetusa**, the Dacian capital in the Orăştie mountains.
101–271	**Roman conquest** of Dacia (completed 106) produces a fusion of cultures: the Daco-Romans, held to be the ancestors of the Romanian people.	**Trajan's Bridge** at Drobeta–Turnu Severin, forts and the ruins of **Ulpa Traiana** show the Roman line of advance. The **Tropaeum Traiani** at Adamclisi commemorates the Roman victory.
271–C9	Goths, Huns, Avars and Bulgars carve successive empires here; Slavs begin to settle from 567.	Inscriptions, coins and burial remains either support the **Theory of Daco-Romanian Continuity** or don't; the debates continue.
896–C13	**Magyars** gradually wrest control of Transylvania from native voivodes; **Saxons** settle there after 1143; and in 1224 migrate into eastern Transylvania.	Indigenous structures – the **Bihara Citadel** near Oradea – and those of the newcomers: eg **Cîrţa Monastery**, the "Passage of Stairs" in Sibiu, and parts of some **walled towns**.
C13	Radu Negru founds the Basarab dynasty and the principality of **Wallachia** south of the Carpathians. Tatars invade Transylvania in 1241 and 1284, giving impetus to the building of walls and citadels.	**Negru Vodă Monastery** founded in 1215 at Cîmpulung, the first Wallachian capital, together with many churches (walled during the C15). That at **Cisnădioara** (c.1200) and **St. Michael's Cathedral** in Alba Iulia are examples of C13 **Romanesque architecture**.

C14	East of the Carpathians, Bogdan Vodă founds the principality of **Moldavia** (1364) with Rădăuţi as its capital.	**Citadels** of **Făgăraş** and **Rîşnov** (rebuilt C15). The Court at **Curtea de Argeş** (c.1370) precedes **Cozia Church** which marks the advent of **Byzantine architecture** in Wallachia. Styles in the north are divergent – eg the wooden Church on the Hill at **Ieud** (c.1364) and Rădăuţi's **Bogdana Church**. Braşov's **Black Church**, the first phase of St Michael's in Cluj, and **Bran Castle** (1377) exemplify Transylvanian **Gothic architecture**.
C15	**Turkish expansion** is checked by Hunyadi in Transylvania, Vlad the Impaler in Wallachia and Stephen the Great in Moldavia. After the 1437 Bobîlna peasant uprising, the Magyar nobility, Saxons and Székely form the **Union of Three Nations** to defend their privileges.	**Bistriţa Monastery** founded in Moldavia (1407). **Hărman**, **Prejmer** and other **fortified Saxon churches**, the **castles at Lăzarea, Poienari and Hunedoara** and the strengthening of the **walls around Sighişoara, Cluj and Sibiu** are all monuments to a period of violence and insecurity. Stephen founds the **monasteries** of **Putna** (1466), **Voroneţ** (1488) and **Neamţ** (1497) in Moldavia.
C16	**Peasant uprising** of 1514. Following the Ottoman and Hapsburg partition of Hungary, Transylvania struggles to stay independent, while Moldavia and Wallachia acknowledge Ottoman suzerainty.	Monasteries of **Arbore, Humor, Moldoviţa** and **Suceviţa** are built; soon, their walls and those of Voroneţ are painted with magnificent **frescoes**.The **Episcopal Church** at Curtea de Argeş (1517) rises above the limitations of Byzantine architecture in Wallachia; while Sibiu's Councillors' Tower and the **Sighişoara citadel** are typical of C16 Saxon buildings in Transylvania.
C17	In 1600, **Michael the Brave** briefly unites Moldavia, Wallachia and Transylvania. Moldavia and Wallachia have a respite from misrule during the reigns of Basil the Wolf (Vasile Lupu, 1633–52) and **Constantin Brîncoveanu** (1688–1714) but later succumb to the **Phanariots**, while Transylvania has its "Golden Age" under Gabor Bethlen (1613–29).	Between the construction of Dragomirna and Cetăţuia monasteries, **Moldavian church architecture** reaches its apogee with the building of Iaşi's **Trei Ierarhi** (1639), covered in intricate stonecarvings. In Wallachia, the monasteries of Arnota, Govora and Polovragi precede **Horez Monastery** (1691–93), the largest, most impressive example of **Brîncoveanu-style architecture**, which also characterizes Sinaia Monastery (1695).
C18	**The Ottomans withdraw** in 1718. Serbs and Swabians settle in the Banat. In 1784 a peasant uprising occurs in Transylvania. The Romanians' petition for political equality is rejected in 1791.	Despite the Creţelescu Church in the Brîncoveanu style, the C18 is more notable for the construction of splendid **wooden churches in** Maramureş at **Rozavlea, Bogdan Vodă,Şurdeşti** – and many **Baroque churches, palaces and cathedrals**, eg in Oradea, Cluj, Sibiu and Timişoara. Huge **Vauban-style citadels** are raised at Arad, Alba Iulia and Oradea.

C19	Magyars revolt against Hapsburg rule and declare the union of Transylvania with Hungary despite Romanian opposition (1848–49). In 1859 **Moldavia and Wallachia** unite to form Romania, while after 1868 the Hungarians pursue a policy of **"Magyarization"** in Transylvania.	In Bucharest, the construction of the Şos. Kiseleff and the Calea Victoriei reflects **French influence**; Manuc's Inn, the Şuţu Palace and many new buildings are founded in the capital and after 1859 universities are established at Iaşi and Bucharest. Sibiu's Podul de Fier and Brukenthal Museum, electric streetlighting in Timişoara, the building of rail lines and a channel through the Iron Gates are all aspects of **modernization** affecting Transylvania. Monumental buildings in Iaşi, Tîrgu Mureş etc embody the era's assertive nationalism; in Wallachia and Moldavia these are in neo-Brîncovenesc style, while in Transylvania and the Banat the Secession (Viennese Art Nouveau) style is common.
1907	**Peasant uprising** in Romania.	Ploieşti oilfields developed by foreign capital. The Mosque at Constanţa is the first **ferro-concrete** structure (1910).
1918	**Union of Transylvania with Romania**; confirmed by the Trianon Treaty (1920) despite Magyar opposition.	**Monumental Orthodox Cathedrals** constructed in Alba Iulia, Tîrgu Mureş, Timişoara, Cluj etc to celebrate the status of "Greater Romania" in the 1920s. In the 1930s, the Royal Palace and the **Arc de Triumf** are built in the capital.
1944	Romania liberated from Nazis.	Damage caused by Allied bombs is rapidly repaired and **high-rise blocks** are built to meet the housing shortage (eg in Ploieşti and Bucharest).
1949	Establishment of Communist Party rule.	Romania's **industrialization** and the style of architecture are strongly **Soviet-influenced** – eg the Casa Scînteii and the first, abortive attempt to dig the Danube–Black Sea Canal using forced labour. The **Friendship Bridge** (completed in 1954) and the **Iron Gates dam** (1971) are both joint ventures with neighbouring socialist countries; while the Galaţi steel mill and the coastal **tourist complexes** have a Western input. The **Danube–Black Sea Canal** is opened in 1984. Subsequent major construction projects included **Otopeni airport**, the **Metro** and the **Centru Civic** in the capital; the Dîmboviţa canal; and Romania's first **nuclear power station** at Cernavodă on the Danube.
1965	**Ceauşescu** becomes leader following the death of Gheorghiu-Dej, and pursues a nationalist economic policy contrary to the wishes of Comecon, which is reluctant to help. This persuades Ceauşescu to seek credit and technical assistance from the West.	
1977	Earthquake in Bucharest.	
1989	**Ceauşescu overthrown**. Romania's first free elections held.	Even before the revolution there was a boom in building churches and private houses in the villages.

ROMANIA'S MINORITIES

While Wallachia and Moldavia are largely monocultural, Transylvania has always been pluralistic and multi-ethnic. Although there is a specifically Transylvanian culture and sensibility common to all the races living there, there are still those who seek to make political capital by setting one race against another. For visitors, of course, this multi-ethnic mix is at the heart of Transylvania's charm.

THE MAGYARS

Transylvania (including the Banat) was ruled by Hungary for several centuries, and when it was united with Rumania after World War I Hungary lost half its population and two thirds of its area. Although Slovakia and Croatia were also lost, it's Transylvania which has always been the focus of Hungarian desires; there are still about 1.6 million **Magyars** or Hungarians in Romania.

The Hungarians had treated their subject peoples badly, denying them their linguistic and cultural rights, and inevitably the Romanians, once they were in charge, behaved in a similar manner. Things became far worse in Ceauşescu's later years, and eventually Magyars began to flee across the border to Hungary, the first refugees from one Warsaw Pact state to another. Around 10,000 fled in 1987 and double that in 1988, when demonstrations in Budapest against oppression in Romania (and especially the systematization programme) played a key part in the movement towards political reform at home. In late 1989 hundreds of refugees were crossing the border every week, despite many more being caught by border guards; in 1990, 17,000 emigrated legally, but numbers have since declined.

Normal civil rights were in theory restored, with Hungarian-language education widely available, but as Magyars asserted their rights there was a reaction in the Romanian community, feeding nationalist parties such as the Party of Romanian National Unity and Vatră Romanească, whose policy is "to make Romanians masters in their own home". These parties kept Iliescu in power, and so new laws were proposed to curtail Hungarian-language education; the Democratic Union of Hungarians in Romania, the largest opposition party, launched a campaign of civil disobedience against this in 1994.

There are in fact three Transylvanian Magyar communities, the Székely and the Csángó to the east, and the regular Magyars who settled later in the west. All remain strong and confident of their cultural identity, and there is little likelihood of a further exodus.

THE GERMANS

In contrast to the endurance of the Hungarian population, there are now few **Germans** left in the country. The Saxon community in Transylvania dates back to 1143, when they were invited to guard the Transylvanian passes by King Geza II of Hungary; they developed a unique culture of their own, and grew prosperous by dominating the trade routes to Asia. They were granted self-government, based on their seven chief towns of Hermannstadt (now Sibiu), Kronstadt (Braşov), Schassbürg (Sighişoara), Klausenburg (Cluj), Mühlbach (Sebeş), Mediasch (Mediaş), and Bistritz (Bistriţa). As the Tatar threat was superseded by that from the Turks, these became fortified cities, while the villages have walled churches, often with storage chambers for food in case of siege. From the eighteenth century, the Saxons (actually of Mosel-Frankish origin) were joined by other German colonists: the Schwaben or Swabians, who moved into the areas of the Banat recently vacated by the Turks, the Landler in Transylvania and Bucovina, and the Zipser in Maramureş.

The population reached a maximum of about 650,000 in the 1930s. After World War II some Germans were expelled from Bucovina and Dobrogea, and 75,000 men and women, accused of pro-Hitler sympathies, were taken for slave labour in the Soviet Union from 1945 until 1950. Many of them had their property confiscated and this was not returned to them after 1989 when land was decollectivized. German law guarantees citizenship to all those of German origin, and from 1967 the then West German government bought up to 10,000 exit visas a year. Thus the Saxons were already slipping away when the revolution came, and around 120,000 left in 1990. Now their culture has almost entirely vaporized, leaving under

20,000 Germans in Romania. After thirty generations, many villages contain just one or two old folks surrounded by Romanians and Gypsies.

THE JEWS

The history of Romania's **Jews** is similar to that of the Germans. There were two communities, the Sephardim, living along the Danube and speaking Ladino, and the Ashkenazim, the Yiddish-speaking Jews spread right across Central Europe, with many in Bucovina and Maramureş. Jews have been in Romania since Roman times, with more coming in the eighth and ninth centuries after the collapse of the Jewish Khazar empire, and also in 1367 and in 1648 when they were expelled from Hungary and Poland. Most settled in Bessarabia and Bucovina, and prospered there; the community peaked around 1924, when it numbered 800,000. Romania was one of the few parts of the world where Jews were allowed to own land and form self-sufficient rural communities.

Although the Turks had treated Jews fairly, independent Romania increasingly treated them as foreigners rather than as citizens, and they began to emigrate, mostly to North America; the literary scholar Moses Gaster, however, went to Britain, and became a professor at Oxford University in 1886, at the age of thirty, and then Chief Rabbi. In 1878 equal citizenship was forced on Romania by the great powers at the Congress of Berlin. The 1907 revolt was strongly anti-Semitic, and was followed by the rise of the Iron Guard and other nationalist parties; during **World War II** the Jewish population was butchered (see box on p.352), leaving only 428,000 Jews in Romania by 1947.

In the glorious new world of Communism, the people were to be one without ethnic distinction, and all national minorities' organizations were disbanded in 1953. However Stalin was always anti-Semitic, and after the purging in 1952 of Romania's Jewish Foreign Minister, Ana Pauker, the climate turned against Romania's Jews again. Ceauşescu was happy to **sell Jews to Israel** for up to $3000 for each exit visa; at least 300,000 had left by 1989, and there remain only about 12,000 now. Moses Rosen, Chief Rabbi from 1947 as well as a parliamentary deputy, performed a dazzling balancing act, travelling to the US every year to argue for the continuation of Much Favoured Nation status in order to gain exit visas for his flock.

Additionally the American Joint Distribution Committee, not allowed to operate anywhere else in Eastern Europe, was able to spend $4m a year on the welfare of Romania's Jewish community. Rosen died in 1994, leaving Romania's anti-Semitism largely unaffected by the revolution.

THE GYPSIES

For most **Gypsies** or Rroma, life is worse today than under Ceauşescu. They are attacked for not working, but also for smuggling and for the other shady deals by which they earn a living. Under Iliescu, state television always focused on Gypsies in opposition demonstrations to discredit the opposition by association; but there has been an equal rise in ethnic consciousness among the Rroma, and there are now five Romani newspapers.

Gypsies left northern India in the tenth and eleventh centuries and arrived in Europe around 1407, at the same period as the Tatar invasions. Almost at once many were enslaved, and, in the sixteenth century, came the first great period of **persecution**, matched only by the Nazi holocaust. In Wallachia and Moldavia Gypsies were divided into two main groups, the *lăieţi* or "members of a horde", free to roam, and the *vătraşi* or settled Gypsies. The latter were slaves, working as grooms, servants, cooks and farm labourers, as well as being musicians. In 1837 the politician Mihail Kogălniceanu, who campaigned on their behalf, wrote: "On the streets of the Iaşi of my youth, I saw human beings wearing chains on their arms and legs, others with iron clamps around their foreheads, and still others with metal collars about their necks. Cruel beatings, and other punishments such as starvation, being hung in the snow or the frozen river, such was the fate of the wretched Gypsy."

Wallachia and Moldavia **freed their Gypsies** between 1837 and 1856: many in fact stayed with their original owners as paid employees, but many also emigrated, reaching Germany in the early 1860s, France in 1867, Britain and the Netherlands in 1868, and North America by 1881. This is usually seen as a direct result of their emancipation from slavery, but the movement west had in fact begun some decades earlier. The economic system that made slavery viable had begun to break down as cheap grain imports from North America flooded Europe, and inevitably the boyars would in any case have cast them off before long.

At least 20,000 Gypsies were **deported to Transnistria** by Antonescu's regime during World War II, and a higher proportion died than in any other European country. The Communist regime confiscated Gypsies' carts and forced them to settle on the edges of villages; in 1956 38 percent of Gypsies over the age of 8 were illiterate, but by 1966 almost all their children at least went to elementary school. The Gypsy population is somewhere between 400,000 and 2 million (of 8 million in Europe) – between 2 and 10 percent of the Romanian population and **Europe's largest minority**. Around 40 percent of them no longer speak Romani and these consider themselves barely Rroma; perhaps 10 percent are still nomadic, although they usually spend the winter camped at a permanent settlement.

There is increasing **discrimination** against Gypsies, and widespread antipathy towards them; given their great increase in numbers and visibility, they are now the universal scapegoats. They have received very little international aid and discrimination against them, particularly in employment, has inevitably pushed many into crime. Perhaps more alarming is the great rise in **crime against Gypsies**; there have been many instances of fights leading to mobs burning down Gypsy houses and driving them out of villages, and at least eight Gypsies have been killed in racist attacks since 1989. In almost every case village authorities have condoned the attacks, police have kept away, and there have been no arrests.

GYPSY CULTURE

The Gypsies left India to escape the caste system, and today their society is divided into clearly defined groups of uniform equality. There are around forty **tribes or groups** in Romania, including the argintari (jewellers), căldărari (tin/coppersmiths), fierari (blacksmiths) and lăutari (musicians). There is also a general division into corturari (nomadic tent-dwellers) and vătraşi (settled).

Gypsy concepts of propriety are, with their language, their most obvious Indian heritage; everything is defined as either wuzho (clean), or marime or mochadi (unclean). **Involvement with non-Gypsies** (gadjé) is seen as risky (especially sharing food or having sex with them), and in particular the upper half of the body is regarded as clean while the lower half is not. Thus upper-body excretions such as spittle are seen as clean and may be used to wash wounds, and upper clothes must be washed separately from lower clothes.

As soon as a girl reaches puberty she must wear a long skirt and a separate top, washed separately and not with men's or children's clothes. Women are not allowed to cook while menstruating or during pregnancy. Women don't cut their hair, which is always bound, and once they are married it must always be covered with a diklo or headscarf. **Marriage** (seen as a cure for epilepsy and mental retardation) takes place in a girl's early teens, bringing an end to her education. Red and green are lucky colours, so a bride wears red and a baby will have a red band on its wrist; black is used only for mourning.

Cutlery and crockery are potentially unclean, so Gypsies eat with their hands and prefer disposable cups and plates; the greatest insult is to refuse someone's food. As in India, to be fat is to be seen as wealthy and lucky, although women also carry their wealth with them in the form of huge Hapsburg gold coins. Friday is a day of fasting, when no animal products are eaten.

OTHER MINORITIES

There are many **other ethnic groups** in Romania, and not only in Transylvania. Around 70,000 **Ukrainians** live in Maramureş and Bucovina, and 45,000 **Russians** (mostly Lipovani) live in the Danube Delta, Dobrogea and Moldavia. Almost as many **Serbs** live at the other end of the country, in the Banat, having fled from Turkish domination in the eighteenth and nineteenth centuries, and there are about 18,000 **Slovaks** in the same area, descendants of colonists brought into the area after the Turks had gone. Muslim descendants of the Turks and Tatars themselves still live on the Black Sea coast, around 23,000 of them, with 10,000 Bulgarians in the same area. In the thirteenth century, the **Armenian** diaspora reached Moldavia, and later moved on into Transylvania, settling in isolated but prosperous communities in towns such as Suceava, Brăila, Constanţa, Dumbrăveni, Gheorgheni and Gherla; now they number perhaps five thousand, almost totally assimilated, although their churches survive, some with Hungarian priests.

The **Aroumanians** are a group of ethnic Romanians who lived in Bulgaria and near Thessaloniki for many centuries as prosperous merchants with their own Romanian-language schools and culture; almost all returned to Romania between the world wars, and they have virtually vanished as a recognizable culture, although their weaving (dark red geometrical patterns on a black background) can still be seen in museums.

RELIGION

As everywhere in the world, ethnic differences are reflected in **religion**; the Romanian majority follows the **Romanian Orthodox** creed, which like the other Orthodox Churches is a hierarchical body not given to free thought or questioning dogma or authority. Under Ceauşescu the Church did everything it was asked to, and positively discouraged dissidence. In Transylvania, and particularly in Maramureş, many Romanians follow the **Uniate** creed (see p.168), which was regarded by the Communists as untrustworthy and was forcibly merged with the Orthodox Church.

The Hungarian population is divided more or less equally between the **Roman Catholic** and **Calvinist** (Reformat) faiths; the Calvinist Church was pretty much under the Communist thumb, but the Catholic Church had the strength to resist and to keep its integrity. The Schwab and Landler Germans are also Roman Catholics, while the Saxons, Catholics when they arrived in Romania, later embraced **Lutheranism**, although a few are Seventh-Day Adventists. In addition about 75,000 Hungarians, mainly around Cluj and Turda, are **Unitarian** (see p.198), and since 1989 the Baptists and newer evangelical churches have been making great gains, mostly among people who are disorientated by change and the loss of certainty and stability in society.

ENVIRONMENTAL AND SOCIAL PROBLEMS

In Romania there is little that really compares with the environmental devastation of wide swathes of southern Poland, the northern Czech Republic, and eastern Ukraine, but even so the country did suffer, and there are many industrial plants that cause immense damage in their immediate neighbourhood. While the bulk of the damage was inflicted during the Communist period, it should be remembered that some of the worst offenders, such as Copşa Mică's carbon-black plant and the Valea Călugărească fertilizer plant (east of Ploieşti), were built in the capitalist period, and the Reşiţa and Hunedoara steelworks and the Zlatna copper smelter date back to the eighteenth century.

Romania's mammoth increase in industrial output over the last five decades – production of steel rose from 280,000 tonnes in 1938 to 14 million tonnes in 1986, and of fertilizer from just 5900 tonnes in 1950 to 1.2 million tonnes in 1986 – was achieved by a total disregard for any considerations other than **maximizing production** as fast as possible. Thus industrial injuries are commonplace, and energy consumption is up to fifty percent more per unit of output than in the West, the most notorious example being the Slatina aluminium smelter, which in 1989 consumed 14 percent of Romania's total electricity production, equal to all domestic consumption. Since then heavy industry has contracted, with a commensurate fall in polluting emissions; road traffic has risen fifty percent since 1990, but still only accounts for a tiny share of Romania's pollution, which is calculated to affect 10 percent of the population, and 20 percent of the country's territory. Rubbish, now estimated at 180kg per capita per year, is a developing problem, as Western-style packaging takes over.

The most polluted sites now are Copşa Mică, Zlatna and Baia Mare, all of which produce acid rain and a cocktail of up to ten heavy metals that run straight into the water system. In **Zlatna**, where a new plant was opened in 1986, sulphur dioxide emissions are above the legal maximum 30 percent of the time and dust emissions 63 percent of the time, while life expectancy in the area is ten years below the average, and falling. In **Baia Mare**, 50,000 tonnes of sulphur dioxide are pumped out every year, together with 3000 tonnes of metal dust, both well over safe levels; amazingly, the industrial zone was built upwind of the residential area, and in a valley subject to thermal inversions which trap the pollution. Almost as bad are the artificial fibre factories of **Brăila** and **Suceava** – the latter giving rise to "Suceava Syndrome", a unique respiratory and nervous complaint that has led to many malformed babies. In 1987, the chemical plant in **Giurgiu** produced clouds of chlorine that floated across the Danube to blanket the Bulgarian town of Ruse, and there are fertilizer and petrochemical plants in Arad, Dej, Făgăraş, Năvodari, Piteşti, Ploieşti and Tîrgu Mureş, all producing illegal levels of hydrocarbons and inorganic compounds. In **Bucharest**, total emissions have fallen by a third since 1989, due to industrial recession; in some industrial areas ammonia levels are still nine times the legal limit and lead two hundred times the limit, but throughout the city nitrous oxides and lead (in car fumes) and dust are the main problems.

Additionally, the **use of fertilizers, pesticides and insecticides** has caused problems, damaging 900,000 hectares of agricultural land and entering the drinking water supply. Many of the country's rivers are now dead; in all 22 percent fall into the poor and bad categories. Fertilizer use has halved since 1989, due to cost rather than environmental awareness, and as a result water quality is improving.

Similarly, the damming of the Iron Gates and the dyking of the Danube flood plain, has led to the **Danube's flow** through the Delta being reduced by 50 cubic kilometres per annum, leading to algal blooms and lower fish yields. In places the river is only oxygenated to a depth of 10m, and the Delta may die unless water flows can be speeded up. Consequently, the **Black Sea** is one of the most polluted areas in the world – toxic wastes, over-fishing, and a one-fifth fall in freshwater inputs combining to disasterous affect. Surfeits of nutrients cause plankton blooms (red tides), leading to loss of light and dissolved oxygen, and thus decimating fish stocks.

At one time Ceauşescu did take an interest in pollution problems, with **environmental protection laws** passed in 1967, 1973 and 1976, and a National Council for the Protection of the Environment created in 1975, although without a budget of its own. The Braşov cement works were closed (after the creation of new capacity elsewhere) and the Bucharest abattoir and incinerator were moved to the outer suburbs. In the 1980s, however, he became more obsessed with expanding industrial capacity, and environmental data became increasingly secret. Water quality has been monitored since 1960, and air quality since 1973; but little use was made of this information before 1989.

After the revolution, a new **Ministry of Waters, Woods and Environmental Protection** was created, with the aim of reducing pollution by a fifth by 1995, and bringing it down to European levels soon after the year 2000. Two ecological parties were set up, gaining 4 percent of the vote in the 1990 elections (half of it in Bucharest), giving them a senator each and twenty deputies between them. An ordinance on atmospheric pollution was passed in August 1993; this means that potential investors can at least calculate future environmental costs, although not as yet past liabilities. A new environment law was passed in December 1995, after great delays. There's now an Environmental Protection Agency in each county, responsible for pollution monitoring and permits. Volunteer groups are growing in number, although they're largely involved in clearing up effects rather than in tackling causes.

Much the same applied to the **protection of historical monuments**, with useful legislation being passed before 1977, when the Historical Monuments Administration was disbanded for daring to oppose Ceauşescu's plans for Bucharest's Civic Centre. There was no effective protection from then until 1989, and many towns have simply been gutted. In February 1990, the Administration for Historical Monuments, Sites and Areas was set up, but again the required legislation is stuck in parliament, and there is no state funding. Most conservation to date has been achieved with funding from the Church, or, in the case of **Saxon monuments**, from Germany. **Biertan** and the **Bucovina and Horez monasteries** have become UNESCO World Heritage sites.

Ceauşescu was also determined to have his own **nuclear power station** at Cernavodă, on the Danube, and chose a 660MW Canadian design rather than that used at Chernobyl and all over the Soviet bloc. However, construction standards were so appalling that a third of welded joints in pipes failed stress tests, and between 1989 and 1996 it had to be almost totally rebuilt. One reactor finally went on line in 1996, saving almost £100m in fuel imports per year.

HEALTH PROBLEMS

As a result, in part, of these environmental conditions, Romania also has serious **health problems**. Socio-economic factors also contribute: bad housing in some parts of Bucharest leads to children suffering three times the level of respiratory disease found in other parts of the city, alcohol-related problems are rising, and in 10 percent of settlements, **water supplies** are under one hundred litres per day per head, with water being cut off for five or more hours a day in major towns such as Caracal, Slatina, Ploieşti, Constanţa, Iaşi, Cernavodă and Craiova. The average family spends 56 percent of its income on food, but their daily **diet** contains on average only 2832 calories (less even than in the late 1980s); 10 percent of children aged 10–14 are anaemic.

In the 1960s, **average life expectancy** was similar to that in Western Europe, but has since fallen behind. It dropped from 71 in 1989 to 69.5 in 1995, behind every European state except Albania and Slovakia, though still seven years longer than in Russia. **Cancer rates** are rapidly overtaking those in Western Europe, with breast cancer doubling in twenty years, and cervical cancer rates six times those in Greece, Italy and Spain. An explosion in lung cancer is not far off, due to a massive postwar rise in smoking. Respiratory diseases are common and the incidence of tuberculosis is the highest in Europe, although it has declined to 81 cases per 100,000. Likewise viral hepatitis, typhoid, polio, tetanus and cholera are all in decline, and there have been no cases of diphtheria since 1990. The main killer, causing 61 percent of deaths, is **cardiovascular disease**, the highest rates in Europe being found in Romania and Bulgaria.

HIV has been present since 1984, but was not officially accepted until 1987; there were 3136 reported cases by the end of 1994, 2900 of them in children under twelve, almost all caused by injections with infected needles in the perverse custom of giving babies blood transfusions to "fortify" them.

In 1967 Ceauşescu introduced his notorious laws designed to boost **Romania's birthrate**; these were briefly effective, but soon fertility began to drop, and continued to do so even as the laws became more draconian. Latest figures show that by 1983 the birthrate was back to its 1966 level of 14.3 per thousand, and had fallen to 10.9 in 1994. Marriage rates, at 6.8/1000 in 1995, were at their lowest level for fifty years. **Infant mortality**, at 21.2 per 1000 live births in 1995, remains very high, almost triple the average for the developed nations of the OECD. This high rate is due to lack of medical equipment, congenital abnormalities (due in part to pollution), and low birth weight, and these also lead to a high mortality rate among children aged 1 to 4.

HEALTH SERVICE REFORM

Romania's **healthcare system** needs fundamental reform: health spending is not a priority for the government, but has risen from 3 percent of GNP in 1990 to 8.2% in 1993. In addition the World Bank is leading a reform project, driven by the urgent need to improve health. Romania has plenty of well-trained **doctors**, and, with the opening of private medical schools, there will soon be an oversupply. However, there is a great shortage of **nurses**, and midwife training was halted altogether between 1978 and 1990. There are still only a thousand **psychologists** in Romania as psychology was seen as subversive under Ceauşescu, and there are no **geriatric specialists** at all, while the geriatric population is soon to double. Likewise social work was abandoned in the 1970s, as its existence implied there were problems in society.

Most of those working in the health service are deeply demoralized, leading to a poor attitude to patients; in theory doctors earn less than half the average salary, but in practice the gifts and backhanders that fuel the system may bring their earnings up to double the average. The system is hierarchical and hospital-centred; there are no job interviews – those doctors qualifying with top marks get prestigious jobs in hospitals while the worst are assigned to local *dispensars* or clinics. These are depressing and underfunded places, usually referring patients to a *policlinic* (for outpatient care) or hospital; this is very inefficient, and a major shift to primary and preventative healthcare (including comprehensive family planning) is essential.

ORPHANS

The result of Ceauşescu's scheme to increase the workforce has been that many women have had children that they could not possibly afford to bring up, and, as is well known, these have been abandoned in dire **state orphanages**, grossly under-staffed and under-funded, with staff so desensitized that children were left to yell and to bang their heads against the wall. Reared with no mental stimulation, it's not surprising that many orphans were diagnosed (at three years old) as mentally handicapped and left without education in "Institutes for the Irrecuperable".

The Western media was saturated with distressing images of these orphanages, causing a massive popular reaction, particularly in Germany, and emergency **aid and volunteers** flooded into Romania. Today, relief agencies focus on long-term strategies with emphasis on training and helping the Romanians to help themselves. Some orphanages have been replaced by family-home-type units, and family support centres have opened in some towns. There are still blackspots – **old people's homes** are even worse than the orphanages, but little work has been done there, and little aid of any kind has reached southern Wallachia.

Childless Romanian couples are reluctant to **adopt** as most orphans are Gypsies and therefore not wanted. However, interest from the West was considerable; at least 10,000 had been adopted by foreigners by July 1991, when adoptions were abruptly halted, in order to prevent the sale of babies. However, there are still cases of babies being bought and smuggled out – in 1994, a British couple were arrested for this, but released from custody after government intervention. In mid-1995, after public panic about paedophile rings and organ theft, a new adoption law was passed, allowing adoptions only through the Romanian Committee on Adoptions in conjunction with a foreign agency; in 1996 there were just twelve adoptions to the UK. One of the first acts of the Constantinescu government was to re-establish a National Committee for Child Protection, incorporating the Romanian Committee for Adoptions, and to

AID AGENCIES

There is still relief work to be done in Romania, but it is best achieved by working through the main established **agencies**, which are gradually absorbing most of the new charities set up in 1990. These work with church bodies and other established structures in Romania, and are coordinated by the **Romania Information Centre** and the **Interdepartmental Commission for Coordination and Support of Humanitarian Activities**.

Contact addresses

Christian Childrens' Fund of Great Britain (Romania), 52 Bedford Row, London WC1R 4LR or FREEPOST WC1R 4BR (☎0171/831 7145).

Interdepartmental Commission for Coordination and Support of Humanitarian Activities (Comisia Interdepartamentala pentru Coordonarea și Sprijinirea Activitaților Umanitare), Str. Ministerului 1–3, Bucharest 70107 (☎01/613.75.44 or 615.02.00 ext 384).

Regional Environmental Centre, B-dul Burebista 1, bl. D15, sc 1, et 7, ap 28, Bucharest sector 3 (☎01/322.85.56, fax 322.85.57).

Relief Fund for Romania, 7th floor, 54 Regent St, London W1R 5PJ (☎0171/439 4052).

Romania Information Centre, Southampton University, England, SO17 1BJ (☎01703/551328); RICIR, Str. Pitar Moş 27, et 2 ap 7, Bucharest sector 1 (☎01/211.37.80).

European Children's Trust, 21 Garlick Hill, London EC4V 2AU (☎0171/248 2424).

Rumänien Info Dienst, Karolingerstrasse 2, 71322 Waiblingen, Germany (☎7183 2089, fax 7183 2089, digitas@aol.com).

World Vision UK, 599 Avebury Boulevard, Central Milton Keynes MK9 3PG (☎01908/841000)

bring laws into line with international norms, giving autonomy to local Directors of Social Services.

Ion Ţiriac (once Boris Becker's coach) is running TV ads to fund an orphanage in his home town of Braşov; these will not raise much money in Romania but are a useful first step in consciousness-raising. Efforts are being concentrated on encouraging people to take orphans home for weekend visits, to give them love and show them life outside the orphanages. The problem of unwanted children remains, and will do so until there is comprehensive family planning, now the object of a huge Phare/Advocacy programme, a joint venture between the EU and the US.

WILDLIFE

Despite Romania's industrial pollution problems, much of the countryside is surprisingly unspoilt, and as you climb up into the hills you enter a world where pesticides and fertilizers have never been used and where meadows are full of an amazing variety of wild flowers – a landscape representative of Europe two or three centuries ago.

HABITAT

One third of Romania is mountain, largely forested, and this is where most of the more interesting flora and fauna are to be found. One third of the country is hill and plateau, with a fair quantity of woodland remaining, and one third is plain, mostly intensively farmed.

The **Carpathian mountains** form an arc sweeping south from the Ukraine and around Transylvania to end on the Danube at the Iron Gates. At lower levels they are mostly covered with oak and hornbeam, with, up to about 1400m, an association of beech mixed with common silver fir and sycamore known as Carpathian Beech Forest (*Fagetum carpaticum*). Spruce begins to appear at about 1000m, and is dominant from 1400m to 1700m. Above this comes the lower alpine zone, characterized by dwarf pine and other stunted bushes, and then, from 1900m, the higher alpine zone of grass, creeping shrubs, lichen, moss and ultimately bare rock.

Elsewhere, particularly on the **Transylvanian plateau**, there is much more

oak and beech forest, although much has been cleared for fields. To the east there are vast grassy steppes, the western end of the immensely fertile Chernozem or "black earth" belt that stretches east for 4000km to Novosibirsk.

In the **southwest** of the country, near the Iron Gates of the Danube, the climate is more Mediterranean, with Turkey and downy oaks, Banat pine and sun-loving plant species on the limestone rocks of the Mehedinţi and Little Retezat massifs.

The **Danube Delta** is a unique habitat, described in detail on p.314. Formed from the massive quantity of sediments brought down the river, it provides an ideal stopping-point for millions of migrating birds, as well as a home for many reptiles and other animals.

Nature reserves have existed in Romania since 1930, and there are now 586 in all, including individual caves, rocks and even trees. The first National Park was created in 1935 in the Retezat mountains; although the Scientific Reservation in the western part of this park was treated by Ceauşescu as a private bear-hunting reserve. The Retezat and Rodna mountains and the Danube Delta have been named as part of UNESCO's worldwide network of Biosphere Reserves, and at least ten other national parks are to be designated as a result of the 1995 Environment Act. These include the Bicaz and Nera gorges, the Cerna valley, and the Apuseni, Bucegi, and Căliman mountains.

FLORA

In springtime, the **mountain meadows** of Romania are a riot of wild flowers, 12 percent of which are endemic to the Carpathians. The timing of this varies with the altitude, so that any time from April to July you should be able to find spectacular scenes of clover, hawkweed, burdock, fritillary and ox-eye daisy covered in butterflies, and, at higher levels, gentians, white false helleborine, globeflower and crocus. **Alpine plants** include campanulas, saxifrage, orchids, alpine buttercup, pinks, and, in a few places, edelweiss.

In the warmer **southwest** of the country, the Turda gorge is an especial sun-trap, with rarities such as *Allium obliquum*, *Aconitum fissurae*, *Hieracium tordanum* and various species of *Dianthus*, while there are other rare varieties of *Hieracium* in the Retezat Scientific

Reservation, and orchids, lilies and Carduus varieties on the limestone of the Little Retezat.

The **Danube Delta** is home to at least 1600 plant species, which fall into three main categories. The floating islets that occupy much of the Delta's area are largely composed of reeds (80 percent *Phragmites australis*), with mace reed, sedge, Dutch rush, yellow water-flag, water fern, water dock, water forget-me-not, water hemlock, and brook mint. In the still backwaters, wholly submerged waterweeds include water-milfoil, hornwort, and water-thyme; while floating on the surface you'll find water plantain, arrowhead, duckweed, water soldier, white and yellow waterlily, frog bit, marsh thistle, and épi d'eau. The river banks are home to white willow, poplar, alder, and ash; while the more mature forests of Letea and Caraorman also contain oak trees, elm and aspen and shrubs such as blackthorn, hawthorn and dog rose. The Romanian peony can be found along the coast nearby.

BIRDS

Permanent residents are relatively rare in the **Danube Delta**, with only around 44 species remaining all year round. These include white-tailed eagle, cormorant, greylag goose, mute swan, griffon vulture, great-crested grebe, bittern, shelduck, mallard and kingfisher. However almost 300 species of birds can be seen here at various seasons, the twin peaks of ornithological interest being from the end of March to early May, and from August to October, when millions of **migratory birds** pass through in all directions: osprey, plovers, arctic geese, cranes and half-snipes from Siberia; saker falcons from Mongolia; and egrets and mandarin ducks from China.

From mid-May to mid-July, another hundred-plus species of birds, most of which have wintered in Africa, come to **breed** here and in the great lakes immediately to the south. Europe's largest colonies of white and Dalmatian pelicans, 60 percent of the world population of pygmy cormorants, and over 16,000 night herons, squacco herons and purple herons nest here, together with marsh harriers, black-winged stilts, glossy ibises, spoonbills, curlews and avocets. The coastal plains attract griffon vultures, short-toed eagles and the hobby.

In **winter**, the number of visiting birds is reduced but still amazing. Main visitors include

most of the European population of great white herons (or egrets), 20,000 red-breasted geese (almost half the world population), 50,000 white-fronted geese, and 30,000 red-crested pochard, with smaller quantities of other ducks such as pintail, goldeneye, wigeon, teal, smew, red and black throated divers and Manx shear water.

Away from the coast, on the **plains** inland, you may still find the great bustard and the calandra lark, the largest European lark, while summer visitors include the stridently coloured roller and bee-eater, the equally exotic-looking hoopoe, the imperial eagle, red-footed falcon and lesser grey shrike.

Other than in the Delta, the biggest and most dramatic birds are usually to be seen in the **mountains**, above all the golden eagle and the raven, while in the **forests** lurk large game birds such as the capercaillie, hazel grouse, and (in the north) black grouse. Easiest to spot are nutcrackers, jays and woodpeckers (particularly the black and three-toed species in conifers, and great spotted, middle spotted and white-backed species in deciduous trees).

The forests are also home to raptors including buzzards, sparrowhawks, hen harriers and eagle owls. Nightingales visit deciduous woods in summer, and you're also likely to see storks, in particular the white stork, whose large nests are characteristically built in the heart of human habitations, on telephone poles and chimneys.

ANIMALS

The largest mammals live in the montane forests. Having been protected under Ceauşescu, for his own personal hunting, there are now five or six thousand **brown bear** in Romania, particularly in the eastern Carpathians. Although they do raid garbage bins in Poiana Braşov and on the outskirts of Braşov, they are generally afraid of humans and will keep well clear unless you come between a female and her cubs in April or May.

The Carpathian **red deer** is found mainly in the northern spruce forests, where the stags' mating cries resound through the valleys in September and October; it is often possible to observe their ritual conflicts from a distance. Above the treeline, the most visible mammal is the **chamois**, the mountain goat which can be seen grazing in flocks with a lone male perched on the skyline to keep watch. **Wild boar** are found in the lower forests (including the Delta), and can weigh 200kg, almost as much as a red deer stag. They appear mostly at night, and can leave a clearing looking as if it has been badly ploughed when they have finished digging for roots. They too have a reputation for aggression when protecting their young in the springtime.

Wolves, though fairly thinly spread, inhabit the hilly forested parts of the country, and the Letea area of the Delta. They are blamed for attacks on sheep and are hunted in winter, when their tracks can be followed in the snow. Smaller forest mammals include fox, wild cat, polecat, marten, weasel, stoat and red squirrel, while otters are found along many rivers, and the Delta is possibly one of the last refuges of the European mink, and also home to enot (or raccoon dog), coypu, muskrat and beaver, all North American species that have escaped from fur farms in the former Soviet Union.

The most frequently seen **amphibia** are salamanders (not unusual after rain), while

snakes include the grass snake, horned adder and (less common) adder. The steppe viper is not extinct, despite reports in Western Europe, but survives in the Delta, where you may also see the European whip snake, the second largest in Europe at three metres in length. The warm weather of the southern Banat and the Delta sandbanks provides a suitable environment for **tortoises** and **lizards**.

Romania's rivers are home to seventy species of **fish**, mainly trout, dace, grayling, barbel and carp. The stiller waters of the Delta shelter another fifty-plus freshwater species, as well as almost twenty species that migrate from the Black Sea to breed; the main channels are home to perch, pike and catfish, and to many types of sturgeon, sterlet and the related sevruga, as well as the Danube mackerel (or Pontic shad) and rare gobies. Most of these species are in decline due to pollution, over-fishing and eutrophication of the water due to algal blooms.

MUSIC

The Carpathian mountains trace a cultural fault-line across Romania that separates Central Europe from the Balkans, sharply dividing the musical styles on either side. Of course such borders are rarely impermeable; the same language is spoken on either side and there is plenty of cultural and musical cross-fertilization. The many strands of Romanian music are extraordinarily varied and archaic, preserving almost archeological layers of development, from the "medieval" music at the extremities in Ghimeș and Maramureș, to the "Renaissance" sounds of Mezőség and the more sophisticated music of Kalotaszeg.

Tours to study Romanian folk **dance** are organized by the Doina Foundation, Aarhuispad 22, 3067 PR Rotterdam, Netherlands (☎10/421 86 22, fax 455 6065), which also helps organize an annual Balkan festival in Zetten and sells flutes, boots, costumes and icons.

THAT OLD TRANSYLVANIAN SWING

If you want to experience a real living European folk tradition, there's no beating **Transylvania**. Home to an age-old ethnic mix, the region's music is extraordinary: wild melodies and dances that are played all night, especially at weddings. Although many Transylvanian villages were collectivized in the Communist

years, their spirit remained relatively resilient to the changes. The region's music, certainly, survived intact, and it's still a part of everyday life. The older people know the old songs and still use them to express their own personal feelings.

The composers Bartók and Kodály found Transylvania the most fertile area for their folk-song collecting trips in the first decades of this century, and they recognized that the **rich mix of nationalities** here had a lot to do with it. Transylvania has been home to Romanians, Hungarians, Saxons, Gypsies and other ethnic groups for hundreds of years. For these communities music is part of their national identity, yet it is also part of a unified and distinctly Transylvanian culture. The Romanian music of Transylvania is closer to Hungarian than it is to the Romanian music in the rest of the country. And the Hungarian music of Transylvania sounds much more Romanian than the music of Hungary proper.

In fact within Transylvania the Romanians and Hungarians share many melodies and dances. It takes a very experienced ear to tell the difference and even then a particular melody may be described as Hungarian in one village and Romanian in another just over the hill. The Romanian dances often have a slightly less regular rhythm than the Hungarian, but often the only difference between one tune and another is the language in which it is sung. There's even a unique recording of an old man from the village of Dimbău (Küküllődombó) singing a song with the first half of each line in Hungarian and the second half in Romanian.

Transylvania is much more **Central European** in character and architecture than the other parts of Romania, and Transylvanian Romanians tend to consider themselves more "civilized" than their compatriots in Moldavia and Wallachia. The music of Transylvania sounds much less Balkan than that from over the Carpathians; it might seem wild and exotic, but it is recognizably part of a Central European tradition with added spice from its geographical location.

The traditional ensemble is a **string trio** – a violin, viola (*contra*) and a double bass, plus a cimbalom (*tambal*) in certain parts of Transylvania. The *primás*, the first violinist, plays the melody and leads the musicians from one dance into another while the *contra* and

CLASSICAL MUSIC

Classical music was lavishly funded by the Communist state, and still has far less elitist connotations than in the West. Main cities have a philharmonic orchestra and/or an opera house, and tickets (available through the local Agenţia Teatrale) are very cheap. Additionally, the Saxon communities have maintained a Germanic tradition of singing chorales by Bach and his contemporaries.

The first important composer of the Romanian national school was **Edvard Cavdella** (1841–1923), who was also a formidable violinist. Little known in the West, his works include the historical opera *Petru Rareş* and the romantic and lyrical *First Violin Concerto*, dedicated to and premiered by Enescu.

Although the composers Bartók, Ligeti and Xenakis were all born on Romanian soil, Romanian classical music remains virtually synonymous with **George Enescu**, born near Dorohoi in 1881. At the age of four he was studying with a local Gypsy violinist, Nicolas Chioru, and at the age of seven he was admitted to the Vienna Conservatoire, where he met Brahms and was present at the premiere of his clarinet quintet. Between 1894 and 1899 he studied under Fauré and Massenet at the Paris Conservatoire, before embarking on a three-fold career as composer, conductor and violinist. His *Romanian*

Rhapsodies were first performed in 1903 and remain his most popular works; as the name implies, they are largely based on Romanian folk tunes. His *Third Violin Sonata* is his best chamber work and has a national flavour. His *First Symphony* (1906) was Brahmsian in style, but, although he remained a neo-romantic, later works also showed experimental features, such as the use of quarter-tones and a musical saw in his masterpiece, the opera *Oedipe*. Begun in 1910, this was finally performed in 1936; it is the most comprehensive treatment of the myth, covering Oedipus's entire life from birth to death, with no classical compression. There is a good modern recording (1989) featuring José van Dam.

By bad luck or bad planning, Enescu spent both world wars in Romania, the first as court violinist to Queen Marie and the second on his farm near Sinaia (in recognition of which the Communists only collectivized two thirds of his land). In between he spent most of his time in Paris, teaching violin at the École Normale de Musique (to Yehudi Menuhin and Ida Haendel, among others), and giving the premiere of Ravel's violin sonata in 1927. His recording, with the young Menuhin, of the Bach *Double Concerto* remains one of the best available.

Again, after World War II he returned to Paris, and even after a stroke in 1954 refused to return

bass are the accompaniment and rhythm sections of the band. The *contra* has only three strings and a flat bridge so it only plays chords, and it's the deep sawing of the bass and the rhythmic spring of the *contra* that gives Transylvanian music its particular sound. Often the bands are expanded with a second violin or an extra *contra* to give more volume at a noisy wedding with hundreds of guests.

WEDDING PARTIES

Music in Transylvania serves a social function – nobody would dream of sitting down and listening to it at a concert. In some areas there are still regular weekly dances, but everywhere the music is played at weddings, sometimes at funerals and at other occasions, including when soldiers go off to the army, and around Christmas.

Wedding parties last a couple of days and often take place in a specially constructed wed-

ding "tent" built from wooden beams and tree fronds. The place is strung with ribbons and fir branches, tables are piled high with garish cakes and bottles of ţuică, and fresh courses are brought round at regular intervals. There's a space cleared for dancing and on a platform is the band of musicians sawing and scraping away at battered old fiddles, and a bass making the most mesmerizing sound. The bride and groom, stuck up on their high table, look a little fed up while everybody else has the time of their lives.

Wedding **customs** vary slightly from region to region but generally the band starts things off at the bride's or groom's house, accompanying the processions to the church and possibly playing for one of the real emotional high spots, the bride's farewell song (*cîntecul miresei*) to her family and friends, and to her maiden life. While the marriage takes place within the church, the band plays for the young people, or those not to Communist Romania, dying in Paris in 1955. He now lies in the Père-Lachaise cemetery; despite his opposition to Communism, the regime nevertheless coopted his name, christening orchestras and streets after him.

The best-known contemporary composer in Romania is the hugely prolific **Anatol Vieru**. He was born in Iaşi in 1926 and has composed in a modern but not avant-garde style, occasionally drawing on folk influences. Several of his works have been released internationally on CD.

Many of Romania's musicians have had more success abroad than in their home country. Puccini's *Tosca* was created by Hariclea Darclée, and Strauss's *Arabella and the Countess in his Capriccio* by Viorica Ursuleac; Julia Varady and Ileana Cotrubas were renowned sopranos in recent years, and the pianist Clara Haskill and violinist Sándor Vegh were Romanian-born. Romania's best-known pianist is **Dinu Lipatti** (Enescu's godson), who had a mercurial talent and suffered an early death in 1950 from leukaemia. In his lifetime he was referred to as "God's chosen instrument". His recordings (just five CDs) have never been deleted, and one of them, made in Besançon just months before his death, is widely regarded as the best-ever live recital disc.

Sergiu Ceilibidache (1912–96) studied in Berlin and in 1945 became conductor *pro tem* of the Berlin Philharmonic until Furtwängler was cleared of Nazi sympathies. He continued as assistant conductor in Berlin until 1952, going on to run the Swedish Radio Symphony Orchestra, the Stuttgart Radio Orchestra, and from 1980 the Munich Philharmonic, making his US debut only in 1984. Described as "transcendentally endowed", although not very interested in music outside the mainstream Germanic repertoire, he was also a perfectionist, demanding up to eighteen rehearsals for some concerts; nevertheless he stopped making studio recordings in 1953. He was also a composer, with four symphonies and a piano concerto to his name.

Contemporary musicians to look out for include the tenor **Alexandru Agache**, the sopranos **Angela Giurgiu**, **Mariana Nicolescu**, **Adina Nitescu** and **Leontina Vaduva**, pianist **Radu Lupu**, violinist **Eugene Sarbu** and the conductors **Cristian Mandel**, **Ion Marun** and **Horia Andrescu**. The violinist **Alex Bălanescu** left Romania in 1959, joining the Arditti Quartet and then in 1987 forming his own **Bălanescu Quartet**, playing works by David Byrne, Kraftwerk, Gavin Bryars and Michael Nyman as well as the established classics. He returned to Romania in 1991, and in 1994 released "Luminiţa" ("Glimmer"; Mute STUMM 124), about the "so-called revolution", featuring drum machine and the sampled voice of Ceauşescu, alongside some fine folk-inflected writing for strings.

invited to the feast, to dance to in the street outside. Once the couple come out of the church there's another procession to wherever the wedding feast is being held – either in the village hall or the "tent" erected at the house of the bride or groom. There the musicians will have a short break to eat and then play music all Saturday night, alternating songs to accompany the feast with dances to work off the effects of the food and large quantities of ţuică. There are even particular pieces for certain courses of the banquet when the soup, stuffed cabbage or roast meat are served.

Late in the evening comes the bride's dance (*jocul miresei*) when, in some villages, the guests dance with the bride in turn and offer money. Things usually wind down by dawn on Sunday; people wander off home or collapse in a field somewhere and then around lunchtime the music starts up again for another session until late in the evening.

With the trend towards larger and larger weddings all sorts of instruments have started to find their ways into bands. Most common is the piano-accordion, which, like the *contra*, plays chords, though it lacks its rhythmic spring. Very often you can hear a clarinet or the slightly deeper and more reedy *taragot* which sounds wonderful in the open air. Sadly, however, because young people have moved away to work in towns, they often demand the guitars, drums and electric keyboards of the urban groups at the banquets – along with appalling amplification, which is increasingly brought in, too, by traditional acoustic bands.

Some band leaders might regret the trend but they are obliged to provide what the people demand. They may play traditional melodies but with the newer instruments the quality of the music is often lost. Some groups stick unswervingly to the traditional line-up, like the marvellous **Pălatca** band, recognized as one of the greatest in Transylvania.

GYPSY BANDS

The band from Pălatca (Magyarpalatka), like most of the village musicians in Romania, are **Gypsies**. In the villages, Gypsy communities all tend to live along one particular street in the outskirts, often called Strada Muzicanților or Strada Lăutari – both of which translate as "Musicians' Street". Gypsy musicians will play for Romanian, Hungarian and Gypsy weddings alike and they know almost instinctively the repertoire required. Children often play alongside their parents from an early age and grow up with the music in their blood.

Playing music can be an easy way to earn good money; the best bands command handsome fees, plus the odd chicken and bottles of țuică. It's also an indication of the value of music in this society that the musicians are not only well rewarded but also well respected. When the old *primás* of the Pălatca band died all the people he had played for in the village came to pay their respects at his funeral.

It's difficult to highlight the best bands – there are dozens of them – but in addition to the Pălatca band, those of the following villages of central Transylvania are excellent (the names are given in their Romanian form with the Hungarian in brackets): Vaida-Cămăraș (Vajdakamarás), Suatu (Magyarszovát), Sopuru de Cîmpie (Mezőszopor), Sîngeorz-Băi (Oláhszentgyőrgy), and Sic (Szék), an almost totally Hungarian village and one of the great treasure houses of Hungarian music.

A glance at the engagement book of one of these bands will show them booked for months ahead. Yet most of them confine their playing to quite a small area as travel is relatively difficult. Some tunes are widely known right across Transylvania but many are distinctly local and a band playing too far from its home village will simply not know the repertoire. It will be interesting to see what happens now that local bands are travelling to Hungary and beyond on tour.

THE HUNGARIANS

There are 1.6 million **Hungarians** in Transylvania and seven million Romanians, but it is the music of the Hungarian minority that has made most impact outside the region. The Hungarians consciously promoted the culture of their brethren in Transylvania to highlight their suffering under Ceaușescu. Hungaroton, the state label, produced a large number of excellent recordings while Budapest-based groups like **Muzsikás** have toured extensively and acted as cultural ambassadors for the music.

Transylvania has always held a very special place in Hungarian culture as it preserves archaic traditions and medieval settlement patterns that have disappeared in Hungary itself. As a minority during the Ceaușescu regime, the Hungarians felt threatened, and there was a deliberate effort to wear their traditional costumes, sing their songs and play their music as a statement of identity, even protest. These days, national costume and dances are much more visible among the Hungarian minority than the majority Romanians (other than in Maramureș).

REGIONAL STYLES

Within the overall Transylvanian musical language there are hundreds of local dialects: the style of playing a particular dance can vary literally from village to village. But there are some broad musical regions where the styles are distinct and recognizable.

Bartók gathered much of his Romanian material in the area around **Hunedoara**. The area is still musically very rich though, strangely enough, a recent musical survey found that virtually the entire repertoire had changed.

Further north is the area the Hungarians call **Kalotaszeg**, home to some of the most beautiful music in the region. This area lies along the main route from Cluj (Kolozsvár) to Hungary and Central Europe, and the influence of Western-style harmony shows itself in the sophisticated minor-key accompaniment – a development of the last twenty years. Kalotaszeg is famous for its men's dance, the *legényes*, and the slow *hajnali* songs performed in the early morning as a wedding feast dies down, which have a sad and melancholy character all their own. One of the best of all recordings of Transylvanian music includes both these forms, featuring the Gypsy *primás* **Sándor Fodor** from the village of Baciu (Kisbács), just west of Cluj. There is also some fine Romanian music in Sălaj county, in the north of this area, which can be heard in the villages or on a very fine Romanian recording of dances from Sălaj (*Jocuri Sălajene*) by a small ensemble from Zalău.

Probably the richest area for music is known to the Romanians as **Cîmpia Transilvaniei** and to the Hungarians as **Mezőség**. This is the Transylvanian Heath, north and east of Cluj – a poor, isolated region whose music preserves a much more primitive feel with strong major chords moving in idiosyncratic harmony.

Further east is the most densely populated Hungarian region, the **Székelyföld** (Székely Land). The Székelys, who speak a distinctive dialect of Hungarian, were the defenders of the eastern flanks of the Hungarian kingdom in the Middle Ages, when the Romanians, as landless peasants, counted for little. Rising up towards the Carpathians, their land becomes increasingly wild and mountainous, and the dance music is different once again, with eccentric ornamentation and very often a cimbalom in the band.

For Hungarian-speakers the songs are fascinating as they preserve old-style elements that survive nowhere else. In one village I heard a ballad about a terrible massacre of the Székelys by the Hapsburgs in 1764, sung as if it had happened yesterday. Fleeing this massacre, many Székelys went over the Carpathians into Moldavia, where they preserved music and customs that are no longer found in the Székelyföld itself. During World War II, 14,000 Székelys were resettled in the south of Hungary. In those outer reaches, the string bands of Transylvania have given way to a solo violin or flute accompanying the dances.

MOLDAVIA AND MARAMUREŞ

The Hungarian occupants of the remote pastoral regions east of the Carpathians are called the **Csángós**. Strictly speaking this is **Moldavia**, not Transylvania, and the music – with its archaic pipe and drum style – sounds wild and other-worldly, ruptured across the divide between Transylvania and the Balkans.

Hungarian records of the Csángós often feature music from the Ghimeş (Gyimes) valley, where you find peculiar duos of violin and *gardon* – an instrument shaped like a cello but played by hitting its strings with a stick. The fiddle playing is highly ornamented and the rhythms complex and irregular, showing the influence of Romanian music. Csángó songs are also of interest to Hungarians for their archaic qualities. The extraordinary Csángó singer **Ilona Nistor** from Oneşti (formerly Gheorghe Gheorghiu-Dej) in Bacău county has a growing reputation.

On the other side of Transylvania, sandwiched between Hungary, Ukraine and the Carpathians, are the regions of **Maramureş** and **Oaş**, both areas of distinctive regional character. Village costumes are not just worn for best but for everyday life and the music includes magic songs and spells of incantation against sickness and the evil eye. You can still find traditional Sunday afternoon village dances, either on the streets or on wooden dance platforms. From birth, through courtship and marriage to death, life has a musical accompaniment.

The music of Maramureş, while recognizably Transylvanian, sounds closer to that of Romanians beyond the Carpathians. As often happens in the highland regions of Romania, here the music is played predominantly by Romanians, not Gypsies. With an instrumental group of violin (*ceteră*), guitar (*zongoră*) and drum (*dobă*), it has a fairly primitive sound, lacking beguiling harmonies and with a repeated chord on the *zongoră* (often played vertically and back to front) as a drone. Hundreds of years ago much of the music of Europe probably sounded something like this.

WALLACHIA

As in Transylvania, most village bands in **Wallachia** are comprised of **Gypsies**: the group is generally named **Taraf** and then their village name. These musicians (*lăutari*) are professionals who play a vital function in village life at weddings and other celebrations: yet their music sounds altogether different from that of their Transylvanian counterparts. The word *taraf* comes from the Arabic and suggests the more oriental flavour of this music. Songs are often preceded by an instrumental improvisation called *taksim*, another name borrowed from the Middle East.

The lead instrument is, as ever, the fiddle, which is played in a highly ornamented style. The middle parts are taken by the *ţambal* (cimbalom), which fills out the harmony and adds a rippling to the texture. At the bottom is the double bass, ferociously plucked rather than bowed Transylvanian style. In the old days you'd always find a *cobza* (lute) in such bands, but their place has given way to the *ţambal*, guitar and accordion. The Gypsies are never slaves to tradition; the young ones particularly are always keen to try new instruments and adopt modish styles. The staple dances are the *horă*, *sîrbă* and *brîu* – all of which are danced in a circle.

In Romanian the word *cînta* means both "to sing" and "to play an instrument", and the *lăutari* of Wallachia usually do both. Whereas in Transylvania the bands play exclusively dance music, the musicians in the south of the country have an impressive repertoire of **epic songs and ballads** which they are called on to perform. These might be specific marriage songs or legendary tales like *Şarpele* (the snake) or exploits of the Haiducs, the Robin Hood brigands of Romanian history. One of the tunes you hear played by *lăutari* all over Romania is *Ciocîrlia* (The Lark), which has also become a concert piece for the stage ensembles. Reputedly based on a folk dance, it's an opportunity for virtuoso display, culminating in high squeaks and harmonics as the solo violin imitates birdsong, followed by the whole band swirling away in abandon on the opening theme.

Considering the wealth of village musicians in Romania it's significant that three of the very few recordings available feature the same *taraf* from the village of **Clejani**, southwest of Bucharest (just south of Vadu Lat station); it's a village of some five hundred Gypsies, almost all professional musicians, whose reputation has spread throughout the area. The appearance of the so-called **Taraf of Haidouks** from Clejani at the 1991 WOMAD festival caused a sensation as they played their wild and unmistakable music into the night and, when finally forced off stage, split into smaller groups to engage in persistent busking for the rest of the festival. Their recordings are extraordinary, packed full of truly virtuoso playing with incredible performances on violin, *ţambal* and accordion. *Taraf de Haidouks* includes the "Ballad of the Dictator" (see box), which also features on the soundtrack of the 1994 film *Latcho Drom*; composed to a traditional melody by the 70-year-old fiddle player Nicolae Neascu, the piece tells of the dramatic fall of Nicolae Ceauşescu – a new spin on the age-old tradition of ballads addressed to the "Green leaf" (*Foaie verde* or *Frunze verde*). Other famous Wallachian Gypsy bands include those from Mirsa, Dobroteşti, Suteşti and Brăila.

THE DOINĂ

The **doină** is a free-form, semi-improvised ancient song tradition. With poetic texts of grief, bitterness, separation and longing, it might be called the Romanian blues. Very often different texts are sung to the same melody, which may then take on a contrasting character. It is essentially private music, sung to oneself at moments of grief or reflection, although nowa-

---

Balada Conducatorului
(Ballad of the Dictator)

Green leaf, a thousand leaves
On this day of the 22nd
Here the time has returned
The one in which we can also live
Brother, live in fairness
Live in freedom

Green leaf, flower of the fields
There in Timişoara
What are the students doing?
Brother, they descend into the streets
Bringing with them banners
And cry "It is finished for the tyrant!"
What are the terrorists doing?
They pull out guns
Brother, they shoot at the people

Green leaf, flower of the fields
What are the students doing?

Into the cars they step
Towards Bucharest they head
In the streets they shout
"Come out, Romanian brothers
Let's wipe out the dictatorship!"

Ceauşescu hears them
His minister calls for
A helicopter which takes him away
What do the police do?
They follow in his steps
They bring him back in a tank
They lock him up in a room
And his trial begins
We take his blood pressure
And the judge condemns him
"Tyrant, you have destroyed Romania"

Nicolae Neascu of the Taraf of Haidouks

days the songs are often performed by professional singers or in instrumental versions by Gypsy bands. Old *doinăs* of the traditional kind can still be found in Oltenia, between the Olt and Danube rivers in the south of the country. This one is typical:

I don't sing because I know how to sing
But because a certain thought is haunting me
I don't sing to boast of it
But my heart is bitter
I don't sing because I know how to sing
I'm singing to soothe my heart
Mine and that of the one who is listening to me.

LOST SHEEP

The pastoral way of life is fast disappearing and with it the traditional instrumental repertoire of the *fluier* (shepherd's flute). But there is one form – a sort of folk tone poem – that is still regularly played all over the country: **the shepherd who lost his sheep**. This song was referred to as early as the sixteenth century by the Hungarian poet Bálint Balassi. I've heard it on the flute in Moldavia, the violin in Transylvania and on the violin and *gardon* in Ghimeş. It begins with a sad, *doină*-like tune as the shepherd laments his lost flock. Then he sees his sheep in the distance and a merry dance tune takes over, only to return to the sad lament when he realizes it's just a clump of stones. Finally the sheep are found and the whole thing ends with a lively dance in celebration.

Some of the professional bands have adopted the lost sheep story and embroidered it so that during his search the shepherd meets a Turk, a Jew, a Bulgarian and so on. He asks each of them to sing him a song to ease his suffering and promises to pay them if they succeed. No one succeeds until he meets another shepherd who plays a *ciobaneasca* (shepherd's dance) and cheers him up. In the end he finds his sheep devoured by wolves.

THE PIPES OF PAN

Romania's best-known musician on the international stage is **Gheorghe Zamfir**, composer of the ethereal soundtrack of the film *Picnic at Hanging Rock*. He plays *nai*, or **pan-pipes**, which are thought to have existed in Romania since ancient times – they're shown in a famous Roman bas-relief in Oltenia. The word "nai", however, comes from Turkish or Arabic, so perhaps an indigenous instrument existed as well

---

EASY LISTENING?

Romania's **pop** speciality is *musică uşoră* or easy music, dreadful stuff out of a 1970s' timewarp, but immensely popular, with big summer festivals in Mamaia (July–August) and Braşov (September). When Romania does get a chance at the Eurovision Song Contest, expect them to sweep the board. **Jazz** is also popular, with a festival in Sibiu.

---

as a similar one brought by professional musicians through Constantinople.

In the eighteenth century "Wallachian" musicians were renowned abroad and the typical ensemble consisted of violin, *nai* and *cobza*. But by the end of the next century the *nai* had begun to disappear and after World War I only a handful of players were left. One of these was the legendary **Fanica Luca** (1894–1968), who taught Zamfir his traditional repertoire. Nowadays, Zamfir plays material from all over the place, often accompanied by the organ of Frenchman Marcel Cellier.

THE BANAT BEAT

The **Banat**, Romania's western corner, is ethnically very mixed, with communities of Hungarians, Serbs, Slovaks, Germans and Gypsies living alongside the Romanians. Its music is fast, furious and a relatively new phenomenon, having absorbed a lot from the *novokomponovana* music of neighbouring Serbia. It's extremely popular, played all the time on the national radio and by Gypsy bands everywhere. Probably its attraction is its fast, modern, urban sound, with saxophones and frequently erotic lyrics. The Silex recording of the **Taraf de Carancebeş** (sic) is a great introduction to this virtuoso style.

THE CEAUŞESCU LEGACY

Nicolae Ceauşescu's 25 years of dictatorship still hang like a dark shadow over Romania. The legacy extends, too, to some of the country's folk music, which was manipulated into a sort of "fakelore" to glorify the dictator and present the rich and picturesque past of the Romanian peasantry from whom Ceauşescu aimed to create the "New Man".

Huge sanitized displays called **Cîntarea Romaniei** (Song of Romania) were held in

DISCOGRAPHY

CDs are marked with an asterisk

TRANSYLVANIAN VILLAGE BANDS

Various *Hungarian Music from Northern Mezőség* (Hungaroton, Hungary). Four LPs featuring music from the villages of Bonţida (Bonchida), Răscruci (Válaszút), Buza (Búza), Fizemul Gherlii (Ördöngösfüzes) and Suartu (Magyarszovát). Collected by Zoltán Kallós and György Martin, these are earthy performances of music that has become all the rage in Budapest.

*Various *La Vraie Tradition de Transylvanie* (Ocora, France). A good selection of peasant music from Maramureş and Transylvania.

*Various *Musiques de Mariage de Maramureş* (Ocora, France). One of the few recordings of Maramureş music, performed by three village wedding bands.

*Various *Romania – Music for Strings from Transylvania* (Chant du Monde, France). A fine collection of dance music played by village bands. Good to see Romanian music in a first-class release like this. Highly recommended.

*Sándor Fodor *Hungarian Music from Transylvania* (Hungaroton, Hungary). Music from Kalotaszeg including some Romanian dances. One of the essential Transylvanian records.

*Mihály Halmágyi *Hungarian Music from Gyimes* (Hungaroton, Hungary). Dance, wedding and funeral tunes played on fiddle and *gardon*. Strange and wild music. A great performance of "the shepherd and his lost sheep" with a running commentary.

*Szászcsávás Band *Folk Music from Transylvania* (Quintana/Harmonia Mundi, France). This is the real thing – a Gypsy band from the predominantly Hungarian vilage of Ceuaş (Szászcsávás). Great recording, wild playing plus some interesting Saxon and Gypsy tunes.

*Taraful Soporu de Cîmpie (Buda, France). From the village of Soporu, one of the fine Gypsy bands from the Cîmpia Transilvaniei.

HUNGARIAN TÁNCHÁZ GROUPS

*Various *Musiques de Transylvanie* (Fonti Musicale, Belgium). This is the best overall introduction to Transylvanian music, with a very good selection of pieces and performances.

*Béla Halmos *Az a szép piros hajnal* (Hungaroton, Hungary). One of the leading musicians of the Budapest tánczház scene with a collection of music from various regions of Transylvania.

*Muzsikás *Máramaros* (Hannibal, UK). A fascinating CD from the top Hungarian group joined by two wonderful old Gypsy musicians on fiddle and cimbalom to explore the lost Jewish repertory of Transylvania, distinguishable by the oriental-sounding augmented intervals in the melody. Also *Blues for Transylvania* (Hannibal, UK), a fine selection of Hungarian music from Transylvania.

*Ökrös Ensemble *Transylvanian Portraits* (Koch, US). Another comprehensive guide to the various styles of Transylvania. The fiddle-playing of Csaba Ökrös on the last track is stunning.

regional centres around the country with thousands of peasants dressed up in costume bussed out to picturesque hillsides to sing and dance. This was filmed, appallingly edited, and shown on television every Sunday (indeed, programmes of this kind, often lushly orchestrated with scores of strings, are still used to fill the odd half-hour gap in the TVR 1 schedule). The words of songs were often changed – removing anything deemed to be religious or that questioned the peasants' love of their labours, and replacing it with bland patriotic sentiments or hymns to peace.

This gave folklore a pretty bad name among the educated classes, though the peasants were hardly bothered by it at all. They just did what they were told for Cîntarea Romaniei and got on with their real music in the villages. The fact is that traditional music still flourishes throughout Romania – probably more than anywhere else in Europe – not thanks to Ceauşescu, but despite him. The isolation of the country and its almost medieval rural lifestyle have preserved traditions that have been modernized out of existence elsewhere.

*Ferenc Sebő *Folk Music from Lőrincréve* (Hungaroton, Hungary). Extraordinarily rich and beautiful music from the Maros-Küküllő (Mureş-Tîrnava) region south of Cluj, with modern players re-creating the music as collected before World War II.

ROMANIAN GYPSY GROUPS

*Taraf de Carancebeş *Musiciens du Banat* (Silex, France). A five-piece band of saxophone, trumpet, clarinet, accordion and bass. Some stunning virtuoso playing, which is enough to explain the popularity of the Banat style.

*Taraf de Haidouks *Taraf de Haidouks* and *Honourable Brigands, Magic, Horses and Evil Eye* (Crammed Discs, Belgium). Both of these are essential recordings of virtuoso playing by Romanian musicians from Clejani in an ensemble of fiddles, accordions, *ţambal* and bass. Their earlier recording (as ***Les Lăutari de Clejani** *Music of the Wallachian Gypsies* (Ocora, France) is another fine, if slightly less colourful, collection of songs and dances.

*Trio Pandulescu *Trio Pandulescu* (Silex, France). This highly recommended trio features hot accordion playing from Vasile Pandelescu plus *ţambal* and bass. Brilliant music-making with delicate moments of real poetry and all the requisite fire.

ROMANIAN VILLAGE RECORDINGS

Various *Ballads and Festivals in Romania* (Chant du Monde, France). A scholarly collection of long ballads and a few dances from Wallachian villages. Good recordings and full texts in French.

*Various *Village Music from Romania* (VDE-Gallo, Switzerland). A three-CD box produced by the Geneva Ethnographic Museum. Archival recordings of specialized interest made by the Romanian musicologist Constantin Brăiloiu in 1933–43 on his travels around Moldavia, Oltenia and Transylvania; with detailed sleeve notes and lyrics.

OTHER RECORDINGS

*Dumitru Fărcaş & Marcel Cellier *Taragot et Orgue* (Disques Cellier 007014). Zamfir's accompanist with the leading player of the clarinet-like taragot.

*Gheorghe Zamfir & Marcel Cellier *L'Ame Roumaine* (Pierre Verany 750002, France). Popular pan-pipe music from Romania's most famous musician, with Marcel Cellier on organ.

*Popeluc *Blue Dor* (Steel Carpet MATS013). Maramureş dancing and drinking music (some recorded live at village bashes), with the odd Irish reel and English song too.

*Various *Roumanie: polyphonie vocale des Aroumains* (Le Chant du Monde, LUX 74803). CNRS/Musée de l'Homme recordings of the Romanians living in Dobrogea, Bulgaria and elsewhere in the Balkans. Hard-core ethnic stuff; melancholy unaccompanied vocal choruses.

*Various *YIKHES: Klezmer recordings from 1907–1939* (Trikont, Germany). "Jewish jazz" – remastered 78s, including a couple of 1910 tracks by Belf's Romanian Orchestra, virtually the only European Klezmer band of the period to have been recorded. Many Romanian musical forms like the *doinä* have been absorbed into the Klezmer repertoire.

Luckily, village systematization didn't progress very far, although the impact of earlier collectivization and forced resettlement of peasants badly affected traditional culture in some of the central provinces. Since the revolution, some musicologists have even hazarded a beneficial effect of Cîntarea Romaniei in reviving ballads, *doinăs* and other forms which were dying out. They are now concerned to get back to the original styles and even to rediscover the Christian dimensions of Romanian folk music.

As Romania slowly catches up with the rest of Europe, its rich musical traditions are likely to disappear. Already it is getting harder to hear traditional bands playing at weddings. At the same time, musicians from Western Europe (such as the Anglo-Maramureş trio Popeluc) are delightedly incorporating Romanian material into their music. Doubtless the music will survive somehow, but the great joy of Romanian music now is its total spontaneity and authenticity.

Simon Broughton

DRACULA AND VAMPIRES

Truth, legends and fiction swirl around the figure of Dracula like a cloak, and perceptions of him differ sharply. In Romania today, schoolbooks and historians extol him as a patriot and a champion of order in lawless times, while the outside world knows Dracula as the vampire count of a thousand cinematic fantasies derived from Bram Stoker's novel of 1897 – a spoof-figure or a ghoul. The disparity in images is easily explained, for while vampires feature in native folklore (see below), Romanians make no associations between them and the historical figure of Dracula, the Wallachian prince Vlad IV, known in his homeland as Vlad Ţepeş – Vlad the Impaler. During his lifetime (c1431–76) Vlad achieved renown beyond Wallachia's borders as a successful fighter against the Turks and a ruthless ruler; his reputation for cruelty spread throughout Europe via the newly invented printing presses (whose pamphlets were the bestsellers of the fifteenth century) and the word of his political enemies – notably the Transylvanian Saxons. At this time, Vlad was not known as a vampire, although some charged that he was in league with the Devil.

VLAD ŢEPEŞ – THE HISTORICAL DRACULA

He was not very tall, but very stocky and strong, with a cold and terrible appearance, a strong and aquiline nose, swollen nostrils, a thin reddish face in which very long eyelashes framed large wide-open green eyes; the bushy black eyebrows made them appear threatening: His face and chin were shaven, but for a moustache. The swollen temples increased the bulk of his head. A bull's neck connected his head to his body from which black curly locks hung on his wide-shouldered person.

Such was the papal legate's impression of **Vlad Ţepeş** – then in his thirties and a prisoner at the court of Visegrád in Hungary. He had been born in Sighişoara and raised at Tîrgovişte after his father, Vlad Dracul, became Voivode of Wallachia in 1436. Young Vlad's privileged childhood effectively ended in 1444, when he and his brother Radu were sent by their father as hostages to Anatolia, to curry favour with the Turkish Sultan. By this move, Vlad Dracul incurred the enmity of Iancu de Hunedoara, prince of Transylvania, who arranged his murder in 1447. His sons were released by the Turks to be pawns in the struggle between their expanding empire, Hunyadi and the new ruler of Wallachia. The experience of five years of Turkish captivity and years of exile in Moldavia and Transylvania shaped Vlad's personality irrevocably, and educated him in guile and terrorism.

Seeking a vassal, Hunyadi helped Vlad to become **ruler of Wallachia** in 1456; but promptly died, leaving him dangerously exposed. Signing a defence pact and free trade agreement with the Saxons of Braşov, Vlad quickly decided that it was also prudent to pay an annual tribute of 10,000 gold ducats to the Sultan while he consolidated his power in Wallachia. For generations there, the boyar families had defied and frequently deposed their own rulers, including Vlad's father and his elder brother Mircea, whom they buried alive.

His method of law enforcement was simple: practically all crimes and individuals offending him were punished by death; and Vlad's customary means of execution was **impaling people**. Victims were bound spread-eagled while a stake was hammered up their rectum, and then were raised aloft and left to die in agony, for all to see. To test his subjects' honesty, Vlad disguised himself and moved among them; left coins in shops and over-compensated merchants who had been robbed; and slew all that failed the test. Foreigners reported the demise of theft, and Vlad symbolically placed a golden cup beside a lonely fountain for anyone to drink from and no one dared to take it away. On Easter Day in 1459, Vlad eliminated the potentially rebellious boyars en masse by inviting them and their families to dine at his palace; guards then entered and seized them, impaling many forthwith while the remainder were marched off to labour at Poienari. In a similar vein, he invited Wallachia's disabled, unemployed and work-shy to feast with him at Tîrgovişte, and asked if they wished to be free of life's sufferings. Receiving an affirmative reply Vlad had them all burnt, justifying his action as a measure to ensure that none of his subjects should ever suffer from poverty or disability.

All this was but a ramp for Vlad's ambition to be the acknowledged ruler of a mighty power, which caused much feuding with the **Saxons** of Braşov, Sibiu and the Bîrsa Land. It began in 1457, when he accused them of supporting claimants to his throne, and decided to end the Saxon merchants' practice of trading freely throughout Wallachia. When they persisted, Vlad led his army through the Red Tower Pass to burn Saxon villages, and had any of their people found inside Wallachia impaled. In 1460 Vlad annihilated the forces of his rival, Dan III, who invaded with the support of Braşov; and on this occasion dined in a garden among the impaled bodies of his enemies, using a holy icon as a dish, according to the *Chronicon Mellicense*. A month later he attacked the Bîrsa Land, and impaled hundreds of townsfolk on Sprenghi Hill within sight of Braşov's defenders before marching off to ravage the Făgăraş region.

At the same time, Vlad plotted to turn **against the Turks** and form alliances with his cousin Stephen of Moldavia, and the Hungarian monarchy. Having defaulted on payments of tribute for two years, and nailed the turbans of two emissaries to their heads when they refused to doff them, Vlad **declared war** by raiding Turkish garrisons from Vidin to Giurgiu. A massive army led by Sultan Mehmet II crossed the Danube into Wallachia in 1462, but found itself advancing through countryside denuded of inhabitants, food and water, "with the sun burning so that the armour of the ghazz-is could well be used to cook kebabs". On the night of June 17 Vlad's army raided the Turkish camp inflicting heavy casualties, and a few days later the demoralized invaders approached Tîrgovişte only to recoil in horror. En route to the capital Vlad had prepared a forest of stakes 1km by 3km wide, upon which 20,000 Turkish and Bulgarian captives were impaled. Shattered by their losses and these terror tactics, the Turks retreated home in disorder.

Dracula's downfall has been attributed to the Saxons, who used every opportunity to support his enemies and defame him throughout Europe. Most likely they forged the implausible "treason note" (in which Vlad purportedly offered to help the Sultan capture Transylvania) – the pretext for Mátyás Corvinus to order Vlad's arrest in November 1462. Until 1475, he was a "guest" at Visegrád, where Mátyás would introduce him to Turkish ambassadors to discomfort them; Wallachia's throne was occupied by Vlad's pliable brother Radu "The Handsome", who had once served as the Sultan's catamite. Released by Mátyás to continue the anti-Turkish struggle, Vlad resided for a year in Sibiu (where the townsfolk deemed it politic to allow him hospitality) and regained his throne in 1476. His triumph was short-lived, however, for Radu offered the boyars an alternative to "rule by the stake" and a chance to placate the Turks, which they seized gratefully. In circumstances that remain unclear (some say that a servant was bribed to slay him), Vlad was betrayed by the boyars and killed. His head disappeared – reputedly sent to the Sultan as a present – while the Impaler's decapitated body was reputedly buried inside the church at Snagov Monastery, where it's said to remain today.

The lack of any inscription on Vlad's tomb and of any portraits of him in medieval church frescoes suggests that attempts were made, for many years afterwards, to erase the memory of Dracula in Romania, although in the Ceauşescu epoch he was rehabilitated as a wise lawgiver and a fighter for national independence. Vlad's cruelties were minimized or forgiven, and apologists argued that impalement was widely practised by the Turks (as Vlad would have seen in his youth), and by Stephen the Great of Moldavia, besides being prescribed in the old Wallachian *Vlastares* penal code. In 1985 Ceauşescu's vile court poet Adrian Păunescu denounced Stoker's novel and the Dracula films as "only one page in a vast output of political pornography directed against us by our enemies", an attack "on the very idea of being a Romanian"; predictably the Hungarians were blamed for creating the vampire myth. Romanians continue to be disgusted by the outside world's sensationalist view of Vlad and of its crass exploitation in tourism.

VAMPIRES

Horrible though his deeds were, Vlad was not accused of **vampirism** during his lifetime. However, vampires were an integral part of folklore in Eastern and Southeastern Europe, known as *vámpír* in Hungarian and *strigoi* in Romanian. Details of their habits and characteristics vary from place to place, but in their essentials are fairly similar. A vampire is an **undead corpse**, animated by its spirit and with a body that fails to decay, no matter how long in the grave. Vampirism can be contagious or people might occasionally be born as vampires, bearing stigmata such as a dark-coloured spot on the head or a rudimentary tail. However a vampire is usually created when a person dies and the soul is unable to enter heaven or hell. The reason may be that the person has died in a "state of sin" – by suicide, for example, or holding heretical beliefs – or because the soul has been prevented from leaving the body. Hanging was a form of death dreaded by Romanians, who believed that tying the neck "forces the soul down outward"; while the Orthodox custom of shrouding mirrors in the home of the deceased was intended to prevent the spirit from being "trapped" by seeing its reflection. As Catholicism and Orthodoxy competed for adherents in the wake of the Ottoman withdrawal from the Balkans, priests also claimed that the cemetery of the opposing church was unconsecrated land, thereby raising the fear of vampires rising from the grave.

Once created, a vampire is almost immortal, and becomes a menace to the living. In Romanian folklore, vampires frequently return to their former homes at night, where they must be propitiated with offerings of food and drink, and excluded by smearing garlic around the doors and windows. Should a new-born baby lie within, it must be guarded until it is christened, lest a vampire sneak in and transform it into another vampire. Two nights of the year are especially perilous: **April 23**, St George's Day (when, as Jonathan Harker was warned in Bram Stoker's novel, "all the evil things in the world will have full sway"), and **November 29**, the eve of St Andrew's Day. On the latter night, vampires rise with their coffins on their heads, lurk about their former homes, and then gather to fight each other with hempen whips at crossroads. Such places were considered to be unlucky, being infested by spirits called *lele* (Man's enemies). In Gypsy folklore, vampires (*mulé*) also live at the exact moment of midday, when the sun casts no shadow. Gypsies must cease travelling, for at that instant *mulé* control

the roads, trees and everything else. Interestingly, Gypsies only fear their own *mulé* – the ghosts and vampires of *gadjé* (non-Gypsies) are of no account.

The greatest danger was presented by **vampire epidemics**. Although in horror films and Bram Stoker's novel, vampires must bite their victims and suck blood to cause contagion, in Eastern European folklore the vampire's look or touch can suffice. A classic account refers to the Austro-Hungarian village of Haidam in the 1720s. There, before witnesses, a man dead ten years returned as a vampire to his son's cottage, touched him on the shoulder and then departed. The man died the next morning. Alarmed by this report and others relating how long-dead villagers were returning to suck their children's blood, the local military commander ordered several graves to be exhumed, within which were found corpses showing no signs of decay. All were incinerated to ashes – one of the classic methods of exterminating vampires. Another epidemic occurred in the village of Medvegia near Belgrade, between 1725 and 1731. A soldier claimed to have been attacked by a vampire while in Greece (where vampire legends also abound), and died upon his return home. Thereafter many villagers swore they had seen him at night, or had dreamt about him, and ten weeks later complained of inexplicable weakness. The body was exhumed, was found to have blood in its mouth, and so had a stake driven through its heart. Despite this precaution there was an outbreak of vampirism a few years later, and of the fourteen corpses examined by a medical commission, twelve were found to be "unmistakably in the vampire condition" (undecayed). In 1899 Romanian peasants in Caraşova dug up thirty corpses and tore them to pieces to stop a diphtheria epidemic, and in 1909 a Transylvanian castle was burned down by locals who believed that a vampire emanating from it was causing the deaths of their children. Only recently, in 1988, outside Niş in southern Serbia, a thirteen year-old girl was killed by her family, who believed her to be a vampire.

Sceptics may dismiss vampires and vampirism entirely, but some of the related phenomena have rational or scientific explanations. The "return of the dead" can be explained by premature burial, which happened frequently in the past. Nor is the drinking of blood confined to legendary, supernatural creatures. Aside from the Maasai tribe of Kenya – whose diet contains cattle blood mixed with milk – numerous examples can be found in the annals of criminology and psychopathology.

BRAM STOKER'S DRACULA

During the eighteenth century, numerous well-publicized incidents of vampirism sparked a **vampire craze in Europe**, with both lurid accounts and learned essays produced in quantity. The first respectable **literary work** on a vampire theme was Goethe's *The Bride of Corinth* (1797), soon followed by Polidori's *The Vampyre*, which arose out of the same blood-curdling holiday on Lake Geneva in 1816 that produced Mary Shelley's *Frankenstein*. Other variations followed, by Kleist, E. T. A. Hoffmann, Mérimée, Gogol, Dumas, Baudelaire, and Sheridan Le Fanu, whose *Carmilla* features a lesbian vampire in Styria.

These fired the imagination of **Bram Stoker** (1847–1912), an Anglo-Irish civil servant who became manager to the great actor Sir Henry Irving in 1878 and wrote a few other novels, all now justly forgotten. In 1890 he conceived the suitably *fin-de-siècle* idea of a vampire novel; initially it, too, was to be set in Styria, with an anti-hero called "Count Wampyr", but once he had unearthed the figure of Vlad Ţepeş during his detailed researches in Whitby Public Library and the Reading Room of the British Museum, the setting moved east to Transylvania, and **Count Dracula** was born. Stoker's fictional Count, who was a Székely, owed something to another historical Hungarian – the "Blood Countess", Elizabeth Báthori, born almost a century after Vlad's death – and was possibly influenced by the "Jack the Ripper" murders which happened a decade earlier in Whitechapel, where Stoker lived for a time while writing his book. Stoker delved deep into Romanian folklore, history and geography, and the book is a masterpiece in its mixture of fantasy and precise settings.

Other books on the same theme followed, but it was the advent of **cinema** and the horror film that has ensured the fame of Dracula. The silent *Nosferatu* is perhaps the greatest vampire film, followed by Béla Lugosi's 1931 *Dracula*, while Hammer's 1958 classic *Dracula* boasted the dream coupling of Christopher Lee as the Count and Peter Cushing as Van Helsing. Coppola's *Bram Stoker's Dracula* is truest to its roots, even going so far as to include the historic Vlad Ţepeş in a prelude.

Dracula buffs might like to contact the **British Dracula Association**, headed by Julia Kruk, 213 Wulfstan St, London W12 0AB (☎0181/749 2694) and Rob Leake, 11 Harriott Close, Greenwich, London SE10 0JP (☎0181/853 1741). Their journal, *Voices from the Vaults*, concerns itself with the Gothic imagination and literature.

BOOKS

The surge in interest in Eastern Europe since 1989, and the particularly dramatic nature of Romania's revolution and its problems since then, have led to several excellent writers visiting in quick succession. In addition there is a wealth of nineteenth-century and early twentieth-century travellers' accounts, although much is out of print. Romanian literature is still under-represented in translation. Publishers details are given in the form (UK publisher/US publisher) where both exist; if books are published in one country only, this follows the publisher's name (eg Serpent's Tail, UK). University Press has been abbreviated to UP. Out of print titles are indicated (O/P).

TRAVELLERS' TALES

PREWAR

Charles Boner *Transylvania: Its Products and its People* (O/P). Long-winded but useful nineteenth-century account: particularly informative on the Saxon and Magyar communities.

Emily Gerard *The Land Beyond the Forest* (O/P). One of the classic nineteenth-century accounts of Transylvania, written by an expatriate Scot. Massive and rambling, but highly informative on folk customs, superstitions, proverbs and the like.

Patrick Leigh Fermor *Between the Woods and the Water* (Penguin, UK & US). Transylvania provides the setting for the second volume in this unfolding, retrospective trilogy, based on Leigh Fermor's diaries for 1933–34, when he walked from Holland to Constantinople. His pre-

cocious zest for history and cultural diversity rose to the challenge of Transylvania's striking contrasts and obscurely turbulent past; the richness of his jewelled prose and the deluge of details are impressive, if not overwelmingly so.

Queen Marie of Romania *My Country* (O/P), *The Country that I Love* (O/P) and *The Story of My Life*, published as *Ordeal* in the US (3 vols; O/P) are all gushingly twee, and fail to convey the forceful character of this Edinburgh lass who won the hearts of Romania's people. Many of the illustrations are lovely, however, and the books do have a certain period charm.

Lion Phillimore *In the Carpathians* (O/P). A fascinating account of a journey by horsecart through the Maramureş and Székelyföld just before World War I, by a proto-hippy who wants nothing but to commune with the mountains and the trees.

Sacheverell Sitwell *Romanian Journey* (Oxford University Press). Motoring around, the Sitwells were both politely appalled, and vaguely charmed, by Romania; but most of all seem to have been relieved that their gastronomic fortunes didn't suffer unduly. Nice colour plates in the original edition.

Walter Starkie *Raggle Taggle* (O/P). After his exploits in Hungary, Starkie tramped down through Transylvania to Bucharest, where his encounters with Gypsies and lowlife are recounted in a florid but quite amusing style. A second-hand bookshop classic, occasionally found with the accompanying record of Starkie playing his fiddle.

Teresa Stratilesco *From Carpathians to Pindus* (O/P). Covers the same ground as Gerard, with an equally sharp eye for quirky details.

POSTWAR

Henry Baerlein, ed. *Romanian Scene* and *Romanian Oasis* (O/P). Two fine anthologies of travellers' tales in which most of the prewar authors listed above are featured. Baerlein also wrote three turgid accounts of his own travels during the 1930s: *Bessarabia and Beyond* (O/P), *And Then to Transylvania* (O/P) and *In Old Romania* (O/P).

Nick Crane *Clear Waters Rising* (Penguin). A walk along the mountain spine of Europe, from Finisterre to Istanbul, including the entire length of the Carpathians – interesting contrasts between life in the mountains of Eastern Europe and the lack of it in the West.

Helena Drysdale *Looking for Gheorghe* (Sinclair-Stevenson, UK). A quest rather than a travel book, although the picture of Romanian life both before and after the revolution is spot-on. A search for a lost friend leads to unsavoury insights into life with the Securitate and finally to a hellish "mental hospital".

Jason Goodwin *On Foot to the Golden Horn* (Vintage/Holt). Not exactly in the footsteps of Leigh Fermor, but nevertheless an engaging and well-informed writer walking from Gdansk to Istanbul in 1990 – almost half the book is in fact set in Transylvania. Very thoughtful, but it's annoyingly hard to work out which are the author's opinions and which those of the characters he meets.

Brian Hall *Stealing from a Deep Place* (Minerva/Hill & Wang). Hall cycled through Hungary, Romania and Bulgaria in 1982 and produced a beautifully defined picture of the nonsense that Communism had become, and of people's mechanisms for coping.

Georgina Harding *In Another Europe* (Sceptre, UK & US). Another cycle tour, this one in 1988. Slimmer than Hall's book but concentrating far more on Romania, with a more emotional response to Ceauşescu's follies.

Eva Hoffmann *Exit into History* (Heinemann/Viking). Not a patch on *Lost in Translation*, her superb account of being uprooted from Jewish Kraków to North America, but this tour of East-Central Europe in 1990 still yields seventy insightful pages on Romania.

Andrew MacKenzie *Romanian Journey* and *Dracula Country* (both O/P). *Romanian Journey's* dollops of history, architectural description and bland travelese wouldn't be so bad if MacKenzie didn't also whitewash the Ceauşescu regime, of which his strongest criticism was that there's "nothing soft" about it. *Dracula Country* is a more admirable book, as it doesn't purport to describe contemporary Romania and assembles interesting facts about folklore and Vlad the Impaler.

Rory MacLean *Stalin's Nose* (Flamingo/Little, Brown). With its wonderfully surreal humour, this is not exactly a factual account, but it is a fundamentally serious book about the effects of World War II and Communism all over Eastern Europe.

Claudio Magris *Danube* (Collins Harvill/Farrar, Straus, Giroux). One of the great travel books of recent years, full of scholarly anecdotes and subtle insights. Magris follows the Danube from source to sea, with side-trips as far as Sighişoara.

Dervla Murphy *Transylvania and Beyond* (Arrow/Charnwood, Ulverscroft). A more serious and analytical book than many of her others, tussling with the problems of immediately post-revolutionary Transylvania and its ethnic tensions in particular. Tellingly, she uses the Hungarian spelling "Rumania" throughout, while other spellings are erratic.

Peter O'Conner *Walking Good: Travels to Music in Hungary and Romania* (O/P). Another Irish fiddler in search of Gypsy music, forty years after Starkie. O'Conner's quest took him to Slobozia, Cojocna and Făgăraş, staying with local people a few years before this became illegal. Entertaining.

Ivor Porter *Operation Autonomous: With SOE in Wartime Romania* (O/P). Porter came to Olivia Manning's Bucharest in 1939 to do the job she gave to Guy Pringle, left in 1941 and returned in December 1943, to be captured at once – this is not only a fascinating account of the 1944 coup (including contacts with the West, covered up until 1989), but is also full of excellent background information on Romania in this period.

Sophie Thurnham *Sophie's Journey* (Warner/Little, Brown). Heart-warming story of work in the orphanages.

Giles Whittell *Lambada Country* (Phoenix, UK). Another cycle trip to Istanbul, at the same time as Jason Goodwin'. Less than a quarter of the book is on Romania, but it's interesting and informative, particularly on Magyar attitudes.

SPECIALIZED GUIDEBOOKS

Kiss Botond *Cartea Deltei* (Fundaţia Aves, Romania). Only in Romanian, but far and away the best guide to the Danube Delta.

Tim Burford *Hiking Guide to Romania* (Bradt/Globe Pequot). Now in a second edition.

Dave Gosney *Finding Birds in Romania* (Gostours, 109 Hammerton Rd, Sheffield S6 2NE, UK). This covers the Danube Delta only.

Informative, but strangely it does not include a checklist of possible species.

HISTORY AND POLITICS

As well as the titles listed below, there's quite a collection of books on the changes of 1989 across Eastern Europe, well worth looking at if you're travelling around the region; they tend to treat Romania as the exception, the only one with a violent revolution. They include **Roger East** *Revolutions in Eastern Europe* (Pinter/St Martin's Press); **William Echikson** *Lighting the Night* (Sidgwick & Jackson/Morrow); **Mischa Glenny** *The Rebirth of History* (Penguin, US & UK); **Mark Frankland** *The Patriots' Revolution* (Sinclair-Stevenson/Ivan Dee); and **Gwyn Prins** *Spring in Winter* (Manchester UP/St Martin's Press). **John Simpson**'s *The Darkness Crumbles* (Hutchinson/Trafalgar), an updated version of his *Despatches from the Barricades*, is less analytical, but has a splendid first-hand account of dodging bullets during the Bucharest street fighting.

Mark Almond *The Rise and Fall of Nicolae and Elena Ceauşescu* (O/P). Very readable account by one of the best academics writing on Romania, though too kind to the sinister Silviu Brucan. Rather wayward footnotes and accents.

Dan Antal *Out of Romania* (Faber, UK & US). An insider's version of the now so familiar story: dreadful oppression under Ceauşescu, and even worse disillusion after the revolution. Well enough told by a sympathetic character.

Ed Behr *Kiss the Hand You Cannot Bite* (Hamish Hamilton/Random House). A good, populist account of the Ceauşescus' rise and fall.

Dennis Deletant *Ceauşescu and the Securitate: Coercion and Dissent in Romania* (Hurst/ME Sharpe). Fascinating coverage of many hidden aspects of Communist Romania.

Terence Elsberry *Marie of Romania* (Cassell/St Martin's Press). A colourful biography of Queen Marie.

Mary Ellen Fischer *Nicolae Ceauşescu: A Study in Political Leadership* (L. Rienner, UK & US). Academic, detailed and readable description of the system created by Ceauşescu that was soon to drag him down.

S. Fischer-Galaţi *Twentieth Century Rumania* (Colorado UP, US). An easy read with good illustrations, this complements Hale's book (see below) by providing more background, and is basically sympathetic to many changes that happened under Communism.

Tom Gallagher *Romania after Ceauşescu: The politics of intolerance* (Edinburgh UP/Colorado UP). The most recent academic study of contemporary Romania, focusing particularly on the issue of nationalism.

George Galloway and Bob Wylie *Downfall* (Futura/Macdonald Futura). Unreliable – Labour MP Galloway was well briefed by Iliescu and his aides and fell hook, line and sinker for their version of events.

Vlad Georgescu *The Romanians: A History* (Tauris/Ohio State UP). The best modern history in translation, although the importance of dissidents under Ceauşescu seems overstated. Georgescu, head of the Romanian Service of Radio Free Europe, died in 1988, but an epilogue covers the events of 1989.

Dinu Giurescu *The Razing of Romania's Past* (World Monuments Fund/US ICOMOS). Describes in painstaking detail the buildings destroyed by 1988 in Ceauşescu's megalomaniac prestige projects.

Julian Hale *Ceauşescu's Romania* (O/P). Readable and informative, albeit dated and overly optimistic.

Dan Nelson *Romania After Tyranny* (Westview, UK & US). A collection of pieces by many of the big names in Romanian studies, but already looking dated.

Ion Pacepa *Red Horizons* (Heinemann/Regnery Gateway). A lurid, rambling "exposé" of the Ceauşescu regime, written by its former intelligence chief (who defected in 1978), describing disinformation and espionage abroad, corruption and perversions among the élite, and much else. Pacepa was deeply involved but reveals little about himself.

Prince Paul of Hohenzollern-Roumania *King Carol II: A life of my grandfather* (O/P). The nephew of the current King Mihai, Paul doesn't deny his grandfather's dreadful personal life, but attempts to rehabilitate him as a statesman placed by fate in an impossible position between Hitler and Stalin: plausible but not ultimately convincing.

Martyn Rady *Romania in Turmoil* (Tauris/St Martin's Press). Wonderfully clear account of Ceauşescu's rise and fall, continuing to the end of 1991, which gives it an edge on the books rushed out in 1990. Recommended.

Nestor Ratesh *Romania: The Entangled Revolution* (Praeger, UK & US). A careful account of the revolution, laying out all the confusion that still surrounds events.

Ion Raţiu *Contemporary Romania* (Foreign Affairs Publications, UK). A generally negative portrayal of the Communist system by an émigré who made a million in Britain and was to return after Ceauşescu's downfall to lead an opposition party.

Mark Sanborne *Romania* (Nations in Transition series; Facts on File, US). A pretty lightweight overview of Iliescu's Romania.

George Schöpflin *The Hungarians of Rumania* (Minority Rights Group, UK). A careful presentation of the evidence on Communist discrimination against the Magyars.

R. W. Seton-Watson *A History of the Roumanians* (Cambridge UP, UK). Although it largely ignores social history and eschews atmospherics, and even the author admits his despair at the welter of dynastic details, it's still the classic English work on Romanian history before 1920. Seton-Watson's *Roumania and the Great War* (1915) and *The Rise of Nationality in the Balkans* (1917) somewhat influenced British policy in favour of the Successor States, and for this reason he attracted great hostility in Hungary.

Christine Sutherland *Enchantress: Marthe Bibesco and her World* (John Murray, UK). A brilliant snapshot of both Romanian and French society and politics in the first half of the twentieth century, and of one of its most charismatic figures, Queen Marie's rival.

John Sweeney *The Life and Evil Times of Nicolae Ceauşescu* (Hutchinson, UK). Not definitive, but worth reading.

Lászlo Tökes *With God, for the People* (Hodder & Stoughton/Lubrecht & Cramer). The autobiography of the man who lit the spark of the revolution and continues to be a thorn in the establishment's side, even as a bishop.

Richard Wurmbrand *In God's Underground* (Living Sacrifice Books, US). The memoirs of a Lutheran priest who spent many years incarcerated at Jilava, Piteşti and other notorious prisons.

FOLKLORE

Romanian books on folklore and ethnography (of coffee-table book dimensions) are cheaper to buy and easier to find in Romania. The illustrations are often great, but many of the books have only garbled or touristic English summaries; however **Ion Milcea**'s *Sweet Bucovina* and **Maliţa & Banateanu**'s *From the Thesaurus of Traditional Popular Custom* (both published by Editura Sport-Turism, Bucharest) are safe recommendations. Massive books on the Saxon communities, beautifully produced in Austria and Germany, include *Die Siebenburgische Karpatenverein* (Wort und Welt, Thaur bei Innsbruck), *Siebenbürgen, ein Abendländisches Schicksal* by H. Zillich (Blauen Bucher) and *Kirchenburgen in die Siebenbürgen* by Hermann and Alida Fabini (Hermann Böhlwas). The best books on the Maramureş churches are *Monumente Istorice şi de Artă Religioasă din Archiepiscopia Vadului, Feleacului şi Clujului* (Episcopate of Vad, Feleac and Cluj) which omits a few interesting places but is pretty definitive; and *Pictura Murală Maramureşeană* by Anca Pop-Braţu (Meridiane).

David Buxton *Wooden Churches of Eastern Europe* (O/P). A learned and thorough tome.

Gail Kligman *The Wedding of the Dead* (California UP, US) and *Căluş: Symbolic Transformation in Romanian Ritual* (Chicago UP, US). The first is a wonderful book if you want to know everything about the anthropology and rituals of one Maramureş village, leud. The second is a slim but interesting anthropological study of the Whitsun Căluş rite, which still lingers in parts of southern Romania.

Katherine Verdery *Transylvanian Villagers: Three centuries of political, economic and ethnic change* (California UP, US). Based on field work west of Sebeş – a duller area than Maramureş, but therefore more broadly applicable than Kligman's book, though not as readable. Verdery's other book, *What was socialism and what comes next?* (Princeton UP, US) also seems dull, but offers fascinating insights.

DRACULA

Vampire literature is now a respectable academic subject, and the centenary in 1997 of the publication of *Dracula* has produced plenty of new material, mostly serious rather than exploitative.

Paul Barber *Vampires, Burial and Death: Folklore and Reality* (Yale UP, US). Proclaims itself as "a scholarly work on human decomposition and historical attitudes to it", which says it all.

Barbara Belford *Bram Stoker: A biography of the author of Dracula* (Weidenfeld & Nicholson/Random House). A more rigorous biography than Farson's, though marred by cod psychology.

Daniel Farson *The Man who wrote Dracula: A biography of Bram Stoker* (Michael Joseph, UK). Entertaining account of the life of the fictional Dracula's creator.

Radu Florescu & Raymond McNally *In Search of Dracula* (Hale/Graphics Society, NY) and *Dracula: A Biography* (Hale/Hawthorn) are founts of knowledge about the Impaler; while McNally's *Dracula was a Woman: The Blood Countess of Transylvania* (Hale, UK) divulges the perverted deeds of Elizabeth Báthori.

Christopher Frayling *Vampyres* (Faber, UK & US). Primarily a study of the vampire theme in literature and broader culture, but also a near-definitive review of the phenomenon itself.

Clive Leatherdale *Dracula: The Novel and the Legend* (Aquarian/Desert Island Books). Is more concerned with the novel than with its Romanian background.

Nicolae Stoicescu *Vlad Țepeș: Prince of Wallachia* (Bucharest) is the standard Romanian biography of the Impaler, whom Stoicescu practically attempts to sanctify.

Bram Stoker *Dracula* (Penguin, UK & US). The Gothic horror original that launched a thousand movies. From a promising start with undertones of fetishism and menace in Dracula's Transylvanian castle, the tale degenerates into pathos before returning to Romania, and ending in a not too effective chase.

ROMANIAN LITERATURE

PROSE

Emil Cioran *On the Heights of Despair* (Chicago UP, US). A key early work (1934, reissued in 1992) by this nihilist anti-philosopher. .

Petru Dumitriu *The Family Jewels, The Prodigals* and *Incognito* (all O/P). A literary prodigy lauded by the Party for his book *Dustless Highway*, Dumitriu fled Romania in 1960 and subsequently published two tales of dynastic ambition, followed by his masterpiece of moral and psychological exploration, *Incognito*, set against the backdrop of the war and the Communist takeover.

Mircea Eliade *Shamanism* (Routledge/Pantheon), *Youth without Youth* (Ohio State UP, US) and *Fantastic Tales* (Forest Books, UK). The first is the most interesting and informative example of the academic work for which he is internationally known. The latter two are fictions which don't quite match his reputation as a magical realist in the South American tradition, although this is partly due to the translation. His *Journals* are published in four volumes by Chicago UP, and *Les Roumains: Précis Historique* (a very slim history) is available in French in Romania.

Norman Manea *On Clowns: The Dictator and the Artist* (Faber/Grove Weidenfeld). Deported to the camps of Transnistria at the age of five, after the war Manea became an engineer and then an increasingly dissident writer, fleeing to the USA in 1986. This collection consists largely of over-intellectual musings on the nature of dictatorship and the subjected populace's complicity.

Herta Müller *The Passport* (Serpent's Tail/Consort). Müller is a Schwab who left Romania in 1987. *The Passport* is a tale, in a distinctive staccato style, of the quest for permission to leave for Germany.

Dumitru Popescu *The Royal Hunt* (Quartet/Ohio State UP). One of a sequence of seven volumes, this novel describes the way in which terror can overwhelm a community. Popescu is perhaps Romania's best-known contemporary novelist, and was president of the Writers' Union before the revolution.

Liviu Rebreanu *Uprising, Ion* and *The Forest of the Hanged* (Peter Owen/Ion Twayne, NY). The trilogy comprises a panoramic picture of Romanian social life from the late nineteenth century to the First World War. *Uprising*, which deals with the 1907 peasant rebellion, shocked Romanian readers with its violent descriptions when it first appeared in 1933.

Elie Wiesel *Night* (Penguin/Discus). Wiesel was born in Sighet in 1928 and was deported to Auschwitz, where his family died, in 1944. After the war he pursued an academic career in the USA and was awarded the Nobel Peace Prize in 1986 for his work interpreting Judaism and the Holocaust. This slim book opens in the ghetto of Sighet, but soon moves to the death camps.

POETRY

George Bacovia *Plumb/Lead* (Minerva, UK). Along with Arghezi, Bacovia is the leading pre-war Romanian poet. Exquisite melancholy. (Sadly, none of Arghezi's work is available in translation.)

Maria Banuş *Demon in Brackets* (Forest Books/Dufour). Born in 1914, Banuş was a left-wing activist through the 1930s and 1940s, but her intimate lyricism remains popular today.

Petru Cârdu *The Trapped Strawberry* (Forest/Dufour). A Romanian-Yugoslav from Vršac, across the border south of Timişoara, Cârdu writes ironic poems in both Romanian and Serbo-Croat.

Ion Caraion *The Error of Being* (Forest/Dufour). A leading poet of the older generation, who composed many of his poems in the camps of World War II.

Nina Cassian *Call Yourself Alive?* and *Cheerleader for a Funeral* (Forest/Dufour). Savagely sensual and wickedly funny work from one of Romania's best poets.

Paul Celan *Selected Poems (1920–70)* (Penguin/Persea). Romania's greatest poet – although all his work is composed in German – and one of the best of the twentieth century. Born in Bucovina in 1920, Celan survived the camps of Transnistria and emigrated to Paris. He committed suicide in 1970.

Mircea Dinescu *Exile on a Peppercorn* (Forest/Dufour). Dissident before 1989, Dinescu was the first to announce the revolution on TV and was briefly coopted onto the FSN Council.

Mihai Eminescu *In Celebration of Mihai Eminescu* (Forest/Dufour) and *Selected Works of Ion Creangă and Mihai Eminescu* (Eastern Europe Quarterly, US). The national poet – it's a scandal that there isn't a paperback of his greatest hits.

John Farleigh ed. *When the Tunnels Meet* (Bloodaxe/Dufour). A great idea – contemporary Romanian poems in versions by contemporary Irish poets, with a corresponding volume published in Romania; Dinescu, Sorescu, and most notably Blandiana interpreted by Heaney. *Sorescu's Choice* (Bloodaxe/Dufour) is a similar collection of younger Romanian poets.

Jon Miloş *Through The Needle's Eye* (Forest/Dufour). A Yugoslav-Romanian now living in Sweden, Miloş writes about universal social and environmental problems.

Marin Sorescu *Let's Talk about the Weather* (Forest/Dufour), *Selected Poems 1965–73* (Bloodaxe/Dufour), *The Biggest Egg in the World* (Bloodaxe/Dufour) and *Censored Poems* (Bloodaxe/Dufour). Hugely popular and respected both before 1989 (when his readings had to be held in football stadiums) and after (when he briefly became Minister of Culture), Sorescu died in 1996. His style is more ironic and accessible than that of many of his contemporaries and makes a good introduction to Romanian poetry. His play *Vlad Dracula the Impaler* (Forest/Dufour) has also been translated.

Nichita Stănescu *Bas-Relief with Heroes* (Memphis State UP, US). Stănescu died aged fifty in 1982, but his prolific work (of which this is a selection) is still very influential.

Ion Stoica *As I Came to London one Midsummer's Day* (Forest/Dufour) and *Gates of the Moment* (Forest/Dufour). A poet of the older generation, now director of the Bucharest University Library, blending old and new influences.

Grete Tartler *Orient Express* (Oxford UP, UK). An excellent Schwab writer, translated by Fleur Adcock.

Liliana Ursu *The Sky Behind the Forest* (Bloodaxe/Dufour). "Carnivorous and tender, majestic and human", a clear insight into her country and its people.

Brenda Walker ed. *Anthology of Contemporary Romanian Poetry* (Forest/Dufour). Features the work of Romania's two best living poets, Nina Cassian and Ana Blandiana.

FOREIGN NOVELISTS

Saul Bellow *The Dean's December* (Penguin/Harper & Row). The repression and poverty of Ceauşescu's Romania is contrasted with the hypocrisy and decadence of American society.

Olivia Manning *The Balkan Trilogy* (Mandarin/Penguin). The TV screening of *The Fortunes of War* made Manning's epic story of thoroughly exasperating characters, initially set in Bucharest, widely known in Britain. The atmosphere of wartime Bucharest is well rendered in exquisite prose, but as an extended study of human relationships it's weakly constructed and eventually wearisome.

Gregor von Rezzori *Memoirs of an Anti-Semite* (Pan/Vintage) and *The Snows of Yesteryear* (Vantage/Knopf). The first is an account of growing up in the largely Romanian city of Czernowitz (Cernăuţi, now in Ukraine); the second is similar but more episodic.

Barbara Wilson *Trouble in Transylvania* (Virago/Seal Press). Inveterate traveller Cassandra Reilly goes to Sovata to investigate a murder, and gets the hots for most of the women she meets. Pretty strong on local colour in other respects.

LANGUAGE

Romanian is basically a Romance language with a grammar similar to Latin. This familial resemblance makes it easy for anyone who speaks French, Italian or (to a lesser extent) Spanish to recognize words and phrases in Romanian, even though its vocabulary also contains words of Dacian, Slav, Greek and Turkish origin, with more recent additions from French, German and English. German is widely understood – if not spoken – in the areas of Transylvania and the Banat traditionally inhabited by Saxons and Swabians; and many educated Romanians have learned the language for professional reasons, although the tendency among students nowadays is increasingly towards English. Foreigners who can muster any scrap of Hungarian will find it appreciated in the Magyar enclaves of Transylvania, but its use elsewhere invites hassle rather than sympathy, which is even more the case with Russian – a language that's greeted with derision by almost everyone except the Lipovani communities of the Delta.

Romanian **nouns** have three genders – masculine, feminine and neuter. **Adjectives** (usually placed after the word they describe) and **pronouns** always "agree" with the gender of the noun. *Mai* and *cel mai* are generally used to make comparatives and superlatives: eg. *ieftin* (cheap); *mai ieftin* (cheaper), *cel mai ieftin* (the cheapest). In Romanian

articles are not always needed: the indefinite article "a" comes before the noun and is *un* for masculine and neuter words, *o* for feminine ones; the definite article "the" is added to the end of the noun: *-a* for feminine words, *-ul* or *-le* for masculine or neuter ones. The plural forms of nouns are slightly more complicated, but tend to end in *-i* or *-le*. **Verbs** are conjugated, so do not require pronouns such as "I" or "you", although these may be added for emphasis.

Pronunciation is likewise fairly straightforward. Words are usually, but not always, stressed on the syllable before last, and all letters are pronounced. However, certain letters change their sounds when combined with other ones. When speaking, Romanians tend to slur words together.

A "o" sound as in done.

Ă "er" sound as in mother; the combinations AU and ĂU resemble the sounds in how and go.

C is like "k" or as in country; except when it precedes certain letters: CE sounds like chest; CI sounds like cheek; CHE like kept; and CHI like keep.

E sounds as in ten; but at the start of a word it's pronounced as in year; while the combined EI sounds like bay or ray.

LINGUISTIC POLITICS

The letter î replaced â when Stalin forced Romania to change the rules to make the language more Slavic in form, although a few exceptions such as România and Brâncuşi were allowed to survive. In 1994 the Romanian Academy decreed that î should revert to â, so that Tîrgu Mureş is officially Târgu Mureş, and Cîmpulung is now Câmpulung.

The rules (to do with whether words have a Latin root, where in the word the letter falls, and whether it follows a prefix) are too complex for most Romanians to follow, and as it is simpler for foreigners to cope with one accent on "i" (î) and one on "a" (ă) – Bîrgău rather than Bârgău, for example – and many signs and maps remain unchanged, we have decided to stick with the old form. However you should be aware of the potential for confusion.

ROMANIAN WORDS AND PHRASES

Basics and Greetings

Yes, no, and	*da, nu, şi*	Good day	*Bună ziua (or Servus)*
Please, thank you	*Vă rog, mulţumesc*	Good evening	*Bună seară*
Sorry, Excuse me	*Îmi pare rău, permiteţi-mi*	Good night	*Noapte bună*
		How are you?	*Ce mai faceţi ?*
Good, bad	*Bun, rău*	What's your name?	*Cum vă numiţ?*
Do you speak English?	*Vorbiţi englezeste?*	Cheers!	*Noroc! (literally Good Luck!)*
I don't understand	*Nu înţeleg*		
Please speak slowly	*Vă rog să vorbiţi mai rar*	Good, that's fine	*Bun, minunat (De acord = it's agreed)*
Please write it down	*Scrieţi, vă rog*		
Say that again, please	*Vreţi să repetaţi, vă rog*	Goodbye	*La revedere (or ciao, pa)*
I, we, you	*Eu, noi, dumneata (tu is informal)*	Bon voyage	*Drum bun (literally "Good road")*
Hello	*Salut*	Leave me alone!	*Lăsaţi-ma în pace!*
Good morning	*Bună dimineaţă*		

Directions and Accommodation

Where? /When?	*Unde?/Cînd?*	Twin beds	*două paturi*
The nearest	*cel mai aproape*	Double bed	*un pat dublu*
A (cheap) hotel	*un hotel (ieftin)*	For one person (alone)	*pentru o persoană (singura)*
Campsite	*loc de campare, popas*		
Toilet	*toaletă, WC (pronounced vay-say-oo)*	Shower, bathroom	*duş, baie*
		There's no water	*Nu curge apă*
Is it far?	*Este departe?*	Hot, cold	*cald/fierbinte, frig/rece*
What bus must I take?	*Ce autobuz trebuie sa iau?*	How much per night?	*Cît costa pentru o noapte?*
Is there a footpath to..?	*Există potecă spre..?*	Is breakfast included?	*Micul dejun este inclus în preţ?*
Right, left, straight on	*Dreapta, stînga, dreapt înainte*	Have you nothing cheaper?	*Nu aveţi altceva mai ieftin?*
North, south, east, west	*Nord, sud, est, vest*	Can you suggest another (a cheaper) hotel?	*Puteni să-mi recomandaţi un alt hotel (un hotel mai ieftin)?*
Have you a room?	*Aveţi o cameră?*		
With, without	*cu, fără*		

Signs

Arrival, departure	*Sosire, plecare*	Ladies' (Gents') WC	*WC femei (bărbaţi)*
Entrance, exit	*Intrare, leşire*	Waiting room	*Sală de aşteptare*
Vacant, occupied	*Liber, ocupat*	Operating, cancelled	*Circulă, anulat*
No vacancies	*Nu mai sînt locuri*	No smoking	*Fumatul oprit (Nefumatori)*
Open, closed	*Deschis, închis*		
Admission free	*Intrare gratuită*	No entry, danger	*Intrare interzisa, pericol*

Requests and Buying

I want (should like)...	*(Aş) vreau...*	Waiter, waitress	*Chelner, Chelneriţa*
I don't want...	*Nu vreau...*	It's finished.	*S-a terminat...*
How much?	*Cît costă?*	Two glasses	*Două pahare (sticle) de bere*
A little (less)	*(Mai) puţin*	(bottles) of beer	
Is there...?	*Există.?*	Same again, please	*Încă un rînd, vă rog*
Have you/do you sell..?	*Aveţi..?*	What's that?	*Ce este acesta?*
Where can I buy..?	*Unde pot să cumpăr..?*	Is it any good?	*Merita?*
Too expensive	*Prea scump*	Bon appétit	*Poftă bună*
What do you recommend?	*Ce îmi recomandaţi?*	Bill, receipt	*Notă, chitanţă*
		When will it be ready?	*Cînd este gata?*

At once, we're in a hurry	*Imediat, noi grăbim*	Will you refund my money?	*Vă rog sa-mi dați banii înapoi?*
What's the rate for the pound/dollar?	*Care este cursul lirei sterling/dolaruli?*	Any letters for me?	*Aveți vreo scrisoare pentru mine?*

Getting Around

Does this bus go to the train station?	*Autobuzul acesta merge la gară?*	Two seats for... (tomorrow)	*Două locuri pentru... (mîine)*
Bus terminal	*La autogară*	I want to reserve a sleeper (couchette)	*Vreau sa rezerva loc de vagon de dormit (cu cușete)*
Beach	*La plajă*		
Into the centre	*În centru*		
Does it stop at?	*Oprește la?*	I want to change my reservation to...	*Aș vreau să schimba rezervă pentru...*
Has the last bus gone?	*A trecut ultimul autobuz?*		
I (want to) go to	*(Vreau să) merg la*	Is this the train for..?	*Acesta este trenul de..?*
Where are you going?	*Unde mergeți?*	Where do I change?	*Unde schimb trenul?*
Stop here (at...)	*Opriți aici (la...)*	Is there a boat from here to...?	*Există curse de vapor de aici la..?*
Is it a good road?	*Drumul este bun?*		
It isn't far	*Nu este departe*	When does the next boat leave?	*Cînd pleacă vaporul următor?*
Crossroads	*Intersecție*		
Bridge	*Răscruce, pod*	Can I rent a (rowing) boat?	*Pot să închiriez o barcă (cu vîsle)?*
Which platform does the train to... leave from?	*De la ce peron pleacă trenul către...?*	How much do you charge by the hour/for the day	*Cît costa ora/ziua?*
When does the train leave?	*Le ce ora pleacă trenul?*		

Time and Dates

What's the time?	*Ce oră este?*	Sunday	*Duminică*
It's early/late	*Este devreme/tîrziu*	January	*Ianuarie*
This morning	*Azi dimineață*	February	*Februarie*
Day, afternoon	*Zi, după masă*	March	*Martie*
Midday, midnight	*Amiază, miezul nopții*	April	*Aprilie*
Evening, night	*Seară, noapte*	May	*Mai*
Today, yesterday	*Azi, astăzi, ieri*	June	*Iunie*
(day after) tomorrow	*(poi) mîine*	July	*Iulie*
Soon, never	*Curînd, niciodată*	August	*August*
Everyday	*În fiecare zi*	September	*Septembrie*
Monday	*Luni*	October	*Octombrie*
Tuesday	*Marți*	November	*Noiembrie*
Wednesday	*Miercuri*	December	*Decembrie*
Thursday	*Joi*	New Year	*Anul Nou*
Friday	*Vineri*	Easter	*Paște*
Saturday	*Sîmbătă*	Christmas	*Crăciun*

Numbers

0	*zero*	10	*zece*	20	*douăzece*	500	*cinci sute*
1	*un, una*	11	*unsprezece*	21	*douăzeci și un(a)*	1000	*o mie*
2	*doi, doua*	12	*doisprezece*	30	*treizeci*	First	*întîi*
3	*trei*	13	*treisprezece*	40	*patruzeci*	Second	*al doilea*
4	*patru*	14	*paisprezece*	50	*cincizeci*	1 kilo	*un kilo*
5	*cinci*	15	*cincisprezece*	60	*șaizeci*	a half	*jumătăte*
6	*șase*	16	*șaisprezece*	70	*șaptzeci*	a third	*o treime*
7	*șapte*	17	*șaptsprezece*	80	*optzeci*	a quarter	*un sfert*
8	*opt*	18	*optsprezece*	90	*nouăzeci*	three quarters	*trei sferturi*
9	*nouă*	19	*nouăsprezece*	100	*o sută*		

G is hard as in gust, except in the dipthongs EG (like sledge); GE (like gesture); GI (like jeans); GHE (like guest); and GHI (like gear).

I is as in feet; except for the vowel combinations IU as in you; IA as in yap; and IE as in yes.

Î (or **Â**) is pronounced midway between the O in lesson and the O in sort.

J is like the "s" in pleasure.

K only occurs in imported words like kilometre.

O is as in soft; except for OI, which is like boy, and OA as in quark.

R is always rolled.

Ş is slurred as in shop.

Ţ is a "ts" sound as in bits.

U sounds like book or good; but UA is pronounced as in quark.

W occurs in such foreign words as whisky and western.

In addition to the following language box, see the specialist vocabularies for eating and drinking (p.37–38) and hiking (p.47), and the glossary (below).

ELEMENTARY HUNGARIAN	
Yes	*igen*
No	*nem*
Please	*kérem*
Thanks	*köszönöm*
Hello	*jó napot, servus*
Goodbye	*viszontlá tásta*
Cheers!	*egeszegedre!*
Where is..?	*Hol van..?*
When?	*Mikor?*
How much is it?	*Mennyibe kerül?*
Cheap	*olcsó*
Expensive	*drága*
Open	*nyitva*
Closed	*zárva*
Hotel	*szálloda*
Station	*palyaudvar, vasú, allomas*

ELEMENTARY GERMAN	
Yes	*Ja*
No	*Nein*
Thanks	*Danke*
Hello	*Güten Tag, Grüss Gott*
Goodbye	*Auf Wiedersehen*
Cheers!	*Prost!*
Where is..?	*Wo ist..?*
When?	*Wann?*
How much is it?	*Wieviel kostet es?*
Cheap	*Billig*
Expensive	*Teuer*
Open	*Offen*
Closed	*Geschlossen*
Station	*Bahnhof*

ROMANIAN TERMS: A GLOSSARY

ALIMENTARĂ food store.

ARDEAL "forested land", the Romanian name for Transylvania.

BAIE bath, spa (plural Băile).

BISERICĂ church; **BISERICI DE LEMN**, wooden churches.

BIVOL buffalo, introduced from India by the Gypsies; **BIVOLARI** are buffalo-drovers (a Gypsy tribe).

BOYAR or Boier, feudal lord.

BUCIUM alpine horn used by shepherds, also known as a Tulnic.

BULEVARDUL (B-dul or Blvd.) boulevard.

CALEA avenue.

CĂLUŞ traditional Whitsun fertility rite performed by Căluşari in rural Wallachia and southwestern Transylvania.

CAPRĂ masked "Goat dance" to celebrate the New Year.

CASĂ house.

CETATE fortress or citadel.

CHEI gorge.

CÎMPULUNG (or Câmpulung) meadow or long field, for which settlements like Cîmpulung Moldovenesc are named.

CLIŞARNITA towered guest house-cum-repository for treasures, found in Moldavian monasteries.

CSÁNGÓ Hungarian "Wanderers" from Transylvania who settled on the Moldavian side of the Carpathians.

DACIANS earliest established inhabitants of Romania, subjugated and colonized by the Romans during the first to fourth centuries AD.

DEAL hill.

DOINĂ traditional, usually plaintive, Romanian folk song.

DRUM road; Drum Naţional highway.

ERDÉLY the Magyar name for Transylvania.

FSN Frontul Salvării Naţional, the National Salvation Front set up as an umbrella front during the revolution and soon transformed into a new government; Iliescu's wing split as the FDSN (Democratic Front of National Salvation) and then the PDSR (Democratic Socialist Party of Romania), while Roman's wing continued as the FSN before becoming the Partidul Democratic (FSN) and then the Social Democratic Union (USD).

GADJÉ Rroma (Gypsy) term for non-Gypsies.

GRADINĂ garden.

GRIND raised area of accumulated silt in the Danube Delta.

GURĂ mouth.

HORĂ traditional village round dance.

HOSPODAR ruling prince of Moldavia.

ICONOSTASIS literally "icon-bearer", decorated screen in an Orthodox (or Uniate) church containing tiers of icons that separates sanctuary from nave and priest from congregation during Eucharist.

JUDEŢ county.

LAC lake.

LEGION or Iron Guard, Romanian fascist movement, 1927–41.

LIPOVANI ethnic group living by fishing and gardening in the Danube Delta, descended from Russian "Old Believers".

LITORAL the coast.

MAGAZIN large store.

MAGYARS Hungarians, roughly two million of whom live in Romania, mainly in Transylvania.

MĂNĂSTIREA monastery or convent.

MOARĂ mill.

MUNTENIA the eastern half of Wallachia, paradoxically not at all mountainous.

NAI pan-pipes.

NAOS nave or central part of an Orthodox church, lying below the central cupola and in front of the iconostasis.

NARTHEX entrance hall of an Orthodox church, often decorated with frescoes.

NATIONS (or *Nationes*) historically, the privileged groups in Transylvania.

NEDEIA village fair or festival characteristic of the mountain regions.

OLTENIA the western half of Wallachia, flanking the River Olt.

PĂDURE a wood.

PAS a mountain pass.

PCR Partidul Communist Roman – until 1989, the Romanian Communist Party. Since reconstituted as the Socialist Party of Labour (PSM).

PEŞTERA cave.

PHANARIOTS Greek administrators, and later rulers of Moldavia and Wallachia during the centuries of Ottoman hegemony.

PIATRA stone or crag.

PIAŢA square; also a market.

PLAJĂ beach.

PLAUR floating reed islands, characteristic of the Delta.

POD bridge.

POIANA glade, meadow.

POPĂ (or Preot) Orthodox priest.

POTECA path.

PRONAOS see NARTHEX.

RĂSCOALA peasant rebellion; usually refers to the great uprising of 1907.

REGAT the "Old Kingdom", as Moldavia and Wallachia were known after they united in 1859.

RÎU river.

ROM (or Rroma) Gypsies, who arrived in Romania in the fifteenth century.

SANCTUAR sanctuary or altar area of a church, behind the iconostasis.

SAT village.

SAXONS name given to Germans who settled in Transylvania from the twelfth century onwards.

SCHWABEN (Swabians) name given to Germans who settled in Banat in the eighteenth century; others who moved to Transylvania at this time are known as Landler.

SECURITATE Communist security police, now reborn as the SRI or Romanian Information Service.

SIEBENBURGEN Saxon name for Transylvania (literally, "seven towns").

ŞOSEAUA (Şos.) long tree-lined avenue.

STÎNA sheepfold.

STRADA (Str.) street.

SZÉKELY Hungarian-speaking ethnic group inhabiting parts of eastern Transylvania known as the Székelyföld.

ŢARA land, country (Romanian); Gypsy encampment.

TÎRG or Târg, market, fair or festival.

VAD ford.

VALE valley.

VĂTAF leader of Căluşari dancers (Romanian); tribal chieftain (Gypsy).

VIRF peak, mount.

VLACHS (or Wallachs) foreign name for the Romanians of Wallachia, Moldavia and Transylvania before the nineteenth century.

VOEVOD voivode or ruling prince of Transylvania or Wallachia.

AN A–Z OF ROMANIAN STREET NAMES

Romania shares in the European tradition of naming its streets, schools and universities after historical personages and dates, and these of course reflect the ruling ideology. Today most of the Communist names, such as Lenin and Gheorghiu-Dej, have gone and been replaced by prewar leaders such as Iuliu Maniu and Octavian Goga, although nineteenth-century liberal-democratic figures such as Brătianu and Kogălniceanu remain acceptable. However, in Oradea, Rîmnicu Vîlcea and Tîrgu Mureş streets have been named after Antonescu, whose status remains unclear, and in Cluj and Tîrgu Mureş streets named after Hungarian heroes such as Petöfi now have Romanian names. The process has continued under Ciorbea, with royal names returning and Republicii falling further from favour.

Vasile Alecsandri (1821–90) poet, playwright and politician.

Theodor Aman (1831–91) painter.

Ion Antonescu (1882–1946) Conducator (war-time dictator).

Tudor Arghezi (1880–1967) poet.

Mareşal Alexandru Averescu (1859–1938) World War I commander.

Nicolae Bălcescu (1819–52) liberal politician, played a leading role in the 1848 revolution.

Gheorghe Baritiu (1812–93) president of Romanian National Party 1884–89.

General Henri Mathias Berthelot (1861–1931) head of the French Military Mission which enabled Romania to survive World War I.

Lucian Blaga (1895–1961) philosopher, poet.

Ion Brătianu (1829–91) liberal politician, who invited Carol I to take the throne. Founder of a political dynasty, including his son **Ionel** or Ion I.C. (1864–1927), prime minister during World War I, **Vintila** (1867–1930), who succeeded his brother Ionel as leader of the Liberal Party, **Constantin** (Dinu; 1866–1953), leader of the Liberal Party from 1933, an ally of Maniu in the war-time opposition, who died in Sighet prison, and **Gheorghe** (1898–1953), who led a pro-Antonescu wing of the Liberal Party and killed himself in Sighet.

Constantin Brîncoveanu (or Brâncoveanu) ruling prince of Wallachia 1688–1714, who generated an artistic renaissance.

George Călinescu (1899–1965) writer.

Dimitrie Cantemir (1673–1723) scholar, ruling prince of Moldavia 1710–11.

Ion Luca Caragiale (1852–1912) Romania's greatest dramatist.

Henri Coanda (1886–1972) aviation pioneer.

George Coşbuc (1866–1918) poet.

Ion Creangă (1837–89) suspended deacon, author of folk tales known to every Romanian.

Alexandru Ioan Cuza ruler of united Wallachia and Moldavia 1859–1866.

Decebal Dacian ruler 87–106 AD.

Constantin Dobrogeanu-Gherea (1855–1920) literary critic, early socialist thinker.

Gheorghe Doja leader of 1514 revolt.

Ion Duca (1879–1933) Liberal prime minister assassinated by Iron Guard.

Mihail Eminescu (1850–89) the national poet.

George Enescu (1881–1955) the national composer.

Octavian Goga (1881–1939) poet, anti-Semitic prime minister 1937–38.

Griviţa (1877) battle in Bulgaria (also **Pleven, Smîrdan**).

Bogdan Petriciu Haşdeu (1838–1907) linguist, historian

Horea (Vasile Nicola-Ursu, 1730–85) leader of 1784 revolt, with **Cloşca** and **Crişan**.

Avram Iancu (1824–72) leader of 1848 revolt.

Iancu de Hunedoara ruler of Transylvania 1441–56, also Regent of Hungary.

Tache Ionescu (1858–1922) leader of Romanian delegation at Paris Peace Conference 1918–20.

Nicolae Iorga (1871–1940) historian, founder of National Democratic Party 1910, prime minister 1931–32, assassinated by Iron Guard.

Panait Istrați (1884–1935) writer.

Mihail Kogălniceanu (1817–91) liberal politician, played a leading role in the 1848 revolution, later Foreign Minister.

Gheorghe Lazăr (1779–1823) writer and educationalist.

General Gheorghe Magheru (1804–80) revolutionary leader in 1821 and 1848–49.

Titu Maiorescu (1840–1917) literary critic, prime minister 1910–12.

Iuliu Maniu (1873–1953) prime minister 1928–30, led anti-German resistance, died in prison.

Arón Márton ((1896–1980) Roman Catholic bishop of Alba Iulia, who opposed the persecution of the Jews in 1944 and of the Uniates in 1949, and was imprisoned in Sighet.

Mátyás Corvinus son of Iancu de Hunedoara, king of Hungary 1458–90.

Samuil Micu or Micu–Klein (1745–1806) co-author of *Supplex Libellus Valachorum* (1791), with **Petru Maior** (1761–1821) and **Gheorghe Şincai** (1754–1816).

Mihai Viteazul ruling prince of Wallachia 1593–1601, also conquered Moldavia and Transylvania.

General Vasile Milea (1927–89) Defence Minister, "committed suicide", ie done away with, on December 22 1989 after refusing to order the army to open fire.

Matei Millo (1814–96) dramatist.

Mircea cel Bătrîn ruling prince of Wallachia 1386–1418.

Constantin Noica (1908–87) philosopher.

Petru Rareş ruling prince of Moldavia 1527–38 and 1541–56.

Ciprian Porumbescu (1855–83) composer.

Emil Racoviţa (1868–1947) founder of bio-speleology.

Liviu Rebreanu (1885–1944) novelist.

Mihail Sadoveanu (1880–1961) novelist, vice-president of Grand National Assembly (1948), president of Union of Writers (1949).

Andrei Şaguna (1809–73) Orthodox bishop, elected leader at Field of Liberty (1848), first president of ASTRA (The Association for Romanian Culture in Transylvania).

Ştefan cel Mare Stephen the Great, ruling prince of Moldavia 1457–1504.

Nicolae Titulescu (1882–1941) finance minister, foreign minister 1932–36, president of League of Nations, hated by the Axis.

Traian Roman emperor 98–117 AD, conquered Dacia 101–107.

Tudor Vladimirescu led 1821 revolt.

Vlad Ţepeş Vlad the Impaler, ruling prince of Wallachia 1456–76.

Aurel Vlaicu (1882–1913) inventor of the metal-bodied aeroplane (1912).

Traian Vuia (1872–1950) Romania's first aviator (1906).

INDEX

In Romania, the custom is to list a, i, s and t after ă, î, ş and ţ respectively; however, we have not distinguished between the two forms. Note also that î has been used instead of ă.

A
Abrud 206
Accommodation 32
Ada Kaleh 116
Adamclisi 327
Ady, Endre 210
Agapia 229
Agnita 151
Airlines
  in Australia and New Zealand 13
  in Britain 4
  in the USA and Canada 10
Aiud 168
Alba Iulia 165–167
Albeşti 147
Alexander the Good 346
Antonescu, Marshal Ion 351
Apuseni mountains 202–211, 292
Arad 294–299
Arbore 250
Arcfu 105
Arieşeni 294
Arnota Monastery 113
Aurora 338
Avram Iancu (Banat) 298
Avram Iancu (Transylvania) 206

B
Babadag 324
Bacău 226
Baia Mare 268–271
Baia Sprie 274
Banks 20
Bars 36
Bartók, Béla 209, 298
Basarabi 327
Basil the Wolf 233
Batiza 280

Beiuş 293
Beliş 208
Berbeşti 275
Beştepe 324
Bicaz (Maramureş) 271
Bicaz (Moldavia) 232
Bicaz Ardelean 233
Biorton 151
Birdwatching 47
Bîrgău valley 215
Bîrsa 298
Bîrsana 280
Bistriţa 214–216
Bistriţa Monastery 112
Blaj 167
Bogdan the One-eyed 244, 282, 346
Books 388–394
Borlova 307
Borşa 283
Botos 261
Băiţa 294
Băile Bálványos 182
Băile Herculane 308
Băile Homorod 179
Băile Miercurea 163
Băile Tuşnad 182
Bran 140
Brâncuşi 113
Brâncuşi, Constantin 110, 111
Braşov 133–139
Breaza 97
Breb 277
Brîncoveneşti 186
Brăila 221
Bucegi mountains 126–133
BUCHAREST 55–88
  Accommodation 61–65
  Arrival 57
  Art Museum (National) 67
  Bars 84
  Băneasa Bridge 80
  Botanical Gardens 78
  Calea Victoriei 70
  Ceauşescus, fall of the 67
  Centru Civic 73
  Cinema 85
  Cişmigiu Gardens 77
  Citadel 76
  Cotroceni Palace 78
  Excursions from Bucharest 88
  Ghencea Cemetery 75
  Great Synagogue 76
  Herăstrău Park 79
  History 57

  History Museum (National) 72
  Listings 86
  Metro map 60
  Music 84
  Nightlife 84
  Palace of Parliament 73
  Piaţa Revoluţiei 66
  Piaţa Unirii 75
  Piaţa Universităţii 76
  Piaţa Victoriei 78
  Restaurants 81
  Royal Palace 67
  Skopţi 80
  Şoseaua Kiseleff 79
  Street names 66
  Theatre 85
  Tourist office 59
  Transport 59
  University 77
  Village Museum 79
Bucium 206
Buciumi 212
Budeşti 277
Buses 7, 27
Buşeşti 271
Buşteni 130
Buzău 224

C
Cabanas 33
Calafat 118
Căciulaţi 88
Călan 173
Călata 208
Călăţele 208
Căldăruşani 88
Căliman mountains 186
Călimăneşti-Căciulata 107
Călineşti 276
Căluşari, festival of 172
Camping 33
Capîlniţa 179
Car rental 31
Caransebeş 306
Caraorman 322
Caraşova 309
Caritas 196
Caving 47
Ceahlău massif 232
Ceauşescu, Nicolae 67, 98, 119, 353–355, 381
Cerna valley 307
Cernavodă 326
Changing money 20
Cheia 98

Children 51
Chilia Veche 320
Chişcău 293
Churches 42
Cîlnic 163
Cîmpeni 203
Cîmpina 96
Cîmpu lui Neag 177
Cîmpulung Moldovenesc 259
Cîmpulung Muscel 103
Cindrel 161
Ciocaneşti 261
Ciolpani 89
Cîrlibaba 261
Cisnădie 159
Cisnădioara 160
Ciucea 209
Cîşliţa 320
Cluj-Napoca 190–200
Constanţa 328–334
Constantinescu, Emil ix, 359
Consulates abroad, Romanian
   16
Copşa Mică 153
Corneşti 275
Corund (Northern Transylvania)
   213
Corund (Szélely Land) 179
Corvinus, Mátáyas 191, 286,
   346
Costineşti 337
Covasna 180
Cozia Monastery 108
Craiova 117
Crime 49
Cristian 162
Crişan 321
Cristuru Secuiesc 179
Crivaia 309
Csángó region 225
Culcea 272
Cupşeni 273
Curtea de Argeş 104
Cuza, Alexandru Ioan 235,
   349
Cycling 31

D
Danube–Black Sea Canal
   326–327
Dej 211
Delniţa 184

Densuş 173
Derşida 213
Deseşti 274
Deva 170
Dîrjiu 179
Disabled travellers 19
Dobrogea, The 326
Doi Mai 339
Dózsa, György 303
Dracula 89, 98, 105, 141,
   148, 150, 346, 384–387
Dragomirna Monastery 249
Dragoş, Prince 247
Drinks 36
Driving 8, 30
Drobeta-Turnu Severin 114
Dubova 116
Durău 232

E
Eforie Nord 336
Eforie Sud 336
Embassies abroad, Romanian
   16
Eminescu, Mihai 240
Enisala 325

F
Făgăraş 142
Făgăraş mountains 144
Festivals 43
Fildu de Sus 208
Flights
   from Australia 13
   from Britain 3
   from Canada 12
   from Ireland 9
   from New Zealand 13
   from the USA 10
   internal 27
Focşani 224
Food 35
Food glossary 37
Football 47
Funar, Gheorghe 191
Fundata 142
Funerals (Maramureş) 276

G
Galaţi 223
Gay issues 50
Geoagiu-Băi 169

Germans 364
Ghelinţa 182
Gheorgheni 184
Gheorghiu-Dej, Gheorghe 353
Gherla 201
Gheţari 206
Ghimeş 226
Gîrda de Sus 206, 294
Girl Fair (Muntele Găina) 206
Giuleşti 275
Giurgiu 119
Glossary 399
Goga, Octavian 210
Goleşti 102
Grigorescu, Nicolae 97
Groza, Dr Petru 294, 352
Gura Humorlui 257
Gura Portiţei 325
Gurghiu 187
Gypsies 365

H
Harghită Băi 179
Hălmagiu 299
Hărman 146
Hărniceşti 274
Haţeg 172
Health 21
Hida 209
Hiking 46
History of Romania 343–360
Hobiţa 113
Hodac 187
Homestay schemes 34
Homorod 147
Horez Monastery 112
Horezu 112
Hotels 33
Hoteni 275
Huedin 208
Humor Monastery 258
Hunedoara 172
Hunedoara, Iancu de 172,
   268, 346
Hunyadi, János *see* Hundoara,
   Iancu de

I
Iaşi 233–242
Ieud 281
Ilganii de Sus 321
Ilieni 180

Iliescu, Ion 356
Ilişeşti 248
Ineu 298
Insurance 17
Iron Gate of Transylvania 115, 174
Iron Guard 235
Istria 325
Iza Valley 280–282

J
Jews 365
Jupiter 338
Jurilovca 325

K
Kalotaşteg culture 209
Karst topography 207
Kazan gorge 116
Kodály, Zoltán 209
Kós Károly 180, 181

L
Lacu Roşu 185
Lake Razim 324
Language 395–398
Lăpuş 273
Lăzarea 185
Lenauheim 298
Leşu 213
Letea 322
Lipova 300
Lipovani, The 314
Lotrului mountains 161
Lugoj 306
Lupescu, Magda 235

M
Magyars 364
Mahmudhia 324
Mail 39
Maliuc 321
Mamaia 334
Mănăsteria Giuleşti 275
Mănăstireni 208
Mangalia 338
Maps 24
Mara 274
Mărăşeşti 225
Marginea 251
Mărginimea Sibului 162

Measurement of the Milk Festival 210
Medgidia 327
Mediaş 152
Merry Cemetery 279
Meziad 293
Michael the Brave 100, 117, 244, 347
Miercurea Ciuc 182
Miercurea Sibului 163
Mihai, King 351, 358
Mihai Viteazul *see* Michael the Brave
Mila 23, 322
Mircea the Old 346
Mogoşoaia 89
Moisei 283
Moldova Nouă 117
Moldova Veche 116
Moldoviţa Monastery 256
Money 20
Mugeni 179
Mureş defile 300
Murighiol 323
Music 375–383

N
Nagybánya School 269
Năsăud 213
Năvodari 335
Neamţ county 227–233
Neamţ Monastery 231
Negreşti 280
Negru Vodă 328
Negru Vodă Monastery 103
Neptun 337
Newspapers 41
Nicoleşti 184
Niculiţel 319
Northern Transylvania 211–216
Nuntaşi 325

O
Ocna Sibului 153
Ocna Şugatag 277
Ocoliş 203
Odobeşti 224
Odorheiu Secuiesc 178
Olimp 337
Olt valley 106
Oneşti 225

Opening hours 42
Oradea 286–294
Orăştie 169
Oraviţa 310
Orlat 163
Orphans 370
Orşova 116
Ostrov 328
Ovid's Island 335

P
Package tours
  from Australia and New Zealand 14
  from Britain 4
  from the USA and Canada 12
Padeş 113
Padiş plateau 207
Painted Monasteries 252–259
Păltiniş 161
Panciu 224
Pecinişca 308
Periprava 321
Petreştii de Jos 202
Petroşani 176
Petru Rareş 347
Piatra Craiului 142
Piatra Neamţ 227
Pietroasa 293
Pîncota 298
Piteşti 100
Ploieşti 94
Plopiş 274
Poiana Braşov 139
Poiana Micului 259
Poienile Izei 281
Police 49
Polovragi 111
Post 39
Potlogi 89
Prahova valley 126–133
Praid 179
Predeal 132
Prejmer 146
Pria 210
Prolaz 309
Public holidays 43
Putna Monastery 254

R
Racîş 209
Rădăuţi 251

Radio 41
Radna 299
Rareş, Petru 244
Rarău massif 260
Rascoala, The 119
Răşinari 160
Reghin 186
Remetea Chioarului 272
Reşiţa 308
Restaurants 35
Retezat mountains 174–177
Rieni 294
Rîmeţ 203
Rimetea 203
Rîmnicu Vîlcea 106
Rîşnov 140
Rodna mountains 283
Rogoz 272
România Mare 214
Romanian language 395–398
Rosetti 322
Roşia Montana 206
Rozavlea 280
Rupea 147

S

Săcălăşeni 272
Săcel 280
Sălciua de Jos 203
Sălişte 163
Sănduleşti 202
Şanţ 213
Săpînţa 279
Sarmizegetusa (Dacian) 170
Sarmizegetusa (Roman) 173
Satu Mare 266
Saturn 338
Satşugatag 275
Scorniceşti 119
Sebeş 163
Semenic 309
Semenic mountains 309
Sexual harassment 50
Sfîntu Gheorghe 180, 323
Sfistofca 322
Sibiel 163
Sibiu 153–159
Sic 201
Sighet Prison 278
Sighetu Marmaţiei 277
Sighetu Silvaniei 213
Sighişoara 148–151

Sîmbata Monastery 145
Şimleu Silvanei 213
Sîmmicolau Mare 298
Sinaia 127
Sînmihaiu Almaşului 209
Sîntă Măria-Orlea 173
Sîntana 298
Sîrbi 213, 277
Skiing 46
Slănic 98
Slon 98
Snagov 89
Soccer 47
Solca 250
Şomcuta Mare 272
Sovata 179
Spas 22
Ştefan cel Mare *see* Stephen the Great
Ştei 294
Stephen the Great 231, 242, 346
Stîna de Vale 293
Strei 173
Suceava 242–249
Suceviţa Monastery 255
Sulina 322
Şuncuiuş 211
Şurdeşti 274
Systematization 90
Székely Land 177

T

Techirghiol 336
Teiuş 167
Telephones 39
Television 41
Tilişca 163
Timiş valley 305–307
Timişoara 300–305
Tîrgovişte 98
Tîrgu Jiu 109–111
Tîrgu Lăpuş 272
Tîrgu Mureş 187–190
Tîrgu Neamţ 230
Tîrgu Secuiesc 182
Tismana 113
Tismana Monastery 113
Tökes, Lászlo 304, 355
Topliţa 186
Tourist offices 23
Trains 6, 26
Transylvanian Heath 200

Tulcea 315–319
Turda 201
Turda gorge 202
Turnul Monastery 108
Tusa 213

U

Uniate Church 168
Unitarianism 198
Uzlina 324

V

Vadu Izei 277
Valau lui Traian 327
Valea Mărului 108
Văleni 208
Vălenii de Munte 97
Vama Veche 339
Vampires 384–387
Văratec 229
Vaşcău 294
Vatra Dornei 260
Vatra Moldoviţei 257
Venus 338
Victoria 324
Vienna Diktat 212
Vîrfurile 294
Visas 15
Viscri 147
Vişeu de Jos 282
Vişeu de Sus 282
Vişeu Valley 282
Vlad the Impaler *see* Dracula
Vlad Ţepeş *see* Dracula
Vladimirescu, Tudor 348
Vlăihiţa 179
Voineasa 108
Voroneţ Monastery 257

W

Web sites 23
Wildlife 372–374
Wooden churches (Maramureş) 272–273

Z

Zăbala 182
Zalău 212
Zărneşti 142
Zimbor 209

direct orders from

Amsterdam	1-85828-218-7	UK£8.99	US$14.95	CAN$19.99
Andalucia	1-85828-219-5	9.99	16.95	22.99
Australia	1-85828-220-9	13.99	21.95	29.99
Bali	1-85828-134-2	8.99	14.95	19.99
Barcelona	1-85828-221-7	8.99	14.95	19.99
Berlin	1-85828-129-6	8.99	14.95	19.99
Belgium & Luxembourg	1-85828-222-5	10.99	17.95	23.99
Brazil	1-85828-223-3	13.99	21.95	29.99
Britain	1-85828-208-X	12.99	19.95	25.99
Brittany & Normandy	1-85828-224-1	9.99	16.95	22.99
Bulgaria	1-85828-183-0	9.99	16.95	22.99
California	1-85828-181-4	10.99	16.95	22.99
Canada	1-85828-130-X	10.99	14.95	19.99
China	1-85828-225-X	15.99	24.95	32.99
Corfu	1-85828-226-8	8.99	14.95	19.99
Corsica	1-85828-227-6	9.99	16.95	22.99
Costa Rica	1-85828-136-9	9.99	15.95	21.99
Crete	1-85828-132-6	8.99	14.95	18.99
Cyprus	1-85828-182-2	9.99	16.95	22.99
Czech & Slovak Republics	1-85828-121-0	9.99	16.95	22.99
Dublin Mini Guide	1-85828-294-2	5.99	9.95	12.99
Edinburgh Mini Guide	1-85828-295-0	5.99	9.95	12.99
Egypt	1-85828-188-1	10.99	17.95	23.99
Europe	1-85828-289-6	14.99	19.95	25.99
England	1-85828-160-1	10.99	17.95	23.99
First Time Europe	1-85828-270-5	7.99	9.95	12.99
Florida	1-85828-184-4	10.99	16.95	22.99
France	1-85828-228-4	12.99	19.95	25.99
Germany	1-85828-309-4	14.99	23.95	31.99
Goa	1-85828-275-6	8.99	14.95	19.99
Greece	1-85828-300-0	12.99	19.95	25.99
Greek Islands	1-85828-310-8	10.99	17.95	23.99
Guatemala	1-85828-189-X	10.99	16.95	22.99
Hawaii: Big Island	1-85828-158-X	8.99	12.95	16.99
Hawaii	1-85828-206-3	10.99	16.95	22.99
Holland	1-85828-229-2	10.99	17.95	23.99
Hong Kong	1-85828-187-3	8.99	14.95	19.99
Hungary	1-85828-123-7	8.99	14.95	19.99
India	1-85828-200-4	14.99	23.95	31.99
Ireland	1-85828-179-2	10.99	17.95	23.99
Italy	1-85828-167-9	12.99	19.95	25.99
Jamaica	1-85828-230-6	9.99	16.95	22.99
Kenya	1-85828-192-X	11.99	18.95	24.99
Lisbon Mini Guide	1-85828-297-7	5.99	9.95	12.99
London	1-85828-231-4	9.99	15.95	21.99
Madrid Mini Guide	1-85828-353-1	5.99	9.95	12.99
Mallorca & Menorca	1-85828-165-2	8.99	14.95	19.99
Malaysia, Singapore & Brunei	1-85828-232-2	11.99	18.95	24.99
Mexico	1-85828-044-3	10.99	16.95	22.99
Morocco	1-85828-040-0	9.99	16.95	21.99
Moscow	1-85828-118-0	8.99	14.95	19.99
Nepal	1-85828-190-3	10.99	17.95	23.99
New York	1-85828-296-9	9.99	15.95	21.99
Norway	1-85828-234-9	10.99	17.95	23.99

around the world

Pacific Northwest	1-85828-092-3	9.99	14.95	19.99
Paris	1-85828-235-7	8.99	14.95	19.99
Poland	1-85828-168-7	10.99	17.95	23.99
Portugal	1-85828-180-6	9.99	16.95	22.99
Prague	1-85828-122-9	8.99	14.95	19.99
Provence	1-85828-127-X	9.99	16.95	22.99
Pyrenees	1-85828-308-6	10.99	17.95	23.99
Rhodes & the Dodecanese	1 85828 120 2	8.00	14.05	19.00
Romania	1-85828-305-1	10.99	17.95	23.99
San Francisco	1-85828-299-3	8.99	14.95	19.99
Scandinavia	1-85828-236-5	12.99	20.95	27.99
Scotland	1-85828-302-7	9.99	16.95	22.99
Sicily	1-85828-178-4	9.99	16.95	22.99
Singapore	1-85828-237-3	8.99	14.95	19.99
South Africa	1-85828-238-1	12.99	19.95	25.99
Soutwest USA	1-85828-239-X	10.99	16.95	22.99
Spain	1-85828-240-3	11.99	18.95	24.99
St Petersburg	1-85828-298-5	9.99	16.95	22.99
Sweden	1-85828-241-1	10.99	17.95	23.99
Thailand	1-85828-140-7	10.99	17.95	24.99
Tunisia	1-85828-139-3	10.99	17.95	24.99
Turkey	1-85828-242-X	12.99	19.95	25.99
Tuscany & Umbria	1-85828-243-8	10.99	17.95	23.99
USA	1-85828-307-8	14.99	19.95	25.99
Venice	1-85828-170-9	8.99	14.95	19.99
Vietnam	1-85828-191-1	9.99	15.95	21.99
Wales	1-85828-245-4	10.99	17.95	23.99
Washington DC	1-85828-246-2	8.99	14.95	19.99
West Africa	1-85828-101-6	15.99	24.95	34.99
More Women Travel	1-85828-098-2	10.99	16.95	22.99
Zimbabwe & Botswana	1-85828-186-5	11.99	18.95	24.99

Phrasebooks

Czech	1-85828-148-2	3.50	5.00	7.00
French	1-85828-144-X	3.50	5.00	7.00
German	1-85828-146-6	3.50	5.00	7.00
Greek	1-85828-145-8	3.50	5.00	7.00
Hungarian	1-85828-304-3	4.00	6.00	8.00
Italian	1-85828-143-1	3.50	5.00	7.00
Japanese	1-85828-303-5	4.00	6.00	8.00
Mexican	1-85828-176-8	3.50	5.00	7.00
Portuguese	1-85828-175-X	3.50	5.00	7.00
Polish	1-85828-174-1	3.50	5.00	7.00
Spanish	1-85828-147-4	3.50	5.00	7.00
Thai	1-85828-177-6	3.50	5.00	7.00
Turkish	1-85828-173-3	3.50	5.00	7.00
Vietnamese	1-85828-172-5	3.50	5.00	7.00

Reference

Classical Music	1-85828-113-X	12.99	19.95	25.99
European Football	1-85828-256-X	14.99	23.95	31.99
Internet	1-85828-288-8	5.00	8.00	10.00
Jazz	1-85828-137-7	16.99	24.95	34.99
Opera	1-85828-138-5	16.99	24.95	34.99
Reggae	1-85828-247-0	12.99	19.95	25.99
Rock	1-85828-201-2	17.99	26.95	35.00

¿Qué pasa?

the perfect getaway vehicle

low-price holiday car rental.

rent a car from holiday autos and you'll give yourself real freedom to explore your holiday destination. with great-value, fully-inclusive rates in over 4,000 locations worldwide, wherever you're escaping to, we're there to make sure you get excellent prices and superb service.

what's more, you can book now with complete confidence. our £5 undercut* ensures that you are guaranteed the best value for money in holiday destinations right around the globe.

drive away with a great deal, call holiday autos now on **0990 300 400** and quote ref RG.

holiday autos miles ahead

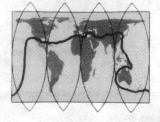